# Freedom to Fiefdom
# Volume One

## (The Descent of Mankind)

by

William Beverley

First published in Great Britain by Schismatic Books
info@schismaticbooks.co.uk

Copyright © William Beverley 2015

The right of William Beverley to be identified as the author of this work has been asserted by him in accordance with the Copyright, Designs and Patents Act 1988.

All rights reserved.

This book is sold subject to the condition that no part of it shall be reproduced, resold, hired out, or stored in a retrieval system in any form, or by any means, without the publisher's prior written consent, and without a similar condition including this condition being imposed on the subsequent purchaser.

ISBN 978-0-9933419-5-3


A copy of the British Library CIP record for this book is available from the British Library.

The story of the Tower of Babel is an allegory in which the world spoke a single language and seemed at ease and united. That was until the vexatious and jealous God of the Hebrews, the first of the Abrahamic Gods, decided it was His prerogative to spoil it for the arrogant earthlings. From Genesis 11 concerning the building of the tower in Mesopotamia we are told:

> ... 6 &7 The LORD said, "If as one people speaking the same language they have begun to do this, then nothing they plan to do will be impossible for them. Come, let us go down and confuse their language so they will not understand each other." ...

Those early Semitic mythologists and scribes, interestingly in Mesopotamia and possibly originally speaking an Akkadian language that pre-dated the Aramaic of the later Hebrews, spun their yarn about human development and the consequences for speech, language, and subsequent civilisation. The Hebrews put the story in writing, and went on to conquer Palestine and make the religion their own of course.

Hypothesis one in this book looks back hundreds of millennia before the story of the Tower of Babel – to the time when human babble really began; to a time when the seeds of discord and ideological servitude were first sown.

**Cover Design:** *The Confusion of Tongues,* An Engraving by Gustave Doré (1865).

# Table of Contents

1 Preface to Volume One......................................................................1
2 Acknowledgements.............................................................................3
3 Provenance and Disclaimer...............................................................4
4 A Warning.............................................................................................5
5 Introduction – What This Book is About.......................................6
   5.1 Real History......................................................................................6
   5.2 Speculative Origins and the Concept of Ethnogenesis..........7
   5.3 Real History and Dangerous Ideologies....................................9
   5.4 Speculative Mechanisms and Hypotheses..............................11
      5.4.1 The Development of Speech and Structured Thinking...11
         5.4.1.1 Speech – A Prerequisite for Ideology..........................11
         5.4.1.2 The Written Word............................................................12
         5.4.1.3 Destiny – Cognitive Dissonance....................................13
         5.4.1.4 Synchronicity....................................................................14
      5.4.2 Corporate Empathy and Corporate Response....................15
      5.4.3 Group Psychopathy – Mob Mentality and Mob Rule........17
         5.4.3.1 Psychopathy and Corruption Today............................19
         5.4.3.2 Psychopathy and Corruption From Recent History...19
         5.4.3.3 Psychopathy and Corruption From Distant History...20
      5.4.4 Social Consequences – Five Hypotheses..............................21
         5.4.4.1 Leveraged Degradation..................................................21
         5.4.4.2 A Brief Overview of the Five Hypotheses...................22
      5.4.5 Hope and Despair Spells Dissident Conflict......................23
         5.4.5.1 Barking, Braying, or Bleating ?......................................23
         5.4.5.2 Catholicism, Zionism, Islamism, Anarchic Blasphemism......23
6 Historical Scope and Granularity – Volume One......................26
   6.1 Introduction...................................................................................26
   6.2 Three Million Years of Humanity.............................................28
      6.2.1 The Lower Palaeolithic – Started circa 3 MYA...................28
      6.2.2 The Middle Palaeolithic – Started circa 0.1 MYA...............29

    6.2.3 The Upper Palaeolithic – Started circa 0.05 MYA.........................29
    6.2.4 Missing Links..................................................................................29
  6.3 Key Events in the British Isles – Palaeolithic and Later........................31
  6.4 Ethno–Cultural Timeline – the Last Ten Thousand Years..................34

# 7 Environmental Milestones.....................................................................35
  7.1 Pangea and Dinosaurs, One Ice Age and Many Glaciations.................35
  7.2 Human Habitation................................................................................36
  7.3 Glaciation Ends But the Ice Age Continues........................................37
    7.3.1 Map – A Possibly United Northern Europe circa 10,000 BC.........39

# 8 Early Ethnocultural Migration and Archaeological Horizons.....40
  8.1 The Earliest People – A People With No Name..................................40
    8.1.1 Flint and Obsidian Distribution in Neolithic Times.....................46
    8.1.2 Map – Inverted Europe to Emphasise Oceanic Continuity..........47
    8.1.3 European Rivers – Global Glue....................................................48
      8.1.3.1 Map – The Rivers of Europe................................................49
  8.2 The Amber Trade – One of the Earliest Land Routes?.......................50
    8.2.1 Map – Lombard Migration From Scandinavia to Italy.................51
    8.2.2 Map – The Much Older Amber Trade Route...............................52
  8.3 The Megalithic Folk 5000 BC – The Earliest Ocean Routes?.............53
    8.3.1 Map – Coastal and River Spread of the Megalithic Culture.........54
  8.4 Corded Ware Culture and Language Roots circa BC 2500.................55
    8.4.1 Map – The Possible Spread of Indo-European Languages...........57
  8.5 The Beaker Folk BC 2800 to 1800, and Normanton Down.................58
  8.6 The Urnfield Culture BC 1200 to 800...................................................58
  8.7 The Bronze Age Collapse circa 1200 BC..............................................59
  8.8 The Legend of Brutus 1100 BC.............................................................60
  8.9 The Picts 1000 BC.................................................................................60
  8.10 Map – Diverse Cultures in a Global Context 1000 BC.....................62
  8.11 The Celts 1000 BC...............................................................................63
    8.11.1 Celtic Domination of Europe.......................................................63
    8.11.2 Celtic Linguistics..........................................................................65
      8.11.2.1 Insular Extant – British Isles and Brittany........................65
      8.11.2.2 Continental Extinct (by circa 4th Century AD) – Europe....65

- 8.11.3 Non-Celts............................................................................65
  - 8.11.3.1 Photograph of a Tarim Basin Mummy...............................67
- 8.11.4 A Celtic Conclusion..................................................................68
- 8.11.5 Map – The Lands of the Celts circa 3rd Century BC....................70

# 9 British Tribes at the End of the Iron Age – Fact or Fiction?........71
- 9.1 Table – British Tribes at the End of the Iron Age..............................74

# 10 The Western Roman Empire and Its Invasion of Britain...........80
- 10.1 Early British Trade Links...............................................................80
- 10.2 Roman Influence on Britain..........................................................81
- 10.3 The Rise and Fall of the Western Romans.....................................82
  - 10.3.1 The Principate......................................................................84
  - 10.3.2 The Dominate......................................................................84
  - 10.3.3 Corpus Juris Civilis...............................................................84
  - 10.3.4 Basilika................................................................................84
  - 10.3.5 Map – Maximum Reach of the Empire Under Hadrian...........85
  - 10.3.6 Map – Threats to the Roman Empires circa 400 AD................86
- 10.4 Table – Roman Emperors and Significant British Events...............88
- 10.5 Countdown to Doom – Seeds of the Holy Roman Empire...........106
  - 10.5.1 Note Concerning the Name "Theoderic"..............................107
  - 10.5.2 Map – Majorian's Final Thrust for Empire 457 AD................108
  - 10.5.3 Map – British Tribes at the Time of the Roman Conquest......109
  - 10.5.4 Map – Initial Roman Objectives – Britain's Currency............110
  - 10.5.5 Map – Further Roman Conquest – Circa 68 AD...................111
  - 10.5.6 Map – Further Roman Conquest – Circa 80 AD...................112
- 10.6 Map – Roman Britain at its End circa 410 AD.............................113

# 11 The Dark Ages – Who Says?......................................................114
- 11.1 Map – British Regions at the Start of Anglo-Saxon Britain............115
- 11.2 Migration Just Before the Time of the Monk Gildas......................116
  - 11.2.1 Map – The Irish, Angles, Jutes, and Saxons Arrive................116
  - 11.2.2 Map – Irish Routes into Wales.............................................117
- 11.3 Britain During the Lifetime of Gildas..........................................118
  - 11.3.1 Map – Circa 540 AD – Britons Already Squeezed Westwards.....118
  - 11.3.2 Map – 600 AD – Even More Saxon Expansion......................119

## 12 The Germanic and Nordic Invasions..................................................120
### 12.1 Jutes, Angles, Saxons, and Frisians..............................................120
#### 12.1.1 Map – Jute, Angle, Saxon, and Frisian Origins..............................121
### 12.2 Vikings, Danes, and Norsemen..................................................122
#### 12.2.1 Map – The Burhs and Other Anglo-Saxon Fortifications...........129
### 12.3 Summary and Conclusion......................................................129
## 13 The Norman Invasion....................................................................131
### 13.1 Introduction...........................................................................131
### 13.2 The English Background..........................................................132
### 13.3 The Invaders and Their Backgrounds.......................................134
#### 13.3.1 King Harald III of Norway...................................................134
#### 13.3.2 Duke William of Normandy................................................134
### 13.4 The Battles Of 1066................................................................135
#### 13.4.1 The Battle of Fulford Gate 20th September............................135
#### 13.4.2 The Battle of Stamford Bridge 25th September......................136
#### 13.4.3 The Battle of Hastings 14th October....................................136
##### 13.4.3.1 Battle of Hastings – Anglo-Saxon Cf. Norman Armies........136
##### 13.4.3.2 Battle of Hastings – Progress..........................................136
##### 13.4.3.3 Battle of Hastings – Endgame........................................137
##### 13.4.3.4 Battle of Hastings – Consequences................................137
### 13.5 Ethnic Cleansing of the British by the Normans.......................138
#### 13.5.1 Map – Displaced Anglo-Saxon Earldoms 1068......................139
#### 13.5.2 Map – Displaced Anglo-Saxon Earldoms 1075......................140
#### 13.5.3 Map – Displaced Anglo-Saxon Earldoms 1087......................141
## 14 Migrant Invasions........................................................................142
### 14.1 Introduction...........................................................................142
### 14.2 The Background – a Poor Starting Point..................................143
### 14.3 Pre-World War Two Migration Into Britain..............................144
#### 14.3.1 British Jews and Russian Jews.............................................144
#### 14.3.2 Romanies and Gypsies of the 14th Century..........................145
#### 14.3.3 Lombardy and the Hanseatic League...................................146
#### 14.3.4 Huguenots (French Protestants) of the 17th Century.............147
#### 14.3.5 Indians of the 17th Century................................................147

14.3.6 Africans of the 18th Century...............................................................147
14.3.7 Germans of the 19th Century...............................................................148
14.3.8 Map – Extent of the Hanseatic League circa 1400.....................149
14.3.9 Miscellaneous Arrivals.........................................................................150
14.4 Post-World War Two Migration Into Britain..........................................151
14.4.1 The West Indies....................................................................................151
14.4.2 India, Pakistan, and Bangladesh....................................................151
14.4.3 Uganda....................................................................................................151
14.4.4 Nigeria and Biafra – Civil War........................................................152
14.4.5 The Balkans, Somalia, Iraq, Afghanistan, Syria.......................152
14.5 The 1951 Refugee Convention – UNHCR 1966 - 67..........................153
14.5.1 Present-Day Refugees and Asylum Seekers in the UK...........154
14.5.2 Failed Applicants Remaining in the UK......................................155
14.5.3 Government Inaction and the Reality – Migration Watch.........156
14.6 Related Acts of Parliament.............................................................................159
14.6.1 Aliens Act 1905.....................................................................................159
14.6.2 British Nationality and Status of Aliens Act 1914...................159
14.6.3 Aliens Act 1919.....................................................................................160
14.6.4 Polish Resettlement Act 1947..........................................................160
14.6.5 British Nationality Act, 1948...........................................................160
14.6.6 Commonwealth Immigrants Act 1962..........................................160
14.6.7 Race Relations Act 1965....................................................................161
14.6.8 Commonwealth Immigrants Act 1968..........................................161
14.6.9 Race Relations Act 1968....................................................................162
14.6.10 Equal Pay Act 1970............................................................................162
14.6.11 Immigration Act 1971......................................................................162
14.6.12 Sex Discrimination Act 1975.........................................................162
14.6.13 Race Relations Act 1976..................................................................162
14.6.14 British Nationality Act 1981..........................................................163
14.6.15 Immigration (Carriers' Liability) Act 1987..............................163
14.6.16 Immigration Act 1988......................................................................163
14.6.17 Dublin Convention 1990.................................................................163
14.6.18 Immigration and Asylum Appeals Act 1993...........................163

14.6.19 Disability Discrimination Act 1995..................................................164
14.6.20 Asylum and Immigration Act 1996..................................................164
14.6.21 Human Rights Act 1998.......................................................................164
14.6.22 Immigration and Asylum Act 1999..................................................165
14.6.23 Race Relations (Amendment) Act 2000.........................................165
14.6.24 Special Educational Needs and Disability Act 2001....................165
14.6.25 Nationality, Asylum and Immigration Act 2002..........................166
14.6.26 Asylum and Immigration Act 2004..................................................166
14.7 Disability Discrimination Act 2005..............................................................166
14.7.1 Equality Act 2006....................................................................................166
14.7.2 Immigration, Asylum and Nationality Act 2006............................167
14.7.3 Equality Act 2010....................................................................................167
14.8 The Complete Anti-Discrimination Framework........................................167
14.9 An Open Door and a Trojan Horse................................................................169
14.9.1 A Numbers Game and an Ethnicity Game.......................................169
14.9.2 What is Hate Crime?...............................................................................172
14.10 Some Immigration Metrics..............................................................................174
14.10.1 Timeline and Numbers........................................................................174
14.10.2 Graph – Net Annual Migration To the UK, 1971 to 2005..........176
14.10.3 Graph – Total Migration In and Out 1975 to 2008.......................176
14.10.4 Seven Key Facts From the Migration Watch Website................177
14.10.5 In Work, Out of Work, In Prison, Illegally Here.........................178
14.10.5.1 Table – Representation in the Criminal Justice System.....179
14.10.5.2 Illegal Immigration Levels.......................................................180
14.11 Riotous Assembly................................................................................................181
14.11.1 Brief History of the Riot Act 1715...................................................181
14.11.1.1 The Original Riot Act 1715......................................................182
14.11.1.2 Amendment – The Criminal Law Act 1967........................182
14.11.1.3 Repeal – The Statute Law (Repeals) Act 1973...................183
14.11.2 List of Principal Riots in Britain.......................................................183
14.11.2.1 Riots in England 12th to 19th Centuries.............................183
14.11.2.2 Riots in England Early 20th Century....................................184
14.11.2.3 Riots in England 1970s..............................................................184

14.11.2.4 Riots in England 1990s..................................................185
14.11.2.5 Riots in England 2000s..................................................185
14.11.2.6 Riots in England 2010s..................................................185
14.11.3 Racially Motivated Violence – 1919 Dock Workers...................186
14.11.3.1 Recent Era Riots..........................................................186
14.11.4 Blair-Brown – New Labour Treachery.....................................186
14.11.5 A Seditious Document...........................................................187
14.11.6 The Reply From the Upper Chamber......................................191
14.11.7 New Labour's Words of Wisdom............................................193
14.11.7.1 Remorseful Reprobates.................................................194
14.12 British Citizenship Awards.........................................................196
14.12.1 Table of Grants of Citizenship 1997 to 2011..............................197
14.12.2 Example Reports Around the Change of Government 2010....197
14.12.3 Immigration Statistics 2010 to 2011 – Blair-Brown Legacy.........199
14.12.4 Table of Grants of Citizenship 1962 to 2010..............................200
14.12.5 Table of Grants of Settlement and Extensions 2009 to 2011......201
14.12.6 Top Ten Nationalities Granted Citizenship in 2011...................201
14.13 Public Attitude..........................................................................202
14.13.1 Immigration – Public Opinion 2009 to 2010.............................202
14.13.2 Immigration – Public Opinion Change 1964 to 2011.................203
14.14 Islamic Racially Motivated Sexual Abuse of Whites....................204
14.15 References Concerning This National Suicide.............................205
14.15.1 A Report Specifically Into the Issues of Abuse at Rochdale.....206

# 15 DNA Studies..................................................................................207
# 16 The Two Thousand Year War – Papal Hegemony.....................209
16.1 Introduction................................................................................209
16.1.1 An Indictment......................................................................216
16.2 The Geography of the Early Church – the Apostolic Sees.............216
16.2.1 Map – The Four Patriarchal Districts or Apostolic Sees............217
16.3 Sources of Information................................................................218
16.3.1 Liber Pontificalis....................................................................219
16.3.2 Papal Apologists...................................................................220
16.3.3 Critics Within the Church.....................................................220

16.3.3.1 Anti-popes ..................................................................... 220
16.3.3.2 Gallicanists .................................................................. 221
16.3.3.3 Conciliarists ................................................................. 221
16.3.4 Critics Outside the Church ............................................... 222
16.4 Heretics and Schismatics ............................................................. 224
16.4.1 Gnosticism – Including the Cathars ................................... 224
16.4.2 Marcionism ....................................................................... 225
16.4.3 Montanism ........................................................................ 226
16.4.4 Docetism ........................................................................... 226
16.4.5 Manichæism ...................................................................... 227
16.4.6 Novationism ...................................................................... 227
16.4.7 Donatism ........................................................................... 227
16.4.8 Arianism ............................................................................ 228
16.4.9 Nestorianism – the Eastern Orthodox Church .................... 228
16.4.10 Chalcedonism – the Western Catholic Church ................. 229
16.4.11 Monophysitism and Monothelitism – the Coptic Church ....... 229
16.4.12 Jansenism ........................................................................ 230
16.4.13 Pelagianism ..................................................................... 230
16.4.14 Valentinianism ................................................................ 231
16.4.15 Eutychianism .................................................................. 232
16.5 Temporal or Spiritual? - the Divine Right of Kings ....................... 232
16.6 Blasphemy .................................................................................. 233
16.6.1 Some Dictionary Definitions ............................................. 233
16.6.2 A Summary of Islamic Interpretation ................................. 234
16.6.2.1 Blasphemy in the Qur'an .............................................. 234
16.6.2.2 Blasphemy in Islamic Law ............................................ 235
16.6.2.3 The Punishment for Blasphemy .................................... 236
16.6.3 Blasphemy Law United Kingdom ...................................... 238
16.6.4 Blasphemy Law Europe ..................................................... 238
16.6.5 Blasphemy Law Worldwide ............................................... 239
16.7 A Selection of Christian Church Fathers ...................................... 239
16.7.1 Eusebius of Caesarea circa 260 to 340 aka Eusebius Pamphili .... 239
16.7.2 Saint Irenaeus of Lyon circa 120 to 200 ............................. 239

- 16.7.3 Saint Ignatius of Antioch circa 50 to 100...........................240
- 16.7.4 Tertullian of Carthage circa 160 to 240.............................240
- 16.7.5 Saint Anthony of the Desert circa 250 to 356, the First Monk....241
- 16.7.6 Saint Athanasius of Alexandria circa 296 to 373, First Orders...242
- 16.7.7 Saint Jerome of Pannonia circa 347 to 420..........................243
- 16.7.8 Saint Ambrose circa 340 to 397 – Victory Over an Emperor.....243
- 16.7.9 Saint Augustine 354 to 430 aka Augustine of Hippo...............244
- 16.8 Anno Domini 32 to 96 – THE POPES START HERE.................245
  - 16.8.1 Context..................................................................245
    - 16.8.1.1 Adversity..........................................................245
    - 16.8.1.2 Martyrs 32 to 96 – or Creative Propaganda ?............245
  - 16.8.2 The Popes of the Period 32 to 96................................246
- 16.9 Anno Domini 96 to 192...................................................246
  - 16.9.1 Context..................................................................246
    - 16.9.1.1 Breathing Space....................................................246
    - 16.9.1.2 Martyrs 96 to 192 – or Creative Propaganda ?..........247
    - 16.9.1.3 Tertullion circa 160 to 240....................................248
  - 16.9.2 The Popes of the Period 96 to 192..............................248
- 16.10 Anno Domini 193 to 235................................................249
  - 16.10.1 Context.................................................................249
    - 16.10.1.1 More Heretics......................................................249
    - 16.10.1.2 Hippolytus circa 170 to 235..................................250
  - 16.10.2 The Popes of the Period 193 to 235..........................250
- 16.11 Anno Domini 235 to 284................................................251
  - 16.11.1 Context.................................................................251
    - 16.11.1.1 Roman Imperial Chaos..........................................251
  - 16.11.2 The Popes of the Period 235 to 284..........................252
- 16.12 Anno Domini 284 to 364................................................253
  - 16.12.1 Context.................................................................253
    - 16.12.1.1 A Christian Emperor of East and West.....................253
    - 16.12.1.2 The Edict of Milan................................................253
    - 16.12.1.3 Church Buildings Appear, the Arian Crisis, Nicaea...........254
    - 16.12.1.4 The Inevitable Issues of Succession........................254

16.12.1.5 The Arrival of the First Foederati - the Franks....................255
16.12.2 The Popes of the Period 284 to 364................................255
16.13 Anno Domini 364 to 401.............................................256
    16.13.1 Context..........................................................256
        16.13.1.1 Deterioration of the Roman West...........................256
    16.13.2 The Popes of the Period 364 to 401.............................257
16.14 Anno Domini 401 to 468.............................................258
    16.14.1 Context..........................................................258
        16.14.1.1 The Sacking of the West....................................258
        16.14.1.2 The Year 410 – Alaric and the Visigoths...................259
        16.14.1.3 The Vandals Arrive in Africa, Gaiseric's First Treaty..........259
        16.14.1.4 The Vandals and the Huns..................................260
    16.14.2 The Popes of the Period 401 to 468.............................261
16.15 Anno Domini 468 to 537.............................................263
    16.15.1 Context..........................................................263
        16.15.1.1 The Beginning of the End and Vice Versa....................263
        16.15.1.2 493 AD – Odovacer is Killed by Theoderic the Great........264
        16.15.1.3 Summary of the Judicial Scope of Theoderic the Great.....264
        16.15.1.4 Map – Theoderic's Confederation 523......................265
    16.15.2 The Popes of the Period 468 to 537.............................265
16.16 Anno Domini 537 to 607.............................................269
    16.16.1 Context..........................................................269
        16.16.1.1 The Gothic War, the Plague, the Lombards..................269
    16.16.2 The Popes of the Period 537 to 607.............................270
16.17 Anno Domini 608 to 800.............................................274
    16.17.1 Context..........................................................274
        16.17.1.1 The Lombards and Franks...................................274
        16.17.1.2 The Donation of Pepin......................................275
        16.17.1.3 The Treaty of Pavia – Birth of the Papal States..............276
        16.17.1.4 The Donation of Constantine................................276
    16.17.2 The Popes of the Period 608 to 800.............................277
16.18 Anno Domini 800 to 891.............................................282
    16.18.1 Context..........................................................282

16.18.1.1 Towards a Holy Roman Empire (HRE)..................282
16.18.2 The Popes of the Period 800 to 891..............................282
16.19 Anno Domini 891 to 962........................................................286
   16.19.1 Context................................................................................286
      16.19.1.1 Lost Direction, the Cadaver Synod.......................286
   16.19.2 The Popes of the Period 891 to 962.............................286
16.20 Anno Domini 962 to 1138......................................................289
   16.20.1 Context................................................................................289
      16.20.1.1 The Holy Roman Empire, the First Emperors.....289
      16.20.1.2 The Investiture Controversy..................................290
      16.20.1.3 Hereward the Wake................................................293
      16.20.1.4 Map – The Papal and Other Italian States 1000..294
      16.20.1.5 Map – Italian States circa Gregory VII and Henry IV.......295
      16.20.1.6 Map – The Southern Italian States in 1112..........296
   16.20.2 The Popes of the Period 962 to 1138...........................297
16.21 Anno Domini 1138 to 1250....................................................308
   16.21.1 Context................................................................................308
      16.21.1.1 The Holy Roman Empire and Papal Interference..............308
      16.21.1.2 Map – Prussian and Other Baltic Tribes circa 1200............310
   16.21.2 The Popes of the Period 1138 to 1250.........................311
16.22 Anno Domini 1250 to 1273....................................................316
   16.22.1 Context................................................................................316
      16.22.1.1 HRE – The Great Interregnum, Papal Materialism..........316
      16.22.1.2 The End of the Hohenstaufens.............................317
   16.22.2 The Popes of the Period 1250 to 1273.........................318
16.23 Anno Domini 1273 to 1337....................................................321
   16.23.1 Context................................................................................321
      16.23.1.1 Enter the Hapsburgs, the Papacy Moves to Avignon.......321
   16.23.2 The Popes of the Period 1273 to 1337.........................321
16.24 Anno Domini 1337 to 1453....................................................326
   16.24.1 Context................................................................................326
      16.24.1.1 Hundred Year War, Western Schism, Papal Atrocities.......326
   16.24.2 The Popes of the Period 1337 to 1453.........................327

16.25 Anno Domini 1453 to 1559 .................................................. 337
  16.25.1 Context ......................................................................... 337
    16.25.1.1 Jesuits, Tudors, and Ottomans ............................... 337
    16.25.1.2 Sir Thomas More's Utopia ...................................... 337
    16.25.1.3 The Hundred Year War End - Peace? - the Italian Wars ..... 338
    16.25.1.4 The Italian Wars ....................................................... 338
    16.25.1.5 Phases in the Italian Wars – Combatants ................ 340
    16.25.1.6 Map – The French - HRE Frontier circa 1470 ......... 341
    16.25.1.7 Map – The Papal and Italian States 1494 ................ 342
    16.25.1.8 War of the League of Cognac – Combatants ........... 343
    16.25.1.9 International Dispositions at This Time .................. 343
    16.25.1.10 Map – The Influence of Genoa – 13th to 17th Centuries. 345
  16.25.2 The Popes of the Period 1453 to 1559 ............................. 346
16.26 Anno Domini 1559 to 1618 .................................................. 360
  16.26.1 Context ......................................................................... 360
    16.26.1.1 1559 Hapsburg Spain Leads Europe ........................ 360
    16.26.1.2 Outcome in the Late 16th Century ........................ 360
  16.26.2 The Popes of the Period 1559 to 1618 ............................. 361
16.27 Anno Domini 1618 to 1700 .................................................. 366
  16.27.1 Context ......................................................................... 366
    16.27.1.1 War, Peace, and Papal Brutality ............................... 366
    16.27.1.2 The Thirty Year War – Combatants ......................... 367
    16.27.1.3 The First Anglo-Dutch War (1652 to 1654) ............. 367
    16.27.1.4 The Second Anglo-Dutch War (1665 to 1667) ......... 368
    16.27.1.5 The War of Devolution (1667 to 1668) .................... 368
    16.27.1.6 The Third Anglo-Dutch War (1672 to 1674) ........... 369
    16.27.1.7 Map – French Attack on the Dutch Republic 1672 ... 369
    16.27.1.8 The Franco-Dutch War – Combatants ..................... 370
    16.27.1.9 The Nine Year War – Combatants ........................... 371
    16.27.1.10 Map – European Powers in 1648 ........................... 372
  16.27.2 The Popes of the Period 1618 to 1700 ............................. 372
16.28 Anno Domini 1700 to 1769 .................................................. 379
  16.28.1 Context ......................................................................... 379

- 16.28.1.1 Bourbon Expansion and Wars of Succession......................379
- 16.28.1.2 The Emergence of Prussia....................................................380
- 16.28.1.3 Map – The Growth of Prussia 1600 to 1795........................381
- 16.28.1.4 The War of Spanish Succession – Combatants..................382
- 16.28.1.5 The War of Spanish Succession – Background..................382
- 16.28.1.6 The War of Spanish Succession – the Two Crowns...........383
- 16.28.1.7 The War of Spanish Succession – the Grand Alliance......384
- 16.28.1.8 The War of Spanish Succession – the War Itself................384
- 16.28.1.9 The War of Spanish Succession – The Peace of Utrecht...385
- 16.28.1.10 The War of Polish Succession – Combatants...................387
- 16.28.1.11 The War of Austrian Succession – Combatants...............388
- 16.28.1.12 The Seven Year War – Combatants..................................389
- 16.28.1.13 Map – Marlborough's Victory at Blenheim 1704.............390
- 16.28.1.14 Map – Europe After the War of Spanish Succession.........391
- 16.28.2 The Popes of the Period 1700 to 1769............................................392
- 16.29 Anno Domini 1769 to 1800...........................................................394
  - 16.29.1 Context..............................................................................................394
    - 16.29.1.1 Towards the French Revolution..........................................394
    - 16.29.1.2 The War of Bavarian Succession – Combatants.................395
    - 16.29.1.3 The Fourth Anglo-Dutch War (1780 to 1784).....................395
    - 16.29.1.4 The 1st Anti-Napoleonic Coalition (1792 to 1797)............396
    - 16.29.1.5 The 2nd Anti-Napoleonic Coalition (1798 to 1802) – I.....396
    - 16.29.1.6 The Anglo-Corsican Kingdom............................................397
  - 16.29.2 The Popes of the Period 1769 to 1800............................................397
- 16.30 Anno Domini 1800 to 1820...........................................................400
  - 16.30.1 Context..............................................................................................400
    - 16.30.1.1 Napoleonic Wars, Congresses and Concerts in Turmoil...400
    - 16.30.1.2 The Carbonari – a Preview of the Fascisti ?.......................401
    - 16.30.1.3 The 2nd Anti-Napoleonic Coalition (1798 to 1802) – II...401
    - 16.30.1.4 The 3rd Anti-Napoleonic Coalition (1803 to 1806)...........401
    - 16.30.1.5 The 4th Anti-Napoleonic Coalition (1806 to 1807)...........401
    - 16.30.1.6 The 5th Anti-Napoleonic Coalition (1809)........................402
    - 16.30.1.7 Map – Butchery of Poland – End of the 18th Century.....403

16.30.1.8 Map – Italian States 1796 – Before Campo Formio..........404
16.30.1.9 Map – The Result of Campo Formio, October 1797........405
16.30.1.10 The 6th Anti-Napoleonic Coalition (1812 to 1814)..........406
16.30.1.11 Maps – Developments Around the Final Conflicts..........406
16.30.1.12 Map – Italian and Regional Powers 1810......................407
16.30.1.13 Map – Rheinbund and Neighbours circa 1812................408
16.30.1.14 Map – Duchy of Warsaw & Free City of Danzig 1814.....409
16.30.1.15 Map – European Powers After Congress of Vienna 1815..410
16.30.1.16 Congress of Vienna and Concert of Europe After 1815......411
16.30.1.17 The Austrian and Emerging Italian Spheres....................411
16.30.1.18 Map – Austrian Pretensions – Northern Adriatic Sea......411
16.30.1.19 Additional Austrian Gains................................................414
16.30.1.20 Great Britain....................................................................414
16.30.1.21 Switzerland......................................................................415
16.30.1.22 Spain................................................................................416
16.30.1.23 France and Portugal........................................................416
16.30.1.24 Sweden, Denmark, and Norway......................................416
16.30.1.25 The Netherlands, the Batavian Republic, and Belgium. .416
16.30.1.26 Russia..............................................................................417
16.30.1.27 Prussia.............................................................................418
16.30.1.28 Map – Prussian Expansion 1807 to 1871.......................419
16.30.1.29 Turkey – The Eastern Question.......................................420
16.30.1.30 The German Confederacy – Seeds of Unity...................420
16.30.1.31 The Spanish Civil War of 1820........................................420
16.30.1.32 The Lasting Legacy of the Period – A Poisoned Chalice. 421
16.30.2 The Popes of the Period 1800 to 1820.......................................422
16.31 Anno Domini 1820 to 1914................................................................424
16.31.1 Context........................................................................................424
16.31.1.1 Napoleonic Era – Concert of Europe – World War One....424
16.31.1.2 Liberty and Emancipation – at Home and Abroad............425
16.31.1.3 Gathering Storm Clouds....................................................426
16.31.1.4 Crimean War 1853 to 1856 – Combatants.......................427
16.31.1.5 The Italian Wars of Independence – An Overview...........427

16.31.1.6 First Italian War of Independence – Combatants..............428
16.31.1.7 Second Italian War of Independence – Combatants..........428
16.31.1.8 A Link Between the German and Italian Unifications.......430
16.31.1.9 Map – States of the Kingdom of Sardinia 1860s..................432
16.31.1.10 Austrian-Prussian or Third Italian Independence War....433
16.31.1.11 Bismarck Lends a Hand.........................................................433
16.31.1.12 Map – German States 1866 – The Deutsche Bund.............435
16.31.1.13 Franco-Prussian War – Combatants......................................436
16.31.1.14 The Papal States, Belligerent Until Italian Unification....436
16.31.2 The Popes of the Period 1820 to 1914............................................438
16.32 Anno Domini 1914 to 1939......................................................................444
16.32.1 Context..............................................................................................444
16.32.1.1 The Great War and the Following Inter-War Years............444
16.32.1.2 Map – Opposing and Neutral Forces – World War One..449
16.32.1.3 Map – Alliances at the Start of World War One..................450
16.32.1.4 Map – The European Powers in 1918....................................451
16.32.1.5 Map – German Losses by the Treaty of Versailles...............452
16.32.1.6 Map – Interpretation of Ethnic Distribution in 1918.........453
16.32.1.7 Map – The Balkans from 1914 to 1992...................................454
16.32.1.8 Table – Human Losses During World War One.................455
16.32.2 The Popes of the Period 1914 to 1939............................................456
16.33 Anno Domini 1939 to 2015......................................................................463
16.33.1 Context..............................................................................................463
16.33.1.1 The Approach to the Second World War..............................463
16.33.1.2 Table – Human Losses During World War Two.................467
16.33.1.3 The Second World War to the Present..................................470
16.33.1.4 Post War Germany......................................................................471
16.33.1.5 Post War Failures........................................................................472
16.33.1.6 Economic Instability..................................................................472
16.33.1.7 Disagreement on Tariffs and Trade........................................473
16.33.1.8 Imperial Guilt Spells Gains for the US and USSR...............474
16.33.1.9 Map – German Partitions in 1947 and Détente in 1990....477
16.33.2 The Popes of the Period 1939 to 2015............................................478

16.33.3 The Centrepiece Behind the Skull Cathedral Altar, Otranto...486
**17 Read All About It – The London Gazette..........................487**
**18 A History of Money and Financial Empire.........................488**
  18.1 A Dissident Preface..........................................................488
  18.2 The Origin and Evolution of Money....................................489
    18.2.1 Prehistoric Speculation................................................489
    18.2.2 Early Monetary Function and Debt...............................491
    18.2.3 The Oldest Evidence – Prehistoric and Early Classical...495
    18.2.4 1st Millennium AD and Medieval Issues........................499
      18.2.4.1 Jewish Hegemony – True or False?......................506
    18.2.5 Further Medieval Developments..................................507
  18.3 The Bank of England – 1694.............................................511
  18.4 The Gold Standard – A Quarter Millennium of Indecision...........514
    18.4.1 Table – Milestones – The Gold Standard Since 1717.....515
  18.5 The Rise (and Fall ?) of the American Economy.....................517
    18.5.1 Introduction..............................................................517
    18.5.2 Colonial Scrip and Independence..................................518
    18.5.3 Freemasonry, Illuminati, and Jewish Influence................519
    18.5.4 From Revolution to Civil War – the Greenback Dollar.....522
    18.5.5 Unstoppable Growth by Attrition – At Home and Abroad...525
    18.5.6 Wall Street – a Forgotten Lesson...................................526
  18.6 Parliamentary and Royal Sequestration of Britain's Wealth..........528
    18.6.1 Saxon Autonomy, Norman Tyranny, and Liberal Irony....528
    18.6.2 Medieval and Post Medieval Changes............................530
    18.6.3 Land Grabbing – the Exploitation of Ireland...................532
    18.6.4 Land Grabbing – English Acts of Enclosure....................533
    18.6.5 Land Grabbing – Highland Clearances in Scotland.........534
    18.6.6 Present-day Privatisation and Retraction of Responsibility...535
    18.6.7 The Crown Estates Today.............................................537
  18.7 Catastrophic Financial Reversals..........................................538
    18.7.1 The Great Tulip Mania 1637.........................................538
    18.7.2 The South Sea Bubble..................................................538
      18.7.2.1 Introduction.......................................................538

18.7.2.2 Map – Spanish Lands in the 18th Century New World......540
18.7.2.3 The Bubble Inflates and Bursts Spectacularly......................541
18.7.3 Ponzi Schemes and Massacres in Palestine................................544
18.7.4 Enron and British Collusion.....................................................547
18.7.5 U.S. Monopolisation – the Death of Bretton-Woods................548
18.7.6 European Defaulters.................................................................550
18.7.7 Global Corporate Collapse – the Great Crash of 2008..............551
18.7.7.1 Minsky-Kindleberger Perspective, Financial Crisis 2008.....552
18.7.7.2 Bubble and Profile One – Oil............................................555
18.7.7.3 Bubble and Profile Two – House Prices............................557
18.7.7.4 Bubble and Profile Three – the Global Stock Markets.......558
18.8 Recession an Ancient Peril - Inflation a New One.........................560
18.8.1 The Keynesian Viewpoint.........................................................561
18.8.2 The Monetarist Viewpoint – e.g. Milton Friedman...................563
18.8.3 Monetarists and Keynesians Crossover.....................................564
18.8.4 Recession in Theory.................................................................566
18.8.4.1 Supply Side Shock – Economics of Factory Production.....567
18.8.4.2 Demand Side Shock – World-view of the General Public..567
18.8.5 Inflation in Theory..................................................................569
18.8.5.1 Cost-push Inflation..........................................................569
18.8.5.2 Demand-pull Inflation.....................................................570
18.8.6 Deflation in Theory.................................................................571
18.8.7 The Savings Ratio and the Paradox of Thrift............................571
18.8.8 Summary of Present-Day Economic Definitions.......................572
18.8.9 Historical Observation and Speculation...................................575
18.8.9.1 Recession in Antiquity.....................................................575
18.8.9.2 Inflation in the Western Isles...........................................576
18.8.9.3 Recession – Old, Inflation – New....................................578
18.8.9.4 Graph – the Historical Lack of Inflation in Grain Prices...579
18.8.10 Present-Day Innovation and Monetary Reform......................582
18.8.10.1 Quantitative Easing........................................................582
18.8.10.2 The Reform Movement..................................................586

# 19 Finance, Politics, and the Media – Hegemony or Conspiracy?.589

19.1 The Rothschilds and Zionism ..................................................590
19.2 More and Yet More Money Changers of Questionable Loyalty.....594
    19.2.1 Frankfurt-am-Main ........................................................594
    19.2.2 Warburg, Swiss Bank Corporation, UBS ........................594
    19.2.3 BNP-Paribas, Bichoffsheim, Goldschmidt ......................594
    19.2.4 Samuel Montague and Company .....................................595
    19.2.5 Sir Edgar Speyer, 1st Baronet 1862 to 1932 .....................595
    19.2.6 George Blumenthal 1858 to 1941 ....................................595
    19.2.7 Lazard Brothers ...............................................................596
    19.2.8 Lazard Group LLC .........................................................596
    19.2.9 Sir James Goldsmith 1933 to 1997 ..................................596
    19.2.10 Helbert Wagg & Co. .....................................................597
    19.2.11 Schroders, President of the World Bank, and Gordon Brown...598
    19.2.12 Salomon Brothers ..........................................................599
    19.2.13 Bear Stearns, Lehman Brothers, Merrill Lynch ............600
    19.2.14 John Key – Prime Minister of New Zealand ................600
    19.2.15 Oppenheimer, De Beers, Anglo-American Corporation .........601
    19.2.16 Goldman-Sachs, J.P. Morgan, Rothschild – Again ......601
    19.2.17 Jacob Schiff ....................................................................603
19.3 The Aga Khan ..............................................................................604
19.4 A Food Scam – the Hebrew-Islamic Alliance ..............................604
19.5 Political Hegemony ......................................................................606
    19.5.1 Jacobins, the Illuminati, Winston Churchill ....................606
    19.5.2 The Bolshevik, Fabian, and Jewish Connection ..............611
19.6 Dodgy Dealing U.K. Style ............................................................616
    19.6.1 Introduction .....................................................................616
    19.6.2 Carbon Credit Trading ....................................................617
    19.6.3 Charities ..........................................................................617
    19.6.4 Quasi Autonomous Government Organisations – Quangos...618
    19.6.5 Think Tanks ....................................................................619
    19.6.6 Gordon Brown, and Think Tank and Charity Exploitation.....619
    19.6.7 Lobbyists .........................................................................620
        19.6.7.1 Definition of Lobbying and Related Matters ....................620

19.6.7.2 Introduction to the Problem.................................................621
19.6.7.3 A Handful of Betrayals........................................................622
19.6.7.4 Lobby Bill – the Passage Through Parliament....................625
19.6.7.5 Lobby Bill – Progress and Prognosis................................626
19.6.8 The Most Corrupt British Public Figures in Living Memory...626
19.6.8.1 The Unique Case of Switzerland...............................628

# 20 The Onset of Egalitarianism and Governance by Statute........629
20.1 Introduction..............................................................................629
20.2 Parliament and the Judiciary - Evolution and Divergence............631
20.2.1 From Antiquity...................................................................631
20.2.2 The Corporation of the City of London..............................634
20.2.3 Norman Change................................................................636
20.2.4 Keepers and Justices of the Peace.....................................637
20.2.5 Commission of the Peace – County Level..........................638
20.2.6 Quarter Sessions..............................................................639
20.2.7 Parish and Village Constables and Religious Loyalty.........640
20.2.8 The Poor Laws and the Marriage Ceremony......................641
20.2.9 Petty Sessions..................................................................642
20.2.10 Municipal Corporations Act 1835....................................642
20.2.11 Social Darwinism 1870...................................................642
20.2.12 The Rise of Liberalism....................................................643
20.2.13 The End of the Courts of Assizes and Quarter Sessions...........644
20.3 The Court Structure Now – Buried Within the EU........................645
20.3.1 www.supremecourt.uk – Terms and Conditions..................646
20.3.2 Appellate Committee of The House of Lords......................646
20.3.3 Supreme Court History......................................................647
20.3.3.1 Supreme Court – Middlesex Guildhall...............................648
20.3.4 Supreme Court References to the EU Court of Justice............648
20.3.5 Diagramme – Secular Estates of the EU............................650
20.3.6 Diagramme – UK Judiciary and New UK Supreme Court.......651
20.4 Principal Acts of Parliament that Shaped Britain..........................652
20.4.1 Charter of Liberties aka Coronation Charter.......................653
20.4.2 The Magna Carta(s) of 1215 and 1225...............................653

    20.4.2.1 Image of an Original Magna Carta.................................653
  20.4.3 The Treason Act 1351..............................................................654
  20.4.4 The Act of Supremacy 1534....................................................655
  20.4.5 The Petition of Right 1628.....................................................655
  20.4.6 The Habeas Corpus Act 1679................................................657
  20.4.7 The Bill aka The Declaration of Rights 1688-1689...............659
  20.4.8 The Act of Settlement 1701....................................................662
  20.4.9 Enclosure aka Inclosure Acts 1773 to 1882............................665
  20.4.10 The Great Reform Act 1832 and the Chartist Movement......669
  20.4.11 The Acts of Union – Scotland 1706 & 1707, Ireland 1800......672
  20.4.12 Act of Union – Scotland 1706................................................672
  20.4.13 Union with England Act 1707...............................................674
  20.4.14 Union with Ireland Act 1800.................................................676
  20.4.15 Act of Union – Ireland 1800..................................................677
  20.4.16 The Human Rights Act 1998.................................................678
    20.4.16.1 The ECHR Judges Look After Themselves !....................687

**21 What the People Say...........................................................689**
  21.1 The People's View of Governance..................................................689
  21.2 The People's View of Personal Well-being.....................................690
  21.3 The Happy Planet Index................................................................691
  21.4 Table – Confidence in Governments Internationally....................692

**22 From Freedom to Fiefdom – Summary and Conclusions.........693**
  22.1 Increasing Sophistication..............................................................693
  22.2 Increasing Governance.................................................................694
  22.3 Humanity's Empirical Phenomena...............................................698
  22.4 Seven Conjectures........................................................................699
    22.4.1 Conjecture 1 The Equivalence of Feudalism and Imperialism...699
    22.4.2 Conjecture 2 Imperial Slipstreaming...........................................700
    22.4.3 Conjecture 3 Imperial Start and Endgame Issues.......................701
    22.4.4 Conjecture 4 Imperial Legacies...................................................702
    22.4.5 Conjecture 5 Imperial Morality and Stamina.............................704
    22.4.6 Conjecture 6 Social Maturity, Confidence, Survivability..........706
    22.4.7 Conjecture 7 Perpetual Warfare..................................................707

 22.5 Five Hypotheses..................................................................708
  22.5.1 Hypothesis 1 – A Tower of Babel........................................709
   22.5.1.1 Introduction – This Book's Front Page Questions............709
   22.5.1.2 Global Front Page News Headlines................................710
   22.5.1.3 Widening the Hypothesis..............................................710
   22.5.1.4 More is Less.....................................................................711
   22.5.1.5 Some Real Figures............................................................712
   22.5.1.6 Wealth Then and Now....................................................712
   22.5.1.7 War and Genocide Then and Now.................................713
   22.5.1.8 Life Expectancy Then and Now.....................................713
   22.5.1.9 Pandemic Then and Now................................................713
   22.5.1.10 Quality of Life Then and Now.....................................714
  22.5.2 Hypothesis 2 – Four Social Mutations and Squalor...................714
   22.5.2.1 The Origins of Governance............................................715
   22.5.2.2 A Social Nadir in Modern Britain..................................717
  22.5.3 Hypothesis 3 – Human Nature and Corporate State Nature....719
   22.5.3.1 Schematic Showing Individual and Corporate Posturing...722
  22.5.4 Hypothesis 4 Part One: Mechanisms of Governance.................723
   22.5.4.1 A System for National Government................................723
   22.5.4.2 Corporate Spirituality....................................................723
   22.5.4.3 A Resource Exchange Mechanism.................................724
  22.5.5 Hypothesis 4 Part Two: Maintaining the Grip..........................724
   22.5.5.1 Political Evangelism........................................................724
   22.5.5.2 Religious Evangelism.......................................................725
   22.5.5.3 Monetary Evangelism.....................................................725
   22.5.5.4 The Tricorn Hat Caricature............................................726
   22.5.5.5 A Nadir of Western Governance....................................727
   22.5.5.6 Dissident Postures Within a Governed Population...........728
  22.5.6 Hypothesis 5 – Armchair Historians.........................................730
**23 A Glossary of Contentious Terms..................................................732**
**24 Bibliography.....................................................................................739**
**25 Internet Index of References and Other Downloads.................751**
**26 A Very English End – Nennius' Wonders of Britain.................752**

26.1 Loch Lomond – River Leven..................................................752
26.2 River Severn – Severn Bore..................................................752
26.3 The Hot Springs at Bath......................................................753
26.4 Salt Springs at Droitwich...................................................753
26.5 Extra Turbulent Severn Bore Locations.....................................753
26.6 Whirlpools Resulting From Severn Bore.....................................754
26.7 Mysterious Source of Fish – Location Now Unknown.........................754
26.8 An Apple-like Fruit Growing on an Ash-like Tree..........................755
26.9 Continuous Wind Emitted by a Cave.........................................755
26.10 The Levitating Altar........................................................756
26.11 The Returning Plank.........................................................757
26.12 Cabal's Cairn...............................................................757
26.13 Amr's Tomb..................................................................758
26.14 Cruc Mawr Tomb..............................................................758

**27 Index to Volume One..........................................................760**

# Note Concerning Images Throughout the Book.

In order to minimise retail cost, maps and other colour images have been reduced to monochrome for this paperback version. All such images are available to download free of charge, in their original colour versions, as a Portable Document Format (PDF) file by emailing to info@freedomtofiefdom.com the precise subject line as follows:

REQUEST F2F ALL IMAGES

Note that the use of an auto-reply facility means that the body of an email with the above subject line will not be read, and, after you have been sent the link, your email address will be discarded.

The PDF file covers both volumes and is supplied without warranty.

It is intended to also make the colour images available as a free eBook, the availability of which will also be confirmed in the response to an email received as described above.

## 1 Preface to Volume One

Some of the Introduction that follows relates to political and philosophical considerations that went into compiling this history book. That introduction will anticipate observations, conjectures, and hypotheses that are justified in greater detail later in the book, therefore, if the going gets tough, then it is suggested that the reader skips to the chapter titled *Historical Scope and Granularity* where the only onset of distress will be that caused by history itself; and history is of course, like justice, blind and neutral.

It is necessary at this early stage to declare that definitions of some terms, that are arguably pejorative, and sometimes just plainly and colloquially acerbic, may be found towards the end of Volume One in the form of a *Glossary of Contentious Terms*. Those words are central to the context of this sometimes angry, and often irreverent book, and such fiery words and expressions should only be used if their meaning is fully understood. Like history and justice, words also are blind and neutral, but it is suggested that those who use them or their derivatives aggressively, and in either a personal sense or to close down debate, are themselves ignorant, insensitive, and ill-informed bigots and-or fools.

Facts also are neutral even when distasteful, but too frequently they are ignored or wilfully abused, and many of the words in the glossary are contentious, especially by association with emotionally charged facts, or in certain contexts. It is a sad reflection that our language and our history can be so misused by accident or by design in order to deceive and coerce, and yet in a wireless world turning in cyberspace, history and historiography are now no longer the sole preserve of academics – the immediacy of the study of history and its lessons are available to all. History is our inheritance and it is non-negotiable.

Concise but comprehensive facts are therefore paramount, and if they are within a rational structure, then the more the better, and while there can be no guarantee of total objectivity when writing about history, it is hoped that the facts presented throughout the two volumes of this book will speak in their own defence, and that they will be heard.

## Preface to Volume One

Despite significant reliance on the internet for information, attempts have been made to avoid any bias towards modern scholastic opinion, and throughout the book reference is frequently made to the works of older historical writers as an adjudication view, the only risk attached to this strategy being the adequate recognition of any opinion, not the accuracy of facts themselves which can be verified by anyone.

This book is an opinionated but uncensored presentation of facts, not filtered opinion *per se,* and the reader may choose to side with any opinion, recent or otherwise, that gives comfort. Rewriting history to make it more "comfortable" is, of course, anyone's prerogative, but both revisionism and conservatism frequently exceed simple scholarly reality checks when in the hands of political and ideological crusaders.

Although this book is about only verifiable fact, it is not without polemics in the form of some candid propositions and angry outbursts, and spontaneous as they may appear, it is to be hoped that they will escape categorisation as either obsequious homily or gratuitous vomit. These outbursts should be quite obvious even to those of a robust constitution. Ignore them if you will.

At this point an acknowledgement must be made of the very real danger of falling into the mode of a pretentious sage writer, otherwise caricatured as a secular prophet, and exemplified by some critics as Thomas Carlyle, who drew the opprobrium of some of his peers for obscuring his message with too much detail. There has to be a fine line between an acceptable polemic and an over-egged didactic pudding, and hopefully the reader will survive the experience of the following chapters.

The next item is more than just a grateful acknowledgement of the many sources, academic or otherwise, without which this book could not have been written – it is intended to highlight the fact that all of the information in the book is available to anyone with internet access, interest, and an open mind. It is followed closely by pre-emptive strikes against academic pomposity and politicisation, opposition to which, as will become clear, is one of the themes of this work.

## 2 Acknowledgements

Grateful thanks are extended to all of the providers of the thousands of internet websites that are listed in the separate *Internet Index* document in "clickable format" (See the chapter in Volume One titled *Internet Index of References and Other Downloads*), and to the contributors to those internet websites.

Apologies are extended to anyone who feels they have been plagiarised by specific omission from this section or by repetition of their own words – such would not have been my intention, nor would it have been done in a cavalier fashion – where cogent expression in open cyberspace has been encountered it has been reused.

Particular acknowledgement goes to the following:

- Search engines and proxies: Google, DuckDuckGo, and Startpage.
- Innumerable political blogs that are indicative of humankind's ideological polarisation and hopelessness.
- Fordham University, New York – books.
- Internet Archive – books and defunct websites.
- Project Gutenberg – books.
- Internet History Source-books – books.
- www.jstor.org – books and periodicals.
- Wiki Commons – maps.
- British History Online – Primary and secondary sources for medieval and modern history.
- Public domain summaries from Encyclopædia Britannica (11th ed.), Cambridge University Press.
- Public domain summaries from Wikipedia.
- Greenwichpast.com – timelines.

## 3 Provenance and Disclaimer

This book contains no knowingly adopted falsehoods and it promotes no extremes. However, because no-one can know the minds of all the authors of the works from which information has been taken, the superfluous statement has to be made that no-one has endorsed this work, and this work endorses no other work unless explicitly stated.

Wherever possible, contentious facts have been verified at a minimum of three unconnected sources, and an assessment of any connection or vested interest has been made by observation of style and presentation, and has been noted as such where relevant.

Reference works of an obviously editorial or censorial nature are generally deprecated, though they may be quoted with a warning if the material seems to have some sort of factual merit. All of the mainstream media without exception fall into this category, along with many historical periodicals and internet websites.

Numbered citations throughout the text are avoided in favour of categorised internet links – there is nothing in this book that cannot be found and verified on the Internet in seconds, and credit must be given to all those who are constructively engaged in cyber-activism. It is hoped that Internet links may serve as acknowledgements of the efforts of the wise, and as a condemnation of those vociferous and bellicose maggots – zombies – that have hijacked so much of the internet and the press for their own self-interest.

## 4 A Warning

This book contains many references to contentious and inflammatory material, and it identifies some examples of extremism from the feral world of internet activism. Some of that material is offensive, and some of it verges on the absurd politically correct *meme* of what is called Hate Crime – once moderated by the straightforward concept of Seditious Libel. Although intended to illustrate the imaginative extremes of man's ideologies, parts of the book might be judged blasphemous by dysfunctional minds, and anyone afraid of the truth should progress no further – some readers will be offended.

Real history is grim, and although it is riddled with hubris and primitive instinct, it is our undeniable heritage and birthright whether we like it or not. History contains nothing of which we should be ashamed or judgemental, or for which we should be apologetic, and yet some are self-indulgent in the futility of apologies for what they see as "the sins of the father". Those apologists may masochistically or naïvely prefer that their nation and ancestors should have suffered more historically, or they may prefer to have played the part of a martyr, but to pathetically wish for a better past is to betray the present and, by weakness, to compromise the future for everyone.

Such wasteful and self-indulgent negativity, concerning what is usually recent history and within living memory, ignores the reality of human nature as discussed in the third hypothesis in this book. The fifth hypothesis in the book then proceeds to relate to a nihilistic corruption of the opportunity to learn from the vengeful and vexatious events of both recent and a more distant history.

An email address and a website support this book in cyberspace.

email: info@FreedomToFiefdom.com

Website: http://www.FreedomToFiefdom.com

# 5 Introduction – What This Book is About
## 5.1 Real History

This is an encyclopaedic reference book in two volumes about real and uncensored global history from the remotest time to the present day, and its aim is to cut through ideological myth, hype, and disinformation. It covers wide-ranging migrations and imperial adventures of many races and dominions over thousands of years – geographically, politically, and financially – and within necessarily limited space an attempt has been made to include detail that is comprehensive yet provocative of further investigation.

The book was initially compiled to rationalise the author's feelings of protest and rage against social injustice, and against widespread cultural destruction during the 3$^{rd}$ millennium; and it was an extensive study of history alongside an indulgent immersion in present-day internet warfare that led to five hypotheses, or interpretations of history and of human psychology, in respect of the author's concept of *the descent of man* and the perception of that descent.

In the context of western democracies, and Britain in particular, tenets throughout English history are comprehensively underwritten by several lists, such as: English and United Kingdom Heads of State; leaders both parliamentary and of the people; and Acts of Parliament.

Worldwide, examples of significant events are provided in an attempt to suggest a "who, what, and when" commentary on the subjects of justice, freedom, and fiefdom, as they relate to the individual. Many pages are watermarked (or blood-marked) by a tide of unease that ranges from disaffection, through dissidence and activism by an individual, to outright mob rebellion at times – often in an inescapable climate of merciless warfare, persecution and treachery, insurrection, and treason; all of it maintained by goading, and bloody repression and revenge on the part of both dissident rebels and the State.

The book contains several historical paradigms, but one chapter in particular acts as an arterial link or central theme, uniting many of the other topics. That chapter begins at the start of what is often referred to as

## Introduction – What This Book is About

the "common era" or the year zero AD, and its title is *The Two Thousand Year War – Papal Hegemony*. It may also be viewed as starting with the transition from the Iron Age to the Romano-British Age, and this particular story contains references to many subsidiary and divergent tales of imperial struggle and betrayal that are presented to a finer granularity in the other chapters on post-Roman history. This single expansive item could be read in isolation, or at least scanned if the detail concerning the Popes for instance is too demanding, though the reader is cautioned against missing the colourful exposure of two thousand years of Papal greed and murderous corruption.

Another broad brush view of European history is suggested by the chapter in Volume Two titled *The War of Frankonian Succession AD 814 to 1945* that highlights the author's perception of almost twelve hundred years of European self-destruction that followed the collapse, due to aristocratic succession issues, of the united Europe of Emperor Charlemagne.

Setting a long-term trend, the united Europe of old excluded Britain, and a comparison of the reasons for Britain's exclusion from that mighty empire, with Britain's struggle during the Second World War, and with the continuing struggle to fully engage with Europe in the 3$^{rd}$ millennium, would make interesting reading, but it is beyond the scope of this book, although only marginally off-topic.

### 5.2 Speculative Origins and the Concept of Ethnogenesis

Returning to the distant past, to a time when the emergence of humanity was barely apparent, it is the author's contention that following the development of a collective sense of kinship that went beyond the immediate family, there have been several step-changes or tipping points that have occurred at different times and in different places around the world, and that it is such uneven social development that has facilitated the imperial ascendancy of one tribe or race over another. This ascendancy created the basis for an inevitable primal sense of racism – that concept and word that at the same time are so beloved and yet loathed by excitable and insecure minds for which judgemental extremes are second nature. In reality, racism is no more, necessarily, than merely a sense of one's own identity that equates to an inescapable self-awareness when it is accentuated by any form of competition with strangers, be that for land, for food, for mates, or in connection with the spread of spiritual and cultural belief; any intelligent mind should be able to distinguish between that and truly psychopathic prejudice and-or acts of race-based hatred.

Such extremes, undesirable as they are, have shown themselves as tribalism and the killing of those of a different clan – even those of the same ethnicity – at least in recorded history, and it might be argued that if we accept the reality of the concept of "race memory", then it follows that atavistic self-awareness favours the Multi-Regional Hypothesis concerning humanity's spread and racial evolution, as opposed to the single-source Out of Africa Hypothesis.

Regardless of such a sensitive debate, it may be deduced that one of the defining tipping points long ago, was when the diversity and populations of pure-blooded autochthonous and distinctive tribes reached a critical mass, and encountered others. Since then, there has been a never ending, running battle between the opposing forces of capricious individuality on the one hand, and on the other a society represented by the more ponderous and manipulative corporate Nation-State; a State that, in order to survive and win, became obliged to adopt imperial ambition, or at least to display a highly competitive bravado among its peer States, as new ones emerged to challenge the older.

Consequent calls to war by demands of fealty or by conscription, and by the imposition of tax increases to meet those challenges, have underlined the differences between the interests of the individual and those of the State from antiquity, and discrepancies between the expected responsiveness of the individual, and the grudging responsibility on the part of a disingenuous container Nation-State, have long been a recipe for continuous dissident unrest and conscientious objection. History has repeatedly shown that when the intensity and intrusion of governance exceeds some acceptable limit, then the disconnect between an individual and the State becomes so great that there is no possibility of consensus without radical change – usually involving revolution and bloodshed.

Ancient corporate identities that warranted the classification of Nation-State would have been initially small-scale but virile unions of clans or tribes, and at later times larger federations of more diverse peoples – the important point being that they had managed to identify a common cause amongst themselves that was strong enough to engender a sense of patriotism and demesne. In some cases, such a corporate identity would lead to a more bombastic nationalism, and to an acquisitive imperialism that would promote a mixture of sometimes outright violent conquest, but in other cases an initially peaceful mass migration. Without distinguishing at this point between conquest and migration, the Phoenicians, Greeks, Assyrians, Hebrews, and Gauls, were typical of the years BC; and the Turks, Vandals, Goths, and Mongols, were typical of the early part of the Common Era, or years AD. See later chapters that identify all known such adventurers and associate them with their often homogenised legacies.

The above concepts of recursive ethnic blending have been expressed by some academics as *Ethnogenesis* – see the definition of Ethnogenesis in the Glossary – and all the above issues are contributory factors to all five of this book's hypotheses.

## 5.3 Real History and Dangerous Ideologies

The historical record clearly shows that over the millennia Nation-States have been rarely parental but oft-times tyrannical; or more ominously, despotic and dictatorial – see the chapter on Greek History in Volume Two for the original concept of tyranny. From such considerations this book makes the assertion that all Nation-State societies today, with their contrived and often excessive regulatory systems based on hierarchy and subservience, are corrupt, procedurally inept, and urgently in need of repair.

Real and holistic history embraces far more than the politically correct and blinkered tales of trivia for school pupils, served up to support the twisted rhetoric of ideological teachers' unions. A true and honest syllabus should include more than the almost exclusively condemnatory history

*Introduction – What This Book is About*

that originated in Britain with the intelligentsia of the highly influential Communist Party Historians Group (CPHG), of which, several members, notably the late Christopher Hill and Eric Hobsbawm, dominated the educational seedbed of the Universities of Oxford, Cambridge, and London, while another CPHG member, E.P. Thompson, along with A.J.P. Taylor who was a member of the Communist Party, dominated the public face of their subject with masterful rhetoric and compelling physical presence for more than fifty years after the Second World War.

As far as is known, those Marxist historians had no specific connection with the well-known Marxist civil servants Guy Burgess, Donald MacLean, and Kim Philby, all of whom defected to the U.S.S.R.; nor with Anthony Blunt, the Soviet agent and talent spotter who was Surveyor of the Queen's Pictures, and who was disgracefully granted immunity from prosecution and allowed to retain his U.K. citizenship; nor with several members of Parliament – people like Labour's John Stonehouse MP and the Conservative Raymond Mawby MP – who were proved to have worked for the communist military intelligence service of the Czechoslovak Socialist Republic, and by association, the U.S.S.R.

Whether connected or not, all of those treacherous ideologues – historians, celebrities, administrators, and government employees alike – supported the quietly insidious *Comintern* (the Communist International Movement) bias of much post-war British mainstream culture, education, and media. Among the most biased media organisations have been the two state-sponsored Public Service Broadcasters – the British Broadcasting Corporation, and its establishment-biased partner Channel 4, closely followed by several iniquitous newspaper groups that were possessed with an apparently chameleon political complexion and capability.

Unsurprisingly, most of the public, the rest of the media, and many other Establishment lickspittles, all swallowed that liberal dosage of medicinal propaganda without so much as a grimace. In spite of any notion of political or moral enlightenment and responsibility, they have become the degenerate and unprincipled bodies – opposed to any public well-being – that were so spectacularly exposed during scandals involving

## Introduction – What This Book is About

parliamentary expenses, hacking, widespread race-based sexual abuse, widespread paedophilia, lobbying, and other diverse disgraces that increased during the first decade of the 3$^{rd}$ millennium. These scandals seemed to rise to a peak during 2011 and 2012, but since then have continued through into 2015 in the United Kingdom with fresh revelations to an unbelievably regular and continuous schedule.

Those despicable and domestic bodies will be identified during the course of the two volumes of this book, together with the world's most dangerous ideologies – ideologies of several types that bind and tyrannise their victims, and that are responsible for tens if not hundreds of millions of deaths, and inestimable misery. Continuing degradation of humanity is an undeniable reality despite all the human rights babble to the contrary.

### 5.4 Speculative Mechanisms and Hypotheses

At this point, a handful of notions will be introduced, some of which may well challenge the reader's credulity. These notions are entirely relevant to any attempt to explore present-day human behaviour that results from conflicts between instinct and social propriety, and to gain an appreciation of any changes in that respect throughout history.

It is the author's contention that adequate contemplation of these earth-shattering anthropological and social developments, and the adoption of a respect for our evolution, can support the task of coming to terms with reality without the invention of religion.

#### 5.4.1 The Development of Speech and Structured Thinking

An arcane subject in itself, and the subject of prodigious and well-informed academic study, the following is a simplistic exhibit that will be part of the evidence presented in support of the book's hypotheses.

##### 5.4.1.1 Speech – A Prerequisite for Ideology

Complex ideologies could only be developed and spread among minds after the development of speech – our mute ancestors can have had no Church or Parliament, and no Central Bank. To support the accurate vocalisation of thoughts, there had to be an intelligent mental framework within which emotions and ideals or goals could be churned over, and be resolved into some sort of memorable tokens that could then be expressed as spoken words. It is assumed that biological mutation of the brain and voice-box simultaneously, or progressively, enabled the evolution of such intelligence and speech, and encouraged the invention of a recognised set of rules governing expression. Those rules – semantics and grammar – ensure that ambiguity can be eliminated, unless ambiguity is intended, because most randomly chosen combinations or sequences of spoken words break the rules and are redundant or meaningless. One can imagine a mixture of humour, quizzical looks, and frustration at times, as conventions slowly became established. The first verbal jokes may well have been accidental, or related to the habit in apes to "smile" in order to convey submission or fellowship; and inane pleasantries may be seen as an attempt to provoke and prolong the disarming politeness of first greetings that is customary among some humans.

### 5.4.1.2 The Written Word

The abstract concept of increased accuracy by increased redundancy can be taken a step further by an appreciation of the utility of the development that followed the emergence of the faculty of speech, and that replaced vocal tradition – the use of a written alphabet to record speech and to capture the speaker's intent in the form of writing.

Putting to one side the complexities of hieroglyphs and pictograms that reflect a fascinating alternative approach to early recording, the English alphabet consists of 26 symbols, from which only a very small percentage of all possible combinations of letters are valid words.

This means that with the extra support of grammatical rules, we can easily spot any mistakes in a written tract, since most "words" composed of random combinations of letters would have no known meaning, and most random combinations of otherwise correctly spelled words would be gibberish. Because of this, written ideas can be distributed with very high precision, and without any doubt as to an author's meaning.

Both well-meaning and ill-intentioned orators now had the perfect tools with which to ensnare followers, and to take control of the direction in which civilisation would develop.

### 5.4.1.3 Destiny – Cognitive Dissonance

As given in the Glossary of Contentious Terms in this book, Cognitive Dissonance is defined as "Confusion due to one's conflicting instincts, beliefs, and opinions." – acc. Leon Festinger, 1956 – and it is suggested that the posture of the central figure on the front cover of this book epitomises such a confounding of the intellect, and an implied resulting instability.

In the context of the objectives of this book, it is further suggested that the character of the players, and the nature of the environment within which the faculty of speech emerged, were absolutely crucial to the relative ascendancy of cultures, and to the outcome of conflicts that would determine the ultimate destiny of civilisation. Sadly, we can only imagine those remote, diverse, and multiple origins. Furthermore, of particular significance is the question of how much of the mindset of the speechless hominin remains with us today after the long evolution of the words and many languages that must have developed from nothing to their current sophistication by common, or "corporate" consent. No one person was responsible for the development of speech, and in that respect at least, we retain and use the corporate expression of our distant ancestors, every time that words form part of our thoughts, and whenever we open our mouths to vocalise those thoughts. The theme of common, or corporate, motivation and expression will be repeated below, and one visible reality of the above suggestions is the very clear "national character" that can be ascribed to cultures ranging from dense rain forests to open steppe lands – racial stereotypes are a long term reality, and they are only disrespectful in the hands of mischievous pranksters.

It may well be that, after all the basic commodities and phenomena of life had been named, and had thereby acquired unambiguous labels, some of the earliest extended use of language and symbols would have arisen in connection with two areas of ambiguity in which rules would have been required to ensure fairness – bartering and primitive gaming – and it is suggested here, that the development of speech outstripped both the development of morality and the ability to control the instinct to cheat if necessary in order to gain a bargain or to win a game.

Maybe such an unfortunate state of affairs is a cosmic inevitability when common sense and instinct become the victim of rules – but the result is that although those ancestral barbaric ambiguous grunts became muted, an association with criminality and cognitive dissonance was now guaranteed for some silver-tongued individuals and for corporate groups with more strength than sense.

Nobody can deny the incongruity of eloquently spoken justifications for brutally punitive Crusades and Jihad throughout history, and nowadays the articulate advocacy of suicide bombings, the beheading of aid-workers, and the carpet bombing of civilians. See the concept of Psychopathy below.

### 5.4.1.4 Synchronicity

The eminent 20$^{th}$ century Swiss psychiatrist Carl Jung wrote a book titled *Synchronicity: An Acausal Connecting Principle* that attempted to rationalise meaningful coincidences that hitherto would have been classified as paranormal if they were not just dismissed as simple coincidence or chance. Jung gave respectability to a concept that might otherwise have been relegated to the world of cranks, and he introduced a new subject into the field of orthodox physics and psychology. The studies and considerations described in that book relate to transient experiences of inexplicable coincidence, and his conclusion was that in addition to the many scientifically explained phenomena, reality consisted of some connections for which we currently have no explanation. He said that when there was no obvious causal connection, then in the case of coincidences of *compelling significance* or meaning there had to be some other explanation.

A couple of examples might be as follows. Firstly, two people independently and spontaneously decide to meet up after a long separation, and discover on meeting that each had just experienced the same event or influence – something with which neither would normally be associated. Secondly, while reading a randomly acquired history book or a novel, and randomly arriving at some event described in the book, an event in real life is experienced that has a direct, unambiguous, and factual relevance to the event in the book, and features on the same day during which the random event was *coincidentally* reached in the book.

Many people have had first or second-hand experience of some such "spooky" coincidence, but neither Jung nor anyone since has been able to conclusively prove or disprove his hypothesis that there is some sort of connection, and it stands, albeit arguably, within the scope of credible science. It is therefore a concept that should be available for reference without incurring ridicule.

### 5.4.2 Corporate Empathy and Corporate Response

It is the author's contention that such transient or brief Synchronicity as suggested by Jung, also should be existential under some conditions as a more persistent Synchronicity – a connecting principle with no readily explicable cause – and that such connection is related to what might be termed Corporate Empathy, the latter being in the present context distinct from the meaning usually attached to the expression by commercial business methodology.

Corporate Empathy or Corporate Response in the context of this book relates to a little, if at all, understood facility by which apparently instantaneous decisions and cooperative responses seem to be made by groups of entities without any obvious cue or chance for the communication of a strategy among possibly thousands of individuals. The most dramatic and large-scale examples are rapid entire-group movements of flocks of birds, and of shoals of fish, that appear to move as one – they seem to achieve complex spatial conformity in the absence of language and without any time to establish a plan of action, and to communicate that plan by whatever means to the entire community. Such coincidental manoeuvres are not transient, and they sometimes continue for periods of time of the order of tens of minutes.

Other examples of more persistent cooperative behaviour in the absence of language as we know it concern the much longer-term organisation and conduct of social insects such as ants and bees, and the specifically strategic positioning of the hunters of herd animals during a hunt by packs of lions and wolves. These examples of unspoken cooperation may last for years.

Another compelling example of protracted Corporate Empathy and Corporate Response, on a much smaller scale and, most significantly, in a context of presumed much reduced sensory perception and expression of "intent", and over lengthy periods of time, is the behaviour of slime moulds that are members of neither the traditional animal nor plant kingdoms, but of a relatively newly defined *Protoctista* Kingdom. Slime moulds consist of thousands of individual disconnected cells that can move and act independently in a way that is not too dissimilar to the locomotion of other micro-organisms. They can do this for a significant period of time compared to the rapid bird or fish movements, but those same microscopic individuals can also physically combine over an extended period of time, and then go on to behave cooperatively in the guise of a *single-minded organism* that has the outward appearance of a small common garden slug.

The mechanism of the cooperative slime mould is currently a mystery, and given the single-celled nature of the individuals, it is difficult to imagine how any "signalling" between those individuals could be resolved by biologists. It is the combination of individual and corporate behaviour that distinguishes them totally from other known lifeforms. Micro-organisms maintain their isolationist sovereignty absolutely, while in higher order lifeforms, virtually all cells have no separate existence. Any speculation concerning the reality of sub-conscious bonding, regardless of the physical scale of the life-forms involved, is left to the reader.

Other quite different types of Corporate Response might be the spread of revolutionary response among the individuals within a previously cowed human population, and the spread of revolutionary fervour by emulation from one Nation-State to another, such as the toppling of many communist regimes of eastern Europe during the last quarter of the 20$^{th}$ century, and the so-called Arab Spring destabilisation of several Nation-States during the first quarter of the 21$^{st}$ century.

Although it can reasonably be argued, in the case of the latter examples above, that external forces and factions were complicit in regime change, the fact remains that the adoption of the changes across a number of Nation-States was, in each case, rapid, total, and comparable, and for a while at least, the new regimes were subsequently characterised by sectarian mob rule and hysteria. In some cases the breakdown of order and its replacement by chaos and inhuman barbarity has been persistent, and this might well be described as corporate insanity, or *Group Psychopathy*, which is the next notion of human behaviour, and one to which at least slime moulds, in their innocence, might be presumed to be immune.

### 5.4.3 Group Psychopathy – Mob Mentality and Mob Rule

At a local tribal level throughout history, and long before the age of electronic social networking, there have been numerous unsavoury cases of group behaviour in the form of witch hunts and lynch mobs – mass actions by a crowd – often murderous actions of which few of the individual participants would be capable in isolated circumstances. Quite separately, in otherwise peaceful crowd conditions, wild stampedes under duress take place, and individuals have been trampled and crushed without malice by an incoherent mob of which they were previously a part. We see recurring manifestations of what might be described as *mass hysteria* in present-day news items, frequently referred to as social *disorder*, whereas in fact they are manifestations of social *order* within the context of the masses involved, and it is common to speak of a Nation-State being ill-at-ease with itself.

Antagonistic and mean-minded mob rule or collective consciousness, within or without government, might be referred to as "Group Psychopathy", and although all of the examples may well involve varying elements of real-world causal stimuli, the mechanism of the linkage among many individuals that produces an unspoken and rapid group response is unknown. It is suggested in this book that humanity remains susceptible to the same mechanisms that are displayed by lower life-forms, and that these mechanisms together with the aberration of Group Psychopathy are largely responsible for the phenomena suggested by the book's five hypotheses, some examples of which are as follows.

When the hue and cry is raised by the politically correct mainstream against some peripheral expression of dissident instinct with which it disagrees, both individual and group psychopathy are evident in the strident and manic behaviour of all varieties of the agents of our governance – politicians, clerics, administrators, and the media – as the dissidents are vigorously denounced, and any balanced debate is triumphantly silenced.

Psychopathy is also evident in the actions of some ideologically frenetic so-called activist groups; and demonstrations, counter-demonstrations, street battles, and pernicious internet warfare are the common result.

Typical examples of issues that are sufficiently emotive to generate such dissident confrontations in Britain and elsewhere relate to:

- National involvement in arguably irrelevant foreign wars.
- Threats to ancient culture due to perceived differences between multiculturalism and nationalism.
- Protests over corporate control of money involving the worldwide "Occupy Movement" for instance.
- Islamification of society and the introduction of Sharia Law into British and European national law.
- Uncontrolled mass immigration and resultant pressure on culture and infrastructure – housing, health, education, policing, and unemployment benefit.

Cancerous and debilitating psychopathy at both group and individual levels, especially among the media and its spokespersons, totally corrupts both the expression of any original dissident message and its comprehension by listeners. This obscuration and suppression of reasonable facts by bellicose rhetoric and by the inappropriate use of contentious terms (see the Glossary) by some people, leads to a resultant cultural anarchy and lost causes for many; and such parliamentary vandalism is pervasive today in all the above typical examples of dissident confrontation.

Psychopathy may be typified at both the individual and the group level as follows.

### 5.4.3.1 Psychopathy and Corruption Today

*"... a personality disorder characterised by a pervasive pattern of disregard for, or violation of, the rights of others. It is defined in different ways, but can involve a lack of empathy or remorse, false emotions, selfishness, grandiosity or deceptiveness; it can also involve impulsiveness, irritability, aggression, or inability to perceive danger and protect one's self."*
– Wikipedia.

### 5.4.3.2 Psychopathy and Corruption From Recent History

*"Power tends to corrupt, and absolute power corrupts absolutely. Great men are almost always bad men."*
– The historian and intellectual Lord Acton 1887.

*"It has often been said that power corrupts. But it is perhaps equally important to realize that weakness, too, corrupts. Power corrupts the few, while weakness corrupts the many. Hatred, malice, rudeness, intolerance, and suspicion are the faults of weakness. The resentment of the weak does not spring from any injustice done to them but from their sense of inadequacy and impotence. We cannot win the weak by sharing our wealth with them. They feel our generosity as oppression."*
– Eric Hoffer, circa mid-20$^{th}$ century.

*"It is impossible to calculate the moral mischief, if I may so express it, that mental lying has produced in society. When a man has so far corrupted and prostituted the chastity of his mind as to subscribe his professional belief to things he does not believe he has prepared himself for the commission of every other crime."*
– Thomas Paine, circa 1776.

*"Corruption, the most infallible symptom of constitutional liberty."*
– Edward Gibbon, circa 1780, in his writings and in his book *The Decline and Fall of the Roman Empire*.

## 5.4.3.3 Psychopathy and Corruption From Distant History

*"Corruption is man's inheritance."*
– Pope Anacletus circa 100 AD, recorded in the book *Day's Collacon: An Encyclopaedia of Prose Quotations*.

*"The more corrupt the state, the more numerous the laws."*
– Tacitus circa 100 AD, in his book *The Annals* (of Imperial Rome).

*"Our earth is degenerate in these latter days; bribery and corruption are common; children no longer obey their parents; and the end of the world is evidently approaching."*
– Anon – Assyrian clay tablet 2800 BC.

## Introduction – What This Book is About

### 5.4.4 Social Consequences – Five Hypotheses

The five hypotheses referred to earlier are previewed below, and towards that end the two volumes of the book embrace many aspects of environmental and socio-political change. The two volumes tell the story of, or at least refer to, most of the world's principal dynastic and imperial conquests and wars, together with allusions to their root causes of ideology, and contention for natural resources. Alternatively, plain adventurism is identified if that seems appropriate.

### 5.4.4.1 Leveraged Degradation

To steal an over-used and cringeworthy commercial expression, it is suggested that the descent of humankind is indicated by a "leveraged" degradation over time of the behaviour of, and of the values held by, sentient beings on earth; and furthermore, that such degradation is aggravated nowadays by globalisation, and that the perception, and the acceptance or denial of that contrived and leveraged degradation by man himself, is an intimate part of the process. Most of the time we are in denial, and dissidence is crushed by a somnambulant status quo.

The use of the expression "leveraged degradation" is intended to convey a sense of the fact that, given our present-day worldly wisdom, and presumed morality, we should now be better behaved than were our distant, and presumed barbaric, ancestors – though that assumes that there is some truth in the proposition that human nature is essentially good. The historical record that follows, however, will be found to negate any assertion of improvement over time, and it is suggested that net global well-being and social integrity in our age, is, on the contrary, far below that pertaining at the dawn of civilisation, and that this is due to ever increasing globalisation with minimisation of the relevance of individuality.

Imperialism is strangely denigrated by many, while, in the same breath, its ugly sister Globalisation is venerated, and the fact that during the 3rd millennium we have increased wealth differentials by contrived international economic events, despite the so-called beneficial consequences for the world of having disposed of Imperialism – complements this book's first hypothesis. All five hypotheses will be expanded at the appropriate point where conclusions are being drawn in the chapter titled *From Freedom to Fiefdom – Summary and Conclusions*.

### 5.4.4.2 A Brief Overview of the Five Hypotheses

Data to support the book's hypotheses is derived from an in-depth and objective study of history, and those five hypotheses that will be developed during the book concern the descent of man and the perception of that descent. They are only very briefly stated here:

1. Global welfare and social integrity in our age is less than that pertaining at the dawn of civilisation, and the downward spiral is marked by a series of tipping points, the first of which was the development of the faculty of speech.

2. The descent of man is a consequence of humanity's social evolution and *social natural selection* – a counterpart to, and a counter-productive consequence of biological mutation and Darwinian natural selection.

3. Belligerent posturing remains a fundamental and determining trait of humanity at both individual and group levels. Enhanced by the faculty of speech, and hampered by ideology, human behaviour can be represented by a very simple syndrome that derives from the ancient theme of the seven deadly sins. As portrayed in many nature films, we inherit belligerence and posturing in undiluted measure from our anthropological ancestors.

4. The paradigm of governance today is corrupt and threadbare, and worldwide it can be reduced to just three aspects: National Government, Corporate Spirituality, and a Currency Mechanism. Unfortunately, as will be shown, these three concepts derive directly from the practical social consequences of the previous two hypotheses concerning social natural selection and belligerent posturing, the provenance of which, guarantees their fallibility and the inevitable shortcomings of all forms of governance.

5. Lessons from history are rarely learned because perception from a comfortable perspective fails to capture essential dynamics, and cannot capture horror. Group Psychopathy compounds the problem.

## 5.4.5 Hope and Despair Spells Dissident Conflict

Potentially benevolent Corporate Empathy when degraded by Group Psychopathy can, and frequently does, ensure that despair replaces hope on the part of the most reasonable of dissident causes, and while there are no doubt some fundamentally good but politically naïve members of society, at best they can only be seen as collateral victims of the struggle between crippling ideology and instinctive creativity.

### 5.4.5.1 Barking, Braying, or Bleating ?

At present in England, though the same can be said for many western democracies, candidates for reform should include Parliament, Government, the Church with its man-made doctrines, the Crown and Aristocracy, and diverse private and public bodies, the latter of which are exemplified by a corrupt and ideologically biased media, and by exclusively self-interested financial institutions. As a final highly influential system that is in need of most reform, the compliant and gullible public itself is indicted; that bloated body that facilitates political correctness, and that variously barks, brays, and bleats with servility and in ignorance, in response to the goading received from the State and its media. That's most of us.

According to internet chatter and blogs, many dissidents today are looking for another more comprehensive Magna Carta, or in the event that recognisable but esoteric remedies already exist, then those frustrated dissidents would like to see the complete dissemination of such remedies and truths, and a thorough demonstration of their viability so that they may be implemented with confidence by an ever wider dissident public; the alternative is the continuing reinforcement and imposition upon the compliant public of discredited systems and values that can only lead to polarisation, disenfranchisement, and social disintegration.

### 5.4.5.2 Catholicism, Zionism, Islamism, Anarchic Blasphemism

To support a break from this miserable spiral, any dissident individual, although intimidated by the State, has a right and a duty to rebel. This right and duty is as valid in England and all the "Western Democracies" today as it was in the fashionably reviled regimes of Libyan and Iraqi dictators, Nazi Germany, Stalinist Russia, Maoist China, or any of the perceived totalitarian tyrannies of the previous two millennia. That catalogue of totalitarian tyranny includes movements such as Roman Catholicism, Judaic Zionism, Islamism, and the author's own category of *Anarchic Blasphemism*, where Anarchic Blasphemism is not just the use of anti-dialectical and bigoted blasphemy law as a weapon by a State or religion, but also the equally reprehensible and deliberate employment of extremist behaviour by an exhibitionist or so-called dissident protester with the apparently sole aim of the public desecration of the beliefs of others.

Although it is arguable that the possibly preposterous nature of those beliefs of others matters not, and that the blasphemous act is free speech and a form of artwork or entertainment for a select audience, the very existence of the argument is just one more example of the hopelessness of humanity in its sophisticated and dogmatic social form.

Anarchic Blasphemism is a form of cultural anarchy, a destructive or at least an ignorant and mocking thrust with few if any redeeming qualities – there is nothing good about a bad taste which is usually a warning to the body of corruption and of impending sickness. The guffaws of some of those in the anarchic blasphemer's audience might easily be confused with a nauseous heaving of their more sensitive neighbours.

Examples of mentally puerile Anarchic Blasphemism displayed by the general public might be: firstly, the Muscovite Pussy Riot of 2012 involving the public desecration of a Russian Orthodox place of worship; secondly, the caricature in popular publications of values that are sacred to some, such as the French Charlie Hebdo satirical portrayals of, among many ideological absurdities, the Muslim Prophet Muhammad, both before the atrocity at the offices of the publication in Paris in January 2015 and just afterwards; and thirdly, the annual Islamic attacks in Britain on the institution of Remembrance Day, and the physical assaults that target its supporters. There are many more examples of the confusion of the right to free speech with the right and appropriateness of response, and the confusion around those arguments is yet another example of the

## Introduction – What This Book is About

hopelessness of humanity, and is beyond any further comment or judgement in this book.

Dissidence therefore, does not necessarily equate to moral right or integrity, but it will be obvious to anyone who studies, with a truly open mind, the complete spectrum of both the mainstream status quo and its opposing activism, wherein lie the stony ideological refuges, in the lank shadow of which lurk the real practitioners of violence and suppression of free thought.

In the virulent world of ideology, some profess opposition to oppression whilst being the real hate practitioners, and some who are accused of oppression are themselves the oppressed. All professed dissidents need to ask themselves whether they are true to the spirit of dissidence, or whether they are merely nurturing a seed for a future ideology that will itself spawn dissent.

*– This book is dedicated to victims of poor or malicious leadership and judgement, everywhere and everywhen. Autumn 2015.*

# 6 Historical Scope and Granularity – Volume One
## 6.1 Introduction

Although this volume deals mainly with the common era, in order to put our present-day existence into an historical context, we begin with a brief description of mainly recent palaeoecological changes and go on to describe an island – Britain – with no border controls, an island that became more and more accessible from about 12,000 years ago. It is suggested that significant numbers of early migrants arrived by sea, those arrivals being part of an enormous loosely integrated though diverse group of Atlantic and Mediterranean coastal cultures – an ancient people of the Atlantic seaboard and elsewhere. Similarly styled Megaliths, burial chambers, and standing stones, that stretch from the Baltic via the Atlantic islands, of which the British Isles are just one part, around the French and Spanish coastlines, and via the Mediterranean Balearic Isles, Corsica and Sardinia, and many more islands en route to the Middle East, are suggestive of a continuity that is likely to be more than 10,000 years old.

All known arrivals up to the Norman Conquest in 1066 AD, the last successful armed invasion of Britain, are covered, and there is a detailed chapter covering subsequent waves of contrived immigration, both ethnically and quantitatively, that at the start of the 3$^{rd}$ millennium are causing cultural and demographic changes on a scale and at a rate that has never been seen anywhere in any of the world's recorded peacetime history.

Reference is made to the interpretation of the results of some DNA studies that suggest Britain's gene pool up to the 3$^{rd}$ millennium has been virtually unchanged for some 8,000 years or so, and that relatively recent arrivals due to racially inclusive invasions, such as Roman, Anglo-Saxon, Germanic, Nordic, and Norman, have made little difference. Differences due to non-racially inclusive Asian and African invasions remain to be quantified.

Such studies are complex and subject to interpretation, and it would be interesting to see how the facts and opinions change during the 3$^{rd}$ millennium.

## Historical Scope and Granularity – Volume One

The historical scope and focal points of this part of the book were originally determined by whatever seemed necessary:

- To characterise and resolve present-day British and Western Democracy.
- To reveal, and to then clarify the development of governance by the state.
- To identify the times at which the State may have departed from an obviously benevolent role.
- To examine notable examples of the State's opposition by the general public.
- To search for warnings from history.

Although the many tribal groups and cultures identified in the following chapters are variously accepted as fact, myth or legend, and a balanced view of the likely truth can only be formed by reference to many sources, fanciful or otherwise, by historical tradition, the above bullet-points can be related to two quite separate, but coincident events.

Firstly, the empowerment of Egbert King of Wessex (AD 802 to 839), the Sovereign of the Royal House of Wessex who was known as the first *Bretwalda* or Ruler of Britain – Britain then being really England and not the British Isles – and secondly, the emergence of the short-lived united continental European empire of Charlemagne, King of the Franks and Emperor of the Romans, who was crowned in 800 AD.

Charlemagne, the Franks, and the Holy Roman Empire are covered in depth in Volume Two, and the first part of Volume One is concerned with British developments.

(Note: "Holy Roman Empire" and "Holy Roman Emperor" may both be abbreviated HRE in future, but the full expression will be used in any event if the context is not clear.)

That start point of circa 800 AD referred to above, however, has been blurred way back to include the arrival of the progenitors of the Wessex Dynasty and their Saxon peers, and also to include one or two early British historians whose writings should not be overlooked. Consideration of some interesting theories concerning the cultural identification of an even earlier arrival of ancestors of the so-called Ancient Britons are postponed to the chapter titled *British Tribes at the End of the Iron Age – Fact or Fiction?* Those theories propose that Phoenicians, and their contemporaries the Trojans, settled in the British Isles about three millennia ago.

Even before any of these possible human arrivals, however, we should acknowledge the physical development, the conquest, and the settlement of our Island that goes back very much further – before the last glaciation that blanketed most of our green and pleasant land in a shroud of white, life-defying and omnipotent climatic censorship – and so, moving back further in time, the next section starts from the point that we currently believe to be the very beginning of human history.

## 6.2 Three Million Years of Humanity

Archaeological names and ages in literature differ according to an author's nationality and geographic area, but also widely among compatible academic sources for no single reason that could be determined, so this section contains an averaged definition for the ages; it's one that seems to fit most descriptions for Britain and western Europe, although it is compiled from several sources, and there is more variation in dates and ages as we go further back in time.

The three divisions within the oldest interval of interest here, the Palaeolithic or Old Stone Age, that started anywhere from 2.5 to 3.5 million years ago (MYA), are as follows:

### 6.2.1 The Lower Palaeolithic – Started circa 3 MYA

Roughly coincident with the start of the Pleistocene Epoch, typically dated from 2.6 MYA, the oldest level of the Palaeolithic is characterised by the emergence of simple stone tools, and this formative age ended about 120,000 years ago after a duration of possibly two or three million years. It may have included the peak age of Neanderthal man, and as described below, it certainly included the beginning of the current Ice Age that technically persists to the present day, having seen several glaciations. See Volume Two.

### 6.2.2 The Middle Palaeolithic – Started circa 0.1 MYA

Starting around 100,000 years ago, the presence of Neanderthal man continued into the Middle Palaeolithic, built from the earlier age, but that version of humanity probably declined during this period of the Old Stone Age that ended about 40,000 years ago. Given uncertainties, and ongoing finds of fossils and artefacts, the Middle Palaeolithic may stretch back well over one hundred thousand years.

### 6.2.3 The Upper Palaeolithic – Started circa 0.05 MYA

At some time during the last 50,000 years the emergence of modern man, Homo Sapiens, was complete - certainly by about 12,000 years ago - although "modern" humans, of whatever sub-species, may have been indulging in acts such as cooking food and using tools, that distinguished them from apes, for 200,000 years, or as far back as the Lower Palaeolithic.

### 6.2.4 Missing Links

Attempts to classify the *Homo* genus in imaginative sub-species, and to link those sub-species with earlier types of hominin genus on the basis of the discovery of just a few fossils and remains, and to then proceed with the introduction of unsubstantiated and contentious theories of human origin and spread based on similarly sparse evidence, are a frivolous academic indulgence that has become a cultural and political weapon. It is, however, a weapon that is of increasingly questionable utility in light of new discoveries as the vastnesses of Siberia, China, and Alaska, with other central Asian and far eastern regions, become more accessible after centuries of archaeological denial and academic neglect.

We can say with certainty that several varieties of human beings, including our own, appeared on the scene at various times during the Pleistocene Epoch, but by the beginning of the current post-glacial Holocene Epoch, that is defined to have begun about 12,000 years ago during the Upper Palaeolithic Age, only our own *Homo Sapiens* remained.

We are therefore, primarily creatures of the Holocene Epoch, from the beginning of which time we see significant megalithic constructions raised, but beyond that very little is certain at the start of the 3rd millennium AD.

## 6.3 Key Events in the British Isles – Palaeolithic and Later

It is important to acknowledge that the present-day Scottish, Welsh, and Irish, identify their own tribal history and Monarchs, and although there is much commonality with the English, there is also a world of parallel development and heritage deserving of dedicated volumes.

An overview of the possible development of humanity that most regions of the British Isles hold in common is as follows, and it is advisable to pause to consider the magnitude and the significance of the potential events of success and failure; of happiness, and of unimaginable trauma, that must have been experienced during each long interval of just one of the many thousands of years. There are approximately fifty human generations in each one thousand year interval, and there is a mixture of acknowledged speculation, and recorded fact, concerning all the dramas that have played out during this epic history, throughout both volumes of this book:

- The first hominins arrived in Britain about 1,000,000 years ago. Some now say as much as 2,000,000 or even earlier.
- Neanderthal settlements were well established 200,000 years ago; they didn't happen overnight, but their origins are obscure.
- The most recent glaciation – the Devensian – began about 100,000 years ago.
- There is solid evidence of the first modern humans, Cro-Magnon Man, one of which, Homo sapiens, appeared in northern Europe circa BC 40,000 to 30,000. Cro-Magnon Man is a loose term for "modern humans", and does not connote a single species – they may well have been around many millennia before this date of 40,000 BC. The subject is currently undergoing change and confusion, with names for "modern humans" such as Homo-sapien neanderthalensis, Homo-sapien Cro-Magnonensis, and Homo-sapien-sapien.
- The Palaeolithic aka Old Stone Age is said to have ended circa 12,000 BC, and Neanderthal Man is assumed to have either

become extinct or to have been absorbed by inter-breeding with other species of Cro-Magnon Man, some time before then.

- The Late Palaeolithic, aka Early Stone Age, is said to have begun circa 10500 BC.
- The end of the most recent glaciation, circa 10,000 BC, was the start of the Holocene Epoch.
- The Mesolithic, aka Middle Stone Age, began circa 9000 BC.
- The arrival into Britain of the first tribes of the Holocene Epoch is placed circa 8500 BC, though sea level changes may have hidden evidence for other earlier migrants.
- Britain became separated from the European mainland just before 6000 BC when Doggerland was inundated, and several land bridges among England, Scotland, Wales, and Ireland were lost.
- The Neolithic aka New Stone Age began circa 5000 BC.
- Evidence of farming appears in Britain between BC 5000 and 4500.
- Accelerating trade, cultural exchanges, and migrant arrivals are noted circa 4000 BC.
- The Bronze Age began in Britain circa 2500 BC.
- The Bronze Age Collapse circa BC 1200 to 1000 (see below) may well have been partly responsible for the rise of Britain and the West, an ascendancy that arguably continued unabated into the 20th century AD.
- The Consolidation of Ancient British Tribes lasted from circa 1000 BC to 43 AD.
- The Roman Invasion and its Collapse defined the period AD 43 to 410.
- The Dark Age of reputed British anarchy and cowardice, and of Scot and Pict predation lasted from circa AD 410 to 495.
- The Germanic, Nordic, and Norman Invasions, enlivened the years from AD 495 to 1200.

- The Emergence of Modern England, and its Parliamentary and Judicial Systems, covered the period from the 13th Century to the Present.
- Cultural expulsions of the Jews for instance, and religious dissident arrivals, such as Protestants, were spread across the 13th to the 17th centuries.
- The English Civil War: Issues began in 1625 AD, War was declared in 1642 AD, English King Charles I was executed in 1649 AD, and the Restoration of the Monarchy took place in 1660 AD.
- Many Wars and World Wars were spread across the entire 2nd millennium, and into the third, from 1000 AD to the present without end.
- The British Empire and Commonwealth is defined to have begun in the year 1497 AD.
- The Collapse of the British Empire and Commonwealth took place from 1945 to 1997 at the behest of the victorious World War Two allies.
- The Multicultural Invasion, and the painful and costly Conversion of Britain, began in 1950 and continues with increasing vigour today.
- Glaciated and undemocratic Governance exists today, driven largely by ignorant and bigoted parliamentarians and lackeys.

## 6.4 Ethno–Cultural Timeline – the Last Ten Thousand Years

Although the interpretation of cultural and dynastic periods is to some extent subjective, an overview might be as follows:

| | |
|---|---|
| Ancient Britons | 8500 BC to 1000 AD |
| Roman Britain | 55 BC to 410 AD |
| Anglo-Saxon Period | AD 519 to 1066 |
| Viking Incursions | 700 to 1100 |
| Norman Conquest Period | 1066 to 1154 |
| Modern Britons Complete | circa 1200 |
| Plantagenet Period | 1154 to 1485 |
| Tudor Period | 1485 to 1603 |
| Elizabethan Era | 1558 to 1603 |
| Stuart Period | 1603 to 1714 |
| Jacobean Era | 1603 to 1625 |
| Caroline Era | 1625 to 1649 |
| The Interregnum | 1649 to 1660 |
| Restoration Era | 1660 to 1685 |
| Georgian Era | 1714 to 1830 |
| (Regency Period | 1811 to 1820) |
| Victorian Era | 1837 to 1901 |
| Edwardian Era | 1901 to 1910 |
| World War I | 1914 to 1918 |
| Inter-war Period | 1918 to 1939 |
| World War II | 1939 to 1945 |
| Modern Britain | 1945 to Present |

## 7 Environmental Milestones

Most of the detail in this book that covers the years before the Palaeolithic Age is contained in Volume Two, but the most recent three million years that incorporate the development of our ancestors – known as hominins – are briefly put into a more distant planetary context below.

### 7.1 Pangea and Dinosaurs, One Ice Age and Many Glaciations

The most recent Ice Age started about 2.58 MYA, and may well last another 100 million years. It's the fourth or fifth Ice Age that we know about in the current incarnation of the earth's tectonic plates during the last 500 million years, the super-continent Pangea having commenced its breakup into the continents of today around 200 MYA. It was the Mesozoic Era, starting 250 and ending 65 MYA, with its periods named Triassic, Jurassic, and Cretaceous that saw the evolution and destruction of the dinosaurs, creatures that straddled the continental diaspora that emanated from Pangea to form the distribution of tectonic plates that we see today.

Tectonic plates are largely recycled every 500 million years or so, and we have little idea how many ice ages may have occurred since the earth's creation about 4,500 MYA, during which time much of the earth's crust has been repeatedly digested and regurgitated along with any evidence. There are portions of the earth's lithosphere known as cratons that are up to four billion years old, and that have survived the subduction and destruction process. They are enormously strong and thick cores, or islands of rock that have been around since the Archaean Aeon (see Volume Two), but their only legacy to the present day is chemical and mineral, most famously diamonds.

Just before the onset of the present 500 million year period, it is estimated that the Snowball Earth period of complete glaciation occurred around 600 MYA, and the oldest symmetrically bodied fossils date back to about that time, although the very oldest fossils have been dated to about 3,500 MYA in the Archaean Aeon, the time when Stromatolites were responsible for changing the world's atmosphere to a relatively oxygen-rich mixture that would favour the development of life as we know it today, but that would spell a toxic extinction for many anaerobic life-forms.

Notwithstanding the above, since Greenland and Antarctica still have colossal ice deposits, logic tells us that the last ice age is still officially in force, and that within an ice age there are many advances and retreats of the ice, and many short-term climatic cycles with their attendant phases of warming and cooling, and variable atmospheric carbon content. Neither were the Snowball earth period, nor a complete change of atmospheric gas, in any way the responsibility of mankind; and just one volcanic eruption can, does, and will continue to negate the futile remedial efforts of decades of New World Order legislation, sympathetic job creation, and taxation.

## 7.2 Human Habitation

The British Isles were first inhabited almost 1,000,000 years ago by early humans, the evidence for that early habitation being revealed by artefacts found very recently (~2009) in East Anglia, and there have been several glacial cycles within the current ice age that would have kept those primitives creeping northwards after the retreating ice face and across newly revealed tundra, and then retreating south again, over and over, in the face of prehistoric climate change. Pretty frustrating if you could take a long term view, but at least they didn't have to face an iniquitous carbon tax and the bizarre notion of actually trading and profiteering from a deprecated attribute. See the sub-section *Carbon Credit Trading* in the chapter titled *Financial, Political, and Media Hegemony*.

There is evidence of Neanderthal human settlement in decorated caves in Derbyshire, England as recently as 45,000 years, although as noted earlier, Neanderthal man may be as old as 200,000 years. Some of the best, and most thought-provoking presentations of information on this subject can be found on the websites of the *Ancient History Of Britain* (AHOB) project.

DNA evidence suggests that modern humans may have arrived in Britain as early as 25,000 years ago, but since that time glacial movements have caused sea level oscillations of around 120 metres or 400 feet, and the significance of this change is two-fold. Firstly, much evidence of coastal settlements – a likely first foothold of the earliest migrants – will have been destroyed, and secondly, there would have been significant cyclical land bridges not only between modern-day France and England, but also from Ireland to Scotland, and possibly from Ireland to other Welsh and English promontories, thus changing totally the coastal potential and attraction for settlement and communication. This contention is supported by discoveries publicised as recently as 2012 concerning the discovery (below present-day sea level) of an 8,000-year-old boat-building complex in the Solent, Hampshire.

## 7.3 Glaciation Ends But the Ice Age Continues

The most recent covering of ice within the glaciations of the current ice age, as localised to Britain, is known as the Devensian Glaciation; other geographic areas on a global scale have other names for the same period, but our ice sheet reached its maximum extent approximately on a line joining Bristol and London about 18,000 years ago. From 14,000 to 13,000 years ago there was a warm period known as the Windermere Interstadial which no doubt caught out some optimistic migrants, because it was followed by another cold stadial called the Loch Lomond Advance that started possibly as quickly as within a decade, lasted an apocalyptic 1,300 years, and ended virtually instantaneously in a decade or so. That most recent icing, or stadial, ended about 11,650 years ago, and since then the world has experienced generally increasing warmth during the current Global Interstadial or Holocene Epoch, although some of the Lake District, and parts of Scotland north of the Clyde were still iced as recently as about 10,000 years ago.

It's likely that the warm Atlantic Gulf Stream would have helped defrost the Western Isles and the Orkneys so that they and their surrounding sea-routes would have been well clear by that time – the start of the Mesolithic. It is Greenland ice cores that have enabled changes over the last 20,000 to 30,000 years to be dated with such precision.

Looking at the artist's impression map below, we can only wonder at the significance of the river delta that may have formed the gulf at the head of the present-day English Channel where the confluence of many rivers would have united many scattered early settlements throughout a physically open and possibly culturally homogeneous Doggerland of northern Europe.

If we consider that the Rhine and the Thames were just two of many rivers that flowed into the gulf from two water sheds, one either side of the land bridge that was present as a result of lower sea levels during the most recent glaciation, then it becomes apparent that the geographic range and the opportunities for the communication of trade and ideas were immense.

That entire region would later be inundated, and would become submerged by hundreds of feet of water by about 6000 BC, leaving only the smallest evidence of human presence in the form of usually small artefacts dredged up in the nets of the fishermen of today, and that is as much as we know at the end of the 2nd millennium, though advances in marine archaeology may hopefully add to that record in the future.

## Environmental Milestones

### 7.3.1 Map – A Possibly United Northern Europe circa 10,000 BC

The massive estuary that would later become the English Channel was once a funnel for any inshore sailor-adventurers that were running before the presumed prevailing south-westerly winds. With sea levels hundreds of feet lower than those of today, the combination of south coast white cliffs with their abundant flint deposits, and the colossal delta formed by the several rivers of which the mighty Rhine and Thames were just a part, must have been an awesome location for social and commercial exchanges.

Map from http://commons.wikimedia.org/wiki/Category:Maps released under CC-BY-SA
http://creativecommons.org/licenses/by-sa/3.0/

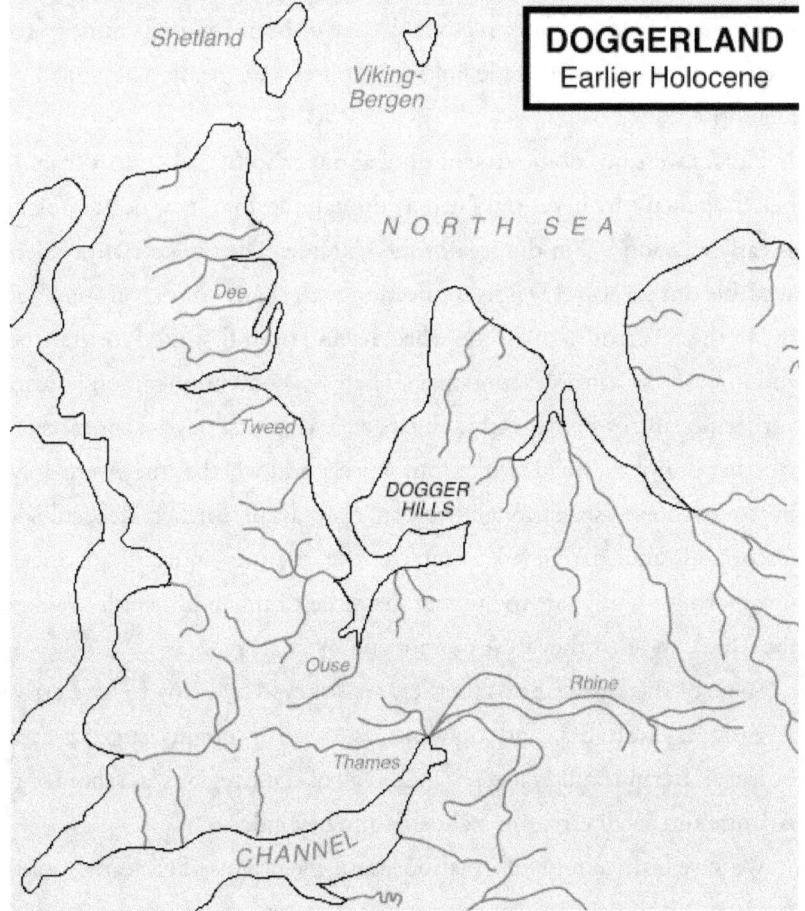

## 8 Early Ethnocultural Migration and Archaeological Horizons
## 8.1 The Earliest People – A People With No Name

So the Holocene that's been with us for about 12,000 years has seen the ice retreat, and the arrival of diverse tribes that intermingled to eventually form a landscape of Ancient Britons. These tribes would have been nomadic hunter gatherers and fishermen, and possibly exiles, adventurers, and restless misfits from a wide area. With the exception of the Doggerland inundation, geography for the most part doesn't change in the short term, and tribal movements are only restricted by wide oceanic barriers, so the earliest dispersal mechanisms among the continents of the northern hemisphere might quite reasonably have been re-used during later migrations, especially if trade links and routes were being maintained and memorised.

Horses were not domesticated until about 2500 BC, as evident from the Bell Beaker culture in central Europe, though this may have begun possibly as early as 4000 BC in the area of the Ukraine. The only certain evidence available during 2015 AD is in connection with chariot burials around 2000 BC in the Siberian steppes, the wheel having been first used for transport about 3500 BC in Mesopotamia. There is contention among various authorities as to whether early vehicles were chariots, wagons, or carts, and whether or not they had two or four wheels, and whether they were drawn by ox or horse; so although we can only await further archaeological discoveries and dating to complete the picture concerning wheeled transport, it is fairly safe to say that the earliest human dispersals pre-dated the wheel, and that they were on foot and by boat.

Some of the earliest British settlers are believed by many to have arrived as early as 8500 BC, and opinions as to their origins suggest Spain, Portugal, Ireland, and France, or indeed all of these regions, as sailors of the Atlantic and Mediterranean seaboards and beyond.

We have little certain information about the origins of the earliest of the Ancient Britons, either in terms of tribal sources, or in terms of dates. All that can be determined are the dates of any enduring archaeological remains, and interpretations of the geographic spread of any common

## Early Ethnocultural Migration and Archaeological Horizons

cultural characteristics, such as pottery styles, burial traditions, and megaliths. From that geographic spread we might infer a degree of ethnic or tribal relationship and similarity, though not identity.

In 2007, carbon dated evidence indicated Mesolithic habitation of Orkney around 7000 BC, and Maeshowe, a large grass covered stone chamber constructed about 2700 BC, impressive enough in its present form, is now thought to be built on the site of an even earlier stone circle; we can only guess the real antiquity of the site, though Maeshowe is reminiscent of Newgrange in Ireland that was built about 3200 BC.

In spite of the temptation to imagine trekkers, dragging their meagre possessions across harsh, trackless wastes, and pushing back the frontiers as was seen during the 17th to 19th centuries (AD) in the New World and Africa, it is very likely that the Mediterranean, Atlantic seaboard, and the enormous network of navigable continental rivers, provided the transport – concurrent maritime mechanisms – for the movements of both people and ideas during the Mesolithic period (circa BC 8000 to 5000), just as they did millennia later for the Celts – whoever the Celts were. See later cautions concerning this word.

DNA studies suggest arrivals into Ireland about 7300 BC of a people from the Iberian (Spanish) region, and it is only reasonable to suppose that they came by sea.

Some historians suggest a catchment area for proto-Britons, that includes all of present-day Europe, the Phoenician states in the eastern Mediterranean, and the southern shores of the Mediterranean, while Dr. Stephen Oppenheimer, a professor of genetics at Oxford University, states categorically that the British derive from a former ice-age refuge in the Basque country.

The perspective of the map below has been altered by inverting it to deconstruct our usual perception of the British Isles as being out on a limb. It emphasises the continuity of the sea lanes and intricate coastal havens from the Baltic and Orkney to the African side of the Straits of Gibraltar; and into and around the entire Mediterranean shoreline. As shown on the subsequent map, the immense coastal water highway is augmented and segmented by short-cuts that are facilitated by an even longer network of principal rivers. A chapter covering pre-Celtic history in Barry Cunliffe's book *The Celts* is explicit on some of these points. Archaeological excavations of prehistoric boats reveal fish hooks of a size that was larger than that required for just river fish, and which date back to the Mesolithic. Those maritime excavations are compelling evidence that our ancestors did not remain on land or were only river bound for 8,000 years. They suggest that the fishermen ventured out to sea as part of an interactive culture that traded tin, copper, gold, salt, and luxury goods etc.; a culture that was widespread along the Atlantic coast thousands of years before the Celts or the Romans arrived.

The Tin Islands for instance, are identified on some versions of Herodotus' map from about 450 BC, see Volume Two, and from their location, those Tin Islands are suggestive of the British Isles, although there are other references to a possibly separate island group named the Cassiterides. Given the duration, and the geographic spread, of the implicitly tin-based Bronze Age, and the age of maritime artefacts found from Iberia to the North Sea, together with diverse historical writings, it is likely that there was more than one region producing tin and lead, well over two millennia ago, and stretching from Iberia, via now lost coastal regions of the Bay of Biscay, such as the ancient Loire estuary, to at least the coasts of Cornwall.

In its entirety, the shallow European continental shelf, much of which would have been exposed 12,000 years ago, certainly holds much historical record, from Dogger Bank and the Solent to southern Spain, but what of the coastline of Africa?

We know of early settlements by variants of the *homo* genus in Morocco 160,000 years ago, and we know of the fabrication of decorative beads from seashells 80,000 years ago, also in Morocco, but there is an inconceivable gap before we see the Phoenicians trading there around 4,000 years ago. Sadly this may be a result of real climate change that desiccated enormous regions particularly within the tropics of Cancer and Capricorn around 4000 BC, creating deserts and a perfect sand-blasting climate to erase all organic remains, and virtually all but buried remains; even those being rendered yet more obscure by shifting sands and rising seas.

No doubt time, the abstract mystery that has been responsible for the concealment of our origins, may in future provide some answers, but the anthropological hiatus that occurred a few millennia BC, and the absence of definite archaeological remains of any western European cultures earlier than megalithic times, have orphaned us in the sense of our being denied a feeling of identity through a well-defined and comforting long heritage before Romano-British times. It might be argued that such a dearth of verifiable roots has inclined us as individuals to the dubious mercies of ideology, and that it has condemned us as a society to the psychology of adolescence until our species matures some more.

For now, it might be informative to indulge in some constructive speculation, and to picture the situation at the southernmost point of Spain 12,000 years ago – a culture and people with acceptably robust and at least inshore sea-going vessels. There would have been complete freedom, and a right to roam in a world with few if any borders. Standing on the prow of what then would have seemed a modern and reliable craft, and with the inscrutable and limitless Atlantic in front of us, and an intricate but ultimately circular and climatically uniform coastline of the Mediterranean inside the Pillars of Hercules behind us, liberty was total, although even in remote times, several millennia BC, there may already have been increasing tribal congestion and a likelihood of conflict over the best natural resources.

What wonders, freedom, and mystique must therefore have been suggested to upwardly mobile tribal groups by the extremes of climate on our right (northwards) and on our left (to the south)? Consider the diversity of fish, coastal variety, and natural harbours with so many river accesses to the interior, that stretched for two thousand miles to the north. Consider temperate forest and seasonal variety just inland of the often crenellated coast to the north of the entrance to the Mediterranean, and past the Pyrenean ridge into the Bay of Biscay, and beyond to the myriad islands of the peninsulas that would eventually become the British Isles after the loss of Doggerland.

If we now look to the south, the contrast is stark. Beyond the westernmost territory of Senegal, we see tropical jungle and a miasma of mangrove swamp that covers about half of the western African coastline across a region that is centred on the equatorial Gulf of Guinea that stretches north and south of present-day Nigeria. Outside of that region, which also contains just about all the principal river estuaries of West Africa, much of the coastline is inhospitable desert, and over all is a relatively tiny continental shelf, and a seasonal endowment of a dry one and a wet one.

It's no wonder that there was, and still is, a huge ethnocultural frontier between Europe and Africa in the west, despite the narrowness of the Straits of Gibraltar.

Moving eastwards into the Mediterranean, and along its southern shore, it would take the lubrication and mediation of the river Nile to encourage significant cultural exchanges via Arabs and Egyptians with the black African interior, one undesirable consequence being the early development of slavery on a commercial scale by Arab merchants, who later would find wider receptive markets in Europe and the Americas.

The notion that the Atlantic ocean was an integral part of human migration may be supported by recent discoveries (2012 AD) in the U.S.A. of man-made tools of French flint, dating back 20,000 years, that are assumed to have been taken there by migrations of palaeolithic tribes at a time when the North Atlantic was frozen, and supply lines based on seal and sea-bird hunting along the southern extent of the ice sheet were possible between Europe and North America. Eskimo or Inuit cultures were quite content with such hardship until the benefits of U.S. commercialism and fast food arrived on their frozen doorstep as recently as two hundred years ago.

Starting circa 20,000 BC, and continuing during the gradual retreat of the ice sheet over the following millennia up to, and then, with likely increased numbers, after the start of the ice-free Holocene Epoch, settlers

## Early Ethnocultural Migration and Archaeological Horizons

would have been drawn north, and the benefits of sea travel would have been highlighted as the coastal and littoral features, and the marine harvest varied every spring. It seems entirely reasonable that each annual revelation of a northern addition to the approaching Holocene coastline that we know today, would have been a renewed stimulus for a land-rush of opportunists, as existing coastal settlements disappeared under rising sea levels, albeit at a slow and adaptable pace over several millennia. Under the effects of that slow inundation, coastal settlers would literally have just floated away to pastures new, and prevailing south-westerly winds would have encouraged a migration northwards, especially with craft that at that time most probably had no way of sailing to windward.

In southern Britain, the earliest evidence of human activity in the Stonehenge area of England dates back to wooden post holes circa 8000 BC – that's pretty close to the time when parts of England were still glaciated, and must presumably indicate one of the earliest settlements – though the settlers' identity remains unknown. Stonehenge itself is thought to have been constructed in phases beginning circa 3100 BC, and the people responsible at that later stage were well enough established to have links across southern England to Wales, where the blue stones were quarried at possibly several sites in the Preseli Hills of north Pembrokeshire. These people certainly pre-dated the Celts, who are understood to have arrived much later. A hardy seafaring race would have seen the task of transporting the huge blue stones (about 60 of them at 4 tons each) by sea from South Wales to one of the south coast ports, and thence as far upriver as possible, in a far different light to the way we puzzle over the issue today, and can only think in terms of wooden rollers over land. Apart from DNA evidence, we can only speculate about the identity of the first arrivals after the ice sheets receded. We do know however, that they had thousands of years in which to spread and establish demographic trends and cultures that would persist beyond their original identity.

### 8.1.1 Flint and Obsidian Distribution in Neolithic Times

It would be interesting to search for any correlation between the distribution of deposits of these minerals that provided the earliest tools, and the distribution of Neolithic settlements, but a detailed study is beyond the scope of this book. Briefly and simplistically:

Obsidian is found wherever there is volcanic activity, and its occurrence is independent of glacial action. This glass-like mineral, found on the surface, would therefore have favoured the concentration of early societies around the volcanoes of the temperate Mediterranean region.

Obsidian is known to have been traded widely across the Aegean islands and into the regions referred to as the Ancient Near East (ANE), and the ready availability of this easily crafted, glass-like material, in the midst of such navigable waters and myriad islands, may well have been one of the main drivers of early habitation. See the section on the Minoan civilisation in the chapter on the Ancient Greeks in Volume Two.

Flint and other forms of crystalline quartz are found in large concentrations particularly in Europe and North America. When glaciers retreat, nodules are often left behind, and due to continuous tidal action and their irregular shape, they tend to arrive higher up on beaches than other more uniformly shaped minerals.

A retreating glacier face was the very condition to be found 12,000 years ago across southern Britain and northern Europe, and flint nodules are found in prodigious quantity throughout Cretaceous chalk cliffs – notably those of the English Channel and southern England – and, significantly, also along the southern shores of the Baltic Sea; the seaside playground of tribes whose descendants would later migrate in large numbers to a future British island after the inundation of Doggerland.

As referred to earlier, the white cliffs near the ancient delta made up by the confluence of the Rhine, Thames, and other European rivers would have been of immense stature at the time of the Doggerland bridge, and the brilliant white chalk would have been a beacon of that precious resource – again in the midst of an easily navigable network of rivers and coastlines.

*Early Ethnocultural Migration and Archaeological Horizons*

As will be seen below, the ancient Amber Trade began in that seaside playground on the southern shores of the Baltic Sea, and one can imagine early hunter-gatherers looking for flints, and being attracted by the totally different qualities of amber deposits.

**8.1.2 Map – Inverted Europe to Emphasise Oceanic Continuity**

So much of the continental shelf would have been exposed 15,000 years ago, that it is difficult to comprehend the limitless marine harvest, and boundless rent-free living space. Britain at that time was joined to continental Europe, and there were probably land bridges among many of the islands of ancient Albion, creating a haven of causewayed refuges. Significant parts of the medium grey area on the map below (the continental shelf) would have been dry land. The British Isles are to the right of the centre of the map, and the leg of Italy is to the left. The Strait of Gibraltar is at the top edge, slightly left of centre. It is suggested that an Atlantic bounty of free land and a limitless marine harvest would have been an irresistible lure to the peoples of the Mediterranean world.

Map Google Earth

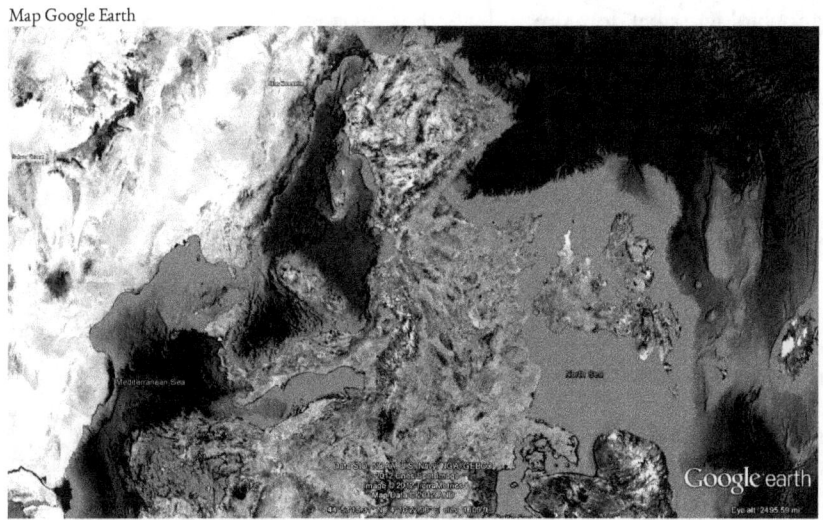

### 8.1.3 European Rivers – Global Glue

When we look, too, at the length and the route of the river Danube for instance, 1,780 miles from the heart of Europe to the Black Sea, we have to marvel at the number of modern states through which it passes, with all their ethnicities and socio-political variants. The Danube was there long before any emergence of statehood, yet it hosts so many, and it might be deduced that far from being of utility for just a state boundary, it may well have been a magnet for migration, settlement, and spin-off settlements since people first developed the boat, before which a safe and timely traversal of such long distances would have been far more challenging.

In their entirety the integral network of European rivers form obvious short-cuts for commerce, such as the several routes taken by the ancient Amber Trade from the Baltic to the Mediterranean, and for the transfer of knowledge among the many and convoluted coastal settlements. It is interesting to speculate on the significance of the differing importance of rivers with respect to whether a river forms just a present-day national frontier, or whether it passes through what might be the heartland of a much older tribal domain; and whether anything can be deduced from that when set alongside records of known political treaties and settlements that were made following international conflicts. See the section on the origins of the Magyars in Volume Two.

Although rivers as geographical barriers are naturally inferior to high mountain ranges or seas, they would nevertheless afford some defensible barrier, and they would have the long term benefits of being a powerful catalyst inviting interaction and of regulating a manageable détente and rapprochement that can only begin during peacetime.

The Danube was a perfect example of this when, as an initial frontier between Roman and Germanic empires of the early 1$^{st}$ millennium AD, it was also the interface across which the Goths and other barbarians would later supplant the failing Western Roman Empire – initially as *foederati*. See later chapters for examples of the *foederati* status that was bestowed when treaties of support for the Roman Empire were signed by "outside" tribes.

*Early Ethnocultural Migration and Archaeological Horizons*

The Don (1,212 miles) and the mighty Volga (2,294 miles) rivers transported Scandinavians thousands of miles beyond their frozen heartlands to the Black and Caspian Seas respectively, and those waterways conditioned the early demographics of the Caucasus that is rivalled only by the Balkans and the Middle East for protracted and destructive ethnic unrest. In an earlier age the Danube would similarly have provided the Celts with a highway to and from the same vast seas to the south-east.

The map below illustrates the significance to the continent of Europe of its river network, that given its land area, is possibly unrivalled in terms of the sheer number of individual rivers and watersheds, and in respect of the directions of travel that were afforded to its ancient migrant populations.

### 8.1.3.1 Map – The Rivers of Europe

Map from European Commission Joint Research Centre - http://ccm.jrc.ec.europa.eu/php/index.php?action=view&id=23

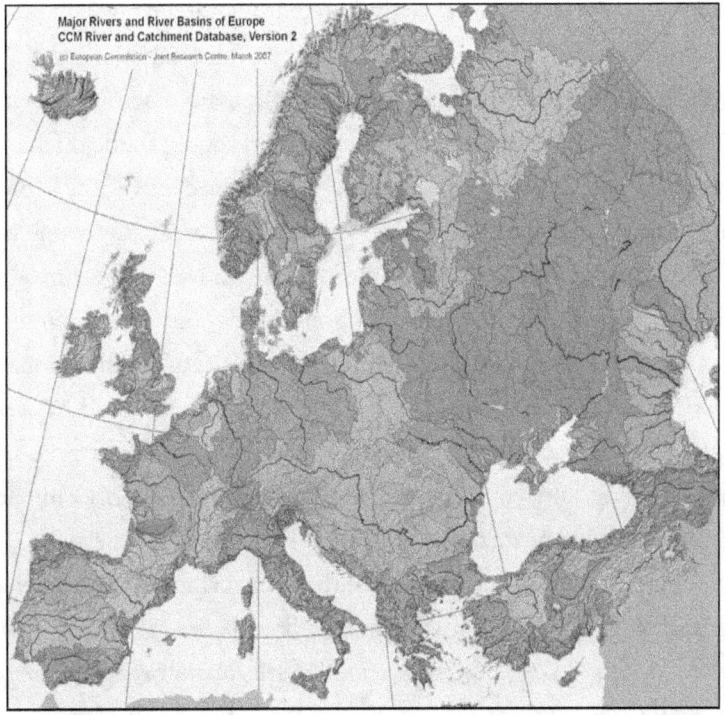

## 8.2 The Amber Trade – One of the Earliest Land Routes?

The amber trade must have had an effect on the migration of peoples in very early times, and the trade is believed to have started as much as 13,000 years ago, the largest deposits in the world being found in the area around Gdansk in Poland. The fossilised deposits of tree sap come from pine forests that were laid down as long ago as the Carboniferous Period, 300 MYA, but most commonly in a form that was suitable for jewellery use, from about 40 MYA. Amber workshops have been found dating back to the Neolithic Period, about 3000 BC, and fashioned goods have been found in remains from ancient Greece, Egypt, and Rome. One or more of these ancient Amber Road trade routes are believed to have been re-established during the latter part of the 1$^{st}$ millennium BC by the Celts after a decline, possibly due to fickle Greek fashions.

The routes, at least in their relatively recent revival, involved significant river commerce originating in the Baltic Sea and passing along the rivers Elbe, Oder, Vistula, Dnieper, and Danube, with many associated potential fabrication sites in Germany. Via connected land routes, traffic reached the Adriatic Sea and Rome, and the trade was taken over by the Romans during the ascendancy of the Roman Empire. This trade is just one more small facet that is indicative of commerce and travel that spanned the whole of Europe including parts of Scandinavia and Russia, and that demonstrates the free and knowledgeable movements of people as long ago as 5,000 years or more, carrying on a craft that even then could have been around for 8,000 years. We have to bear in mind these awesome time-spans when imagining and considering the so very slow, and discriminating migrations of our ancestors, the early peoples of Europe and beyond.

The amber trade is said to have been the principal form of commerce in imperishable goods between North and South. See *The Geographical Journal* Vol. 66, No. 6 (Dec., 1925), *Prehistoric Routes Between Northern Europe And Italy Defined By The Amber Trade*, by J.M. de Navarro.

The two maps on the next page indicate a close relationship between the two routes of human endeavour.

*Early Ethnocultural Migration and Archaeological Horizons*

## 8.2.1 Map – Lombard Migration From Scandinavia to Italy

Map from http://commons.wikimedia.org/wiki/Category:Maps released under CC-BY-SA
http://creativecommons.org/licenses/by-sa/3.0/

Early Ethnocultural Migration and Archaeological Horizons

## 8.2.2 Map – The Much Older Amber Trade Route

Map from http://commons.wikimedia.org/wiki/Category:Maps released under CC-BY-SA
http://creativecommons.org/licenses/by-sa/3.0/

*Early Ethnocultural Migration and Archaeological Horizons*

## 8.3 The Megalithic Folk 5000 BC – The Earliest Ocean Routes?

The distribution of early sea-borne peoples implied in the earlier sections covers much of the Mesolithic and Neolithic western world, including the larger Mediterranean islands such as Sicily, Corsica, and Majorca; and their megaliths provide the best identity for these otherwise unknown peoples. Their efforts and legacy are spread over thousands of years, and thousands of miles – a macro-achievement – and at a micro level their DNA is still with us today as described later.

Their probable technical achievements are worthy of note in connection with an overview of their arrival in the British Isles, and to do that we have to look to records from other historical civilisations that left behind written records. Much speculation is possible, but proof of a link between distant cultures and the Ancient British culture is harder to find. The attributes of megalithic structures is one possible link, particularly their spatial design. This can be examined in terms of orientation and dimensions; orientation is widely accepted now as being strongly tied to solar and lunar observations, and dimensions have more controversially been linked to the Megalithic Yard that is discussed in detail in Volume Two of this book.

The distribution of mankind around the coastlines of Europe, and probably throughout the river network at this early time is illustrated on the map below.

*Early Ethnocultural Migration and Archaeological Horizons*

## 8.3.1 Map – Coastal and River Spread of the Megalithic Culture

Map from http://commons.wikimedia.org/wiki/Category:Maps released under CC-BY-SA
http://creativecommons.org/licenses/by-sa/3.0/

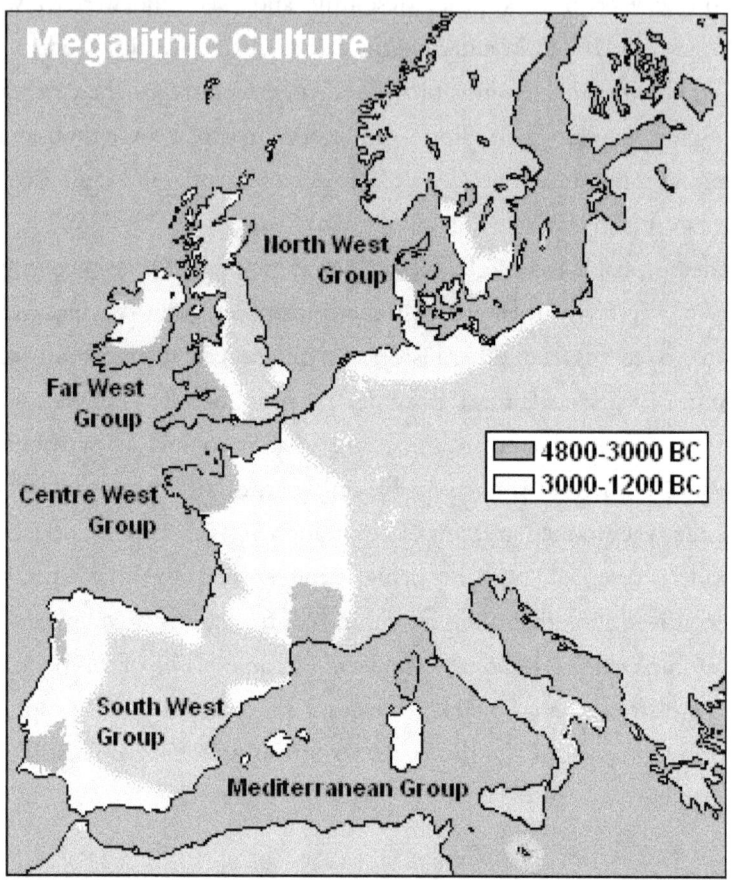

Corsica, Southern France, western areas of Spain, Brittany, and several coastal regions of the British Isles – notably the Southwest – possess apparently related megaliths from the earlier period, 4,800 to 3,000 BC.

The lighter areas indicate the later spread of that ancient and communicative culture that began some 7,000 years ago, while recent discoveries are pushing the beginnings back as far as 12,000 years ago or more.

## 8.4 Corded Ware Culture and Language Roots circa BC 2500

As nomadic ways of life gave way to more settled tenure of a given place, evidence of cultural characteristics in the form of buried remains became more persistently recorded in deliberate burials and middens, and it has been found convenient to use such characteristics to define way-points, or Archaeological Horizons during the course of social development, though it is important to bear in mind that there can be no implication of ethnic or tribal origins of a people from such artefact-related cosmetics and behaviour. Notwithstanding that caveat, one such metric that includes the British Isles within its scope, is the spread of Corded design work on pottery. There are other older Archaeological Horizons, such as the Cardial Culture, aka Impressed Ware Culture circa 6000 BC, and a Linear Pottery Culture circa 5000 BC, but although these two specific cultures reached the Atlantic, they are not as yet recorded in Britain.

The huge area covered by these implied cultural links stretches from the Dutch North Sea, through Scandinavia and the Baltic, as far east as the Volga river to the north of the Caspian Sea, and as far south as the Carpathian and Alps mountain ranges. There has been some detailed research in Poland and the Baltic states, and there are clear links between the Corded Ware and Beaker Cultures, though perhaps the only inference that can reliably be made, is reinforcement of the concept of well-established and protracted communication of ideas and trade commodities over enormous distances at this very early period; and given the ingress of seas and rivers, it is highly likely that such trade routes would have included the territories along the Atlantic seaboard, including Britain. The area covered by this culture is considered to overlap, in the eastern parts, the region that sourced the earliest forms of Indo-European language, from which came the following ten language roots:

- Celtic – the British Isles, Spain, France, and Europe as far as central Turkey.
- Germanic – England, Scandinavia, and Central Europe to as far as the Black Sea.

- Italic – Italy, Portugal, Spain, France, and Romania.
- Balto-Slavic – Baltic: Latvia and Lithuania. Slavic: eastern Europe, Belarus, Ukraine, and Russia.
- Balkan – The Balkans and western Turkey.
- Hellenic – Greece, the Aegean Islands, and Mediterranean coastal lands as a result of Alexander the Great.
- Anatolian – Anatolia, Asia Minor, and Turkey.
- Armenian – Armenia and eastern Turkey.
- Indo-Iranian – Iran, Kurdish Iraq, Turkey, India, Pakistan, and Afghanistan.
- Tocharian – The Tarim Basin of Xinjiang in western China.

There is, of course, nothing to link the evolution of Indo-European languages with the specific Corded Ware and Beaker Cultures, but the coincidence of such an extensive geographical range of connected peoples, and the imperative to communicate at least for purposes of trade at this time, would support the idea that culture and possibly language can spread without necessarily involving a whole-scale migration of peoples.

*Early Ethnocultural Migration and Archaeological Horizons*

## 8.4.1 Map – The Possible Spread of Indo-European Languages

Map from http://commons.wikimedia.org/wiki/Category:Maps released under CC-BY-SA
http://creativecommons.org/licenses/by-sa/3.0/

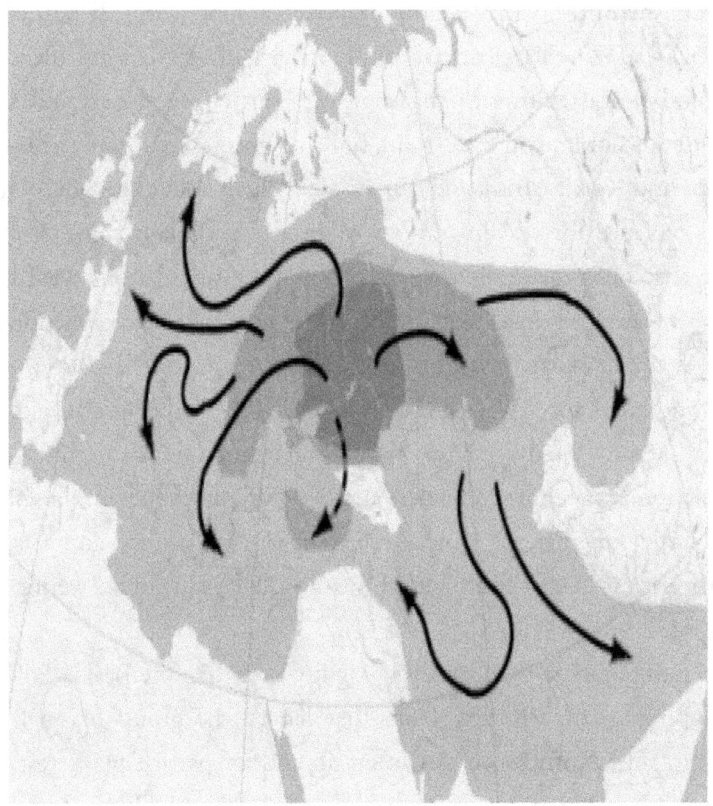

## 8.5 The Beaker Folk BC 2800 to 1800, and Normanton Down

One of the earliest known named people (named by historians that is) to arrive in the British Isles were the Beaker Folk, more correctly termed Bell-Beaker Folk. Whether an actual people arrived, or whether just the style of commodity and culture of that time was carried by traders and simply imported is not known for certain, but something was spread throughout Europe and North Africa, and it arrived in Britain about 2000 BC. There is some evidence for real migrations of people, although some historians argue that only culture is transferred and that populations were largely stable by the Iron Age. Regardless of opinion, the Beaker phenomenon indisputably happened well before the Iron Age, and its practitioners are real contenders for a place among our ancestors. Other useful questions would be: how many arrived as a percentage of the existing indigenous population at the time; and where and how did they mix with those earlier inhabitants of ancient Albion. Ongoing DNA studies and futuristic improvements in that field may be the most likely way of answering those questions.

Contemporary with, or possibly slightly later than the Beaker Folk were developments on Salisbury Plain that led to the group of earthworks known as the Normanton Down group and, of particular interest, Bush Barrow. Excavated at various times since circa 1800 AD, intricate gold and amber objects have been unearthed that alone defy the suggestions that the people of the time were uncultured barbarians.

## 8.6 The Urnfield Culture BC 1200 to 800

People of the Urnfield culture (circa 1000 BC) of the late Bronze Age derived from the Beaker Culture and preceded the Celts with whom they overlapped in time and geography. They were characterised by cremation of the dead, internment of ashes in urns, and by the adoption of tumuli that came into use during the Middle Bronze Age, circa 1600 BC. Their characteristics could easily be viewed as Celtic or at least proto-Celtic and, while of great interest in terms of European cultural history, their wider significance is tiny compared to global cultural diversity that existed even at this early period.

It is a sad reflection that such diversity with distinctness of local character should become, after many millennia of evolution, abhorred and opposed by the liberal eugenicists of the late 2nd and early 3rd millennia AD, for whom so-called multiculturalism and bland uniformity are an ideal.

## 8.7 The Bronze Age Collapse circa 1200 BC

The Bronze Age in Britain had started circa 2000 BC and it saw both development and destruction on a large scale. Opinion varies concerning the distribution and chains of events, though there is evidence of all imaginable negative influences, ranging from natural catastrophes, such as volcanoes and earthquakes, to civil conflict within, and invasion from without. Interactive cultures had already existed for millennia, and it may well be that colonial and subsequent ex-colonial dynamics, along with regime change, were at play even then, in much the same way as the symptoms that we see nowadays in connection with the collapse of infrastructure and the growth of dysfunctionality throughout Africa and the Middle East, and the subsequent transfer of that dysfunctionality back into the imploding imperial European sources by immigration.

From whatever source, much of the destruction occurred around the eastern Mediterranean from Egypt to northern Anatolia in present-day Turkey where the Hittite empire was centred, then further on into the region between the Black Sea and the Caspian Sea where the Maykop Culture had existed since possibly 4000 BC, and eastwards through Mesopotamia – mostly present-day Iraq. Sea-going bandits and pirates were responsible for much inter-racial conflict, and two Aegean islands, Crete and Cyprus, are cited by some as pirate bases. As a group, these piratical nuisances, wherever they were based, are referred to as Sea Peoples, but they were almost certainly not just one racial group. Additionally, the causes of the Bronze Age Collapse may well have involved a hiatus in trade or a recession, to be expected as a consequence of widespread piracy anyway, and if so, such a loss of trade and peaceful contact would have at the very least given the collapse added momentum.

## 8.8 The Legend of Brutus 1100 BC

Brutus, the great-grandson of the Trojan warrior Aeneas, is said by Nennius in his book *Historia Brittonum*, and by others (see below chapter *British Tribes at the End of the Iron Age – Fact or Fiction?*), to have come to Britain circa 1100 BC and named the land after himself. He is also reputed to have driven out the Picts, implying that the Picts were here much earlier than the time suggested by other documentary evidence. Much, though not all of Nennius' writings are relegated by modern historians to the rank of myth, and one might say therefore that the Brutus theory has been selectively rubbished because it doesn't fit. See also the works of Gerald of Wales and modern writers such as the respected W. M. Flinders Petrie F.R.S. for more possibly balanced detail and opinion.

## 8.9 The Picts 1000 BC

It's very difficult to know where to put the Picts in this introduction, because although the earliest written evidence of named Picts is from Roman references in the 3$^{rd}$ and 4$^{th}$ Centuries AD, there was, as alluded to above, already an identifiable people and culture in Scotland, or in the vernacular, Alba, long before that, and those Albans and the early Hibernians across the seas to the west were certainly distinct from the Celts, whoever the Celts may be.

The Picts are said to have been spread throughout Ireland which is believed to have been a more local source of migrant waves, and they may have arrived as early as 1000 BC; if so, they retained their identity for nearly 2,000 years, being ultimately just absorbed by the Irish and the Scots, and by the Anglo-Saxons during the 9$^{th}$ century AD. The Picts have been referred to as *Cruithni* by their contemporaries throughout the islands and regions of the British Isles, and until that eventual, perhaps inevitable absorption, they were possibly the most rebellious and furious force ever to migrate into the region.

Spread throughout central Scotland and into the islands, this early people, who spoke a non-Indo-European language, employed original and distinctive art forms that were used for body decoration and that were also cut into rocks as animal shapes and spirals, and worked into metal. Such art-forms are also found throughout Spain, France, and Ireland – not forgetting the Basque country. Later, the Picts appear to have adopted Celtic culture and art-forms which complicate the picture even more.

Unusually in Britain, the Picts were a matrilinear society, where entitlement to the crown passed through the bloodline of the mother, and this alone sets them apart from most other tribal groups. Orkney Islanders were specifically acknowledged as a seafaring race by the Romans, and the Pictish navy was renowned for its attacks against the Roman forces of occupation.

According to *The History of the Kingdom of Ireland* by Nathaniel Crouch, aka Richard Burton, circa 1640 to 1725, who was an English bookseller, publisher and writer with a shop in London:

> "... [Some time after the death of St. Patrick around 490 AD] ... Next, the five sons of Dela from Greece came hither, and utterly routed the giants, being before weakened by their own dissension, and then divided the country into five provinces, as they are at this day, fixing a stone in the midst of the country, to make the division more equal; but at length ambition prevailing, one of these sons, named Slanius, subdued his other brethren, and reigned alone, but was interrupted in his new dominion by an army of Scythians, who invaded the land, and after them the Britons, and then the Scots under Gathelus, as is afore-mentioned, came from Spain, and fixed here, reigning a great while in peace, till the Picts came thither out of Scythia under Roderick, being accidentally cast ashore upon those coasts, who were brought before the king of Ireland, to whom Roderick thus spake ... Scythians we are, even Picts of Scythia...".

Crouch was not recognised as an historian, but as a bookseller he would have had access to many more original and antiquarian tomes than are in circulation today, but the fact that he wrote for a non-academic audience has been used to disparage his work. It's difficult to know whether to take his writings as legend or at least partially factual.

Towards the end of the Roman occupation, the Picts of Scotland were more precisely identified as two tribes – northern highlander Caledonians and the southern Maetae. Their fate is covered later.

## 8.10 Map – Diverse Cultures in a Global Context 1000 BC

Map from http://commons.wikimedia.org/wiki/Category:Maps released under CC-BY-SA
http://creativecommons.org/licenses/by-sa/3.0/
Author: Thomas Lessman

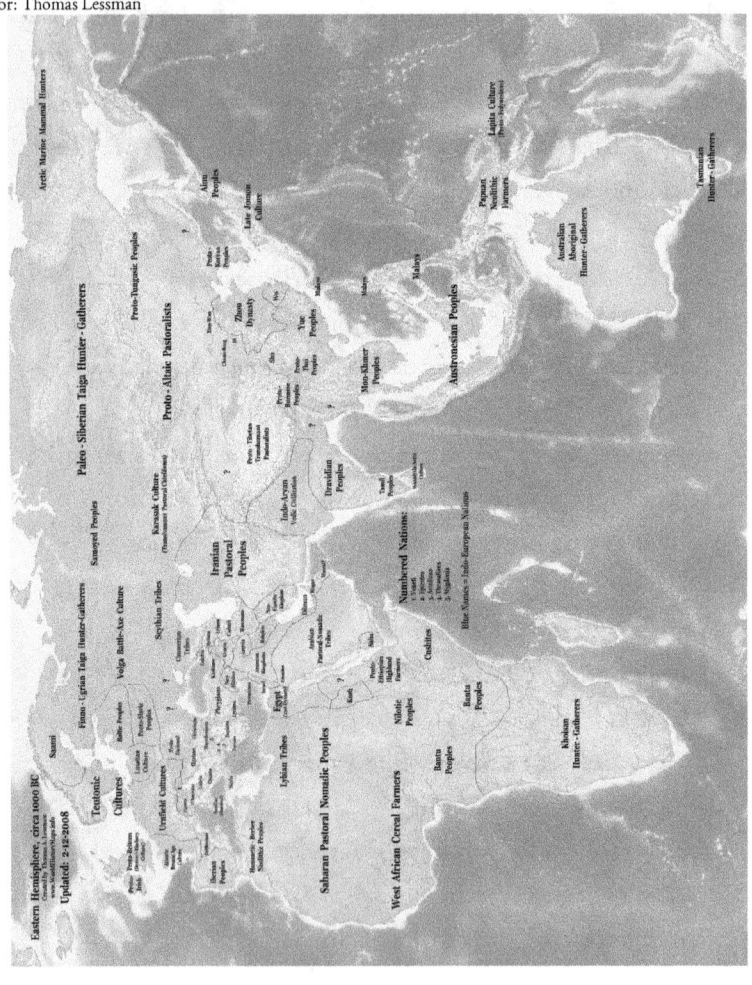

## 8.11 The Celts 1000 BC

The word Celt is without doubt a catch-all for many diverse peoples. Celtic peoples of the present day can be only loosely modelled on the Celts of the 1st millennium BC, even if DNA indicates a relationship. We do not know for certain what racial or cultural traits they had, and their contemporary Gauls may or may not be the same people.

Celts, Gauls, and "Barbarians" were all pretty much the same to the Romans despite their tribal diversity; and pedigree was of no consequence. Conquest and the allocation of *Civitas* and later *Foederatus* status was the imperative.

Since the subject of the Celts is contentious to some, and romantically revered by many, and since the Britons at the time of the Roman Conquest were most certainly Celtic by nature and heritage, in order to gain confidence in whatever precise interpretation we put on that phrase, it is advisable to spend some time to establish whatever reliable facts we can that might lead to verification and further investigation. In addition to the following selective and attributable detail, there is an almost endless potential for further Celtic studies in the form of the history of tribal developments along the waterways and ancient highways of the whole of Europe during the two millennia BC, but in any event, and without doubt, the Celtic empire is a substantial part of British ancestry.

Therefore, the word Celt will be used throughout this book as if it is a given fact, and it is hoped that no outrage is caused to the romantic or the academic. Julius Caesar's *De Bello Gallico and Commentaries*, will give a flavour of contemporary Roman opinion, and several other books in the bibliography, and other sources on the internet may be cross-referenced by the reader.

### 8.11.1 Celtic Domination of Europe

The Celts dominated Europe during the Iron Age (circa 800 BC to 43 AD), having their origins circa 1200 BC at the end of the Bronze Age, just before the emergence of the *Hallstatt Culture* in a region stretching from present-day Austria to the Czech Republic – exactly at the headwaters of some of Europe's biggest rivers – the Elbe, Oder, and principally the

Danube. There was a second Celtic upsurge in 450 BC known as the *La Tène Culture* in the region of present-day Switzerland – also at headwaters – in this case the Rhine and the Danube. It is surely of significance, and no coincidence, that the newly emergent dominant cultures in these regions had links via navigable waterways to the, even then, ancient civilisations on the Atlantic, Baltic, and Mediterranean.

It must be noted that there is some disagreement among historians about the degree of integration of diverse Celtic tribes in respect of both language and culture, and some academics maintain that not all tribal members of the *La Tène* and *Hallstatt* cultures and their derivatives were truly Celtic. For the purposes of this book such differentiation is out of scope, though note that the British, Irish, and Brittany forms of the Celtic language are termed Insular, and they are alive to this day, whereas the variants in the rest of the Celtic empire are termed Continental and they are all now dead languages. These aspects are expanded later.

In 475 BC the Celts defeated the non-Indo-European Etruscans at the Ticino river in the Po valley, Italy. Unfortunately the Etruscan soothsayers known as *Augurs* that watched bird patterns obviously missed that one. In 390 BC the Celts defeated an Indo-European Rome, that also misused their Augurs, and in 279 BC they defeated the Greeks. These were not just one-off Pagan on Pagan battles, the Romans and Greeks received a severe and repeated pasting for a while. At the height of their power, circa 300 BC, settlements were established as far away as Poland, the Ukraine, and historic Galatia in the central plains of Turkey. Their prowess, but also their beastly behaviour as perceived by the civilised Romans and Greeks, is documented by many writers of the ancient world, and a short list of the more well-known historical writers, Greek and Roman, that refer to either the Celts or just the world of the Celts at the time is given in Volume Two as an overview, and as a key to further reading. Some long dead authors' words are now represented only by fragments, but there are nevertheless many full and voluminous texts freely available via the internet, and links are provided. See the chapter in Volume One titled *Internet Index of References and Other Downloads*.

*Early Ethnocultural Migration and Archaeological Horizons*

### 8.11.2 Celtic Linguistics

Apart from enduring cultural art-forms, the only absolutes concerning the Celts are linguistic characteristics, and they can be fairly scientifically described.

Celtic linguistic characteristics fall into two broad categories, and a deeper analysis of their syntactic and semantic commonalities, coupled with their distribution and persistence supports belief about the movement of peoples. See references for further detail on this complex subject, but briefly, the two categories are as follows.

### 8.11.2.1 Insular Extant – British Isles and Brittany

Goidelic languages: Irish, Manx, and Scottish Gaelic.

Brythonic languages: Breton, Cornish, and Welsh.

### 8.11.2.2 Continental Extinct (by circa 4$^{th}$ Century AD) – Europe

Celtiberian: Northern Spain.

Gaulish: Much of Europe and as far as Galatia in Turkey.

### 8.11.3 Non-Celts

One particular instance of oft-suggested Celtic manifestation needs to be dismissed. This involves the so-called Celtic Mummies or Cherchen Men found in Xinjiang, China who were certainly not Celts. They may well have the physical appearance and tartan sartorial elegance of imagined Scottish or Celtic tribes, but they pre-date what we conventionally assume to be the Celts by as much as one or two thousand years. Some of the mummies date from circa 1800 BC and have Caucasian features, and the fact that possibly western settlers should be found so far east at such an ancient time is no less intriguing and possibly more so, since the further back in time we go, the less credence or respect we generally give in terms of sophistication and mobility. To put it another way, the more primitive we consider the people to have been, the more likely we are to regard them in a patronising way as Noble Savages, just what some Greeks and Romans did in their time to the Celts. These Tarim mummies are now believed to be of the Indo-European Tocharian peoples who were eventually driven out of the Xinjiang province of China by about 800 AD by the Uyghurs. Closely identified with the Yuezhi people, who were also Indo-Europeans, the

Tocharians / Yuezhi arrived in north-west India about 30 AD and are believed to have formed the Kushan Empire that included the area of present-day Kashmir, where to this day there are many uncharacteristically fair skinned people of uncertain pedigree. A mystery indeed, and exactly where these racially European people originally came from, and how they got thousands of miles from their likely homeland is not known. Though not Celts, they may well have had a common ancestor; some suggest the Scythians, a name associated by some with early migration to Britain, and some suggest other peoples of the Persian region. It may be that wider DNA studies over the next several decades will solve these fascinating unknowns.

In fact, possibly co-incident with the Celtic expansion, there was an outpouring of marauders from a region stretching east and north of the Black Sea as far as the Russian Steppes. Among this group were the Scythians (8$^{th}$ century BC to 2$^{nd}$ century AD) and the Sarmatians (5$^{th}$ century BC to 4$^{th}$ century AD), with at least the Scythians being mentioned in various historical chronicles about arrivals in ancient Britain. Romantic representations of Picts, Celts, Scythians, and Sarmatians, all similarly dressed, and all armed to the teeth for Armageddon abound on the internet, and there are clear associations among these similar yet diverse peoples in the minds of many amateur historians of today.

As indicated in later chapters in Volume Two about the empires from the Asian Steppes and the Chinese borders, the Tarim Basin is far to the east of European regions, and is presently part of China's Xinjiang province, with borders among several present-day principalities, such as Kazakhstan, Tibet, and India. The almost 4,000-year-old presence in these regions of Caucasian people challenges much of what we normally assume about our ancestors and their possibly near relatives.

*Early Ethnocultural Migration and Archaeological Horizons*

## 8.11.3.1 Photograph of a Tarim Basin Mummy

Photo – Sir Marc Aurel Stein 1914

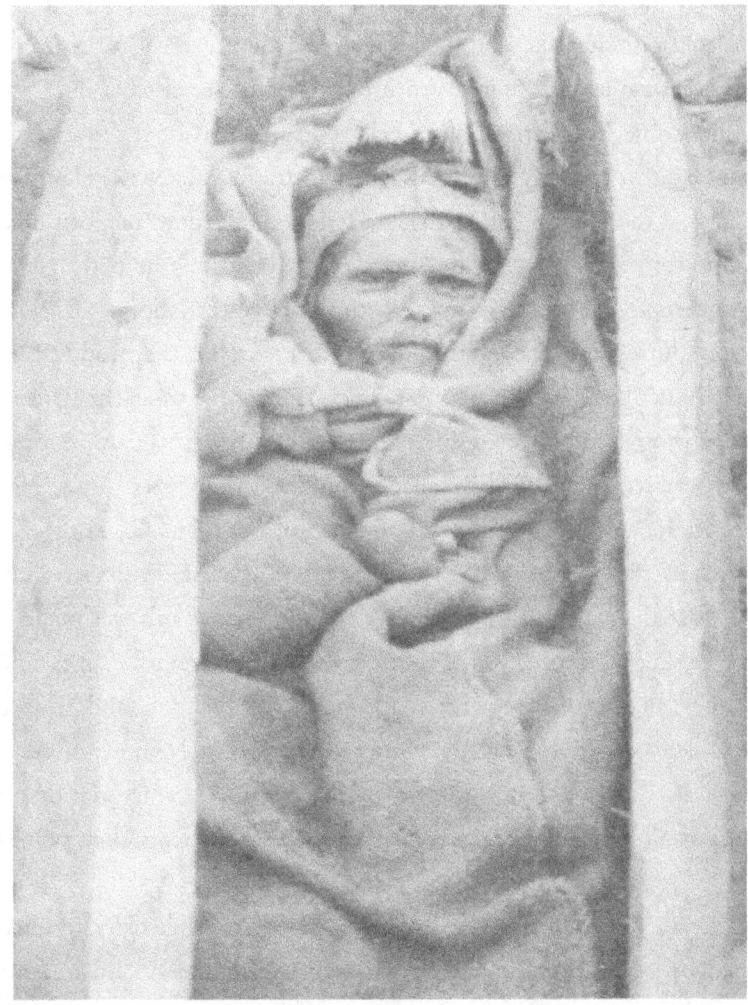

### 8.11.4 A Celtic Conclusion

As a single identifiable culture or civilisation, the Celts were frequently in trouble for pan-European ideological alliances and advances that the Romans just did not like, and such was a pretext for Caesar's initial attempt at invasion or at least a punitive venture against Britain in 55 BC. This was a year after some British tribes were believed to have assisted the sea-faring Veneti Gauls of Brittany to resist Roman aggression. Likewise, Hannibal's invasions of the Roman sphere that started in 218 BC drew in albeit mixed support from a range of Celtic and Gallic tribes while he had to battle many others to gain passage from North Africa to the Rhone valley. That invasion during the Second Punic War between Carthage and Rome, started in the Iberian peninsula after which Hannibal crossed the Pyrénées, passing through the Celtic-Gallic lands on his way to the Alps for the surprise attack on the Romans from the north. So, after initial confrontations between Hannibal and mainly southern Gauls they had formed a partial alliance circa 218 BC, and it was about 160 years later, circa 55 BC, that the agreement between Celts and Veneti Gauls was made – a considerable period of possible Celtic co-operation against Rome. There was, after all, the common Roman enemy throughout, and it seems reasonable to believe that offshore Celts and continental Gauls would have had at least some small notion of common cultural identity and destiny. We just don't have any written records of such affinity from their point of view.

By the end of the Iron Age when the Celts as a possible federation were decidedly past their best, many of the 20 or so tribes in Britain were well enough differentiated to strongly identify with local tribal names such as Boadicea's Iceni, but to acknowledge a common cause just didn't seem within their grasp. Maybe they were content with identity at a tribal level, or maybe they had already experienced confederation followed by divisive devolution, such as the many yet to come worldwide in later centuries, and didn't like the idea at the very time that lasting unity was needed.

It was the Romans who left the most substantial written records, and they wanted revenge on the barbarians at whose hands they had suffered in previous centuries. Hence, and this is only one of many pan-European scenarios of Roman atrocity, we see recorded in the British context by the Romans themselves, the persecution and massacres of Druids that happened under the Roman butcher Suetonius Paulinus – cause alone for some serious early British dissent. The further vile abuse of the family of Boadicea by the Romans, and the Britons' tragic failure in their attempts at revenge compare with desecrations throughout the Gallic and Slavic lands during World War Two at the hands of the 20th century dictators, but they are beyond the scope of this text.

**Epitaph**: a tragic-heroic, at least virtual, federation, that was ultimately doomed by its own querulous nature that really does add credibility to the aphorism *"united we stand, divided we fall"*. Assuming we accept Roman accounts of course.

*Early Ethnocultural Migration and Archaeological Horizons*

## 8.11.5 Map – The Lands of the Celts circa 3rd Century BC

Map from https://en.wikipedia.org/wiki/ Category: File released under the terms of the GNU Free Documentation License

**Key:**

X = Maximum Celtic expansion by the 270s BC – The British isles, much of continental Europe, and central Anatolia (present day Turkey)

The six commonly-recognised 'Celtic nations' which remained Celtic speaking throughout the Middle Ages are: Brittany, Wales, Cornwall, Isle of Man, Ireland, and Scotland.

Areas that remain Celtic-speaking today are confined to the extremities of those six regions, and are shown as the darkest tone on the above map.

## 9 British Tribes at the End of the Iron Age – Fact or Fiction?

The table below represents the scope and character of the tribes of the British Isles at the beginning of the 1st millennium AD, see also maps in the next chapter. Those tribes were documented, according to widely held present-day belief, only by the Romans, and such a latinised account rendered by the victors must be regarded with whatever objectivity we may choose to credit them, given the barbarous and vengeful treatment dished out to so many of their victims who had resisted military occupation during the Roman hegemony. These civilised Romans were a people that had razed and ploughed the city of Carthage and then salted the ground so that nothing would grow, and who cut off the hands of defeated Gauls. The inglorious nature of the Romans of both their Eastern and Western Empires will become apparent in subsequent chapters when, for example, it will be seen that half of their emperors died of unnatural causes, most commonly assassination by their peers, and where mutilation by blinding, and the cutting off of noses and ears was commonplace.

Concerning the accuracy of historical record, Roman cartographers did indeed make some gross mistakes in the relative positioning of some of the regions of Wales, England, Ireland, and Scotland, and some of their categorisations of tribes cannot be verified at all. So much so, that there is a view by some historians that confused and erroneous inferences may have been made by both the Romans and their Greek predecessors in respect of the names, and concerning the principal characteristics, of both suggested confederations and individual tribes. One example is that the Belgae may have been an alliance of some sort, and not a specific tribe. So the information we have must be regarded as a best estimate.

There is however, much richness in the *Matters* of the regions (see the section titled *The Dark Ages – Who Says?*), and inclusion of the true magnificence of Welsh and Irish-Scottish history, and a discussion of whether it is just legend or fact, is beyond the scope of this book. Except that is, to make reference to one manuscript that is rarely aired, and never part of British History curricula in our schools. That manuscript is known as Jesus College MS LXI. A relatively recent translation of this obscure manuscript exists as a more easily-read parallel of Geoffrey of Monmouth's *Chronicle of the Early Britons*. Other versions of such a British Prehistory appear under the name *Brut Tysilio*, and in works by Gildas and Nennius; and the whole subject is enmeshed in historiographic uncertainties and academic contention around the *Brutus* theory of the settlement of the British Isles some three or four millennia ago. See the chapter in Volume One titled *Internet Index of References and Other Downloads*.

If it is a true proposition that both MS LXI and Geoffrey of Monmouth's books, that also appear under the names *Historia Regum Britanniae* and *The History of the Kings of Britain*, derive from an earlier factual source, then not just the root, but the whole of British culture and the perception of our heritage is infinitely more interesting than merely impersonal, opaque, and mute, ages of stone, bronze, and iron. Furthermore, the imputation by many historians that the Romans were the first people of real significance, and that their British predecessors were just barbarians with no real pedigree, would be proven to be a blatant rewriting of history for reasons that can only be described as ideological and academic sloth. It may be that the real answer lies somewhere between these extremes. The reader is directed to recent DNA research referred to in the section titled *DNA Studies*, and to the implications in the chapter on the origins of the Greeks in Volume Two.

A reading of William Cooper's relatively brief *Chronicle of the Early Britons* including its compelling footnotes concerning geographic and other synchronisms is highly recommended, along with a paper titled *Neglected British History* by W. M. Flinders Petrie F.R.S.

In addition to the two renowned Roman historians Titus Livius aka Livy who wrote in the early 1st century AD, and Claudius Ptolemaeus aka Ptolemy who wrote during the middle of the 2nd century AD, there was a Greek named Pytheas of Massalia who is believed to have visited the British Isles during the 4th century BC. He was later referred to by yet another Greek historian, Diodorus Siculus, who wrote circa the middle of the 1st century BC; but even before that, as referred to in the chapter titled *The Earliest People – A People With No Name*, the Greek Herodotus wrote

*British Tribes at the End of the Iron Age – Fact or Fiction?*

circa 445 BC referring to the British Isles as the Tin Islands or, contentiously, as the Cassiterides.

Yet another fascinating theory concerning the development if not the origin of British tribes however, relates to evidence for trade links with, and cultural influences from the Phoenicians, who are accepted by just about all historians as having visited these shores around the 5th century BC. Further detail is beyond the current scope and the reader is recommended to view the online book with its challenging but compelling theories:
http://www.jrbooksonline.com/pob/pob_toc.html

## 9.1 Table – British Tribes at the End of the Iron Age

| Region | Tribe | Synopsis |
|---|---|---|
| Caledonia | Caereni | Mentioned by Ptolemy, but not much more known. They were possibly sheep farmers of the remote north-west corner of Scotland, Sutherland. Possibly closely linked with their similar named neighbours Carnonacae and Creones. |
| Caledonia | Caledonii | A Roman catch-all name for many tribes beyond their normal campaign reach. Described as extremely hardy and red-haired, some may have been Pictish. |
| Caledonia | Carnonacae | See Caereni. |
| Caledonia | Cornovii | Known to Ptolemy, they were centred in the remote north around Caithness, and may have been Pictish. |
| Caledonia | Creones | See Caereni. |
| Caledonia | Decantae | Mentioned only briefly by Ptolemy, they are believed to have inhabited the firths of Moray and Cromerty. |
| Caledonia | Epidii | Possibly related to the Damnonii, they occupied islands and regions west of the Clyde estuary. |
| Caledonia | Lugi | Mentioned by Ptolemy, but not much more known, they are believed to have been located in the region of the Moray Firth. |
| Caledonia | Smertae | Mentioned by Ptolemy, they were located in the far north, just below the northernmost tribe, the Cornovii, in Sutherland. |
| Caledonia | Taexali | Beyond Antonine's Wall in the Grampians, not much is known. |
| Caledonia | Vacomagi | Mentioned by Ptolemy, they were in the region of the river Spey, and may have been Pictish. |
| Caledonia | Venicones | Beyond Antonine's Wall in the Tayside region, not much is known, possibly Pictish. |

*British Tribes at the End of the Iron Age – Fact or Fiction?*

| Region | Tribe | Synopsis |
|---|---|---|
| Hibernia | Autini | aka Uaithni or Auteini, centred in western Ireland, they were known to Ptolemy. |
| Hibernia | Brigantes | Probably associated with the confederation just over the water, the Hibernian Brigantes were located in south-east Ireland. |
| Hibernia | Cauci | Mentioned by Ptolemy, it is interesting that along with their neighbours the Menapii, two similarly named tribes existed in Germany and Gaul. |
| Hibernia | Concani | Other than their inclusion on some maps, nothing is known. |
| Hibernia | Coriondi | In south-east Ireland, they may have been associated with similarly named tribes in both the southern and northern British mainland. |
| Hibernia | Darini | In north-eastern Ireland, they may have been associated with the tribes that populated Scotland. |
| Hibernia | Eblani | Located in the region of Dublin, probably between the rivers Boyne and Liffey. |
| Hibernia | Erdini | Mentioned by Ptolemy, but not much known, they are believed to have been located in the north-west around Donegal Bay. |
| Hibernia | Gangani | Mentioned by Ptolemy, a possibly ancient people located in the south-west around the river Shannon. There is a tribe with the same name in Wales. |
| Hibernia | Iverni | Mentioned by Ptolemy, they are thought by some to be very ancient early settlers of the island, and may have provided the basis for the name Hibernia. They are believed by others to be related to the Belgae of the British mainland and of the European continent. Both views may be valid. |
| Hibernia | Menapii | Indicated by Ptolemy as the earliest settlers of the Waterford region. |

| Region | Tribe | Synopsis |
|---|---|---|
| Hibernia | Nagnatae | Known to Ptolemy, they are believed to have occupied the counties Mayo, Sligo, and Fermanagh, stretching from the west, north-eastwards into Ulster. |
| Hibernia | Robogdii | In the north, they may have been synonymous with the Dal Riata who with others of the group known as *Scotti* went on to populate northern regions of Scotland. |
| Hibernia | Usdiae | aka Vodiae, aka Udiae, located in County Cork in Munster, they were known to Ptolemy, and believed to have been early settlers of the land. |
| Hibernia | Uterni | Southernmost coast and adjacent to the Iverni on maps, but no detail available. They may have been synonymous with the Iverni. |
| Hibernia | Velabri | Mentioned by Ptolemy, located in County Kerry in the far south-west. They are thought by some to be ancient relatives of some of the early settlers from Iberia. |
| Hibernia | Vennicnii | Possibly related to the Venicones, a tribe that may have arrived in Ireland from Fife, Tayside, and who were possibly Pictish. |
| Hibernia | Voluntii | Believed to have occupied the whole of Ulster at one time. Ptolemy's works suggest they are synonymous with the Ulaidh or Uluti from which the name Ulster is derived. |
| Middle England | Corieltavi / Coritani | Compliant association of tribes of livestock farmers. In pre-Roman times they minted their own coins at Lincoln and were later associated with Leicester. Hostilities concerning the Brigantes were common. |
| Middle England | Cornovii | In pre-Roman times they may have occupied the Wrekin Hill Fort, but other than sharing their name with a Caledonian tribe, not much is known. They were later centred at Wroxeter. |

*British Tribes at the End of the Iron Age – Fact or Fiction?*

| Region | Tribe | Synopsis |
|---|---|---|
| Middle England | Dobunni | A large pro-Roman tribe of the Cotswold area, and the regions to the north and west. They minted their own coins before the Roman invasion, and were wealthy agriculturalists. Initially centred at the Bagendon Hill Fort, they later had a capital at nearby Cirencester. |
| Northern England | Brigantes | A confederation of many tribes centred on the Pennines, but stretching into many of the present-day surrounding counties. Variously at peace and war with the Romans. |
| Northern England | Carvetii | Broke away from the Brigantes circa 100 AD to resume what was possibly an earlier independent existence. Settled around Carlisle. |
| Northern England | Parisi | Possibly related to the same named tribe in northern Gaul, they shared burial practices not found among other British tribes. Situated in east Yorkshire. |
| South-east England | Cantiaci | Capital at Canterbury, they had strong links with Gaul, and for a time were linked with the Trinovantes and the Catuvellauni. |
| South-east England | Catuvellauni | Associated for a period with the Trinovantes and Cantiaci in respect of much of their cultural domestic behaviour. They shared at one time a capital at Colchester, but their original centre was Saint Albans. |
| South-east England | Iceni | Wealthy, coin-minting people, initially indifferent to Roman rule, and centred at Thetford and Snettisham, East Anglia. Later collaboration with the Romans, a move to Norwich, and then subjugation, led to the famous uprising under Boudicca at the time that Roman forces were diverted to massacre the Druids of Mona. |

| Region | Tribe | Synopsis |
|---|---|---|
| South-east England | Trinovantes | Associated with the Catuvellauni and Cantiaci in respect of much of their cultural domestic behaviour. They shared at one time a capital at Colchester, becoming dominant there under Roman occupation. |
| Southern England | Atrebates | Powerful, and minting their own coins, they were associated with the continental Atrebates tribe in present-day Belgium. They were early clients of Rome and were instrumental in the causes of the Roman invasion of 43 AD under Claudius. |
| Southern England | Belgae | Imperfectly understood, they had a capital at Winchester, but may have been a confederation of tribes with similar cultural and linguistic traits to the Belgae on the continent. |
| Southern England | Regni | Imperfectly understood, they had a capital at Chichester, and may have been linked with the Atrebates. |
| Southern Scotland | Damnonii | Centred around Glasgow and Strathclyde, and beyond Hadrian's wall, little is known. |
| Southern Scotland | Novantae | Little known, they were probably sandwiched between the Picts and Romanised tribes to their south. Possibly located south of Strathclyde. |
| Southern Scotland | Selgovae | Further north than the Forth estuary and beyond Hadrian's wall, little is known. |
| Southern Scotland | Votadini | Occupying a region between Northumberland and the Forth around Edinburgh, they were probably a confederation of several tribes and distinct in several respects from other neighbouring tribes. Later becoming known as the Gododdin, they may have been in existence for more than a thousand years before the Roman invasion. |

*British Tribes at the End of the Iron Age – Fact or Fiction?*

| Region | Tribe | Synopsis |
|---|---|---|
| South-west England | Cornovii | Believed by some to be a member of the Dumnonii – see below. They were not identified by Ptolemy, but from other sources there is a suggestion that they may have had a fortress at Tintagel. |
| South-west England | Dumnonii | Possibly King Arthur's tribe. Capital Exeter, largely unaffected by Roman occupation. They were linked to Armorica, the province in Brittany that spoke the same dialect. During the later Saxon predations, many of the Dumnonii and their associated tribes fled to Armorica seeking refuge and taking with them the name that would become Bretagne or Brittany. |
| South-west England | Durotriges | Resisted Romanisation. They minted coins and had a capital at Dorchester, with several other hill fort centres. |
| Wales | Deceangli | Warlike tribe of north Wales and Anglesey aka Mona, they resisted the Romans, and as the centre of the Druid faith they were the victims of a massacre by the Romans under Gaius Suetonius Paulinus circa 60 AD. |
| Wales | Demetae | Relatively peaceful, they were an agricultural tribe based at Carmarthen. Strong links with the Bretons of Armorica. |
| Wales | Gangani | Warlike tribe of north-west Wales, they resisted the Romans. Associated with the Irish tribe of the same name. |
| Wales | Ordovices | Warlike tribe of west and mid Wales, they resisted the Romans. Associated with resistance under Caractacus, they were eventually pacified by Agricola circa 80 AD. |
| Wales | Silures | Furious resistance to Roman occupation, their centre was at Caerwent east of present-day Newport in Wales. |

# 10 The Western Roman Empire and Its Invasion of Britain
## 10.1 Early British Trade Links

Britain had been trading with various cultures in Europe since at least 500 BC, as suggested by the inclusion of the Tin Islands on some versions of Herodotus' maps at that time, but most likely in tin at least for an even longer time, possibly since circa 1500 BC according to some sources.

Other commodities, such as hunting dogs, jewellery, mineral resources, tools, and armaments, may have been traded in the wake of migrant movements since 10,000 BC or so, and the Romans were quite familiar with Britain as a trading nation. It was not a backwater of primitives.

There were three declared Roman initiatives to take control of Britain during a one hundred year period, and they are as follows:

- 55 BC Julius Caesar – inconclusive expeditions.
- 40 AD Caligula – abortive planning in Gaul, no invasion.
- 43 AD Claudius – Romanisation began.

When the Romans finally arrived in Britain in 43 AD they were surprised to find the British using chariots like those that had been developed in the Hallstatt and La Tène Celt societies hundreds of years previously. Yet academic wisdom and convention is that Britain at this time had no roads, and that the Romans built the Fosse Way, Watling Street, etc.

These roads connected long established British tribes that had existed for possibly thousands of years, and that in spite of the occasional punch up, probably over border disputes, cattle rustling and philandering, were very much inclined to agreements and alliances if not overall peace, though it has to be conceded that it was inter-tribal warfare that induced the treacherous Trinovantes of Essex to side with the Romans against the main British opposition, the Catuvellauni, during the first attempted Roman invasion in 55/54 BC. A wide infrastructure nevertheless suggests wide cooperation, and notwithstanding British tribal differences, much of the terminology for road technology and transport used by the Romans was not Latin but of Celtic origin – the word chariot, for instance, is derived

## The Western Roman Empire and Its Invasion of Britain

from the Celtic language of the Gauls – a bit of a give-away, and a slip-up by the Roman propaganda machine.

It is surely more likely that the Celts built the first roads throughout their comprehensive, yet loosely bound, pan-European confederation and, as said by some academics, that they taught the art of road building to the Romans, who may well have added to the technology, but certainly did not invent it. Celts pre-date Romans by roughly one thousand years.

Further evidence for the use of chariots and other road transport, on roads that must have been more than *"... slushy clay"* as some historians maintain, comes from both recent studies and historical narrative that puts the first wheeled carts at about 3500 BC and covering an area from the Atlantic Coast to the Caspian Sea. It is only reasonable to assume that during a period of possibly more than *three thousand years* the users of road transport would have done something to make their traffic smoother and faster; and in support of this, there is indisputable evidence of contrived improvements to human thoroughfares in the form of wooden-surfaced track-ways dating back six millennia in Somerset (the Sweet Track), and in ancient London (present-day Greenwich). Although believed to be mainly walkways, they demonstrate an adaptability and will to make progress.

### 10.2 Roman Influence on Britain

So, from loose commercial ties over many centuries, Britain became more directly affected (it was invaded!) during the last few decades of the Roman Republic, and the first 400 years or so, the heydays, of the Western Roman Empire. The previously self-reliant, rather loose, and sometimes turbulent confederation of British tribes was, like all Roman clients, drawn into prolonged international adventurism in general, and the supply of combatants and resources in support of the continuous conflicts of the ruling empire. When the Western Roman Empire collapsed however, Britain was left marginalised, softened, without much military will or strategic prowess of its own, and surrounded by some rather angry Scottish Picts, Irish Hibernians, Irish Scotti, and predatory pirates from Germanic and Nordic tribes that had been kept on the fringes of the Roman Empire for many decades. All these opponents of the now civilised British were, of course, still very streetwise.

## 10.3 The Rise and Fall of the Western Romans

A summary of Roman interference in British affairs would not be complete without at least a thumbnail overview of the three historical periods of overall Roman influence and authority in Europe.

The three phases of Roman ascendancy are:

- The Roman Monarchy (BC 753 to 508).
- The Roman Republic (BC 508 to 27).
- The Roman Empire (Western BC 27 to 480 AD, Eastern AD 285 to 1453).

From about 753 BC to 508 BC a series of kings comprised a Roman Monarchy about which very little written detail remains; this is partly due to the reputedly destructive ravages of the Gauls and Celtic peoples circa 390 BC, a time when commercial trade links with, and cultural awareness of the most distant western outposts of Europe would have been common. See later detail in Volume Two concerning the geographical reach of the Ancient Greeks and Phoenicians.

Beginning in about 508 BC, the period that was known as the Roman Republic was a time of much conflict, including expansion throughout Italy, and frequent civil and governmental treachery involving coup d'etat and assassination. Circa 390 BC, following a rapid recovery from the sacking of Rome by the Gallic Senones led by Brennus, there were successive wars with foreign cultures, such as the Samnite (southern Italian), the Pyrrhic (Greek), the Punic (Carthaginian), and the Gallic (French). These wars involved some of the best known and legendary but ultimately defeated leaders like Julius Caesar, Pyrrhus (with his Pyrrhic victories), Hannibal, and Vercingetorix. It was during the republic period that the enduring iconic and emblematic S.P.Q.R. logo appeared – **S**enatus **P**opulus**Q**ue **R**omanus meaning "The Senate and People of Rome".

## The Western Roman Empire and Its Invasion of Britain

The end of the Roman Republic began with a spate of foreign campaigns and internal rivalries around 100 BC, involving such well-known names as Pompey, Crassus, and Spartacus, and that peaked during the years 54 BC to 52 BC when, even by Roman standards, excessive governmental corruption and violence provoked Julius Caesar to cross the river Rubicon with a veteran army in 49 BC and put to flight the incumbent Pompey. To enter Rome at the head of an army, albeit unopposed, was considered illegal and intimidating. One of Julius Caesar's other achievements at this time was the destruction of the Great Library at Alexandria when he burned his own ships and unintentionally set the whole town ablaze in 48 BC.

Caesar now became a dictator, manipulating the Senate and changing laws to increase his personal power until he was assassinated in 44 BC by a group led by Gaius Cassius and Marcus Brutus, though this only prolonged the internal struggles until the suicide of Mark Anthony and Cleopatra VII in 31 BC, and the final emergence in 29 BC of Gaius Octavian.

The derivation of Octavian's full honorific name is worthy of note. He was born Gaius Octavius Thurinus, but was adopted as Gaius Julius Caesar in his uncle Julius Caesar's Will in 44 BC; he was finally proclaimed as the first Emperor in 27 BC – Gaius Julius Caesar Augustus – "Augustus" meaning "revered one" or "majestic". Augustus is an honorific title, not a name.

The emergence of the Augustus saw the start of 207 years of Roman Peace or *Pax Romana* when it is said that the Roman Empire expanded by relatively peaceful means. Those peaceful means included the invasion, subjugation, and indiscriminate murder of many Ancient Britons, the mitigation of which should possibly be a crime in itself, not unlike later controversies about the denial of genocide and Holocaust concerning the Jews, Armenians, and several other cultures of the 20th century.

It is convenient to divide the duration of the expansionist Roman Empire into periods as follows.

### 10.3.1 The Principate

From 27 BC to 284 AD the first period is characterised by the presentation of the State as a continuation of the Republic, the Senate retaining significant power. It started with Gaius Octavian (aka Augustus), and ended in a confusion of concurrent claimants, some of whom were baseless usurpers. This period was set entirely within the Western Empire, and the Eastern Empire had not yet been formalised.

### 10.3.2 The Dominate

Simpler to define, it began with Emperor Diocletian in 284 AD, and ended in 518 AD with Emperor Anastasius I. The Dominate was of a more monarchical character, with an increased number of Emperors and Caesars at the helm, and this period saw the split of empire, loss of the western part, and confirmation of Christianity as the state religion.

### 10.3.3 Corpus Juris Civilis

This period continued, solely and entirely, in the Eastern Empire from 518 with Emperor Justin I, ending in 867 with Emperor Michael III. The period saw the development of the Justinian Code of legal conventions and definitions that influenced legal practices throughout Europe, and to some extent, at least academically, down to the present day. It also promulgated laws imposing Christianity and proscribing paganism under pain of death.

### 10.3.4 Basilika

This period continued from 867 with legal system developments under Emperor Basil I and his successor Emperor Leo VI; it ended with the destruction of the Eastern Empire under Emperor Constantine XI in 1453. It was characterised by amendments to the Corpus Juris Civilis, by then written in Greek, and employed in order to accommodate historical developments that had occurred since Justinian's Code that had been originally written in Latin some 400 years earlier. This Basilika period relates entirely to the Eastern Empire, the Hellenisation of which was now complete, and the regime became truly known and characterised as the Byzantine Empire.

## 10.3.5 Map – Maximum Reach of the Empire Under Hadrian

Map from http://commons.wikimedia.org/wiki/Category:Maps released under CC-BY-SA
http://creativecommons.org/licenses/by-sa/3.0/

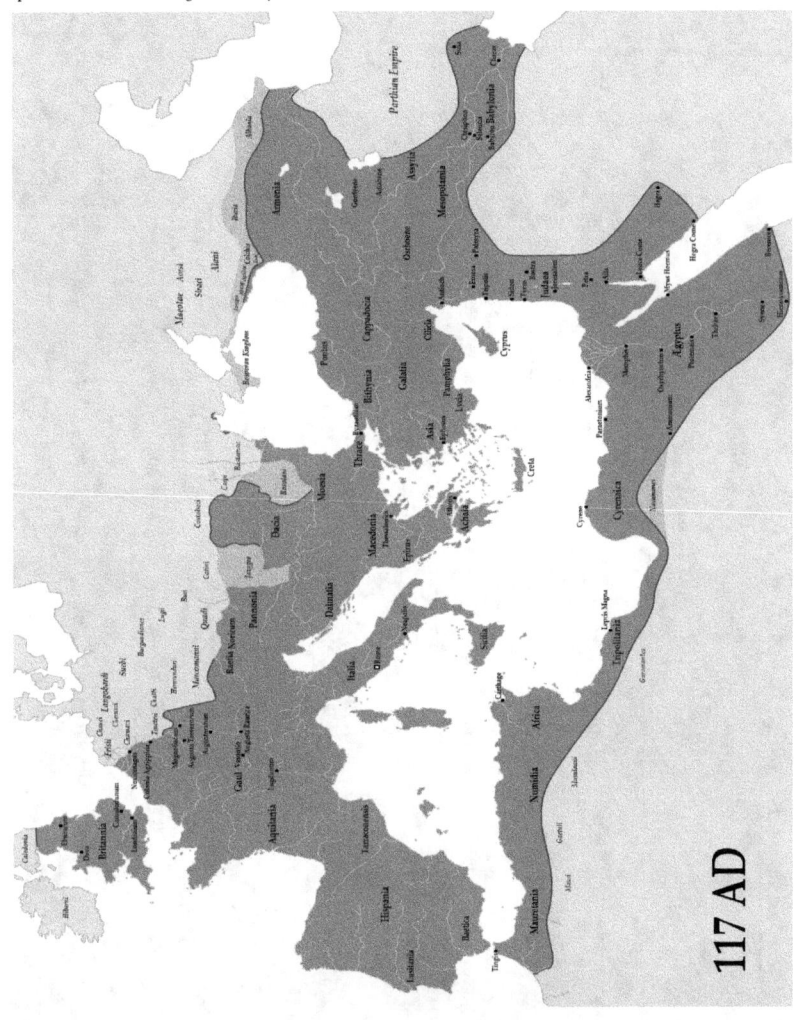

## 10.3.6 Map – Threats to the Roman Empires circa 400 AD

Map from http://commons.wikimedia.org/wiki/Category:Maps released under CC-BY-SA
http://creativecommons.org/licenses/by-sa/3.0/

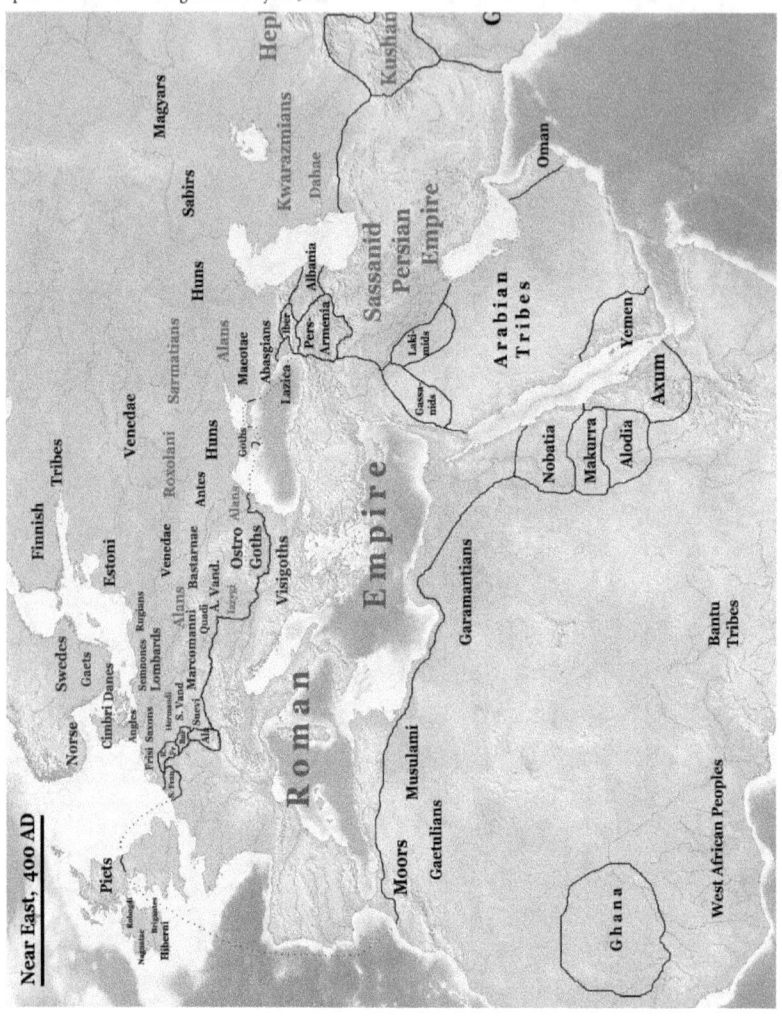

## The Western Roman Empire and Its Invasion of Britain

The summary table below should be enough to demonstrate the overall instability of Roman governance, and the lack of popularity abroad of its ambassadors and of its leadership. That lack of popularity even writhed periodically within its own contemporary and diverse population; this is in spite of considerable triumphalist achievements. Of around 130 openly appointed emperors and co-emperors, some 66 were murdered by their peers or their own military, and still others died in uncertain circumstances including likely political assassination, declared dead in battle, and through disease. Hardly an Empire at peace with itself, and yet it is consistently and unquestionably represented, quite falsely, throughout western European educational curricula as a light among Pagan and barbaric darkness.

The following table is provided to cross-reference some of the more significant events of the time, many of those events also being described in the books of the historical British and Anglo-Saxon chroniclers that are detailed in Volume Two. The table also supports the above ideas about fitness or qualification to govern. The sequence of events that occur as the Western Empire collapses and the Eastern Empire emerges, and the events that befall the quite separate Holy Roman Empire as it evolves from the quarrels of the Franks should be a warning from history. The unbelievably dysfunctional leadership, and the rank profligacy of the Byzantine Empire as it lays itself open to takeover and violation by Islam in the shape of the Ottomans one thousand years later should be a similar warning from history.

## 10.4 Table – Roman Emperors and Significant British Events

**NB.** Many of the events in this table are cross-referenced in the chapter in this book, Volume One, titled *The Two Thousand Year War – Papal Hegemony*, and in the chapter in Volume Two titled *The Eastern Roman or Byzantine Empire 330 to 1453 AD* – this table does contain several references to emperors of the partly concurrent Eastern Roman Empire.

| Dates, Emperor(s), Fate, Comments and Romano-British Issues ||
|---|---|
| **First Triumvirate 59 BC to 44 BC** ||
| Gaius Julius Caesar, Marcus Licinius Crassus, and Gnaeus Pompeius Magnus. This loose political alliance of the three dictators led to their own deaths and the collapse of the Republic as follows: Marcus Licinius Crassus died in battle 53 BC. Gnaeus Pompeius Magnus was assassinated in Egypt seeking refuge from Julius Caesar in 48 BC. Gaius Julius Caesar was assassinated in the Senate 44 BC. The end of the Roman Republic now began, and its death throes would last from 44 BC to 27 BC. ||
| **Second Triumvirate 43 BC to 33 BC** ||
| Gaius Octavian, Marcus Aemilius Lepidus, and Marcus Antonius aka Mark Antony. This legally convened leadership saw the death of the Roman Republic, and the turbulent birth of the Roman Empire under Gaius Octavian. This was the time of Mark Antony's well-known liaisons with the Ptolemaic Dynasty of Egypt and Cleopatra VII. See later chapter in Volume Two titled *The Ancient Greek Empire*, from which that Ptolemaic Dynasty arose. ||
| 33 BC to 27 BC Gaius Octavian | Period of conflict among the members of the Second Triumvirate, and a transition to the eventual victory of Gaius Octavian and his move from Consul to Emperor; he was given the new honorific title "Augustus". |
| **Start of the Julio-Claudian Dynasty** ||
| 27 BC to AD 14 Augustus (Gaius Octavian) | Died from natural causes. **British Context: There were complex tribal alliances within Britain, and varying sincerity regarding tribute to Rome.** The British King Cunobelinus (late 1st century BC to circa 43 AD) and his son Caratacus of the Catuvellauni in south-east England are said to have provoked the Roman conquest under Claudius, by their war with two other British tribes, the Roman vassals the Trinovantes and the Atrebates. |
| AD 14 to 37 Western Emperor Tiberius | Probably died from natural causes, though possibly **assassinated.** |

## The Western Roman Empire and Its Invasion of Britain

| Dates, Emperor(s), Fate, Comments and Romano-British Issues | |
|---|---|
| AD 37 to 41 Emperor Caligula | **Murdered** by the Praetorian Guard. **British Context:** 39 or 40 AD. Caligula received a fugitive Briton from the Catuvellauni tribe, and mounted a punitive but farcically unsuccessful invasion of Britain that never left the shores of Gaul. |
| AD 41 to 54 Emperor Claudius | **Poisoned** by his wife Agrippina, the mother of Nero. **British Context:** 51 AD Caratacus was treacherously captured and delivered to Rome by Queen Cartimandua of the northern British Brigantes. Due to his dignified deportment in captivity, Caratacus and his family were pardoned and lived thereafter in Rome. |
| AD 54 to 68 Emperor Nero | Nero was declared an enemy of the state by the Senate, and **committed suicide** with a slave's assistance. **British Context:** circa AD 60 Boudicca (aka Boadicea), Queen of the Iceni, led a confederation of the Iceni, the Trinovantes, and others in an initially successful, but ultimately disastrous revolt against the Romans. The tragic story ended with victory to the Roman governor, Gaius Suetonius Paulinus at the Battle of Watling Street circa AD 61. Circa AD 63 Joseph of Arimathea visited Glastonbury. |
| **Year of the Four Emperors (Civil War) – Galba, Otho, Vitellius, and Vespasian** | |
| AD 68 to 69 Emperor Galba | **Murdered** in a plot created by Otho because he did not adopt Otho as his son and successor. |
| AD 69 Emperor Otho | **Committed suicide** in an attempt to end the civil war. |
| AD 69 Emperor Vitellius | **Murdered** in favour of Vespasian. |
| **Start of the Flavian Dynasty** | |
| AD 69 to 79 Emperor Vespasian | Died from natural causes. **British Context:** The Conquest of Britain was completed by the initial subjugation of Wales and Scotland AD 71 to 84, though there would never be sustained peace. |
| AD 79 to 81 Emperor Titus | Died from natural causes or possibly **assassinated** by Domitian. |
| AD 81 to 96 Emperor Domitian | **Assassinated** by others in the ruling elite. |

| Dates, Emperor(s), Fate, Comments and Romano-British Issues ||
|---|---|
| **Start of the Nervan-Antonian Dynasty** ||
| AD 96 to 98 Emperor Nerva | Died from natural causes. Proclaimed emperor by the senate. One of the *Five Good Emperors* – a term coined by Machiavelli that distinguished between good rulers that were specifically adopted, and most of the remainder who inherited the office. |
| AD 98 to 117 Emperor Trajan I | Died from natural causes. One of the *Five Good Emperors*. Regnal I is added throughout this book to distinguish him from the later Emperor Trajan Decius. |
| AD 117 to 138 Emperor Hadrian | Died from natural causes. One of the *Five Good Emperors*. **British Context: Construction of the 73 mile Hadrian's wall was begun around the start of his reign, and finished in 128 AD.** |
| AD 138 to 161 Emperor Antoninus Pius | Died from natural causes. One of the *Five Good Emperors*. AD 142 Construction started of 39 mile long Antonine's wall. Finished circa AD 154. |
| AD 161 to 169 Emperor Lucius Verus | Died from natural causes. Co-emperor with Marcus Aurelius |
| AD 161 to 180 Emperor Marcus Aurelius | Died from natural causes. He was a Stoic – believing in the calm acceptance of life because it is fated. His book *The Commentaries* is in the public domain. One of the *Five Good Emperors*. |
| AD 175 Emperor Avidius Cassius (Usurper) | **Murdered** by his own army. Successful military leader, usurped title on mistaken news of death of Marcus Aurelius. He ruled only in Egypt and Syria. |
| AD 177 to 192 Emperor Commodus | **Assassinated.** His reign was characterised by currency devaluation, political strife, and personal public acts of debasement and perversion. Considered by some to have commenced the **Decline of the Roman Empire.** |
| **Start of the Year of the Five Emperors and the Severan Dynasty** ||
| AD 193 Emperor Pertinax | **Murdered** by the Praetorian Guard after he failed to fully meet their demands. Proclaimed emperor by the senate. |
| AD 193 Emperor Didius Julianus | **Executed** on the orders of the Senate and his successor Septimius Severus. Proclaimed emperor by the Praetorian Guard after the title of Emperor was auctioned. |

## The Western Roman Empire and Its Invasion of Britain

| Dates, Emperor(s), Fate, Comments and Romano-British Issues ||
|---|---|
| AD 193 to 194/195 Emperor Pescennius Niger (Usurper) | **Killed fleeing after defeat.** Usurper, proclaimed emperor by Syrian troops, defeated in battle by Septimius Severus. |
| AD 193/195 to 197 Emperor Clodius Albinus (Usurper) | **Committed suicide, or was killed after defeat, along with his wife and family.** **British Context: He was proclaimed emperor by British troops, but after several successes was defeated in battle by Septimius Severus.** |
| AD 193 to 211 Emperor Septimius Severus | Died from natural causes. Proclaimed emperor by Pannonian troops, he was accepted by the senate and posthumously restored with the honour of Pertinax. |
| AD 198 to 217 Emperor Caracalla (nickname, a type of Gallic hooded cloak.) | **Assassinated** on the orders of his successor Macrinus. **British Context: He was proclaimed co-emperor with his brother Publius Septimius Geta while in York during a campaign against the Britons.** Born as Lucius Septimius Bassianus, and described by Edward Gibbon in *The History of the Decline and Fall of the Roman Empire* as *"the common enemy of mankind"*, he is widely considered to have been the cruellest and worst emperor of all, having ordered wholesale massacres and also personally murdering his younger brother, so it is said, in the arms of their mother. |
| AD 209 to 211 Emperor Geta | **Assassinated** on the orders of Caracalla, his brother and co-emperor. |
| AD 217 to 218 Emperor Macrinus | **Executed** on the orders of Elagabalus. |
| AD 217 to 218 Emperor Diadumenian | **Executed** at the age of 10. Junior co-emperor under his father Macrinus. |
| AD 218 to 222 Emperor Elagabalus (nickname, a Romano-Syrian deity) | **Murdered** at the age of 18, by his army with Roman Emperor Alexander Severus' grandmother's support. Born as Varius Avitus Bassianus, he was proclaimed emperor by the army, but became so depraved that he was eliminated. |
| AD 222 to 235 Emperor Alexander Severus | **Murdered** by his army after perceived weakness while trying to buy peace from invading German tribes. Born Marcus Julius Gessius Bassianus Alexianus. |

## The Western Roman Empire and Its Invasion of Britain

| Dates, Emperor(s), Fate, Comments and Romano-British Issues | |
|---|---|
| **Principal Rulers during the Crisis of the 3rd Century** | |
| AD 235 to 238 Emperor Maximinus Thrax aka Emperor Maximinus I | **Murdered** by the Praetorian Guard following unexpected hardships while suppressing a revolt by senators; he had been proclaimed emperor by the army, but never went to Rome. The first of the Barracks Emperors – Emperors by virtue of military connections, of which there were 14 in a space of 33 years, he began the **Crisis of the 3rd Century**, a period of military anarchy that enhanced the already started Decline. |
| AD 238 Emperor Gordian I | **Committed suicide** after his son Gordian II's death. Proclaimed emperor in Africa. With his son, he opposed Maximinus for one month before their defeat. |
| AD 238 Emperor Gordian II | **Killed** during the Battle of Carthage, fighting a pro-Maximinus army. He had been proclaimed co-emperor with Gordian I. |
| AD 238 Emperor Pupienus | **Brutally murdered** with his co-emperor by the Praetorian Guard in favour of Gordian III. Pupienus and Balbinus were initially co-emperors and presided over the defeat of Maximinus, but distrusted each other and failed to see their impending assassination. |
| AD 238 Emperor Balbinus | **Brutally murdered** – See Pupienus above. |
| AD 238 to 244 Emperor Gordian III | Death unclear probably **murdered** by Philip the Arab. |
| AD 244 to 249 Philip the Arab | **Killed in battle** by Decius, he was proclaimed emperor after the death of Gordian III. He is believed to have been sympathetic to Christians, and may have been the first Christian emperor. |
| AD 249 to 251 Emperor Trajan Decius | **Killed in battle** with his son and co-ruler Herennius Etruscus. He initiated much persecution of the Christians that led to unrest and divisions. **British Context: circa 250 Saxon piracy along the east coast of Britain and Brittany in France increases at this time, prompting the strengthening of coastal defences.** |
| AD 251 to 253 Emperor Gallus | **Murdered** by the army in favour of Aemilianus, he had been proclaimed emperor by them after Decius' death. |
| AD 253 to 260 Emperor Valerian | **Died in squalid captivity** after Persian treachery, defeat, and torture – he was the only emperor to become a prisoner of war. He had been proclaimed emperor by the army. |
| AD 253 to 268 Emperor Gallienus | **Probably murdered** by his own generals, he was a junior co-emperor under Valerian until 260 when Valerian was captured by the Persians. |

# The Western Roman Empire and Its Invasion of Britain

| Dates, Emperor(s), Fate, Comments and Romano-British Issues | |
|---|---|
| AD 268 to 270 Emperor Claudius Gothicus | Died from smallpox. Proclaimed emperor by the army. |
| AD 270 Emperor Quintillus | Cause of death unclear. He proclaimed himself emperor. |
| AD 270 to 275 Emperor Aurelian | **Murdered** by the Praetorian Guard. Proclaimed emperor by the army. The Great Library at Alexandria was, again, seriously damaged when Aurelian was suppressing an Egyptian revolt. 70,000 books were lost. |
| AD 275 to 276 Emperor Marcus Claudius Tacitus | Possibly died of fever or **assassinated**, he was the last emperor elected by the Senate. |
| AD 276 to 282 Emperor Probus | **Murdered** by his own soldiers in favour of Carus. He had been initially proclaimed emperor by an eastern army. |
| AD 282 to 283 Emperor Carus | Believed to have died from natural causes, he had been proclaimed emperor by the Praetorian guard. He was peacefully succeeded by his two sons. |
| AD 283 to 285 Emperor Carinus | Cause of death is debated, but it is likely that he was **killed by a member of the army in revenge for the seduction of his wife**. Carinus was the son of Carus and co-emperor with his brother, Numerian. Carinus had the reputation of being one of the worst of the emperors. |
| AD 283 to 284 Emperor Numerian | Cause of death is uncertain, possibly disease, but he was probably **murdered**. The son of Carus, he was co-emperor with Carinus. The possible assassin was publicly blamed, condemned, and executed on the spot by the new Emperor Diocletian. |

| |
|---|
| **Dates, Emperor(s), Fate, Comments and Romano-British Issues** |
| **Principal Usurpers during the Crisis of the 3rd Century**<br>These 26 usurper Emperors all received the title, but did not achieve greatness. Virtually all were **murdered or killed in power struggles.**<br>AD 240 Emperor Sabinianus<br>AD 248 Emperor Pacatianus<br>AD 248 to 249 Emperor Jotapianus<br>AD circa 250 Emperor Silbannacus<br>AD 249 to 252 Emperor Priscus<br>AD 250 Emperor Licinianus<br>AD 251 Emperor Herennius Etruscus<br>AD 251 Emperor Hostilian<br>AD 251 to 253 Emperor Volusianus<br>AD 253 Emperor Aemilian<br>AD 260 Emperor Saloninus<br>AD circa 260 Emperor Ingenuus<br>AD 260 Emperor Regalianus<br>AD 260 to 261 Emperor Macrianus Major<br>AD 260 to 261 Emperor Macrianus Minor<br>AD 260 to 261 Emperor Quietus<br>AD circa 261 Emperor Mussius Aemilianus<br>AD 268 Emperor Aureolus<br>AD 268 to 270 Emperor Claudius Gothicus<br>AD 270 Emperor Quintillus<br>AD 271 Emperor Septimius<br>AD 275 to 276 Emperor Tacitus<br>AD 276 Emperor Florianus<br>AD 280 Emperor Julius Saturninus<br>AD 280 Emperor Proculus<br>AD 280 Emperor Bonosus |
| **Gallic Empire 260 to 274**<br>The separatist region, consisting of present-day Britain, France, Germany, and parts of Spain, was an opportunistic movement that started during the crisis above, and was ended by Aurelian (see above). The usurper emperors below may well have been regional officials attempting secession.<br>**British Context: Britain was part of this uprising, and given the regions involved, it is interesting to speculate on a possible Celtic under-current of concerted resistance.** |

| | |
|---|---|
| AD 260 to 268 Emperor Postumus (Usurper) | Usurper, eventually **killed by his own troops.** |
| AD 268 Emperor Laelianus (Usurper) | Usurper defeated and **killed by Postumus.** |
| AD 269 Emperor Marius | **Murdered** by the army after they elected him. |

## The Western Roman Empire and Its Invasion of Britain

| Dates, Emperor(s), | Fate, Comments and Romano-British Issues |
|---|---|
| AD 269 to 271 Emperor Victorinus | **Murdered** by the army after they elected him. |
| AD 270 to 271 Emperor Domitianus II (Usurper) | Little is known about his life, rise to power, or death. |
| AD 271 to 274 Emperor Tetricus I | Believed to have died from natural causes. After the death of Victorinus he was elected by the rebel army which he later betrayed to Aurelian to save his own life. |
| **Britannic Empire 286 to 296** **British Context:** The isolated separatists in Britain lasted for 10 years and were finally defeated by Emperor Constantius Chlorus, the father of Emperor Constantine (The Great). | |
| AD 286 to 293 Emperor Carausius | His removal from office was ordered by Emperor Maximian (see below), and he was **assassinated** by his minister of finance, Allectus. **British Context:** A Gaul from the region of present-day Belgium, Carausius declared himself emperor of Britain and northern Gaul on the strength of his support by various legions and mercenaries, and his successes at sea against Saxon pirates along the coast of Britain, Brittany, and Normandy. Again, it is interesting to speculate on a possible Celtic under-current of concerted resistance. |

| Dates, Emperor(s), Fate, Comments and Romano-British Issues |
|---|
| **Tetrarchy and Constantinian Dynasty**<br>Emperor Diocletian's reforms following the Crisis of the 3rd Century involved the definition of the Tetrarchy – 2 Augusti, each with a subservient Caesar. Although notions of Eastern and Western Empires were really evolutionary until the end of the reign of Emperor Theodosius in 395 when the empires did irrevocably separate, Rome ceased to be the administrative capital and was replaced by 4 distributed centres of government:<br>Eastern Region<br>Nicomedia (present-day Izmit in Turkey) became the capital of Augustus Diocletian.<br>Sirmium (present-day Sremska Mitrovica near Belgrade in Serbia) became the capital of Caesar Galerius.<br>Western Region<br>Mediolanum (present-day Milan) became the capital of Augustus Maximian.<br>Augusta Treverorum (present-day Trier in Germany) became the capital of Caesar Constantius Chlorus.<br>**Map – Geography of the Tetrarchy – Starting in 293 AD**<br>Map from http://commons.wikimedia.org/wiki/Category:Maps released under CC-BY-SA http://creativecommons.org/licenses/by-sa/3.0/<br><br>As noted earlier, the 3rd century was also the time of the greatest extent of the Western Empire. |

| AD 293 to 296<br>Emperor<br>Allectus | **Killed** in battle against the forces of Constantius Chlorus that were sent to liberate the Britons. Allectus had declared himself emperor after killing his predecessor, Carausius.<br>**British Context: End of the Britannic Empire, and 36 years of consistent dissidence and rebellion by at least regionally Celtic peoples.** |
|---|---|

## The Western Roman Empire and Its Invasion of Britain

| Dates, Emperor(s), Fate, Comments and Romano-British Issues | |
|---|---|
| AD 284 to 305 Emperor Diocletian *Eastern Empire* His Caesar (as part of the Tetrarchy) was Galerius | **Abdicated,** he had been co-emperor ('Augustus') with Maximian. He was declared emperor by the army after Numerian's death. 285 AD Diocletian sowed the seed for the later split into Eastern and Western Empires by dividing the imperial administration between East and West. 303 AD Diocletian began the persecution of Christians. **British Context: Saint Alban's martyrdom occurred sometime between 209 and 304, and despite that uncertainty, he is recognised as the first British martyr. In 304 AD, the second and third of the British Christian martyrs, Saints Julius and Aaron died.** |
| AD 286 to 305 Emperor Maximian *Western Empire* His Caesar was Constantius Chlorus | **Abdicated,** he had been co-emperor ('Augustus') with Diocletian. |
| AD 305 to 306 Emperor Constantius Chlorus *Western Empire* His Caesar was the later Emperor Severus II | Died from natural causes. He had been a junior co-emperor ('Caesar') under Maximian, later becoming co-emperor Augustus with Galerius after Maximian's abdication. **British Context: Constantius Chlorus died at York, England. In 305 he made war on the Picts, claiming victory and the title *Britannicus Maximus*.** |
| AD 305 to 311 Emperor Galerius *Eastern Empire* His Caesar was the later Usurper Emperor Maximinus II | Died from natural causes while fading from office. He had been a junior co-emperor ('Caesar') under Diocletian, later becoming co-emperor Augustus with Constantius Chlorus after Diocletian's abdication. |
| AD 306 to 307 Emperor Severus II *Western Empire* | **Executed** by Maxentius, he had been made a junior co-emperor ('Caesar') under Constantius Chlorus, becoming Augustus after Constantius' death. |

*The Western Roman Empire and Its Invasion of Britain*

| Dates, Emperor(s), Fate, Comments and Romano-British Issues | |
|---|---|
| AD 306 to 312 Emperor Maxentius *Western Empire (Partial control)* | **Defeated in battle** by Constantine I and drowned trying to escape. He was the son of Maximian, and had been proclaimed Augustus by the Praetorian Guard. |
| AD 306 to 312 (Battle for Accession) Reigned to 337 Emperor Constantine I *Eastern and Western Empires* | Died from natural causes. He was proclaimed Augustus by the army in 306. He defeated Maxentius in 312 and converted to Christianity, issuing (with the support of Licinius) the Edict of Milan in 313 that promoted tolerance of all religions. Constantine's many un-Christian-like actions are held by many to demonstrate the primarily opportunistic nature of his conversion. **British Context: He was born at York, England, the son of Constantius Chlorus.** |
| AD 308 to circa 310 Emperor Domitius Alexander (Usurper) *Africa and Sardinia only* | **Executed by strangulation** after defeat in battle by Maxentius. He had proclaimed himself emperor in Africa. |
| AD 308 to 324 Emperor Licinius (Usurper) *Eastern Empire* | **Executed by hanging** after being deposed by Constantine I. He had been appointed Augustus by Galerius, and became sole Augustus in the East circa 312 AD. Frequently in a state of civil war with Constantine. |
| AD 311 to 313 Emperor Maximinus II (Usurper) *Partial control in both Eastern and Western Empires* | **Committed suicide** after defeat in battle by Licinius. He had been made a junior co-emperor ('Caesar') under Galerius, becoming Augustus after his death. |
| AD 316 to 317 Emperor Valerius Valens (Usurper) Licinius' lackey *Eastern Empire partial* | **Executed** by Licinius after having been appointed co-Augustus by Licinius. |

*The Western Roman Empire and Its Invasion of Britain*

| Dates, Emperor(s), Fate, Comments and Romano-British Issues ||
|---|---|
| AD 324<br>Emperor Sextus Martinianus (Usurper)<br>*Western Empire* | **Executed** after being deposed by Constantine I. He had been another co-Augustus appointed by Licinius.<br>324 to 330 New Rome was built at Byzantium, and in 330 AD, **Constantine moved the seat of the Empire** from Nicomedia (present-day Izmit) which was east of the Bosphorus to this new city – Constantinople. |
| AD 337 to 340<br>Emperor Constantine II<br>*Territorial Jurisdiction Variously affected by Christian Sectarianism* | **Killed in battle against his brother** Western Emperor Constans I.<br>The son of Constantine I, he was co-emperor in a fractious alliance with his brothers.<br>**The largely sectarian issues among the sons of Constantine the Great arose less than 25 years after the ecumenical Edict of Milan in 313. So much for peace in their time.** |
| AD 337 to 361<br>Emperor Constantius II<br>*Territorial Jurisdiction Variously affected by Christian Sectarianism* | Died of fever.<br>The son of Constantine I, Constantius II was co-emperor in a fractious alliance with his brothers. |
| AD 337 to 350<br>Western Emperor Constans I<br>*Territorial Jurisdiction Variously affected by Christian Sectarianism* | **Killed by Magnentius troops.**<br>The son of Constantine I, Constans I was co-emperor, also in a fractious alliance with his brothers.<br>See further detail in this volume, in the chapter titled *Saint Athanasius of Alexandria circa 296 to 373 – 1st Orders* and in the *Table of the Life and Death of the Byzantine Empire* in Volume Two, in the chapter titled *The Eastern Roman or Byzantine Empire 330 to 1453 AD*. |
| AD 350 to 353<br>Emperor Magnentius (Usurper)<br>*Territorially Britannia, Gaul, and Hispania* | **Committed suicide.** Usurper, proclaimed emperor by the army and defeated by Constantius II. |

| Dates, Emperor(s), Fate, Comments and Romano-British Issues ||
|---|---|
| c. AD 350 Emperor Vetranio (Usurper) *Western Empire (briefly)* | **Abdicated** and died from natural causes. Proposed by Constantina, the sister of Constantius II, he proclaimed himself emperor against Magnentius. He was recognised by Constantius II, but was then peacefully deposed. |
| c. AD 350 Emperor Nepotianus (Usurper) *Territorially Rome only* | **Executed** after being defeated by Magnentius. He had proclaimed himself emperor against Magnentius. |
| AD 361 to 363 Emperor Julian *Eastern and Western Empires* | **Killed in battle** against the Sassanid Empire (Greater Persia), he had been made Caesar by his cousin Constantius II, then proclaimed Augustus by the army. Known as Julian the Apostate, he rejected Christianity in favour of Paganism (Neoplatonism). **Early Frankish tribes were permitted to settle in Europe** (Belgian Salian and Ripuarians etc.) in exchange for treaties of alliance. |
| AD 363 to 364 Emperor Jovian *Eastern and Western Empires* | Died from natural causes or **poisoning**. Jovian was proclaimed emperor by the army after the death of Emperor Julian, but he went on to suffer humiliating defeats by the Persians, and serious territorial losses. He reinstated Christianity. |
| Start of Valentinian Dynasty, West 364 to 392, East 364 to 378 ||
| AD 364 to 375 Emperor Valentinian I *Western Empire* | Died from natural causes. He had been proclaimed emperor by the army after Jovian's death. Co-emperor with his brother Valens. |
| AD 365 to 378 Emperor Valens *Eastern Empire* | **Killed in battle**. He had been made co-emperor in the East by his brother Valentinian I. Defeats by the **Goths, Visigoths**, and Persians hastened the end of the Western Empire. |
| AD 365 to 366 Emperor Procopius (Usurper) *Eastern Empire (partial)* | **Executed** after being defeated by Valens. Having retired from public life, Procopius proclaimed himself emperor, it seems, as a last resort, after rumours were spread that he was a threat to the successors of Emperor Julian and Emperor Jovian. |

## The Western Roman Empire and Its Invasion of Britain

| Dates, Emperor(s), Fate, Comments and Romano-British Issues | |
|---|---|
| AD 367 to 383<br>Emperor<br>Gratian<br>*Western Empire, then Whole Empire* | **Assassinated**. Son of Valentinian I, he was a junior Augustus (West) from 367, Senior Augustus (West) from 375, and Senior Augustus (Whole Empire) from 378 after the death of his uncle, Emperor Valens. His half-brother Valentinian II was co-emperor from 375. He lost territory and was perceived as fawning towards the enemy.<br>**Gratian was the last Roman Emperor to lead a campaign across the Rhine.**<br>**Orthodox Christianity became dominant during his reign.**<br>**The use of foreign barbarians as mercenaries in the Roman Army increased from this time, and is considered to have been a major factor in the decline of the Western Empire.** |
| AD 375 to 392<br>Emperor<br>Valentinian II<br>*(Puppet under Theodosius I)*<br>*Western Empire* | Deposed and **hanged** in suspicious circumstances, possibly by the Frank, General Arbogast (Flavius Arbogastes) who served Theodosius I. Valentinian II was the son of Valentinian I, and he came to power as an infant, a tool of the army. |
| AD 383 to 388<br>Emperor<br>Magnus<br>Maximus<br>(Usurper)<br>*Western Empire (partial)* | **Deposed and executed.** He was commander of Britain when, outraged by Gratian's displays of weakness and toadying, he crossed to Gaul and was proclaimed emperor by the army. At one time recognised by Theodosius I, he entered Italy and was defeated and executed by him.<br>**British Context: After his death, there was no further Roman imperial activity in either northern Gaul or Britain except for one possible campaign by Flavius Stilicho, a highly ranked General. See below.** |
| c. AD 386 to 388<br>Emperor Flavius<br>Victor<br>(Usurper)<br>*Western Empire (partial)* | **Executed** by the Frank, General Arbogast, on the orders of Theodosius I. The son of Magnus Maximus, he had been proclaimed an Augustus by his father. |
| AD 392 to 394<br>Emperor<br>Eugenius<br>(Usurper)<br>*Western Empire (partial)* | **Executed** by Theodosius I after defeat in battle. He had been proclaimed emperor by the army under Arbogast who committed suicide.<br>**It has been said that Eugenius was the last hope for the Pagan religion to oppose the rise of Christianity in Europe, since although he was a Christian, he was the last Roman Emperor to support the philosophy of Roman Polytheism.** |

| Dates, Emperor(s), Fate, Comments and Romano-British Issues ||
|---|---|
| **Start of Theodosian Dynasty 392 to 457** ||
| AD 379 to 395 Emperor Theodosius I *Eastern and Western Empires* | Died from natural causes. Made co-emperor for the East by Gratian when threats from several barbarian quarters were increasing along with Roman defeats.<br>**The last Roman Emperor to rule over a unified Roman Empire.**<br>**He admitted Visigoths as residents within the Empire.**<br>381 Start of Christian persecution of Paganism.<br>389 to 391 Paganism is banned and attacked, including such acts as extinguishing the eternal fire in the Temple of Vesta in the Roman Forum, and the disbanding of the Vestal Virgins.<br>391 Theodosius ordered the destruction of Pagan monuments and records at the Great Library at Alexandria.<br>**British Context: Sometime during the period 396 to 398 there was a naval campaign by General Flavius Stilicho against the Picts, and on land an attempt was made to quell invasions by the Scotti and the Saxons.** |
| AD 383 to 408 Emperor Arcadius *Eastern Empire* | Died from natural causes. Appointed co-emperor with his father Theodosius I.<br>**Sole emperor and Augustus for the East from January 395.** (Augustus as referred to earlier was an honorific title meaning "Majestic One".)<br>A weak emperor, he was dominated by others.<br>**399 Arcadius ordered the final destruction of all remaining non-Christian temples.** |
| AD 393 to 423 Emperor Honorius *Western Empire* | Died from natural causes. Appointed Augustus for the West, at the age of 8, by his father, Theodosius I.<br>**Sole emperor and Augustus for the West from January 395 at the age of 10.**<br>A weak emperor, a consul from the age of 2, he was dominated by others, among them Flavius Stilicho. Stilicho was famously **half Vandal and half Roman**, and he was a capable general who was eventually expelled and executed, partly as a result of his failure to deal with the British revolts. During the first years of the 5$^{th}$ century, his reign saw increasing invasions by **Visigoths, Ostrogoths, Alans, Suevi, Vandals, and Quadi;** and the movement of the capital from Milan to Ravenna.<br>**British Context: 406 to 407 Revolts in Britain.**<br>**410 Rome is sacked by the Visigoths under Alaric.**<br><u>**Britain becomes isolated from Rome, and is expected to organise its own defence.**</u> |

*The Western Roman Empire and Its Invasion of Britain*

| Dates, Emperor(s), Fate, Comments and Romano-British Issues |
|---|
| **Usurpers of the Western Empire during the Crisis at the start of the 5th Century**<br>Relatively short-lived and **mostly defeated in battle or executed.**<br>AD 407 Emperor Constantine III<br>AD 409 Western Emperor Constans II (Not to be confused with Byzantine Emperor Constans II, 641 to 668)<br>AD 409 Emperor Priscus Attalus<br>AD 409 Emperor Maximus<br>AD 411 Emperor Jovinus<br>AD 412 Emperor Sebastianus<br>**British Context:** In 407 Emperor Constantine III was proclaimed emperor in Britain. He was defeated by Emperor Constantius III (who was only briefly emperor in 421), and he became a priest in 411. After being given safe conduct, Constantine III was killed by Constantius III, and Britain became further isolated. A secular historian, Procopius of the 6th century, considered to be the last major historian of the ancient world, wrote of Britain at this time *"...from that time onwards it remained under [the rule] of tyrants."* |

| | |
|---|---|
| AD 408 to 450 Emperor Theodosius II *Eastern Empire* | Died from natural causes. Son of Arcadius, he became emperor at the age of 7 when Arcadius died. He oversaw the completion of significant fortifications of Constantinople, promoted Christianity, and started a war with the Persians that ended in a draw when the Eastern Empire was under attack by the **Huns**. Significant tribute in gold was paid to the Huns during his reign. |
| AD 421 Emperor Constantius III *Western Empire* | Died from natural causes. Son-in-law of Theodosius I; appointed co-emperor by Emperor Honorius, he had played a significant role since about 410. His sudden death in 421 was a major blow to an empire under severe threat. |
| AD 423 to 425 Emperor Joannes *Western Empire* | Defeated and **executed after torture** by Theodosius II in favour of Valentinian III. Proclaimed Western Emperor via the civil service, he tolerated Christianity. He attempted, unsuccessfully, to use **Huns** to defend the Western Empire against the Eastern Roman Empire. |
| AD 425 to 455 Emperor Valentinian III *Western Empire* | **Assassinated**, he was the son of Constantius III and was appointed emperor by Theodosius II. After a period of major loss of empire in Gaul, Spain, Africa, and around the Mediterranean, and after unbearable taxation, he had one success, and a huge one at that. Albeit with enormous help from the Visigoths and several other barbarian tribes, he was the Roman Emperor that saw the **defeat of Attila the Hun in 451**. Foolishly, Emperor Valentinian then murdered the Roman General Flavius Aetius who had been chief of staff during the campaign against Attila. Considered profligate, Valentinian III was probably murdered in revenge for adulterous relationships. |

## The Western Roman Empire and Its Invasion of Britain

| Dates, Emperor(s), Fate, Comments and Romano-British Issues | |
|---|---|
| AD 450 to 457 Emperor Marcian *Eastern Empire* | Died from natural causes. Appointed by the sister of Theodosius II, he was generally successful for the Eastern Empire, but having cancelled tribute payments to Attila the Hun, he seems to have stood by and watched the subsequent destruction of the Western Empire. |
| **The Beginning of the End for the Western Roman Empire** | |
| AD 455 Emperor Petronius Maximus *Western Empire* | **Murdered** – stoned by a Roman mob after fleeing Rome when faced with invasion by the **Vandals and Alans**. He proclaimed himself emperor after the death of Valentinian III, but lasted only 11 weeks. He had been responsible for several political assassinations and had divided Rome's leadership. 455 Rome was sacked by the Vandals. |
| AD 455 to 456 Emperor Eparchius Avitus *Western Empire* | **Believed murdered** while remaining a perceived threat after being deposed. He had been allied with the **Ostrogoth and Visigoth King Theoderic I**, and was proclaimed emperor by Theoderic's son, King Theoderic II, but was eventually deposed by the senate at the instigation of Flavius Ricimer, who was a Romanised German military leader (a **Suevi**). Ricimer was considered characteristic of several barbarian commanders who had been paid in attempts to save the doomed Western Empire. |
| AD 457 to 461 Emperor Flavius Majorian *Western Empire* | **Executed after torture**, by the manipulative Ricimer, by whom he had been appointed. Somehow uniting diverse **mercenaries** for support, he fought successfully for a time against Alemanni, Franks, Goths, Vandals, Burgundians, and Visigoths. The net was being drawn tight, and he is considered **the last emperor to have made a serious attempt to re-establish Roman dominion in the West. See the map below.** |
| AD 461 to 465 Emperor Libius Severus *Western Empire* | **Executed** by Ricimer, he was a religious and pious puppet who had been installed by Ricimer. **British Context: Britain had now been abandoned for 50 years.** |
| AD 467 to 472 Emperor Procopius Anthemius *Western Empire* | **Executed** by Ricimer, by whom he had been appointed, he was more capable than his predecessor and maintained links with the Eastern Empire. However, the infiltration of barbarians into all levels of Roman political and military life, and the machinations of Ricimer, prevented any successful defence by the **now fragmented indigenous Roman faction**. |
| AD 472 Emperor Anicius Olybrius *Western Empire* | Died from natural causes. Appointed by Ricimer, he was a puppet with little interest in anything other than religion. |

*The Western Roman Empire and Its Invasion of Britain*

| Dates, Emperor(s), Fate, Comments and Romano-British Issues | |
|---|---|
| AD 473 to 474 Emperor Flavius Glycerius **Western Empire** | Little is known of his life or death. Ricimer being dead, he was appointed by Ricimer's nephew, Gundobad, and deposed by Julius Nepos at a time when the Empire faced the terrifying prospect of invasion by a combined army of **Ostrogoths and Visigoths**. He later became Bishop of Salona. |
| AD 474 to 480 Emperor Julius Nepos **Western Empire** | **Murdered** in 480 by his own soldiers, possibly with the connivance of his predecessor, Glycerius, now the Bishop of Salona. Nepos had been appointed by Emperor Leo I of the Eastern Empire. He was deposed by Flavius Orestes, the father of Romulus Augustus in 475, but was still recognised as the lawful emperor in Gaul and Dalmatia until his death. **The Western Roman Empire is considered by some to have persisted until the death of Emperor Nepos in 480.** |
| AD 475 to 476 Emperor Romulus Augustus **Western Empire** | **Abdicated.** Ruled and died in relative obscurity with no recognition by the Eastern Empire, and little practical achievement of any kind, having dominion over only parts of the Italian peninsula. Deposed by Flavius Odoacera, a German soldier who became the first King of Italy. **The Western Roman Empire is considered by many to have ended in 476, others as seen above say 480.** Flavius Odoacera continued to pay notional lip service to Julius Nepos, and after Nepos' death, to the Eastern Emperor, Flavius Zeno Augustus; but after treacherous behaviour on all sides, Odoacera was eventually murdered by the Ostrogoth, King Theodoric the Great, who had been appointed King of Italy by Zeno in the hope that the Ostrogoths would leave his Eastern Empire alone. This was a black mark against the otherwise noble Theodoric the Great. \*\*The Western Empire was finally accepted by the Eastern Empire as having been lost to Germanic tribal leadership in 526 AD. Fragmentation of the whole Italian region at the hands of Visigoths, Lombards, Franks, later medieval European Nation-States, and not least the Catholic Popes, would continue until the re-unification of Italy in 1861. **British Context: When the Western Roman Empire finally folded, all chances of any aid to the Romanised Britons were lost. Pict and Scotti predations from the north, and Germanic invasion and colonisation from northern mainland Europe were already underway as detailed in later chapters.** |

## 10.5 Countdown to Doom – Seeds of the Holy Roman Empire

**400 AD.** During the first years of the 5$^{th}$ century, the reign of Emperor Honorius saw increasing invasions across the Rhine and from regions yet further to the east by Visigoths, Ostrogoths, Alans, Suevi, Vandals, and Quadi. The principal regent to the young Emperor Honorius, the renowned and high-ranking General Flavius Stilicho, was himself half Vandal.

**410.** The capital of the failing Western Empire had already been moved to Ravenna, but Rome still remained politically and iconically of great significance. After a couple of years of failed negotiations and duplicity by weak Roman leadership, the Visigoths under their leader, Alaric, sacked Rome, and then departed to settle in south-west Gaul (Aquitaine, France).

**455.** Rome was more comprehensively sacked by the Vandals, and the same year the Ostrogoth and Visigoth, King Theoderic II, was behind the appointment of Emperor Eparchius Avitus.

**457.** Emperor Majorian was appointed by a Romanised German, Flavius Ricimer, and a mercenary army was used to defeat Theoderic II and retake parts of the empire. His brief reign of just four years saw most of Spain and southern France back in Roman hands, and some penitent Visigoths, Burgundians, and Suevi recommitted to *foederati* status.

**461 to 474.** The native German, Ricimer, and his nephew, Gundobad, executed and appointed emperors at will, and infiltrated the civil and military with various so-called barbarians. Emperors Flavius Majorian, Libius Severus, Procopius Anthemius, Anicius Olybrius, and Flavius Glycerius were all proxies for the ineligible (by birth) Ricimer. Only Glycerius avoided being murdered.

**474.** Emperor Leo I of the Eastern Empire stepped into the fray in his final year as emperor, and proclaimed his nephew, Julius Nepos, Emperor of the West. Nepos made peace with the Visigoths further west, but failed to make peace with the Vandals (and associated Alans), who had a powerful navy and were running pirate raids from the north African coast against interests of the Western Empire. The Vandals, under their leader Geiseric (aka Genseric), had made a separate peace around the year 435 with

## The Western Roman Empire and Its Invasion of Britain

the Eastern Empire. Duplicity and distrust between East and West was further evident when Nepos was finally disposed of, with the connivance of the Senate, in 480.

**475.** Flavius Orestes, the head of the military, and part German, and previously at the court of Attila the Hun, unconstitutionally proclaimed his 12-year-old son, Romulus Augustus, emperor, and forced Nepos to retreat to Dalmatia from where he continued as nominal emperor with recognition by the Eastern Emperor Flavius Zeno.

**476.** Flavius Orestes failed to pay his mostly mercenary Germanic army, and Romulus Augustus was deposed by the mercenaries' chosen leader, Flavius Odoacera (a German soldier) aka Odovacer, who became the first King of Italy. Flavius Orestes was executed and his son, Romulus Augustus, disappeared into obscurity.

**480.** Nepo was murdered as part of a conspiracy consisting of some uncertain blend of Glycerius, Odoacera, and Zeno.

**493.** After several years, Flavius Odoacera, who had continued with the approval of Zeno and the Senate, and who achieved military and diplomatic victories, became too successful, so that the treacherous Zeno arranged for Theoderic the Great and the Ostrogoths to replace him. Odoacera was murdered by Theoderic as the two shared a meal, and the orgy of death was extended to as much of his army and family as could be found.

Thus was laid the basis for the evolution of the Frankish and Holy Roman Empires over the next several hundred years. There is much more on this in later chapters in Volume One and Volume Two.

### 10.5.1 Note Concerning the Name "Theoderic"

Theoderic I (circa 393 – 451 AD), a Visigothic king, was renowned for his contribution to the victory over Attila the Hun at the Battle of the Catalaunian Plains – albeit posthumously.

Theoderic II (circa 426 – 466 AD), a son of Theoderic I, was infamous for killing his older brother in order to become king of the Visigoths. After his defeat by Emperor Majorian, circa 458, he was in turn killed by his younger brother.

*The Western Roman Empire and Its Invasion of Britain*

Theoderic the Great (circa 454 – 526 AD) was an Ostrogothic king who had been raised in the court of the Eastern Roman Empire, and who rose to high rank in the west after the Western Roman Empire disintegrated. His strength was instrumental in maintaining order during the transition towards the Germanic (later Holy) Roman Empire.

### 10.5.2 Map – Majorian's Final Thrust for Empire 457 AD

Map from http://commons.wikimedia.org/wiki/Category:Maps released under CC-BY-SA
http://creativecommons.org/licenses/by-sa/3.0/

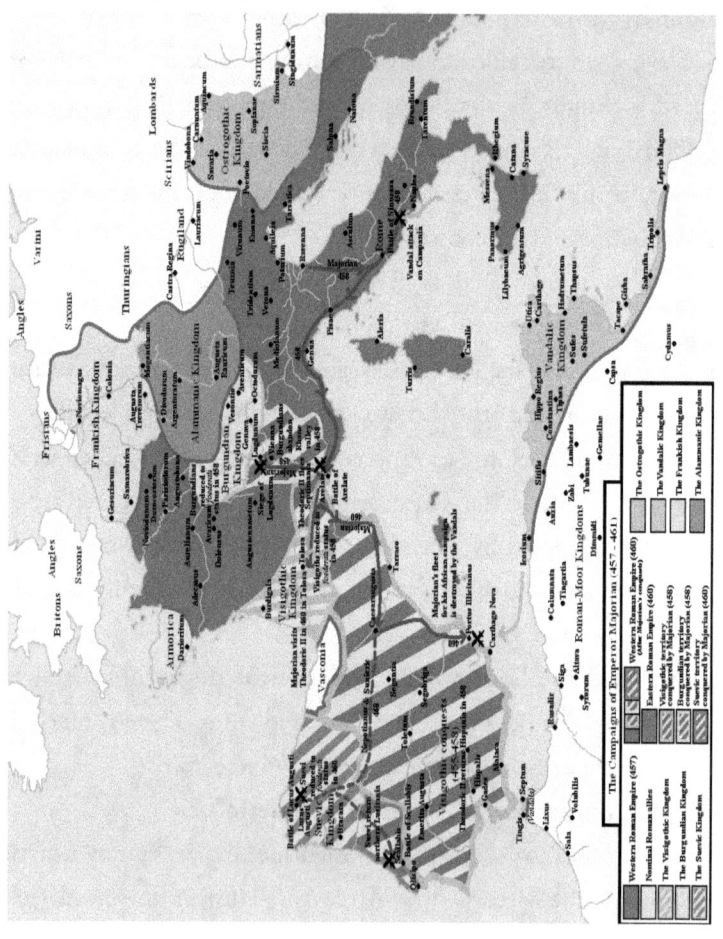

## 10.5.3 Map – British Tribes at the Time of the Roman Conquest

1 Mainly Goidelic.
2 Mainly Pictish.
3 Mainly Brythonic (British) areas.

Maps from http://commons.wikimedia.org/wiki/Category:Maps released under CC-BY-SA
http://creativecommons.org/licenses/by-sa/3.0/

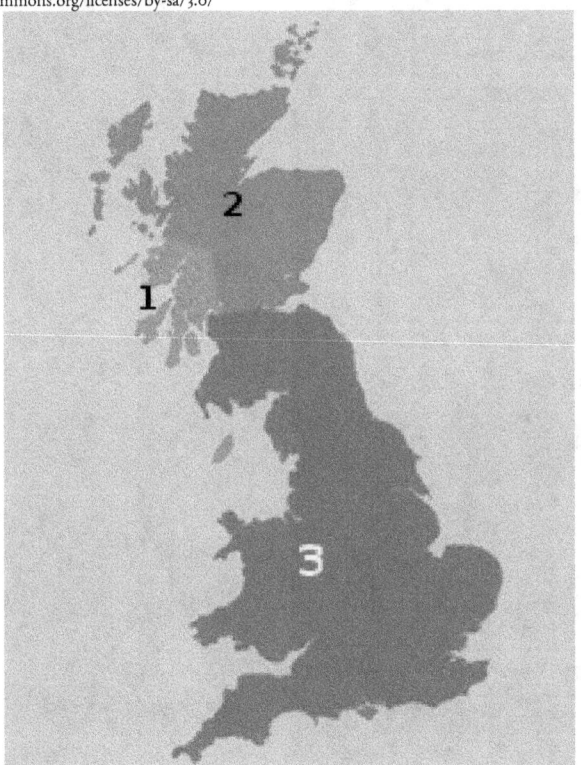

Before the Continental invasions the British Isles were the result of 5,000 years, or more, of possibly slow integration. With only contentious written records however, the image above may be too simplistic, and it should not be taken as indicative of any united governance, although after many millennia there may well have been considerable inter-tribal "cultural unity".

*The Western Roman Empire and Its Invasion of Britain*

## 10.5.4 Map – Initial Roman Objectives – Britain's Currency

Maps from http://commons.wikimedia.org/wiki/Category:Maps released under CC-BY-SA
http://creativecommons.org/licenses/by-sa/3.0/

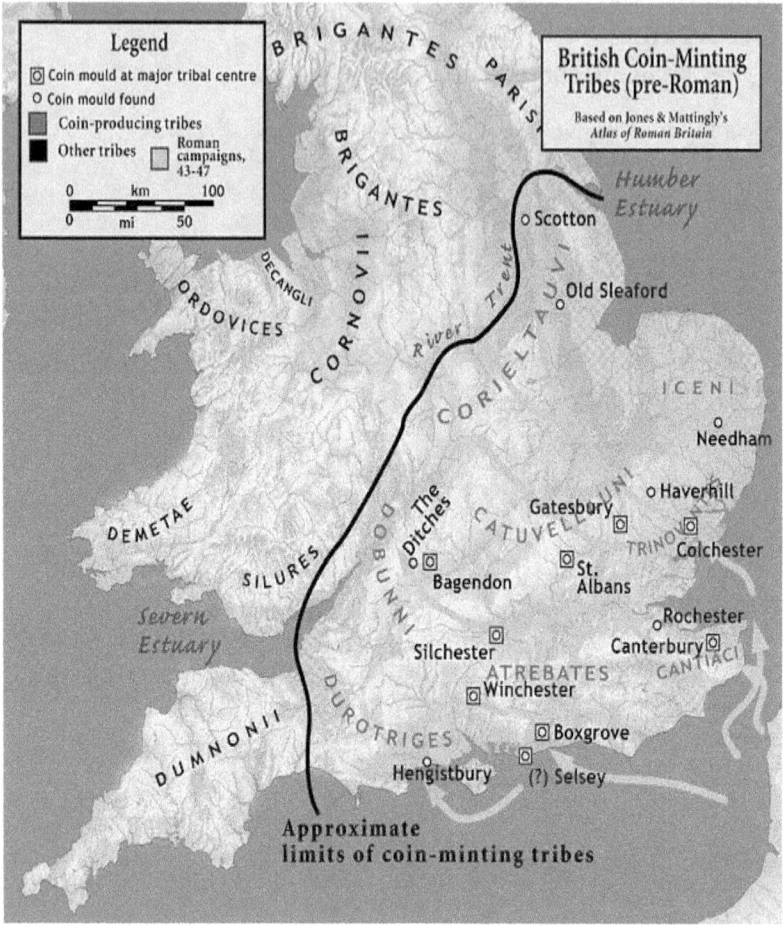

Minted coins and the implication of commerce further support notions of peaceful co-existence among Ancient British tribes that had coalesced from diverse arrivals over thousands of years. Name-calling and overt prejudice, such as the Roman use of the broad derogatory term "Barbarian" to disparage all those on the margins of their dominion, would nowadays be unacceptable. One might well wonder why an oppressor bent on conquest and theft, coming from a region that would later invent the scourge of fascism, should be venerated today as a civilising influence.

# The Western Roman Empire and Its Invasion of Britain

III

## 10.5.5 Map – Further Roman Conquest – Circa 68 AD

Maps from http://commons.wikimedia.org/wiki/Category:Maps released under CC-BY-SA
http://creativecommons.org/licenses/by-sa/3.0/

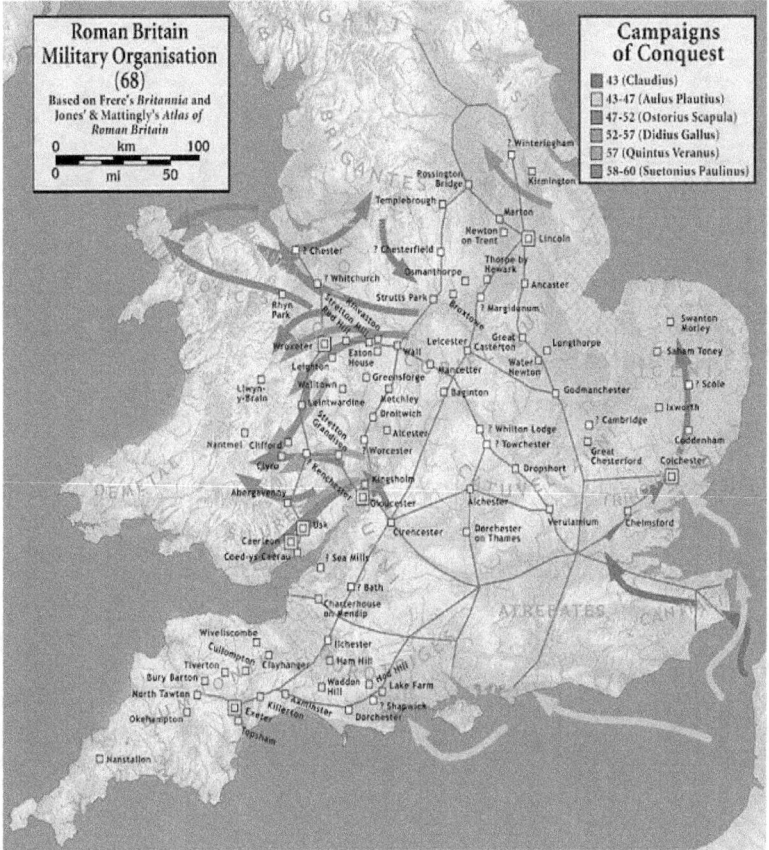

Note that roads such as the Fosse Way and Watling Street were in use as highways among British tribal centres long before the Romans arrived in 43 AD. Therefore to attribute these highways to the Romans is highly questionable. Together with the Britons' minted currency, those routes also suggest free travel and trade among the tribes, with the implication of a pre-Roman *Pax Brittanica*.

## 10.5.6 Map – Further Roman Conquest – Circa 80 AD

Maps from http://commons.wikimedia.org/wiki/Category:Maps released under CC-BY-SA
http://creativecommons.org/licenses/by-sa/3.0/

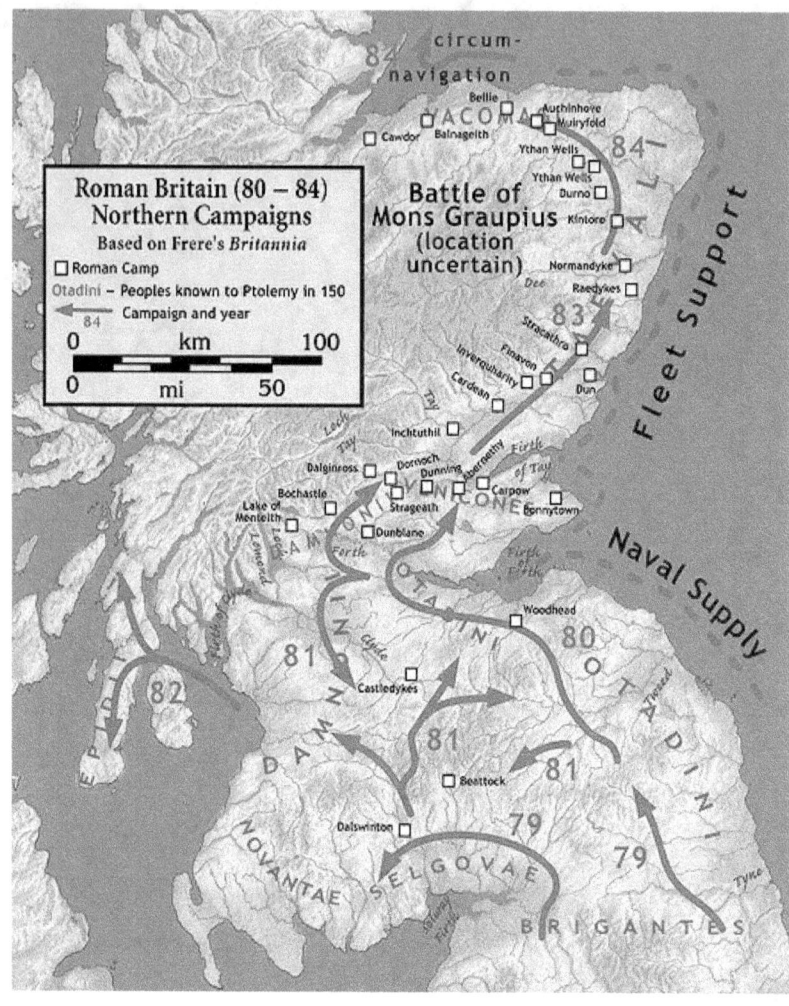

## 10.6  Map – Roman Britain at its End circa 410 AD

Map from http://commons.wikimedia.org/wiki/Category:Maps released under CC-BY-SA
http://creativecommons.org/licenses/by-sa/3.0/

## 11 The Dark Ages – Who Says?

From the 4th to the 6th centuries AD, Irish tribes, at that time named *Scotti*, crossed into Scotland from Ulster in the north to become the Scots. Thus began the ethnic dilution or absorption of the Picts who were squeezed by those Scotti in the west, and by the Northumbrian Anglo-Saxons in the east. In spite of several successful battles, by the time of the Norman Conquest the Picts had ceased to exist as a separate culture or race; they left very little to identify a tenure of possibly thousands of years, though a contributory factor could have been rising sea levels throughout the Mesolithic period, to which, in their possible early history as seafarers, they would have been vulnerable at least in coastal areas that saw sea levels rise 30 metres, with tidal and wave action able to destroy even stone constructions over the millennia. Bede does impart some lasting memory of the Picts by referring to their language as being distinct from Welsh and Gaelic:

> "...This island at present, following the number of the books in which the Divine law was written, contains five nations, the English, Britons, Scots, Picts, and Latins, each in its own peculiar dialect..."

Further south, during the 4th and 5th centuries AD, there were significant movements of Irish tribes into Wales and Cornwall, probably from the kingdom of Munster, and via Leinster as shown on the map below. Lasting and quantitative evidence of this particular migration was left in the form of the extent of the distribution of Ogham inscriptions on stone monuments around the shores of the Irish sea and on the Isle of Man. Outside Ireland they are mostly to be found in Pembrokeshire in Wales, and throughout Cornwall, but there is also evidence that the culture spread through central southern England as far as Reading, Silchester, and even London.

*The Dark Ages – Who Says?*

The true nature of the times can best be appreciated through the writings of monks and other commentators that are catalogued under the classification of "Matters of Britain", and a small number of similar "Matters" from the cultures of Ancient Greece, France, and Rome, several of which are referenced in chapters in Volume Two.

## 11.1 Map – British Regions at the Start of Anglo-Saxon Britain

Map from http://www.gutenberg.org/etext/16790 Public Domain

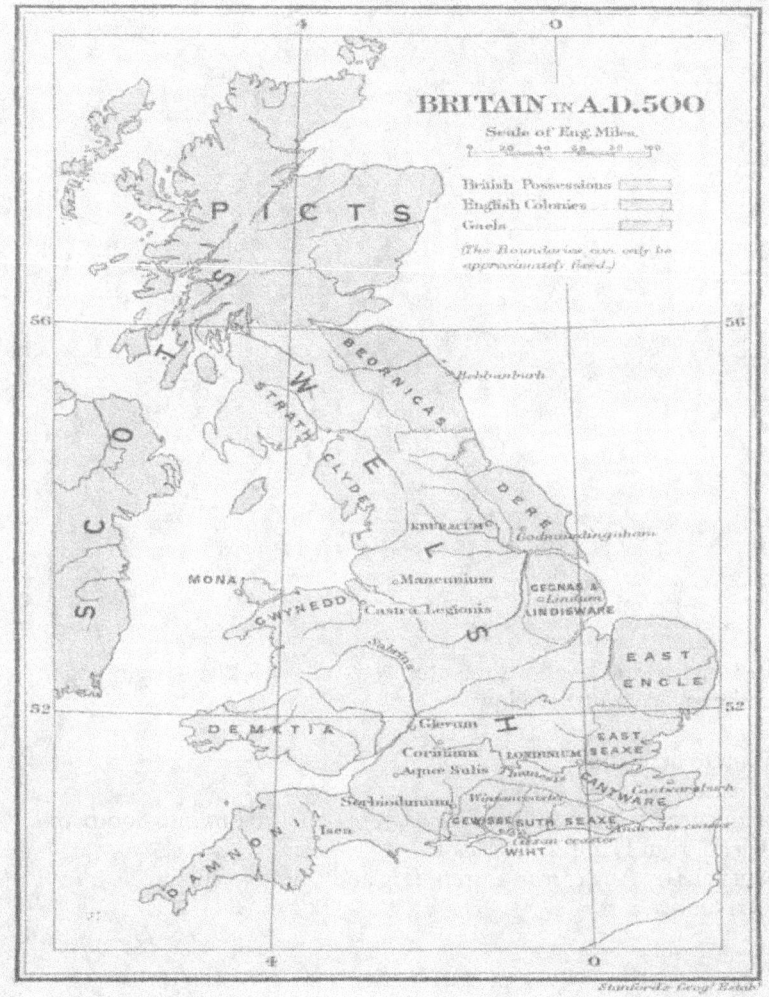

Gaels = Scots & Picts, English Colonies were in the east, British possessions were: Central England, Wales, The Southwest (Welsh on the map).

## 11.2 Migration Just Before the Time of the Monk Gildas
### 11.2.1 Map – The Irish, Angles, Jutes, and Saxons Arrive.

Maps from http://commons.wikimedia.org/wiki/Category:Maps released under CC-BY-SA http://creativecommons.org/licenses/by-sa/3.0/

The invasion arrows above are interpreted anti-clockwise beginning in Southwest Scotland as follows:

Irish-into Scotland.
Irish into Wales.
A sequence of Saxons, Jutes, Saxons, Jutes, and Saxons into Southern England from Hampshire to Essex.
Incursions by Angles into Eastern England from Norfolk to Northumberland.

# The Dark Ages – Who Says?

## 11.2.2 Map – Irish Routes into Wales.

Maps from http://commons.wikimedia.org/wiki/Category:Maps released under CC-BY-SA
http://creativecommons.org/licenses/by-sa/3.0/

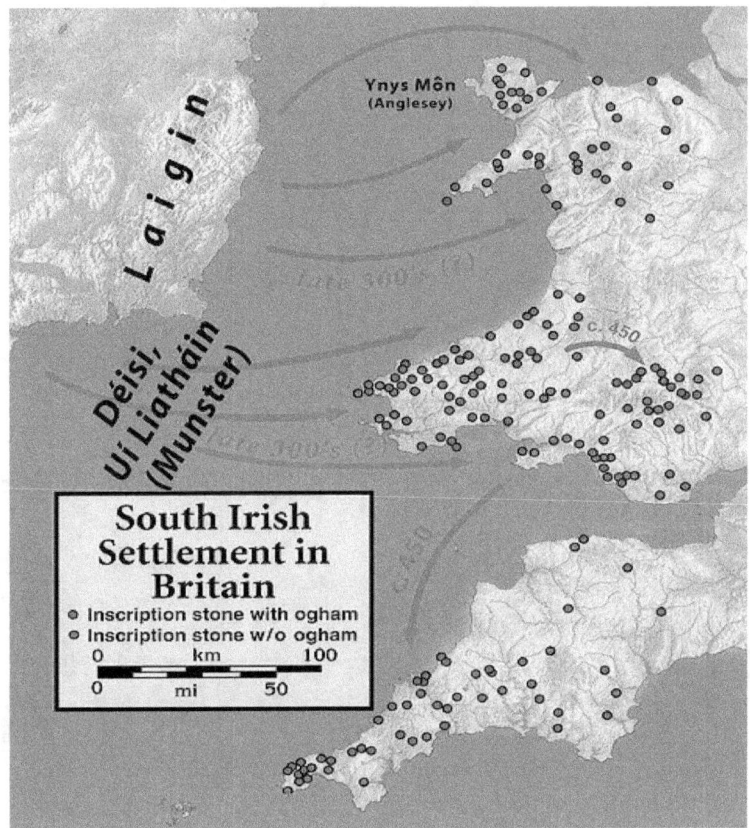

## 11.3 Britain During the Lifetime of Gildas
### 11.3.1 Map – Circa 540 AD – Britons Already Squeezed Westwards

Maps from http://commons.wikimedia.org/wiki/Category:Maps released under CC-BY-SA
http://creativecommons.org/licenses/by-sa/3.0/

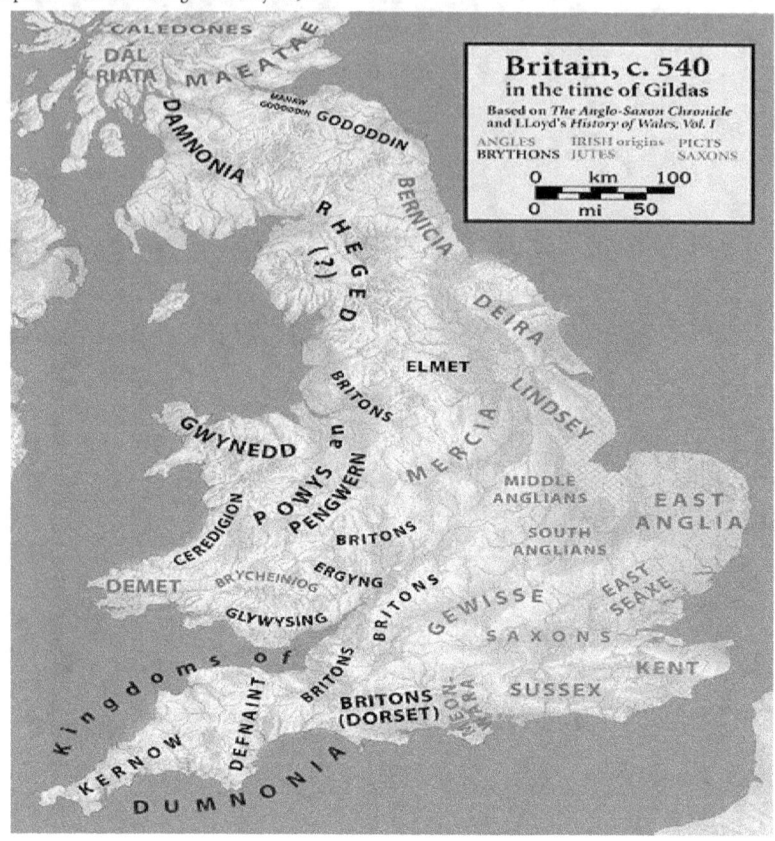

## 11.3.2 Map – 600 AD – Even More Saxon Expansion

Maps from http://commons.wikimedia.org/wiki/Category:Maps released under CC-BY-SA
http://creativecommons.org/licenses/by-sa/3.0/

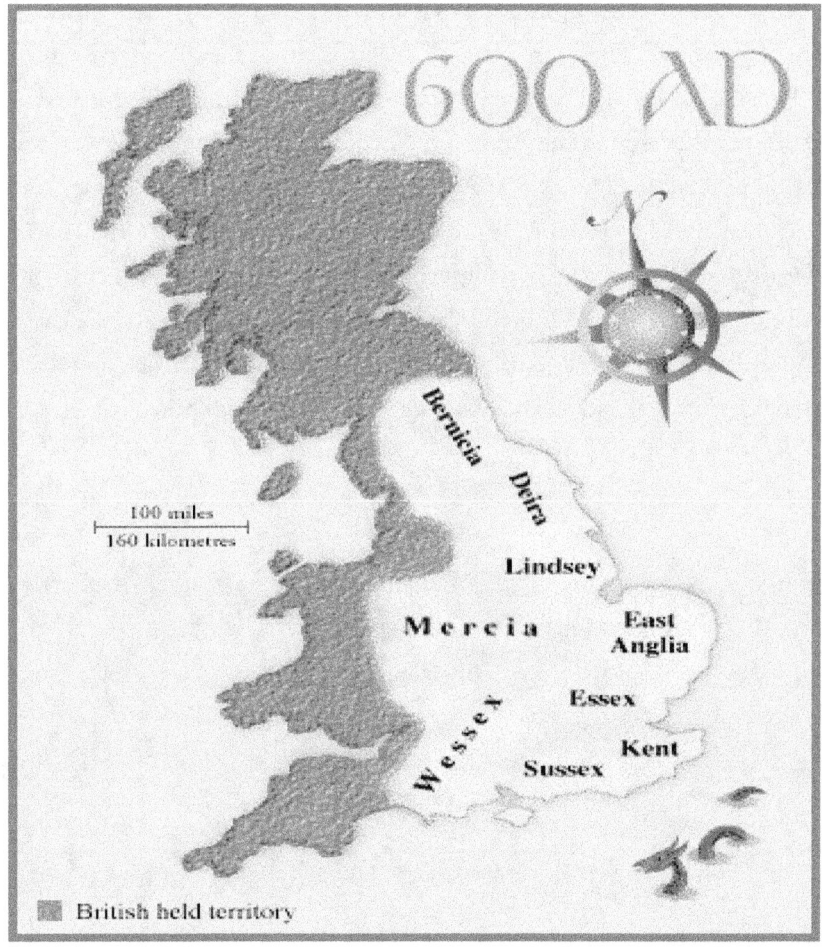

## 12 The Germanic and Nordic Invasions
## 12.1 Jutes, Angles, Saxons, and Frisians

This Germanic group of peoples is also referred to as a group of tribes – the *Ingaevones*. There are various spellings, and they were part of a Germanic culture that developed, spread out, and became differentiated as separate tribes around the Baltic and North Seas. The term *Ingaevones*, was used in Pliny the Elder's book, *Naturalis Historia* or *Natural History*, and was also quoted by Hector Munro Chadwick in his book *The Origin of the English Nation* (1907). The Ingaevones may well be descendants of the tribes that long before had collected flint and amber along the southern shore of the Baltic Sea – tribes that many generations earlier may have traded with Britain across the now forgotten Doggerland Bridge.

See next page.

## The Germanic and Nordic Invasions

### 12.1.1 Map – Jute, Angle, Saxon, and Frisian Origins

Map from http://commons.wikimedia.org/wiki/Category:Maps released under CC-BY-SA
http://creativecommons.org/licenses/by-sa/3.0/

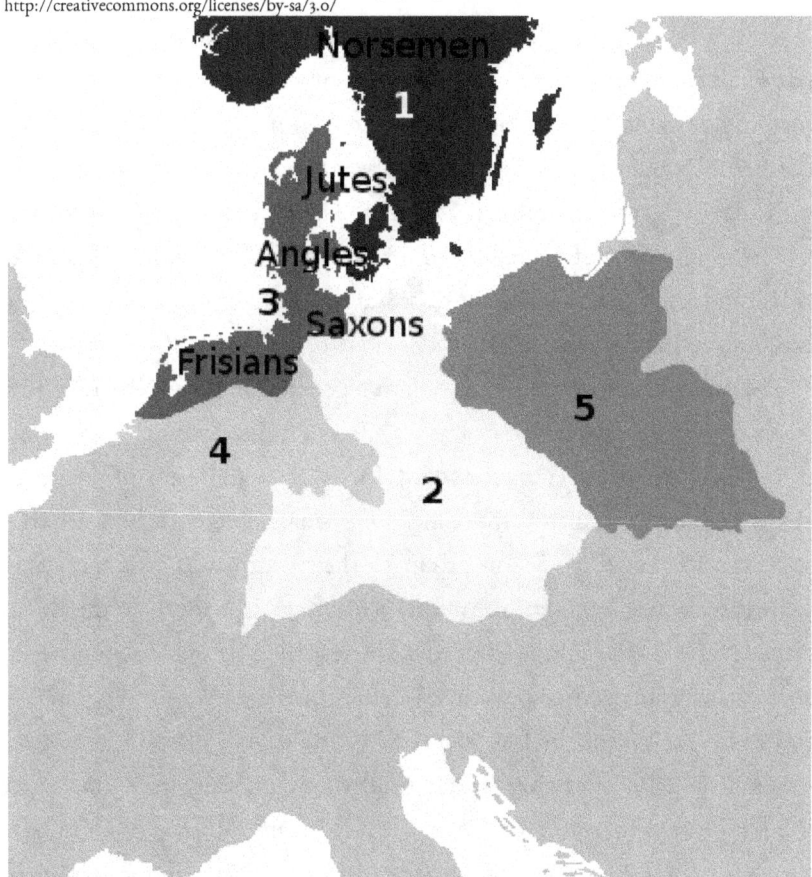

1 North Germanic
2 Elbe Germanic (Irminonic)
3 North Sea Germanic (Ingvaeonic)
4 Weser-Rhine Germanic (Istvaeonic)
5 East Germanic

## 12.2 Vikings, Danes, and Norsemen

Culturally and ethnically little different to the peoples previously identified as Jutes, Angles, Saxons, and Frisians, who were collectively known as the Anglo-Saxons, the Vikings comprised people from just a bit further north than the Anglo-Saxon regions, but still within present-day northern Denmark, plus Sweden, Norway, and the many surrounding islands of the Baltic Sea and the North Sea. Their identity as a single force is said by some to be just a romantic innovation of the last couple of hundred years, and certainly the present-day Scandinavian principalities did not exist fifteen hundred years ago.

They were unquestionably all sea-faring peoples, and they were used to a harsh climate. They followed a strong Pagan belief system, with richly embedded concepts of courage and loyalty to kin, as did many of the tribes along the southern Baltic shoreline. One small difference between the Vikings and the Anglo-Saxon group to their south, was that there was some east to west pressure from other invasive groups south of the Baltic on the Anglo-Saxon lands and people, whereas the Vikings could not really claim that sort of external pressure as an incentive to explore and expand. It was quite the reverse in fact, since the Scandinavian diaspora, explored more later, pushed eastwards and southwards creating trade links and founding the embryonic Rus nation which became Russia. It seems that they wanted trade and dominion to the east by river and land, but initially at least, just booty to their west by sea, which they generally got in abundance, forming settlements later on in Ireland, northern England, and Normandy in France.

The notable part of the Viking phenomenon ran from about AD 700 to 1066 and a little beyond, and in the case of the British Isles, the whole adventure was really a protracted struggle, between in many cases historical rivals and related tribes, to see who could get control of Britain, and specifically England. The Norman Danes eventually won out in 1066 after having morphed into the plain "Normans".

The Viking influence was prodigious, but after an overview here, only British related details will be of interest. As a rough guide to the overall

## The Germanic and Nordic Invasions

spheres of interest and influence, the Norwegians travelled north and west, out into the North Atlantic to colonise Scotland, Ireland, Wales, the Shetland and Faroe Islands, Iceland, and Greenland; the Swedes travelled east, into Finland, Ukraine, Estonia, Latvia, Lithuania, Poland, and Germany, and they founded the original version of Russia at Kiev, as well as venturing along the Dnieper and Volga rivers to the Black Sea and Caspian Sea. The Danes meanwhile, plagued England with the Danelaw, and settled in Normandy, France.

There was no rigid barrier to the co-existence of tribes or families in any of those areas in any general or national sense, though vendettas and rivalries would have ensured a healthy competitiveness. Viking influence overall, with varying persistence of their sometimes precarious settlements, extended to: North Africa, Italy, Constantinople and the Middle East, North American northerly coasts, and Newfoundland and Labrador in Canada. From the late $11^{th}$ to the early $13^{th}$ centuries, they provided mercenary services as the Varangian Guard to the Emperor of Byzantium, but later faced stiff competition from Anglo-Saxon refugees, displaced from England following the Norman Conquest.

**789.** The Vikings first came to England as raiders, and they hit the Dorset coast at possibly Wareham or Portland.

**793.** Lindisfarne aka Holy Island off the Northumbrian coast was the scene of a terrible slaughter and the robbery and destruction of valuable religious relics.

**794.** The locals, being prepared after the previous year's outrage, repulsed a raid near Jarrow which, together with the effects of a devastating storm, resulted in the raiders staying away for 40 years. The residents of Jarrow had good reason to defend the town since the Monastery of Saint Paul, once the home of the Venerable Bede, was reputed to have been the only centre of learning in Europe north of Rome. This is referred to by Simeon of Durham in his *History of the Kings*.

**835.** A furious wave broke on the shores of the peaceful island, with fleets of up to three or four hundred ships entering the English river system. For thirty years England was constantly a victim to short lived incursions.

**852.** Poor Saxon organisation allowed the Danes to over-winter on the Isle of Thanet in Kent, and possibly gave them the idea of staying just a little longer.

**865.** Following further greedy, weak, and meek leadership by the British Romano-Christian elite, and after a more robust and increased resistance to external pressures in their home territory in continental Europe, a more sustained and confident Danish invasion of Northumbria and Eastern England was launched, to be met initially by utter confusion and lack of spirit by many of the defenders. The monasteries and other religious repositories were brimming with riches and consumables that had been elicited in the name of the faith from the church's flock, and the ecclesiastic regimes were ripe and possibly deserving of a wake-up call. The onslaught was to continue until 954 AD.

**866.** A very small military reversal occurred when King Ælle of Northumberland defeated and captured the Viking, Ragnar Lodnok, and according to historical Scandinavian stories, had him cast into a snake-pit, while, watched by the King, more adders were thrown onto him while he sang until he died. This military reverse was indeed short-lived, since a large army – the Great Army – led by Ivar "the Boneless", son of Ragnar Lodnok, that had landed in East Anglia the previous year, now made its way north by land and sea, and during 867 York and the whole of Northumbria were taken, and Whitby Abbey was destroyed. These wins were followed by the defeat of the East Anglians in 869, and by the conquest of most of Mercia during the three years from 874 to 877.

Northumbria and the north of England were now lost forever by the Anglo-Saxons to the Danelaw – the word denoting both the geographical area and the customs of the people – and the Midlands were in a state of thrall. Wessex alone was unconquered, and Ivar the Boneless went on to become King of Dublin, dying in 872, but not before an Irish branch of the Vikings was well established – the Hiberno-Norse.

## The Germanic and Nordic Invasions

An account of the sacking of pre-Viking York, written about 150 years after the event, was made by Simeon of Durham who said:

> *"... The army raided here and there and filled every place with bloodshed and sorrow. Far and wide it destroyed the churches and monasteries with fire and sword. When it departed from a place it left nothing standing but roofless walls. So great was the destruction that at the present day one can scarcely see anything left of those places, nor any sign of their former greatness..."*

Further detail can be read in Simeon of Durham's *History of the Kings of England*, that is a part of *The Historical Works of Simeon of Durham*, translated by the Reverend Joseph Stevenson, in *The Church Historians of England Volume III Part II*. It should be noted that Simeon of Durham is not held in the highest regard by modern historians, and the correct attribution of these works is in question, with two other possible authors mentioned by the translator and more recent scholarly researchers.

**870.** The Danes carried the fight south to Wessex, and the Saxon, Alfred of Wessex was crowned in the year 871 at Winchester.

**871 to 878.** The struggle went back and forth between Alfred and the Danes until in 878 Alfred, being heavily outnumbered, made a strategic withdrawal from his stronghold at Chippenham, Wiltshire, and fled south. It was after an earlier defeat by the Danes at Wilton in 871 that Alfred had decided to pay the Danes money to keep the peace, the forerunner of Danegeld that became more and more common and costly in the 10$^{th}$ century, and that, like any surrender to blackmail, was just appeasement and foolish.

**878.** In March, Alfred (later to become the Great), King of Wessex, hid in the marshes of the Somerset Levels and built a fortress at the Isle of Athelney – a base from which he carried out guerilla raids on the Danes. It was during this time that he was reputed to have burned some cakes that he was supposed to be watching, earning himself a scolding from the dame of the household.

**878.** By May, Alfred had formed an army from among the folk of Somerset, Wiltshire, and Hampshire. They gathered at the now lost Egbert's stone – east of the forest of Selwood at Brixton, but which some say is near the much later (1772) monument known as Alfred's Tower, 4 or 5 miles west of Bruton in Somerset, and the conscripts, or maybe volunteers, are romantically said to have arrived along the ridgeways of the three counties. It must be remembered that the population were possibly descendants of arrivals possessed with an equally ferocious fighting ability to that of the Danes, and the Anglo-Saxons had a homeland to defend.

The battle was joined after about 20 miles marching to the north, and Alfred's abiding Greatness was assured when they surrounded and forced surrender on the Viking army at the Battle of Ethandun, present-day Edington, near Westbury. After the battle, thought by some to be commemorated by the more recent Westbury White Horse, the Viking leader, Guthrum, and several more prominent military figures in the Danish army were persuaded to convert to Christianity at Wedmore, to sign up to a peace treaty, and then to just go home to East Anglia where their jurisdiction was known as the Danelaw. The Danes retained East Anglia and the North, while Wessex had part of the Midlands and the South, but not Cornwall where Britons still clung to the vestige of an ancient empire.

Following the victory of 878, Alfred acted to create a kingdom that could be successfully defended and held against further invasion. To achieve this, his principal legacies were the system of Burhs or Burghs – fortified towns, an expanded standing army instead of just an on-call militia, and a strengthened navy. The Burh system took advantage of existing walled towns whose foundations and walls he strengthened, some of those sites dating back to the Bronze Age when similar strategies had taken advantage of the landscape. Burhs were widely scattered to provide a refuge no more than 20 miles from any less-fortified habitation, and the whole population had an interest and an obligation to maintain the fortifications. Hilltops, ports, and religious centres were used, and the resulting network also became a commercial network. This all cost money of course, and so the administrative system known as the Burghal Hidage was developed under Alfred and his immediate successors in order to identify the Burhs themselves, and to specify expectations of tax yields in terms of acreage or *hidage* of associated lands. One hide was expected to support one household, and depending on productivity, would have been about 20 acres. The military yield in the form of soldiery and other personnel to support the Burh strategy was also reckoned in terms of hides; one soldier with his equipment for every 5 hides, and one auxiliary per hide. In times of crisis, the civil population with whatever resources they could carry or herd, retreated to the Burhs, which then acted like defensive squares from which the invaders could be harried while also being largely denied local produce. The comparative security of the Burhs made them ideal for hosting Royal Mints for the production of coinage, and for its control by the agents of the Sovereign.

In 1897 the English historian F. W. Maitland, particularly renowned for his contribution to legal history, made reference to a medieval document, roughly dated to the early 900s AD, and titled the 'Burghal Hidage'. The document listed thirty-three fortified towns or Burhs throughout Wessex, and also identified taxes, and the way the required strength of men-at-arms was calculated to maintain the defence of a given stronghold. Overall, there is powerful evidence to support the legendary achievements of Alfred the Great in the development of coastal and inland defensive networks, and the creation of an infrastructure and organisation to maximise their effectiveness.

Several years of skirmishing throughout Wessex validated the Burh system when the Danes, after causing serious trouble starting in 891, were eventually forced to give up during 896. With increased security in the British Anglo-Saxon sphere came more cultural output, as a part of which Alfred's reign began the production of the Anglo-Saxon Chronicle that would be updated over the next two or three centuries. It was written not in Latin as was customary, but in Old English, and a small introductory extract from this fascinating public domain document is given below. It is believed to have been King Alfred the Great who personally commissioned the Chronicle circa 890, but it would continue to evolve for several generations with the language of expression changing from the original Anglo-Saxon, to the last entries circa the middle of the 12th century being what is described as Middle English.

A translation by Rev. James Ingram (London, 1823), with additional readings from the translation of Dr. J.A. Giles (London, 1847) is as follows:

> "...The island Britain is 800 miles long, and 200 miles broad. And there are in the island five nations; English, Welsh (or British), Scottish, Pictish, and Latin. The first inhabitants were the Britons, who came from Armenia, and first peopled Britain southward. Then happened it, that the Picts came south from Scythia, with long ships, not many; and, landing first in the northern part of Ireland, they told the Scots that they must dwell there. But they would not give them leave; for the Scots told them that they could not all dwell there together; "But," said the Scots, "we can nevertheless give you advice. We know another island here to the east. There you may dwell, if you will; and whosoever withstandeth you, we will assist you, that you may gain it." Then went the Picts and entered this land northward. Southward the Britons possessed it, as we before said. And the Picts obtained wives of the Scots, on condition that they chose their kings always on the female side; which they have continued to do, so long since. And it happened, in the run of years, that some party of Scots went from Ireland into Britain, and acquired some portion of this land. Their leader was called Reoda, from whom they are named Dalreodi (or Dalreathians). Sixty winters ere that Christ was born, Caius Julius, emperor of the Romans, with eighty ships sought Britain. There he was first beaten in a dreadful fight, and lost a great part of his army...".

*The Germanic and Nordic Invasions*

Armenia is generally accepted as meaning Armorica, which could have implied anywhere from Iberia, north through Gaul, and as far as Brittany.

### 12.2.1 Map – The Burhs and Other Anglo-Saxon Fortifications

Map from http://commons.wikimedia.org/wiki/Category:Maps released under CC-BY-SA
http://creativecommons.org/licenses/by-sa/3.0/

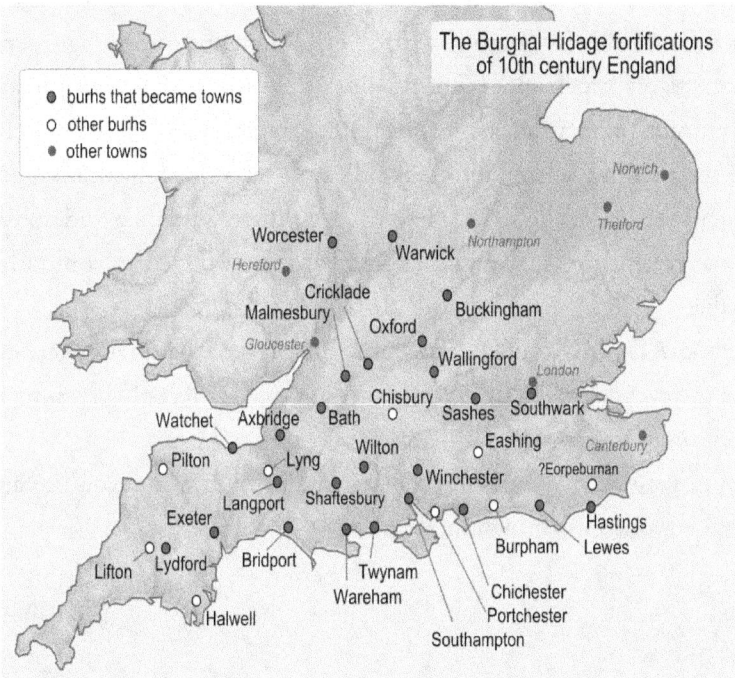

### 12.3 Summary and Conclusion

The Viking invasions were instrumental in provoking the unification of England during the Dynasty of the House of Wessex, eventually under Alfred the Great, and later after a temporary defeat by the Danes during the period 1013 to 1042, under Harold Godwinson of the Restored House of Wessex in 1066.

It was in that fateful year of 1066, after all the armed struggles, and after all the internal cultural and so-called religious enlightenment in the face of Pagan iconoclasm, that the unified Anglo-Saxons were destined to ultimately and irrevocably fall victim to the unrelenting Norseman invasion attempts. This final time the threat was not from across the North

Sea but from a build-up across the English Channel of the Nordic family branch in Normandy.

As eloquently expressed in the book *Millennium* by Tom Holland, the close of the 1st millennium had been a time of great political and cultural significance to the population of Europe; superstitions, premonitions and expectations held by our ancestors one thousand years ago were understandably much more fanciful than were those of the supposedly more rational population that existed at the start of the 3rd millennium – where we are now. In spite of mankind's 1500 years of sophistication and enlightenment since the so-called Dark Ages, there was still a widespread irrational fear of the Y2K bug that was not just restricted to computing anomalies.

In 1000 AD, one wonders how much more were the English on edge during the events leading up to the worst imposition of lasting tyranny to befall the island?

Events just sixty-six years into the new millennium would confirm and surpass everyone's worst nightmares.

# 13 The Norman Invasion
## 13.1 Introduction

This event was a lead-in and an introduction to the nature of much of the 2nd millennium. England's ultimately relatively stable and prosperous Anglo-Saxon period, following the Viking predations, was to be replaced by a barbarous Norman regime of conquest, carpet bagging, and ethnic cleansing. Its unpleasantness and royal excess were certainly responsible for nurturing the seed of the English, and later British and colonial constitutions and their durability. British foreign policy, essentially based on opposing any other ascendant power in Europe in order to maintain peace and stability, was conceived and would be grown in the succeeding few centuries.

The so-called Dark Ages, even at the time of William the Conqueror (aka William the Bastard, so nicknamed due to birth not to behaviour) were a distant memory, and the Charter of Liberties and its successor Magna Carta were inconceivably far ahead in the 13th century; they would be the first attempts to set out a contract between the Monarch and the People that would restrict the whims of the monarch, and that would grant rights to the people. The People in return, in that far future, would agree to be ruled by the Crown.

Meanwhile, at the start of the 2nd millennium in Normandy the loose concept of feudalism had matured, a concept that had first evolved during the Roman crisis of the 3rd century when deteriorating civil order had forced many into contracts of serfdom with land owners in order to find protection. Feudalism, that vile oppressive system that is still apparent in the 3rd millennium, was now an established and accepted practice of the Normans. In Norman society, the subjects of the Monarch, that is to say the People, consisted of Lords, Vassals, and Serfs; there was no reliably structured parliament or constitution, and deference and obligation among the levels of society derived purely from the possession of land, grants of tenure, and the provision of military services when required. Underpinning it all, were: Common Law; oaths among the Monarch, Lords, and vassals; and the cruel exploitation of a vast and voiceless powerhouse that did all the productive work – the mass of serfdom – that were kept in penal subjugation by a Lord's retainers, and who had small chance of escaping from their lowly status. The Feudal system was a veritable nursery school of dissidence and it was coming to England.

## 13.2 The English Background

From the first Germanic arrivals, led by Cerdic in 519 AD, the land had been a battleground among: the original Britons, Welsh, Picts, and Scots; and the newly arrived Jutes, Frisians, Angles, and Saxons. It seems that at some time or other just about everyone had fought everyone else, had intermarried, and had generally culturally cross-pollinated. From the first Viking raids in 789 AD until the last in 1066, the continuing battles became more simply identifiable as Anglo-Saxons versus the Vikings, and ultimately a struggle between the Houses of Wessex and Denmark, while the aboriginal Britons were culturally marginalised, and isolated in Cornwall and parts of Wales and Scotland.

That view, however, may well be too simplistic, and there are contra theories that a large number of quiet, original, resident Britons persisted in all regions, trading and assimilating among successive military waves of adventurers, who, although in a minority, exerted their influence by violence, intimidation, and a disproportionate entry in the annals of history. So in reality, those aboriginal Britons were almost certainly genetically integrated with the wider British population by this time

At the beginning of 1066, Edward the Confessor, the Anglo-Saxon King of England, was close to death, and without a hereditary or otherwise publicly acknowledged heir; his upbringing had been in Normandy and he was inclined to things Norman, rather than Viking. It might be useful to get an overview of the royal turbulence and dynastic changes around this time. The cultural ascendancy, occasioned by what was effectively civil war, is indicated by the alternations of the reigning monarchs and their often brief periods of tenure as shown in the table below.

## The Norman Invasion

| Period | Dominion | Monarch |
|---|---|---|
| 978 to 1013 | Wessex | Æthelred the Unready (first reign). |
| 1013 to 1014 | Denmark | Sweyn Forkbeard. |
| 1014 to 1016 | Wessex | Æthelred the Unready (second reign). |
| 1016 | Wessex | Edmund Ironside. |
| 1016 to 1035 | Denmark | Cnut (aka Canute). |
| 1035 to 1040 | Denmark | Harold Harefoot. |
| 1040 to 1042 | Denmark | Harthacnut. |
| 1042 to 1066 | Wessex | Edward the Confessor. |
| 1066 | Wessex | Harold Godwinson. |
| 1066 | Wessex | Edgar the Ætheling. Proclaimed, but never crowned. |
| 1066 to 1087 | Norman | William I, aka William the Bastard, aka William the Conqueror. |

During this period of turbulence the Anglo-Saxon interest in England was secured to Cnut by his appointment of Godwin as earl of Wessex, and by Godwin's second marriage to Cnut's sister-in-law, Gytha. An excellent account of the complexities of the extended families may be read at the following two websites:

http://www.medievalhistory.net/page0008.htm

http://orthodoxwiki.org/Harold_of_England

Earl Godwin had a foot in each camp, having helped Cnut's son, Harold Harefoot, to the throne, and then also having ensured Edward's succession and the positioning of his own daughter, Edith, as Edward's queen. However, Edward's inclination to things Norman, and a disregard for his own people at times, led to the temporary banishing in 1051 of Earl Godwin and his sons, Harold, Tostig, Gyrth, and Leofwine, and the sending to a convent of his Queen Edith. Edward however, was not a military leader, and he was forced to pardon the Godwins after only a year, and to hand over virtually all state powers to Harold Godwinson, retaining for himself only religious interests, and holding Godwin's youngest son, Wulfnoth, as hostage to the agreement.

Therefore, when Edward the Confessor died on January 5th, 1066, he left a widow and Queen, Edith, who was the sister of Earl Godwin's son Harold; and so it was this Harold Godwinson – brother-in-law of the recently deceased King Edward, and someone of rank who already wielded state power – who now claimed to have been anointed by Edward in the presence of Queen Edith. This was a compelling claim by a powerful lord, and it was quickly approved by the Witan.

## 13.3 The Invaders and Their Backgrounds

### 13.3.1 King Harald III of Norway

King Harald of Norway had gained the nickname *Hardrada* – Ruthless or Hard Ruler – and he believed that he had a claim to the throne of England because of a treaty between his predecessor, Magnus I of Norway, and King Harthacanute of England. That treaty proclaimed succession by either one of them to both kingdoms in the event of the death of one of them without an heir, but, although Harthacanute died first, Magnus had not been able to take England which allowed Edward the Confessor to take power. So, when Magnus died Hardrada teamed up with Harold Godwinson's own brother, Tostig, and was determined to take the crown. Landing in early September 1066 with a force of about 15,000 men from some 300 ships, they plundered York and the nearby coastline, and arrived at Stamford Bridge where they expected to receive favourable peace terms from King Harold Godwinson. King Harald of Norway had learned his trade as a mercenary for emperor Michael IV of the Byzantine Empire, and he was a formidable opponent.

### 13.3.2 Duke William of Normandy

Viking supremacy in Normandy had been established in 911 AD when Rollo, who was baptised Robert following his defeat by the French King Charles III, was granted leave to settle in the region around Rouen as a Fiefdom or Duchy in order to defend it and the Seine approach to Paris against further Viking raids. Feudal systems, described more later, arise in societies that have insufficient governance or bureaucratic infrastructure to maintain a fully integrated Nation-State under arms, and it was natural for the emergent Norman identity to adopt such a system, which, although alien to Nordic concepts, was already prevalent throughout the Frankish Empire. There were many conflicts among local and external claimants to power, and although Guillaume (William) of Normandy as the 7th leader of the Normans became Duke in 1035 when he was only 7 or 8 years old, it wasn't until 1063 that he finally became the undisputed Norman leader. This was largely due to the support of the King Henri I.

The approval in England of the English King Harold Godwinson by the Witan was deeply resented by Duke William of Normandy who was distantly related to Edward the Confessor, and who claimed that in 1051 it had been promised that he would have the throne of England when Edward died. He additionally claimed that Harold Godwinson had sworn fealty to him in 1064, and this propaganda, whether fact or fiction, was later recorded in the Bayeux Tapestry.

William accordingly assembled an army to invade England, including elements from several regions including Flanders and Brittany.

Footnote to this background: DNA studies suggest that the Norman invasion of England was predominantly not Nordic, but French in ethnic terms, and that it served to actually diminish the Scandinavian gene base of Britain, albeit slightly.

## 13.4 The Battles Of 1066

### 13.4.1 The Battle of Fulford Gate 20th September

This was the first of a series of related battles that would culminate in the Norman invasion of Britain. It was fought at Fulford near York where, after strong resistance and bloody fighting, it resulted in victory for the invading alliance and the occupation of the regional centre and Archbishopric of York. The invasion force comprised the Norwegian King Harald III aka Harald Hardrada, and the fifth columnist, the traitorous Saxon, Tostig Godwinson, who was the brother of the English King Harold. The defending home side, for the Kingdom of England, comprised the Earls Morcar of Northumbria and Edwin of Mercia, and it was this defeat of the Saxons that drew English King Harold north to repel the invaders, thereby allowing another set of invaders, the Normans, to make an unopposed landing in the south where they had ample time to set up a solid defensive camp, well-stocked with just about every provision that could be commandeered from miles around and with no resistance.

### 13.4.2 The Battle of Stamford Bridge 25$^{th}$ September

The English army under King Harold Godwinson was force-marched to do battle at Stamford Bridge, and within a week of the losses at Fulford Gate, they totally destroyed the invading army including its leaders, King Harald and Tostig. Of their 300 ships, only 24 were permitted to depart, taking mainly the surviving wounded and Harald's son. The Viking (Nordic variety) influence in England was now stabilised, and there would be no further lasting incursions. An ironic final Saxon victory.

The victorious but seriously battered and weakened army now had to march back more than 250 miles to the south coast to do battle against the settled and rested Norman invaders.

### 13.4.3 The Battle of Hastings 14$^{th}$ October

### 13.4.3.1 Battle of Hastings – Anglo-Saxon Cf. Norman Armies

|         | Foot | Archers | Cavalry |                                              |
|---------|------|---------|---------|----------------------------------------------|
| Norman  | 4500 | 1700    | 2200    | Virtually all trained, including mercenaries. |
| English | 7500 | 0       | 0       | All infantry with no specific expertise.     |

In spite of recruiting some fresh forces in London and having in their ranks some 2,000 dedicated and loyal to the death troops, the mostly part-time Saxon soldiers were outnumbered by fresh Normans who had plenty of time to fortify defensive positions and to gather into their compounds all the local produce needed to sustain themselves and their pack and combat horses, and to deny any surplus to the Saxons.

### 13.4.3.2 Battle of Hastings – Progress

The battle took place at Senlac Hill, six or seven miles from Hastings, on October 14$^{th}$, and it was the last decisive battle to result in a conquest of England. The Norman strategy was firstly to attack with a barrage of arrows, to follow up with a disruptive infantry assault, and to capitalise on the scattering of the defensive lines by a cavalry charge, while the English defensive strength lay in a formidable shield wall uphill from the attackers, from which javelins stones and a variety of missiles could be rained down on the Normans. In fact both a Norman infantry and a cavalry charge were repulsed, and there were reports that at one point William himself had been unhorsed. As so often happens though, lack of discipline can lead to unexpected reversals, and after one hour of intense fighting when the Normans had suffered some serious casualties, the Saxons broke ranks and abandoned the shield wall to pursue the hated invader.

Seizing the opportunity to launch a fresh attack, the Norman archers quickly struck over the broken shield wall at the troops in the rear, immediately killing or seriously wounding King Harold and many within his senior ranks. Believing the battle to be lost, the part-time militia or *fyrd* element broke and fled, and the field was taken by William the Conqueror.

### 13.4.3.3 Battle of Hastings – Endgame

Following the battle William expected tribute to be paid by the English, but whether from an expectation of further battles and maybe expulsion of the French, or just lack of leadership, this did not take place, so he remained in the Hastings area, resting his forces before advancing on London.

### 13.4.3.4 Battle of Hastings – Consequences

The Norman Conquest forced the entry of the English into mainstream Europe, with an English monarch who was also a Duke of part of France, and a thorn in the side of the French King. The course of English history was to change from its earlier centuries of defensive and ecclesiastical activity, to a major involvement with the Crusades, a foreign policy that became increasingly confrontational with any other ascendant European power, and particularly Anglo-French rivalry that would last for 800 years until the Entente Cordiale of 1904, though hostility towards European ascendancy continues even into the 21$^{st}$ century.

Domestically, the conquest was to lead initially to poverty and hardship for the majority, with widespread examples of genocide and ethnic cleansing that would cause an Anglo-Saxon diaspora. Eventually, assimilation and synthesis, as in previous millennia, would lead to a stable new Britain, but only after many centuries of bitterness and numerous factional wars.

## 13.5  Ethnic Cleansing of the British by the Normans

The progress of the Norman takeover is best seen on the maps below, but those simple illustrations of a bygone demographic do not capture in any way the horror wreaked by the Normans in an initially unwarranted slaughter by fire and the sword, of civilians of all ages as the invader conducted a northwards sweep of hundreds of villages and towns, the larger ones being Oxford, Warwick, Leicester, Nottingham, Derby, Lincoln, and York; few were spared, and the surrounding fertile farmlands were also despoiled.

Following a few successful responses in the form of more or less guerilla operations by combined English and Danish forces, and diverse bands of locals, the death of a Norman Earl and several hundred Norman soldiers at Durham in January 1069 led to a short-term climax of the escalating Norman aggression. This orgy of genocide and destruction was known as the Harrying or Harrowing of the North, and it lasted at least over the winter of 1069-1070, during which the destruction of crops, livestock, and land was calculated to complement the slaughter by denying any survivors both sustenance and shelter.

An indication of the nationwide scale and intensity of the Norman destruction was captured in the Domesday Book that was recorded in 1086, and persistent evidence of the iron fist approach would go on to be exemplified by the construction of something like 1,000 castles that would be hammered into the hitherto pastoral and peaceful landscape in less than one hundred years. Ironically, those foreboding fortifications would be used as an equivalent, but with an aggressive and anti-Anglo-Saxon agenda, to the defensive Burghs of Alfred's day, the Burghs having been innovated two hundred years earlier in an altogether different world.

# The Norman Invasion

## 13.5.1 Map – Displaced Anglo-Saxon Earldoms 1068

Map from book: William the Conqueror and the Rule of the Normans (1908) by Frank Merry Stenton

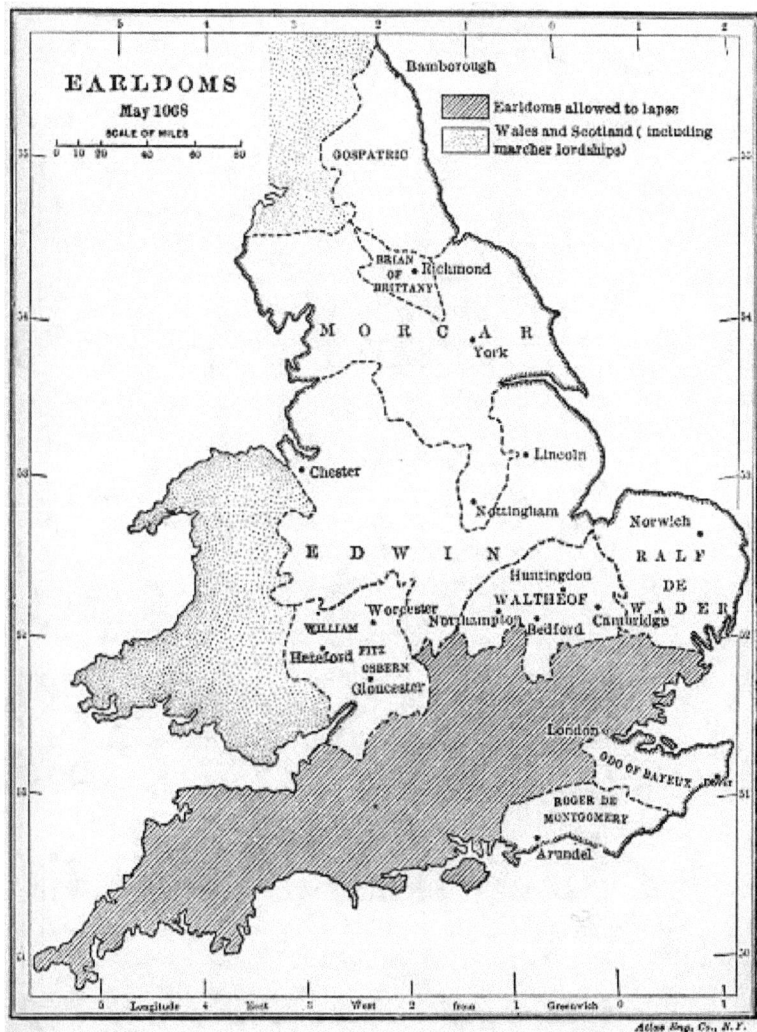

## 13.5.2 Map – Displaced Anglo-Saxon Earldoms 1075

Map from book: William the Conqueror and the Rule of the Normans (1908) by Frank Merry Stenton

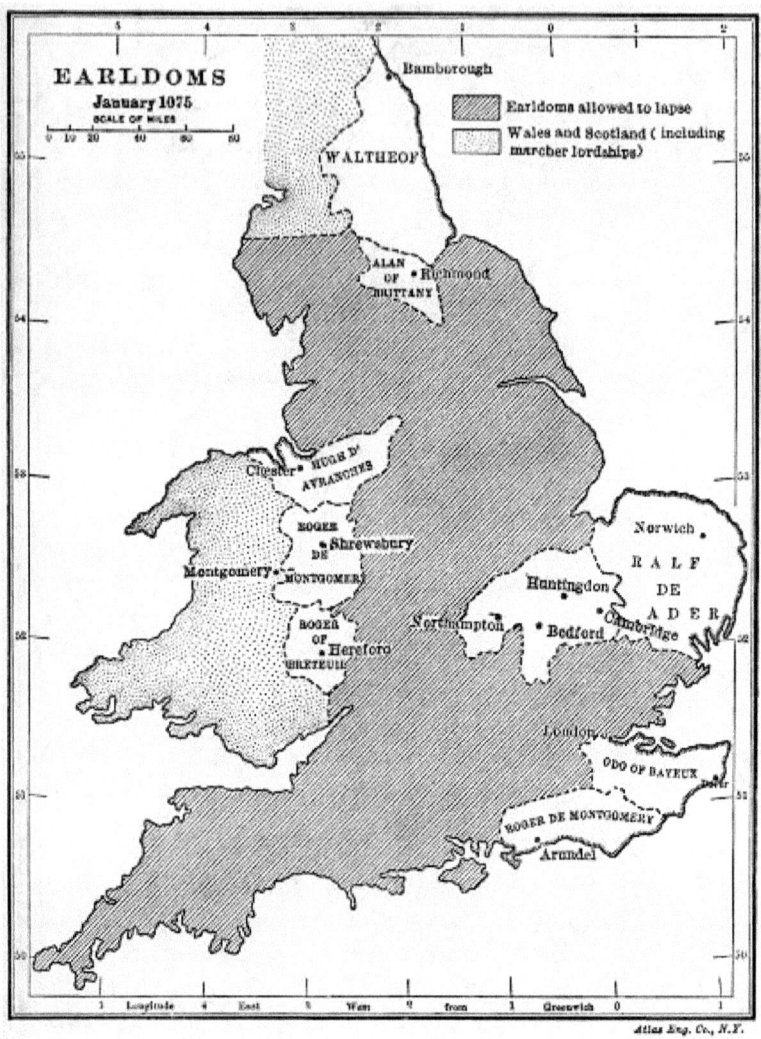

## 13.5.3 Map – Displaced Anglo-Saxon Earldoms 1087

Map from book: William the Conqueror and the Rule of the Normans (1908) by Frank Merry Stenton

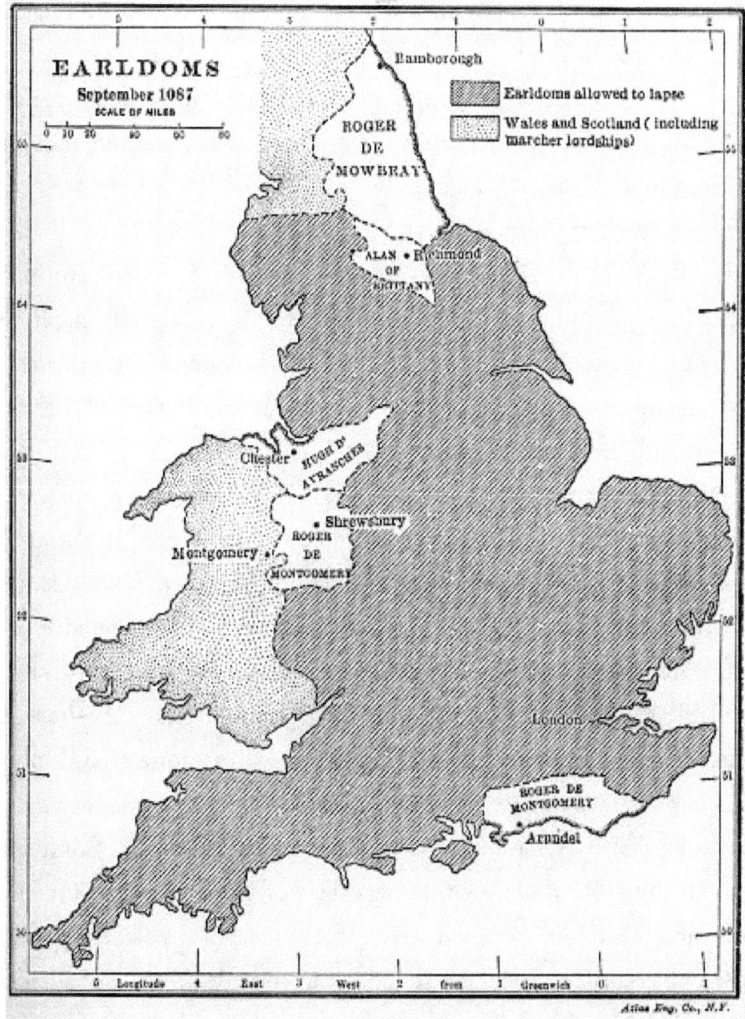

# 14 Migrant Invasions
## 14.1 Introduction

This chapter is intended to illustrate the range of the sources of migrants and the changes in the rates of immigration into what had, by medieval times, become a relatively settled Christian culture with a well-integrated population, and with genetic roots that dated back some ten thousand years. See the chapter on DNA later.

After the earliest unknown arrivals that most probably came to these islands as part of an aquatically nomadic Atlantic Seaboard culture as suggested earlier, and that was possibly from the Iberian peninsula, itself a cross-roads between northern Africa and the Mediterranean, all inward migration up to the end of the 1st millennium AD had been of predominantly northern European stock – in itself a huge and constantly vulnerable and varying melting pot. The salient point is that all these early migrations occurred over an immense timescale, into a recently glacier-free and relatively empty land, and that the rate of arrivals allowed adequate opportunity for successive generations to assimilate ethnic differences, and to mitigate tribal conflicts with newcomers; or at least to establish identifiable and acknowledged territorial boundaries that reflected resources, and that respected local traditions. Cross-border raids would always have been a danger to peace, and their extent, together with any sensitivities that may have existed towards miscegenation are completely unknown to us. We do know that regardless of whether tribal differences were regarded as ethnic, planned inter-tribal marriages or partnerships were almost universally regarded as strengthening confederations and alliances, and we also know that there was enough peace to enable the fulfilment of the desire to develop art and culture.

Against a background of increasing population it would be interesting to speculate on how changes were made to the presumably unspoken methods and primitive protocols of establishing or acknowledging territory for newcomers, as farming developed and spread among communities, and the percentage of farmers increased while the percentage of hunter-gatherers decreased.

On the other hand, the contrast between those spacious times and today's overcrowded cities would be depressing in the extreme, and many do indeed find it difficult to remain factual when confronted by demographic and cultural paradigm shifts, such as the sudden and massive, obviously inter-ethnic alien migrations of the 20th and particularly the early 21st centuries. That difficulty in remaining factual applies to all parties involved in the debate, and this chapter aims to make a decisively clear and irresistibly forceful cut through mainstream and liberal lies and self-deception. Anyone who believes that immigration to wealthy nations is in any sense an answer to world poverty and misery should watch "Immigration, World Poverty and Gumballs" on Youtube: https://www.youtube.com/watch?t=1&v=LPjzfGChGlE

All we can do is to remove our blinkers, be they political or delusional, and open our eyes to the facts of today. There is nothing conjectural or bigoted about doing that.

## 14.2 The Background – a Poor Starting Point

In reality of course, even historical tribal differences have never been completely resolved, and territorial limits in respect of common land and reasonably sized private lands have never been honoured. Those two failures are evidenced down to the Post Medieval Period (circa 1547 AD) by persistent skirmishes among the so-called Ancient Britons at the time of the Roman invasion, by the ensuing inter-tribal treachery of Briton against Briton that assisted the ongoing Roman cause and subsequent Anglo-Saxon takeover, and by later land enclosures and disenfranchisement of the general population following the Norman Conquest and the harrowing of the Saxons.

Furthermore, it is undeniable in the Modern Age (post 1901 AD), whether in the microcosm of inner-city deprivation and gang-culture competition, or in the macrocosm of territorial aggrandisement over natural resources, or in the tiny mindset of political and religious sectarianism, that an easily provoked hostility persists. The need for Civil Rights marches in Britain in the latter part of the 2$^{nd}$ millennium and the frequency of heavily policed street demonstrations during the 3rd millennium (when they aren't banned) are testament to a barely suppressed state of civil war that is exacerbated by an inadequately serviced population, and by congested cultural anarchy.

This apocalyptic and immortal spectre of tribalism needs little invitation to emerge, and it does so with undiminished frequency and ferocity to display its primordial bestiality as either the cause of, or the corollary of, conflict that has not ceased, and that realistically will never cease – neither inter-nationally nor inter-tribally – whatever agreements and protocols are signed, and with whatever accompanying fanfare. We can see that fact from historical repetitions across all empires and within all administrations; heads continue to roll, and fingers and lives continue to get burned – as will become apparent by the end of the two volumes of this book.

## 14.3 Pre-World War Two Migration Into Britain

> *"More people have now migrated to the UK in a single year (2010) than did so in the entire period from 1066 to 1950, excluding wartime."*
>
> – http://www.migrationwatchuk.com

### 14.3.1 British Jews and Russian Jews

The Jewish population of Britain is one of the oldest immigrant communities, and it has fluctuated due to specific invitations and expulsions, starting from the 1st millennium AD when one of the first skills-specific waves was recorded just after the Norman invasion. This was at the invitation of Duke William the Conqueror for business and banking or financial reasons. Estimates suggest a total Jewish population up to about 6,000 by the 13th century, around which time they were persecuted and expelled, albeit peacefully and with travel concessions, during the reign of King Edward I.

Until the 1970s this culture was the only significant non-Christian representation in Britain.

At the start of the 19th century there were estimated to be 10,000 Jews in Britain, and by 1914, due to the Russian pogroms of 1881, this had risen to about 120,000, many living in ghettos in London's East End.

The World Zionist Organisation, that had started in 1897, came to greater prominence in the 1920s and was led by Chaim Weizmann, who went on to become the first President of Israel after its formation in 1949. The beginning of the drive for a Jewish homeland had been given impetus by the Balfour Declaration of 1917 which had been authored by the British Foreign Secretary, Arthur Balfour, who was a Conservative under the wartime coalition government of David Lloyd-George. Weizmann had known Balfour since about 1910 when he (Weizmann) was a lecturer in Chemistry at the University of Manchester, and Balfour was his local MP. It is said that the Balfour Declaration was promoted in part as recognition of his friend Weizmann's contribution to the war effort, a coincidence without which, Middle-Eastern history might have been different in many respects.

By the end of the Second World War Jews in Britain no longer lived in inner-city ghettos and new arrivals moved straight into a suburban environment, after which the population seems to have risen to a peak of about 300,000 in 1991.

The 2001 Census indicated that there were 266,740 Jews in Britain, and this has since increased to 275,000 in 2005, and to 280,000 in 2008.

### 14.3.2 Romanies and Gypsies of the 14th Century

Since the 14th century or possibly a little earlier, and originally numbered in the hundreds, Roma Gypsies were commonly found working with horses, and as travelling hawkers and handymen. Estimates have always been difficult to determine because of their itinerant and reclusive nature, but modern sources put the number of recently arrived Central European Roma at more than 100,000, with an additional population of mixed Irish and Gypsy travellers, comprising historical arrivals and their families, of about 300,000. Other sources put the combined total at between 300,000 and 500,000.

### 14.3.3 Lombardy and the Hanseatic League

After the expulsion of the Jews around the end of the 13th century, the Lombards, who were established money lenders and bankers in Italy, and particularly at the wealthy trading centre of Venice, were responsible for an influx of London-based money traders that continued into the 16th century. We can trace the principles of the Fractional Reserve Banking System back to the Lombards, and most probably back to the Jewish Goldsmiths who preceded them at the end of the 1st millennium; condemnations of usury were, after all, mentioned in the Bible one thousand years before that, but more of this subject later.

From further north the Hanseatic League, see map below, was formed for the mutual support of its members, who were a loose confederation of Guilds or *Hansa* and who were commercial traders, not Nation-States. In the absence of the protection of a centralised German State, this militant trade body looked after itself and, when required, it assembled its own armies and armed shipping, trading mainly through northern Germany and among the ports on the Baltic Sea. At that time, from roughly the 12th or 13th to the 17th centuries, in spite of the Holy Roman Empire, Germany was still a frequently changing mixture of hundreds of Principalities with no guaranteed law enforcement and, as will be seen in later chapters, there was a background of almost constant warfare somewhere or other. The League involved at one time more than one hundred and fifty trade associations, and their relevance to British immigration was due to a tax incentive whereby merchants could take advantage when trading, even as residents in England, of the tax-free status of the Cologne Hansa. This tax-free status had been conferred on the Cologne Hansa by English King Henry II in the middle of the 12th century, and that dispensation would be expanded to include other members of the increasing Hanseatic League one hundred years later under English King Henry III. This was perhaps a vision of the lack of accountability for tax, in the nation of source, that we see in the 3rd millennium.

Hansa traders were largely eliminated at the end of the 16th century, though memories of their commercial power linger and frequently provide material for political debate concerning the EU.

http://www.hartford-hwp.com/archives/60/039.html

http://www.economist.com/news/europe/21590934-britain-excavates-old-alliance-europes-liberal-free-trading-north-new-hanseatic-league

### 14.3.4 Huguenots (French Protestants) of the 17th Century

The wider subject of the Huguenots is covered in another chapter in Volume Two, but in summary, up to 50,000 Protestant asylum seekers from France arrived in Britain during the 16th and 17th centuries, many of them being silk workers and weavers who settled in London, notably Spitalfields. By the late 18th century, the rise of the silk industry abroad had caused such issues with industrial relations in the London silk industry that the 1801 Spitalfields Acts were belatedly passed to regulate working conditions, and to try to protect the home industry. It was too little too late, and most of the Huguenot community moved away from London, and integrated into the wider English communities, the only remaining traces nowadays being surnames with more or less similarity to French names after their spelling became Anglicised over the generations.

### 14.3.5 Indians of the 17th Century

Early arrivals of Indians, or Lascars as they were known, began with their recruitment as sailors and clerks into the East India Company during the 17th century, with later diversification into domestic servants both male and female. By the middle of the 19th century there were more than 40,000 in Britain, and by the start of the 20th century the figure had risen to around 70,000.

### 14.3.6 Africans of the 18th Century

Gradually increasing from Elizabethan England up to the end of the slave trade in 1807, it has been estimated that there were about 15,000 black Africans in Britain, virtually all made up of slaves who were brought into Britain by the slavers themselves, or as military recruits remaining in the British army that fought against the American Republicans during their

War of Independence. At this time they were mostly domestic servants, or they were destitute, and only a few made it into the middle-class. From the 18th to the 20th centuries there would have been small communities around docklands where they could find manual work, and during the two World Wars of the 20th century numbers increased with military service from the British colonies. There was a population of possibly 20,000 by 1945.

### 14.3.7 Germans of the 19th Century

As noted in an earlier chapter, one of the largest waves of immigration into England was the arrival of the Germanic group of peoples termed *Ingaevones* that settled as Anglo-Saxons during the 5th and 6th centuries, and who largely displaced the older Ancient Britons. In the early 18th century several thousand Germans were displaced from the German Principality known as the Palatinate of the Rhine by the French, and they were invited to England by its last Stuart Monarch, Queen Anne (1702 to 1714).

From census figures, by 1861 there were about 28,644 German immigrants of this more recent period, and that figure had increased to 53,324 by 1911. Severe reaction by the authorities as a result of a fear of fifth columnists or spies during World War One led to the harsh deportation of even long-term residents, most of whom spoke no German, and the population dropped to about 20,000 by 1918. Germans were found in all parts of the working population.

## 14.3.8 Map – Extent of the Hanseatic League circa 1400

Map from http://commons.wikimedia.org/wiki/Category:Maps released under CC-BY-SA
http://creativecommons.org/licenses/by-sa/3.0/

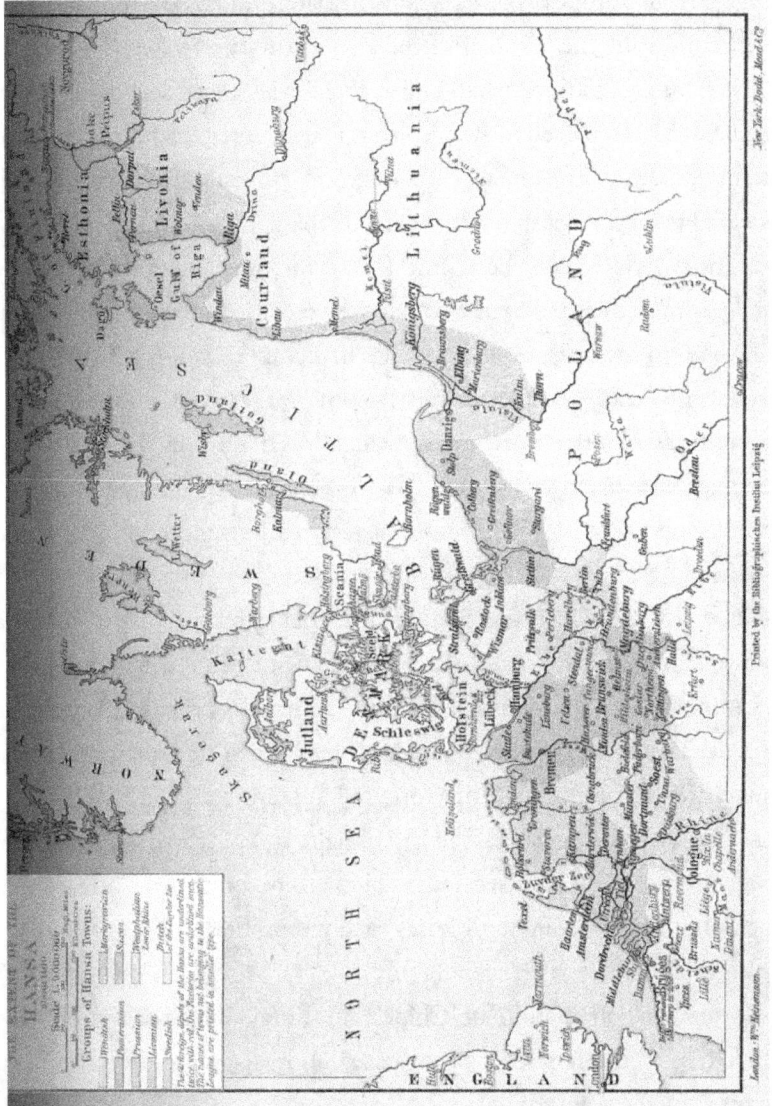

### 14.3.9 Miscellaneous Arrivals

A few thousand German and Italian Prisoners-of-War, and civilian refugees from European conflicts and Russian revolutionary unrest arrived in Britain during the first half of the 20$^{th}$ century up to 1945. Later in the 1940s, as more countries fell under the Soviet dictatorship of eastern Europe, refugees arrived in Britain from many sources including the more distant Ukraine, and one particular group consisting of 157,000 Poles benefited from the Polish resettlement Act 1947.

Chinese have always been just about the smallest ethnic group of immigrants, with only about two hundred recorded in Britain in 1871 just after the Opium Wars. As will be seen in Volume Two, the First Opium War (1839 to 1842) and the Second Opium War (1856 to 1860) resulted in disgracefully punitive settlements being forced on China during those years, and associated civil unrest was responsible for revenge attacks on Chinese and European Christians that resulted in hundreds of thousands of deaths.

Some say, not as mitigation of Imperial excesses, that China had followed an almost isolationist trade policy with Britain, France, and the U.S.A., and China is regarded by some as having provoked the cynical drugs trade that was effectively used to break down trade barriers, and to gain territorial concessions in the form of long-term leases.

Migrations of refugees at the time might be compared with later less dramatic migrations that, again, resulted from commercial realignments when one of those long-term leases finally ran out and Hong Kong was returned to Chinese sovereignty in July 1997.

By 1911 the population of Chinese in Britain had risen to thirteen hundred, and the 1991 Census suggested about 157,000. That would be increased by the events of 1997.

## 14.4 Post-World War Two Migration Into Britain
### 14.4.1 The West Indies

The beginnings of larger-scale specific group immigrations can be dated from the arrival of almost five hundred black Africans from the Caribbean West-Indies aboard the ship *MV Empire Windrush* on 22$^{nd}$ June, 1948. That beginning was prompted by so-called skills shortages that became apparent after 1945, although the requirement is commonly quoted as being due to the need to fill jobs that the British were too lazy or too fussy to take. This was followed by many more such group migrations, with annual figures rounded and summarised as follows:

- 1949 to 1951 less than 1,000 per year.
- 1952 and 1953 an average of 2,000 per year.
- 1954 about 10,000.
- 1955 about 25,000.
- 1956 about 26,000.
- 1957 about 22,000.
- 1958 about 17,000.

In 1957 the total population was about 100,000, and the 1991 Census put the black population at 890,727.

### 14.4.2 India, Pakistan, and Bangladesh

In 1939 the Indian population of Birmingham was about one hundred. Following Indian and Pakistani Independence and Partition in 1947, the total population of immigrants from both these new Nation-States of the Indian sub-continent in Britain in 1955 had risen to about 11,000.

In 1991 the Census indicated about 840,000 Indians, 477,000 Pakistanis, and 163,000 Bangladeshis.

### 14.4.3 Uganda

Another source of group immigration was the exodus of 80,000 Asians from Uganda in 1972 when they were expelled by the Ugandan President and madman, Idi Amin Dada, the self-proclaimed "King of Scotland". 30,000 descendants of the original Indians who had settled in Uganda came to Britain, the rest dispersing on British passports around the world, with very few returning to India. The result of the expulsions was the whole-scale destruction of Ugandan businesses when Amin's nominated new African owners were unable to cope.

### 14.4.4 Nigeria and Biafra – Civil War

This proxy war lasted for two and a half years, from 1967 to 1970, and although it was fought on African soil, nominally between Nigeria and a breakaway region called Biafra, it was really about Oil and First World interests, which guaranteed adequate finance for the introduction of mercenaries. Nigeria was supported by the unlikely bed-fellows of the United Kingdom, China, and the Soviet Union; and opposing them in support of Biafra were France, South Africa, and Israel. The diverse tribal complexities of Nigeria, and the further belligerents in addition to those listed above are of no interest to us here, beyond noting that it was a war in which civilians suffered as much as the military, or more so, and the result was two millions dead on each side, and a tidal wave of more than three million refugees in Biafra alone. While there is no easily available evidence of significant numbers of refugees arriving in Europe other than to Portugal, that had been on the Biafran side, this war has to be noted as a mark of the awful depths to which the Nigerian regime descended. This civil war may rank as one of the most heinous conflicts of the 20$^{th}$ century for at least three specific reasons: Firstly, because of the civilised world's involvement; secondly, because of Britain's contribution by constructing the intrinsically divisive, nightmare nation of Nigeria in the first place; and thirdly because of the corruption of commercial interests.

Many refugees from later Nigerian atrocities and ethnic and sectarian conflicts within that perpetually divided nation would arrive in Britain over the following four decades and into the 21$^{st}$ century.

### 14.4.5 The Balkans, Somalia, Iraq, Afghanistan, Syria

Co-incident with all the other established migration drivers were: the Balkan wars from 1991 to 1999; a totally dysfunctional Somalia that has been destroyed by continuous civil war ever since Somaliland declared itself an independent republic in 1991 – a conflict that continues to the present;

the wars in Iraq of 1990 to 1991, and 2003 to 2011; and the war in Afghanistan from 2001 to 2014. All of these wars have led to many hundreds of thousands of refugee immigrants arriving in Britain.

In the case of the Somalis, no-one has any accurate idea of numbers because many have arrived via other European countries where they could not settle, and where, in their own words, they were subjected to bureaucracy and isolation among non-black ethnicities. The UK Border Agency only settled into its current form in 2008, and issues of inadequate performance by its various component parts during its evolution before that time, both in the UK and at ports of departure, removed the proper recording and control of such EU leapfrogging cases, and allowed them, after arrival in Britain, to simply disappear into their insular communities.

The best estimate that was made by the Council of Somali Organisations, based in the U.K., is that there are between 350,000 and one million Somalis in Britain. As will be shown later, of all immigrant groups they have the lowest rate of employment.

### 14.5 The 1951 Refugee Convention – UNHCR 1966 - 67

Refugees internationally are protected by the 1951 convention that began solely in relation to post-war Europe, but which was extended globally in 1967 after it was enshrined by Resolution 2198 (XXI) of the United Nations as the Convention and Protocol Relating to the Status of Refugees under the United Nations High Commission for Refugees (UNHCR) in 1966 to 1967. The Introductory Note from the Protocol is presented below for interest.

For the full document see: http://www.unhcr.org/3b66c2aa10.pdf

> *"Grounded in Article 14 of the Universal Declaration of Human Rights 1948, which recognizes the right of persons to seek asylum from persecution in other countries, the United Nations Convention relating to the Status of Refugees, adopted in 1951, is the centrepiece of international refugee protection today. The Convention entered into force on 22 April 1954, and it has been subject to only one amendment in the form of a 1967 Protocol, which removed the*

*geographic and temporal limits of the 1951 Convention. The 1951 Convention, as a post-Second World War instrument, was originally limited in scope to persons fleeing events occurring before 1 January 1951 and within Europe. The 1967 Protocol removed these limitations and thus gave the Convention universal coverage. It has since been supplemented by refugee and subsidiary protection regimes in several regions, as well as via the progressive development of international human rights law."*

### 14.5.1 Present-Day Refugees and Asylum Seekers in the UK

The particularly emotive subject of asylum seekers, and the issue of the distinction between genuine asylum seekers and economic migrants, has become more prominent since the wars and unrest relating to Somalia, Iraq, Afghanistan, the Arab Spring, and the Balkans. The African continent as a whole, meanwhile, continues in poverty, disorder, and dictatorship; and its proximity around the Mediterranean ensures that it will always be a source of economic migrants. An overview from one or two sources follows.

According to the BBC, from 1998 to 2000 the following groups of asylum seekers arrived:

- 45,000 from Africa.
- 22,700 from the Indian sub-continent.
- 25,000 from Asia.
- 12,000 from the Americas.

Of those above arrivals and other unidentified groups, approximately 125,000 were allowed to settle in the UK in 2000.

As this book goes to press in Autumn 2015 a confused picture unseen since the end of the Second World War is being painted. Stretching from the English Channel throughout Europe and, via the Balkans, as far as the southern coastline of the Mediterranean Sea and eastwards into the Middle East, many hundreds of thousands of people are on the move. The mass of humanity ranges from genuine refugees from the Syrian Civil War that began in 2011, but that has become exacerbated by the anarchic death cult known as Islamic State or "ISIL", to economic migrants from Sub-Saharan Africa that are gathered at Calais in France and attempting illegal entry into Britain daily with the objective, declared by many, of obtaining benefits. The latest numbers of all groups are expected to exceed one million and they are scheduled for resettlement throughout Europe, there being a total absence of support for their accommodation by Arab countries.

### 14.5.2 Failed Applicants Remaining in the UK

According to the Daily Mail newspaper, during a three month period over the summer of 2012, 29,100 asylum seekers arrived. That equates to an annual rate of 116,400, which would be close to the highest figure in the nation's history; and in November 2015, despite government commitments to control the issue, the annual net rate of immigration had increased to a staggering figure in excess of 330,000.

Ninety per cent of asylum seekers in 2012 were assessed as having no valid case, but only 3,565 were returned home, and the newspaper expresses that figure as an indication that for every successfully blocked inappropriate asylum attempt, eight more arrive. Home Office figures from which these indicators are derived, do not include illegal immigrants, a figure estimated to be 60,000 a year, who just disappear into existing communities.

The organisation Migration Watch is an immigration and asylum think-tank chaired by Sir Andrew Green, a former Ambassador to Saudi Arabia. It also has supporting consultancy from a Professor of Demography at Oxford University, David Coleman. Migration Watch is virtually a lone voice with credentials that presents factual information, predominantly from the Government Office For National Statistics, to stand in opposition to vastly outnumbering cries in the media and academia in support of the ideology of continuing and even increasing immigration. Migration Watch, as a result of its presentation of uncomfortable facts, has attracted the predictable hints that it is "right-wing and dangerous", and some academics have implied that it is unfair that it has a platform with a credible presentation, if such credibility is not available to the proponents of mass immigration. Given the colossal imbalance of rhetoric and subliminal indoctrination that is churned out daily by the equally dangerous "left wing and liberal" media, press, and university spokespersons, one can only wonder at their lack of confidence in what they themselves, the pugnacious proponents of multiculturalism, have achieved in the 3rd millennium. It is the multiculturalism lobby that raised the question of fair representation, even though they unquestionably already have a disproportionate voice.

The detail below is an assessment covering the period 1997 to 2004, and it is taken from the following internet article:

http://www.migrationwatchuk.org.uk/Briefingpaper/document/108

### 14.5.3 Government Inaction and the Reality – Migration Watch

1. The government have avoided putting a figure on exactly how many asylum seekers whose claims have failed remain in the UK. They say that, as they cannot provide a precise figure, they will not provide one at all.

2. However, it is possible to make an independent estimate, based entirely on Home Office data, by taking the number of initial decisions made and subtracting those granted asylum (either initially or on appeal) and those granted exceptional leave (or humanitarian protection or discretionary leave). This gives the number of asylum seekers whose claims have failed. From this we can subtract those who have been removed or have left under the Voluntary Return Programme to give the number of asylum seekers whose claims have failed but for whom there is no evidence of departure.

3. This methodology has some minor flaws. It will count as failed asylum seekers those who have not exhausted their rights of appeal or for whom there has been insufficient time to start or complete removal proceedings. But the opposite will obtain at the beginning of the period so, over a long timescale, these two sets of problems should broadly cancel each other out.

*Migrant Invasions*

4. The following are the resultant numbers for the period 1997 to 2004:

| a. | Initial decisions made | 499,000 |
|---|---|---|
| b. | Granted asylum at initial hearing | 52,000 |
| c. | Granted asylum on appeal | 61,000 |
| d. | Granted exceptional leave, discretionary leave or humanitarian protection | 72,000 |
| e. | Asylum claim rejected (i.e. a-b-c-d) | 314,000 |
| f. | Removed | 75,000 |
| g. | Failed but not removed (e-f) | 239,000 |

All numbers in the table above have been rounded to the nearest thousand and all exclude dependants. All data is from the Home Office Asylum Statistics annual volumes for 1997 to 2003 and quarterly volumes for 2004.

5. A small number of asylum claims will also have been allowed at further appeals to the Tribunal or at judicial review. Data for these is incomplete but the numbers are small – in 2001 for instance there were 475 further appeals accepted at the tribunal and 260 at judicial review. Allowing 1,000 acceptances a year over the 8 year period would reduce the number of failed asylum seekers remaining in the UK down to 231,000.

6. Dependants have only recently been separately counted in Home Office data. They will have added somewhere between 20% and 30% to the claimant count. The total of asylum seekers and their dependants remaining in the UK whose claims have failed will therefore be in the order of 287,000 to 300,000.

7. The Home Office claim that some asylum seekers leave the country after their claim has failed without notifying the authorities and without being picked up in the International Passenger Survey. This is possible but counter-intuitive. When compiling Internal Migration Statistics they assume that 10% of failed claimants leave the country quietly in this manner. Even allowing for this would only reduce the number of failed claimants remaining in the UK from 231,000 excluding dependants by

31,000 (i.e. 10% of 314,000 – see paragraph 4) to 200,000. Adding dependants on to this would give between 240,000 and 260,000 failed asylum seekers and their dependants remaining in the UK.

8. These figures take no account of those whose asylum claims failed prior to 1997 and who remain in the UK.

9. Our conclusion therefore is that 250,000 is, if anything, an underestimate of the number of failed asylum seekers remaining in the UK. Furthermore, over the period, only about one in four (24%) of failed cases have been removed.

10. The status of some of those whose claims have failed has since been regularised through the amnesty announced by the former Home Secretary, David Blunkett, on 24 Oct 2003. This granted Indefinite Leave to Remain (ILR – effectively settlement) to all applicants who applied for asylum before 2 October 2000 and had at least one dependant child born before that date and still under 18. The government have declined to say how many people have so far qualified for this amnesty (House of Lords answer 4713 of 11 Nov 2004). Their press briefing at the time mentioned 50,000.

Since the recommendations of a House of Lords report, The Economic Impact of Immigration in 2007 to 2008 that is covered in some detail below, monthly reports by the Office For National Statistics have become available for anyone to read who is interested in the facts. With back numbers, they are available at the following website (put all of the text in the link below on one line in a browser):

http://www.ons.gov.uk/ons/search/index.html?pageSize=50&sortBy=none&sortDirection=none&newquery=Migration+Statistics+Quarterly+Report

## 14.6 Related Acts of Parliament

By the 1960s, the government decision implied by its British Nationality Act of 1948, that would have allowed all members of the Commonwealth to enter and stay in Britain without restriction, simply had to be amended; the consequences in any single country, let alone one that was still not fully recovered from a world war, were unthinkable. After it was realised that as many as one billion citizens – British passport holders and their dependants in the Commonwealth – would have been entitled to reside in Britain, the ill-considered ideological proposal was amended by the Commonwealth Immigrants Act 1962 and by subsequent Acts.

It is reasonable to consider that virtually all of the later Anti-Discrimination Acts, whatever the nature of discrimination, stemmed from the issues first raised by aliens and immigration, and a list of the Acts covering more than one hundred years, with the Long Titles of those that have so far been digitised, is provided here as an indication of the determination with which the British nation has attempted to defend its borders while accommodating the world. Due to the incomplete digitisation of Acts of Parliament at the website below, one or two variants of Acts from the early 20$^{th}$ century may have been omitted, though it is believed that there are enough for the present context. The notes below of whether or not an Act has been digitised may, of course, have changed since this chapter was written. See website:

http://www.legislation.gov.uk

### 14.6.1 Aliens Act 1905

Not digitised. The first such Act to be passed in peacetime, it is generally accepted as being a response to Jewish immigration that accelerated from about 1880.

### 14.6.2 British Nationality and Status of Aliens Act 1914

Royal Assent 7$^{th}$ August, 1914.

*"An Act to consolidate and amend the Enactments relating to British Nationality and the Status of Aliens."*

### 14.6.3 Aliens Act 1919

Royal Assent 23rd December, 1919.

*"An Act to continue and extend the provisions of the Aliens Restriction Act, 1914."*

### 14.6.4 Polish Resettlement Act 1947

Royal Assent 27th March, 1947.

*"An Act to provide for the application of the Royal Warrant as to pensions, etc., for the military forces to certain Polish forces, to enable the Assistance Board to meet the needs of, and to provide accommodation in camps or other establishments for, certain Poles and others associated with Polish forces, to provide for their requirements as respects health and educational services, to provide for making arrangements and meeting expenses in connection with their emigration, to modify as respects the Polish resettlement forces and past members of certain Polish forces provisions relating to the service of aliens in the forces of the Crown, to provide for the discipline and internal administration of certain Polish forces and to affirm the operation up to the passing of this Act of provision previously made therefore, and for purposes connected therewith and consequential thereon."*

### 14.6.5 British Nationality Act, 1948

Royal Assent 30th July, 1948.

*"An Act to make provision for British nationality and for citizenship of the United Kingdom and Colonies and for purposes connected with the matters aforesaid."*

### 14.6.6 Commonwealth Immigrants Act 1962

Royal Assent 18th April, 1962.

*"An Act to make temporary provision for controlling the immigration into the United Kingdom of Commonwealth*

*citizens; to authorise the deportation from the United Kingdom of certain Commonwealth citizens convicted of offences and recommended by the court for deportation; to amend the qualifications required of Commonwealth citizens applying for citizenship under the British Nationality Act, 1948; to make corresponding provisions in respect of British protected persons and citizens of the Republic of Ireland; and for purposes connected with the matters aforesaid."*

## 14.6.7 Race Relations Act 1965

Royal Assent 8th December, 1965.

Title apparently not available via UK Government offerings over the Internet.

Although it also set up the first Race Relations Board, the first Act was considered inadequate since it covered only discrimination in public places and did not cover housing or employment. In spite of the potentially useful Section 6 that covered *incitement*, and despite repeated requests, the Act does not appear to be available on the government's website, whereas all other searched Acts returned results. The government website is: http://www.legislation.gov.uk/ukpga

Details on this Act were subsequently located as part of the publication *The Modern Law Review, Vol. 29, No. 3 (May, 1966)*, available via subscription (free) at the excellent facility: http://www.jstor.org

## 14.6.8 Commonwealth Immigrants Act 1968

Royal Assent 1st March, 1968.

*"An Act to amend sections 1 and 2 of the Commonwealth Immigrants Act 1962, and Schedule 1 to that Act, and to make further provision as to Commonwealth citizens landing in the United Kingdom, the Channel Islands or the Isle of Man; and for purposes connected with the matters aforesaid."*

### 14.6.9 Race Relations Act 1968

Royal Assent 25th October, 1968.

> "An Act to make fresh provision with respect to discrimination on racial grounds, and to make provision with respect to relations between people of different racial origins."

### 14.6.10 Equal Pay Act 1970

Royal Assent 29th May, 1970.

> "An Act to prevent discrimination, as regards terms and conditions of employment, between men and women."

### 14.6.11 Immigration Act 1971

Royal Assent 28th October, 1971.

> "An Act to amend and replace the present immigration laws, to make certain related changes in the citizenship law and enable help to be given to those wishing to return abroad, and for purposes connected therewith."

### 14.6.12 Sex Discrimination Act 1975

Royal Assent 12th November, 1975.

> "An Act to render unlawful certain kinds of sex discrimination and discrimination on the ground of marriage, and establish a Commission with the function of working towards the elimination of such discrimination and promoting equality of opportunity between men and women generally; and for related purposes."

### 14.6.13 Race Relations Act 1976

Royal Assent 22nd November, 1976.

> "An Act to make fresh provision with respect to discrimination on racial grounds and relations between people of different racial groups; and to make in the Sex Discrimination Act 1975 amendments for bringing provisions

in that Act relating to its administration and enforcement
into conformity with the corresponding provisions in this Act."

### 14.6.14 British Nationality Act 1981
Royal Assent 30th October, 1981.
> "An Act to make fresh provision about citizenship and nationality, and to amend the Immigration Act 1971 as regards the right of abode in the United Kingdom."

### 14.6.15 Immigration (Carriers' Liability) Act 1987
Royal Assent 15th May, 1987.
> "An Act to require carriers to make payments to the Secretary of State in respect of passengers brought by them to the United Kingdom without proper documents."

### 14.6.16 Immigration Act 1988
Royal Assent 10th May, 1988.
> "An Act to make further provision for the regulation of immigration into the United Kingdom; and for connected purposes."

### 14.6.17 Dublin Convention 1990
Not digitised, this was the first EU attempt, covering twelve member states, to define responsibility for processing asylum seekers.

### 14.6.18 Immigration and Asylum Appeals Act 1993
Royal Assent 1st July, 1993.
> "An Act to make provision about persons who claim asylum in the United Kingdom and their dependants; to amend the law with respect to certain rights of appeal under the Immigration Act 1971; and to extend the provisions of the Immigration (Carriers' Liability) Act 1987 to transit passengers."

### 14.6.19 Disability Discrimination Act 1995

Royal Assent 8th November, 1995.

*"An Act to make it unlawful to discriminate against disabled persons in connection with employment, the provision of goods, facilities and services or the disposal or management of premises; to make provision about the employment of disabled persons; and to establish a National Disability Council."*

### 14.6.20 Asylum and Immigration Act 1996

Royal Assent 24th July, 1996.

*"An Act to amend and supplement the Immigration Act 1971 and the Asylum and Immigration Appeals Act 1993; to make further provision with respect to persons subject to immigration control and the employment of such persons; and for connected purposes."*

### 14.6.21 Human Rights Act 1998

Royal Assent 9th November, 1998.

*"An Act to give further effect to rights and freedoms guaranteed under the European Convention on Human Rights; to make provision with respect to holders of certain judicial offices who become judges of the European Court of Human Rights; and for connected purposes."*

This single Act wrote into UK law the European Convention on Human Rights, and some say it has done more to encourage integration than any other piece of legislation. This is one area, however, where even New Labour governmental officers might argue among themselves particularly in connection with counter-terrorism initiatives that were about to be elevated to dizzy heights following the impending 2001 New York World Trade Centre atrocity. Many believe that the European Convention on Human Rights was more ideologically driven than well-designed. Undeniably, it has been responsible for inappropriate grants of asylum at the expense of genuine applicants, and it has been the cause of many miscarriages of justice in the name of political correctness. Furthermore, for decades British Legal Aid budgets administered by the Legal Services Commission have been largely consumed by immigration cases prosecuted by ethnic minority lawyers.

### 14.6.22  Immigration and Asylum Act 1999

Royal Assent 11th November, 1999.

> *"An Act to make provision about immigration and asylum; to make provision about procedures in connection with marriage on superintendent registrar's certificate; and for connected purposes."*

There were also additional regulations concerning homelessness and support during 1999.

### 14.6.23  Race Relations (Amendment) Act 2000

Royal Assent 30th November, 2000.

> *"An Act to extend further the application of the Race Relations Act 1976 to the police and other public authorities; to amend the exemption under that Act for acts done for the purpose of safeguarding national security; and for connected purposes."*

### 14.6.24  Special Educational Needs and Disability Act 2001

Royal Assent 11th May, 2001.

> *"An Act to amend Part 4 of the Education Act 1996; to make further provision against discrimination, on grounds of disability, in schools and other educational establishments; and for connected purposes."*

### 14.6.25 Nationality, Asylum and Immigration Act 2002

Royal Assent 7th November, 2002.

> *"An Act to make provision about nationality, immigration and asylum; to create offences in connection with international traffic in prostitution; to make provision about international projects connected with migration; and for connected purposes."*

### 14.6.26 Asylum and Immigration Act 2004

Full name: Asylum and Immigration (Treatment of Claimants, etc.) Act 2004

Royal Assent 22nd July, 2004.

> *"An Act to make provision about asylum and immigration."*

This Act also covered trafficking.

## 14.7 Disability Discrimination Act 2005

Royal Assent 7th April, 2005.

> *"An Act to amend the Disability Discrimination Act 1995; and for connected purposes."*

### 14.7.1 Equality Act 2006

Royal Assent 16th February, 2006.

> *"An Act to make provision for the establishment of the Commission for Equality and Human Rights; to dissolve the Equal Opportunities Commission, the Commission for Racial Equality and the Disability Rights Commission; to make provision about discrimination on grounds of religion or belief; to enable provision to be made about discrimination on grounds of sexual orientation; to impose duties relating to sex discrimination on persons performing public functions; to amend the Disability Discrimination Act 1995; and for connected purposes."*

## 14.7.2 Immigration, Asylum and Nationality Act 2006

Royal Assent 30th March, 2006.

*"An Act to make provision about immigration, asylum and nationality; and for connected purposes."*

## 14.7.3 Equality Act 2010

Royal Assent 8th April, 2010.

*"An Act to make provision to require Ministers of the Crown and others when making strategic decisions about the exercise of their functions to have regard to the desirability of reducing socio-economic inequalities; to reform and harmonise equality law and restate the greater part of the enactments relating to discrimination and harassment related to certain personal characteristics; to enable certain employers to be required to publish information about the differences in pay between male and female employees; to prohibit victimisation in certain circumstances; to require the exercise of certain functions to be with regard to the need to eliminate discrimination and other prohibited conduct; to enable duties to be imposed in relation to the exercise of public procurement functions; to increase equality of opportunity; to amend the law relating to rights and responsibilities in family relationships; and for connected purposes."*

## 14.8 The Complete Anti-Discrimination Framework

Enforcement of judicial process and the overall implementation of social change, of which the law is only a part, are a result of several factors including Acts of Parliament, the creation of Commissions or Quangos, and ongoing Inquiry-generated Reports. In 1999 for instance, following the Macpherson Report that suggested institutional racism was widespread, there were major changes to all areas of law enforcement including the Police and Immigration Control, and their methods of operation. This was driven by the 2000 Race Relations (Amendment) Act, and there was much further anti-discrimination legislation covering several subjects between 2000 and 2010, culminating in the 2010 Equality Act.

Stepping back in time though, the Race Relations Board was set up following the 1965 Race Relations Act, and the Community Relations Commission was set up after the 1968 Race Relations Act, both being superseded by the Commission for Racial Equality (CRE) that was set up following the Race Relations Act of 1976. It would have been encouraging if the issue of Quango definition and its funding could have been settled without further uncertainty and cost to the public, but that was not the end of the evolutionary pattern. The CRE was regarded with suspicion by many in the judiciary and in government, with Lord Denning, Master of the Rolls, likening its potential powers to "...the days of the inquisition." It would be thirty years before there was another major change.

Following the Equality Act of 2006, the Equality and Human Rights Commission (EHRC) commenced in October 2007 and combined the interests of the Community Relations Commission, the Equal Opportunities Commission (gender equality) and the Disability Rights Commission, and it is said today that issues of immigration and integration are again being obfuscated when they were once in clearer view.

The Nine Protected Grounds of the EHRC for reference are:

- Age.
- Disability.
- Gender.
- Race.
- Religion and Belief.
- Pregnancy and Maternity.
- Marriage and Civil Partnership.
- Sexual Orientation.
- Gender Reassignment.

## 14.9 An Open Door and a Trojan Horse

There are many sources of quantitative data, of assumed accuracy, about immigration into the United Kingdom, and even more sources of subjective and ideological commentary concerning concepts, such as skills shortages, demographic decline, and the desirability of diversity and enrichment. Sadly, other than opinion polls that appear to have been totally ignored by all governments since 1964, there is only silence when it comes to estimating what were the wishes of the British nation for massive ethnic and cultural change before the event was imposed. Political election manifestos of all mainstream parties have strangely always avoided the subject, and any party members who voiced opposition were silenced, e.g. Enoch Powell who was sacked from Cabinet by the late Sir Edward Heath for giving a speech, and Conservative Party Monday Club members who were pejoratively labelled as members of "The Nasty Party" and racists. There has never been any meaningful debate, and even though at the time of Enoch Powell's "Rivers of Blood" speech in 1968 at Birmingham when it was established via a national poll that **more than 70% of the British people agreed with his concerns**, he and his speech are nowadays referred to as *"...infamous and offensive"*, even on the U.K. Government's outsourced National Archives website. Dishonourable and bigoted, subliminal propaganda today by a government appointed body.

### 14.9.1 A Numbers Game and an Ethnicity Game

In fifty years, in the absence of any referendum or consultation, non-British ethnicity – non-white in plain language – has risen from less than 1% to more than 12%, the greatest increases having occurred as a result of non-mandated and ideological social engineering (eugenics) policies during the New Labour Government of 1997 to 2010. This was against a background devoid of any policy of integration other than the distribution of unemployed immigrants among the nation's cities, towns, and villages. This was underhanded and deceitful, if not treasonable, and it would be interesting to see the result of any private prosecution for Treason against the likes of Tony Blair, Gordon Brown, Jack Straw, and David Blunkett.

Judgement has in fact been implied by the public through polls suggesting that, although they (the public) suffered from the sort of subliminal propaganda issued by government and the media during the 1990s as implied above, there was in fact a later dawning which was evidenced by a negative perception during the 2000s. Respondents to the question of whether immigration and race relations are one of the most important issues facing the nation were 5% affirmative in 1999, 46% affirmative in 2007, and, following the catastrophic tenure of Blair-Brown that mercifully ended in 2010, an estimated 75% affirmative in 2012. That increasing concern, expressed too late, most certainly does not speak of increasing integration and decreasing tension with time as multiculturalist ideologues would like to believe. It is quite the reverse, as demonstrated by the phenomenon of "white flight" from cities and from the nation.

The lack of any policy of integration over fifty years has resulted in the perfectly understandable clustering of many cultures and communities into their own socially and ethnically defensive, frequently inner-city locations, making any prospect of significant integration into British culture and the wider community even more remote – and why should there have ever been any expectation otherwise? The whole issue is a numbers game, it is an ethnicity game, and it is a comfort game – the comfort taken by well-off misguided champagne socialists and conservatives who are far-removed from the cultural coal-face.

More recently it has become a much more sinister religious game, and integration could only ever have been achieved with a positive programme and with limited numbers with which to deal. Roy Hattersley, the MP and deputy leader of the Labour Party from 1983 to 1992 is recorded as saying: *"...Integration without limitation is impossible; equally, limitation without integration is indefensible."*

The list of Acts of Parliament above tells the tale of disjointed British policy on immigration and integration. It started as defensive measures, and became one of enforced race relations and the imposition of anti-discrimination laws as a result of one or two examples of small-scale homespun rioting; but British policy was mainly derived from watching events unfold in the United States during the 1960s, where civil rights activists and college unrest were often in the news for all in Britain to watch with trepidation; and all this, in spite of the much longer history of American multiculturalism. More recent government initiatives to justify immigration have revolved around the financial benefits to the nation, but these have been comprehensively demolished by a House of Lords report – *Select Committee on Economic Affairs, 1st Report of Session 2007-2008, The Economic Impact of Immigration*, covered below.

In addition to the Acts of Parliament, the British response to mitigate the risk of race riots was an initiative on a broad front through all government agencies. Visibility of ethnic minorities was ensured by the unspoken encouragement of their inclusion in broadcasting, out of all proportion to their representation in society; there was positive discrimination and there were changes in local government and police employment and working practices; the school curriculum, particularly in respect of history and social studies, was adjusted; the Commission for Racial Equality was created; and whenever there were race riots because the foregoing had little or no effect in its intended target area, there were government sponsored Inquiries such as the Scarman Report into the Brixton Riots of 1981, and a general suggestion that it was white society that had failed to accommodate ethnic minorities!

While there may have been some truth in the suggestion that, over the decades, natives who were on the front-line of change were exhibiting symptoms of a reactive tribalism (and what on earth did the remote and academic government in its ivory tower expect?), that tribalism most certainly did not amount to an extent that warranted the creation of a blame culture and the attribution of a sense of guilt. But this is exactly what did happen and continues to happen. The white general public, or natives, and particularly any dissident within the mainstream media, have been brow-beaten and pushed into a position from which there could be no questioning of government competence, or its treachery, or other failings in the preceding decades that were the real causes of an irretrievably broken society.

With such a sense of implied guilt firmly established, and with left wing domination of, significantly, the National Unions of Journalism and Teaching along with virtually all others, any questioning of immigration, or any expression of concern at cultural loss from an undeniable and rapid ethnic overload would instantly be met with apoplectic cries of "racist!" and "institutional racism!"; and all further debate would be suppressed. The problem lies as much with the cowardice and self-delusion on the part of the "silent majority", as with the bellicose ideologue.

### 14.9.2 What is Hate Crime?

After 2012 we now see hate laws which are an attempt to extend state control to cover ignorant or careless expression and bad deportment that has not yet manifested itself as an otherwise indictable felony. The danger is that it will not be applied even-handedly, but in accordance with a ubiquitous politically correct and timid psychology. We may be only a small step away from thought crimes, but perhaps Hate Crime legislation can also be used to combat all discriminatory actions, and to reinforce open discussion, irrespective of race, creed, or colour; though disgracefully, there has not been a very good start. The legislation has not helped in the recent cases of clear hate crime in association with sexual predation and paedophilia by gangs of virtually exclusively Islamic Asian men against white girls; the issues that were being highlighted by several organisations for months and even years beforehand, were being simultaneously ignored by a Police force that can only be described as devoid of any integrity or moral standards, and totally undeserving of their badge of office. Prejudicial and deliberate inactivity in that office should rank as Hate Crime by the Authorities by default, but there has been absolutely no visible retribution against the officers concerned that are of all ranks, and from whom there has been no sign of contrition.

To clarify the subject of Hate Crime and its prevalence, an extract follows that is taken from the Home Office website on the matter: http://homeoffice.gov.uk/crime/hate-crime/

*"Hate crime involves any criminal offence which is perceived, by the victim or any other person, to be motivated by hostility or prejudice based on a personal characteristic. The definition covers five main strands, in particular - disability, gender-identity, race, religion or faith and sexual orientation. Legislation has been in place for a number of years to protect victims from such hate crimes, including offences for those who intend to stir up racial hatred, and those who commit racially and religiously aggravated offences or engage in racist chanting at football matches. New criminal offences have also been introduced in recent years to reflect the seriousness of hate crime, including enhanced sentencing.*

*On 13 September 2012, the Home Office published statistics on hate crimes recorded by the police in England and Wales for the first time. In 2011/12, 43,748 hate crimes were recorded by the police, of which:*

- *35,816 (82 per cent) were race hate crimes*
- *1,621 (4 per cent) were religion hate crimes*
- *4,252 (10 per cent) were sexual orientation hate crimes*
- *1,744 (4 per cent) were disability hate crimes*
- *315 (1 per cent) were transgender hate crimes*

*Race hate crimes accounted for the majority of hate crimes recorded in all police forces."*

It appears that the long established, but hazy offence of Seditious Libel is no longer adequate to protect the nation – or is the Hate Crime legislation just intended to obfuscate the issue of an individual's right to free speech? Such intended suppression of rights might well be the case, because, whilst targeted and unwarranted offence towards any individual is, of course, reprehensible, we are equally told that there is no mitigation of a so-called Hate Crime, even though all of the issues in connection with an indictment for generalised writing or speeches may be totally true. In other words we are not permitted to voice certain truths.

## 14.10 Some Immigration Metrics

As stated earlier, there are many sources of numerical information on migration, and the next few items concern some of those metrics and their interpretation.

### 14.10.1 Timeline and Numbers

**1982 to 1983.** From government statistics these years mark the first recorded transition from long-term net emigration from Britain to net immigration. As summarised below those years also show the top three migrant nation sources and targets.

**1982.** Immigrants from Germany, the U.S., and France. Emigrants to Australia, the U.S., and South Africa. Net emigration of about fifty thousands.

**1983.** Immigrants from the U.S., Australia, and Germany. Emigrants to the U.S., Australia, and Bahrain. Net immigration of about seventeen thousands.

**1994.** A similar pattern with only small average net immigration involving the same nations that featured for 1982 and 1983 persisted until this year.

**1994 to 1998.** Those same nations were responsible during this period for an average net annual immigration of about eighty thousands.

**1998 to 2001/2002.** average net annual immigration was about one hundred and sixty thousands, the countries remaining broadly similar to those above.

**2003.** India joined the top three source countries for immigration.

**2004.** India was the top source, with total net annual immigration now more than two hundred and sixty thousands.

**2005 to 2009.** Poland and India were the top two source nations with an average total net immigration of more than two hundred and fifty thousands every year in this period.

**2010.** India and Pakistan were the top two countries, with Poland third, as sources of net annual immigration of two hundred and fifty thousands.

*Migrant Invasions*

The above detail is graphically shown at the following website:
http://www.neighbourhood.statistics.gov.uk/HTMLDocs/dvc123/index.html

Other representations from government figures are presented in the graphs below, though the net outflow in the second figure, shown between 1991 and 1993, is not seen in any other data.

Figures reported in the media in May, 2011, resulting from a publication by the U.K. Government Office For National Statistics showed that the ethnic minority population had risen by 40% in the eight years from 2001 to 2009, and in 2011 stood at 9.1 million. One in six Britons now are non-white. The reason for the accelerated growth is the addition of higher birth rates in the ethnic minority population and, one would assume, the unstated factor of white flight in an international context, as a component of emigration. Birth statistics for 2008 in London for instance, showed that 55% of births were to women born outside the UK, the majority being African and Asian.

Another report in May, 2012, stated that during the ten years between 1999 and 2009 there was a net immigration of two million, which represents a 70% increase in the foreign-born population in recent times. In actual numbers it is a change from 3.8 million in 1993 to 6.9 million in 2008 – more than 12% of the United Kingdom's population.

## 14.10.2 Graph – Net Annual Migration To the UK, 1971 to 2005

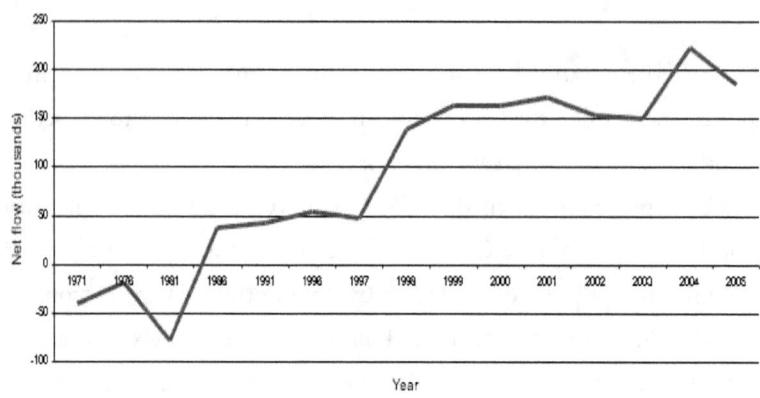

## 14.10.3 Graph – Total Migration In and Out 1975 to 2008

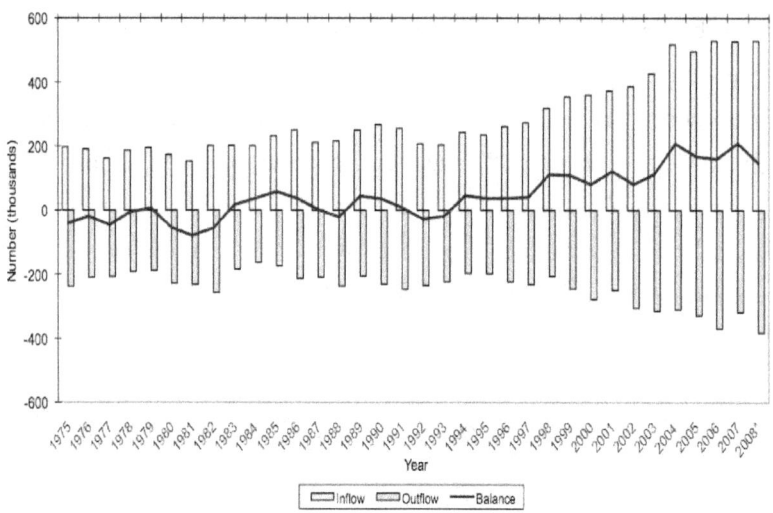

### 14.10.4 Seven Key Facts From the Migration Watch Website

(Website, Revised April 2012).

Author's Note – there is no relationship between any of the figures below and ethnicity or the source of immigration. Demographic change due to unequal birth rates among British communities is a separate issue.

- Net immigration quadrupled to nearly 200,000 a year between 1997 and 2009. In 2010 it was 252,000 and in 2015 it was over 330,000.
- Over 3 million immigrants have arrived since 1997.
- Migrants arrive almost every minute; they leave at just over half that rate.
- We must build a new home every seven minutes for new migrants.
- Britain is already, with the Netherlands, the most crowded country in Europe.
- The population of the UK will grow by over 7 million to 70 million in the next 16 years, 5 million due to immigration – that is five times the population of Birmingham.
- To keep the population of the UK, already more than 64.5 million in 2015, below 70 million, net immigration must be reduced to around 40,000 a year. It would then peak in mid-century at about 68 million.

NB. The figures above have been amended upwards due to increased net immigration during the course of writing this book. For up-to-date figures on a rapidly changing subject, the reader should refer to:

http://www.migrationwatchuk.org/statistics-population-country-birth

It should be noted that the BBC and other mainstream media organisations in 2015 no longer use the term "immigration" in their reporting. They choose instead the ambiguous and less sensitive term "migration" with an occasional concession that it is "net", but without specifying that it is inbound.

## 14.10.5 In Work, Out of Work, In Prison, Illegally Here

Since 2004 the character of immigration has changed from previously being sourced largely from the Third or Developing World, of which the predominant home nations were either sub-Sahara African or within the Indian sub-continent, and which were seeking permanent residence in Britain, to being sourced by large numbers of temporary workers from the expanded EU that saw two significant instances of accession in 2004 and 2007.

In 2004 the A8 countries: Estonia, Latvia, Lithuania, Poland, The Czech Republic, Slovakia, Slovenia, and Hungary, plus Malta and Cyprus joined, and in 2007, Bulgaria and Romania were added. All restrictions against the 2004 entrants, which in the U.K. were mainly in respect of welfare issues, were dropped by 2008, but are believed to remain in force against Bulgaria and Romania.

An illustration of the degree of ideological bias at play around this time of EU expansion is in the comments variously made through organs such as the Guardian newspaper that white immigration from the EU would be a bad thing because it would reduce the numbers of non-white immigrants able to enter the country, and thereby reduce the degree of diversity and enrichment. From such a eugenic point of view, one must assume that if ten million French or German white Europeans had been transplanted into the U.K., it would have been more permissible to express dismay and outrage at such social engineering.

The significance in terms of cultural impact is that, because of the vastly increased EU sources, the percentage of non-white immigration is reduced, and that a greater percentage of immigration is for a shorter period, and more focussed on specific employment. This suits the stated government preference for immigrants to reduce skill shortages. A counter to this apparent improvement though, is that immigrants have lower employment rates overall, than UK-born people. A summary of some comparative employment detail is as follows.

*Migrant Invasions*

Immigrant men have broadly similar employment rates, while women have much lower employment rates, e.g. family-building Muslim women 25%.

In 2010 employment rates among male workers in the U.K. varied as follows:

- Migrants from the A8 EU Countries 90% employed.
- Other non-UK EU countries 76%.
- India 81%.
- Australia 86%.
- UK-born men 75% – This figure presumably includes all ethnic groups, and is therefore probably skewed by the fact that nearly 50% of Black males are unemployed.
- Pakistan and Bangladesh, probably less than 50%. Figures are not obvious. "Significantly lower" said one source, and 46% and 42% respectively were estimates from another.
- Somalis. Their rate of employment is unknown but is believed to be the lowest of any immigrant group. It may be as high as 35%. For emphasis that is to say that only 35% of them may just possibly be employed.

## 14.10.5.1 Table – Representation in the Criminal Justice System

According to the Ministry of Justice, via the Office For National Statistics, the variations among ethnic groups for apprehension, indictment, and incarceration indicate seriously disproportionate representation of Black, Asian, and Mixed groups, and that fact must indicate either a failing in the legal system and society's use of that system, or a failing in the groups themselves:

Proportion of individuals at different stages of the Criminal Justice System (CJS) process by ethnic group compared to the general population of England and Wales – see below:

|  | White | Black | Asian | Mixed | Chinese or Other | Not Known | Total Numbers |
|---|---|---|---|---|---|---|---|
| Population aged 10 or over 2009 | 88.60% | 2.70% | 5.60% | 1.40% | 1.60% | - | 48,417,349 |
| Stop and Searches (s1) 2009 / 10 | 67.20% | 14.60% | 9.60% | 3.00% | 1.20% | 4.40% | 1,141,839 |
| Arrests 2009 /10 | 79.60% | 8.00% | 5.60% | 2.90% | 1.50% | 2.40% | 1,386,030 |
| Cautions 2010 (1) | 83.10% | 7.10% | 5.20% | - | 1.80% | 2.80% | 230,109 |
| Court order supervisions 2010 | 81.80% | 6.00% | 4.90% | 2.80% | 1.30% | 3.20% | 161,687 |
| Prison population (including foreign nationals) 2010 | 72.00% | 13.70% | 7.10% | 3.50% | 1.40% | 2.20% | 85,002 |

Note 1. Data is based on ethnic appearance and therefore does not include the Mixed category.

These figures were eclipsed by the release of data during 2014 that indicates that 20% of male inmates in Young Offender Institutions are Muslim, and that 42% of all inmates are from black and minority ethnic communities. This is drastically disproportionate to the believed percentage mix in the general population, but the director of the Prison Reform Trust could only say that it was "a big increase" and that "the reasons were unclear".

## 14.10.5.2 Illegal Immigration Levels

It has been estimated that about 620,000 or approaching 10% of the foreign-born population in Britain are here illegally. That is a significantly higher proportion than that estimated to exist in the two other most closely modelled EU countries, Germany and France. See:

http://www.migrationinformation.org/Feature/display.cfm?ID=600

## 14.11 Riotous Assembly
### 14.11.1 Brief History of the Riot Act 1715

The Act was introduced as a response to widespread unrest during unpopular tax increases under the Whig Government of the time. The Riot Act could be read out by an officer of the law, after which, failure to disperse would become an arrestable felony. To attest the validity of the reading, the words 'God save the king' were necessary.

Under section 1 of the Act, it must be proved that:

- twelve or more persons;
- present together;
- used or threatened unlawful violence (all charged must use);
- for a common purpose; and that
- the conduct of them (taken together);
- was such as to cause;
- a person of reasonable firmness;
- present at the scene;
- to fear for his personal safety.

It also followed that:

- Each of the persons using unlawful violence for a common purpose is guilty of riot.
- It is immaterial whether the 12 or more use violence or threaten it simultaneously.
- A common purpose may be inferred from conduct.
- It is an offence which may be committed in private as well as in public places.

The words that were required to be delivered in a loud voice, and as near to the rioters as possible were as follows:

> *"Our sovereign Lord the King chargeth and commandeth all persons, being assembled, immediately to disperse themselves, and peaceably to depart to their habitations, or to their lawful business, upon the pains contained in the act made in the first year of King George, for preventing tumults and riotous assemblies. God save the King."*

The "Reading of the Riot Act" worked very well, and protesters of all ages, including women and children, could then be beaten, shot, and bayoneted, with immunity from prosecution, and law-abiding bystanders could also join in the fray. Any survivors were then hanged or transported at the will of a sometimes indisputably inhuman judge. The Riot Act was applied with a vengeance, and it made no difference if protests were peaceful or socially justifiable.

### 14.11.1.1 The Original Riot Act 1715

Royal Assent – Passed in 1714, took effect in 1715.

> *"An Act for preventing tumults and riotous assemblies, and for the more speedy and effectual punishing the rioters".*

### 14.11.1.2 Amendment – The Criminal Law Act 1967

Royal Assent 21st July, 1967

> *"An Act to amend the law of England and Wales by abolishing the division of crimes into felonies and misdemeanours and to amend and simplify the law in respect of matters arising from or related to that division or the abolition of it; to do away (within or without England and Wales) with certain obsolete crimes together with the torts of maintenance and champerty; and for purposes connected therewith."*

### 14.11.1.3 Repeal – The Statute Law (Repeals) Act 1973
Royal Assent 18th July, 1973

> *"An Act to provide for the reform of the statute law by the repeal, in accordance with recommendations of the Law Commission and the Scottish Law Commission of certain enactments which, except so far as their effect is preserved, are no longer of practical utility."*

### 14.11.2 List of Principal Riots in Britain

This is a comprehensive though possibly incomplete list of disturbances that have been classified as Riot, with those related to issues of immigration or race, either as the prime cause or as spread by imitation, emphasised in **bold**.

#### 14.11.2.1 Riots in England 12th to 19th Centuries

- 1189 Massacre of the Jews
- 1196 Poor Riot
- 1355 Saint Scholastica Day Riot
- 1381 Peasants' Revolt
- 1517 Evil May Day
- 1668 Bawdy House Riots
- 1710 Sacheverell Riots
- 1736 Edinburgh
- 1769 Spitalfield Riots
- 1780 Gordon Riots
- 1791 Priestley Riots
- 1793 Bristol Bridge Riot
- 1809 Old Price Riots
- 1816 Spa Fields Riots
- 1816 Ely and Littleport Riots
- 1819 Peterloo Massacre
- 1830 Swing Riots
- 1831 Queen Square Riots (Bristol)
- 1832 Days of May

1838 Battle of Bossenden Wood

1896 Newlyn Riots

### 14.11.2.2 Riots in England Early 20th Century

1907 Brown Dog Riots

1910 Tonypandy Riots

**1919 Dock Workers Race Riots**

1919 Epsom Riot

1919 Birkenhead Police Officer's Riots

1919 Battle of George Square, Glasgow

1919 Battle of Bow Street

1919 Luton Peace Day Riots

1932 Old Market Riot (Bristol)

1932 Birkenhead Unemployment Riots

**1936 Battle of Cable Street**

**1958 Notting Hill Race Riots**

**1962 Dudley Riot**

### 14.11.2.3 Riots in England 1970s

1970 Garden House Riot

**1975 Chapeltown Race Riot**

**1977 Battle of Lewisham**

**Riots in England 1980s**

1980 Saint Paul's Riot

**1981 England Riots**

**1981 Brixton Riot**

**1981 Chapeltown race Riot**

**1981 Toxteth Riots**

**1981 Moss Side Riot**

**1981 Handsworth Riots**

**1985 Handsworth Riots**

**1985 Brixton Riot**

**1985 Broadwater Farm Riot**

1987 Chapeltown Race Riot
1989 Dewsbury Race Riot

### 14.11.2.4 Riots in England 1990s
1990 Poll Tax Riots
1990 Strangeways Prison Riot
1991 Meadow Well Riots
**1991 Handsworth Riots**
**1991 Dudley Riots**
**1992 Hartcliffe Riot (Bristol)**
**1995 Manningham Riot**
**1995 Brixton Riot**

### 14.11.2.5 Riots in England 2000s
**2001 England Riots**
**2001 Bradford Riots**
**2001 Oldham Riots**
**2001 Harehills Riot**
**2005 Birmingham Race Riots**
2009 G-20 London summit protests

### 14.11.2.6 Riots in England 2010s
2010 UK Student Protests
2011 Stokes Croft Riot (Bristol)
**2011 England Riots – Widespread**

### 14.11.3 Racially Motivated Violence – 1919 Dock Workers

Possibly the earliest significant racially motivated violence, if not exactly riots, occurred in 1919 just after the post-war return to civilian life of hundreds of thousands of men looking for work. In several docklands around Britain the relatively small communities of Black, Asian, Arab, and Chinese were seen as posing a threat to British jobs and to the availability of housing for the expanding indigenous workforce, and many were abused and attacked, with a small number of fatalities.

#### 14.11.3.1 Recent Era Riots

A final note should be the acknowledgement of a changed or additional dimension to riots since 2001, after which time Islamic *radicalism* has given rise to justifiable concern by people of all communities. Note that the term *radicalism* has now completely replaced the term *fundamentalism* in the media since the latter might imply a real link to religion, whereas the former can be read as mitigation.

Riots of the 21st century are no longer simply divided along racial lines, though such unrest persists, but now involve resistance to the spread of Islam; that spread being literally high-profile by the building of mosques for instance. Further detail can be found from internet links (see the chapter in Volume One titled *Internet Index of References and Other Downloads*) and by simple searches using the names and implied contexts above.

### 14.11.4 Blair-Brown – New Labour Treachery

Quite distinct from any humanitarian motive there had been a very successful attempt by New Labour towards the end of the 20th century, as described by one of their own, Andrew Neather, in October 2009: *"...to rub the right's nose in diversity...."* This was an example of ideological national suicide during the last decade of their damaging and scurrilous term of office from May 1997 to May 2010 – a period that should live in infamy, and not least for its give-away of the nation's gold reserves that quadrupled in value shortly thereafter.

That regime was responsible for the contrived and profligate attempt at the destruction of a nation's identity, and it has been suggested that one of

Labour's objectives was to maximise third world immigration into Britain in order to irrevocably change the character of the nation, and to theoretically improve their own chances of re-election by the resultant increase in grateful, new, and Labour-inclined arrivals. This is evident from the above commentary by Neather, who back then at the start of the new millennium had been a New Labour speech writer and advisor to Tony Blair, to Jack Straw, and to David Blunkett, and who had been a confidant throughout the highest echelons of Labour Party power; but it is also apparent from comments made by other Labour MPs and ministers, and from various documents. Their actions were nothing short of a eugenics policy. Racism and racists are endemic in the New Labour Party and across all its adherents, together with any of the offshoot divisions of their apologists in the Liberal Democratic and Conservative parties.

### 14.11.5 A Seditious Document

These scurrilous motives have been suggested by several sources, and they appear to be supported by the rewriting of a particular document as it passed through draft and development stages. That document, for which the drafts have been dragged into the public domain by a Freedom of Information request, was initially a Restricted Policy document titled *Preliminary Report on Migration*, dated 11th July, 2000. All of these documents are freely available on the internet from the U.K. Government Cabinet Office:

http://www.cabinetoffice.gov.uk/resource-library/freedom-information-release-migration-economic-and-social-analysis

Although the draft policy document at first had no named author, there is a footnote during section 2, The economic theory of migration, against a paragraph that runs as follows:

> "Another conceptual trap is the view of "the immigration decision" as a one-off. In practice, people migrate, for economic, family, or other reasons; they may initially intend to stay temporarily and then return or move on to a third country, or to settle; 4 in any case, they may subsequently

*change their minds and do something else. Globalisation increases the number and complexity of these flows: for this reason, we refer wherever possible to migration and migrants, rather than immigrants."*

The footnote 4 in the passage above, then for some bizarre reason states: *"The team leader for this project has "migrated" [according to the standard definition – moved between countries, intending to stay at least a year] four times since 1992, and will do so again in August 2000".*

The section and footnote together are of such fatuous and pointlessly pathetic character that one wonders if it was merely the truculent product of thinking out loud, and one that was not really intended for any sort of audience at all. The document is riddled with such inanities and shocking adolescent immaturity and naïvety. But wait, it gets even better.

A second draft document emerged in October 2000 titled Migration: An Economic and Social Analysis, and it was sub-titled on the front cover as: *A joint research study by the Home Office Economics and Resource Analysis Unit and the Cabinet Office Performance and Innovation Unit (PIU).*

That document spoke of *economic* and social objectives of *immigration*. Various sections in this document that were removed before its release into the public domain as a third version are very telling. The sections removed or edited for public consumption were as follows:

- All of the several references to *social* policy and objectives of immigration have been removed from the issued document.
- References to *the difficulty of halting or reversing economic migration* have been removed from the issued document.
- An initial statement that *Migrants are reasonably successful* has been altered to state instead *Migrants have mixed successes*.

- The statement *Migrants are not disproportionately involved in crime* has been deleted altogether.
- Another removal consisted of a potentially damaging, by its admission, but actually a fatuous, unsubstantiated, and in fact unprovable piece of nonsense: *The more general social impact of migration is very difficult to assess. Benefits include a widening of consumer choice and significant cultural contributions; these in turn feed back into wider economic benefits.*

All the above edits and two final exclusions conclude the demonstration that the document had an agenda that needed softening, the last two significant items to be chopped being:

- There would be a *legal channel for low-skilled migration*.
- A post-entry migration policy would be designed to *ensure that migration does indeed contribute to the Government's economic and social objectives*.

The third and final (as far as we know) version of the document has been sanitised and made digestible for those with a strong constitution. It is finally issued with the same title as the draft – *Migration: An Economic and Social Analysis*, and this time it credits its authors. The caveat on the front cover that one sees before anything else *"The views expressed in this report are those of the authors, not necessarily those of the Home Office (nor do they reflect government policy)"* does raise a question as to the integrity, purpose, and point of the exercise when the first drafts were clearly stated as the responsibility of *"PIU / Home Office"*, and *"Cabinet Office / PIU"*.

To remove any doubt concerning the Cabinet Office and its provenance, along with that of its document, the following is a verbatim extract from the Cabinet Office website:

http://www.cabinetoffice.gov.uk/content/about-cabinet-office:

> *The Cabinet Office* ***sits at the very centre of government,*** *with an overarching purpose of making government work better.*
>
> ***We support the Prime Minister and the Cabinet, helping to ensure effective development, coordination and implementation of policy and operations across all government departments.*** *[Author's font emphasis]*
>
> *We also lead work* ***to ensure the Civil Service provides the most effective and efficient support to Government to help it meet its objectives.*** *[Author's font emphasis]*

- *Cabinet Office ministers*
- *Cabinet Office Board*
- *Cabinet Office structure*
- *Freedom of Information*
- *Consultations*
- *Plans and performance*
- *Working for the Cabinet Office*
- *Supplying the Cabinet Office*

Even over the limited period of the evolution of this seminal document that appears to have driven Labour immigration policy, it was becoming evident from their edits, that the initially rose-tinted views of the authors were adjusting towards reality. They also prove that the committee did not start out with a neutral frame of mind, but with an expectation and assumption that the document could be made to fit an assumed ideology.

The whole thrust and flavour of this series of Labour Party policy documents is at best insensitive and ignorant – a trite and immature academic political thesis that is out of touch with the real world. When set alongside that real world – a world of falling education standards and broken families; a reality of youth unemployment figures across all ethnic groups; real housing shortages; a disproportionate presence of some ethnic groups in the Criminal Justice System; real social unrest and tension among all ethnic communities; and last but not least in the light of real pressures on the NHS and schools, the document is at worst treasonable. It is the result of a blindly venal and bigoted multicultural mindset – one of trying to justify more immigration without being able to completely leave an ideological cuckoo land and see reality, and even in the run-up to the General Election in spring 2015, during television interviews, the New Labour leadership was still unable to accept that there has to be an upper limit on immigration.

Many of the propositions in that document from the start of the 3$^{rd}$ millennium are facile and naïve conjecture, and their insubstantial, wishful propositions concerning positive aspects of immigration simply do not scale in reality. Yet their policy has been implemented, and as the authors well knew, and even stated before back-tracking, the situation cannot be reversed.

Furthermore, the political intention of the cabal behind the document *Migration: An Economic and Social Analysis* is indisputably indicated by the phrase above *"... **to ensure the Civil Service provides the most effective and efficient support to Government to help it meet its objectives.**"* That is to say, they want to ensure that the theoretically apolitical Civil Service adopts their political ideology to even possibly act on their behalf after they have been consigned to history.

Anyone who doubts the reality of the treason only has to look at the rate of Citizenship Grants in a section below, where the correlation between New Labour and rate increases from **37,000 per annum** to as high as **204,000 per annum** is plain to see.

### 14.11.6 The Reply From the Upper Chamber

Although New Labour propagated the lie that uncontrolled mass immigration was good for the economy, the final parliamentary word on the sorry subject goes, for now at least, to the Higher Chamber – The House of Lords – that took a different view and produced a document titled *The Economic Impact of Immigration* during 2007 and 2008, admittedly with more hindsight than the Cabinet Office committee, but hopefully also with better foresight and a more balanced intellect.

The first paragraph in the document's abstract states:

> *"Immigration has become highly significant to the UK economy: immigrants comprise 12% of the total workforce— and a much higher proportion in London. However, we have found no evidence for the argument, made by the Government, business and many others, that net immigration —immigration minus emigration—generates significant economic benefits for the existing UK population."*

There is much more, and the document goes on to negate much of the accepted rhetorical stance and nonsense of the Blair-Brown Government at the start of the 21st century, and it raises many questions. The document is freely available on the internet at:

www.publications.parliament.uk/pa/ld200708/ldselect/.../82/82.pdf

The last paragraph before the Lords' recommendations, still within the abstract of the eighty plus pages of the document is:

> *"Our overall conclusion is that the economic benefits to the resident population of net immigration are small, especially in the long run. Of course, many immigrants make a valuable contribution to the UK. But the real issue is how much net immigration is desirable. Here non-economic considerations such as impacts on cultural diversity and social cohesion will be important, but these are outside the scope of our inquiry."*

They have declared that the economic benefits are minimal, but they do not have the integrity to even hazard a guess at the overall wisdom of immigration.

### 14.11.7 New Labour's Words of Wisdom

Finally, just a few extra nails in the Blair-Brown coffin were supplied by discredited New Labour MPs as follows:

In 2003, the then home secretary, David Blunkett, said there was *"...no obvious upper limit"* to the number of people who could come into Britain. So it's back to 1948 then perhaps?

Labour MPs were unable to speak against the abuses that they recognised because so many Labour seats, including Jack Straw's, depended on Asian votes.

Labour (shadow in 2012) immigration spokesman Chris Bryant, said:

> *"...There is another argument which people worry about and it is that this country is too full. I don't subscribe to that view, I find that an odd argument...."*.

He said this after many in his party, including the party leader at the time, Ed Milliband, and Chris Mullin, acknowledged the disgraceful mishandling of immigration during the Blair-Brown years, and yet he was still able to make such a naïve pronouncement when Britain is one of the most densely populated countries in the world. The statistics on overcrowding in terms of extreme jobless Somalis and Pakistanis for instance, along with housing, welfare, and education pressures are there for anyone to see. This is a politician who would like to think he is in a government in waiting.

Ignorant they may be, but they cannot claim ignorance as an excuse since there have been many polls of public opinion over the years. One taken in 2007 by Ipsos-MORI, for instance, found that 76% said immigration should be much tougher (64%) or stopped altogether (12%). The same poll found that as many as 68% agreed that there were already *too many* immigrants in Britain. But no doubt this is racism, and from the graphs in the section *Public Attitude* below, it would seem that Britain has been a nation of foul racists since at least 1964.

### 14.11.7.1 Remorseful Reprobates

Unexpected further admissions in respect of the possibly treasonable activities of the Blair-Brown New Labour Government appeared during 2012 and 2013.

These were made by a Marxist literary critic, Peter Hitchens, and the ex-spin doctor and Prime Minister Blair's one-time closest advisor, Lord Mandelson. It might be argued that all of these parasites should be stripped of their employment prospects, and of any honorary titles if not their livelihood, for their squalid behaviour, and for the misery they have inflicted on mainly elderly people who were abandoned in a wasteland of both immigrant and liberal white English ideologically-driven multicultural hostility and psychological brutality.

The literary critic and Marxist, Peter Hitchens, was cynically published on 1st April, 2013. There is certainly some sort of fool involved and his words can be read at the following website:

http://hitchensblog.mailonsunday.co.uk/2013/04/how-i-am-partly-to-blame-for-mass-immigration.html

In case an attack of shame or a denial causes the website to be censored, an extract from this monstrous story is as follows:

> 'When I was a Revolutionary Marxist, we were all in favour of as much immigration as possible. It wasn't because we liked immigrants, but because we didn't like Britain. We saw immigrants – from anywhere – as allies against the staid, settled, conservative society that our country still was at the end of the Sixties. Also, we liked to feel oh, so superior to the bewildered people – usually in the poorest parts of Britain – who found their neighbourhoods suddenly transformed into supposedly 'vibrant communities'. If they dared to express the mildest objections, we called them bigots. Revolutionary students didn't come from such 'vibrant' areas (we came, as far as I could tell, mostly from Surrey and the nicer parts of London). We might live in 'vibrant' places for a few (usually

*squalid) years, amid unmown lawns and overflowing dustbins. But we did so as irresponsible, childless transients – not as homeowners, or as parents of school-age children, or as old people hoping for a bit of serenity at the ends of their lives...."*

On 14th May, 2013, the former minister Lord Mandelson admitted that Labour deliberately engineered mass immigration. Between 1997 and 2010 net migration to Britain totalled 2.2million.

His words can be read at the following website:

http://www.dailymail.co.uk/news/article-2324112/Lord-Mandelson-Immigrants-We-sent-search-parties-hard-Britons-work.html

Similarly, a small extract is as follows, though it falls far short of the dreadful reality of the consequences of his venal abuse of both his position and of the nation. From the security of his undeserved, privileged existence, he admitted, as if it was some sort of prank:

*"Immigrants? We sent out search parties to get them to come... and made it hard for Britons to get work..."*

In an earlier age it might have been suggested that such swine that admit responsibility for the misery of national cultural anarchy deserve nothing less than capital punishment for treason against the State and its people.

## 14.12 British Citizenship Awards

If one was inclined to believe in conspiracy theories, then trying to find data at the Home Office series of websites might in the first few attempts be confirmation of one's worst imaginings. Just about all the information is there somewhere, however, but it is not presented in a consistent manner and requires some familiarisation. Some data has been archived and needs to be searched differently to that which has been judged current, and some of those current periodic reports omit certain information. Trends over long intervals are recorded, but the clarity that would be obvious in a simple series of consistent monthly or quarterly reports can be buried in too much raw spreadsheet information. There is even an admission or two that records have not been ideal and, given the politicisation of staff, one might reasonably conclude that such poor record-keeping was no accident.

The detail presented below is an accurate extraction from a number of Home Office sources, all of which are cited. The first presentation of data is from individual downloads by year, some being archived, some not.

### 14.12.1 Table of Grants of Citizenship 1997 to 2011

| Year | Citizenship Grants |
|---|---|
| 1997 | 37,000 |
| 1998 | 54,000 |
| 1999 | 55,000 |
| 2000 | 82,000 |
| 2001 | 90,000 |
| 2002 | 120,145 |
| 2003 | 124,315 |
| 2004 | 140,795 |
| 2005 | 161,780 |
| 2006 | 154,095 |
| 2007 | 164,635 |
| 2008 | 129,375 |
| 2009 | 203,790 |
| 2010 | 195,130 |
| 2011 | 177,878 |

Former Indian and Pakistani nationals have accounted for the largest numbers of grants in almost every year from 2001. The exception was 2007 when former nationals of Pakistan accounted for the fifth highest number of grants. Together, former Indian and Pakistani nationals accounted for a quarter (25%) of grants in 2011.

### 14.12.2 Example Reports Around the Change of Government 2010

These examples are of particular interest because they cover the transition from the end of the New Labour Government to the beginning of the Conservative Government in May 2010. The paragraphs that follow are verbatim extracts from Home Office sites. Occasional differences between figures in tables and figures in paragraphs are Home Office issues of consistency.

Example Source:

http://www.homeoffice.gov.uk/publications/science-research-statistics/research-statistics/immigration-asylum-research/control-immigration-q4-2010/control-immigration-q4-2010?view=Binary

**25th February, 2010.** The total number of citizenship decisions made in 2009 was 215,005, an increase of 55 per cent compared to 2008 (138,465). The number of decisions made in 2009 has recovered from the comparatively low level in 2008 when staff resources were temporarily transferred from decision-making to deal with administration of an increase in new applications. This followed the publication of the green paper *The Path to Citizenship: Next Steps in Reforming the Immigration System* in February 2008. The number of persons granted British citizenship in 2009, compared to 2008, rose by 58 per cent from 129,375 to 203,865.

**25th November, 2010.** The number of persons granted British citizenship in the UK fell by 740 to 197,135 in the year to 30th September, 2010, compared to a year earlier. Grants of British citizenship have shown a broadly rising trend since 2007, increasing from 126,310 in the year to September 2008; and to 197,870 in the year to September 2009.

**24th February, 2011.** The number of persons granted British citizenship in the UK fell by 4 per cent to 195,130 in 2010 compared to 2009 (203,790). However, grants of British citizenship are above the levels seen in the period 2005 to 2007, which ranged between 154,000 and 165,000

**26th May, 2011.** The number of persons granted British citizenship in the UK fell by 1 per cent to 195,410 in the year to March 2011, compared to a year earlier. Grants of British citizenship have shown a broadly rising trend since 2007, increasing from 151,805 in the year to March 2007; and to 197,845 in the year to March 2010.

Around this time, reports took a new format and the next quarterly report initially seemed to be a circular reference devoid of any data.

**Q2 25th August, 2011.** Immigration Statistics, April to June 2011. *'Further and more detailed analysis, including information on grants of*

*British citizenship and extensions of stay, can be found in the Immigration Statistics, April – June 2011." [?No data could be found?]*

April to June 2011, seems to have been removed from the record, but further confusing data from the end of 2011 into 2012 was then found via the following:

http://www.homeoffice.gov.uk/publications/science-research-statistics/research-statistics/immigration-asylum-research/

The following quarterly sets of figures apparently indicate how the annual rate of grants of citizenship was changing at the time.

**Q3 released 24ᵗʰ November, 2011.** Immigration Statistics for the period July to September 2011, suggest that 179,613 people were granted British citizenship in the year ending September 2011. That was 9% fewer than in the previous twelve month period (197,051). The fall was mainly due to fewer grants based on marriage, and fewer grants to children related to British citizens.

**Q4 released 23ʳᵈ February, 2012.** Immigration Statistics for the period October to December 2011, suggest that there were 177,878 grants of British citizenship in the year ending December 2011. This confirmed the trend of the previous quarter and indicated 9% fewer than in the previous twelve month period (195,046), again mainly due to fewer grants based on marriage and to children related to British citizens.

**Q1 released 24ᵗʰ May, 2012.** Immigration Statistics for the period January to March 2012, suggest that there were 175,298 grants of British citizenship in the year ending March 2012. This was 10% fewer than in the previous twelve month period (195,369), yet again mainly due to 10,979 fewer grants based on marriage and to children related to British citizens.

### 14.12.3 Immigration Statistics 2010 to 2011 – Blair-Brown Legacy

This is another example of data for the significant government transition period from New Labour to Conservative, presented in a different but fairly comprehensive format, and again verbatim from the Home Office site. It is clear proof of the result of the last decade of Brown's New Labour treason – the intent to reduce the proportion of white Britons as much as possible. See the following website reference:

http://www.homeoffice.gov.uk/publications/science-research-statistics/research-statistics/immigration-asylum-research/immigration-q2-2011/immigration-q2-summary

The Home Office table below graphically shows the changing rate of grants of British citizenship and the arrest in 2010, with the change of government, of the New Labour contrived upward surge.

http://webarchive.nationalarchives.gov.uk/20130128103514/http://www.homeoffice.gov.uk/publications/science-research-statistics/research-statistics/immigration-asylum-research/immigration-brief-q2-2011/citizenship

### 14.12.4 Table of Grants of Citizenship 1962 to 2010

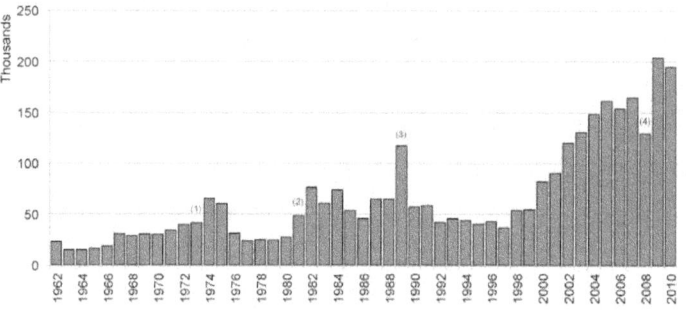

The number of people granted settlement, as distinct from citizenship, reached a record 241,000 in 2010 (including dependants), and this increase in 2010 was particularly due to rising numbers of grants on a discretionary basis relating to a backlog of cases of asylum – a clear admission of lack of motivation to protect the nation, and subsequent procedural abrogation. In addition, work-related grants of settlement reached a record 84,000 in 2010, reflecting high numbers admitted for work purposes five years earlier. However the latest data, for the year to June 2011, showed an 8% fall in grants of settlement (208,000), with decreases in both the work and the family categories.

195,000 people were granted British citizenship in 2010, slightly lower than the record 204,000 in 2009, but more than double the level a decade

## Migrant Invasions

earlier. Nearly half (48%) of the grants were on the basis of residence – a quarter for children related to British citizens and nearly a quarter (24%) based on marriage. The latest figures show that this slight decline continued in the year to June 2011.

There is evidently still an open door to relatives of the original Citizenship Grant, and headline statistics taken from the Home Office website suggest the Conservative Government has made very little progress towards reducing the influx.

### 14.12.5 Table of Grants of Settlement and Extensions 2009 to 2011

Table notes (1) below, Calendar year 2010 compared with 2009.

|  | Year to June 2011 | Year to June 2010 | Percentage change |
|---|---|---|---|
| Before entry visitor visas issued | 1.6 million | 1.4 million | +15% |
| Admissions (journeys) (1) | 101.5 million | 101.4 million | +0% |
| Extensions – grants | 304,585 | 321,969 | -5% |
| Settlement – grants | 207,824 | 226,084 | -8% |
| Citizenship – grants | 185,663 | 197,896 | -6% |

### 14.12.6 Top Ten Nationalities Granted Citizenship in 2011

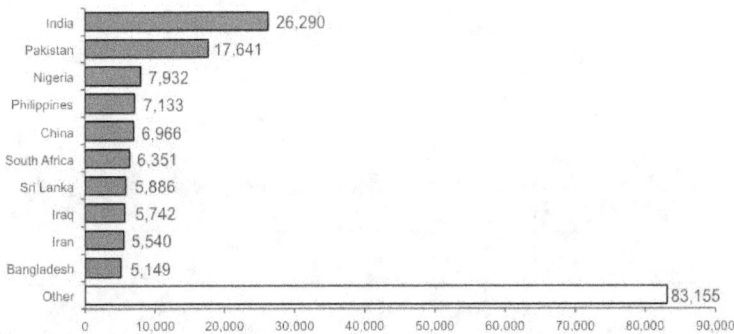

|  |  |
|---|---|
| India | 26,290 |
| Pakistan | 17,641 |
| Nigeria | 7,932 |
| Philippines | 7,133 |
| China | 6,966 |
| South Africa | 6,351 |
| Sri Lanka | 5,886 |
| Iraq | 5,742 |
| Iran | 5,540 |
| Bangladesh | 5,149 |
| Other | 83,155 |

**That is a total of 177,785 during the period of so-called Tory commitment.**

### 14.13 Public Attitude

Another independent body that collates immigration data is known as the Migration Observatory, based at the Centre on Migration, Policy and Society (COMPAS) at the University of Oxford, and they have produced a document titled *Public Opinion toward Immigration: Overall Attitudes and Level of Concern* that is freely accessible at their website: http://www.migrationobservatory.ox.ac.uk/

Even many foreign-born respondents believe immigration should be reduced, with significant overall response being *"Reduced a Lot"*.

#### 14.13.1 Immigration – Public Opinion 2009 to 2010

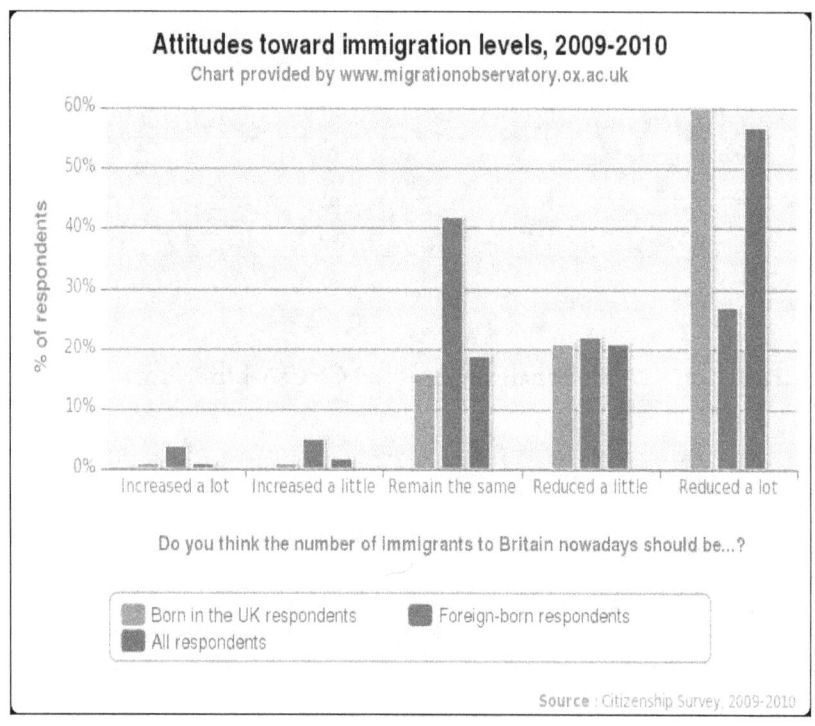

And in case that is considered too narrow a snapshot in time, a further series of polls is condensed into the illustration below of changes of opinion over forty-five years or so since 1964 – very little change in fact when allowances are made for slightly differing techniques used to gather data. The reader is referred to the internet document for more information:

http://www.migrationobservatory.ox.ac.uk/

### 14.13.2   Immigration – Public Opinion Change 1964 to 2011

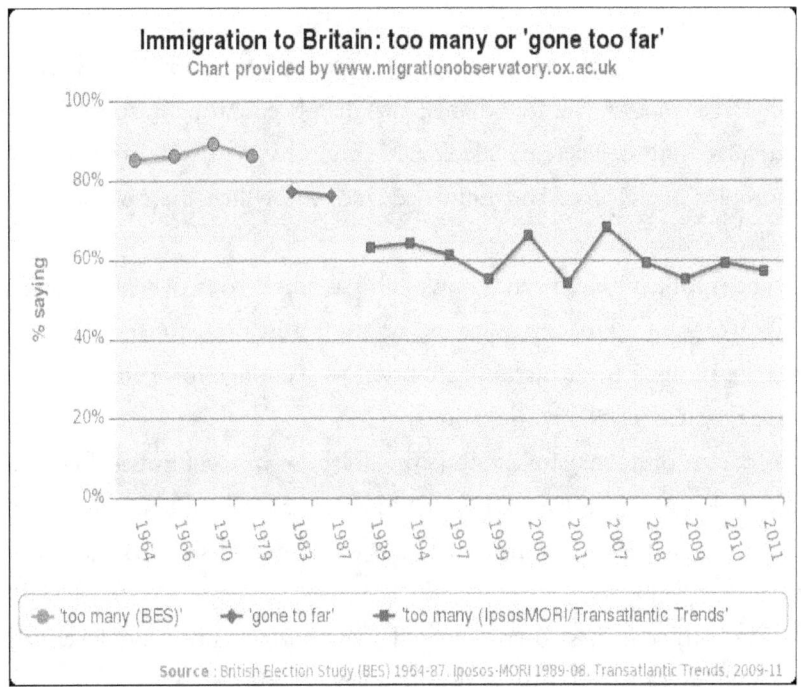

The wishes of more than 60% of the population, and this allows for something in excess of ten million immigrants, are constantly ignored by a self-centred ideological minority that manages to infect most of society with a malaise of complacency, to the extent that despite the United Kingdom Government's clear abdication of responsibility, the mainstream political parties are returned to power time after time.

## 14.14 Islamic Racially Motivated Sexual Abuse of Whites

This is being carried out by Pakistani gangs, and there has been an Establishment cover-up. The item belongs in this chapter because it is a direct consequence of unfettered immigration.

The disgraceful issue has grown without restraint because of cowardly political correctness at many levels of our national administration, and it has reached its horrific proportions because of tolerance and active encouragement of cultural change that has been brought about by an extremist and belligerent, ideological minority – a minority with a disproportionate voice and influence, and one which has no place in a civilised society.

The problem has been known about since 2003 when a council employee was told to keep quiet and attempts were made to sack her, but it was not brought to the nation's attention with enough force and shame to make repeated headlines until 2014.

One can only imagine the scale of the abuse that continued for more than 10 years, and the lives that have been irrevocably blighted.

Police and police commissioners did nothing, and silenced those who raised their voice.

The problem has been exposed with prosecutions at Rochdale, Rotherham, Oxford, Reading, Birmingham, Aylesbury, and London; and it is depressing in the extreme to consider the many other large cities with similar populations of criminally inclined and culturally sponsored predators that have not been brought to justice.

Estimates of 1,400 victims are accepted as being a considerable understatement. See the references below.

The perpetrators are large numbers of Pakistani men who use, in many cases, the excuse that their religion compels them to abuse the infidel. These vile abusers have then been actively abetted by social and police workers by their failure to respond and act when presented with very clear evidence for many years.

This is one more example of the elimination of our historic freedom and dignity by those in positions of trust and power – infidels, in the guise of white Englishmen and Englishwomen, have been too cowardly to defend the young womenfolk of their own Nation-State, and their apologists must stand with them.

This indictment includes all those who feel that the subject has been exaggerated or is too sensitive to be highlighted.

## 14.15 References Concerning This National Suicide

http://www.homeoffice.gov.uk/publications/science-research-statistics/research-statistics/immigration-asylum-research/immigration-q2-2012/citizenship-q2-2012

http://www.homeoffice.gov.uk/publications/science-research-statistics/research-statistics/immigration-asylum-research/control-immigration-q4-2010/control-immigration-q4-2010?view=Binary

http://webarchive.nationalarchives.gov.uk/20110218135832/http://rds.homeoffice.gov.uk/rds/stats-release.html

http://www.homeoffice.gov.uk/publications/science-research-statistics/research-statistics/immigration-asylum-research/immigration-tabs-q2-2012/citizenship-q2-2012-tabs

http://www.homeoffice.gov.uk/publications/science-research-statistics/research-statistics/immigration-asylum-research/immigration-q2-2012/citizenship-q2-2012

http://www.migrationobservatory.ox.ac.uk/briefings/uk-public-opinion-toward-immigration-overall-attitudes-and-level-concern

http://www.migrationinformation.org/feature/display.cfm?ID=736

http://www.sovereignty.org.uk/features/articles/immig.html

http://en.wikipedia.org/wiki/Historical_immigration_to_Great_Britain

http://www.sovereignty.org.uk/features/articles/immig.html

http://www.migrationinformation.org/feature/display.cfm?ID=736

http://www.migrationinformation.org/Feature/display.cfm?ID=600

http://www.migrationinformation.org/charts/blair-fig1-may07.cfm

http://www.migrationinformation.org/charts/uk-jul09-fig1.cfm

http://www.migrationpolicy.org/pubs/UK-countrystudy.pdf May 2012

http://www.migrationwatchuk.com/Briefingpaper/document/48

http://en.wikipedia.org/wiki/Immigration_to_the_United_Kingdom_%281922-present_day%29

http://www.nationalarchives.gov.uk/museum/item.asp?item_id=50

http://www.researchasylum.org.uk/?lid=1304

http://en.wikipedia.org/wiki/Expulsion_of_Asians_from_Uganda

## 14.15.1 A Report Specifically Into the Issues of Abuse at Rochdale

http://www.rochdale.gov.uk/council_and_democracy/policies,_strategies__reviews/reviews/independent_review_of_cse.aspx

## 15 DNA Studies

A final word on the pre-medieval settlement of Britain concerns opinions as a result of DNA studies, and I restrict this to one example, though there are many references and opinions to be found on the internet, including one that Scots are closely related to the Berbers of North Africa.

Bryan Sykes is a former Professor of Human Genetics at the University of Oxford and a Fellow of Wolfson College, Oxford. In his 2006 book *Blood of the Isles*, he examined British genetic clans, and a précis follows:

The genetic make-up of Britain and Ireland today is very much as it was in the Neolithic Period, and much as it was in the Mesolithic period. This applies to whatever tribal, cultural or ethnic name we use, and we should really just refer to them all as Cro-Magnon. The Basques are the same in this respect as the British and Irish, and some examples of genetic influences are:

1. Central European Celts made minimal contribution to the genetic make-up. Most of Britain's Celtic input came from the Atlantic seaboard of western Europe.
2. Picts were not an obviously separate ethnicity, and people from two principal Pictland areas, Tayside and Grampian, show no significant difference to the rest of Britain.
3. Anglo-Saxon contribution to the genetic make-up of England is under 20 percent of the total, even in southern England.
4. The Vikings (Danes and Norwegians) made a substantial contribution in central, northern, and eastern England – the ancient Danelaw. In the Orkney and Shetland Islands it is about 40 percent. This shows that the Vikings engaged in large-scale settlement.
5. The Norman contribution was only about 2 percent. Given their Norseman origins, this should raise some questions, such as how one might distinguish between the French and Nordic DNA

influence resulting from the Norman Conquest given the existing Nordic DNA presence throughout England.

6. There are only sparse traces of the Roman occupation, almost all in southern England.

So we are still genetically a mixture of the first Mesolithic inhabitants combined with Neolithic settlers who came by sea via Iberia and possibly ultimately from the eastern Mediterranean.

A final observation is that the female line shows a certain degree of mixture of original Mesolithic inhabitants and later Neolithic arrivals from Iberia, while the male line correlates more strongly with the later Neolithic arrivals from Iberia. Another way of putting it is that the earlier males succumbed to *social natural selection* (author's expression), which is about as tongue-in-cheek as using the expression *Genghis Khan effect* (Bryan Sykes's expression.)

# 16 The Two Thousand Year War – Papal Hegemony

Advance conclusion:

> *The Balance of Power is rarely, if ever, the long-term Balance of Success – neither militarily nor economically. There has never been a persistently successful and supreme empire based solely on the Nation-State, although there is compelling evidence for the persistent retention, and even the continuing growth, of influence and control by Global-Elites in all areas of governance.*

– Freedom to Fiefdom, 2015.

## 16.1 Introduction

Empires have come and gone since the earliest written records, and from even older archaeological remains one might argue that expansion and domination of adjoining territory has always been a characteristic of ambitious, survival-minded tribes. Indeed, even the lower orders of animals mark their territory and defend it against newcomers, and frequently seek to expand into that of their neighbours. So, to those who would criticise empire, one might ask the question what is or what was its alternative? What would they have in its place given the state and nature of the human character? Absorption into the empire of another perhaps?

Empire is an attempt to pre-empt war and to increase wealth and security by absorbing potential adversaries, and it is suggested that as empires contract, the consequences of war are greater than during imperial expansion or during their stable lifetime. Treaties between empires have rarely, if ever, lasted the test of time, and the more sophisticated that empires become, the more susceptible they are to fluctuations and extremes of the three aspects of governance to which allusion was made at the start of this book – National Government, Corporate Spirituality, and a Currency Mechanism.

To complement the current chapter, Volume Two of this book contains a tabulated look at all known empires and their relevance to Britain, and then covers in great detail those historical empires and their European derivatives that have had the greatest effect – notably the Roman, Frankish, Holy Roman, Papal, and various Islamic hegemonies.

Much of Europe's self-destruction is covered within those chapters, alongside the tale of several geopolitical and financial empires and hegemonies that suggest lessons from history – chiefly, the always fatal ones concerning: firstly, divisions among Nation-States in the face of common external threats; secondly, internal fragmentation that is frequently seen in the form of issues of aristocratic succession; and thirdly, international conflicts resulting from such internal succession issues that escalate to "Wars of Succession" among Nation-States which often have overlapping dynastic Royal Families.

Just about all empires and imperial adventurism are driven by leaders that follow an ideology, sometimes a spiritual or religious one, sometimes an economic one, but in any event at least one that is associated with the concept of destiny, even if only in their own minds. A minority of successful empires were driven by territorial or wealth aggrandisement alone, but these were either very short-lived, e.g. the Huns (about eighty years), or they have become clandestine and for the most part have escaped the clutches of all but the fact or fiction of conspiracy theorists. Reputed examples of the latter are the covert Rothschild extended dynasty and their descendants at one extreme, or any of the many overt global corporations of the world's financial centres at the other, falsifying their accounting in terms of the source of revenue and its quite differently declared locale for tax purposes. A host of such corporations were pursued for immoral tax evasion in Britain during 2012 and are the subject of ongoing legislative change. The immorality lies in the failure to return that tax portion that might benefit the country where the revenue was earned – the criticism being valid as long as the principle of taxation is accepted in the first place, of course.

In terms of religious ideology, Europe is a region inhabited by peoples who were not chosen by God – neither by the Jewish Yahweh, nor the Muslim Allah. Europeans are a subject people, respectively *Gentiles* and

*Kafirs* (variously spelled) to those who follow the two Middle-Eastern Abrahamic religions that share the prophets of the (biblical) Old Testament, and yet hate each other with an intensity that could barely be imagined by a Buddhist or a Pagan for instance. Although there are many translations of both the Bible and the Koran aka Qur'an, two references to non-believers, according to the faiths of Jew and Muslim, are as follows:

From the King James Bible, Deuteronomy 7:6, we are told of the Jew-Gentile relationship:

> *"For thou [the Jews] art a holy people unto the Lord thy God; the Lord thy God hath chosen thee to be a special people unto Himself, above all people [the Gentiles] that are upon the face of the earth."*

From the Qur'an, 25:77, we are told of the Muslim-Kafir relationship:

> *"Say to the kafirs [non-Muslims]: My Lord [Allah] does not care for you or your prayers. You have rejected the truth, so sooner or later, a punishment will come"*

So Europeans are fair game for financial exploitation, and physical abuse and murder by the followers of those two rigidly barbarous and self-centred sects as is written down in their Holy Books that were handed down by their God. And yet, perversely, millions of Europeans have renounced their own ancient Pagan religions and embraced the third Abrahamic sect (that was second in historical terms) known as Christianity, and that has been led, as will be shown below, by a more often than not, despotic and corrupt Pope. The Popes are the only pan-European leaders to emerge during a time-span of two thousand years, and they have declared their interest and intent in both secular and spiritual hegemony over all the component wannabe vassal states of Europe. For the whole two thousand years the Popes have failed to unite states, they have frequently instigated wars to divide them, and they have frequently celebrated atrocities. Their "spiritual" hegemony has ensured that the concept of Pagan religions has been derided and has been made the butt of jokes and the recipient of far more sinister attacks over the millennia. Abrahamic assaults are based firstly on the whimsical, comforting presumption that reality most likely involves the superintendency of a monotheistic super-being – a god – based on nothing more than hearsay of other humans; and secondly on the almost heteronymic notion of heresy which is used as an excuse to inflict the most hideous and uncharitable forms of death and torture on those who dissent.

This chapter was not originally contrived as an assault on Europe's adopted religion, Christianity. It was begun as a profile of the behavioural characteristics of the Bishops of Rome, the earthly bosses of the organisation that purports to be responsible for the Christian faith, for its interpretation down to the minutest detail, for its practice, and for its promulgation and enforcement.

Behaviour is determined by a combination of innate human nature and the environment, and a study of the transient popes and their enduring closet-Empires, both secular and spiritual, cannot be undertaken without some reference to chapters in both volumes of this book that cover parallel transient Empires that, by their intrusive and usually superior force, have necessarily affected the Papal Empire and its aspirations.

This chapter therefore, is about far more than the Roman Catholic popes, but it's worth stressing that, as far as popes are concerned, they are the leaders of the Western Church at Rome alone. A top man such as the Pope, for whom there is no higher authority on earth, is said to be Autocephalous or Supreme, but within the geographically diverse Eastern Orthodox Church, there are many other similarly ranked supreme heads of churches with titles such as the Patriarch of Constantinople, the Catholicos of Armenia (that one has Patriarchs under him), and the Patriarchs of Alexandria, Antioch, and Jerusalem. Because Antioch was the very first Christian mission post, (Saint Peter was a bishop there before he went on to Rome), several of the orthodox churches like to have their own Patriarch

## The Two Thousand Year War – Papal Hegemony

of Antioch, so there are several at Antioch. There was once a Latin Patriarch of Antioch too; he was an exile from the time of the crusades, and he used to be resident in Rome, but the Roman Church gave up on that title and one or two others in 1964, and they were all abolished.

The diversity (enmities!) among all these factions began with schisms from the very earliest times, and grew to what is known as the Great East-West Schism that took more solid form in about 1054 when Rome and Constantinople excommunicated each other. There had been a badly missed opportunity during the 6th and 7th centuries when a political and religious union could have been ratified. It had been based on the concept of the Pentarchy, which was an older Roman administrative notion, that with some cooperation and compromise might have unified the four original Apostolic Sees at: Rome, Alexandria, Antioch, and Jerusalem; with a fifth, Constantinople, added because of its duality with Rome. A See was a diocese or mission founded by one of the Apostles. Squabbling and bickering among the sacred representatives of God on earth ensured the stillbirth of the Pentarchy, and set the stage for immediate divisions and consequent future weakness in the face of external threats such as the Vandals and Islam. Festering distrust of motives, and jealousy of trade successes among the various principalities and cultures within the Christian sphere, served to invite calculated Christian-on-Christian atrocities such as the Fourth Crusade that sacked Constantinople and the coastal Christian city of Zara on the Adriatic – a classic case of Christian butchering Christian.

So this chapter is centred on the western popes, because it is they who have had, and still have immediate relevance to the historic and current governance of western democracies. However interesting may be the Eastern Orthodox Churches and all their variants, there is just too much of that religious confederation to cover in detail, and their relationship is shown by references throughout several chapters of both volumes of this book.

One thing that Popes and Patriarchs of all sects do have in common though, and that does affect us all, is their utter commitment to both geopolitical and spiritual hegemony, and interference in the governance of the world and its people. As will be seen below, concessions to freewill in terms of belief have ebbed and flowed over the last century or so but, prior to that, even members of the same faith who were marginally off-side were either mutilated if they were lucky, or, if unlucky and unrepentant, burned at the stake.

**The claim of total and unquestionable Papal temporal rule over the whole of Italy was only reluctantly relinquished in 1929.**

Now a history of the aspirations of the popes in terms of cameo biographies might be a little dry for most people, though that is in fact how this chapter first began. After a while, however, it became apparent that these popes are no ordinary mortals, or maybe that should read, these popes are just very ordinary mortals. Sometimes, after a very casual inspection, and virtually always after a more detailed investigation, they are seen to possess all the weaknesses of humanity at large, and, given their calling and position, one might have expected better. Indeed, the Catholic Encyclopaedia's coverage of the character of the popes, and the prelates and lower minions they controlled, would have us believe that high expectations were in fact the reality, whereas even allowing for a liberal measure of atheistic Catholic bashing, there is overwhelming and damning evidence that can be presented in opposition to their exalted status.

From the obscurity (and likely much medieval and post-medieval invention) of the lives, martyrdoms, and godliness of the elaborately clad early bishops and popes, through to the present day with its equally elaborately clad effigies, there is an uninterrupted record of greed for power, and corruption of the soul and of the flesh. Misdemeanours and worse were endemic throughout their organisation, both temporal and spiritual, and their congregations were expected to fund the circus, and to support adventurism that was frequently of a military character. Therefore, instead of just a route through mediocre cameo biographies, of which there are still a large number, the last two millennia of papal hegemony is

*The Two Thousand Year War – Papal Hegemony*

mapped and interspersed with junctions and lateral connections to other manifestations of Empire, both ideological and physical, that inevitably will confuse the itinerary.

The Papal Empire has been in existence for nearly two thousand years, its population is over 1.1 billion people, and it is one of the wealthiest global organisations on the planet, with half a million employees and probably more than a trillion pounds in real estate and art treasures. It is not possible to predict with any certainty where it will be in one thousand years' time, but it could yet play a role in the short term against the rise of militant Islam and its penetration, not just of Europe, but of every culture – but only if it (the Roman Catholic Church) isn't throttled by the modern mainstream miasma of cultural anarchy.

We may be able to get an idea of its future utility and prospects in this respect by looking at its past record – a record that is presented over the next several sections of this chapter. The indictment presented below, however, that is the result of this author's assessment of papal conduct, does not bode well for Western Christianity.

## 16.1.1 An Indictment

In support of the themes of this book, the Roman Catholic Church and all of its internationally spawned variants and sects, including Protestantism, stand in the dock accused on the following counts:

1. Conquest by intimidation and the threat of eternal damnation.
2. The destruction of the spiritual belief of countless autonomous regions.
3. The financial exploitation of those regions.
4. The fomenting of wars of attrition that have killed hundreds of millions of people.
5. Failing to unify those regions.
6. Sexually abusing and exploiting many thousands of their subjects of all ages.

Evidence will be provided.

## 16.2 The Geography of the Early Church – the Apostolic Sees

Returning to the earliest days of the Roman Catholic Church, the four Patriarchal Districts, or Apostolic Sees beyond Rome, are rendered on the map below as:

1. Constantinopolis – Constantinople.
2. Antiochia – Antioch.
3. Hierosolyma – Jerusalem.
4. Alexandria – Alexandria.

Comparing that whole region of once peaceful and *potentially* stable ecclesiastical, albeit exploitative rule with the disasters that subsequently befell it, and with the heinous obscenities that continue to plague it today, one has to wonder what God is playing at.

## 16.2.1 Map – The Four Patriarchal Districts or Apostolic Sees
These were the districts Beyond Rome.
https://ia802509.us.archive.org/27/items/0TitlePageWilkinsonsAtlasClassica/ Public Domain

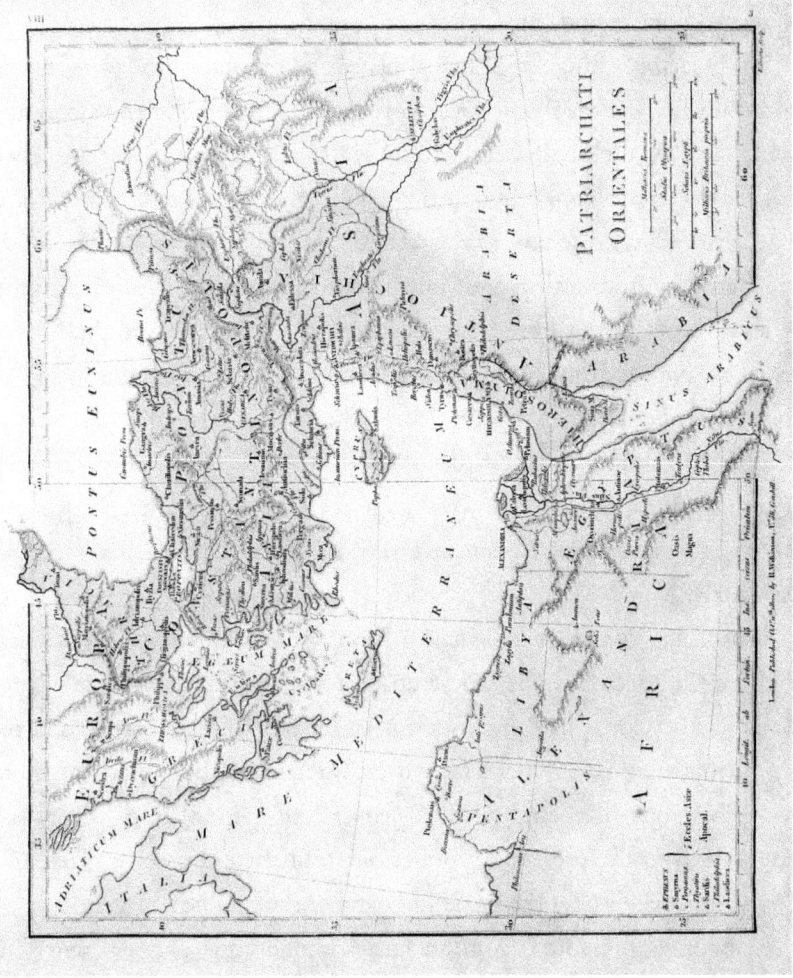

## 16.3 Sources of Information

In an attempt to remain objective, it will be useful to identify the sources of information to be used, and to state whether those sources are or were, pro-pope or anti-pope.

For objective listings of principal players to the end of the 6th century, an invaluable work is A Dictionary of Christian Biography and Literature to the End of the Sixth Century AD, with an Account of the Principal Sects and Heresies (1911), compiled by William C. Piercy and Henry Wace. The latter was a Protestant academic and cleric who, one would hope, was motivated by historical interest not partisan propaganda. Another useful series of books is the Ante-Nicene Fathers (ten volumes), and the Nicene and Post-Nicene Fathers (Series One and Series Two, each consisting of fourteen volumes) that together cover the period from the start of the Church to about the 9th century AD. From all these books can be seen opinions and comments that were made at the time of events, not just the edited and subsequently sanitised versions presented from a sectarian perspective.

Broad biographical detail is taken from two relatively modern sources: the pro-Catholic Catholic Encyclopaedia (1913) and the allegedly pro-Catholic Encyclopaedia Britannica (1911). One or two cited internet sources are further used to supplement and cross-reference the periods of those two Encyclopaedias, and also to cover the period from their last publication to the present. Information from these sources is given as a *précis* immediately after the name and dates of the specific papacy.

Opinion is presented from an anti-Catholic critic and ex-Franciscan monk, Joseph McCabe (1867 to 1955), who wrote more than 200 books, and who lectured extensively. Further reference may also be made to any relevant views from Protestants and secularists, and to the "Matter of Britain", such as the writings of Pelagius and Beda.

### 16.3.1 Liber Pontificalis

Even the *Liber Pontificalis* – a listing of the early popes that is accepted by many as being a piece of Catholic propaganda, probably compiled in the 6th or 7th century to establish the authenticity of the papacy, does not attempt to put dates against the first eighteen pontiffs from Peter to Urbanus I. The dates against those first eighteen popes below are from the encyclopaedias, also of dubious impartiality, and from modern internet compendia that seem to just follow the encyclopaedias. Henry Wace's ...*Dictionary*... is more hesitant about accepting specific dates for many of the characters in his impressive tome, so the dates of many of the popes and events described below have to be viewed with an open mind. In order to get a feeling for the sanctimonious episcopal hegemony of the *Liber Pontificalis*, particularly towards Constantinople and the Eastern Church, and coming at a time when the Acacian Schism (explained below) of the early 6th century would have been fresh in the memory, if not on-going, one only has to read the first few lines of the introduction to the venerable list. An extract from the *Liber Pontificalis* is shown below.

> "The bishopric of Rome, favored [sic] by circumstance in many ways over the bishoprics of other cities, is fortunate also in this, that it possesses records dating almost from the age of its venerable foundation. The equally ancient sees of Jerusalem, Antioch and Alexandria have no memorials earlier than the catalogues of bishops which were set down by the historian Eusebius in the fourth century. Constantinople can trace its episcopal line no further back than the seventh century. On the other hand, Rome, for a variety of reasons which are still matters of controversy, was regarded as a peculiarly faithful custodian of apostolic tradition ; the sequence of its bishops from Peter, the apostle, was cited even as early as the second century as guarantee of its claim to transmit the pure doctrine unalloyed."

### 16.3.2 Papal Apologists

Roman Catholic enthusiasts, be they scholars or just members of the worldwide congregation, deny distasteful historical fact when and where at all possible, and minimise the significance of what's left. There are both blatant omissions and historically dubious additions in much of the commonly available Catholic literature. Among the internet sources used in compiling the sometimes pejorative detail in this book, are the Dictionary and Encyclopaedias referenced above, and those indicated by many more links. See the chapter in Volume One titled Internet Index of References and Other Downloads. Church organisations such as Ultramontane Societies – fanatics that believe in the supremacy of Catholicism over Civil jurisdiction, and the infallibility of the Pontiff – and individual Catholic Clergy are not identified, but historical scholars are named.

### 16.3.3 Critics Within the Church
#### 16.3.3.1 Anti-popes

Many of the historical anti-popes identified below had a lot to say against the Church and its Bishop of Rome (The Pope) during their lifetime, and present-day anti-popes do exist, not just the fringe crackpots frequently found in California. One such anti-pope was the French Archbishop Marcel Lefebvre who died in 1991. In 1970 he founded the Society of Saint Pius X, whose members are traditionalists, opposing liberalisation resulting from the Ecumenical Council, Vatican II, that took place from 1962 to 1965. Although not officially titled Anti-Pope in any of the Catholic Encyclopaedias or Catholic-Hierarchy listings, he was excommunicated by Pope John Paul II in 1988 as a Schismatic for appointing four bishops, and the reason for his excommunication was "for doctrinal rather than disciplinary reasons"; the four bishops that Lefebvre appointed were also excommunicated. Lefebvre was, however, posthumously re-instated in 2009 along with the surviving "gang of four" bishops. The Society of Saint Pius X has a very professional website and they are also involved in worldwide missionary work.

In the chapters about the Popes of the period that follow, the existence of an anti-pope during the reign of an official pope will be indicated by "Cf." – meaning "compare and contrast with" – just after the name of the traditionally accepted pope.

### 16.3.3.2 Gallicanists

Gallicanism is the belief that countries should be able to organise themselves independently of the Pope. The Gallic does apply to France where it originated in the 14$^{th}$ to 15$^{th}$ centuries at the time of the Western Schism. Advocates included Bishop Pierre d'Ailly (1350 to 1420), who also produced a map for Columbus, and his contemporary, French University academic Jean Gerson. There were many others during the next few centuries, and the papacy did not have it all its own way.

### 16.3.3.3 Conciliarists

Conciliarism is the belief that the Ecumenical Council as a whole is infallible, not necessarily the individual Pope. Additionally in the extreme, that an Ecumenical Council might depose a pope. Closer to home geographically, William of Ockham, (circa 1287 to 1347) asserted that only the Church as a whole was free from error, not the Pope or even the Council. He was, of course, excommunicated. An example of changing views on the subject of Conciliarism is shown by the following sequence:

1. The principle was agreed at the prestigious Council of Constance that was convened from 1414 to 1418, mainly to deal with the Western Schism. Even the limited accommodation of Conciliarism implied a liberalisation of thought.
2. Conciliarism was condemned at the Fifth Lateran Council, (1512 to 1517), thus threatening liberalism.
3. Papal Infallibility was specifically affirmed by Blessed Pius IX in 1870, so liberalisation was reversed and Conciliarism was, thereby, finally defeated 450 years after it had first been implied.

That is just one sequence that demonstrates the capricious nature of self-interested popery and theologians, and there are numerous examples throughout Catholic literature from the earliest times to the present day that reveal how they revel in trying to belittle and demean their own contemporary Christians.

### 16.3.4 Critics Outside the Church

This category of dissident includes some anti-popes, the 19th-20th century ex-cleric and scholar Joseph McCabe, miscellaneous Protestant and ecumenical organisations, renowned philosophers and thinkers, such as Bertrand Russell, and atheist organisations, such as the Secular Society, Humanist Society, and innumerable internet blogs. There are dozens of links – see the chapter in Volume One titled *Internet Index of References and Other Downloads*.

Some critics of the Catholic Church suggest that the records of the first three or four centuries are unreliable and are likely to have been creatively enhanced by more recent papal or at least Catholic authorities to bolster the numbers of martyrs claimed, and to improve the record of progress made acquiring early converts. There is indisputable evidence that many of the early Christians were susceptible to apostasy in the face of persecution, and may therefore be judged as poor quality or half-hearted Christians. When it comes to martyrs, it's also a fact that Pagans were martyred during alternating periods of mandated Christianity, so illustrations of the Colosseum hosting feeding time at the zoo and other barbaric spectacles may have in fact portrayed a very ecumenical or mixed diet, not just Christian victims. Indeed the majority of the gore-fests involved not dissidents but gladiatorial contests and animal baiting – sometimes notable for the variety of exotic beasts, and at other times remarkable for the sheer numbers involved.

Other criticisms of at least the early Church include:

1. The popes of the first four or five centuries were mostly without character (visit the Vatican site for detail, i.e. there is no detail), and the same observation applies to many since.
2. For the early Church there was ipso facto a lack of Christian tradition, but the tradition and habit that soon developed

involved an excess of Pagan and contemporary Mithraic styled ceremonial procedure and sartorial grandeur that was adopted for no reason other than pomposity and the self-aggrandisement of the Pope and the clergy. They simply adopted the fancy garments that most impressed them. Mithras was an ancient Persian god and the object of worship of a secretive and mystical group that was contemporary with the Christians of the first two or three centuries in Rome, but of which the origins at this time are unknown. The advocates of Mithraism are believed to have worshipped in caves – just like the early Christians – and one has to wonder how much influence and culture might have been exchanged between the two. Mithraism disappeared as quickly as it had arisen when Constantine the Great opted for Christianity circa 330 AD.

3. Divisions were caused by language differences: Pagan Latin-speaking Romans, contrasted with Christian Hebrew- and Greek-speaking apostles and later evangelists. The Eastern Church would, of course, become Hellenised, thus further increasing the ethnocultural bigotry.

4. There were many cases and varieties of immorality, and rivalry that descended to murder.

5. Too many nepotistic despots and materialistic family dynasties occupied the Lateran Palace and Vatican for centuries, and they were more interested in increasing the acreage of their own estates and the Papal States than the real welfare of the faithful.

6. Too many of the Catholic fathers, popes included, lived in a state of arrogant denial of the abominations of their predecessors; such denial and a culture of apologetics continues to the present day.

7. The Pope aspires to the control of not just the spiritual being of individuals, but to the control of the State, Government, Parliament, Monarchy – the totality of the Governance of mankind – as the infallible representative of God on Earth.

8. The Pope brooks no dissent, and admits no freedom to follow any other religion.

## 16.4 Heretics and Schismatics

A simple-minded layman might be forgiven for regarding the Catholic Church's condemnation of, and subsequent actions against any of the dissidents covered below, as a sadistic attempt to impose its will without mercy on people who were only following their conscience; the evidence being the horrible deaths of millions that equal those resulting from any other despotic regime throughout history. That any person of goodwill could go along with such crimes against humanity beggars belief, but it is worse than that, since it happened repeatedly in multiple jurisdictions, and was tolerated and encouraged at all levels of the clergy.

It is important to bear in mind that, as Henry Wace says, all heretics are schismatics, but not all schismatics are heretics.

### 16.4.1 Gnosticism – Including the Cathars

Gnostic: *"Having knowledge, or rich wisdom"*.

Although the academic interpretation of Gnosticism is still evolving, it can be said with confidence that Gnostic beliefs at the time of the early Christian Church derived from those that were present during the $1^{st}$ century BC, and that they centred on ideas of the interaction of good (spiritual) and evil (material) forces, a form of Dualism, that in turn derived from older religions, such as Zoroastrianism, and the philosophical ideas of ancient Greeks such as Pythagoras and Plato. In other parts of the world, Gnosticism was and is associated with diverse religions and belief systems, but in the current context of Roman Catholic reach, the thoughtful, often ascetic adherents of Gnosticism were not even necessarily unchristian, and many fervently held much of the Christian faith. That was all of no consequence to an ideologically aggressive $4^{th}$ century Pope who was just beginning to form ideas of temporal control and empire; and the Catholic Church became determined to eradicate the Gnostics as heretics, and also to destroy all record of their heresy so that very little is known today. This lack of written detail is exacerbated by the fact that the practitioners of Gnosticism believed that to write down beliefs was to demean and corrupt those beliefs by their materialisation. British and Gallic Druids felt the same way, and we have also been denied a full appreciation of their culture by the actions of themselves and their oppressors, the slightly earlier Romans. After the Gnostic people's destruction around the 4$^{th}$ century, by a virulence greater than that supposedly directed by the Pagan Romans towards the early Christians, more Gnostics appeared around the 10$^{th}$ century just north of the Byzantine Empire. This time they were known as the Cathars, and again they were mercilessly hounded further north and into France, where as Cathars and Albigensians they were butchered and burned in true Catholic style, as part of a Crusade against them from around 1208 to 1255 – a Crusade and act of murderous extermination that was organised and celebrated by His Holiness Pope Innocent III.

One piece of the Gnostics' mindset that might have been of interest to the popes was their rumoured possession of esoteric knowledge that would bring salvation from this world and entry to the next. Such knowledge and understanding was clearly deficient in the Papal ideology that seemed more intent on simply contriving the untimely departure from this world of many of its victims, with no clear destination.

### 16.4.2 Marcionism

Marcion of Asia Minor, on the southern coast of the Back Sea, was the son of a bishop and was born about 110 AD. He was mainly known for his rejection of Judaic scripture and his restricted list of acceptable gospels. Marcionites believed that Jesus was the son of a good God, not the stern and vexatious one of Judaism and the Old Testament. Marcionite Gnostics associated those old Judaic testaments and scrolls with the Demiurge god of much older philosophies, and with the Material deity of other Gnostics. In 144 Marcion was declared a heretic or, more precisely as leader of the movement, a heresiarch; and his real crime was that he decided which texts, out of all those acknowledged by Christians, should be preserved and venerated, and which texts should be disposed of. In truth, this crime was only relative since that is precisely what subsequent Orthodox Christians did, only there were more of them and they had a different opinion of what to keep and what to throw out.

### 16.4.3 Montanism

Named after Montanus, a 2nd century self-acclaimed prophet in the Anatolian region of Asia Minor – most of present-day Turkey – Montanism was an ascetic Christian sect of men and women as equals. Though little real detail is known, it is believed that they advocated some sort of mixture of ecstatic and charismatic Gnosticism and self-development. Elevation to the status of prophet was open to all, and at its height, the heresy had spread around the Mediterranean coastline, and into Gaul. Their big mistake was to reject the need for clergy and the increasingly rich trappings and pretensions of popery, so that the full and vengeful weight of the Church and its scholars was directed at their destruction. Their extermination was eventually complete by about the 7th century, and one of the chief opponents of Montanism, who had at one time actually flirted with that heresy, was the renowned Catholic writer Tertullian, of whom more later.

### 16.4.4 Docetism

This belief had arisen within several sects and also as a component of Gnosticism and other heresies. It answers for some the dilemma of how God could die, as in the death on the cross of the Messiah Jesus. Docetism holds that because God cannot die, therefore Jesus didn't die, and the semantic mechanisms to explain this depend on what other faith or belief is held by the heretic in question. In the case of Gnosticism, the existence of the physical Christ was said to be just an illusion; there was no other choice for them since, as summarised above, their principal belief was "physical bad", "spirit good", so the good Jesus on earth had to be an illusion, and an illusion can't die. In the case of other beliefs and heresies, the principal belief was that Jesus was actually a man with a divine spirit, and that the spirit departed at the last minute; so again the spirit didn't die, and it could come back for the resurrection. Although that may seem to be the basis of Christianity to many onlookers, Catholic martinets would go to war if it seemed that the wrong form of words were being used.

### 16.4.5 Manichæism

Manichæism started about the middle of the 3rd century as the philosophy of the Persian, Mani. It was a blend of Gnostic dualism, Zoroastrianism, and Mani's native Babylonian cultural myth and legend that may have had its roots in ancient Sumeria. With Christian and Buddhist influences, it was one of the largest religions of the time, and a serious rival to all conventional faiths, not just to Orthodox Christianity. Including an aversion to dependence on a single, localised prophet for salvation (e.g. Jesus or the later Muhammad), it survived for more than a thousand years, and spawned other gnostic sects, such as the Paulicians, Bogomilists, and the Cathars aka Albigensians. It has also been compared with Mongolian Tengriism.

### 16.4.6 Novationism

Novation, a Roman priest, opposed the Pope in 251 and refused to baptise those who had lapsed when faced with persecution. He became elected as an anti-pope and was excommunicated by Pope Cornelius, and then declared a heretic. He was possibly martyred under the persecutions of Emperor Valerian I (253 to 260). Novationism reappeared as Donatism, and later still was a part of the expression or statement of purity and rebellion against the corrupt Catholic Church made by the Cathars.

### 16.4.7 Donatism

The heresy was propounded by Donatus who is presumed to have been born around 275 AD, and who was of the African Church. It was a heresy also held by many others of the clergy including bishops, and it specified the need for the clergy to be whiter than white. It further stated that administration of the sacrament could be done by any fallen clergy only if they were first re-baptised, and some extreme Donatists went further by saying that there was in fact no way back for the fallen. There had been many fallen clergy when they surrendered their sacred Christian texts rather than be killed during the persecutions of Diocletian (284 to 305), Bishop Felix of Aptunga in the African Church being alleged as one such, and he had consecrated the new Bishop of Carthage to the annoyance of Donatus and his friends. Emperor Constantine I himself instituted an investigation into the affair at which Felix was exonerated, but that wasn't the end of the matter. The continued expression of the Donatists' rage, along with the re-baptising that Donatists advocated, together with the militancy of a queue of volunteer martyrs, drew the ire of the orthodox Church, notably Saint Augustine who was one of the leading lights in western Catholic theory. In spite of the big names involved, the controversy lasted a couple of centuries, even withstanding the ravages of the Vandals in the early 5th century, but it had disappeared by the time Islam swept all before it along the northern African coastline during the 7th century.

### 16.4.8 Arianism

Arianism was promulgated by Arius, an Alexandrian religious leader, early in the 3rd century, and it was one view of the relationship among the three parts of the Holy Trinity, and of the implied divinity of the prophet Jesus. It is important to bear in mind that the cultural climate, within which early Christianity flowered, was overwhelmingly Hellenistic, with its traditions of classical Greek academia, such as logic and rhetoric; and there was never going to be a meek acceptance of anyone's dogma, whatever their credentials, without some debate and exploration of all the angles.

The central beliefs of Arianism are that Jesus did not always exist, that he was created by God, and that logically he is therefore separate. This belief was condemned at the Council of Nicaea that instead declared the orthodox belief to be an equally constituted trinity of God the Father, God the Son, and God the Holy Ghost. Or something like that.

Arianism was nevertheless adopted by persons of all Roman social levels, including Emperors, and by subsequent barbarian leaders, and the subject would be hotly debated at synods and ecumenical councils for centuries to come.

### 16.4.9 Nestorianism – the Eastern Orthodox Church

Nestorius, a Patriarch of Constantinople, believed that Christ had separate human and divine attributes, whereas the opposition under the Papal banner also believed Christ's nature was twofold, but that it was manifest as a holistic combination. It is said that Nestorius, who was from Syria, was too preoccupied with his Syrian roots, and that he did not enter into the spirit of light-hearted doctrinal debate, but instead escalated the argument into a major issue concerning the ecclesiastical constitution of the Church itself. There was a high-level attempt to resolve the differences when the originally sympathetic Byzantine Emperor Theodosius II called a council at Ephesus in 431, but the stridency of the opposing bishops forced Theodosius to reverse his position and depose Nestorius. So this heresy had now become far more significant to all of them than just a semantic spat, and Chalcedonian Christianity resulting from a further Council of Chalcedon in 451 AD, would become the basis of the Papal Church, and the opposite Nestorian view would become the basis of the Eastern Orthodox Churches. The difference persists to the present day.

### 16.4.10 Chalcedonism – the Western Catholic Church

Opposing Nestorianism (see above) the Catholic Chalcedonian view is that Christ's nature is twofold but that it is manifested as a holistic combination.

### 16.4.11 Monophysitism and Monothelitism – the Coptic Church

Coptic is synonymous with Egypt.

Monophysites of the 5th and 6th centuries were a third way compared to the Nestorians and Chalcedonians, since they believed that Christ was singly and wholly divine. The Christian Egyptian Copts, and those of the Jacobite Church of Syria and other regions of the Middle East and Asia, subscribe to this indisputably Christian doctrine, and yet individuals who put their head above the parapet and said as much were vilified and persecuted, not just by neighbouring Muslims, but by their fellow Christians.

Monothelites attempted in the 7th century to reconcile Monophysitism with orthodoxy by saying something apparently very reasonable such as "Okay, we now accept that Christ had two natures, but we reckon he actually only had one divine will – how about that?". This approach was accepted by Pope Honorius I (625 to 638), but it was then declared as a heresy in 649 at the Lateran Council in Rome, and again in 681 at the sixth ecumenical council at Constantinople.

### 16.4.12 Jansenism

During the period 1640 to 1801, and therefore prevalent much later than the heresies above, Jansenism related to the theories of Cornelis Jansen (1585 to 1638) who was born in eastern Holland. His philosophy emphasised predestination and the necessity of divine grace if there was to be any change to a person's fate, and the philosophy went on to deny the existence of free will, and to maintain that human nature is not capable of doing good because of the devastating effect of Original Sin, and consequent human depravity. Now that may not seem too different to official Catholic doctrine (or Protestant for that matter), but a glance at the entry in Encyclopaedia Britannica should be enough to convince anyone of the utterly politically correct meanderings of Catholic writers in general, and in particular around this subject over the centuries; with its on-going innovative gobbledygook during an attempt, as the hole gets deeper and darker, to explain a preposterously complex absurdity, including Semi-Pelagianism and Double Predestination. This is nothing short of ecclesiastical scrabble in an attempt to outdo and bamboozle the opposition – especially if the central papacy didn't come up with the idea first.

Unsurprisingly, the heresy was strongly opposed by the Jesuits, the very group against which Jansen had been motivated to speak in the first place. Jansenists have been likened to present-day evangelical "happy-clappy" Charismatic sects, sometimes speaking in tongues that they claimed to understand.

### 16.4.13 Pelagianism

Pelagius (circa 355 to 425) was an English monk who thought Saint Augustine was being too pessimistic about the essential sinful nature of even a newly born infant, so he came up with the idea that human nature is actually intrinsically good, and that salvation can be achieved without divine intervention. It may be that, yet again, there was an imputation that the intimidating foghorn evangelism of the clergy might not be quite as necessary for the salvation of the masses as the clergy would like it to be, but for whatever occupational or ideological reason, Pelagianism was condemned by the Churches of both East and West as a heresy, at the Third Ecumenical Council in Ephesus in 431. A watered down version, Semi-Pelagianism, was again condemned at the Council of Orange in 529, and although instances of organised Pelagianism did not occur after the 6th century, the doctrinal issues raised by Pelagius continue to reverberate and to be debated to the present day, with added concepts to tax the Catholic intellect, such as Limited Depravity and Total Depravity.

The Venerable Bede would later report on some weasel words describing Pelagius – those Christian words were spat out by one of Saint Augustine's disciples, Saint Prosper of Aquitaine, who lived circa 390 to 455 and poetically said of Pelagius:

> "A scribbler vile, inflamed with hellish spite,
> Against the great Augustine dared to Write;
> Presumptuous serpent! from what midnight den
> Durst thou to crawl on earth and look at men?
> Sure thou wast fed on Britain's sea-girt plains,
> Or in thy breast Vesuvian sulphur reigns."

Present-day mainstream media, with all its vituperative character assassination, would struggle to beat it.

Pelagius had made the mistake of recognising widespread corruption and depravity in the early Church (at the time of Saint Augustine), and he suggested the concept that man's own free will could be a starting point towards achieving spiritual grace, rather than relying on God's grace to kick start the process. Pelagius opposed the absurd concept of original sin and he brought down the wrath of Augustine and his sycophants.

## 16.4.14 Valentinianism

Valentinus aka Valentinius (circa 100 to 165) was believed to have come from the coastal region of Egypt, and to have studied at Alexandria where he was initially an orthodox Catholic, beginning his Gnostic involvement around the time of the end of the reign of Emperor Hadrian (117 to 138), and continuing into that of Antoninus Pius (138 to 161) when it developed oriental and Latin versions, and spread through Syria, Asia Minor, Gaul, and also became common in Rome. To the great dismay of contemporary commentators, such as Irenaeus and Tertullion, it mutated as it spread, but in common with other Gnostic sects, it always tried to maintain a direct lineage back to a specific apostle. In Valentinus' case that apostle was Saint Paul.

Specific doctrine relating to various mutations of this heresy is said to be difficult to differentiate, though there is enough information for anyone wanting to become a Gnostic in the references – see the chapter in Volume One titled Internet Index of References and Other Downloads. Valentinus is one of the main sources for the inspiration and resurgence of Gnosticism in the New Age of the 20th and 21st centuries, which gives him a claim to spiritual fame to rival that of Saint Peter himself.

### 16.4.15 Eutychianism

Eutychianism is broadly the same as Monophysitism described above, but it is more correctly restricted to the Armenian heretics. It was Eutychian who was allegedly responsible for the death of Saint Flavian, Archbishop of Constantinople, as described later in this chapter.

## 16.5 Temporal or Spiritual? - the Divine Right of Kings

This absurd piece of privileged and sycophantic Court hubris and mumbo-jumbo is yet another club to keep the masses in a state of subservience by elevating the monarch to the level or thereabouts of, if not God the Father, then a lesser god. The concept is found at the root of monarchies worldwide, and its use as a self-serving hoax ought to be obvious to everyone.

Its European provenance, firstly in respect of *primacy* - the relative godliness of Pope and King - can be traced back to Pope Gregory VII, who in 1081 wrote a letter to the bishop of Metz on that subject, in which he claimed that the Catholic aka Universal Pope had higher authority than a regional king. In 1302 Pope Boniface VIII issued a Papal Bull, the *Unam Sanctum* making the same claim, which in essence says that Christ gave his disciple Peter *"the keys to the kingdom"*, and instructed him to "feed his sheep." Furthermore, Christ had told Peter to *"watch over his flock"*, and the argument by Boniface finishes with the logic that, because Peter was the very first pope and not a king, then popes must trump kings.

By extension, God-fearing kings in medieval times told their God-fearing subjects that the King was next-in-line to God's representative on earth, and that he was therefore answerable to God and not to the general public. Acceptance of this outrageous and preposterous royal bluster by the minions or general public is one more indication of the consensual bondage that consigns them to the realms of Fiefdom, thereby robbing them of Freedom.

The idea of the Divine Right was scrapped in Britain following the realities of the English Civil War (1642 to 1651), and the subsequent Glorious Revolution (1689), after which the monarch was answerable to the parliament of the people, and not to God. Throughout Europe, however, some Huguenot and Lutheran aristocratic acolytes, including Luther himself, still clung, in their insecurity and unashamed revulsion of the peasantry, to the idea that their Crown, if its flavour was Protestant, derived some sort of legitimacy from God.

## 16.6 Blasphemy
### 16.6.1 Some Dictionary Definitions

Three groups of definitions of blasphemy, with their internet sources, follow:

http://dictionary.reference.com/browse/blasphemy

1. An impious utterance or action concerning God or sacred things.
2. An act of cursing or reviling God. Judaic.
3. Pronunciation of the Tetragrammaton (YHVH) in the original, now forbidden, manner instead of using a substitute pronunciation such as Adonai. Judaic.
4. The crime of assuming to oneself the rights or qualities of God. Theological.
5. Irreverent behaviour toward anything held sacred.

https://en.wikisource.org/wiki/Catholic_Encyclopedia_(1913)/Blasphemy

1. Blasphemy (Greek blaptein, "to injure", and pheme, "reputation") signifies etymologically gross irreverence towards any person or thing worthy of exalted esteem.

http://www.thefreedictionary.com/blasphemy

1. A contemptuous or profane act, utterance, or writing, concerning God or a sacred entity.
2. The act of claiming for oneself the attributes and rights of God.
3. An irreverent or impious act, attitude, or utterance, in regard to something considered inviolable or sacrosanct.

### 16.6.2 A Summary of Islamic Interpretation

The nature of blasphemy according to this aggressively murderous doctrine that is nowadays proselytised by the venomous rantings of so-called religious leaders, and that is unarguably spread and enforced by war and terror, is presented as a summary of documents of which there are many on the internet. One such example can be found here:
http://www.ltakim.com/articles/Blasphemy.pdf

### 16.6.2.1 Blasphemy in the Qur'an

The Qur'an states that a wide range of unacceptable behaviour constitutes blasphemy, and examples are:

- Apostasy.
- Cursing the name of the God or his prophet.
- Disrespectful behaviour towards other religious figures, beliefs, and customs, including apostles, prophets, or angels.
- False claims to religious knowledge or claiming to be a prophet.
- Expressing religious opinion that is at variance with normative Muslim views.

All of the above may be varied according to a Muslim's feelings at the time – his proclivities – but the Qur'an tells Muslims not to blaspheme against others and to avoid those who blaspheme against Islam. The Qur'an itself does not prescribe punishment for blasphemy, but punishment is prescribed for those who wage war against Islam. Specific punishment is determined by Islamic scholars and jurists.

### 16.6.2.2 Blasphemy in Islamic Law

There are variations among countries and among schools of law, but specifically, in addition to the general examples above, the following blasphemies that include blasphemy against artefacts may be identified:

- Drawing any picture of the Prophet Muhammad or of any other prophet, or making any film that features a prophet.
- Publishing unofficial translations of the Qur'an.
- Stating that Muhammad's parents were not Muslims.
- Finding any fault with Islam.
- Finding any fault with something in the Muslim community.
- Praying that Muslims should become something else.
- Being alone with anyone of the opposite sex who is not a relation by blood.
- Writing the name Muhammad on a toilet wall.
- Believing in the transmigration of souls or reincarnation.
- Denying that there is a life after death.
- Expressing any atheistic or secular beliefs or distributing such beliefs.
- Touching a Qur'an or anything that has touched a Qur'an if you are non-Muslim.
- Damaging a Qur'an or any other book that is of importance to Islam.
- Spitting at the wall of a mosque.
- Setting up any icon between oneself and God, and using that as an intermediary to God.
- Failing to conform to the rules prescribed for Ramadan.

Specifically in Somalia:
- Watching films or listening to music.

Specifically in Indonesia:
- Describing Islam as being an Arab religion.
- Reciting Muslim prayers in any language except Arabic.
- Saying that it is unnecessary to pray five times a day.
- Suggesting that the Qur'an contains lies.
- Whistling during prayers.

Specifically in Malaysia:
- Practising yoga.
- Using any words that are used by Muslims if you are non-Muslim.

Specifically in Bangladesh:
- Laughing at Islamic customs.

### 16.6.2.3 The Punishment for Blasphemy

There is variation in interpretation of the terms associated with blasphemy and apostasy. Furthermore jurists do not all agree as to what constitutes blasphemy, and although there is no specific temporal punishment in the Qur'an itself, any Muslim can regard blasphemous behaviour by anyone as an attack on Islam, or the waging of war on Islam, and can therefore raise the strong possibility of execution. Although there is no certain agreement among jurists on specific punishments, the punishment for blasphemy is covered by the *Kitab al-Hudud* – a Muslim juridical text.

The penalties for blasphemy vary according to jurisdiction, examples being, fines, imprisonment, flogging, amputation, or beheading, but there is no binding agreement among jurists on the use of the death penalty.

The Muslim juridical text *Kitab al-Hudud* translates as *The Book Pertaining to Punishments Prescribed by Islam* and it can be inspected here:

http://www.islam-universe.com/Saheeh_Muslim/17.htm

Having introduced uncertainty, and the impression that there might be some humanity among Islamic jurists, the following prescriptions are found among the writings of the jurists that consequently have the extra-judicial power of life and death over every single human being on the planet – regardless of nationality or belief:

> "Muslim blasphemers are considered apostates and will be condemned to death.
> Non-Muslim blasphemers are not considered apostates but will be condemned to death."

An 8th century jurist, Malik ibn Anas, whose beliefs are still referred to nowadays, states:

> "Whether Christian or Muslim, they must not be granted the chance to repent and shall be subject to immediate execution. Female offenders shall be punished but will be given the chance to repent and not be executed."

See reference:
http://lostislamichistory.com/the-scholar-of-madinah/

Sunni and Shi'a are in agreement about blasphemy, but Shi'a extend the blasphemy to include insults against their Twelvers (historical Imams), and against Fatima, the daughter of Muhammad.

Regardless of any theory, everyone is familiar with the reality that both Muslim-mob and Muslim-loner action, justified by the Muslim "religion" or ideology, frequently leads to the inhumane and extra-judicial killing and maiming of people for no offences whatsoever, and for offences that in any objective and mature human context are trivial. Islamic religious culture is simply unacceptable to Western civilisation that has its own vast shortcomings to resolve without the imposition of the medieval mindset of someone else. Yet for some unfathomable reason the English psyche is allowing the continuing construction of mosques, and the Islamic sectarian takeover of schools, that together will increase the prevalence of what might be seen as a medieval scourge throughout Britain, and that will inevitably lead to further atrocities committed by Muslims in English communities.

> *"To attempt to disassociate the disciples of Islamic radicalisation from the vehicle of their radicalisation is specious and delusional, if not treasonable."*

Tony Blair, several other leading politicians, and members of the clergy have done this after every Muslim atrocity.

### 16.6.3 Blasphemy Law United Kingdom

The Common Law offences of blasphemy and blasphemous libel in England and Wales were abolished in the Criminal Justice and Immigration Act 2008, to be replaced by a series of Hate Speech and Hate Crime laws.

With the abolition of criminal libel, seditious libel, and obscene libel, by the Coroners and Justice Act 2009, many naïvely celebrated the arrival of free speech.

### 16.6.4 Blasphemy Law Europe

Within Europe 8 out of 45 countries have blasphemy laws, and 35 have laws against the defamation of religion in general, or hate speech against religious practitioners. The 8 countries with blasphemy laws are:

1. Denmark.
2. Germany.
3. Greece.
4. Ireland.
5. Italy.
6. Malta.
7. The Netherlands.
8. Poland.

## 16.6.5 Blasphemy Law Worldwide

According to a survey in 2012 by the Pew Research Center's Forum on Religion and Public Life, 198 countries were asked if there was any level of government penalisation of the categories below, with the following result:

There were no such laws in 104 countries, but some form in 94 countries. That is to say, therefore, that 47% of the world's nations that were studied punish the expression of free speech in the respects below.

- Blasphemy is punished in 32 countries – 16% of the 198.
- Apostasy is punished in 20 countries – 10% of the 198.
- Defamation of religion, including religious hate speech, is punished in 87 countries – 44% of the 198.

The Pew Research Center study can be found here:

http://www.pewforum.org/Government/Laws-Penalizing-Blasphemy,-Apostasy-and-Defamation-of-Religion-are-Widespread.aspx

## 16.7 A Selection of Christian Church Fathers
### 16.7.1 Eusebius of Caesarea circa 260 to 340 aka Eusebius Pamphili

He was an advocate of Arianism and he wrote several acclaimed books including an *Ecclesiastical History* and a more general historical *Chronicle* that are available for download; those books provide relevant and succinct timelines of other historical persons and events. Eusebius was a Catholic bishop who took part, as an Arian, in the seminal Council of Nicaea in 325 AD, that was chaired by Emperor Constantine I by whom Eusebius had been invited to present his case. Eusebius lost the battle, reluctantly renounced his Arianism, and accepted the Nicene Creed; he also penned a eulogy to Constantine just for good measure.

### 16.7.2 Saint Irenaeus of Lyon circa 120 to 200

Born into a Christian family in Asia Minor, little is really known of him other than that he condemned the beliefs of others because they did not agree with his own. He wrote a book *Against Heresies – Adversus Haereses* that can be found on the internet (See the chapter in Volume One titled

*Internet Index of References and Other Downloads*), and he was particularly vitriolic about the Gnostic Valentinians (see Valentinus above). He is believed to have become Bishop of Ludunum (Lyon, France), and it is said, though without evidence, by Jerome (see below) and others, that he was martyred under the Roman Emperor Septimius Severus, but this may be another example of the martyr hype that permeates Catholic literature.

Neither Tertullian, nor Hippolytus, nor Eusebius, among many others mention any such martyring according to Henry Wace.

Irenaeus is described by some as a polemicist as if he was a rarity, but other than by a detailed analysis of specific pronouncements it seems difficult to separate one theologian from another; they all seem equally fanatical and convinced of the reality of their faith.

Quite apart from issues of faith, however, Irenaeus' book *Adversus Haereses* was considered to be the best description of Gnosticism until some ancient codices known as the Library of *Nag Hammadi* were found in 1945.

### 16.7.3 Saint Ignatius of Antioch circa 50 to 100

A Syrian, he became the third Bishop of Antioch, and there are compelling arguments both for and against his reputed martyrdom in the Colosseum at Rome during the reign of Emperor Trajan I (98 to 117). Records from the time are rare, and yet he is said to have been the child held by Jesus as described in Mark 9:36 – so it's no surprise that much of his biography quickly became tradition. The culture and value of martyrdom surrounded and is believed to have encouraged the development of the legend of Ignatius, being further strengthened by the facts that, after all the Saviour was martyred, and that gospels specifically relating to the Passion originated in Syria and the region of Antioch. To be martyred was to be assured of sainthood without the need to have been associated with miracles.

### 16.7.4 Tertullian of Carthage circa 160 to 240

Believed to be the son of a Roman Centurion and to have been trained as a lawyer and a priest, he became a formidable polemicist and defender of the faith after his conversion to Christianity around 192. He outspokenly rebutted accusations of cannibalism and incest that were made against Christians at that early time, and with strong Orthodox views, he was the first Christian to write in Latin, widely condemning heretics. Many of his works are available on the internet, one of his major works being against the contemporary Marcionites. It may have been his disillusionment with the factious and fractious nature of the Church, or it may have been down to his exposure to new ideas due to his wide ranging studies that drew him to the Montanist movement, but it was a commune of the Montanists just outside Carthage, present-day Tunisia, that he eventually joined, and not much more was heard of him. All his works were condemned by the Catholic Church by the 6th century, and so he had no chance of canonisation and remained just plain old Tertullian.

### 16.7.5 Saint Anthony of the Desert circa 250 to 356, the First Monk

He was born into a wealthy Coptic family in Upper Egypt and at about eighteen, on the death of his parents, he gave all his possessions to the poor, consigned his sister to the care of a neighbour, and disappeared into the desert to become a hermit. After decades of wandering he acquired a following that disrupted his lonely meditations, and he diplomatically tried to avoid them by retreating further into the desert. It may have been the solitude that did it, but at one point he decided he would become a martyr, and he went to visit the Christians of Alexandria that had been imprisoned under probably the persecutions of the usurper Maximinus II, who we saw in an earlier chapter had partial control in both the Eastern and Western Empires during the period 311 to 313. Although Anthony the monk, contrary to the law about monks appearing in court, did appear in court on several occasions, effectively challenging the authorities to martyr him, he was unsuccessful in his pacifist suicide mission and withdrew to a remote oasis. It was there that he remained for the rest of his long life, and where his followers later built the Monastery of Saint Anthony the Great, about two hundred miles south-east of Cairo, not far from the Red Sea. It remains to this day, and is possibly the oldest monastery in the world, with Saint Anthony considered to have been the very first monk – just about all subsequent orders emulate his ascetic life and austere monk's clothing.

After his death, and on his last instructions, he was buried in secret to avoid veneration of his earthly form.

### 16.7.6 Saint Athanasius of Alexandria circa 296 to 373, First Orders

From an already Christianised family in Alexandria, he was mentored by the Patriarch of Alexandria and eventually succeeded him as Patriarch. He led the ultimately successful debate against Arianism at the Council of Nicaea, and went on to write prodigiously in favour of Orthodoxy, but not without opposition from the Arians that involved violence on both sides, clashes, and conspiracies. During the years circa 336 to 366 he was exiled five times as a result of charges of misdemeanours from within the Church, or as a result of a change of regime that accompanied a change of Emperor. In addition to the official banishments, he was obliged to flee into asylum on several occasions to escape hostile crowds who were after his blood.

Athanasius was certainly not a universally popular man. For example, he was first exiled by Constantine I but returned to Alexandria on Constantine's death, only to be exiled shortly after by Constantine's son, Eastern Emperor Constantius II, even though at this time Athanasius was under the protection of Constantine's other son, Western Emperor Constans I. Athanasius would later describe the Arian Constantius II as a precursor of the Antichrist, and Constans I would later kill their other brother, Constantine II, in battle, and then be assassinated himself by his own troops. This was the legacy and climate of the revered Christian Constantine I – the Great.

For Athanasius there was much more excitement, but summarising, he was exiled for a third time by Constantius, a fourth time by Emperor Julian (The Apostate), and a fifth time by Emperor Valens. Between the reigns of the Emperors Julian and Valens, he had been invited back by Emperor Jovian to write a summary of the Christian Catholic faith, and overall he had what might be described as an interesting life. He had also been acquainted with Saint Anthony and wrote *The Life of Anthony* around 365, commending it to distant monks, thereby contributing to the new concept of Monks in Orders.

### 16.7.7 Saint Jerome of Pannonia circa 347 to 420

Otherwise known as Eusebius Hieronymus, he was educated in Latin and Greek at Rome, and was from either Pannonia or Dalmatia to the north-east of the Adriatic Sea. During his student days he was apparently very unchristian-like and wild, and is said to have *"offended every part of the community"* and to have referred to *"the dainty, luxurious, and rapacious clergy"*. For a while he later favoured a life of privations and discomfort as a penance and the perceived way of increasing his spirituality, but by 380 he had become a bishop at Antioch, and shortly after that a member of the court of Pope Damasus I in Rome. After pointing out the fragmented and archaic nature of Christian texts to the Pope he was commissioned to do something about it, and after discovering that existing Greek texts were unfathomable, he first set out to learn Hebrew so that he could improve and make new, rationalised translations from the original Old Testament sources. This does raise the question of what the Church had been using up to this point that enabled such in-depth assertions about what was, and what was not a heresy. He finally produced a Latin translation of the Bible that would last for centuries, and he is recorded as one of the pre-eminent Doctors of the Church. Life was not all sweetness though, and within a few years he was drummed out of Rome because of his bad tempered contrariness and confrontational behaviour, and amid allegations of an improper relationship with a rich widow named Paula, an event strongly denied by modern apologists. He spent his last years in a hermit cell near Bethlehem making and writing out many more translations, and penning attacks on heresies, though life in his hermit cell cannot have been too bad, since he was frequently host to the widow Paula, who it is said, kept him in good style and enabled him to expand his collection of books. To be fair to Jerome, he did eventually sell his own estate in Pannonia - Dalmatia to help fund the continuing work at their Monastery and Convent.

### 16.7.8 Saint Ambrose circa 340 to 397 – Victory Over an Emperor

From an eminent Roman Christian family, he was educated in law at Rome and was an unbaptised Governor and magistrate, though a declared

Christian. By popular acclaim, even from Arians, he was made Bishop of Milan in 374 – Milan at that time being the capital of the Western Empire under Emperor Valentinian I. Despite his initial support from the Arians, and against some high-level Arian opponents throughout the clergy and up to Imperial level, he managed with some serious political manoeuvring to rule against them at the Synod of Aquileia in 381, thereby suppressing the heresy for a brief time. He continued for the rest of his life to confront Arianism and to encourage the persecution and elimination of Pagans. He took ambassadorial roles in connection with just about all the Emperors of both East and West, and called Emperor Theodosius I to account, making him accept several months of penance for his massacre of 7,000 civilians at Thessalonica in 390. This achievement is of particular significance as an example of the growing power of the papacy. His successes mark him as another of the principal Doctors of the early Church.

### 16.7.9 Saint Augustine 354 to 430 aka Augustine of Hippo

From a not very wealthy family, with a Christian mother and Pagan father in the African province of the empire in present-day Algeria, he was enabled to study rhetoric at Carthage by the charity of a neighbour. Starting as a student, he had a son during a thirteen year relationship with a woman, and was later baptised with his son by the Ambrose referred to above. He was a low-level Manichean aka Manichaean for a while and was Bishop of Hippo from 397 until his death. His high ranking as a Church father is due: to his work as a bishop in creating Christians in the province; to his opposition to the heresies of the Arians, Donatists, Manichaeans, and Pelagians; and not least to his enormous written legacy of dozens of books, letters, and even later books about his own earlier books by way of explanation and clarification. There are, of course, many tributes and biographies about him, and other than a general damning of anyone who furthers, in the name of spirituality, the inquisitorial barbarity against so-called heretics, there does not seem to be any bad press in his respect. He died in 430 at Hippo while it was besieged by the Vandals.

## 16.8 Anno Domini 32 to 96 – THE POPES START HERE
### 16.8.1 Context
#### 16.8.1.1 Adversity

Using the summary of Roman Emperors of the West in an earlier chapter, a not quite arbitrary first period of 32 AD to 96 AD has been defined for the popes, that is, Saint Peter's arrival in Rome under Western Emperor Tiberius, through to the start of the Nervan–Antonian Dynasty (the period of the Five Good Emperors) that began with Emperor Nerva. We'll look at what the Encyclopaedias have to say, identify the commentators of the time and see what they had to say, and then see what a modern era critic who cites manuscripts (usually abbreviated to MSS by historians) has to say.

Of a total of ten Roman Emperors during this first period, including such notables as Caligula, Nero, and Vespasian, only one died of natural causes – the other nine were either assassinated or committed suicide. Not a pleasant background. The language of Rome was Roman Latin, and the language of the Christian immigrants and itinerants was predominantly Greek. There were no churches, and it is likely that meetings were mainly held in the open, frequently cemeteries it seems, and in the catacombs – tunnels cut into the surrounding soft rock, sometimes being natural cave systems formed by water erosion. As mentioned earlier there is an interesting historical and geographic coincidence of Christianity with the much older mystical Mithraic sect, such that both found themselves in similarly challenged circumstances for one or two centuries, and it is difficult to believe that the two sects did not interact in some way.

#### 16.8.1.2 Martyrs 32 to 96 – or Creative Propaganda ?

Melito of Sardis, a prominent 2nd century Christian bishop from Asia Minor, writing in the reign of Marcus Aurelius, knew of no imperial persecutors except Nero (54 to 68 AD) and Domitian (81 to 96 AD).

Tertullian expressly denied that Vespasian (69 to 79 AD) was a persecutor, and Eusebius of Caesarea (circa 260 to 340 AD) expressly asserted that Vespasian did no harm to the Christians.

### 16.8.2 The Popes of the Period 32 to 96

**Saint Peter (32 to 67).** Originally named Simon, he was born at Bethsaida, believed to have been a small town north of the Sea of Galilee on the present-day Israeli - Jordanian frontier. Following his time as a disciple of Christ, Pope Peter was effectively a missionary to Rome and was martyred there under Emperor Nero, probably by crucifixion upside-down as one of the scapegoats for the fire that destroyed much of Rome while Nero legendarily fiddled.

The Council of Jerusalem was held circa 50 AD, and this was the forerunner of later Ecumenical Councils

**Saint Linus (67 to 76).** Thought to be responsible for the decree that women should cover their heads in church.

**Saint Anacletus (Cletus) (76 to 88).** Believed to have been a Roman, he is said by some to have been martyred, but that is not mentioned by Wace, and not much is known except that he may have promoted a clean-shaven appearance for the priesthood.

**Saint Clement I (88 to 97).** Reputedly, though by no means historically proven, martyred by Emperor Trajan I by being thrown into possibly the Black Sea attached to an iron anchor. This legend is believed to have originated no earlier than the 9th century according to Wace, and does not exactly fit with the impression of Trajan gained from his correspondence with Pliny (see below).

### 16.9 Anno Domini 96 to 192

### 16.9.1 Context

### 16.9.1.1 Breathing Space

This is the period during the largely more beneficial time of the Emperors – only two out of eight emperors were assassinated – starting with Emperor Nerva (96 to 98) whose predecessor Domitian (81 to 96) had been assassinated, and who had carried out some, though not too severe, persecutions against the sometimes rebellious Jews as "descendants of David" rather than specifically against Christians. This period ends just after the death of Marcus Aurelius (161 to 180), a stoic who was not expressly anti-Christian, though neither was he averse to seeing them executed on occasion; the extent of such events is not clear but certainly was not of epidemic proportions. The general historical view is that, possibly as a deterrent, accusations were made much more often than the actual imposition of any punishment, and that the number of court cases was maximised by the existence of a class or group of paid informants – *Delatores* – who received their remuneration from the courts. This papal period is extended to 192 AD to include Marcus Aurelius' son, Commodus, who was reviled for his murderous bombast, and was assassinated.

### 16.9.1.2 Martyrs 96 to 192 – or Creative Propaganda ?

Conversations between Pliny the Younger (circa 61 to 112) and Emperor Trajan I (98 to 117), and commentaries by Eusebius, Tertullian, and others suggest that the only martyrs certainly known by name as having suffered under Trajan are two bishops, Simeon of Jerusalem and Ignatius of Antioch. An extract from Trajan's response to a letter he received from Pliny does not suggest an excessively despotic nature:

> "...You observed proper procedure, my dear Pliny, in sifting the cases of those who had been denounced to you as Christians. For it is not possible to lay down any general rule to serve as a kind of fixed standard. They are not to be sought out; if they are denounced and proved guilty, they are to be punished, with this reservation, that whoever denies that he is a Christian and really proves it – that is, by worshipping our gods – even though he was under suspicion in the past, shall obtain pardon through repentance. But anonymously posted accusations ought to have no place in any prosecution. For this is both a dangerous kind of precedent and out of keeping with the spirit of our age".

The implication is that martyrs chose their own fate for the sake of their religion, conceptually no different, one might argue, to suicide bombers that are an almost daily feature of news broadcasts during the 21$^{st}$ century, and that also act in the name of an Abrahamic religion. Regardless of the validity of that comparison, all of those who chose death received the posthumous commendation of Martyr from their comrades, and they all had expectations of reward for their entirely selfish actions. They also had options.

### 16.9.1.3 Tertullion circa 160 to 240

Tertullion was described above but to recap, he was a Christian historian, theologian, and commentator from Carthage, and he was significant because he wrote in Latin – prodigiously and at an early stage. Much of his work is freely available on the internet – see the chapter in Volume One titled *Internet Index of References and Other Downloads*.

### 16.9.2 The Popes of the Period 96 to 192

**Saint Evaristus (97 to 105).** Little known.

**Saint Alexander I (105 to 115).** Said originally to have been martyred by decapitation during the reign of Emperor Trajan I, it is now accepted that he was confused with another Alexander. Excavations of Roman catacombs during the 19th century, however, may have identified the site of the burial of the real martyred Alexander and other potential, though not proven, martyrs.

**Saint Sixtus I (115 to 125).** Also called Xystus I Roman, he decreed that only holy ministers could touch sacred vessels; that bishops needed Apostolic Letters to authenticate themselves in their home dioceses; and that during Mass priests should join the congregation in reciting certain parts of the liturgy.

**Saint Telesphorus (125 to 136).** Believed to have been a Greek, he introduced the Christmas midnight Mass, and specified that Easter celebrations should take place on a Sunday. Possibly martyred for being too successful at gaining converts.

**Saint Hyginus (136 to 140).** Little known, possibly Greek. Talk of Heresies was beginning to enter the records at this time.

**Saint Pius I (140 to 155).** Little is known about Pius, but there was much of significance happening during his lifetime. There is more reference in old manuscripts (ref. Wace) to visits to Rome by Gnostics, such as Valentinus, and by heretics including Marcion as described above.

Marcion was the son of a bishop, and is believed to have been a bishop himself. He advocated episcopalian principles – church government by bishops – and to restate the earlier summary, he was puritanical in his rejection of Judaism, the Old Testament, and anyone and anything of this earth or beyond that smacked of old and conservative celebrity. Later followers of his doctrine have also been described as Gnostics – another simplistic description of them might be: people who relied on esoteric knowledge and philosophy, with a sprinkling of mysticism to get them to God – an approach that long preceded Christianity. As noted earlier, the dualism (focus on Good and Evil) of the Marcionites flourished for a few hundred years.

**Saint Anicetus (155 to 166).** A Roman, possibly martyred, though there is no reference in Henry Wace, and the encyclopaedias acknowledge the scarcity of reliable information at this time.

**Saint Soter (166 to 175).** His benevolence is implied in letters from the time.

**Saint Eleutherius (175 to 189).** Of Greek origin, there is a contentious suggestion that he received a letter from the British King Lucius requesting that he be accepted as a Christian. Nennius' *Historia Brittonum* from circa the 9th century also references a Lucius, and there is a similar legendary suggestion of early British links in the Book of Llandaff aka the *Liber Landavensis, Llyfr Teilo*. Both of these fascinating books are available freely from the internet.

## 16.10  Anno Domini 193 to 235
### 16.10.1  Context
#### 16.10.1.1  More Heretics

The year 193 starts the next period, and in the context of the Western Roman Empire it was the Year of the Five Emperors which was followed by the Severan Imperial Dynasty that lasted until 235. In respect of the last four popes of this group, one has to wonder if the Church was correct in its attribution of the terms *Pope* and *Anti-pope* or whether they had got it the wrong way round.

#### 16.10.1.2 Hippolytus circa 170 to 235

Hippolytus was a member of the clergy, and, because his writings were sometimes critical of the Church and the popes, he was elevated, in popular opinion at least, to the position of anti-pope to the Bishop of Rome at that time – Zephyrinus. He produced many works, one of which was titled *The Refutation of All Heresies*, but he is nevertheless reputed to have been martyred in spite of that work, though there is still controversy about that. Various sources imply that there was more than one Hippolytus associated with ecclesiastical developments and records, and this is just one more example of the dangers in many assumptions about the era, particularly those that lead to ideological assertions. Some say he was torn apart by wild horses, others that he died in the mines of Sardinia, and yet others that he died after returning from Sardinia. For examples of sources to read online etc., see the chapter in Volume One titled *Internet Index of References and Other Downloads*.

### 16.10.2 The Popes of the Period 193 to 235

**Saint Victor I (189 to 199).** From the African territories, he is thought to have introduced Latin into the previously mainly Greek material. More incidents of heretics including the Montanists – a new-age type group led by Montanus and two prophetesses who thought the second coming was imminent, and believed that once fallen, a Christian couldn't be redeemed. They influenced several later Gnostic sects.

**Saint Zephyrinus (199 to 217).** Marcionism had been firmly denounced as heresy by this time, but other heresies proliferated, and there was much persecution under Emperor Severus (193 to 211).

**Saint Callistus I (217 to 223).** Cf. Saint Hippolytus. Callistus and the following three popes were opposed by Saint Hippolytus, anti-pope (217 to 235/236). Callistus was renowned for losing church funds, trying to run away, and fighting in a synagogue. He is said to have been exiled to the mines in Sardinia, but according to Hippolytus he escaped by taking advantage of an amnesty granted by Emperor Commodus in response to a request by Commodus' Christian mistress, Marcia. Callistus apparently managed this at his own entreaty although his name was not among those due for release. Callistus is said to have died in 223, and the tradition is that he was *"...scourged in a popular rising, thrown out of a window of his house in Trastevere, and flung into a well."* This is believed to account for the fact that no epitaph has been found to Callistus in the papal crypt, and it must place doubt on his entitlement to Sainthood.

**Saint Urban I (222 to 230).** Nothing at all is known for certain about Urban, neither whether he was actually martyred, and therefore deserving of his Sainthood, nor where he was interred. Various historians and records differ, and even though the Church was certainly internally riven by schism as a result of Hippolytus, and one would suppose incriminating notes were being taken, and additionally the early clergy were enjoying an otherwise peaceful period under Emperor Severus at this time, there does not seem to be any authenticated, cross-referenced record of Urban. In respect of his canonisation, one has to consider the highly likely possibility of falsified or propagandist recording at a later date.

**Saint Pontain (230 to 235).** Said to have been effectively martyred under Emperor Maximinus Thrax, he was actually exiled to Sardinia, and it is thought that this meant to the mines where, if true, he would certainly have suffered. However, the only evidence for his having died in a way that would have qualified for martyrdom is from the possibly discredited *Liber Pontificalis*, and the existence on his epitaph in the catacombs of the word *Martur* – added it has to be said in different writing to the rest of the epitaph.

## 16.11 Anno Domini 235 to 284
### 16.11.1 Context
#### 16.11.1.1 Roman Imperial Chaos

Starting with the reign of Emperor Maximinus Thrax (235 to 238), the abysmal character of the Roman Empire continued in unabated imperially corrupt fashion through the crisis of the 3$^{rd}$ century until the Tetrarchy began under Emperor Diocletian in 284. During this disastrous interval of less than one hundred years, out of sixty-four Roman Emperors, more than fifty were assassinated or committed suicide, with several more being killed in battle.

### 16.11.2 The Popes of the Period 235 to 284

**Saint Anterus (235 to 236).** Pope for 40 days, and said to have been martyred, but again, only by the much later Liber Pontificalis, which even the Catholic Encyclopaedia says may be unreliable.

**Saint Fabian (236 to 250).** As an unknown farmer visiting Rome, he was selected for Pope when a dove settled on his head. He was martyred under Emperor Decius. It is interesting that of Fabian, Wace says:

> *"It is remarkable that, though the Roman calendar designates all the first 30 bishops of Rome except two as saints and martyrs, Fabianus is the first,* except *Telesphorus and Pontianus, whose martyrdom rests on any good authority"*

There would now be a vacancy for pope for around eighteen months.

**Saint Cornelius (251 to 253).** Cf. Novatian. Opposed by the Anti-Pope Novatian (251 to 258), Cornelius was possibly martyred under the persecution of Emperor Gallus. He is referred to as a martyr by the Orator Cyprian, and by Saint Jerome who was described above. Wace, however, says that with almost the whole Church of Rome, including many that had already denied the faith under previous persecutions and had been readmitted, known as *Libellatici* or *Lapsi*, he took refuge at Centumcellae in Etruria, and that it is doubtful that he died by violent means. It has been estimated that there were up to 50,000 Christians in Rome at this time, so there was either a very big exodus, or a lot of leaderless *Libellatici* left in Rome, and another possibly undeserving Saint on the books.

**Saint Lucius I (253 to 254).** Roman, he was exiled under Emperor Gallus and returned under Emperor Valerian. He died just before Valerian's persecutions began in 257, but whether or not he was martyred (decapitation has been mooted) is not entirely certain.

**Saint Stephen I (254 to 257).** Roman - Greek, he was decapitated by Emperor Valerian's troops. He had taken a softer line towards those seeking readmission to the faith after denying it under threat of death.

**Saint Sixtus II (257 to 258).** Possibly Greek, he was martyred by decapitation along with several others under Emperor Valerian's persecutions.

**Saint Dionysius (260 to 268).** Probably Greek, he is remembered for sending funds to rebuild churches that had been destroyed by the Goths, and to ransom captives held by them. In 260 AD Emperor Valerian was taken prisoner and eventually killed by the Persians, and his successor, Gallienus, ended the persecutions and recognised the legality of the Christian Church. A milestone.

**Saint Felix I (269 to 274).** Roman, he is believed to have been involved in more conflicts with so-called heretics, and with deliberations on the way the Mass should be conducted on the anniversary of the death of martyrs. He was erroneously recorded as having been martyred.

**Saint Eutychian (275 to 283).** Little known.

## 16.12 Anno Domini 284 to 364

### 16.12.1 Context

#### 16.12.1.1 A Christian Emperor of East and West

This was a time of great divergence and the beginning of what would become a new Church in the East when the Roman Empire split its administration between Rome and Constantinople. Diocletian became the Eastern Emperor from 284 to 305, and Maximian became the Western Emperor from 286 to 305.

Following the split into East and West, the Constantinian Dynasty began under Constantius Chlorus in 305 and ended after the brief apostasy of Julian the Apostate (361 to 363) and the short reign of Jovian (363 to 364), but during this time it was the reign of Constantine the Great that is most well known. Taking over from his father, Constantius Chlorus, in 306, he began his struggle for control of the Empire, spending most of his time, until his death in 337, reuniting and then defending the reunited Eastern and Western Empires against usurpers from within.

#### 16.12.1.2 The Edict of Milan

The Edict of Milan of 313, generally dated to January of that year, promoted religious freedom and the restoration of sequestered goods and

Christian peoples to their homes; it was issued by Emperor Constantine, then ruler in the West, and Emperor Licinius, then ruler in the East, but was, however, hardly a recipe for total peace. Licinius would be deposed and hanged by Constantine in 324, and of the eight holders of the office of Augustus during the period from Constantine's accession in 306 to his death in 337, some of them being usurpers, only one, Eastern Emperor Galerius (305 to 311), died of natural causes.

### 16.12.1.3 Church Buildings Appear, the Arian Crisis, Nicaea

During the imperially and pontifically hectic years of 312 to 337, the first church buildings had begun to appear, and in 313 the first blatantly open council or synod was held at the Lateran Palace; and all of this, combined with the Edict of Milan suggested an early 4$^{th}$ century liberalisation. However, if there were any expectations of freedom of thought, then they were very much premature, for just a decade later, circa 323 or 325, it was the time for Arius of Alexandria to give rise to the Arian crisis, the severity of which could hardly be imagined from such a simple and logical suggestion that *"God preceded and created the Son, therefore must have been of a different substance"*. In 325 the Council of Nicaea was called to resolve this dreadful Arian heresy, and the conclusion after much debate was that: *"God and the Son are equal. Same substance"*. It was never going to be as simple as that, as several centuries would demonstrate.

### 16.12.1.4 The Inevitable Issues of Succession

Following the death of Constantine the Great in 337, the Western Empire would be doomed by his dysfunctional descendants and their fratricidal conflict and degeneracy. In a climate of weak imperial leadership, comprising sometimes infant heads of state, and profligate regent empresses, and with the centre of government elsewhere (Milan, Ravenna, Constantinople), there was a perfect opportunity for temporal adventures by the leaders of the Church.

So, in spite of the efforts of Constantine the Great, in 340 his son, Emperor Constantine II, was killed fighting his brother, Western Emperor Constans I, who was in turn killed by a usurper, Emperor Magnentius, in

350. By the end of the Constantinian Dynasty in 364, only three emperors had died of natural causes during a sequence of eight emperors.

### 16.12.1.5 The Arrival of the First Foederati - the Franks

Finally, towards the end of this current batch of pontiffs, around the year 362, and almost unnoticed among the disappointing strands of Constantine's legacy, a confederation of tribes were allowed to settle as foederati during the reign of the born again Pagan, Julian the Apostate, in a remote and relatively insignificant region of northern Gaul. That region was next to the windswept and stormy, cold and grey North Sea, and the confederation was known as the Franks. They would assert themselves with a vengeance in a couple of centuries' time.

### 16.12.2 The Popes of the Period 284 to 364

Saint Caius (283 to 296). Also called Gaius Benevolent, he was fortunate to have lived during a brief peaceful interlude. His depiction as a martyr is controversial. According to Wace, a 6th century manuscript says he died in peace, and only after Beda was martyrdom suggested.

**Saint Marcellinus (296 to 304).** He was Roman, and there is controversy about whether he survived the persecutions of Diocletian or whether he was martyred, the uncertainty being due to the fact that there were several self-seeking attempts by his contemporaries, and later by others, to rewrite history. During Marcellinus' tenure, the first Christian nation, Armenia, was identified in 301 AD. Constantine had not yet experienced his epiphany of course.

**Saint Marcellus I (308 to 309).** Cf. Heraclius. He instituted harsh treatment of recalcitrant Christians who tried to save their necks by denying their faith under persecution, and was eventually exiled and reputedly punished with severe and menial tasks by Emperor Maxentius. There is again controversy about the real detail surrounding him, made more obscure by the fact that, after persecutions by the State, the Christian Church itself persecuted its own according to how they had stood up to the State; and sometimes this self-persecution led to anarchy and death. Anti-pope Heraclius in 309 or 310 was also recorded in the context of how returning apostates were treated, but different sources report his stance ambiguously. It seems that he was eventually exiled along with Eusebius when Emperor Maxentius tried to rid the empire of the intemperate, battling Pontiffs.

**Saint Eusebius (309 to 310).** Not to be confused with the historian, Eusebius of Caesarea (263 to 339), Eusebius the Pope was Sardinian and was involved in the sometimes violent disagreements among papal factions. After only about four months in office he was exiled by Emperor Maxentius (Partial Western Empire 306 to 312) because he was causing too much unrest, and he died in Sicily.

**Saint Miltiades (311 to 314).** A Roman from the African territories, he benefited from the arrival of Emperor Constantine who installed him in the Lateran Palace that remained the principal papal residence until the Avignon Papacy that began in 1309 – almost 1,000 years later. This early and factual donation by Constantine may well have given later papal officials the idea for the preposterous *Donation of Constantine* that will be described in its full absurdity later.

**Saint Sylvester I (314 to 335).** Little known, though he did not attend the First Ecumenical Council of Nicaea in 325. The church's reputation was enhanced at this time while Constantine the Great was in power.

**Saint Marcus (336).** Little known, Roman. It is suggested that burials were now beginning to take place at ground level rather than in the catacombs.

**Saint Julius I (337 to 352).** Roman, it was during the tenure of Pope Julius I that the serious doctrinal controversy termed Arianism arose more strongly.

**Liberius (352 to 366).** Cf. Felix II. Exiled and then recalled, he became embroiled in the Arian controversy. Opposed by Anti-Pope Felix II (355 to 365).

## 16.13 Anno Domini 364 to 401
### 16.13.1 Context
#### 16.13.1.1 Deterioration of the Roman West

The Valentinian imperial dynasty, starting in 364, again saw eight emperors, and again only one died of natural causes, the rest being mainly executed. This was followed by the slightly more settled, but none the less vicious period of the Christian Emperor Theodosius I the Great (379 to 395), ruler of a united Empire of East and West who was also a Christian bishop. Theodosius was wheeled out of retirement to be initially co-emperor of the East by the inexperienced Emperor Gratian (367 to 383) who was having difficulties with mainly Goth barbarians; he would eventually be assassinated for his failures. Theodosius was termed Great because he satisfied Catholic tastes concerning the enforcement of Christianity, not because of noteworthy external military successes, and in the year 380 a law was passed ordering everyone to adopt the Catholic faith as specified by Constantine the Great at Nicaea. In fact, quite apart from any public good, Theodosius was involved in internal civil wars, and widespread persecution of pagans: denial of a place of worship and practice, the destruction of ancient iconography and sacraments, even the extinguishing of the eternal fire in the Temple of Vesta. He established the use of the name "Catholic" Christians and succeeded in imposing Trinitarianism over Arianism. In spite of these successes his legacy and that of his two weak sons – Emperor Arcadius of the Eastern Empire and Emperor Honorius of the Western Empire – was firstly fratricidal division and susceptibility to corruption, and secondly the encouragement of a military structure that was riddled with potentially disloyal barbarians who had yet to feel like true stakeholders. So, confounding the short-term epithet Great, the reality was that, on the ever contracting fringes of the Empire, settlement rights as *foederati* were bestowed on more, and yet more immigrant Goths, Burgundians, and of great future significance, the Franks who settled in Gaul. Although they would turn out to be an asset in time, all these wild and tribal adventurers would contribute in the immediate future to the collapse of the degenerate Roman secular world, and the perpetuation of a separate and distinct Papal Power that was just itching to diversify into the secular.

### 16.13.2 The Popes of the Period 364 to 401

**Saint Damasus I (366 to 383).** Cf. Ursicinus. Spanish, he came to power allegedly amidst violence when his supporters killed those of his rival, Ursicinus, who then became anti-pope (366 to 367). Anti-Pope Ursicinus had been favoured by the previous pope, Liberius, who had been opposed by an anti-pope who favoured Damasus, so the whole business is decidedly suspicious. It was also a time of more widespread conflict when the Eastern Empire saw a resurgence of paganism that led to civil wars and the eventual reunification of East and West under Christianity, but with rivalry between Rome and Constantinople. Pope Damasus I is renowned for his restoration work on the catacombs in order to make them accessible by pilgrims, and the commissioning of writings and engravings in a style known as Damasine Character.

**Saint Siricius (384 to 399).** Believed to have left a wife and children in order to become pope. He faced more heretical suggestions, one from a monk Jovinian who thought that celibacy and abstention from good food and wine was not a good idea and not necessary. Jovinian was supported in this view by a few nuns. Pope Siricius is credited with having issued the first Papal Decretal that could be validated as genuine, and he was actively opposed to the Manichean heretics.

**Saint Anastasius I (399 to 401).** Roman, he faced issues with the works of earlier heretics such as Origen, a prolific writer and accomplished scholar from Alexandria, who actually did much to develop ideas and to articulate ecclesiastical theory. Pope Anastasius I insisted that the clergy and the Deacons should stand bowed during the reading of the gospels.

## 16.14  Anno Domini 401 to 468

### 16.14.1  Context

#### 16.14.1.1  The Sacking of the West

The court of Emperor Arcadius (reign 383 to 408) at Constantinople had surrounded itself with Goths who were steadily dispensing with their old barbaric ways, and from whom physical vigour and an aspirant intellectual vitality was a refreshing change and good for the Eastern Empire. Honorius, after beginning Western rule at Milan as a mere 10-year-old without his father, but with General Stilicho as guardian, moved to Ravenna around the year 404, where natural defences were better and where his weakness was mitigated by a dynastically advantageous marriage

# The Two Thousand Year War – Papal Hegemony

to Stilicho's daughter. Tragically for many thousands, Emperor Honorius had nothing of his father Theodosius' strength though maybe all of his debatable wit.

Since 401, General Stilicho had twice halted the advance through Italy of the Visigoths under Alaric, who was not just a passing barbarian but a favoured Goth and declared Master-General of Eastern Illyricum, and who had been acting on behalf of Eastern Emperor Arcadius. Unbelievably, in 408 Emperor Honorius had Stilicho and his family executed, and he incited the butchery of thousands of women and children of the families of Goths that were serving in the Western Empire's military. The natural consequence of this masterstroke was a defection of many thousands of Goths from Honorius' legions to those of Alaric. The way was now open for the sacking of Rome.

### 16.14.1.2 The Year 410 – Alaric and the Visigoths

After one or two sieges and postponements the nightmare finally became reality in 410. The city of Rome was gutted by fire and it is said that just about anything of value that was moveable was taken, leaving a city of penniless refugees. It was the first such catastrophe since the Gauls, under their leader Brennus, had raided the city eight hundred years earlier in 387 BC. To make matters worse, in this climate of desperation and weakness, and under a secular administration of stupidity and treachery, the Pope and his ecclesiastical authorities were able to pass several decrees and laws that would actually increase papal wealth by imposing fines and sequestrations for anything that could be considered a heresy; and there were to be further taxes on the masses – when the masses could be found among the devastation, of course, – but there would be exemptions for bishops and the clergy.

Naturally, and coming as no surprise, the Pope Innocent I and his entourage of such exempt bishops and the clergy were at Ravenna during the troubles at Rome.

### 16.14.1.3 The Vandals Arrive in Africa, Gaiseric's First Treaty

About the year 428 AD Gaiseric (aka Genseric) and his tribe of fifty thousand or more Vandals crossed the straits of Gibraltar from Spain into

North Africa and pillaged their way east. The Vandals were Christians of the Arian sect and had sworn to rid their conquered territories of all those of the Nicene Creed, which they did without mercy, although they are said to have given the defeated clergy a chance to depart. In the year 435 Gaiseric signed a treaty to become one of the Empire's *foederati*, but this did not stop him taking Carthage from the Empire by force in 439.

### 16.14.1.4 The Vandals *and* the Huns.

It seems that some of the Goths were the lesser of the evils facing Rome around this time, and that for several years they had been integrating of their own free will into Roman culture to some extent, but for the Romans suddenly to be confronted with the Vandals and at the same time the even worse axis of Huns – as seen in another chapter in Volume Two, a Hun Confederation with their own diverse legions of supporting tribes – it must have seemed like the end of the world, as indeed it very soon would be as shown by the following timeline:

**440.** Gaiseric has virtually destroyed the Catholic Church in Africa, and now crosses into Sicily.

**441.** Another treaty is signed between Gaiseric on behalf of the growing Vandal Empire, and Emperor Valentinian III for the Western Roman Empire, giving the Vandals much of North Africa.

**451.** The horrific Battle of the Catalaunian Plains, believed to be near Chalons, northern France, was the swansong of the Western Empire, and certainly changed the course of European history from what it might have been under a Hunnish Dynasty – see detail under Saint Leo I, aka Pope Leo I, aka Leo the Great (440 to 461) below.

**452.** Attila the Hun is dissuaded from attacking Rome.

**455.** Gaiseric the Vandal is invited by the widow of Valentinian to take Rome but is requested to show moderation. So, although refraining from burning the city, Gaiseric organised fourteen days of total sacking and carried off booty and slaves, including the Empress and her daughters, back to Carthage which was his centre of operations.

**460.** The Vandals defeat the Western Romans under Emperor Majorian.

**468.** The Vandals defeat the combined Western and Eastern Romans under Emperor Basiliscus.

See the separate chapters on the Roman Empires of the West (Volume One) and East (Volume Two) for full detail.

### 16.14.2 The Popes of the Period 401 to 468

**Saint Innocent I (401 to 417).** Pope Innocent I confronted the controversy resulting from the philosophy of the heretical Pelagius, who advocated free will and who opposed the concepts of predestination and original sin. Innocent's papacy came at a very significant time with Christianity having been the religion of choice for the Imperial Court for nearly a century. As indicated above, the empire at this time was divided between the two sons of Theodosius, with Western Emperor Honorius based in Ravenna because it was more defensible than Rome. Two years after Innocent I became pope in Rome he moved to Ravenna as well.

**Saint Zosimus (417 to 418).** Known for his fiery temper during his handling of many controversies. Pope Zosimus was in regular contact with missionary outposts in Gaul.

**Saint Boniface I (418 to 422).** Cf. Eulalius. Violently installed as Pope and opposed by Anti-Pope Eulalius (418 to 419). Pope Boniface I continued to oppose Pelagianism and just managed to retain authority over the region known as Illyricum on the eastern side of the Adriatic and covering the states recently known as Yugoslavia, and Greece and the Balkans generally. The Patriarch of Constantinople also claimed Illyricum, and the region remained a flashpoint between the two Empires and their divergent churches. Boniface is the pope who invited Gaiseric and the Vandals into Africa and who ruled that a slave needed his master's consent to be ordained.

**Saint Celestine I (422 to 432).** Roman, most famously known for sending Saint Patrick to Ireland. Although not attending personally, Pope Celestine I sent representatives to the First Council of Ephesus in 431 where the heretical Nestorians were condemned, particularly vociferously, by Eutyches of Constantinople who went on to become labelled a heretic himself for similarly semantic nit-picking in a strident manner.

**Saint Sixtus III (432 to 440).** Before becoming pope he was a supporter of the Pelagian heresy. Known for building works in Rome and for the continuing battle of wits for Illyricum. Pope Sixtus III is also noted for his involvement in the heresies of both Nestorianism and Pelagianism, though it is said that reluctance to pass judgement may have been mistaken for sympathy.

**Saint Leo I the Great (440 to 461).** In 451 near Châlons-en-Champagne, which is about 100 miles east of present-day Paris, the Battle of the Catalaunian Plains had stopped the advance of the Hun under Attila, and it is said that *"... one hundred and sixty thousand corpses littered the plains...."* The forces of the Roman General Aetius, and the Visigothic King Theoderic I, were victorious, albeit with the death of Theoderic, and in 454 the Huns' erstwhile subject tribes within their confederation rebelled and finished the job by destroying the Huns under Attila's son, Ellac, at the Battle of Nedao in the area known as Pannonia, just north of the Dalmatian coast of the Adriatic in the south-west of present-day Hungary. Attila had died in 453, but one of his last acts in 452 had been to march towards Rome, and he thereby unwittingly hastened the development of Venice by causing the local population to flee into the lagoon to construct fortified islands. It was Pope Leo I (Leo the Great) who went to Mincio near Lake Garda, northern Italy, to persuade Attila to desist from sacking Rome; and without force of arms, but almost certainly with a financial inducement, he was successful. Leo was also remembered for construction works and spiritual unification of the church. The Monophysite heresy arose during his papacy following the Council of Chalcedon in 451, and he was continually obliged to contend with the Nestorians, Pelagians, Manichaeans, Priscillianists, Eutychianism, and the ever active Arian factions and foreign nations. A very complex brew of opposing heretical ideas about the one true God.

One triumph that Leo very modestly does not mention in his own writings is his reputed saving of Rome from the Vandals and Gaiseric in 455 when, by some unspecified means, some sources say that he induced the barbarian not to sack the city. This has to be set against the detail above from other sources that say that, if not sacked, Rome was certainly well and truly bagged along with its Empress.

Pope Leo I was the first non-martyred pope to be buried in the Church of Saint Peter in Rome, constructed during the reign of Constantine the Great just over one hundred years earlier.

**Saint Hilarius (461 to 468).** This Sardinian continued the work of Saint Leo I, but bad times were approaching with barbarian infiltration of the army and the Senate. It was just before Pope Hilarius' papacy, while he was still a Deacon, that the Archbishop Flavian of Constantinople was attacked and murdered by Christian ideological rivals, a priest named Eutyches (of Eutychianism fame) along with an accomplice. Hilarius was obliged to flee the Council at Ephesus where the assault had taken place and to travel incognito to avoid what he suspected might also have been his own fate.

## 16.15 Anno Domini 468 to 537
### 16.15.1 Context
#### 16.15.1.1 The Beginning of the End and Vice Versa

In 472 there were effectively two kingdoms in Italy. They were ruled by Emperor Anthemius in Rome and Count Ricimer in Milan. Quite separately, in Constantinople, there was Emperor Flavius Zeno 474 to 475, followed by Emperor Basiliscus 475 to 476, and then again the return of Emperor Flavius Zeno 476 to 491 who in 482 attempted to heal the rift between the Chalcedonians and the Monophysites by the presentation of the reason-based Henotikon act of union. All he achieved by this was further acrimony and anger that an Eastern Emperor should have had the temerity to become involved at all, and the result was the thirty-five year Acacian Schism between the Eastern and Western Christian Churches.

At this time the Western Imperial Court was particularly dysfunctional and degenerate as it faced the approach of its dissolution and its metamorphosis into the Kingdom of Italy under the Goths. That regime change would lead to a couple of centuries of strong leadership under the Goths, and temporary enlightenment in what had become a very dark age for many decades under the Romans.

This factual and demonstrable historical reality is far from the usually portrayed immediate "Dark Age" that is traditionally taught as accompanying the arrival of the barbarians.

The prerogative to really darken the spirit, by destroying education, by diverting wealth into rich trappings that would attract further sackings, by neglecting city defences against such future invasion, and by the creation of a nepotistic and ignorant self-serving hierarchy, would be left to a long line of monstrously undesirable popes.

### 16.15.1.2  493 AD – Odovacer is Killed by Theoderic the Great

Odoacer aka Odovacer, who was most probably an Ostrogoth of Germanic descent, had taken Ravenna from the last Western Roman Emperor Romulus Augustus, and had become King of Italy, though see the chapters on the Roman Empires for detail concerning Emperor Julius Nepos' brief continuation. Theoderic, who was also an Ostrogoth but raised in Constantinople, had a serious grudge against Odovacer because of an earlier treachery against Theoderic's *comites* or honourable supporters, sometimes misleadingly translated as henchmen. In revenge, after taking Ravenna on behalf of his Byzantine patron, the Eastern Emperor Flavius Zeno, Theoderic slew Odovacer "... *with a single sword-stroke* ...." See the freely available book, *Theoderic the Goth, the Barbarian Champion of Civilisation*, by Thomas Hodgkin, D.C.L.

Sadly, Theoderic's descendants were relatively dysfunctional, and following an all too brief Gothic enlightenment, to which Ravenna owes much of its architectural and artistic heritage, those descendants would contribute to some of the worst days of Rome's history.

### 16.15.1.3  Summary of the Judicial Scope of Theoderic the Great

Theoderic the Great was originally of the royal Amal family of Ostrogoths and, after being brought up in Constantinople, he returned to his people as King of the Ostrogoths (471 to 526). The mutual respect between himself and the Byzantine Court under Emperor Flavius Zeno, and Theoderic's victory over Odovacer, led to him taking the titles Ruler of Italy (493 to 526), Regent of the Visigoths (511 to 526), and Viceroy of the Eastern Roman Empire. He was a leader of integrity and honesty though not literate, and Ravenna flowered architecturally; public works, such as sanitation being massively improved during his time.

### 16.15.1.4 Map – Theoderic's Confederation 523

Map from http://commons.wikimedia.org/wiki/Category:Maps released under CC-BY-SA
http://creativecommons.org/licenses/by-sa/3.0/ Author: Vortimer

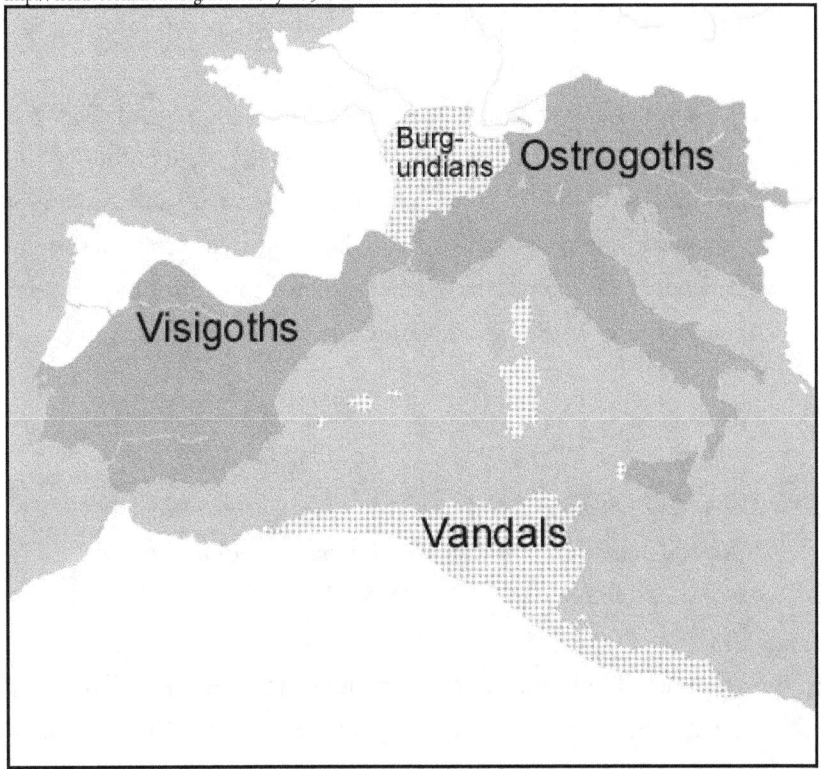

### 16.15.2 The Popes of the Period 468 to 537

**Saint Simplicius (468 to 483).** This pope had to maintain stability during the troublesome period of the end of the Western Empire, and he was obliged to witness the arrival of the Arian Flavius Odovacer (aka Odoacer) as King of Italy. The Eastern Empire was also in turmoil with Basiliscus ousting the Eastern Emperor Zeno in 476. Zeno eventually returned in 477, but throughout Pope Simplicius' tenure there was spiritual and temporal turmoil.

**Saint Felix III (II) (483 to 492).** Roman, his time was fully occupied with managing heresies and controversies, specifically factionalism that was due to Eutychianism and Monophysitism, referred to earlier, both of which relate to the interpretation of the nature of the components of the Holy Trinity. The squabble between the two bishops, Pope Felix of the West and Patriarch Acacius of the East, led to Felix deposing and excommunicating Acacius in 484, and Acacius eliminating Felix from the eastern iconography. The Acacian Schism had started and it would last until 519.

**Saint Gelasius I (492 to 496).** A Berber, and something of a cleric, it was said that he was charitable, and that he asserted papal authority and increased tensions between the Eastern and Western Churches. Not surprising when one reads in Wace that he obliged an errant returning Bishop Misenus of Cumae to declare against that bishop's previous Acacian accomplices in the Eastern Church, and in true Christian style that he:

> "condemned, anathematized, abhorred, and for ever
> execrated Dioscorus, Aelurus, Peter Mongus, Peter Fullo,
> Acacius, and all their successors, accomplices, abettors, and all
> who communicated with them."

This nature of forgiveness and understanding (!) is the basis of the early Catholic Church of Rome – quite contrary to the record of Christ's biblical teachings.

**Anastasius II (496 to 498).** Chiefly associated with the continuing great ideological or doctrinal schism between the Pope and his opposite number in the East, Acacius, the Ecumenical Patriarch of Constantinople. He also spoke out against Traducianism, the belief that the soul is inherited from one's parents. In 451 at the ecumenical council of Chalcedon, it had been decided that Christ had both a divine and a human nature. A letter that was attributed to Anastasius that purported to congratulate King Clovis on his conversion to Christianity, has subsequently been identified as a 17th century forgery. King Clovis of the Salic aka Salian Franks is noted as the founder of the Merovingian Dynasty that just preceded the Carolingian Empire which was the pinnacle of the Franks' unification of continental Europe. It would have been a feather in any Pope's cap to have been the successful missionary at the heart of such a conversion.

**Saint Symmachus (498 to 514).** Cf. Laurentius. A Sardinian born Ostrogoth Pagan, he was a very unlikely candidate for pope – though he had been baptised Christian of course. He was opposed by Anti-Pope Laurentius (498 to 505). Both Pope Symmachus and Anti-pope Laurentius were the first popes to practise Simony, named after Simon Magus, a Samaritan sorcerer at the time of the apostles. Simony was the quite unacceptable practice of bribing officials of the Church or State to gain advantage of some kind, and it included nomination for office – including that of pope. King Theoderic the Great was active at this time and was called on to arbitrate in the sometimes violent, and fatal struggles among the two popes' supporters.

**Saint Hormisdas (514 to 523).** Believed to have been from a wealthy Italian family, he was preoccupied with the Acacian Schism that had started under his predecessors. In 519 Eastern Emperor Justin I reaffirmed the canons of Chalcedon, but as yet there were no issues or confrontation with Theoderic who subscribed to the contrary Arian belief.

**Saint John I (523 to 526).** A frail individual from Tuscany, he was the first pope to visit Constantinople after being so ordered by Theoderic to try to gain some relaxation of the decree against the Arian sect that had been issued by Eastern Emperor Justin. On his return to Ravenna however, in spite of his actual success in Constantinople, Theoderic had him imprisoned on suspicion of conspiring with Justin, and Pope John I died there, possibly from fatigue suffered on the journey, or possibly from privations in prison. That act is out of character for most of Theoderic's behavioural record, and it is a black mark for the Goth if true. John's death in these circumstances was apparently adequate cause for his canonisation.

**Saint Felix IV (III) (526 to 530).** The regnal numbering system gets complicated here due to popes and anti-popes of the same name. Felix IV was actually the third true pope of that name. The Order of Saint Benedict was started about 529 and this would lead to the enormous network of Benedictine Abbeys and monks.

**Boniface II (530 to 532).** Cf. Dioscorus. An Ostrogoth by birth, his appointment was significantly helped by the patronage of Athalaric, the grandson of Theoderic. He was opposed by Anti-Pope Dioscorus (530), both pope and anti-pope were consecrated on the same day.

**Pope John II (533 to 535).** The first pope to adopt a different name as Pope – he was Roman and born Mercurius, that name being known as a Theophoric name that involved taking the name of a god for good luck. Simony was coming along nicely by now, with all sorts of sacred relics and ceremonial accessories being trafficked, as well as an inclination to entertain bribery for office.

**Saint Agapetus I (535 to 536).** Also called Agapitus I, he was Roman and born into a family of Christian activists. Only reigning for 10 months he nevertheless achieved recognition and canonisation by both western Roman Catholic and eastern Orthodox churches. Arian divisions, conflicts with the Vandals in North Africa, and threats from the Eastern Empire continued during this time, though it is said that embassies from Agapetus achieved much despite the state of constant bickering between the two Roman Empires concerning fine points of doctrine.

**Saint Silverius (536 to 537).** He was the son, at least the one admitted to during wedlock, of Pope Hormisdas. In 536 the Byzantine General Belisarius was peacefully accepted into Rome but, the following year, when the city was besieged by the Goths, the General exiled Pope Silverius and, on the orders of the Eastern Empress Theodora, brought over from Constantinople a replacement Pope, Vigilius, who was promised the papacy if he would secretly undertake to disallow the Fourth Ecumenical Council of Chalcedon. That Council had proclaimed *against* the heresy of Eutyches and the Monophysites (they believed that Christ was singly and wholly divine) to which the Empress subscribed. Or so it seemed.

There is much controversy about this beyond the scope of these cameo productions and the reader is directed to the internet for further detail, though one last summary of the seemingly nonsensical semantic infighting is that the underlying cause was a difference in interpretation, by all parties, of the Latin and Greek representations of the concepts of person – *persona*, and nature – *natura*.

It is very tempting to imagine the participants all meaning the same thing, but that being over-anxious to score political points, they went for character assassination of their opponent, and one of the cheapest ways to achieve this was to play the "heretic card" – much like the malignant use of the "racist card" nowadays.

## 16.16  Anno Domini 537 to 607
## 16.16.1  Context
### 16.16.1.1  The Gothic War, the Plague, the Lombards

Ascendancy Note: The Lombards, the Franks.

During the so-called Gothic War that continued from 535 until about 554, Rome changed hands two or three times among the Goths, and Generals Belisarius and Narses of the Byzantine Empire. Rome was sacked again, and ethnically cleansed (actually depopulated) in 546/547 by the last but one Ostrogoth, Totila. The strictly time-boxed Gothic War may well be said to have ended in 554, but anarchy and unrest continued unabated throughout Italy as newly arrived tribes and native Italian tribes fought for the best territory. The Lombards had the strongest identity, see the next grouping of popes, but in summary, from about 550 to 600 they took advantage of the weakened condition of Italy to conquer most of it, and it was during this relatively easy takeover that in 592, while they were on their way to extract more bounty from Rome, that they were halted after negotiations with the first Benedictine Pope – Gregory I. He was also termed Great, but more on that later. Significantly, a spiritual leader had achieved a temporal settlement that had eluded the Byzantine Empire. One more step along the way to temporal power for the papacy, but there were short term repercussions as will be seen later.

The Plague of Justinian during the years 541 to 542 was virtually a worldwide pandemic that was responsible for the deaths of some 20 to 30 million people, and the impoverishment of countless more. DNA studies indicate that China was the original source of that particular strain of the bacterium, a benefit no doubt of early globalisation. After about 750 AD, the plague would lie low until the Black Death of the 14th century.

### 16.16.2 The Popes of the Period 537 to 607

**Vigilius (537 to 555).** Vigilius was the first Byzantine pope and his reign spanned most of the almost twenty years of the Gothic War. When Pope Vigilius had a chance to breathe, he became involved in the controversies and heresies that had challenged the faith since its inception, and he also had to confront a new one – the Three Chapters issue. Briefly, this was an attempt to anathematize the writings of three diverse bishops, and it attracted strident opinion from all levels of political and ecclesiastical hierarchies. An Anathema, a word of Greek origin, was originally an offering to the gods, or something put to one side as sacred. It later became associated with something cursed or banished. It was during this papacy that the most severe yet epidemic of plague broke out – the Plague of Justinian described above.

**Pelagius I (556 to 561).** From a noble Roman family, he was supported by the Eastern Emperor Justinian, and this alone, coupled with some shifts of opinion, alienated him and the papacy from many in Europe for several decades. This cannot have been helped by his construction of a church to celebrate the defeat of the last Ostrogoth, King Teia of Italy, by the Byzantine General Narses, an Armenian eunuch who was favoured in the Eastern Empire Court. The Franks would now extend their gradual and hesitant ascendancy to the Italian sphere.

**Pope John III (561 to 574).** Another noble Roman, he saw the death of Justinian I and invasions of Italy by the Lombards, originally a southern Scandinavian people. An attempt to keep General Narses, who had been ordered back to Constantinople, in Italy to help fend off the Lombards only resulted in civil unrest against the hated eunuch who had been hiking taxes from his retirement home in Naples.

**Benedict I (575 to 579).** Little known during the time of the Lombards' pillaging.

**Pelagius II (579 to 590).** Pelagius aggressively promoted celibacy, witnessed the Christianisation of the Spanish Visigoths, and died from the

Plague that hit Rome in 590. He had unsuccessfully tried to bribe both the Lombards and the Franks to stay away, and had appealed to the Christianity of Frankish rulers; but eventually it was the Lombards who paid the Franks to go home and leave Italy to the Lombards. It was the Lombards who would later become so deeply involved in banking.

**Saint Gregory I the Great (590 to 604).** The first Benedictine Pope. From a wealthy Roman family that had already weathered the storms of the Gothic-Byzantine-Nascent Barbarian Wars, Gregory I was said to be a highly educated, compassionate, and deeply spiritual Pope. It is interesting to note that on learning of his nomination for pope, he wrote to the Byzantine Emperor Maurice (aka Mauricius 582 to 602) begging to be relieved of the duty; but his letter was apparently intercepted by the Prefect of Rome who ensured that the Emperor saw a different letter requesting confirmation, and that he (Emperor Maurice) issued the necessary ratification. The particularly interesting point here is that it was the Emperor, and an Eastern one at that, who appointed the Pope, and that it was entirely expected and accepted by Gregory, not the reverse as would later be most strongly demanded by the papacy right up to the 19th century.

Soon after his accession he is said to have pronounced that the Roman Church was:

> "like an old and violently shattered ship, admitting the waters on all sides, its timbers rotten, shaken by daily storms, and sounding of wreck".

Seemingly in support of this, Henry Wace states that *"No reigns of popes had been so inglorious as those of Gregory's immediate predecessors, Vigilius, Pelagius I., Benedict, and Pelagius II."*

One of Gregory's first acts was to replace secular members of the papal staff with monks and clergy, and he went on to gain the reputation of being a reformer and a prodigious letter writer. Gregorian Chant was named in his honour in the regions of the Franks from about the 9th century, and it is said that a biography of Gregory was penned in distant England at the

Abbey of Whitby before he had been adequately and posthumously venerated in Rome, which suggests that there may have been some reason such as a greater local experience and understanding of the realities surrounding Gregory that would account for that delay.

It was certainly at Gregory's instigation that the Christianisation of Britain had been started by Saint Augustine in 597, and Gregory identified the needs of both Canterbury and York as centres to support the spread of the faith. That was a significant spiritual outreach. There had, however, been even more significant achievements in another sense closer to home when, in 592, he single-handedly managed to mitigate the damage done to Rome and its surroundings (not yet Papal States) by the Lombards under their Arian King Agilulf (reign 590 to 616), after neither Emperor Maurice nor his agent in the West, the Exarch (Governor) of Ravenna, Romanus, had succeeded in halting the Lombards' advance. By his successful negotiations with the Lombards he had demonstrated his capacity and his right to temporal power. In 599 he brokered yet another peace between the Lombards and Emperor Maurice, further increasing his credibility as a statesman and ruler. He further demonstrated his ecclesiastical administrative - corrective reach by opposing the heresy of Donatism in Africa and the sin of Simony in Gaul.

It will now be instructive to look at some other accounts of Gregory the Great.

Firstly he wrote more than eight hundred letters during his time as Pope, and many apparently contain ill-tempered and aggressive language, specific examples being related to that unilateral attempt in 592 to achieve a peace settlement with the Lombards, and his handling of later written exchanges with Romanus the Exarch of Ravenna and the Exarch's superior, the Byzantine Emperor Maurice. These led to serious troop movements and to the brink of conflict between Ravenna and the insubstantial and infant Papal States, for which a defined extent and temporal title of ownership was still evolving. It is believed that Gregory's settlement with the Lombards actually involved a significant payment to stay away, though it was obviously not big enough since they returned for more a few years later.

An indication of his ill-temper and lack of compassion concerns the fate of one of his colleagues, best told by a direct quote from Wace:

> "A monk, Julius, who had been a physician and had attended Gregory himself, night and day, during a long illness, being himself dangerously ill, confided to a brother that, in violation of monastic rule, he had three pieces of gold concealed in his cell. This confession was overheard, the cell searched, and the pieces found. Gregory forbade all to approach the offender, even in the agonies of death, and after death caused his body to be thrown on a dunghill with the pieces of gold, the monks crying aloud, 'Thy money perish with thee'".

Perhaps the worst alleged example of his character relates to his relationship with, and his acceptance of, the Imperial usurper, Phocas, who deposed and executed Emperor Maurice along with his five sons, his brothers, father, and many supporters, forcing Emperor Maurice to witness the executions of his family first. Pope Gregory sent Phocas an obsequious greeting after the event which begins *"Glory be to God on high"* and ends *"Let the heavens rejoice and the earth be glad."* Even if he was ignorant of the full facts, he followed it up some months later by rejoicing that *"... the night of tyranny has ended in a day of liberty."* Phocas' takeover was the first such violent overthrow in the Eastern Empire, and it is believed that, although generally popular because of tax cuts, he went on to kill thousands in order to maintain control of an empire increasingly beleaguered on all borders.

Emperor Phocas (602 to 610) was, of course, himself executed in miserable fashion by his successor Heraclius (610 to 641).

Joseph McCabe had this to say about Pope Gregory's likely knowledge of the circumstances surrounding the atrocities of Emperor Phocas, and on the subject of the fate of the next pope:

> "Instead of the Pope being dependent upon casual and distorted news from Constantinople, as his apologists say, he had had as representative in that city one of the most accomplished of the Roman clergy, and this priest, Sabinianus, was elected to succeed him. He so execrated the name of Gregory and denounced his vandalism that there was a common belief in Rome that, after seventeen months of reign, the ghost of Gregory visited him in the night and slew him. It is more likely to have been one of Gregory's monks."

**Sabinian (604 to 606).** Uncharitably remembered as profiteering from the sale of corn during famine. He reversed some of his predecessor's monastic appointments by appointing secular clergy (priests and bishops, as opposed to monks and abbots) to a number of posts.

**Boniface III (607).** Made initial attempts to reform the papal election procedure by banning discussion of a successor during a pope's lifetime, and also banning the selection until the previous pope had been buried for three days.

## 16.17 Anno Domini 608 to 800
### 16.17.1 Context
#### 16.17.1.1 The Lombards and Franks

A trade in amber from the Baltic to the Mediterranean countries had already been existent for millennia, possibly since the Mesolithic age when the Lombards from southern Scandinavia arrived by a similar route in the north-eastern area of post-apocalyptic Italy in the mid-6th century. Spreading round the northern Italian plains with the Alps to the north, and then heading south, by about the year 680 they had taken most of Italy from the Goths and the Byzantine Empire, with small areas left at Rome and Ravenna, the toe of the Italian peninsula, Sicily, and Sardinia. Corsica

*The Two Thousand Year War – Papal Hegemony*

was taken about 725. Fragmentation of Lombard power into wilful Duchies would deny them absolute control of Italy, and would assist their piecemeal integration with other interested parties over the next century or so. They were a very adaptable and creative people and by the end of the 8th century all traces of their original paganism, customs, and fashions had become Christianised (largely Arian) and civilised with morality, art, and learning that exceeded that of their opponents.

Against a background of hostility and constant skirmishing among the Lombards, Byzantines, and the ascendant Franks, the earlier years of this crucial period saw the temporal power of the popes very gradually begin to acquire what would develop over the next three or four centuries into a temporal determination and lust for wealth and power that would last for nearly a thousand years.

In 756 three events, two genuine and one counterfeit, contributed to the provision of a basis for the papal claim to temporal power over what would come to be termed the Papal States aka the Republic of Saint Peter aka the Church States, and what is known in Italian as the *Stati Pontifici* or *Stati della Chiesa*. They comprised a fluctuating range of territories of mainly central Italy, over which the Pope would have varying degrees of sovereignty from 754/6 to 1870.

### 16.17.1.2 The Donation of Pepin

The first of the three events was the Donation of Pepin that involved the transfer of title of the Exarchate of Ravenna to the Pope by the Frankish Pepin III (Pepin the Short) who had just defeated the Lombard King Aistulf (variously spelled), and conquered the region around Ravenna. Aistulf himself had only taken Ravenna a few years earlier from what had been, in spite of its proxy leadership, an ultimately Byzantine interest and a bolt hole for the Pope. So instead of absorbing Ravenna into the Frankish Empire it was turned over to the Pope who also received from Pepin undisputed title to the Republic of Rome. This genuine donation was re-stated and confirmed by Charlemagne some decades later, and it can be considered a significant milestone in the founding of the Papal State and the establishment of a temporal as opposed to a spiritual dominion for the Pope.

### 16.17.1.3 The Treaty of Pavia – Birth of the Papal States

The second event was the Treaty of Pavia (756 AD) which compelled King Aistulf to relinquish yet more territories in northern and central Italy; and so the Papal States were born, stretching from the Tyrrhenian Sea (Roman west Italian coast ports) east and north to the Adriatic Sea where they linked up with Ravenna.

### 16.17.1.4 The Donation of Constantine

About this time the third event also hit the scene. It was known as the Donation of Constantine, but it was a forgery from the hand of some anonymous cleric in Rome. This most definite example of audacious papal carpet-bagging cited Constantine the Great as having granted to the Papacy, in addition to a list of pompous superlative titles:

1. Supremacy over the sees or dioceses of Alexandria, Antioch, Jerusalem, and Constantinople – in other words the rest of the Pentarchy, Rome also being one of that ancient administrative confederacy.
2. All the churches of God in the whole earth.
3. Landed estates in Judea, Greece, Asia, Thrace, Africa, Italy, and on various islands.
4. And finally, apparently for the popes' personal delectation, (the document named Pope Sylvester and his successors), Constantine the Great also granted a crown, a tiara, imperial garments, the city of Rome, and all the provinces, places and cities of Italy, and the western regions.

One or two of the more greedy popes tried to make use of this utter nonsense, even though it was suspected of being a forgery from medieval times. It is now universally accepted as such, but one has to say it was a good try, though just a tad too greedy.

## 16.17.2 The Popes of the Period 608 to 800

**Saint Boniface IV (608 to 615).** The second Benedictine Pope, he received the first Bishop of London in Rome, who returned with letters addressed to the Archbishop of Canterbury, to King Ethelbert – *Bretwalda* (see earlier chapters), and to the English people.

**Saint Deusdedit (Adeodatus I) (615 to 618).** He initiated the use of lead seals to authenticate Papal Charters or Decrees. The lead seals, or *bullae,* gave rise to the term "Papal Bull" – of which much in an idiomatic sense would be seen during the following centuries. Pope Adeodatus I is also remembered for charitable and selfless acts to relieve suffering after an earthquake, and after a plague of leprosy.

**Boniface V (619 to 625).** From Naples, he was instrumental in the Christianisation of England, and as mentioned by Beda, he sent letters of exhortation to several figures throughout England.

**Honorius I (625 to 638).** Emissaries were sent to Wessex and Ireland. He subscribed to Monothelitism that says that Christ has only one divine will and not both a divine and a human will. For taking this standpoint he would later be anathematised – he was actually condemned as a heretic by the Sixth General Council in 680/1.

**Severinus (640).** A benevolent Roman who abhorred Monothelitism, he was eventually worn down by his conflict with Emperor Heraclius of Constantinople who was a Monothelite.

**John IV (640 to 642).** From the region of Dalmatia (Croatia and the east coast of the Adriatic Sea), Pope John IV saw Slavic invasions of that land, and he attempted to defray damage by sending money for rebuilding, and for the settlement of ransom demands.

**Theodore I (642 to 649).** Greek, born in Jerusalem. Mainly known for his conflict with the Patriarch of Constantinople over the heresy of Monothelitism.

**Saint Martin I (649 to 655).** From Umbria, central Italy, he was keen on the use of Encyclicals (church letters that were more informal than Bulls) to propagate decisions made at Lateran Councils or Synods. His persistent opposition to the Monothelite line of the Byzantine Emperor

Constans II led to his abduction by Byzantine agents, mistreatment, and death in exile in the present-day region of the Crimea (annexed by the Russian Confederation in 2015), at that time still a part of the about-to-contract Eastern Empire.

**Saint Eugene I (655 to 657).** Roman, and after a timorous start with recollection of his predecessor's fate, he did take a stand against the threats of Byzantine Emperor Constans II and was saved from similar exile by the defeat of Constans II by Islamic forces of the Rashidun Caliphate, specifically their victory over Constans at the naval Battle of Phoenix (ancient Phoenicus of the Phoenicians), on the Lycian coast of southern Turkey in 655.

**Saint Vitalian (657 to 672).** Relations with England were improved when Theodore of Tarsus was accepted in England as Archbishop of Canterbury, but the Archbishop of Ravenna on his doorstep declared himself and the See of Ravenna independent. He was supported in this by Byzantine Emperor Constans II who, of course, took any chance to oppose the papacy at Rome. The Synod of Whitby in 664 was a watershed when the English Church resolved that it would decide not just trivial issues, such as when to celebrate Easter, and how a monk should cut his tonsure, but significantly that it would follow the Roman Catholic Church and not the Irish and Celtic traditions that were enshrined in practices at Iona. Vitalian is traditionally believed to have seen the introduction of organ music into churches.

**Adeodatus (II) (672 to 676).** Little known beyond the facts that he was involved in the discipline followed by monks, and that he continued the opposition to Monothelitism.

**Donus (676 to 678).** Little known, though the Archbishop of Ravenna returned to the Roman fold.

**Saint Agatho (678 to 681).** Little known, but during his tenure the Sixth Ecumenical Council took place at Constantinople in 680, and the Monothelite heresy was almost resolved.

**Saint Leo II (682 to 683).** Sicilian, he confirmed the outcome of the Sixth Ecumenical Council that also anathematised Pope Honorius I for being so heretical as to accept the tenets of Monothelitism, and in so doing, laid a basis for arguments against Papal Infallibility. The Ravenna Archbishops were further incentivised to remain with Rome by the abolition of tax on their ecclesiastical garment, the Pallium – a band of white lambs' wool, the equivalent of the Eastern Orthodox Omophor.

**Saint Benedict II (684 to 685).** Roman and a benevolent pope, his tenure saw many churches restored in Rome.

**John V (685 to 686).** Syrian, and the first of a series of eastern origin. Pope John V, significantly, was the first pope to be consecrated without the specific approval of the Eastern Emperor, despite which departure from the norm, East-West relations were improving significantly.

**Conon (686 to 687).** Sicilian, he was a compromise between military and clerical factions. Irish missionaries visited Rome.

**Saint Sergius I (687 to 701).** Cf. Theodore and Paschal. Syrian - Sicilian. In 689 King Caedwalla of Wessex was baptised in Rome. The Exarch of Ravenna, still a nuisance, looted the old Basilica of Saint Peter. An *Exarch* is somewhere between a *Bishop* and a *Patriarch*, and in the Italian context, it really represented an unwelcome outpost of the Byzantine Empire and its Orthodox Church. Sergius was opposed by Anti-Pope Theodore and Anti-Pope Paschal, Paschal eventually being charged with witchcraft.

**John VI (701 to 705).** Greek from Ephesus, (western coast of Turkey), he is credited with dissuading the Lombards from further despoiling the region and Rome in particular. Wilfred of York, an energetic veteran of the heady Synod of Whitby days, was continually falling out with both kings and clerics, and he visited Rome at the age of 70 to seek assistance from Pope John VI in once more regaining his *See* after yet another expulsion. He returned with letters of support for King Ethelred of Mercia, and managed to acquire enough of his possessions to spend a peaceful retirement. Papal authority was clearly taken seriously even in far-off Britain.

**John VII (705 to 707).** Pope John VII was from a Greek background, and there was détente with the Lombards, but although he was one of the

Byzantine Papacy, there was no lessening of hostilities between himself and the Byzantine Emperor Justinian II – aka the Slit-Nosed.

**Sisinnius (708).** Syrian, and probably not from the aristocracy, there was very little income to the papacy. He is said to have improved defences against both the Lombards and Saracens.

**Pope Constantine (708 to 715).** Syrian or Assyrian and fluent in Greek, he was the last pope to visit Constantinople until Paul VI in 1967. It was during 710 that a bizarre event is alleged to have taken place when the Exarch of Ravenna, John III Rizocopo, was on his way back to Ravenna from Naples where he had landed with troops, presumably on the orders of the Byzantine Emperor Justinian II (the Slit-nosed). This Christian Exarch apparently stopped at Rome and slit the throats of several papal officials. One explanation for this is that he was attempting to plunder the Pope's Treasury.

**Saint Gregory II (715 to 731).** A noble Roman, he immediately set about repairing the city walls, mindful of the threats of Lombards and the new threat from the south, the Muslims. He curried favour with the Franks who were already beginning to reverse the Islamic threat in France and would later do so in Spain. This was also the beginning of the Iconoclast issues that would continue for many years and further divide East and West when unity was needed more than ever. There were several visits from some of the more distant Catholic outposts, such as England and Germany.

**Saint Gregory III (731 to 741).** Syrian background, the papacy was dominated by conflicts with the Lombards and opposition to the Iconoclastic controversy in the Byzantine Empire under Emperor Leo III the Isaurian. Continuing support was given to England and the conversion of Germanic regions.

**Saint Zachary (741 to 752).** Continuing the issues of the last two or three popes, he additionally interfered in Frankish affairs by encouraging regime change in the form of the deposing of the Merovingian King Childeric III, and his replacement with the first Carolingian, Pepin the Short.

## The Two Thousand Year War – Papal Hegemony

**Stephen II (752).** Because he died before being consecrated many authoritative lists omit him.

**Stephen III (752 to 757).** In 751, Ravenna had fallen to the Lombards, and the Byzantine Empire was beset by Bulgars to the north, and by the Abbasid Muslims to the south and east. To gain some security and peace, Pope Stephen successfully petitioned the Franks under Pepin the Short, who nevertheless had to twice force the Lombards, under their leader Aistulf, to stop plundering Italy. It was in 754 that the Donation of Pepin was inaugurated, and in 756 that the established peace was consolidated by the declaration by Pepin that the Pope had full control and rights to a central swathe of Italy to be known as the Papal States. The Pope was now a temporal as well as a spiritual leader – a major development.

**Saint Paul I (757 to 767).** Roman, his tenure was almost entirely concerned with juggling relationships among the Franks, Lombards, and Byzantines, and with the really important questions, such as the veneration of images or icons, and the movement of relics of previous popes into safe locations. For detail on the progress of Islam and the Byzantines at this time see other chapters in Volume Two on both the Eastern Roman Empire and the Islamic Caliphates. In 760 there was rumour of Byzantine plans to invade by land and sea, and letters inviting surrender were sent to Ravenna and Venice.

**Stephen IV (767 to 772).** Cf. Constantine II and Philip. A Sicilian Benedictine monk, he was elected amidst barbarity, murder, and mutilation among his supporters and those of the opposing anti-popes, Anti-Pope Constantine II and Anti-Pope Philip. The unpleasantness continued throughout his reign, terminating with the strangling of the Pope's treasurer, Sergius, by the Pope's chamberlain, Paulus Afiarta. This was sometime after Afiarta had already had both Sergius and Sergius' father, Christophorus, blinded. These events are sanitised in most of the Catholic literature.

**Adrian I (772 to 795).** The son of a Roman noble, his reign was the longest until Pius VI in the late 18th century. The Lombards again invaded the Pope's territory under their King Desiderius, but this time the Franks arrived with Charlemagne and settled the matter by exiling Desiderius to an Abbey in France, and by declaring Charlemagne King of the Lombards. The Pope furthered his temporal ambitions by issuing the first papal coin, and he ingratiated himself with the Franks by dating documentation with reference to the reign of Charlemagne, instead of the previous system that made reference to the Eastern Emperors. An interesting relatively parochial and remote event, was the elevation of the English diocese of Lichfield to an archdiocese in 787. This was to balance the power of the Church between the kingdoms of Mercia and Kent, and the request had been made by some English bishops and King Offa of Mercia. To ratify the event, Pope Adrian sent Bishop Hygberht of Lichfield a Pallium, a sheepskin ceremonial band.

## 16.18 Anno Domini 800 to 891

### 16.18.1 Context

#### 16.18.1.1 Towards a Holy Roman Empire (HRE)

The Franks are covered in detail in other chapters in Volume Two and so they are only briefly cross-referenced here.

In the year 800 Charlemagne, as King of the huge empire of the Franks, was crowned Emperor of the Romans in Saint Peter's Basilica, Rome, on Christmas Day. At this time, in the age of a *New Roman Empire*, an Emperor of the Romans was not yet referred to as a *Holy* one, and he wasn't Roman; he was a Frank. It was all an attempt to gain credibility by ingratiating oneself with the Pope, and yet among the sons of Charlemagne, the seeds of discord that would lead to the fragmentation of the Franks' empire were already planted, long before that *Holy* sanctification would be sanctioned.

### 16.18.2 The Popes of the Period 800 to 891

**Saint Leo III (795 to 816).** Of non-noble birth, he was accused of various crimes by supporters of the previous pope, and those supporters made an attempt in 799 to gouge out Pope Leo's eyes and rip out his tongue. Rescued part way through the mutilation, Pope Leo III actually made a full recovery, and Charlemagne arrived in Rome to ensure peace and protection for the Pope. With Charlemagne no doubt glowering in the background, Leo voluntarily made a declaration that all accusations against him were false, and he commuted the death sentences that had been passed on those who had committed grievous bodily harm against him. Charlemagne's reward was to be crowned Roman Emperor on Christmas Day 800. The Byzantine Empress at the time was powerless to do more than protest.

With Charlemagne's backing, Leo settled various disputes among English kingdoms and the Church, but he reversed the previous pope's decision about Lichfield, which reverted to just a normal diocese by 803.

Yet another heresy had to be refuted, and this time it was Adoptionism. It had already been condemned as a heresy by Pope Victor in the $2^{nd}$ century, and seen from a non-religious viewpoint it was just a semantic spat about whether Jesus as God inherited his nature (and was generated) singly from God, or whether as man his existence was also by adoption and grace. This time it had appeared in Spain, and the distance from Rome, as well as Muslim influences, were blamed for its resurrection.

**Stephen V (816 to 817).** Son of a Roman noble, he continued the previous pope's polices and crowned the son of Charlemagne as Frankish Carolingian King and Roman Emperor Louis the Pious (814 to 840).

**Saint Paschal I (817 to 824).** Pope Paschal was a Roman, and when Emperor Louis the Pious wanted his eldest son crowned as King Lothair I of Italy (818 to 855), it was Paschal who crowned Lothair as King in Rome.

Lothair's later years would see fratricidal and patricidal strife within the empire, but before that he had time to take Pope Paschal to task over a rich Abbey that the Pope had appropriated for himself. A group of Roman nobles, taking courage from this, revolted, but they were quickly put down, and harsh punishment was meted out, several eminent nobles and clerics being first blinded, and then beheaded within the Papal Palace. The private secretary of Louis the Pious, a scholar named Einhard aka Eginhard, wrote that it was said by some that the deeds were commanded by Pope Paschal himself. When an inquiry into the outrage was launched by King Lothair, the Pope would not consent to be examined, but by way of explanation is reported to have said that no murders had been committed, but that there had been just a few executions of traitors. Not surprisingly therefore, his papacy is remembered for, and sullied by, intrigue, blindings, and beheadings, within his own retinue and also just after his death. The Roman people would not have him buried at Saint Peter's, and one has to wonder how he ever came to be a Saint.

Lothair went on to be part of the fragmentation of the Frankish Empire that would lead to divisions and conflict in Europe that have lasted to the present day. The outbreak of iconoclasm in the East in 814 led to many refugees seeking asylum in the West, and all were accommodated in the expanding monastic and church buildings that Paschal commissioned.

**Eugene II (824 to 827).** He was appointed with the support of the nobility and the Franks, against the preferences of the clergy. Frankish influence succeeded in reinstating many noblemen and returning lands confiscated under previous regimes. Eugene attempted to raise the educational standards of the clergy, was charitable towards the poor, and he continued to advance the very painful process of converting the distant Nordic peoples – much of that bloody Christian evangelism being at the point of the sword – as begun by Charlemagne.

**Valentine (827).** Another nobleman, he was enthroned before even being ordained a priest. There were rumours that he was actually the son of Pope Eugene II, and he had been elected as Pope not by the clergy but largely by the nobility. He was dead within 40 days, before he had a chance to be authenticated by the Emperor.

**Gregory IV (827 to 844).** Again from the nobility, and again, elected by the nobility, he was embroiled in the Frankish succession issues among Emperor Louis the Pious and his sons from different marriages. Gregory's involvement resulted in confrontations with the Frankish bishops, and there were threats of excommunication on both sides. At the Treaty of Verdun in 843, Louis' eldest son, the perfidious Lothair, eventually inherited the most, and he became Emperor Lothair I of the Romans, King of Bavaria, King of Italy, and King of Middle Francia – a vast central belt separating present-day France and Germany, and stretching from the North Sea to the Mediterranean. The territory of Lothringen (Lorraine) within Middle Francia was named after him. His two brothers and one half brother variously inherited the rest of Europe and all of its peoples.

**Sergius II (844 to 847).** Cf. John VIII. Of noble Roman stock, and from a family that eventually supplied three popes, he was elected by nobles over the popular choice who ended up as Anti-Pope John VIII. There was a serious Saracen raid that defiled two basilicas, Saint Peter's and Saint Paul's, but failed to take Rome itself.

**Saint Leo IV (847 to 855).** A popularly elected Roman of the Order of Saint Benedict, he improved defences, and saw the defeat at the Battle of Ostia in 849 of a large Saracen naval force that was believed to have sailed from Sardinia. The allied Christian fleet consisted of united forces from Rome, Naples, Amalfi, and Gaeta just north of Naples; there had also been a convenient storm at the time.

**Benedict III (855 to 858).** Cf. Anastasius. Benedict was opposed by Anti-Pope Anastasius, who actually had Benedict imprisoned for a short while, but although Anti-Pope Anastasius enlisted the support of the Franks, Anastasius did not prevail. The future Alfred the Great and his father, King Ethelwulf, visited Rome at this time.

**Saint Nicholas I (The Great) (858 to 867).** A very capable pope from a noble family, he advocated the supremacy of the papacy over all, including monarchy. At this time the strangely named Pseudo-Isidorian Decretals raised their head – a set of believed false documents – written by Frankish clerics. They purported to date back centuries and to have set precedents advantageous to the clergy and particularly bishops. A veritable scandal if popes were implicated.

**Adrian II (867 to 872).** A nobleman, he was subservient to Emperor Louis II in matters of a temporal nature. He had a wife and daughter before election as Pope, but they were abducted and murdered in 868. At this time the Eastern Empire was just about completely Hellenised.

**John VIII (872 to 882).** A capable Roman reformer, he suffered incursions by Saracens, and complained of their colonisation of southern Italy. He received envoys from England that was suffering at the hands of the Danes at a time when young Alfred (not yet Great) was something of a disappointment. Pope John VIII wrote Alfred a letter urging him to do better.

**Marinus I (882 to 884).** The son of a priest he was unfortunate to co-exist with the useless Roman Emperor Charles the Fat who contributed nothing positive in spiritual or temporal matters. English King Alfred the Great succeeded in gaining the respect of the Pope and the removal of taxation from the Anglo-Saxon community in Rome.

**Saint Adrian III (884 to 885).** Roman, there is little of note.

**Stephen VI (885 to 891).** Roman, he had to use his own family's money to combat famine when the Papal Treasury was bare. Saracen troubles continued, and Anglo-Saxon pilgrims are recorded as donating Peterspence, known in Anglo-Saxon as "Romescot" in order to help replenish the coffers.

## 16.19 Anno Domini 891 to 962
### 16.19.1 Context
#### 16.19.1.1 Lost Direction, the Cadaver Synod

The period was characterised by further divergence from "Christian principles", and saw divisions among the descendants of Charlemagne that would result in the splitting of the Frankish Empire into three, profligate and Licentious Popery, and the emergence of Papally sponsored feudalism at the Abbey of Cluny – a nauseous form of self-maintaining social slavery that blights humanity to the present day.

### 16.19.2 The Popes of the Period 891 to 962

**Formosus (891 to 896).** Having had a turbulent and controversial life as pontiff, his greatest significance was achieved when his corpse was disinterred and put on trial in full papal regalia in 897 by Pope Stephen VII. The rotting corpse was accused of perjury and various other crimes, a Deacon was appointed to respond, and the corpse was eventually stripped, mutilated, clad in layman's clothes, and thrown into the river Tiber. The event is known as the Cadaver Synod.

**Boniface VI (896).** A Roman who came to power during a riot, he had already been twice deprived of office as a priest and as a sub-deacon. He died in uncertain circumstances, possibly of gout, 15 days after election. In 898 his election was nullified.

**Stephen VII (896 to 897).** Election of this Roman is unclear though probably by patronage of the nobility. He is remembered only for the Cadaver Synod described earlier, and after a public outcry he was strangled.

**Romanus (897).** Italian, he lasted a few months and was deposed by a Roman faction; he was possibly made a monk.

**Theodore II (897).** Another brief Roman papacy, he lasted 20 days but was considered pious and worthy. He reversed the clerical sackings of Stephen VII, and reburied the corpse of Formosus.

**John IX (898 to 900).** Italian, he reinforced the rehabilitation of Formosus, and the condemnation of Stephen VII. Against Germanic opinion, Pope John IX advanced recognition and support for Slavs in the form of the Church of the Moravians. German-Slav hostility is deep-rooted, and it would take more than papal mediation to lance that boil.

**Benedict IV (900 to 903).** A Roman with a brief but commendable reign, he is considered to have begun a dark period of the papacy which was due to short tenure and controversial circumstances, though such were the circumstances of the previous six popes it seems.

**Leo V (903).** Cf. Christopher. Little known, except that Pope Leo V was deposed after two months, imprisoned and executed, possibly by Anti-Pope Christopher who took the throne 903 to 904, though see below.

**Sergius III (904 to 911).** Roman, he is reputed to have executed the two previous combative popes as a kindness. He is also rumoured to have had an affair with the reputed whore or temptress, Marozia, that resulted in a son who would become Pope John XI, though this is understandably denied by Catholic commentaries.

**Anastasius III (911 to 913).** Roman, little is known though significantly at this time the Nordic Rollo and the Normans were introduced to Christianity – and the Christianity of their descendant William the Conqueror would do absolutely nothing to ameliorate the atrocities that would be meted out to the Christians in Britain after 1066.

**Lando (913 to 914).** Little known.

**John X (914 to 928).** Roman, and although vilified by later historians, it seems likely that he worked hard to unify Italy, and that he was active in evangelising widely through Europe. In spite of this he and his brother are believed to have been murdered in prison.

**Leo VI (928).** There is little of note concerning Pope Leo VI.

**Stephen VIII (929 to 931).** Believed to have been supported like several previous popes by the reputed whore or temptress, Marozia, circa 900. Little else of note.

**John XI (931 to 935).** Son of the above-mentioned Roman courtesan - temptress Marozia, his father may have been Pope Sergius III. The Patriarch of Constantinople received a Pallium, seemingly an unusual honour to such a rival. Of great significance he endowed the Congregation of Cluny that would become a major source of enlightenment and reform.

**Leo VII (936 to 939).** A Roman priest, Pope Leo VII is believed to have started his ecclesiastical career as a Benedictine monk, most of note were grants of privileges to monasteries, particularly the Abbey of Cluny.

**Stephen IX (939 to 942).** Roman, though controversially (and generally accepted as unlikely) he is reputed to have been German and to have died after mutilation by supporters of the Roman ruler at the time, Alberic II. He was certainly involved in rivalries among the Frankish aristocracy.

**Marinus II (942 to 946).** Little of note.

**Agapetus II (946 to 955).** Roman, he was virtuous and began, or at least began to think about, the process of reversing the venal and corrupt period known as the *Saeculum Obscurum* – the dark period that began with Benedict IV – or, as it was satirically known, the Pornocracy.

**John XII (955 to 963).** Born Octavianus or Octaviano, this individual must be just about the nadir of popery. He was the son of the Patrician or Bourgeois leader, Alberic II of Spoleto (912 to 954), who ruled Rome from 932 till his death. Pope John XII was variously described as coarse and immoral, living in the Lateran Palace that was likened to a brothel and a stables – when he wasn't involved in an orgy he was usually out hunting.

He was also a seventh generation descendant of Charlemagne who would have been turning in his grave.

Emperor Otto I of Germany (reigned 962 to 973) aka Otto the Great was requested to defend this Pope against King Berengar II of Italy, and in return, Otto was subsequently crowned Emperor of the Romans, a tradition that would evolve into the Holy Roman Emperor being also the current King of Germany. Pope John, now doubting his ability to contain Otto, toadied up to a diverse axis of opposing forces – Berengar's son, Adalbert, the still unpredictable Magyars of Hungary, and the Byzantine Emperor. Otto discovered the plot, entered Rome and replaced Pope John XII with Pope Leo VIII, but after Otto had left to fight Adalbert, John succeeded on his second violent attempt to turn the tables and ousted Leo who fled. The revenge that Pope John XII now wreaked on the opposition who were not quick enough or sensible enough to flee was swift and bloody: a deacon had his right hand severed, a bishop was scourged, and another palatine official lost his nose and ears. And those were the noted ones. The last laugh was to be on Pope John XII who, just before Otto returned to fry him, died in circumstances described as *"... paralysis while in the act of adultery..."*, but it is said by observers at the time that he died as a result of wounds received during a severe beating by the aggrieved husband.

## 16.20 Anno Domini 962 to 1138

### 16.20.1 Context

#### 16.20.1.1 The Holy Roman Empire, the First Emperors

There were three Frankish-Nordic Roman Imperial dynasties as opposed to Pontifical dominions during this period; they were the Ottonian (Saxon) Dynasty, the Salian (Frankish) Dynasty, and the Supplinburger Dynasty of Lower Saxony.

As a rough approximation, during the years 962 to 1138 the first Emperors used only Heraldic Seals as official and ceremonial identification; the more flamboyant Coats of Arms did not appear until it became necessary to find some way of identifying one armoured Knight from another, and this practice became apparent during the years of the English

Plantagenets that followed English King Henry I who died in 1135. In the case of the Roman and later Holy Roman Emperors and their Knights, Coats of Arms appeared during the Hohenstaufen Dynasty that began in 1138.

Further to the north of Europe there were issues between England and Normandy concerning the Norman Conquest of 1066, and within the Holy Roman Empire there were Saxon Rebellions from 1073 to 1075, and from 1077 to 1088. Those rebellions were opportunistic attempts to wrest control from the incumbent King of Germany and Roman Emperor Henry IV, and they were a major cause of Henry's weakness during his epic struggle with Pope Gregory VII, exemplified by Henry's act of contrition at Canossa – see below. The rebels were mainly Saxons from northern Germany and Swabians from a region near Basle where the present-day Swiss, French, and south-western German borders all come together. The Swabians' distant ancestors were the Suevi or Suebi tribe that had merged with the Alemanni and Frankish confederations about five hundred years earlier, and that had experienced something of a diaspora, leaving not much more than their name which, despite a similarity, does not seem to be evidenced by any accepted etymological linkage with the word Swiss.

The Alemanni and Franks' legacy to posterity, however, would be considerably more, since the rendering of their names gives us the names by which Germany and France are known today in both their own, and other diverse languages.

### 16.20.1.2 The Investiture Controversy

This issue was of great significance in respect of the nature of, and the relationship between, the authority of a pope and that of a nation's secular ruler. It will be examined here in three parts.

The end of the 1st millennium, although just an arbitrary point on our historical timeline, was nevertheless of great symbolic importance to a people driven by superstition and increasingly by religion. Many expected a second coming and many others expected the end of the temporal world. Tom Holland's excellent book, *Millennium*, referred to earlier, is dedicated to the subject.

**Firstly, the facts of the origin of the controversy:**

The controversy arose from a disagreement between Pope Gregory VII and the King of Germany cum Holy Roman Emperor Henry IV about who had the right to nominate and invest church officials. Accepted procedure up to this point was that appointments could be made by a monarch, and Pope Gregory was seeking to stop this, nominally as part of reforms against widespread simony. Simony, as seen earlier, was bribery for office, and the sale of relics and ceremonial ware – it was becoming big business for the officers of a money-hungry Papacy.

The reality was that this dressed up reform was one more step along the road to total Papal Supremacy, and the events in 1077 at Canossa, northern Italy, surrounding the self-abasement of Emperor Henry IV, who was made to stand in snow for days before being absolved of an excommunication, together with a papally inspired rebellion against him by his princes, are very different to the treatment that would have passed between a pope and a secular ruler two or three centuries earlier.

The German King and Emperor Henry IV seemingly had no choice but to grovel before Pope Gregory VII so that the nod might then be given by the Pope to the King's countrymen to re-establish their loyalty to their secular king – the Holy Roman Empire had been wilfully and successfully destabilised by a pope, and it appeared that Pope Gregory VII was in control.

**Secondly, the effect of these facts on immediately succeeding generations of Popes and Monarchs:**

After a second excommunication, Henry had taken enough, and he entered Rome by force of arms in 1084 and deposed Pope Gregory VII in favour of an anti-pope who would be more sympathetic to the Empire. Papal Supremacy was, after all, not yet a certainty. Henry could not kill the controversy just like that however; although for a while at least this issue did seem to have been resolved at the Concordat of Worms in 1122. By that Concordat a new pair of protagonists, Emperor Henry V and Pope Calixtus II, agreed a compromise – the Emperor would be present as a judge during the selection of new bishops and abbots, but it would be bishops who would then invest such newly consecrated clergy in respect of their religious power. After all that procedural rigmarole concerning religious duties, the Emperor would then invest them in respect of their secular or temporal role.

**Thirdly the underlying agenda and its longer term future:**

There is much more documentation about this subject in the form of erudite analysis, but from a survey of readily available information, history's judgement on the matter seems to be clouded by the partisan politics of clerical and secular historians, and it is proposed here to look for further fallout from that 11th century Henry-Gregory fight as it appears during the rest of this chapter. It will assuredly be seen to continue to happen in different guises and with different actors, but always because of agitation for more acceptance of Papal Supremacy – a supremacy, one might think, that should not be any different to the concept of Royal Supremacy – except for the fact that "King" was originally a primitive title taken by physical might, whereas "Pontiff" should stem from the benevolence of Christ, and this was, and still remains, a relatively new concept, given the many millennia of human settlement. It was a concept that faced an uphill battle against an entrenched and battle-hardened status quo.

So the next step in the religious revolution, the extension of the Mysteries and Ecclesiastes of that second Abrahamic religion, Christianity, to overlay the very fabric of peaceful and well-established secular governance, was beginning to require an increasingly militaristic papacy, and a militarism with all the subterfuge and willingness to deal death that is necessary in any armed struggle.

It will be seen very shortly that there was a voracious and vigorous appetite and a virile spirit in the Vatican – an insatiable and gluttonous *gourmand* that was quite willing to take part in the literal arms race, and to take whatever combative steps were necessary to achieve Papal Supremacy – the gloves were off, don't miss most of the next batch of popes as they descend into the abyss.

### 16.20.1.3 Hereward the Wake

A final note concerning the context of the years 962 to 1138 should recognise the heroism of Saxon resistance to William the Conqueror aka William the Bastard, and in particular an individual who no doubt characterises many of his sadly unknown kinsmen and women who were murdered by the Normans.

That representative of all the "Unknown Soldiers" of the time was Hereward the Wake, and he made a stand against William the Conqueror and his foul legions in the Fen regions of eastern England after his father and brother were murdered, and his lands were taken, in 1070. Danish King Sweyn Estridsen aka Estrithson, lent support to the revolt against French rule but, after some small successes, the uprising was crushed by the Normans on the Isle of Ely after the resistance movement was betrayed by a scheming and unprincipled local monk, the Abbot Thurstan of Ely, who treacherously showed the Normans the way through the marshes to the stronghold of the heroic Saxon freedom fighters.

The ultimate fate of Hereward the Wake is not known for certain, and accounts vary from his continued resistance to his capture and subsequent execution. Almost a millennium later there are many references to his exploits, both on the internet and in contemporary writings from history such as the *Anglo-Saxon Chronicles*, the *Book of Ely*, the *Domesday Book*, and the *Deeds of Hereward the Saxon*.

## 16.20.1.4 Map – The Papal and Other Italian States 1000

Map from http://commons.wikimedia.org/wiki/Category:Maps released under CC-BY-SA
http://creativecommons.org/licenses/by-sa/3.0/ Author: MapMaster

*The Two Thousand Year War – Papal Hegemony*

## 16.20.1.5 Map – Italian States circa Gregory VII and Henry IV

This map illustrates the range of factions in the Italian arena at the time of the confrontation between Holy Roman Emperor Henry IV and Pope Gregory VII that took place in 1077 at Canossa, located in northern Italy roughly near the letter "M" in Marca di Toscana on the map below.

Map from http://commons.wikimedia.org/wiki/Category:Maps released under CC-BY-SA
http://creativecommons.org/licenses/by-sa/2.5/   Author: MapMaster

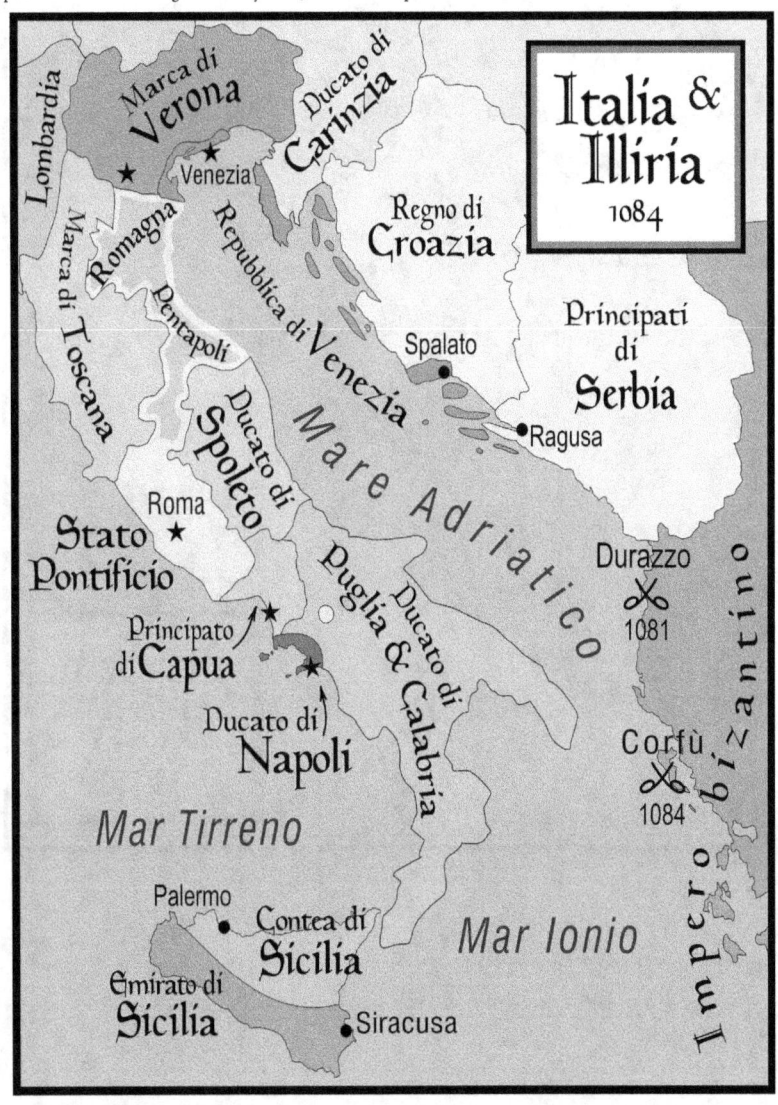

## 16.20.1.6 Map – The Southern Italian States in 1112

Map from http://commons.wikimedia.org/wiki/Category:Maps released under CC-BY-SA
http://creativecommons.org/licenses/by-sa/3.0/ Author: MapMaster

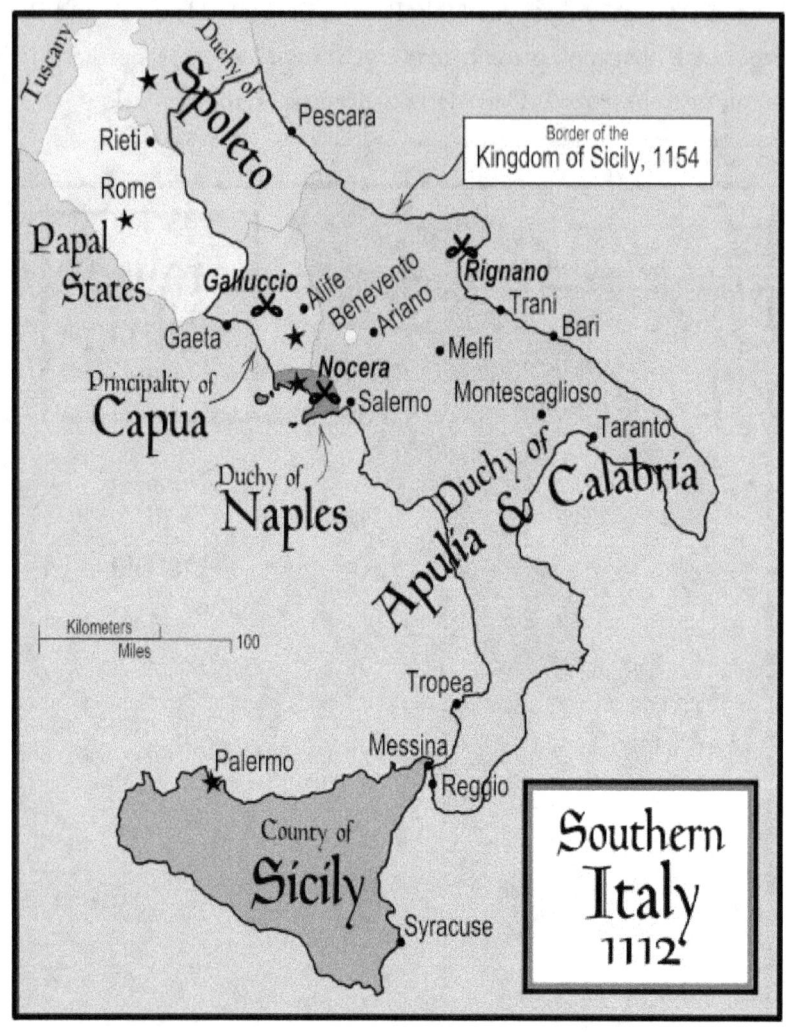

## 16.20.2 The Popes of the Period 962 to 1138

**Leo VIII (963 to 965).** He was Roman and, as described above, he was an anti-pope during the years 963 to 964 against Pope John XII. With Emperor Otto I's patronage Leo was able to become Pope Leo VIII during the years 964 to 965 after ousting Pope Benedict V as described next.

**Benedict V (964).** A Roman of very short tenure, he was elected by the people but after only one month he was deposed by Emperor Otto I and Anti-Pope Leo VIII. He was exiled to Germany where he died in 965 or 966. At the dethroning ceremony the new Pope Leo VIII had personally torn off his Pallium, and had broken a staff or sceptre over Benedict's head for good measure.

**John XIII (965 to 972).** Roman nobility and initially a bishop, there is little of note other than him being deposed and subsequently reinstated after Emperor Otto I, once again, threatened to come to Rome and sort things out. Various decrees and outcomes of Synods that had been held in France and England were confirmed.

**Benedict VI (973 to 974).** Cf. Boniface VII. Roman, he was imprisoned just after Emperor Otto I died, and then, just when an emissary was sent from the new Emperor Otto II to secure his release, he was strangled by the future Anti-Pope Boniface VII who was in league with someone named "Crescentius the Elder".

**Benedict VII (974 to 983).** Cf. Boniface VII. A Roman noble and bishop, he was popularly elected by the clergy and the people with the patronage of Otto II. He was in favour of reform, and a synod in his time outlawed Simony. Anti-Pope Boniface VII continued as anti-pope (974 and 984 to 985) and actually took power in Rome for a while, again most likely in league with Crescentius the Elder who died 984.

**John XIV (983 to 984).** Cf. Boniface VII. Italian and previously the imperial chancellor under Emperor Otto II. It was very unfortunate for him that Otto II died just after the papal consecration and Emperor Otto III, who was only three years old when he became Emperor, was therefore unable to continue to offer papal protection. Anti-pope Boniface VII who was in exile in Constantinople now returned, and most likely with the help of Crescentius the Younger (son of the elder), who was now a Roman Patrician, Pope John XIV was deposed and consigned to the dungeons of Castel Sant'Angelo (aka the Mausoleum of Hadrian) where he shortly died from starvation, or by more explicit murder.

It was at this time, concerning the uncertainties around Pope XIV and his successor, that an error in the regnal numbering of Popes with the name John arose. A later attempt to correct the issue by renumbering all the popes in the range John XV to XIX was partially successful, but the retention of the later Pope John XXI, meant that there was no Pope John XX.

**John XV (985 to 996).** A descendant of the Roman nobility with a reputation for bribery and cronyism, much of his time was taken up with arbitration among the clergy and royalty, including an issue between Saxon King Æthelred and Richard of Normandy. Settlement of diplomatic relations between England and Normandy at this time would lead to family ties that would ultimately give the future William Duke of Normandy, "the Conqueror", a claim to the English throne, with catastrophic results for Anglo-Saxon England and the English. In 993, the pope declared the first ever papal canonisation (as opposed to canonisation by popular acclamation) of Bishop Ulrich of Augsburg in connection with his influence on the victory in 955 at the Battle of Lechfeld. That battle had been the turning point against Magyar invasions in Europe.

**Gregory V (996 to 999).** Cf. John XVI. The first German pope, he was a grandson of Emperor Otto I and he was loyal to Emperor Otto III who was his cousin! He was opposed by the Italian-Greek Anti-Pope John XVI (997 to 998), but the papal family business didn't mess about, and the anti-pope was eventually mutilated by blinding, the cutting off of his nose and ears, and the ripping out of his tongue. In case that wasn't enough he was degraded in public by being seated back to front on an ass and then paraded through the streets. As a reprise, the Castel Sant'Angelo was besieged, and that continuing nuisance, Crescentius the Younger, was executed and then strung up in a gibbet on a high hill in Rome in 998.

**Sylvester II (999 to 1003).** From the Auvergne, he was the first French pope and highly educated, though equally highly superstitious of the impending new millennium. He promoted teaching and the re-introduction of scientific instruments and method that had been lost for centuries, and-or had been developed by Arab culture e.g. Arab numerals. He became the teacher of Emperor Otto III but, with Otto, fled from Rome to Ravenna in 1001 when the nobility and people revolted. Otto III died on his third attempt to retake Rome in 1002. Pope Sylvester II managed a return to Rome but died in 1003. He is reputed to have invented the pendulum clock, although this is conventionally attributed to the Dutch scientist, Christiaan Huygens, in 1656.

**John XVII (1003).** Roman, but little known since he died after only six months.

**John XVIII (1003 to 1009).** Believed subordinate to Roman nobility, principally the Crescenti family, he also had to contend with: firstly, challengers to the last of the Ottonian Dynasty – Roman Emperor Henry II; secondly, ravages of plague; and thirdly, Sardinian Saracens pirating off the west coast of Italy in what is termed the Tyrrhenian Sea – the Mediterranean bounded by Sardinia, Italy, and Sicily – an area of increasing commercial interest for the aspirant temporal Papal States, and a region of spiritual dominance on its doorstep taken for granted by the Vatican.

**Sergius IV (1009 to 1012).** A Roman shoemaker, there is argument about whether or not he was controlled by the nobility, though he did strengthen resistance to the Patrician, John Crescentius, by favouring German influence. Most significantly, he issued a Papal Bull that called for the elimination of Islam from the Holy Land. This followed the destruction by the Fatimid Caliphate in 1009 of the Church of the Holy Sepulchre in Jerusalem, the site of Golgotha where the crucifixion of Christ is believed to have taken place.

**Benedict VIII (1012 to 1024).** Cf. Gregory VI. A noble Roman, he was initially opposed by Anti-Pope Gregory VI in 1012, but gained the support of Emperor Henry II. Benedict went on to subjugate the Crescenti family, defeat the Sardinian Saracen, and ally himself with the Normans who were just beginning their colonisation of southern Italy.

**John XIX (1024 to 1032).** Brother of the previous pope, he had been a consul and layman, and so was made a bishop to qualify him for Pope. In 1024 he continued allegiance to the successor of Emperor Henry II, Emperor Conrad II, who was crowned in Rome. Reversing his initial decision to accept a large bribe to recognise the Patriarch of Constantinople, this pope was complicit in setting the scene for the Great Schism between East and West that developed in 1054.

Poland was brought within the papal sphere at this time.

**Benedict IX (1032 to 1045).** He appears on the list of popes three separate times, because he was twice deposed and restored. He was only 12 when he inherited the throne according to some, 18 or 20 according to others. He was profligate, immoral and just about as unchristian as might be imagined. He was accused of murders, rapes, and adulteries, and was most probably bi-sexual, holding orgies in the Lateran Palace. Forced out of office in 1036, he managed to return, assisted by Emperor Conrad II. There was another brief expulsion in 1044 when Pope Sylvester III had an equally brief tenure until Pope Benedict returned in 1045, only to sell the papacy to his godfather and resign the same year to get married.

**Sylvester III (1045).** Cf. Gregory VI. Pope Sylvester III was considered by some to have merited the title Anti-Pope Sylvester III, although it was Anti-Pope Gregory VI who is most commonly accorded that honour – yet another example of the total lack of clarity and therefore lack of indisputable integrity at the top of the Catholic Church.

**Benedict IX (1045).** He sold the papacy to his godfather who became Gregory VI.

**Gregory VI (1045 to 1046).** Cf. Sylvester III, as above, arguably anti-pope (1045).

**Clement II (1046 to 1047).** In 1046 this ludicrous mess had to be sorted out by the intervention of the German King and Roman Emperor Henry III. At the Council of Sutri in December of that year, it was declared that Pope Benedict IX and Pope Sylvester III were immediately deposed and that Pope Gregory VI should resign. Conveniently to hand was a German bishop who was crowned Pope Clement II to fill the vacuum. Clement in turn facilitated the coronation of Emperor Henry III by crowning him at Rome. In his short reign he was active against Simony. Clement died in 1047 during his return to Rome from a trip to Germany, and was interred at Bamburg Cathedral, Germany. He is the only pope to be buried north of the Alps.

**Benedict IX (1047 to 1048).** Benedict's final brief seizure of the throne. His end is uncertain though some suggest he finally sought atonement and died a penitent.

**Damasus II (1048).** A Bavarian originally known as Poppo, he was initially turned away by the Roman nobility in favour of the rank Pope Benedict IX (again). At this snub, the anger expressed by the Emperor Henry III was enough to get Poppo on the throne. He died of malaria after only 23 days.

**Saint Leo IX (1049 to 1054).** From a noble family near Colmar in the present-day Alsace, he had to first rebut yet another takeover attempt by Pope Benedict IX. He was a reformer of both church practices and finances, but most of his problems were in the south of Italy, where the Normans were behaving badly towards their colonial subjects who were mainly Greek. Duplicity on the part of the Normans led to military conflict, and in 1053 the Greeks and the Pope were defeated at the Battle of Civitella aka the Battle of Civitate though the Pope as spiritual leader of the Normans was treated magnanimously. After tears and pleas by the crafty Normans for forgiveness, Pope Leo IX recognised their rights by conquest to Calabria and Apulia, the toe and heel of Italy, and he was allowed to return home where he died shortly afterwards.

It is at this juncture that the nominally one Roman church split as a result of what is known as the East-West Schism or Great Schism, though in practice the church had been divided for some time as the Catholic West and the Orthodox East. An emissary was sent from Pope Leo IX to the Byzantine Patriarch Michael I Cerularius to discuss the subject of what has since been accepted as a forged decree – the Donation of Constantine –

that unambiguously gave authority over Rome and the Western Empire to the Pope and his successors, and the schism was formalised by the Patriarch's rejection of this. Pope Leo IX died in the middle of this ruckus, but his emissary, Cardinal Humbert of Silva Candida, declared a bull that excommunicated the Patriarch, and the Patriarch responded with a bull that excommunicated the Cardinal, and one might suppose, in the absence of a living pope, the papal successors as well. The two Churches were sundered as a result of many seemingly important differences, such as celibacy among the priesthood, the *filioque* – whether the Holy Ghost proceeded from God and his son (the Western, Latin version), or just from God (the Eastern, Greek version), and the vital issue of whether to use leavened or unleavened bread in the Eucharist.

The ball had not just been dropped, it had been kicked out of court. Later pope-inspired Crusades would butcher the Byzantine population, and the Byzantine Empire would continue as a potentially military threat to the Papal States and Italy, while in the meantime the Islamic Caliphates, though not without their own divisions, continued to build among the islands of the Mediterranean Sea, and throughout the sands and oases of the vast hinterlands of the Black and Caspian Seas – those ancient lands of earlier Hittite, Assyrian, and Babylonian civilisations, and through which Alexander the Great had adventured more than a thousand years previously.

**Victor II (1055 to 1057).** Variously described as Bavarian or Swabian (of the ancient Suevi tribe), both being in southern Germany, he was a kinsman of, and on good terms with, Emperor Henry III. The relationship was so good that Henry would later entrust his 6-year-old son, the future Emperor Henry IV, and the regency to Pope Victor II. He was a reformer, particularly against Simony and priests' use of concubines.

**Stephen X (1057 to 1058).** From the aristocracy of Lorraine, north-east France, he was preparing to make war on the Normans, but died after a reign of only about seven months.

**Nicholas II (1058 to 1061).** Cf. Benedict X. Nicholas II was opposed by Anti-Pope Benedict X, an anti-pope who was actually elected first in circumstances that are believed to have involved bribery and violence. Pope Nicholas II from the French Savoie reversed the previous pope's intentions of attacking the Normans by allying with them to attempt the expulsion of the Muslim from Sicily. He officially added Sicily and Capua (north of Naples) to the Norman territories, supported the reforms of the earlier Pope Victor II, and stiffened resistance to manipulation by Roman nobility, by introducing electoral reform.

**Alexander II (1061 to 1073).** Cf. Honorius II. From Milan he was active in reforms regarding Simony and celibacy. After receiving a representative from Duke William of Normandy, he gave his blessing to William's bid for the throne of England and sent him a papal ring plus an edict to the clergy reinforcing the position. He was briefly opposed by Anti-Pope Honorius II who had the support of the regency of Emperor Henry IV, and who by violence and force of arms had occupied part of the Basilica of Saint Peter for a few weeks in 1062. Agreement with the court of Emperor Henry IV was restored when there was a change of regent who was supportive of Pope Alexander II, though the anti-pope continued to fester and make trouble. That trouble was made in strength from the Castel of Sant'Angelo until about 1064, and after that just vocally until Honorius died in 1072.

**Saint Gregory VII (1073 to 1085).** – Cf. Guibert (aka Clement III). Gregory VII from Tuscany, and the following three popes were opposed by Anti-Pope Guibert (aka Anti-Pope Clement III 1080 to 1100) who was appointed by Emperor Henry IV in an attempt to reassert his authority over the increasing Papal Supremacy that had him twice excommunicated. Known as Hildebrand before his coronation as Pope, Gregory had been prominent in reforms and papal politics for several years. Possibly his two most important contributions were firstly, while he was pre-pontiff Hildebrand, the alliance with the Normans that was ratified by the Treaty of Melfi in 1059; and secondly, during his role as Pope, the establishment of the College of Cardinals and its exclusivity in the electoral process.

Gregory's Treaty of Melfi from 1059 could not have lasted forever of course, and presumably forgetting the 25-year-old agreement with the

Pope, the Normans sacked and burned many parts of old Rome in 1084 when they left their campaign against the Byzantine Empire in the Balkans, in response to a call from Pope Gregory VII who was at the time stuck in the Castel Sant'Angelo and besieged by Emperor Henry IV. See the map of the Italian States at this time below.

Although Gregory VII was beatified (declared blessed in heaven) by Pope Gregory XIII in 1584, and canonised (declared a Saint) in 1728 by Pope Benedict XIII, it has to be noted that against him there have been accusations of misdeeds such as necromancy, torture and murder, started by his contemporaries and repeated through the ages by opponents of Catholicism. That the negativity may well have been in itself malicious is self-evident, and against that negativity Pope Gregory VII was certainly the origin of huge reform; but he was also the author of the Investiture Controversy that would make him many enemies and confound good relations between aristocratic and papal parties for centuries.

**Blessed Victor III (1086 to 1087).** Cf. Guibert (aka Clement III). A Lombard aristocrat from Benevento, north-east of Naples, he was better known for his achievements as the monk Desiderius and as a fine Abbot of Monte Cassino when he was probably involved in mediation with the Normans at the time of the Battle of Civitate during the reign of Pope Leo IX. He resisted elevation to the papacy, and was eventually dragged to the throne. He was an ardent reformer but less fanatical than his predecessor. A final attribution to him, that ultimately may not have evolved in the most favourable light, is the Crusades. Some link the beginning of the Crusades and the "Crusade Paradigm" to Blessed Victor's sponsorship and despatch of the Banner of Saint Peter on a military venture to the Islamic settlement at Tunis in order to acquire ongoing Tribute for the papacy, and to secure the release of Christian slaves. The army sent on this Mahdia Campaign in 1087 was a confederation of forces from Rome, Genoa, Pisa, and Amalfi. It was successful enough to obtain plunder, and it should have laid a framework for a future unified front against Islam. That successful experimental venture had been without Norman support which would have enhanced the fighting capacity significantly.

## The Two Thousand Year War – Papal Hegemony

It's tempting to link Desiderius' character, if not necessarily his legacy, with the poem *Desiderata* by Max Ehrmann – *"Go placidly amid the noise and the haste..."*, though it has to be remembered that there was at least one other Desiderius of repute, Desiderius Erasmus Roterodamus, otherwise known as Erasmus of Rotterdam, circa 1466 to 1536. It is, however, highly unlikely that either the "Blessed" pope or the "Erudite" monk were uppermost in the mind of Ehrmann as he sought his own sense of grace.

**Blessed Urban II (1088 to 1099).** Cf. Guibert (aka Clement III). From the champagne region of France, he initiated the First Crusade. He was a continuing reformer with decrees concerning simony, celibacy of the clergy, and by involvement in the Investiture Controversy and the consequent ongoing antipathy towards Emperor Henry IV. His start in Rome was only made possible with the help of Norman forces with whom he had been reconciled after a Norman civil war in Sicily. Once he had arrived on the doorstep of Rome, mutual excommunications and unpleasantness stretched armed conflict out over some days before Urban was triumphant and could enter Saint Peter's. He established some support in Europe from Countess Matilda of Tuscany and the Welf or Guelph Dynasty against Emperor Henry IV, but wavering fortunes in Europe soon led Anti-Pope Clement III to retake Rome in 1089 while Urban was in the south, and it was three years before Urban could retake the throne. Over the next few years, Urban worked tirelessly, whipping up support for Crusades, calling many synods and councils, and building support and papal consensus – between 1095 and 1097 French King Philippe I was excommunicated twice for adultery, and Urban yet again had to do battle against Anti-Pope Clement III to retake the Castel Sant'Angelo in 1098. The same year he received Saint Anselm of Canterbury with grievances about English King William II (Rufus), who, in Norman fashion, had been pillaging church and people in a most irreligious way. Pope Urban II died in July 1099 but failed to hear the news of the fall of Jerusalem to the Crusaders the same month.

**Paschal II (1099 to 1118).** Cf. Theodoric, Aleric and Maginulf (aka Sylvester IV). A Benedictine monk from Tuscany, in the first few years of his reign he settled the investiture controversy in England for a while, but not France. In 1101 the first Synod of Cashel was held in Ireland, followed by the successful Synod of Ráth Breasail in 1111, again held in Ireland, and this continued the development of the Church in Ireland, at this time formalising changes from a monastic church to one oriented towards the diocese or parish. In the same year, 1111, Paschal was kidnapped by Emperor Henry V and harshly treated in prison for two months before he gave in, conceded much territory and income, and agreed to crown Henry at Saint Peter's, which he did, only to see the clergy of the Hildebrand tradition force the excommunication of Emperor Henry V in 1112, and reverse the concessions of land and wealth that were said to have been extorted, and therefore invalid.

The reference to "Hildebrand" concerns the comparison of the vigorous style of Pope Gregory VII, whose birth-name was "Hildebrand", with that of a legendary and feisty Nordic character. That vigorous style had been exhibited at Canossa as described earlier.

This latest imperiously impertinent slap in the face of an Emperor caused another visit to Rome by Henry that resulted in the hasty exit of Pope Paschal who only returned when Henry had departed in 1118 shortly before the Pope's death. Emperor Henry V was in fact subsequently anathematised not just in Italy but more widely for his actions throughout a papacy that in medieval times had been uncharacteristically long.

Pope Paschal faced various conflicts of office, and he was also opposed by Anti-Pope Theodoric (1100), by Anti-Pope Aleric (1102), and by Anti-Pope Maginulf (Sylvester IV, 1105 to 1111). In spite of all his trials however, he is still credited with holding together the Church throughout Europe and beyond.

Two final points of interest are: firstly, the appointment of the first bishop in America, an Icelander, Erik Gnupsson, who became Bishop of Greenland and Vinland, a region believed to correspond to present-day Newfoundland; and secondly, a bull confirming the Order of the Hospital of Saint John of Jerusalem that later became known as the Order of Knights Hospitaller.

**Gelasius II (1118 to 1119).** Cf. Bourdin (aka Gregory VIII). From Capua, southern Italy, he was harassed by Holy Roman Emperor Henry V and was initially physically beaten and stamped on by Roman imperialists, so that in spite of Norman protection he was frequently on the move during his brief tenure. At one point he had to flee in a galley down the river Tiber while under fire by stones and arrows. He died at Cluny in France, having spent little time in Rome. He was opposed by Anti-Pope Bourdin aka Burdin (Gregory VIII).

**Callistus II (1119 to 1124).** Cf. Gregory VIII. A wealthy Burgundian aristocrat, he is said to have had good connections with royal families in Germany, France, England, and Denmark which allowed him to settle the Investiture Controversy at the Concordat of Worms in 1122. He also overcame the Roman imperialist problem, exemplified by the Frangipani family that had been a thorn during previous papacies, and, with Norman help, Anti-Pope Gregory VIII was imprisoned where he died without further trouble. The power and reach of the papacy at this time can be sensed from attendance at the First Lateran Council called in 1123 to confirm the Concordat of Worms. There were almost three hundred bishops and six hundred abbots. On a more parochial note the Book of Llandaff is referenced at this time in communications from Bishop Urban of Llandaff in Wales to the Pope. The book is in the public domain and describes various events of interest in a Welsh and British context from the end of the Western Roman Empire to medieval times. See the chapter in Volume One titled *Internet Index of References and Other Downloads*.

**Honorius II (1124 to 1130).** Cf. Celestine II. From a humble family in north-east Italy, he was elected amidst fighting between two noble families, the Frangipani and the Pierleoni, during which the original candidate was wounded and violently ejected from the throne that he had already taken. The reluctant Honorius honourably resigned but was quickly re-elected, and the ejected pope became Anti-Pope Celestine II. Various conflicts with diverse heads of state and principalities now ensued but, fortuitously, a compliant Roman Emperor Lothair III replaced the childless Emperor Henry V.

(NB. Some sources identify this Lothair as Emperor Lothair II because he was the second emperor of that name, but the third Lothair to have contributed significant land to the empire).

Pope Honorius preferred the newer Augustine tradition of monastic habit and so, to at least assert his authority and in order to best the Benedictines, one Abbot of Monte Cassino was excommunicated and another forced to resign to make way for Honorius' choice. Honorius subdued the rebellious city of Benevento and skilfully established an alliance with the Norman King Roger II of Sicily. He also settled several disputes among monastic, clerical, and aristocratic factions, throughout France, Brittany, England, Scotland, Wales, and Denmark. In other theatres of conflict he supported Norman efforts against the Moors in Spain, and in 1129 he called the Council of Troyes which approved the newly postulated order of Knights Templar, for which Bernard of Clairvaux was commissioned to identify the Order's rules. Prodigious and mainly successful achievements in a six year papacy.

## 16.21 Anno Domini 1138 to 1250
### 16.21.1 Context
#### 16.21.1.1 The Holy Roman Empire and Papal Interference

The Hohenstaufen family ruled for most of the period 1138 to 1250 and began the use of Heraldic Coats of Arms.

German King Conrad III (life 1093 to 1152) was the first King of Germany of the Hohenstaufen Dynasty, but he was not an Emperor. After opposition to Roman Emperor Lothair III (1133 to 1137) Conrad took the title King of Germany in 1138.

Emperor Frederick I Barbarossa (life 1122 to 1190) – Red Beard – was a nephew of Conrad III and the first Hohenstaufen Roman Emperor, having been elected King of Germany in 1152, crowned Roman Emperor in 1155 by Pope Adrian IV, and for the first time receiving that additional title *Holy* in 1157. He died during the Third Crusade in 1190.

For more information on the Hohenstaufens see the chapter in Volume Two on the Holy Roman Empire.

Papal political aspirations were evidenced in 1246 when Henry Raspe of Thuringia, Central Germany, known as "The Papist King" became anti-king against German King Conrad IV for whom he had previously been regent in 1242. Raspe had initially being confirmed as a Thuringian Landgrave by Emperor Frederick II in that year, 1242, a Landgrave being a noble directly responsible to the Emperor; and Raspe had only become eligible for that esteemed position of guardian of Thuringia, by leap-frogging over his young nephew who was the real heir to the position. This appointment had been made to get more mature support for Emperor Frederick II, and it would have been particularly useful after Frederick had fallen out with Pope Innocent IV, and had received a Papal ban in 1245. The Pope's goading of Henry Raspe however, was successful in creating divisions, and in appealing to Raspe's self-interest, although that Papal prodigy died soon afterwards in 1247.

This was also the time of Thomas Aquinas, circa 1225 to 1274, who was considered by some to be the ideal monk and Catholic philosopher, notably with his "five proofs of God's existence" that would be the basis for the condemnation of any dissenters as heretics, and an excuse for more Papal cruelty. See detail concerning William of Ockham in Volume Two.

One final item of news at this time was the Treaty of Christburg in 1249 that settled a peace between the Roman Catholic Order of Teutonic Knights and the Pagan Old Prussian residents. The Catholic Teutonic Knights were in fact militant missionary invaders and who had been attacking the Prussian Baltic territories. The treaty never really held and this First Prussian Uprising could be seen as the emergence onto the world stage of an identity that would fully mature during the 1860s when the Prussian Otto von Bismarck would weigh in to wage wars of aggression to create the Second Reich of the German people. See the map below showing Prussian and other Baltic tribes circa 1200 AD.

### 16.21.1.2 Map – Prussian and Other Baltic Tribes circa 1200

Map from http://commons.wikimedia.org/wiki/Category:Maps released under CC-BY-SA
http://creativecommons.org/licenses/by-sa/3.0/ Author: MapMaster

Note also the location of Lake Peipus (top right) that would soon be immortalised by Alexander Yaroslavitz Nevsky's heroic resistance to a papally inspired crusade in 1242. See further detail in the section on the Russian Empires in Volume Two.

### 16.21.2 The Popes of the Period 1138 to 1250

**Innocent II (1130 to 1143).** Cf. Anacletus II and Victor IV. Roman, and from a well established family he was involved in considerable European mediations and appointments. In 1131 King Lothair III of Germany was crowned for the second time as King of the Romans at Liege. He had been King of Germany since 1125 after triumphing over a Hohenstaufen rival, Frederick II Duke of Swabia, and in 1133 Lothair was crowned yet again, this time as Emperor Lothair III in the Lateran Palace. Emperor Lothair requested in 1134 that Hamburg should be at least clerically responsible for Denmark, Sweden, Norway, and Greenland, and this was done. In return no doubt, he agreed to assist the Pope in the Iberian theatre where Portugal was at this time seeking independence from Spain as a Monarchy, and Innocent acted as mediator. He was opposed by Anti-Pope Anacletus II (1130 to 1138), who had been supported by the Norman King Roger II of Sicily, and by Anti-Pope Victor IV (1138).

**Celestine II (1143 to 1144).** Little is known and there is little of significance during his six month reign, though he did have a preference for the Plantagenets of England as opposed to the incumbent English King Stephen of Blois, and he had an aversion to Norman King Roger II of Sicily. He is on the other hand the first pope to feature on a controversial list of prophesies published (with some retrospective entries) in 1590 by a Benedictine historian, Arnold de Wyon, but attributed to the 12th century Saint Malachy who was Bishop of Armagh, Ireland. With suggestions by many that it was a 16th century forgery, and held by others that Nostradamus was the real source, the Prophecies of Saint Malachy are highly controversial material and perhaps of special interest given that the 21st century Pope Benedict XVI is listed as the penultimate pope who will be succeeded by someone described as Peter the Roman who will oversee the end of days. There have been many attempts to demonstrate the validity of the prophesies, but just like the very religion, around which the whole issue rotates, it is a matter of personal opinion, belief, or faith – or just a result of the attraction and fascination of arcane material.

**Lucius II (1144 to 1145).** From Bologna, north-east Italy, there were just too many forces in opposition. He had been forced to concede to Norman King Roger of Sicily after unsuccessful armed opposition to him. 1144 saw the start of the Commune of Rome, an attempt to re-establish a republican government as an alternative to nepotistic parties of the nobility, and which was allied to the Roman Emperor and not ruled by the Pope. Finally, during armed conflict with the noble families of Rome, he led an assault and was hit by a stone, an injury from which he shortly died.

**Blessed Eugene III (1145 to 1153).** A Cistercian monk from Pisa, he was respected by all, but nevertheless spent much of his time away from Rome, either voluntarily or forced. The Second Crusade was announced in the period 1145 to 1147, and disastrously dragged on until 1149. The Synod of Kells took place in 1152, continuing the reform of the Church in Ireland, and Emperor Frederick I Barbarossa was elected King of Germany, also in 1152. One year later, the influential Saint Bernard of Clairvaux, who deserves a book to himself, died the same year as Blessed Eugene in 1153.

**Anastasius IV (1153 to 1154).** Roman, he is remembered as a peacemaker and the restorer of the Pantheon.

**Adrian IV (1154 to 1159).** An Englishman from Abbots Langley, he may well have seen the beginning of troubles that would plague Ireland for centuries. In 1152 Emperor Frederick I Barbarossa was elected King of Italy and in 1155 Holy Roman Emperor, and it was about this time that Adrian reputedly issued a bull, known as the *Laudabiliter*, that may or may not have been at the request of John of Salisbury, whom he met at Beneventum, southern Italy in 1156. The Bull and letters of the time supposedly called for the Angevin English King Henry II to invade Ireland and restore good Catholic order. Whatever the truth of the matter, the Normans did continue their westward invasion through Wales, and launched an expeditionary force of knights into Ireland in 1169; English King Henry II followed in person in 1171. Some four centuries later when the Church of England had split from the Church of Rome, a new basis to legitimise hegemony over Ireland was needed, so there was a Crown of Ireland Act in 1542 that enabled the Protestant English King Henry VIII to lay claim to the throne of Ireland. Those troubles would continue to the present day.

Finally, an ironic story has to be noted of the targeting of the Norman King William I of Sicily ("The Bad") by an alliance of Pope Adrian IV, Emperor Frederick I, Byzantine Emperor Comnenus, and Sicilian rebels opposed to William. After initial successes involving many Greeks and diverse mercenaries, in-fighting and pay disputes caused the alliance to fall apart, with William of Sicily increasing his holdings and his papally approved title to them, and with even wider rifts among the papacy and both Emperors.

**Alexander III (1159 to 1181).** Cf. Octavius (aka Victor IV), Pascal III, Callistus III, and Innocent III. From Siena, north central Italy, he inherited a diplomatic mess. After further disagreements, Emperor Frederick I Barbarossa was excommunicated within a year or so of Alexander's coronation. On his doorstep in 1167, the Battle of Monte Porzio between the Rome Commune and the nearby City State of Tusculum with the support of Barbarossa, saw the Rome Commune defeated but grievances created that would lead to papally sponsored atrocities later. Although Pope Alexander III was opposed by Emperor Frederick I and his papal upstarts Anti-Pope Octavius (Victor IV) (1159 to 1164), Anti-Pope Pascal III (1165 to 1168), Anti-Pope Callistus III (1168 to 1177) and Anti-Pope Innocent III (1178 to 1180), he survived for seventeen years and finally, with the Lombard League, vanquished Barbarossa at the Battle of Legnano in 1176 and sealed peace with the Treaty of Venice in 1177. This period was also known as the time of the Wars of the Guelphs and Ghibellines. Other events of the time included the laying by the Pope of the foundation stone for the Cathedral of Notre Dame, Paris, during the reign of French King Louis VII; the martyrdom of Saint Thomas Becket aka Saint Thomas à Becket at the hands of agents of English King Henry II in Canterbury Cathedral in 1170; and the Second Synod of Cashel, known as part of four reforming synods relating to the Church in Ireland, which was held in 1172 at the request of English King Henry II and which purported to give further credence to the notion of Papal and English dominion over Ireland.

**Lucius III (1181 to 1185).** Italian, and from the republic of Lucca, north-west Italy, he continued frosty relations with Emperor Frederick I refusing to crown his son and successor, Emperor Henry VI.

Pope Lucius III's great and unforgettably diabolical achievement to his everlasting shame was the issuing of a decree against heresies, and the declaration that anyone failing to join in the purging of such heresies would suffer a similar fate. Inquisitions and internal Crusades were initiated that resulted in the most grisly deaths of many thousands – in the name of Christianity. The most well-known Christian groups that were anathematised at this time were Cathars, Paterines, Josephists, Waldensians, and Arnoldists. The full text of the Bull can be read in the book *The History Of The Christian Church*, by William Jones.

Perhaps this pope's epitaph should more aptly read "Lucius aka Lucifer".

**Urban III (1185 to 1187).** From a noble Milanese family, the conflict with Emperor Frederick I continued, with papal communications north of Italy being seriously restricted by blockades in the Alps imposed by Emperor Frederick. 1187 saw the defeat of the Crusaders by the Ayyubid Dynasty forces of Saladin at the Battle of Hattin, the shock of which is said to have led to the death of the Pope.

**Gregory VIII (1187).** From a noble Italian family in Benevento, he reigned for less than two months but attempted a reconciliation with Emperor Frederick I, mediated to settle issues between the strategic ports of Pisa and Genoa, and began the Third Crusade.

**Clement III (1187 to 1191).** This Roman was more acceptable to the citizens of Rome, so domestic issues were settled. More widely there were again rifts. Emperor Frederick I (Barbarossa) died in 1190 on the way to the Crusade and consequent grief hit the German contingent badly, with many going home, while Barbarossa's son, Emperor Henry VI, became Holy Roman Emperor. Norman King William II of Sicily ("The Good") had died childless shortly before in 1189 and so to Pope Clement's consternation the Sicilian throne was claimed by marriage by Emperor Henry VI, raising the possibility of the encirclement of the Papal States. When the Sicilians with Clement's support therefore proclaimed Tancred as *Sicilian* King of Sicily, Tancred being the illegitimate son of an earlier Sicilian Duke, another international crisis was born.

**Celestine III (1191 to 1198).** Born into the noble Roman Orsini family, he should probably best be remembered along with the nefarious Emperor Henry VI for their consent to the razing and butchery of the previously pro-Henry town of Tivoli, aka Tibur aka Tusculum. The outrage was principally perpetrated in 1191 by the good folk of the neighbouring previously anti-Henry Rome Commune, no doubt still smarting from their defeat in 1167 at the Battle of Monte Porzio when the Pontiff was Pope Alexander III.

Pope Celestine III was criticised for delaying the excommunication of Duke Leopold of Austria who had kidnapped English King Richard I the Lionheart during his forced land crossing after being shipwrecked in 1192; and Emperor Henry VI, who was believed to be behind the imprisonment and ransom demand, at the very least should have been immediately threatened with excommunication. The ransom has been roughly equated to £2billion in the 21$^{st}$ century. Duke Leopold was eventually excommunicated in 1193 but not before collection of the ransom was well underway. The final sour note against the Pope in this theatre occurred with the death of Tancred of Sicily and the successful acquisition in 1198 of the title King of Sicily for Emperor Henry VI's young son and successor, Holy Emperor Frederick II. In order to curry favour with other power blocs, in 1191 Celestine had confirmed a new military Order – the Teutonic Knights, and he enthusiastically reaffirmed support and patronage of the Knights Templar and the Knights Hospitaller.

**Innocent III (1198 to 1216).** He was responsible for the butchery of the Albigenses, a dissident heretical French sect. He restricted the authority of the Welf (or Guelph) Dynasty's Emperor Otto IV, and in fact excommunicated him in 1215, although the Pope at this time was notionally a nominee of the Welfs. See also the First English Barons' War 1215 to 1217 at the time of Magna Carta.

**Honorius III (1216 to 1227).** Reconciled with the Emperor Frederick II who was crowned by him.

**Gregory IX (1227 to 1241).** Gregory followed the example, in respect of cruel persecutions, that had been set by the Hohenstaufen Holy Emperor Frederick II. Gregory actually hated Frederick, and had swiftly excommunicated him in 1227 after the emperor failed to begin a scheduled crusade due to an epidemic among the imperial troops and that even affected the Emperor himself. Gregory called Frederick an Antichrist, and then with the objective of enhancing his own Christian credentials, the good Gregory furthered the burning of heretics, notably the Albigenses, and then excommunicated Frederick II for the second time in 1239. It was Gregory IX who was responsible for the crusade against the Russians that saw Alexander Nevsky's rise to fame through battles that culminated in the one on a frozen Lake Peipus in 1242. See elsewhere in both volumes.

**Celestine IV (1241).** From Milan, he reigned for 17 days. Little of note.

### 16.22 Anno Domini 1250 to 1273
### 16.22.1 Context
#### 16.22.1.1 HRE – The Great Interregnum, Papal Materialism

There is something of interest associated with all four of the popes of this brief interlude.

Firstly, concerning the Imperial Hohenstaufen Dynasty of the Holy Roman Empire (HRE), it has to be said that both it, and the well-educated, multi-lingual, immensely powerful and widely esteemed (then and by historians since), if sometimes cruel, Holy Roman Emperor Frederick II, were brought low by a scheming Pope Innocent IV, Frederick's erstwhile friend. Frederick was understood to have remarked, whether seriously or not, that Moses, Christ, and Muhammad were three impostors, and such blasphemy would not have endeared him to any of the religious leaders then or now.

Frederick had been fighting on several fronts and against several factions for some years to re-establish Imperial control of various principalities in Italy, and simultaneously the Pope wanted to expand the Papal States as much as possible. There was particular animosity between Frederick and

## The Two Thousand Year War – Papal Hegemony

the Papal States due to their being on opposing sides during the destructive War of the Lombards (1228 to 1243), which was effectively a civil war in the Kingdoms of Jerusalem and Cyprus, and which saw previously allied Crusaders slaughtering each other. Emperor Frederick II's successes therefore, along with his general popularity, made him a target for the expansionist popes of the period.

Emperor Frederick II died in 1250, having in 1235 deposed his own eldest son because of his rebellious disruption on several occasions of Frederick's plans. That eldest son, who was additionally imprisoned by his father, was German King Henry VII (1220 to 1235) among other titles, and he is not to be confused with Holy Roman Emperor Henry VII (circa 1275 to 1313).

Frederick's second son, Conrad, was therefore made German King Conrad IV (circa 1235/7 to 1254) among other titles, and he was expected to become Holy Roman Emperor. Pope Innocent IV's ban on Frederick and his deposing of Conrad in 1245, however, led to usurpers or anti-kings and continuing conflicts throughout Italy that were never completely resolved, so that when Conrad died of malaria in 1254 the titles King of Germany and King of the Romans, and therefore Holy Roman Emperor, would lie unclaimed until a Hapsburg (Holy Roman Emperor Henry VII) would arrive to claim them in 1273.

### 16.22.1.2 The End of the Hohenstaufens

Because there was no Holy Roman Emperor during this period, it is apposite to identify the continuation to extinction of the Hohenstaufen line as Kings of Sicily at this time. Dates are regnal, not lifetime, and the following were all Kings or "almost Kings" of Sicily, sometimes jointly holding the title. Only one or two examples of their possibly numerous other honorific titles are given:

1. Sicilian King Henry I 1194 to 1197, he was also Holy Roman Emperor Henry VI from 1190 to 1197.
2. Sicilian King Frederick I 1198 to 1250 – he was also Holy Roman Emperor Frederick II from 1220 to 1250.
3. Sicilian King Henry II 1212 to 1217, he was not an emperor.

4. Sicilian King Conrad I 1250 to 1254 – he was also German King Conrad IV 1237 to 1254, but not an emperor.
5. Sicilian King Conrad II the Younger 1254 to (de facto 1258), (de jure 1268) – he was also King Conrad III of Jerusalem, and he was executed at the age of 16 in 1268 by Charles of Anjou after allying with the Saracens. Conrad II the Younger was the last of the Hohenstaufens.
6. Manfred 1258 to 1266 was regent of Sicily for Conrad II above. Manfred was killed in battle by Charles of Anjou, also after allying with the Saracens.
7. Charles of the House of Anjou 1266 to 1282 – he was also Neapolitan King Charles I (King of Naples). Sicily would henceforth remain outside the Holy Roman Empire until Holy Roman Emperor Charles V would absorb it into the dynasty of the Hapsburgs in 1516. See below under the next several popes for further controversy surrounding the identity of the "King of Sicily" at this time.

## 16.22.2 The Popes of the Period 1250 to 1273

**Innocent IV (1243 to 1254).** From an aristocratic Genoese family, he took the throne after an eighteen month gap in the papacy, and fearful of imperial duplicity, fled to Genoa from where he assessed his support, eventually moving to France for added security. He raged against Emperor Frederick II, but also against the Hohenstaufens as a whole, and in 1249 ordered a Crusade against Frederick. After Frederick's death in 1250 he continued the war against the imperial successors and felt strong enough to return to Rome in 1253. Rather naïvely he sent a letter to the Mongol Emperor in 1245 asking him to stop killing Christians and suggesting that he should become one himself. The Mongol reply was a demand for submission by all of Europe's leaders including the Pope himself. Pope Innocent IV continued his scheming to eliminate Imperial occupancy of Sicily by offering the papal fiefdom of Sicily to Richard of Cornwall who was the younger brother of English King Henry III, then to Charles of

## The Two Thousand Year War – Papal Hegemony

Anjou, and finally to Edmund, the second son of English King Henry III. They all initially refused, though it seems Edmund eventually accepted the challenge just before the Pope died. Eventually Innocent tried to find an accommodation with Conrad II the Younger and his Regent Manfred, and after apparently succeeding, Manfred reversed his position and with Saracen helpers, defeated a Papal army at the Battle of Foggia in 1254. In a wider context, Manfred also supported Ghibelline (pro-Imperial) communes in Tuscany.

Overall, Pope Innocent IV was involved with foreign issues in, or missions to: Portugal, England, France, Germany, Prussia, Austria, Hungary, Russia, Armenia, and Mongolia, but he is said to have allowed corruption to set in at home – in some cases with complicity.

A final note and comment on the "humanity" of Pope Innocent IV concerns his legacy to succeeding generations in the form of the Papal Bull *Ad extirpanda* that authorised torture as a tool to help the Inquisition obtain confessions from heretics.

**Alexander IV (1254 to 1261).** From a Roman aristocratic family that had already supplied Pope Innocent III and Pope Gregory IX, he first of all confirmed the Sicilian fiefdom to the Plantagenet Edmund aka Edmund Crouchback, son of English King Henry III, in return for a fat payment that led to unrest in England when Henry tried to raise the payment by taxing the English. English King Henry III was very free with the people and land of England, having given the very wealthy and income-producing Cornwall to his brother Richard as a birthday present. Unrest at his latest scam developed into a full scale civil war, the Second English Barons' War 1264 to 1267, the protesters being led by Simon de Montfort, and the Royalists by Henry's first son, Edward, later English King Edward I aka Longshanks aka the Hammer of the Scots.

Pope Alexander IV tried unsuccessfully to unite the Eastern and Western Churches and to organise a Crusade against the Tatars and Mongols who in 1259 were raiding Poland. An example of this pope's inhumanity was the instigation of the Inquisition in France. Of further English significance at this time was the unlikely election of Richard of

Cornwall to the position of King of Germany in 1256 and to that of Holy Roman Emperor in 1257 at Aachen. In reality he mainly settled for the rich pickings from his Cornish estates and had very little, if any, effect as a Roman Emperor. Feckless English aristocratic and governmental disinterest in the affairs of Europe would seem to be an ancient trait.

**Urban IV (1261 to 1264).** The son of a French cobbler from Troyes, he inherited the results of the weakness of his predecessor in a turbulent international climate. The Sicily problem had not been resolved and was still in the hands of the Hohenstaufen, Manfred, with his Saracen supporters; the disgraceful Latin Empire (1204 to 1261) at Constantinople, that had been created by the participants of the Fourth Crusade, was finally ended when the Greeks took it back; and inter-City civil conflicts were rife throughout Italy as a result of differences between the Guelph (pro-Pope) and Ghibelline (pro-Emperor) factions.

The pope died shortly before the results of his two-faced scheming with the opposing Manfred and Charles of Anjou, the latter being the youngest of five children of French King Louis VIII (the Lion), could be seen and taken to a satisfactory conclusion.

**Clement IV (1265 to 1268).** A French soldier and lawyer with two children, this pope from the Languedoc was more a man of the world than many of the popes. Charles of Anjou arrived in Rome and, after sorting out a contract with the Pope, defeated and killed Manfred of Sicily at the Battle of Benevento in 1266. Naples opened its gates to him and he went on to defeat Conrad II the Younger at the Battle of Tagliacozzo, central Italy, in 1268. Conrad was beheaded the same year in Naples for treason – he had after all made an alliance with the Saracens against the Pope. The Angevin Empire, with both French and English lineage, now had a serious Mediterranean foothold. In the last two years of his reign Pope Clement IV was in contact with the Mongol leader Abaqa, then resident in Persia, who had proposed an alliance of the Eastern and Western Roman Empires with the Mongols to resist Muslim invasions.

In true papal and Roman Catholic tradition, however, another opportunity to unite Europe was thrown away.

## 16.23 Anno Domini 1273 to 1337

### 16.23.1 Context

#### 16.23.1.1 Enter the Hapsburgs, the Papacy Moves to Avignon

- The significance of the rise of the Hapsburg Dynasty cannot be overstated.
- The War of the Sicilian Vespers began in 1282 and would run until 1302.
- The Papacy was moved to Avignon in France.

### 16.23.2 The Popes of the Period 1273 to 1337

**Blessed Gregory X (1271 to 1276).** From northern Italy, he was eventually elected after a three year gap with no pope while he was on Crusade – the ninth – in Palestine. He made attempts to resolve the schism with the Eastern Church and exchanged emissaries with the Mongol Empire or Ilkhanate in nearby Persia, though the aspirant alliance against the Muslims never really realised its potential. Rudolph I began the Hapsburg Dynasty in 1273, becoming King of Germany and Holy Roman Emperor.

**Blessed Innocent V (1276).** From the Savoie region of France which was at that time part of the Holy Roman Empire, he died after only five months and is remembered for his enthusiasm for reunification with the Eastern Church, a project that ended with his death – yet another chance to combine ecclesiastical and possibly military forces was lost.

**Adrian V (1276).** From Genoa, he died after only five weeks, but is remembered from his pre-papal time in England, where it is said that his name featured on the oldest known example of English Statute Law – the Statute of Marlborough from 1267. Not to be confused with the English Pope Adrian IV (1154 to 1159).

**John XXI (1276 to 1277).** Probably from Portugal, he was buried alive when a private room he had constructed collapsed on him. As described above under John XIV, an error in the numbering of popes with the adopted name John meant that there was no Pope John XX.

**Nicholas III (1277 to 1280).** The son of Roman nobility, he ensured his own comfort by spending hugely on the Lateran Palace, the Vatican, and a new country residence, and he advanced several members of his own family through the papal hierarchy. Pre-empting the later more notorious Spanish Inquisitor Generals, he had been the principal inquisitor under Pope Urban IV. His highly debatable positive contributions included the attempted continuation of diplomatic and cultural links in 1278 with the Tatars and Mongols, despite their obviously unchristian behaviour, with the aim of penetrating both Persia and China to spread Christianity by the sword. At the end of his reign in 1280 he was involved in the brokering of a settlement between Roman Emperor Rudolf of Hapsburg and Charles of Anjou that involved a marriage between the two families and the donation of a couple of fiefdoms, including their peoples, to Charles.

**Martin IV (1281 to 1285).** From a landed family in the Île de France, he was elected with the patronage of Neapolitan King Charles I aka Charles of Anjou aka King of Sicily. Under obligation to return the favour, he excommunicated the Byzantine Emperor Michael VIII who had retaken Constantinople for the Greeks back in 1261. This excommunication was intended to further Charles' ambitions for another Latin Empire in the East and possibly even wider domination of the Mediterranean. As a result of already simmering resentment in Sicily that was both stoked by Spanish King Peter III of Aragon, a remaining relative of the earlier Manfred of Sicily, and fanned by the work of agents of the Byzantine Emperor, the War of the Sicilian Vespers began in 1282 and was set to run until 1302. Thousands of French residents of Sicily were massacred and several European states would be drawn into the twenty years war. In a rage, the French Pope Martin excommunicated Spanish King Peter III of Aragon, declared Aragon forfeit, and tried to start a Crusade against Peter, but it was all a waste of time, and the Pope was obliged to leave Rome, dying shortly afterwards.

**Honorius IV (1285 to 1287).** Only slightly less antagonistic than his predecessor, this pope from a rich noble family was related to Pope Honorius III. He initially resisted all attempts to resolve the issues of Sicily and Aragon, but just before his death, after approaches by the English King Edward I, he began a process that might lead to a solution under his successors. Additionally, rapprochement with the Germans led to the announcement that February 1287 would see the coronation of Holy Roman Emperor Rudolf of Hapsburg at Saint Peter's, but German internal strife prevented Rudolph's departure. Military advantage against the Muslims that could have been established by acting on yet another missive on the subject from the Mongols in 1285 was lost by bureaucratic ineptitude on the part of the papacy.

**Nicholas IV (1288 to 1292).** A seemingly weak individual from the central Adriatic coast of Italy, he failed to crown Rudolph Hapsburg and he facilitated the continuation of the controversy over the titles King of Naples and King of Sicily by ineffectively crowning Charles II of the House of Anjou as such in 1289. In reality, Spanish King James II (The Just) of Aragon continued in the role until 1296. Nicholas did send missionaries as far as the Mongols, the Tatars, and the Chinese.

**Saint Celestine V (1294).** Following a two year gap due to factional (Guelph and Ghibelline) and family (Orsini and Colonna) conflicts, and because of the inability to decide a successor, Celestine was reluctantly enthroned. He proved to be a bureaucratic bungler; he was totally unsuited to the job, and was most probably an innocent victim. He tried to resign and disappear back to his origins as a hermit, only to be cruelly dragged back by his successor, and imprisoned in awful circumstances where he shortly died. A hole in his skull suggests his death under the following pope may not have been natural.

**Boniface VIII (1294 to 1303).** From a noble Roman family, he made the ridiculous and uncharitable claim that for salvation all persons had to be subject to the Pontiff. In 1295, and still new to the job, he ordered that there should be a peace settlement between German King Adolph of Nassau (1292 to 1298), and his ally English King Edward I in their dispute with French King Philippe IV (1285 to 1314), over claims to various Duchies, and he went on to quarrel with many who paid him any attention. He was not to be trusted, and against the Colonna family in 1298, he razed not just their residence, but their home city as well, and scattered salt on the site after it had surrendered without a fight, and after he had guaranteed that he would spare them. He interfered unsuccessfully in disputes among factions, city states, and Nation-States, and he liberally excommunicated those who opposed him, declaring forfeit, all those principalities that displeased him. His own disputes with King Philippe IV would ultimately be his undoing when, following a series of Bulls relating to taxation and Papal Supremacy, he was surprised by the arrival of a large force, led by agents of the French King, at his papal residence at the historical retreat of Anagni in the hills outside Rome. Conflicting descriptions suggest either that he was beaten to within an inch of his life, and that he committed suicide in bizarre circumstances, or that he simply died about a month later of melancholy, or from a grief-induced fever. The reputation and memory of this violent brute, like that of several other popes, has certainly suffered by depictions of him in purgatory, created by his contemporary, Dante, and later illustrated by Gustave Doré.

**Blessed Benedict XI (1303 to 1304).** From Treviso, north-east Italy, he was reconciled with French King Philippe IV and he absolved the Cardinals of the Colonna family. He did not forgive the agents responsible for the assault on his predecessor at Anagni, and they were excommunicated and summoned before a papal tribunal. Before this could take place he died, it is believed from poisoning, and possibly by command of the excommunicates, led by Guillaume de Nogaret, an agent of French King Philippe IV, who would later play a leading role in other confirmed atrocities.

**Clement V (1305 to 1314).** French-born, from Aquitaine, he chose coronation at Lyons, France, under the gaze of French King Philippe IV. He elected a number of French Cardinals and moved the papacy to Avignon in France. A pattern was emerging. In 1306 Pope Clement revised and revoked previous Papal Bulls to gain favour with the French king and his agents, among them, Guillaume de Nogaret referred to above. Following unsuccessful earlier attempts to combine the Templars with the Hospitallers, on Friday, 13th October, 1307, a date that would live forever more in conspiracy theory and superstition, the Order of Knights Templar were led to grisly slaughter and dissolution, and their finances were appropriated by the French Crown; their French estates were given to the Order of Knights Hospitaller.

In spring 1309 the papacy had already been at historic Poitiers in France for some time for security reasons, and it was now moved via Carpentras to Avignon where it would remain until 1377.

German King Henry VII of Luxembourg became Holy Roman Emperor in 1312, the interregnum having lasted since the death of Holy Roman Emperor Frederick II in 1250. Sadly, Holy Roman Emperor Henry VII died within a year, and it is said that his death dashed the hopes of the Ghibellines and Dante for strong German government of Italy and the Empire.

In a British context, certain strictures against King Edward I were relaxed, and after King Edward II was on the throne in 1307, the Archbishop of Canterbury was allowed to return to his *See* after earlier allegations by Edward I of treason. In 1306, Scottish King Robert I aka Robert the Bruce, was excommunicated for his part in the murder that had taken place in Greyfriars Kirk, Dumfries, earlier that year, of John Comyn aka Lord of Badenoch, who had been a supporter of English King Henry III. In 1305 and 1307 yet more missions from the Mongols seeking an alliance against the Muslims were ignored, and the possibility of massively improved military resistance was thrown away.

**John XXII (1316 to 1334).** Cf. Nicholas V. From Cahors, France, he was enthroned after a two year interregnum, and was involved throughout the papal empire. There was particular antipathy from the Pope towards Holy Roman Emperor Louis IV of Bavaria for sheltering heretics, and generally for supporting someone other than himself, Pope John XXII. This antipathy was complicated yet again by more disturbances among the Guelphs (papal) and Ghibellines (imperialists).

1326 saw the end of the war against the Cathars in the south of France by their brutal murder under the direction of Jacques Fournier (later becoming Pope Benedict XII) who was made a Cardinal for his atrocities.

Pope John XXII was opposed by Emperor Louis IV's nominee for pope, Pietro Rainalducci of Corbario, who became Anti-Pope Nicholas V, and who was installed in Rome during a brief invasion of Italy by Louis in 1328, which although unsuccessful long-term, ensured that John XXII had to stay in Avignon.

Among a host of other dissident clergy at this time, William of Ockham, the English Franciscan monk, was excommunicated in 1328, and with others he took refuge with Duke Louis of Bavaria who was the son of Emperor Louis IV, and whom the dissidents had supported during a scandal concerning the Duke's bigamous marriage that had been arranged to spread the territories of the House of Wittelsbach to include the Tyrol.

A final example of John XXII's ideological bigotry was his condemnation as heresy in 1329, of the writings of the respected German mystic and philosopher, Meister Eckhart, an admonition that he formalised in a Papal Bull.

## 16.24 Anno Domini 1337 to 1453
### 16.24.1 Context
#### 16.24.1.1 Hundred Year War, Western Schism, Papal Atrocities

- Hundred Year War (1337 to 1453).
- Brigandage and the Free Companies of France.
- In England in 1352, treason was defined by statute for the first time.
- In 1362 English replaced French as the national language of England.
- The period of the Lollards.
- The Golden Bull of 1356: a very comprehensive specification of electoral procedures – who, how, where, and when – that was to be followed when identifying a new Emperor.
- The Western Schism began in 1378, following the end of the Avignon papacy in 1377.
- Avignon Pope Clement VII (1378 to 1394).
- Avignon Pope Benedict XIII (1394 to 1417).

*The Two Thousand Year War – Papal Hegemony*

- Third Pope Alexander V (1409 to 1410).
- Western Schism Ends 1417.

During the 14<sup>th</sup> century France was plagued by brigands and marauding militia, many of which were termed "Free Companies", and Pope Innocent sought to fortify the Palais des Papes, though that prudent measure was not soon enough, and he was obliged to pay protection money to avoid a catastrophe.

### 16.24.2 The Popes of the Period 1337 to 1453

**Benedict XII (1334 to 1342).** From Toulouse, he initially wanted to return the papacy to Rome, but factional divisions there, and opinion from others prevented it. In 1339 he began construction of the massive and imposing Palais des Papes in Avignon that remains to this day an irresistible magnet to pilgrims and tourists. He is said to have been an honourable and kind man, vilified only for his natural corpulence and political naïvety, though confounding that is the fact that he tried to get the English King Edward III to adopt the Inquisition, and he encouraged its use against heretics everywhere. He is therefore directly responsible for historical atrocity. Before giving up in 1337, the Pope tried three times to reconcile an apparently willing Emperor Louis IV of Bavaria, but each time he was thwarted by French King Philippe VI, which led to Louis allying with English King Edward III against France. Pope Benedict XII overall was used and abused by the French King, but he did find some consolation by assisting Spanish resistance to an Islamic invasion in 1339.

**Clement VI (1342 to 1352).** From a wealthy aristocratic family in the Limousin region of France, he is possibly best remembered for the Black Death that occurred between 1347 and 1350 during his reign and that killed up to two-thirds of the population of Europe, the Middle East, and Asia. He remained in Avignon and supervised care of the afflicted and dying. He continued the excommunication of Emperor Louis IV until the latter died in 1347 – Louis' successor being crowned Holy Roman Emperor Charles IV in 1355. Pope Clement was a self-confessed lover of fine foods, music and rich tapestries; he issued a Papal Bull in support of indulgences (religious contrition, not his own consumption); he condemned the prevalent persecutions of Jews for being responsible for the plague; and he appointed twenty-five, mostly French, Cardinals twelve of them his relatives. Unsurprisingly, he is said to have spent much of the papal treasure.

**Innocent VI (1352 to 1362).** From Limoges, and educated at Toulouse as a Professor of Civil Law, he is highly regarded. He is credited with largely facilitating the Treaty of Brétigny, signed in May 1360 between English King Edward III and French King John II, that ended the initial part of the Hundred Years War that started in 1337 and would persist until 1453. In 1355 he approved of the coronation of Holy Roman Emperor Charles IV in Rome, but insisted that the Emperor didn't stay around afterwards – which he didn't. Some later annoying unilateral actions by Charles concerning ecclesiastical matters were tolerated in a climate of much needed goodwill and a little peace.

**Blessed Urban V (1362 to 1370).** A son of the aristocracy and from the Languedoc, he was a patron of the arts and learning but also maintained a military posture with some success. His missions were widespread, reaching as far as China.

He was largely unsuccessful in his laudable attempts to turn round the ravages of the Free Companies and point them in the direction of the King of Hungary, at that time in need of mercenary support against invasions by the Turks. An Englishman, Sir John Hawkwood, was one of the most well-known leaders of a Free Company, though it's understood that he did turn his army to more legal conflicts. In 1367 and 1368 the Pope was in Rome where he carried out renovations in an attempt to prepare for a possible return of the papacy from Avignon, but in spite of much civic restoration he was eventually obliged to return to Avignon after yet another chance to unite the church and military power of the Eastern and Western Empires was missed. His open support for the French king during the renewed hostilities between England and France alienated him from the English.

In 1369, England under John of Gaunt, who was the third son of King Edward III, was again at war with France under the French King Charles V; and the Black Prince, the eldest son of Edward III, was leading a campaign against Spain under the Spanish King Henry II of Castile. However, by the year 1374, having been weakened by the Plague, England would have suffered serious reverses. It's no surprise that attempts by Pope Urban V to reconcile the warring factions and organise another Crusade, this time against the Turks, failed – not least because French King John II aka French King "John the Good", who was to have led it, died a prisoner in London in 1364 after his capture by the Black Prince at Poitiers in 1356. Another blow to the chances of a united defence against the ravages of Islam, this time firmly the responsibility of England.

**Gregory XI (1370 to 1378).** Cf. Robert of Geneva (aka Clement VII). From Limoges, France, he had to contend with heresies throughout Europe, particularly that of John Wycliffe, whose followers were known as the Lollards and who translated the Bible into the English vernacular of the time. Pope Gregory XI tried to return to Rome from Avignon, but general hostilities there, and specific hatred of him by the Florentines, who, as an entire city with all their possessions had been excommunicated and outlawed, prevented any enduring expression of the papacy. During this period Gregory's papal legate, Robert of Geneva, who would become the future Anti-Pope Clement VII, was responsible for the massacre of the 4,000 inhabitants of a small village, Cesena in north-east Italy, during the War of the Eight Saints 1375 to 1378 that was led by the Republic of Florence. It is said that one of Gregory's worst faults was his inability to understand that the imposition of French Cardinals on the Italians just was not going to work – several of those Cardinals were in fact his relatives. He was the last French pope.

**Urban VI (1378 to 1389).** This Neapolitan monk was ushered into power without proper election, while a Roman stooge in pope's clothing was being shown to a braying mob who were demanding a Roman pope. The potentially invalid pope was the last to be elected from outside the College of Cardinals, and he was opposed by a Frenchman at Avignon, Robert of Geneva, who was Anti-Pope Clement VII from 1378 to 1394. It was this conflict that caused the Great Western Schism that lasted from

1378 to 1417 and that saw a rival pope in Avignon, and eventually a total of three concurrent popes.

In the lawless climate of central Italy, and with a change of ruler of the Kingdom of Naples, Pope Urban VI suddenly found himself besieged for a while in 1385 in the castle of Nocera in that Kingdom. The besieger was the kingdom's new ruler, Neapolitan King Charles III, who was also King of Jerusalem, King of Hungary, and also an Angevin aka Plantagenet. Rescued in the nick of time by a couple of courageous Barons, Urban, like other popes before him, fled to Genoa, where he gained some comfort by having several of his Cardinals tortured to death for opposing him. During the next few years he sallied forth through Italy at the head of an army looking more like the bellicose head of a Free Company than a pope, and it is said that either he died from injuries sustained when he fell off his mule while on campaign, or that he was poisoned.

**Boniface IX (1389 to 1404).** Cf. Baldassare Cossa (aka John XXIII). From a long-established Neapolitan baronial family, he resided in Rome (or when necessary elsewhere, such as Assisi or Perugia) and had the support of Germany, England, Hungary, Poland, and most of Italy, whereas Avignon at this time was supported by the Holy Roman Empire and the rest of Europe; the two popes, of course, excommunicated each other. It's interesting but unsurprising to note that throughout the Schism, Scotland was in the opposite camp to England.

The Kingdom of Naples was next on the agenda for a decade of papally sponsored unrest as follows:

**1389. The French Pope** Clement VII (aka Robert of Geneva see above) crowned the French Prince Louis II of Anjou, as King of Naples.

Since 1386 however, a certain Ladislaus (9 years old) was already the rightful heir of Neapolitan King Charles III who also had other territorial dominions and honorific titles, and in 1390, with his mother, Margaret of Durazzo, as Regent, they were forced to flee when Louis II of Anjou entered Naples.

**1390. The Roman Pope** Boniface IX crowned Ladislaus King of Naples, and with his support, war began.

## The Two Thousand Year War – Papal Hegemony

**1399.** The war ended with Ladislaus as the victor, and it was during 1399 that the sects known as the Albati or Bianchi appeared in southern France and Italy. Clad in white gowns with a red cross on the back, and with faces covered, they chanted and sometimes self-flagellated. On reaching Rome, after initially being accepted by the authorities, Boniface IX had their leader burned at the stake as an example.

Boniface rebuilt and fortified much of the infrastructure of Rome including the Castel Sant'Angelo and many bridges. England, that had previously been one of the strongest supporters of Rome against Avignon, now rebelled against the corrupt papal practice of giving *benefices* (e.g. freehold properties in England!) to its own favourites in the papal sphere, and a general cynicism that was held by clergy, Crown, and the public towards the papacy was aided by John Wycliffe's preaching and publications. Such resentment towards a papal affiliation with Mammon would spread to other European satellites of Rome over the next century or so. Boniface IX is thought to have been opposed by Baldassare Cossa (later Anti-Pope John XXIII) who had links to bands of brigands before his time as elected anti-pope.

**Innocent VII (1404 to 1406).** Cf. Baldassare Cossa (aka John XXIII). From a humble Neapolitan background, he achieved very little. In 1405 a nephew that he had appointed as a Cardinal had eleven members of the opposition murdered in his own home and then callously thrown into the street. The populace, being rightly incensed, forced the Pope to flee, which in turn prompted the arrival of the King of Naples, Ladislaus, to his rescue. Duplicity and political ambition on the part of Ladislaus led to his occupation of the Castel Sant'Angelo from where he only returned home after being excommunicated. Throughout these troubles the monarchies of France and Germany together with their clergy and academics had been encouraging a resolution of the Great Schism, but unrest in the Papal States had conspired to prevent any reasonably secure transit that would have allowed attendees to get to any of the councils. The blame for this was placed, at least partly with justice, at the feet of Pope Innocent VII. Again, he was opposed by, or at least had to contend with, the unpleasantness of

Baldassare Cossa who would later become Anti-Pope John XXIII – enthroned for the period 1410 to 1415.

**Gregory XII (1406 to 1415).** Cf. John XXIII. From a noble Venetian family, he was elected on the promise that he would resign his seat if the Pope in Avignon would do the same, this so that a new, single pope of unification could then be elected. Although in 1406, on notice of Gregory's willingness for the arrangement, Benedict XIII from Avignon appeared to go along with the principle, it seems that in the event neither would commit, and so in 1409, as a result of negotiations among Cardinals of both camps, the Council of Pisa (led by Baldassare Cossa) was convened, at which both popes were declared deposed and replaced by a single, new Pope Alexander V. There are, of course, no prizes for guessing that the two incumbents refused to budge, and so the problem was now worse, with three popes all claiming that they were the representative of God on earth. Alexander has been described even by Catholic sources as *"A homeless beggar-boy in a Cretan city, knowing neither parents nor relations"* and yet he achieved high academic honours at Oxford and Paris.

It was now Baldassare Cossa's moment, and when Pope Alexander V died suddenly, ten months into his reign and while he was with Baldassare Cossa, Cossa stepped into the breach to become Pope John XXIII from 1410 until 1415. Any thoughts that poison might have been involved would, of course, be a conspiracy theory.

All three popes had widespread support, but John XXIII had probably the most, with France, England, Bohemia, Prussia, Portugal, and some of the Holy Roman Empire. Added to an obviously powerful international axis, he also had support from several Italian principalities or city states, such as Venice and Florence. It was Pope John XXIII who introduced the Medici Bank as the official guardians of the papal purse.

So we return to Gregory XII who lasted until 1415, which was just long enough to see the start of the Council of Constance in 1414 (it went on till 1418) that disposed of the Three Popes Controversy and realised the triumphant election of Pope Martin V in 1417. Two other outcomes from this holy council are worth noting. Firstly, the diabolically dishonourable burning at the stake in 1415 of Jan Hus after he was summoned under the safe passage of a Letter of Indemnity to answer for his beliefs. Secondly, there were unsuccessful attempts to broker a solution to the conflict between the Polish-Lithuanian Commonwealth and the Teutonic Knights. The end of the Byzantine Empire under the heel of the Ottoman Empire was approaching, and everyone's attention was focussed on a lot of Papal Bull.

**Martin V (1417 to 1431).** Cf. Clement VIII, Benedict XIV (there were two of them at this time). From just outside Rome, he was one of the immensely powerful Colonna family with aristocratic siblings who wielded power and control and who were not just figureheads. His first act was to reinforce the authority and credibility of the Chancery – the collectors of money. This was followed by a series of international agreements or *concordats* that were described by some as vague, and that were separately and presumably secretly negotiated with his individual supporter nations.

On Pope Martin's arrival, Rome was virtually uninhabitable as a result of unrest and the Plague, and he set up massive restoration projects and appointed many of his family to administrative posts, any charges of nepotism being mitigated, it is said, by a general shortage of qualified candidates. His most nefarious act must have been the Papal Bull in 1420 to exterminate the followers of Jan Hus and John Wycliffe, and other peripheral Bohemian heretics, and which led to the Hussite Wars that afflicted mainly Bohemia and Moravia. That war or series of wars between 1419 and 1436 had religious, national, and social threads, and was a foretaste of European repression and revolution that would last for five hundred years.

With respect to the anti-popes, Anti-Pope John XXIII submitted in 1415 after accepting another post, and a Spaniard, Anti-Pope Clement VIII, whose reign from 1423 to 1429 is not trivial, was strangely elected to follow the deposed Anti-Pope Benedict XIII (not to be confused with the later official one) and to maintain an Avignon claim with some Spanish influence while it was wanted by any of the regional monarchies.

In 1425, yet another "anti-anti-pope", Anti-Pope Benedict XIV (again, not to be confused with the later official one) made a bid for power on the basis that the current set of "popes" were a product of corrupt lobbies, and bizarrely, and in part secretly, he functioned during the period 1424 to circa 1430, at a time when there was some intrigue concerning Joan of Arc who lived from 1412 to 1431.

So in reality, the end of the Great Schism was followed by a series of minor schisms, just at a time when all support should have been unified and directed to the southern and eastern borders, where the sabre-rattling din from the Ottomans and other Turks was nearing a crescendo. Instead, the Papal and other European states were in an internal orgy of atrocities and ideological conflict.

**Eugene IV (1431 to 1447).** Cf. Felix V. From a wealthy Venetian family, his domestic reign is characterised by ecclesiastical reform and struggle, and by civil wars in Italy among the powerful families – at one point in 1434 he had to flee in disguise down the river Tiber and take refuge in Florence. Later internal bickering and wrangling led to Eugene excommunicating the delegates to the Council of Basel in 1438; the Council responded by declaring Eugene deposed, and by putting Amadeus of Savoy as Anti-Pope Felix V, in his place. Felix V reigned during the years 1439 to 1449 and was the last true anti-pope, though they continue to abound to the present day wherever a group of fanatics, usually Catholics and commonly in the U.S.A., decide to appoint their own Papa. Pope Eugene continued as Pontiff Proper in spite of the above, and is judged to have surmounted the issues of the Council of Basel. As a result of *Decrees* (Pope absent) and *Bulls* (Pope present) emanating from a series of councils, held on-the-move due to the unrest and political threats, in Siena, Basel, Ferrara and Florence, a number of achievements were nevertheless made.

A short-lived union with the Greeks of the Eastern Church was agreed in 1439 and this was followed by other briefly held eastern flavoured unions-agreements-dispensations with Churches and previously considered heretical sects of: Armenia, the Jacobite Church of Syria, the Semitic Maronite Christians, and the Nestorian Christians that had their roots in

## The Two Thousand Year War – Papal Hegemony

the Persian Sassanid Empire, which, as seen elsewhere in this book, was the last pre-Islamic Persian Empire from 224 AD to 651 AD.

When scrutinised in detail however, the apparent accommodations of the above sects do not indicate any humility or ideological flexibility on the part of the Catholic Church. Their rigid doctrine is exemplified by a statement put out after the Council of Florence, part of those referenced above, that had been called by Pope Eugene IV, and that was held overall during the years 1438 to 1445. A Bull was issued that was directed at the Copts in general and the Syrian Jacobites and others specifically, clarifying the issue of Salvation Outside the Church.

From the Bull of union with the Copts, Session 11, 4th February 1442:

> *"...For in less than three years our lord Jesus Christ by his indefatigable kindness, to the common and lasting joy of the whole of Christianity, has generously effected in this holy ecumenical synod the most salutary union of three great nations. Hence it has come about that nearly the whole of the east that adores the glorious name of Christ and no small part of the north, after prolonged discord with the holy Roman church, have come together in the same bond of faith and love. For first the Greeks and those subject to the four patriarchal sees, which cover many races and nations and tongues, then the Armenians, who are a race of many peoples, and today indeed the Jacobites, who are a great people in Egypt, have been united with the holy apostolic see..."*

and later:

> *"...The holy Roman Church believes, professes, and preaches that "no one remaining outside the Catholic Church, not just pagans, but also Jews or heretics or schismatics, can become partakers of eternal life; but they will go to the everlasting fire*

*which was prepared for the devil and his angels (Matt. 25:41), unless before the end of life they are joined to the Church. For union with the body of the Church is of such importance that the sacraments of the Church are helpful to salvation only for those remaining in it; and fasts, alms-giving, other works of piety, and the exercise of Christian warfare bear eternal rewards for them alone. And no one can be saved, no matter how much alms he has given, even if he sheds his blood for the name of Christ, unless he remains in the bosom and the unity of the Catholic Church..."*

Too late, Pope Eugene IV did try to unite Europe in resisting the Turks that were outside the gates of Constantinople and a significant part of papal income was pledged to a Crusade that came to nothing when the papal alliance was annihilated at the Battle of Varna on the western Black Sea coast of Bulgaria in 1444.

It is only historical justice to remind ourselves at this point of the Venetian treachery that occurred many times throughout that geographically small republic's enormous influence. It was at this time, in connection with the campaign of the Hungarian, John Hunyadi, in support of Pope Eugene's Crusade, that Hunyadi led a combined Hungarian and Polish force, already outnumbered, against the Ottomans with the promise of Venetian support to deny the Ottomans a crossing of the Bosphorus. As he made his way to Varna, the Venetians, in a direct volte face, actually ferried the Ottomans across the Bosphorus for the fee of one gold coin per person, and although the ensuing Battle of Varna in 1444 was a defeat for the Hungarians, it was prevented from being a rout because of Hunyadi's stewardship. In spite of the loss of thousands, many more escaped, and the Ottomans were sufficiently depleted to be obliged to postpone operations into Europe. No thanks to the treacherous and venal Venetians.

## 16.25 Anno Domini 1453 to 1559
### 16.25.1 Context
#### 16.25.1.1 Jesuits, Tudors, and Ottomans

- France formed an alliance with the Ottoman Empire.
- 1540 Licence was granted to the Society of Jesus aka the Jesuits.
- 1541 Ignatius Loyola (1491 to 1556) was elected first General of the Jesuits.
- Nikolaus Kopernikus (1473 to 1543).
- King Henry VIII(reign 1509 to 1547).
- King Edward VI (reign 1547 to 1553).
- Cardinal Thomas Wolsey, died at Leicester in 1530, probably mercifully, while on his way from York to London to answer a charge of treason.
- Sir Thomas More was beheaded in 1535 for his principled defiance of the Court of King Henry VIII.
- King Henry VIII's flagship the *Mary Rose* sank.
- Lady Jane Grey of England 1553.
- English Queen Mary I (1553 to 1558).
- English Queen Elizabeth I (1558 to 1603).
- Vienna was besieged on two occasions during this period:
    1. In 1485 during the war between the Duchy of Austria and the Kingdom of Hungary (1477 to 1488).
    2. In 1529 by the Ottomans during their war with, amongst others, the Hapsburgs (1521 to 1718).

#### 16.25.1.2 Sir Thomas More's Utopia

Only a brief reference to the work of Sir Thomas More (1478 to 1535) is made here, but his thought-provoking book can be easily accessed at no cost. His work is of cultural if not dissident value, since he was in reality both a proponent of, and a victim of unrelenting and unforgiving ideology. His nemesis was the volatile polemical climate created by his own Roman Catholic dogma and the mutually exclusive ecclesiastical pragmatism that was driven by the extra-marital affairs of King Henry VIII. The flames of passion and hatred were enthusiastically fanned by the king's sycophantic and vile extended Court, of which More himself was a significant part.

More's sentence for treason, only brought about by his own obstinacy, was that he be hanged, drawn, and quartered, but it was mercifully commuted to a swift beheading. Links are provided in the *Internet Index*.

### 16.25.1.3 The Hundred Year War End - Peace? - the Italian Wars

The Hundred Year War (1337 to 1453) seemed to be over, but the rather inappropriately named Italian Wars that lasted from 1494 to 1559 would be almost as devastating for just as wide a range of contestants, only the battlegrounds would be geographically, more or less, restricted to Italy.

The mid-16$^{th}$ century was also the beginning of a series of wars that are still in the process of academic categorisation. Known as the Northern Wars, it seems that the difficulty is due to a continuing partisan bias by historians from the derivative modern States concerning exactly who experienced the first war. Belligerents included Russia, Sweden, Poland, and Lithuania just for starters – a continuation of old grievances and a chance to keep the pot boiling for a few more centuries.

### 16.25.1.4 The Italian Wars

Briefly summarising what has been the subject of dedicated books, the period 1508 to 1516 saw shifting alliances during the continuation of the Italian Wars.

In 1454 after the horrors of the Hundred Year War, by way of recognising their vulnerability to aggression by the larger European sovereign powers, a twenty-five year treaty was agreed among a subset of the geographically smaller Italian states: the Republic of Venice, the Duchy of Milan, the Republic of Florence, later on the Papal States, and the albeit larger Kingdom of Naples. They called themselves the *Italic League* or *Most Holy League* and managed to stay united long enough to successfully make French King Charles VIII (1483 to 1498) think twice about conquering Italy in 1494/1495 after an inconclusive battle at Fornovo in July, 1495, forced the French to return home. This cessation of hostilities

*The Two Thousand Year War – Papal Hegemony*

would not last however, and Italy's failure to unite as an all-encompassing Nation-State would now lead to the Italian Wars.

It started with a complete mutation of the Italic League aka Most Holy League into the League of Cambrai that would initially pit itself against an isolated Venice. Capricious Italian ambitions made sure that such a clear battle line would not last, and the first two year bout was followed by a change of loyalty by the Papal States in 1510 at the behest of Pope Julius, this time against the French. Still not happy bed-fellows, as everyone became more concerned about France, there were even more dramatic changes of allegiance in 1511 that led to the French King Louis XII being beaten by the Swiss in 1512 at Milan, and again in 1513 just west of Milan. This was not the end of the war however, and Pope Julius' dreams of a united Italian Kingdom led by the Papal States remained unfulfilled due to the partisan ambitions of most of the principal European powers that all wanted a piece of Italy, or as a minimum to see that their rivals did not succeed. From the Papal point of view, France was gone for now, but it had been replaced by several other predatory powers, and a summary of the belligerents in the different phases at this time is as follows (note the complex, shifting allegiances of the Papal States, the Holy Roman Empire (HRE), and Spain, while England and Scotland were relatively late entrants).

### 16.25.1.5 Phases in the Italian Wars – Combatants

**1508 to 1510**

Papal States, France, Duchy of Ferrara, HRE, Spain

*versus*

Venice

---

**1510 to 1511**

France, Duchy of Ferrara

*versus*

Papal States, Venice

---

**1511 to 1513**

France, Duchy of Ferrara

*versus*

Papal States, Venice, Spain, HRE, England, Swiss mercenaries

---

**1513 to 1516**

France, Duchy of Ferrara, Scotland, Venice

*versus*

Papal States, Spain, HRE, England, Duchy of Milan, Swiss mercenaries

## 1516 The Peace of Noyon

## The Two Thousand Year War – Papal Hegemony

## 16.25.1.6 Map – The French - HRE Frontier circa 1470

Map from http://commons.wikimedia.org/wiki/Category:Maps released under CC-BY-SA
http://creativecommons.org/licenses/by-sa/3.0/ Author: Marco Zanoli

### 16.25.1.7 Map – The Papal and Italian States 1494

Map from http://commons.wikimedia.org/wiki/ Public Domain

### 16.25.1.8 War of the League of Cognac – Combatants

The 1526 Peace Treaty of Madrid was reneged upon by the French King Francis I as soon as he returned to France after his captivity by Emperor Charles V following the Battle of Pavia in 1525 – described later.

---

#### 1526 to 1530 League of Cognac (War)

Holy Roman Empire, Genoa

*versus*

France, Papal States, Venice, Florence, England (from 1527), Milan

---

#### 1529 The Peace Treaty of Cambrai

See detail below during the papacy of Clement VII (1523 to 1534).

### 16.25.1.9 International Dispositions at This Time

Sardinia had been ruled by the House of Aragon from 1323 to 1516 after which it came under the direct rule of Spanish King Carlos I aka Holy Roman Emperor Charles V aka Holy Roman Emperor Karl V. It then remained under Spanish rule until 1713 so its governance was little affected by any of the events leading up to the Peace of Cateau-Cambrésis.

Corsica's history was a little more involved. It had been a territory within the Republic of Genoa in 1282, it was under the dominion of the House of Aragon from 1296 to 1434, and it was under French rule from 1553 to 1559. It was returned to the Republic of Genoa by the terms of Cateau-Cambrésis that was ratified in 1559.

By that treaty of 1559 the Duke of Savoy regained Savoy and added most of Piedmont to his inventory, but France gave up all its claims to territory in the Italian peninsula which left the Hapsburg Dynasty of Spain as the major player in Italy.

France did retain a miscellany of scattered principalities elsewhere: the small annexe or Marquisate of Saluzzo in the Piedmont area north of Italy; Calais that had been taken from England in 1558; and three annexed Dioceses known as "The Three Bishoprics" – Metz, Toul, and Verdun – that in the confusion and exhaustion of 1559 seemed overlooked by Emperor Charles V's successor, Emperor Ferdinand I, although they had been identified as a strategic group by French King Henry II in 1552. The area would become a killing ground during World War One.

In the central European region a large principality, roughly equivalent to present-day Burgundy and known then as Franche-Comté, had been transferred from Austria to Spain a couple of years earlier; this was retained by Spain. Further south, in the Italian arena, Spanish King Felipe II received specifically targeted control of the previous battlegrounds of Milan, Naples, and Sicily; and he gained a strange concoction of a few fortified cities in Tuscany including part of the island of Elba. That unlikely concoction was collectively titled the "State of Presidi", and it had been derived mainly from the defeated Republic of Siena.

The reality of Spanish control in Italy, and the continuation of the nominal independence of states such as Savoy, Venice, and the Papacy, would be tested in future centuries.

It is worth noting at this time just how powerful the Italian city States and diverse small republics could be. Venice is well-known as a powerful naval force, but the possibly lesser known Republic of Genoa was of arguably greater significance; it would be from the Sardinian-Genoese region that the Kingdom of Sardinia would eventually provide the discipline and drive for cohesion that would unify Italy. The map below illustrates the enormous influence of the Republic of Genoa, from where several of the forthcoming popes hailed.

## The Two Thousand Year War – Papal Hegemony

### 16.25.1.10 Map – The Influence of Genoa – 13th to 17th Centuries

Map from http://commons.wikimedia.org/wiki/Category:Maps released under CC-BY-SA
http://creativecommons.org/licenses/by-sa/3.0/ Author: Kayac1971

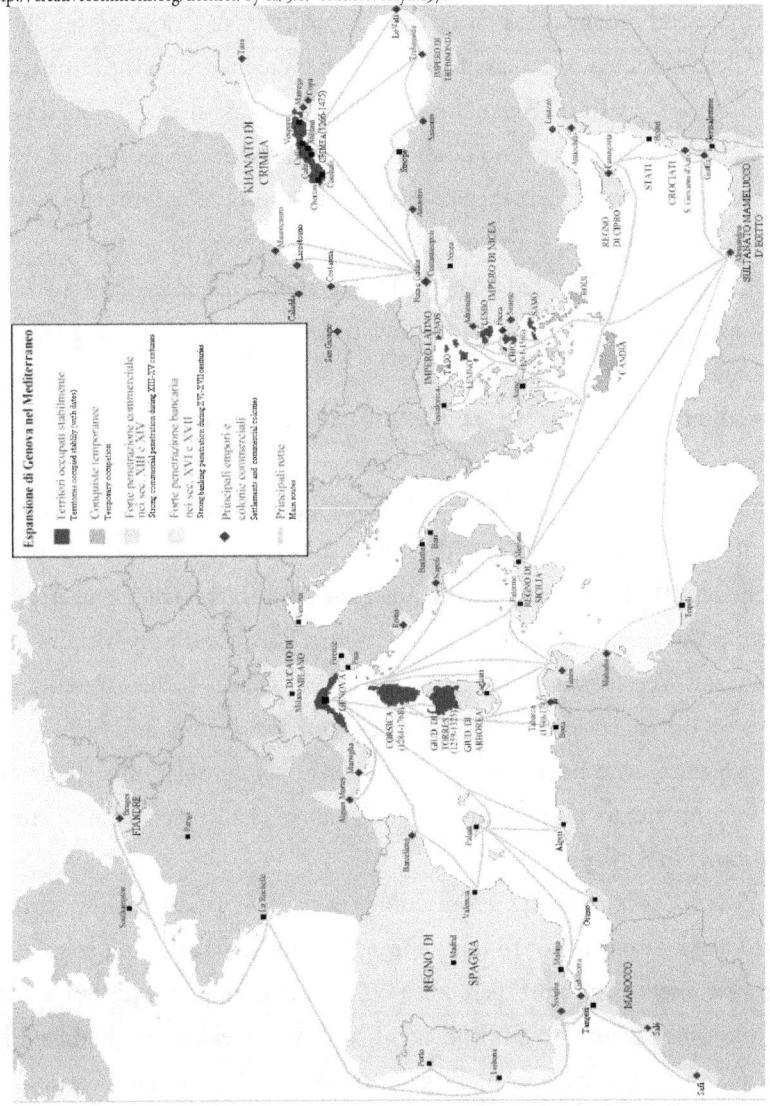

### 16.25.2 The Popes of the Period 1453 to 1559

**Nicholas V (1447 to 1455).** From the region of Genoa, he made further good progress renovating the infrastructure of Rome, both utilities and defences. He was a man of learning and is credited with the translation of many works from Greek and the foundation of the Vatican Library. Much of its early content no doubt came from Greek refugees fleeing from the Ottomans who had taken Constantinople in 1453, and much else was ransacked from other European repositories that were judged risky in the hands of the uncultured. He tried once more, unsuccessfully, to rally Europe against the Turk who was now in Constantinople, a great grievance to him.

**Callistus III (1455 to 1458).** A Spanish nobleman from Valencia, eastern Spain, virtually his whole time was spent attempting to create a unified front against the Turks. The catalogue of failures is lamentable – most were unwilling to pay the taxes to fund any venture, Emperor Frederick III of Germany hated Ladislaus of Hungary, Genoa and Aragon were at war, England and France were at war, Portugal simply withdrew its fleet, and Venice was more interested in commerce. Callistus eventually became distracted by more conflicting claims on Naples and Sicily (The Two Sicilies), and he dropped the ball. The only consolation at this time was a great victory over the Turks at Belgrade in 1456 and continued strong resistance in Albania.

**Pius II (1458 to 1464).** From a noble but ageing Tuscan family, he tried hard like his predecessor to unify Europe against the Turks, but in spite of profuse offers of support there was no significant progress. Pius was a man of the world before his enthronement, with two illegitimate children and accusations against him of general moral laxity. He wrote an autobiography, a novel or two, and some historical works.

**Paul II (1464 to 1471).** Venetian and a nephew of Pope Eugene IV, he was apparently vain and said to wear rouge, yet a recluse and extravagant spender on personal adornment. Although pursuing opposition to the Turks, he was as unsuccessful as his predecessors, and in 1470 the city of Negropont on the Greek Aegean coast fell, largely as a result of Venetian temerity that resulted in the demotion and exile of the Venetian leader of the fleet.

**Sixtus IV (1471 to 1484).** From Genoa, he is remembered for diverse contributions to Rome: the Sistine Chapel and Vatican Library, and with the introduction of artists for those tasks, the instigation of the Renaissance; much renovation of churches and utilities such as water distribution; and increased fortifications.

He encouraged the Spanish Inquisition with a Papal Bull in 1478 that got the process underway after a couple of years, but he later regretted its excesses. He declared a Crusade against the Turks and raised funds but the results were disappointing. On the subject of papal supremacy, he denounced French King Louis XI because he insisted that royal consent had to be given before any papal decree could be issued in France. Concerning nepotism, he was responsible for prosecuting a war between Venice and nearby Ferrara in north-east Italy because he wanted to give Ferrara to his nephew. There were several allegations of sexual laxity and deviation made against him, but no corroborated detail.

**Innocent VIII (1484 to 1492).** From Genoa, but with Greek-Roman ancestors, his reign started amidst civil and clerical unrest. His half-hearted attempts to get a Crusade underway against the Turks may be explained by the undeniable bribe that he received from the Turkish Sultan to keep the Sultan's brother in captivity.

This time was just about in the run-up to the period known as the Little Ice Age that was characterised by unusually cold and wet weather, crop failures, famine, and crime waves. One of Pope Innocent's remedies was to issue a Bull against witches and witchcraft, initially in Germany in 1484. A book written by the two appointed witch-finders, Heinrich Kramer and Jacobus Sprenger, titled *Malleus Maleficarum* meaning *Hammer of the Witches* ( see the chapter in Volume One titled *Internet Index of References and Other Downloads*) no doubt went on to guide other witch-finders and to cause misery to thousands of innocent women and family members. Witch hunting is believed to have persisted until as recently as the early 19$^{th}$ century.

In 1485/1486 he called for Crusades against the Waldenses and Hussites, and in 1491 he was overjoyed to witness the retaking of Granada that confirmed the reconquest of Spain from the multitude of previous Islamic sects and Caliphates. In England he supported the claim to the English throne by the first Tudor, English King Henry VII after he had taken it following his defeat of English King Richard III at Bosworth Field in 1485.

Finally, concerning Simony, he made good business himself from auctioning newly created positions within the papal hierarchy, but in 1489 he hypocritically condemned to death two officials who were forging and selling Papal Bulls.

**Alexander VI (1492 to 1503).** From Valencia, Spain, Rodrigo's uncle was Pope Callistus III, and Rodrigo, who had already served under several popes, had been given the Bishopric of Valencia on his uncle's accession. This was after all the Borgia family, to give them their secular name, and Rodrigo had changed his surname to Borgia by virtue of his mother being Pope Callistus' sister. Just days before Pope Innocent XIII died, Rodrigo had managed to get the rank of Valencia upgraded to metropolitan so that his own rank automatically tracked it and he became an archbishop. As a result, when Rodrigo became Pope it was his son, Cesare Borgia, a 17-year-old student, who took the archbishopric and they managed to keep it nicely in the family for two more ownership changes.

Pope Alexander VI is said to have begun his reign in a more honest way than the previous pope, but events about to unfold stagger belief. He began to allocate land and fiefs to relatives, and when he ran out of available fiefs, he proposed to create them from the papal states and from the Kingdom of Naples. Initially poised for a war involving complex alliances among Italian states and pretenders, and including Neapolitan King Ferdinand I and French King Charles VIII, it was in 1493 that Alexander changed tack by arranging a marriage to reconcile himself with Ferdinand I. He also created a number of Cardinals to gain ascendancy in the Sacred College of Cardinals, of which new additions one was his now 18-year-old son Cesare, and another was the brother of one of his mistresses.

## The Two Thousand Year War – Papal Hegemony

When the Neapolitan King Ferdinand I (of Naples) died in 1494, and the French King Charles VIII made an official claim on that kingdom, Pope Alexander VI made a further volte-face and gave the French king permission to pass through Rome on his way to take Naples. To reduce a long farce to fit this cameo presentation, the Pope had second thoughts and even appealed to the Ottomans to come to his aid and repel the French, but his pathetic pleas were to no avail and Charles VIII entered Rome with his troops at the end of 1494. Alexander narrowly avoided being justifiably deposed and charged with Simony by Charles by the expedient of creating another Cardinal from a bishop that he knew had influence with Charles.

Resistance to the French from Naples was non-existent and the French took the kingdom easily, only to retreat during 1495 as a result of widespread European opposition expressed via "The Holy League" – of several versions this one was the league against France. That opposition had begun when the French entered Italy, and it was the start of the Italian War of 1494 to 1498 that saw France set against: the Holy Roman Empire; the Pope with a miscellany of smaller Italian states ( Naples, Venice, Spain, and, for most of the time, Milan); and England that joined the League in 1496.

In 1499 Charles' successor, French King Louis XII, occupied Milan and Genoa, and Louis' next objective, now with the consent of Pope Alexander VI, was Naples. This would only be possible by compromising on its partition between himself (Louis) and Spanish King Ferdinand V, but the eventual squabbling between France and Spain over the division of booty and the allocation of authority ultimately and unsurprisingly developed into open hostilities and warfare in 1502.

Possibly the most preposterous action of Pope Alexander VI, though it was only an extension of earlier such Bulls, was to issue a Bull, the *Inter caetera*, that granted exclusively to Catholic Monarchs and heirs of the Crown of Castile, all the lands to the west and to the south of a pole-to-pole line 100 leagues west and south of the Azores or Cape Verde Islands. This would have included all of the North and South American continents, and did not seem to require any actual presence to establish rights, neither did it take into account the rights of any existing residents.

On a brighter note, Raphael and Michelangelo among many other artists worked in Rome at this time, although overall the legendary and earthly Borgia scandals and the warmongering by Pope Alexander VI's son, Cesare Borgia, would eclipse any notes of enlightenment, and would provide sufficient detail for another book – as would the futile attempts of more recent Catholic scholars to defend Cesare's actions.

**Pius III (1503).** From the Republic of Siena, Italy, this elderly and well-educated, but frail and gout-afflicted Cardinal managed election after Cesare Borgia had been ejected from the environs of Rome and the conclave. He survived only twenty-six days and died either of an ulcer or poisoning.

**Julius II (1503 to 1513).** From Genoa, he became known as the Fearsome or the Warrior Pope. He was a manipulative master and ensured his election, it is believed, by bribery of other Cardinals. It was this man who encouraged French King Charles VIII to invade the Kingdom of Naples earlier, and from whom Pope Alexander VI believed an indictment for Simony might arise when the French entered Rome at the end of 1494. Pope Julius quickly exerted control over Cesare Borgia, and reconciled the Orsini and Colonna factions; he then set out to eliminate Venice from its control of several Italian states.

At he end of 1503 it was Pope Julius II who gave English King Henry VIII the dispensation needed to enable him to legally marry Katharine of Aragon who had previously been married to Henry's brother and heir to the throne, Arthur, the eldest son of English King Henry VII. The heir apparent, Arthur, had died six months into the marriage, and it was Katharine's denial of consummation of that marriage that would enable the dispensation at this time, but that would be cited as invalid by Henry when he took a fancy to Anne Boleyn two decades later.

By 1506 Julius had, with difficulty and by making concessions, managed to ally himself with two old enemies of the papacy – France and the Holy Roman Empire. With some successes he had also begun preparations to push the Doge of Venice back into his lagoon. 1506 was also the year of the founding of the papal protection militia known as the Swiss Guard.

## The Two Thousand Year War – Papal Hegemony

**Leo X (1513 to 1521).** A Florentine son of the wealthy and powerful Medici and Orsini families, the child who was born with a silver spoon in his mouth was tonsured at the age of seven, made an Abbot at the age of eight, owned the Abbey of Passignano when he was nine, and when he reached the ripe old age of eleven he was given the famous Abbey of Monte Cassino. He was a Cardinal at the age of thirteen and it would be surprising if he had turned out to be anything but selfish.

Corpulent and indolent, he enjoyed good living and expensive banquets, and he was visually recorded on canvas or wood by Raphael; the image is not particularly flattering. It is said that by 1515, only two years into his reign, the Vatican Bank was virtually empty, and this was after an unusually large inheritance from the previous pope.

Pope Leo X is reputed to have declared:

*"It has served us well, this myth of Christ"*

and although denied or misrepresented by present-day Catholic apologists, Leo's decidedly unchristian utterance was recorded by his secretary, Bembo, along with the Pope's taste for sodomy.

Leo's greatest achievement was probably the wrecking of the peace that existed in 1516, partly by his nepotistic attempts to create a central Italian kingdom for his relatives. The French King Louis XII's successor, French King Francis I, had returned across the Alps to Italy and he defeated the Swiss Confederation at Marignano near Milan in 1515. The subsequent peace treaty, The Peace of Noyon in 1516, had ceded Naples to Spain and Milan to France, and France had additionally been granted powers by the Pope to nominate candidates to head abbeys and priories in France. Although this kept France on-side, it was inimical to the clergy and would resonate badly for many years.

In 1517 a group of Cardinals conspired to poison their venerated Pope, the representative of Christ on Earth, resulting in the execution of the leader and the imprisonment of the others, while in the same year the War of Urbino was another distraction in which the previous Duke of Urbino, with the aid of Venice, tried to retake his Duchy. Mainly mercenary armies were involved on both sides, and when the Duke's money ran out, a compromise peace was arranged and the Duke retired.

Apart from his failure to unite an impressively mooted European alliance of forces from the Holy Roman Empire, France, England, Spain, and Portugal to oppose the Ottomans, it was in the year of our Lord 1517, on October 31st, that Pope Leo X witnessed a civil event that would give rise to another enemy that would eat away at the Catholic Church and create internal divisions within Europe – Martin Luther read his Ninety-Five Theses on the absurd nonsense of indulgences at a church in Wittenberg, Germany. After all, it was Halloween, and the "un-dead" and evil spirits were only to be expected.

If we wanted to be charitable to this odious and duplicitous dilettante, the Pope that is, it might be said that some of his spending was charitable, and that the assassination attempt against him by his own clergy, plus the assault by Martin Luther, distracted him from the real sanctity of his position and the responsibility he had to his church; but then it seems that his overarching worldliness and villainy was attached to him from birth.

When Holy Roman Emperor Maximilian I died in 1519, his successor could have been French King Francis I or Spanish King Carlos I, and Pope Leo X juggled the two and even managed an alliance with both contenders at the same time. In 1519 he signed a treaty with Francis I against the successful new Holy Roman Emperor Charles V but in 1521 he made a defensive alliance with Charles V with the real intention of eliminating the French from the whole of Italy.

In 1520 at the Field of the Cloth of Gold near Calais, English King Henry VIII and French King Francis I had met to discuss an alliance, but Henry was already leaning towards Charles V.

Carlos I, the first King of Spain (because Castile and Aragon were united) aka Holy Roman Emperor Charles V (or Karl V) was a Hapsburg, and he was a force to be reckoned with. He was originally from Ghent in Flanders, and he was also the Duke of Burgundy, which gave him, in addition to the Palatinate of Burgundy itself, Holland, Belgium,

*The Two Thousand Year War – Papal Hegemony*

Luxembourg, parts of present-day France, the Kingdom of Naples, several Mediterranean islands, and much of the New World in the Americas. He ruled an area of Europe, the extent of which had not been seen since Emperor Charlemagne, and with others he had already been the nemesis of the French. He would later repeat the humiliation of the French King Francis I at the vital Battle of Pavia in 1525.

Thomas Wolsey was an English Cardinal at this time, living at Hampton Court Palace with his mistress, Joan Larke, with whom he had two children.

At the end of Leo's time, in 1521, the Ottomans, in spite of a treaty of peace for three years that had been signed with the Hungarians in 1519, went on the offensive again and captured Belgrade. They were now poised to strike into Europe, and their eyes were on the gates of Vienna, upstream on the Danube.

**Pope Leo X was the last pope to appoint an Emperor.**

**Adrian VI (1522 to 1523).** From a humble background in Utrecht, Holland, he was the last non-Italian pope for nearly five hundred years. At the start of his reign in 1522, hoping for a united resistance to the Ottomans who in that year had taken Rhodes, he was obliged in 1523 to become part of the axis consisting of the Holy Roman Empire, England, and Venice, against France, and one of the ironies of history was that he had been the tutor of the Holy Roman Emperor, and may therefore have unwittingly contributed something of great importance to the *ethos* of the Imperial approach. His brief reign was opposed not by any identifiable anti-pope, but by "hyenas" in the Roman ranks, clergy, and townsfolk, who were indelibly stained by the previous pope, and who could only mock the courageous efforts of Adrian the outsider.

**Clement VII (1523 to 1534).** From the Medici family of Florence, he was younger and much more wily, though maybe not necessarily more worldly-wise, than his predecessor. Seeing the French victory at Milan in 1524, he changed his support from the Emperor to the French, but when the French were in turn defeated at the Battle of Pavia in 1525, he shifted back to the Imperial side. He had already incurred the displeasure of powerful Roman families, but Clement's fate was sealed when he changed sides yet again in 1526 back to French King Francis I who, on his release, reneged on the concessions he had made while in captivity in Madrid by Holy Roman Emperor Charles V.

Charles V called Clement a wolf, and mercenary troops of the Emperor were allowed to sack Rome for a week in the spring of 1527 with all the horrors of a barbarian sacking. Clement fled after six months captivity in the Castel Sant'Angelo, and he could only return to a ruined city in 1528. Meanwhile, after a success at Genoa, the French suffered plague and defeat at Naples, where they lost much of their army including commanders, and then withdrew to sign the Treaty of Cambrai in 1529, which was essentially a restatement of the earlier Treaty of Madrid (see below), except that Francis was allowed to keep Burgundy.

This pervasive Roman and Italian anarchy of the time is held partly responsible for the English Reformation that was formalised by the English Act of Supremacy in 1534, an Act almost of impatience that might be said to have been provoked by a number of events between the years 1527 and 1534, such events being: spurned requests for an annulment of King Henry VIII's marriage to Katharine of Aragon; Henry's marriage to Anne Boleyn; the birth of the future English Queen Elizabeth I; the appointment of Thomas Cranmer – a friend of the Boleyn family – as Archbishop of Canterbury (he did receive his Pallium); and last but not least the Pope's excommunication of both King and Archbishop. All these things contrived to divert a very welcome ecclesiastical income from the Pope to King Henry VIII, and to encourage the severing of diplomatic relations between England and Rome.

The French King Francis I, while in captivity in Madrid at the hands of Holy Roman Emperor Charles V, and via the 1526 Treaty of Madrid, gave up any claim to Italy or Burgundy, but when released he retracted and formed the League of Cognac, managing to involve Henry VIII from 1527 by the Treaty of Hampton Court that was negotiated between Thomas Wolsey and the French ambassador.

## The Two Thousand Year War – Papal Hegemony

It was at this point, that the Republics of Venice and Florence, with the Papal States, were set alone against the Holy Roman Empire, but by 1530 only Florence remained, suffering defeat in August of that year; the illegitimate Duke who now gained Florence was Alessandro de Medici, thought by more recent historians to be the son of Pope Clement VII.

It was Pope Clement VII who commissioned Michaelangelo to paint The Last Supper in the Sistine Chapel.

**Paul III (1534 to 1549).** From the already wealthy Farnese family of the Papal States, Pope Paul III was welcomed by the Romans as one of their own at a time of great depression and civil dilapidation. He had four illegitimate children, increased the family fortune immensely, built himself a palace and a villa, appointed his grandsons as Cardinals, and had his portrait painted by Titian. He appropriated lands to create Dukedoms for his grandsons, and increased taxes to levels that caused rebellion.

In an ecumenical context, the reforms and precepts resulting from the Council of Trent, that was convened to identify ways of countering the Protestant movement, were the most significant developments for the Catholic Church for centuries, even down to the present day. The Council ran from 1545 to 1563, and to complement ideological rhetoric exchanged with the Protestants, several new religious orders were created to act as agents in the sometimes clandestine and politico-religious cold war that was frequently not so cold; among these were the Capuchins, Barnabites, Theatines, Jesuits, and Ursulines.

A resurgence of the Italian Wars occurred again when the Duke of Milan died and the son of Emperor Charles V, Spanish King Felipe II, inherited the title. It was too much for the French to accept, and this time the battle lines and the fighting took an extra unpleasant turn for Europe when France was actually allied with the Ottomans against the Holy Roman Empire in 1536. The Ottomans attacked Venetian and other Italian possessions in the Adriatic for a while, and France retained Turin, but not much else had changed when the Truce of Nice signalled the end of the war in 1538 – Emperor Charles V and French King Francis I refusing to actually meet, and leaving negotiations to Pope Paul III.

Emperor Charles V continued the fight against the Ottomans, but a combined allied flotilla of Genoan, Venetian, Spanish, Papal, and Maltese vessels was defeated by a smaller Ottoman fleet under Hayreddin Barbarossa at the Battle of Preveza in September, 1538, which led to a peace treaty between Venice and the Ottoman Empire in October, 1540, that ceded various Venetian islands and other possessions in the Aegean and Adriatic to the Turks.

The Truce of Nice was never going to hold, and in spite of further negotiations, in person this time, between Charles V and Francis I during the period 1538 to 1540, no progress was made and a stand-off ensued. Charles V was attempting an invasion of North Africa during 1541, and French King Francis I, out of a sense of fellow feeling when it came to Muslims, waited to see the outcome. Charles' failure was the opportunity for Francis with Ottoman support to attack in such diverse regions as Luxembourg in the north and Perpignan in the south, and after negotiations between Emperor Charles V and English King Henry VIII that were rather difficult due to their religious differences, England, fearing French interference in Scotland, entered the war on the side of the Holy Roman Empire in 1543.

Northern Europe was now ablaze, complicated by the divisions of the Reformation, and a joint French-Turkish fleet was on the point of taking Nice after a siege in the south, following which the Turks were given the French city of Toulon as a base for eight months. By mid 1544 this theatre of war had been abandoned, the Turks returning to Constantinople and the French moving north in response to what turned out to be a very brief and wasteful invasion of France by England and the Holy Roman Empire. The outcome of this failure was a premature peace treaty between the Empire and France – the duplicitous and partially secret Peace of Crépy in 1544, whereby each ceded various claims around Europe, and Francis finally gave up on Naples and agreed to help Charles suppress Protestantism with an attack on Calvin's enclave at Geneva, and also to oppose both England and the Ottomans.

## The Two Thousand Year War – Papal Hegemony

Emperor Charles V thereby left England with a land army bottled up in Calais and Boulogne to continue alone against France, and, in a cunning tactic, France now invaded England in 1545, landing in Scotland, on the Isle of Wight, and in Devon. These mainly fleet actions however, saw accidents on both sides, including the loss of King Henry VIII's flagship the *Mary Rose*, and after the many long years of attrition, both France and England were beggared by the time the Peace Treaty of Ardres was signed in June, 1546.

Elsewhere in Europe, Charles V was fighting the Schmalkalden League of Protestant German principalities with successes on both sides during active combat in 1546 and 1547. This was followed by a period of resolution of differences that involved several steps known as the Augsburg Interim of 1548: firstly, a sort of fudge of both prohibition and acceptance of Protestantism; secondly, The Peace of Passau in 1552 that gave some Protestant freedoms and released earlier prisoners; and finally, The Peace of Augsburg in 1555 that achieved complete recognition of Lutheranism and made provision for its adoption by the ruling aristocracy. The downside was that the people, according to their choice of belief, were expected to migrate among principalities and resettle, if necessary, in a region where their beliefs predominated. Sectarianism was now enshrined in law.

It was during the confusion and distractions above that in 1545 Pope Paul III went along with Imperial warfare against the Protestants by supplying troops and finance, while quietly trying to get two Italian Duchies for his son. During frosty and petulant relations between Pope and Emperor, the Pope's son was assassinated in 1547 and the Pope believed it was with the connivance at least of the Emperor. In 1538 Pope Paul renewed the excommunication of King Henry VIII, this being the last time the papacy would bother about it. The Pope died the following year, partly it is suggested, as a result of the stresses caused over the death of his son and the coincident bad relations with the Emperor.

**Julius III (1550 to 1555).** A Roman scholar of the law and theology, he achieved little more than a reputation for nepotism and the spreading of sexual innuendo concerning a youth that he took from the streets and elevated to the rank of Cardinal. Having failed in political ambitions, he is said to have retreated to his luxury residence from where he made occasional ineffective forays into the milieu of the reform movement associated with the Council of Trent.

Of interest in an English context is the brief restoration of the Catholic Church during the reign of English Queen Mary I ("Bloody Mary"), half-sister of Queen Elizabeth I ("Good Queen Beth").

It was Elizabeth's sister, the vile Queen Mary I who, in 1553 following the tragically brief reign of King Edward VI, instigated the burning of 300 Protestants at the stake.

**Marcellus II (1555).** Variously described as coming from Tuscany, Siena, or the Papal States, he died after less than a month in office.

**Paul IV (1555 to 1559).** A Neapolitan nobleman, he indulged in prolific nepotism and lost the respect of the people. He promoted a brother and nephews to military positions that they then abused, and he allied with the French, living to see the folly of that. He rejected the claim to the English throne by Queen Elizabeth I on the basis that she was illegitimate, and he strengthened the Inquisition, banned Protestant books and translations of the Bible, stopped Michelangelo's pension, and ordered that the nudes in "The Last Judgement" in the Sistine Chapel should be painted more modestly (it didn't happen). In 1555 he issued a canon (a papal law) that created the Roman Ghetto, within which Jews were obliged to live, being locked in at night and having to wear something that identified them as Jews – a yellow hat for men, and shawls for women. Overall he is characterised by his aggressive austerity.

In an international context his reign saw the end of the Italian Wars, with the last conflict, known as the Hapsburg-Valois War, lasting from 1551 to 1559. French King Francis I died in March, 1547, and he was succeeded by his son King Henri II who decided to again attempt to best the Hapsburgs and become the leader of Europe.

French King Henri II was spurred on when the Genoese soldier of fortune, Andrea D'Oria, succeeded in getting a foothold in Tunisia for Emperor Charles V in 1550, and the turn of the French began with an allied

## The Two Thousand Year War – Papal Hegemony

Ottoman rampage via the islands of Malta and Gozo, and the siege of Tripoli in 1551 where about 5,000 Christian slaves were taken for sale in the Turkish markets. By 1553 the French had given Christian people and their lands to the Ottoman Turks, and King Henri II had the strategic island of Corsica for himself. French duplicity and treachery towards European peoples could apparently sink no lower.

On the continent of Europe battles raged between 1552 and 1556, with French King Henri II supported by German Protestants who were more opposed to their own German Catholics than specifically in favour of the equally Catholic Henri. A treaty (Vaucelles) was signed between Spanish King Felipe II and French King Henri II in February 1556, but although it didn't last, by this time the protagonists were getting worn out.

Complications grew when Emperor Charles V gradually abdicated his territories over the years 1554 to 1558 and the Holy Roman Empire was split into two; the first part under his son who became Spanish King Felipe II was the axis of Spain, The Netherlands, Naples, Milan and the Spanish Americas; the second part under his brother who became Holy Roman Emperor Ferdinand I consisted of diverse German principalities, Austria, Slovenia, Bohemia, Hungary and Croatia, Ferdinand eventually receiving full title to what was now a reduced Holy Roman Empire in 1558.

At this time, near the end of yet another long war, fighting among Spaniards, Austrians, English, and French became more prevalent in the western areas of Flanders, Calais, The Netherlands, Belgium, and Luxembourg. By 1559 the coffers were empty and these European armies were at a standstill, which made possible The Peace of Cateau-Cambrésis which was signed between English Queen Elizabeth I and French King Henri II on the 2$^{nd}$ April, and between Henri II and Spanish King Felipe II on the 3$^{rd}$ April, 1559. Sixty-five years of Franco-Spanish hegemony in Italy were ended.

Before summarising the outcome of that Sixty-five Year War, it is important to note the effects on the European Slave Trade of the French alliance with the Ottomans. In addition to the reference above, in 1558, the Ottoman fleet raged along the Italian coast with apparently little strategic objective or effect except for the sacking of Sorrento near Naples, at this time still part of the Spanish territories in southern Italy. 3,000 captives were taken at Sorrento, and further into this slaving expedition that was facilitated by France, the Balearic islands just off continental Spain were similarly pillaged and a further 4,000 people were taken for the Turkish slave markets. So between 1551 and 1558, in this theatre alone, more than 12,000 Europeans (including the 5,000 that were taken after the siege of Tripoli in 1551) were sold into Islamic eastern slavery with the help of France; and these were just the largest individual harvests. Countless more had been taken or butchered, and so, five years after their previous apparent nadir, France had descended even further.

## 16.26 Anno Domini 1559 to 1618

### 16.26.1 Context

#### 16.26.1.1 1559 Hapsburg Spain Leads Europe

- 1603 Scottish King James VI inherited the English throne as English King James I, an event known as the Union of the Crowns.
- An Eighty Year War began during this period. It would become a Dutch War of Independence (1568 to 1648).
- Other players of the time were:
- English Queen Elizabeth I (1558 to 1603).
- Galileo Galilei (1564 to 1642).
- Johannes Kepler (1571 to 1630).

#### 16.26.1.2 Outcome in the Late 16$^{th}$ Century

For the French there was an improvement over the situation in which they found themselves at the start of the 16$^{th}$ century, with gains of territory and an increase in their ranking in terms of international respect as an equal world power. The downside for the French was a complete failure to get any foothold in Italy, and the fact that they were still surrounded by the Hapsburgs who possessed Spain and also a huge area of present-day Germany. Lurking in the background was the prospect of a conflict with an unfettered Protestantism that would divide France for centuries. See the section on the Huguenots that is a part of the chapter in Volume Two titled *The Holy Roman Empire (800 or) 962 to 1806*.

In the case of the Hapsburgs, as a dynasty with two heads ruling both Spain and the Holy Roman Empire, the wars had weakened them by introducing disunity as a result of the separate inheritance of sovereignty, compounded by fragmentation into religious regions with inconsistent papal authority.

For the Kingdom of Spain under Spanish King Felipe II, the result was infinitely better: Spain enjoyed undisputed dominance of Italy; it had achieved successful rapprochement with the French by the marriage of the Spanish King Felipe II (following the death of his first wife English Queen Mary I) to the daughter of French King Henri II; and it was continuing to expand into American territories.

Conversely, England was in a bad situation at this time with no foothold in continental Europe and with a seriously damaged reputation. This would have to change or invasion by one or more European super-powers would surely follow within decades.

### 16.26.2 The Popes of the Period 1559 to 1618

**Pius IV (1559 to 1565).** From Milan, he was possibly related to the Medicis of Florence though much less prominent. He was the opposite in temperament to his predecessor, and he immediately gave amnesty to Pope Paul IV's antagonists and had that pope's nefarious nephews executed. Although nepotistic, he restarted the Council of Trent, and among extremely opposed delegates he unified and reformed the Catholic Church, bringing the twenty-fifth and final session of the Council to a close. Although the turmoil caused by the Reformation was by no means over, and the Catholic Church had lost many of its adherents, three hundred years would elapse before another such council was convened to settle matters of Church doctrine and practice.

Conditions in Rome at the time were poor, and though Pope Pius IV continued reconstruction and renovations, the budget was not helped by a papal obligation to help finance the war against the Turks who at this time were pushing through Hungary. The Franco-Ottoman alliance is of great significance at this time, and with the Holy Leagues is the subject of separate overviews.

**Saint Pius V (1566 to 1572).** From Lombardy, he was from a noble but impoverished family. He was pious, and enforced the decrees of the Council of Trent, augmenting these with his own generosity to the poor, and displaying personal behaviour that was in accordance with his time as a Dominican. He supported the Scottish Queen Mary I – Mary Queen of Scots aka Queen Mary Stuart, and he backed insurrections in England, such as one that failed in the north of England in 1569 that was led by the Earls of Northumberland and Westmorland; also the Ridolfi Plot that was an attempt in 1570 to prepare the way for Scottish Mary by assassinating Queen Elizabeth I. After that failure the Pope issued a Papal Bull that excommunicated Elizabeth and further interfered in England's affairs by encouraging all English Catholics to help depose her. In 1571 Pope Pius V organised another Holy League to confront the Ottomans initially in the eastern Mediterranean, and it met with great success at the Battle of Lepanto the same year. His dream at this time was to unite all European forces to oppose the advance of Islam, but sadly he died while just beginning to formulate real plans.

On the domestic front he improved the water supply and sanitation of Rome, and further afield he helped with the cost of fortifications at Valletta, Malta.

**Gregory XIII (1572 to 1585).** From Bologna, and originally an academic of the law, his name was given to the calendar he commissioned to replace the Julian Calendar – the Gregorian Calendar – an international standard at the present time. It was no doubt formulated with contributions from the great renaissance thinkers and with worldwide wisdom to which Europe was increasingly becoming exposed. The story of the acceptance of the calendar is worth a book by itself – it was only adopted by Greece for example, in 1923. Pope Gregory continued the hope of Saint Pius V for a European alliance against the Ottomans and the other diverse Islamic forces, but he was frustrated in this by divisions within

Europe, such as separate treaties involving Venice and Spain, and by the ongoing Franco-Ottoman European treason. He furthered remote missions to India, China, and the Philippines, and even saw conversions of aristocratic magnates or *Daimyos* in Japan.

Pope Gregory XIII used his ranks of Jesuits and other politico-religious orders to combat Protestantism and to further the geopolitical ambitions of the papacy; an example being the landings of nearly one thousand troops in Ireland during the years 1578 and 1579 to help with potential rebellion and prepare for a possible Spanish - Spanish Netherlands invasion. It would be a decade before anything was to come of this.

An English connection worthy of note is his pre-papal role as a tutor of the future Cardinal Reginald Pole who was the last Catholic Archbishop of Canterbury, and whose patron at one time was King Henry VIII. Pole was made a Cardinal under Pope Paul III in 1536 and Archbishop of Canterbury under Pope Paul IV in 1556, the latter post being held by him for only two years, while also about this time he was Chancellor of both Oxford and Cambridge Universities.

Pole, a second cousin of "Bloody Mary" (English Queen Mary I), was a prominent and dangerously powerful but vulnerable individual, and in the tit-for-tat heretical burnings and beheadings during the reigns of the half-sisters Mary I and Elizabeth I, Reginald Pole's family were monstrously persecuted, imprisoned and executed. His mother, after protesting her innocence, is described as being hacked to death by an inexperienced executioner as she tried, while screaming, to escape the scaffold after the first blow failed to remove her head.

**Sixtus V (1585 to 1590).** From the Papal States, he has been said by some to have had Croat or Slavic ancestry. He inherited a lawless countryside with apparently thousands of brigands, all of whom were shortly and mercilessly eliminated. In 1585 he declared Henry of Navarre aka King Henri IV to be a heretic due to his conversion to the Huguenot Protestant persuasion.

Finding the papal coffers empty, Sixtus acquired significant gold and silver reserves by cost cutting and taxation, while at the same time spending on infrastructure, religious buildings, and sanitation. He reiterated the excommunication of English Queen Elizabeth I, offered a large sum to Spanish King Felipe II to help with the Armada (fortunately for the Pope's budget it was contingent on the Armada actually landing), and to that end instructed the (ex-pat) English Cardinal Allen to prepare a document to be used during the occupation to bring to justice the Queen and anyone else who was opposed to the Pope. Allen, like many other Jesuits, had received an English university education where they had become radicalised, and from where they moved to complete their preparations for undercover work to seminaries in Rome or other Catholic enclaves such as the seminary or English College at Douai in northern France.

The failure of the Armada in 1588 saw Allen and no doubt many other English Jesuits obliged to remain in Rome from where they would continue an opposition in exile. The overall process of such radicalisation of the priesthood was considered part of the grand strategy of the Counter-Reformation, but it was really more than that, being a root and branch mobilisation of Catholic resources. It is interesting to compare the work and the contextual results of the 16$^{th}$ century Roman Catholic Seminary with that of the 21$^{st}$ century Islamic Madrasah.

Despite the apparently benevolent rule of Pope Sixtus V, his statue in Rome was torn down by the mob as soon as he died.

**Urban VII (1590).** The son of a Genoese nobleman and of the sister of a Roman Cardinal, having made a genuinely benevolent start he died after only thirteen days, the shortest reign of any pope.

**Gregory XIV (1590 to 1591).** From Lombardy, his main activity during another brief reign, and with encouragement from Spanish King Felipe II, was to support the French League in its opposition to Henry of Navarre aka Good King Henry, or to give him his crowned title, French King Henri IV. For more information see the section on the Huguenots that is a part of the chapter in Volume Two titled *The Holy Roman Empire (800 or) 962 to 1806*. Pope Gregory XIV funded the Catholic faction and issued instructions to the French to renounce their King or face the direst consequences, so he may justifiably be considered responsible for the actions of one François Ravaillac, a Catholic fanatic, who murdered the good King Henri IV in 1610. Pope Gregory XIV had spent his brief reign in bad health, suffering from malaria and possibly dying from a gallstone.

**Innocent IX (1591).** A lawyer from Bologna, he had already been heavily involved in papal governance during Gregory XIV's reign due to that pope's frequent infirmity, and he continued the same policies.

**Clement VIII (1592 to 1605).** From a historic Florentine family, and born at Fano, north-east Italy, he had a background in the law and was noted for hard work. In 1592 he immediately got to work eliminating banditry among the lowlife, and indicting among the nobility various alleged criminal acts of debatable authenticity, making sure that his own family expropriated the possessions of those executed.

He had heretics burned at the stake, including in 1600, Giordano Bruno, a Dominican friar and scientist, who proposed that the universe was populated with many stars and habitable worlds with intelligent beings. Another infamous issue concerned the papal sanction for the butchery of the entire family of an alleged notorious wife beater and child abuser, Francesco Cenci, who was murdered, according to testimonies extracted under torture in the Pope's dungeons, by members of his family who could take no more. The Pope and his family were the beneficiaries of the confiscated estates.

In 1592 his anti-Semitic legislation included a Papal Bull forbidding Jews living in a community in Avignon from selling new goods, and in 1593 he reiterated Pope Pius V's earlier decree that restricted Jews to living in the cities of Rome, Ancona, and Avignon.

In 1593 King Henri IV appeared to reject his Calvinist stance and return to the Catholic fold, and in 1595 when Clement thought Henri really meant it, he absolved him, which conveniently got Henri onside to deter any aggression in the Italian theatre that might possibly come from Spain or the Empire – Spain was already at war with France in 1595. Henri's absolution also gave the Pope confidence to expand his own possessions by marching into the vacant state of Ferrara after its Duke had died without an heir in 1597. Clement's international success didn't stop there, and in

1598 the Treaty of Vervins between Spain and France that was brokered by the Pope's emissary, a Medici, increased his credibility still further.

Only the Republic of Savoy now remained at war with France in what is known as the Franco-Savoyard War aka the War of Saluzzo (a French annexe in the Savoy region) that peaked in 1600 and 1601 after its Duke was defeated by Henri in 1599. It was now a confirmed peacemaker Pope that brokered yet another deal, The Treaty of Lyon in 1601 by which France, Spain, and Savoy settled all their differences with some exchange of territories between France and Savoy.

Keeping in with the Holy Roman Emperor, Clement gave him valuable assistance, both financially and with troops, in the Hungarian theatre against the Turkish Ottomans.

**Leo XI (1605).** Pope Leo XI was a Florentine with connections to the Medicis, he was strongly opposed to nepotism but died after less than four weeks on the throne.

## 16.27 Anno Domini 1618 to 1700
### 16.27.1 Context
#### 16.27.1.1 War, Peace, and Papal Brutality

- The period was characterised by Bourbon-Hapsburg Rivalry.
- Ascendancy Note: France.
- Fading Power: Spain.
- The Thirty Year War.

The Thirty Year War (1618 to 1648) was really a series of wars that were notionally ended by The Peace of Westphalia in 1648 which was also instrumental in ending what can be regarded as an Eighty Year War – the latter being specifically to do with Dutch independence from Spain – the Dutch War of Independence (1568 to 1648).

In 1648 at the end of that protracted period of warfare the population of Europe had shrunk from thirty million souls to twenty millions; and not unlike the continuous nature of conflict and ignored lessons during and just after the Hundred Year War, the Peace of Westphalia was followed in less than a generation by the Franco-Dutch War (1672 to 1678) and the Nine Year War (1688 to 1697) – the English Glorious Revolution having coincided with the start of that Nine Year War in 1688.

Other players of the time were:

- Johannes Kepler (1571 to 1630).
- Galileo Galilei (1564 to 1642).
- John Locke (1632 to 1704).
- Spanish King Felipe IV (1605 to 1665).
- Spanish King Carlos II (1661 to 1700).

### 16.27.1.2 The Thirty Year War – Combatants
This sectarian war would grind on from 1618 until 1648.

---

**Protestant States and Allies**

Sweden, France (1635), Bohemia, Denmark-Norway (1625 to 1629), Saxony, United Provinces, Electorate of the Palatinate, Brunswick-Lüneburg, England (1625 to 1630), Scotland, Brandenburg-Prussia, Transylvania, Hungarian Anti-Hapsburg Rebels, Zaporozhian Cossacks, Ottoman Empire

*versus*

**Roman Catholic States and Allies**

Holy Roman Empire, Catholic League, Austria, Kingdom of Hungary, Kingdom of Croatia, Spanish Empire, Denmark-Norway (1643 to 1645)

---

### 16.27.1.3 The First Anglo-Dutch War (1652 to 1654)
With the East India Companies of both England and the Dutch Republic competing for world trade, and Dutch opportunism during England's Civil War, the English Commonwealth under the Lord Protector Oliver Cromwell sought to shift the balance back in its favour by

introducing a Navigation Act in 1651 – protectionism that required the carrying of English goods destined for the American colonies in particular, to be done by English ships. A further benefit would be an increase in England's inventory of merchant ships that might be commandeered in wartime.

The First Anglo-Dutch War was declared by England in 1652, and after gains and losses by both sides, with England's larger fleet generally winning, the war was ended by the Treaty of Westminster in 1654.

### 16.27.1.4 The Second Anglo-Dutch War (1665 to 1667)

By now a monarchy again under English King Charles II, England's unprovoked seizure in 1664 of New Amsterdam, later renamed New York, and its attacks on Dutch trading posts in Africa, led to the second war that briefly drew in the German principality of Münster on England's side in 1665, and France on the side of the Dutch United Provinces during the English plague and Great Fire year of 1666. Land-based conflicts were limited, and the results of naval battles were mixed, though a notable Dutch triumph was their raid on the English river Medway when several English ships were destroyed at anchor at Chatham in 1667. Although the war was quickly ended the same year by the Treaty of Breda, a wider context of unrest and scheming between France and England would lead to a resurgence and the spreading of the conflagration.

### 16.27.1.5 The War of Devolution (1667 to 1668)

The brief War of Devolution was a consequence of French attempts to impose a rule of succession that was sometimes employed regionally in the Spanish Netherlands, and that stipulated the superiority of a claim by a daughter of an earlier marriage to that of a son by a later one. In this case French King Louis XIV started the war with the premise that such a rule of succession ought to also be enforceable at a national level such as the change of the head of a sovereign state. He furthermore demanded that his wife, Marie-Thérèse, should be the one to succeed her father, Spanish King Felipe IV (1605 to 1665), to the title of Spain's territories in the Netherlands instead of Carlos El Hechizado – Charles II the Mad, who was her half-brother and also younger. As mentioned elsewhere, Louis was of the

House of Bourbon, and Carlos aka Charles II, was a Hapsburg, so rivalry was virtually genetic – literally so in the case of Carlos, the dysfunctional product of aristocratic in-breeding.

The French invaded present-day Flanders, and after an agreement between France and the Holy Roman Empire to carve up the territory between them, but with the threat of opposition and further war from an alliance of England, Spain, the Dutch, and Sweden, the Treaty of Aix-la-Chapelle in 1668 was hastily signed to prevent any widening of the conflict.

The Treaty of Aix-la-Chapelle left France with many of the border towns that we see today, such as Armentières, Douai, and Lille, and some towns that would later become part of Belgium, such as Charleroi, Kortrijk (Courtrai), and Tournai. Conflict between the two cultural claimants to these areas, Walloons (French) and Flamands (Flemish), would continue to result in deaths into the second half of the 20th century, and to keep alive political claim and counter-claim into the 21st.

### 16.27.1.6 The Third Anglo-Dutch War (1672 to 1674)

This war was part of the wider conflict better known as the Franco-Dutch War, as detailed below.

### 16.27.1.7 Map – French Attack on the Dutch Republic 1672

Map from http://commons.wikimedia.org/wiki/Category:Maps released under CC-BY-SA
http://creativecommons.org/licenses/by-sa/3.0/

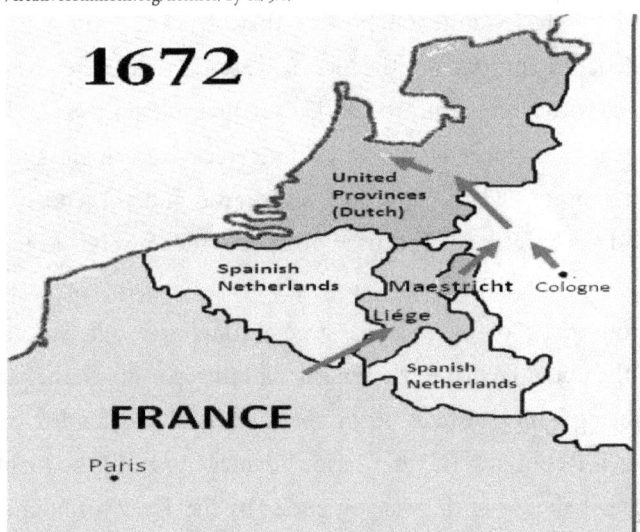

### 16.27.1.8 The Franco-Dutch War – Combatants

Although it appeared to be relatively short-lived, just six wasteful years from 1672 until 1678, it was, of course, a part of the much longer European wars of self-destruction.

---

France, England, Sweden, Bishopric of Münster, Archbishopric of Cologne

*versus*

Dutch Republic, Holy Roman Empire, Spain, Brandenburg

---

At the start of the period, in the spring of 1672, England under English King Charles II joined France under French King Louis XIV and declared war on the Dutch Republic, more correctly known at that time as the Republic of the Seven United Provinces. England's contribution, except for a moderate military contingent including the future Duke of Marlborough, was in the form of its navy, while the majority of land forces were supplied by the continental powers that struck up through the Spanish Netherlands and in from the Germanic states that lay to the east. A resurgence of Dutch forces on land and at sea after initial losses, and the entry to the war in support of the Dutch of forces from Spain and the Holy Roman Empire, led to England's withdrawal and the end of the Third Anglo-Dutch War in February 1674 by the Second Peace of Westminster.

Another four years of often static siege warfare saw relatively little change from the initial French territorial gains in the Spanish Netherlands, that region being quite distinct from the successfully defended more northerly Dutch Republic, and after serious damage to both the finances and the morale of all parties the war was ended by the Treaty of Nijmegen in 1678 which left France as the overall, albeit small-scale winner.

From England's point of view a serious rapprochement with the Dutch would now be most welcome. There was internal English division between a Protestant Parliament and a Catholic Monarchy, and a flirtation had commenced with William of Orange that within a decade would lead to the Glorious Revolution.

### 16.27.1.9 The Nine Year War – Combatants

Another nine years of killing from 1688 to 1697.

---

Dutch Republic, England, Holy Roman Empire, Spain, Piedmont-Savoy, Sweden, Scotland

*versus*

France, Irish Jacobites, Scottish Jacobites

---

The conflict above spanned the papacies of Blessed Pope Innocent XI, Pope Alexander VIII, and Pope Innocent XII, (see below).

### 16.27.1.10 Map – European Powers in 1648

Map from http://commons.wikimedia.org/wiki/Category:Maps released under CC-BY-SA
http://creativecommons.org/licenses/by-sa/3.0/

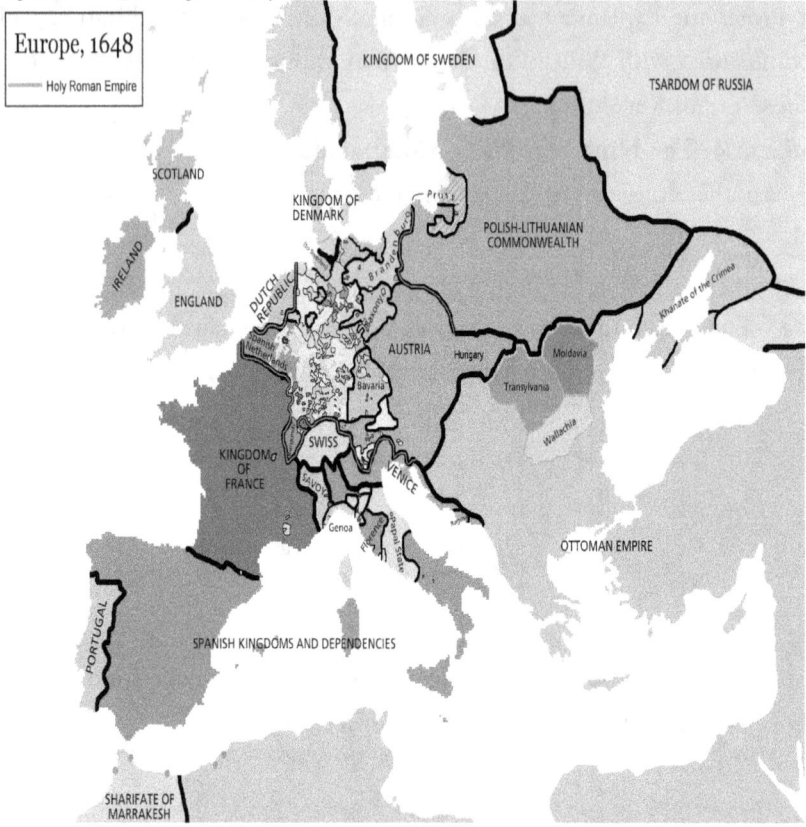

### 16.27.2 The Popes of the Period 1618 to 1700

**Paul V (1605 to 1621).** Born in Rome into the Borghese family from Siena, he had the reputation of being an authoritarian lawyer, and most of the issues of his reign seem to relate to disagreements with other Italian states, mainly Venice, and in respect of the accountability of the clergy to secular law.

Internationally, relations with England were understandably frosty following The Gunpowder Plot of 1605, but in response to a visit from a Samurai, missionaries were sent to Japan in 1615. Universally accepted as being just about as nepotistic as all the other popes, he nevertheless achieved much in respect of church restoration, and at least something in respect of public works.

**Gregory XV (1621 to 1623).** He was from an aristocratic Bolognese family, and nepotistic ecclesiastical and military appointments, and awards of Dukedoms, began in earnest right at the start of his reign, though he did also institute electoral reforms. He was educated by Jesuits, and he maintained an interest in them while not becoming overtly involved in international politics except, that is, when it came to financing the elimination of Protestants, and prosecuting the defence against the Muslims; he did help the King of the Polish–Lithuanian Commonwealth against the Ottoman Empire.

In 1623 his was the last decree against witchcraft – the death penalty was now to be enforced only when it was proved (!) that there was a link with the devil and that deaths had actually resulted from that diabolical link. To strengthen the papacy's evangelical ambitions, in 1622 Gregory established the "Congregation of Propaganda Fide", otherwise known as the "Sacred Congregation for the Propagation of the Faith".

**Urban VIII (1623 to 1644).** The son of a wealthy Florentine nobleman and merchant, he too was educated by Jesuits, and he began his reign with a clutch of canonisations and beatifications, followed by the customary orgy of nepotism that enriched and empowered his family to a fabulous extent. His twenty-one year reign fell entirely within the Thirty Year War, a horror during which he did nothing compassionate for his flock, although in a possibly sinister vein, the "Sacred Congregation for the Propagation of the Faith" emerged as nothing less than a plan for world domination by whatever means, and Pope Urban VIII expanded its worldwide scope from that established by his predecessor, founding in 1627 a training college to support and further enhance the initiative.

Other events of note were as follows: In 1633 he summoned Galileo to Rome to recant his heretical heliocentric ideology; a few years later he deregulated the missionary trade to China and Japan so as to include Orders other than just the Jesuits; and in 1626 he began a series of military adventures against other Italian states and families that would see many killed in fighting and by execution, and that would last until the end of the Wars of Castro during the next pope's reign in 1649 – Castro was the name of an Italian city that was destroyed during Papal military campaigns, see below.

Urban VIII is said by some to have been the last pope to go to war, and the last to indulge in territorial aggrandisement, but the actions of some of his successors would seem to refute this. In pursuit of his last warlike fling, he created arms factories, fortified castles and infrastructure, and he even established an arsenal in the Vatican.

Overseas, in 1640 Portugal became independent of Spain and the Spanish Hapsburg Dynasty, at that time personified by the Spanish King Felipe III, and in order to placate Spain, Pope Urban VIII and Pope Innocent X both refused approbation to any bishop nominated by the new monarch, Portuguese King John IV of the Braganza Dynasty.

**Innocent X (1644 to 1655).** Another Jesuit educated law academic, he was from Rome and a descendant of Pope Alexander VI. Early in his reign he was involved in a spat with France when three brothers (nephews of Pope Urban VIII) of the wealthy and influential Barberini family fled to the protection of Cardinal Mazarin in Paris after the Pope brought charges against them of stealing public funds. The three brothers, a mixture of ranks comprising Cardinal, Archbishop, and military commander, had been the recipients of the nepotistic benefices of Urban VIII. The latest Pope, of course, confiscated their property, but after the French parliament rebuked him, and after Cardinal Mazarin threatened to invade the Papal States, the Pope backed down and was more or less reconciled with the Barberini, especially when his niece married into the wealthy family.

During the reign of Innocent X, the Peace of Westphalia was signed over a six month period during 1648, bringing to an end not just the complex Thirty Year War (Geo-Religious: Hapsburgs, France, Spain, Catholic, Protestant, Bohemia and more...), but also the longer eighty or so years of conflict known as the Dutch War of Independence from 1568 to 1648 (Geo-Religious: Spain, Netherlands, England, Huguenots, and multiple principalities...).

The Dutch Republic was now sovereign, and opposing religious beliefs were, at least for now, more respected if still not universally accepted.

During the English civil war of 1642 to 1649 that equally affected Ireland, the Pope fed the flames with money and armaments for Ireland in an attempt to reinstate Catholic supremacy there, only to see no immediate progress when the Parliamentarians were victorious. Ongoing religious and cultural strife would, of course, continue to the present day.

Pope Innocent X's final warlike act in 1649 was to destroy the town of Castro in the Duchy of Parma over unpaid returns on investments and the alleged murder of the Bishop of Castro. Elsewhere however, in continuing belligerent mood, he issued a Bull that attempted to nullify the parts of the Treaty of Westphalia that he thought didn't suit the Catholic agenda.

His final Bull of note was in 1653, and it was against Jansenism, an heretical movement started in the Low Countries (Netherlands) and France as a result of a manuscript by Cornelius Otto Jansen that was published in 1640, a couple of years after his death. It is too complex to do it justice in a brief summary, and all that can be said here is that the Jansenists believed that the Catholic Counter-Reformation had gone too far in the opposite direction to the equally flawed arguments of Luther on issues such as original sin, grace, and divinity. The Jansenists, although Catholic, seemed to be suggesting that the Counter-Reformation had fallen into the mindset of the Pelagian heresy (one of the first dissidents in this book), and that the Jesuits and even the Pope needed to shape up and remember the roots of the early church.

**Alexander VII (1655 to 1667).** From one of the most powerful families in Italy, the Tuscan Chigi bankers, he was related to Pope Paul V, and was an academic in law, theology and philosophy. The prime minister of the government of French King Louis XIV at this time was the same Cardinal Mazarin who had already crossed swords, almost literally, with the Pontiff in his pre-papal days, and relations with France were strained throughout. Having started with an apparent aversion to nepotism, he succumbed to the temptation by the second year, and showered his relatives with papal and civil positions, palaces, and estates.

Pope Alexander VII was a strong supporter of the Jesuits, encouraging them against the Jansenist heresy in France, and in return for papal help that had been given to the Venetians against the Ottomans, the Pope managed to get the Jesuits accepted back into Venice from where they had been expelled in 1606.

He ensured that the *Index of Forbidden Books* contained prohibitions of the works of the heliocentricists, and, unbelievably, such entries would persist until 1835.

**Clement IX (1667 to 1669).** From a noble Tuscan family, he was educated by the Jesuits and seems to have been genuinely and selflessly against nepotism and all forms of personal gain.

Internationally he was successful in brokering a peace at the end of the War of Devolution (1667 to 1668) between Spain and France. That papal achievement had been made during a year or so of negotiations (1668 to 1669) at the Treaty of Aachen, where the international peacekeeping force was the Triple Alliance of England, Sweden, and the Dutch Republic aka United Provinces, the latter being the forerunner of the present-day Netherlands.

Louis XIV's claim to the Spanish Netherlands during that war had been thin to non-existent, and he was obliged by the peace treaty to return all of his gains. The area would eventually manifest itself as sovereign Belgium, and the armed conflict alluded to earlier between its French speaking Walloons and Dutch speaking Flamands would continue to the present day.

Pope Clement IX has been regarded as one of the most "pleasant" of all the popes, but he was to die in sadness when the Venetian fortress of Heraklion, aka Candia on the island of Crete, fell to the Ottoman Empire in 1669 after some twenty-one years of siege. It is reckoned to be one of the longest sieges ever.

The Pope's grief at this juncture was increased because for years he had been trying to alert and unite Europe in respect of the threat and, had he been successful in that, Crete may have continued in Christian hands instead of becoming an Ottoman vassal state for the next two hundred years.

**Clement X (1670 to 1676).** From long established Roman nobility, he pronounced a considerable list of canonisations and beatifications in his second year. Little else is of note apart from some controversies about the level of tax on imports into Rome, and questions about his financial support of the King of Poland in his struggle against the Ottomans. It would not be long before the Polish would be instrumental in saving Europe from Islamic invasion at the Gates of Vienna in 1683.

**Blessed Innocent XI (1676 to 1689).** Blessed Innocent XI was the son of a nobleman from Como, Lombardy, and he was educated in law aka jurisprudence by the Jesuits. He immediately set about reforming the ministries (the Papal Curia), eliminating nepotism, and prescribing frugality and abstinence; and within a short time the papal accounts were in the black. His puritanical posture, however, was taken to extremes when he closed theatres and temporarily stopped operatic performances.

In 1685 he provoked particularly the French by abolishing the right of asylum by which foreign embassies in Rome could shelter anyone being prosecuted under papal law, a dispensation that had been abused for many years.

In 1687 he reluctantly condemned the latest heresy of Quietism, a sort of meditative or introspective state of Grace that might lead to a better understanding of God. Although it was not a new idea but something stretching back centuries to earlier mystics, it was its recent reappearance as a Christian philosophy that rankled with the Roman Catholic who knew better.

French King Louis XIV was intent on consolidating *royal* control over the appointment of senior clergy in regions of France to the detriment of that of the Pope but, when the Pope complained, Louis ingratiated himself by revoking the Edict of Nantes (covered in Volume Two), and giving the Huguenots a severe beating. Further disagreements, however, led to a small French force invading Pope Innocent's palace. The estrangement concerning France and the Vatican was increased still further by controversy over the appointment of an archbishop for Cologne in 1688 that resulted in Louis XIV annexing Avignon and its resident papal representative. That representative, responsible for both political and ecclesiastical matters, was known as the *Nuncio*.

Probably fortunately, French Louis' principal supporter, the decidedly Catholic English King James II, was removed from the scene in 1688 by the Glorious Revolution, the event that saw the arrival in England, by invitation, of William of Orange who was decidedly Protestant. A potentially damaging confrontation between Pope and French King therefore fizzled out, and it has strangely been suggested that Pope Innocent may have funded the overthrow of English King James II because he disagreed with his imprudent attempts to re-establish Catholicism. A Papal loan was indeed made to William of Orange, but its connection with that specific political outcome is contentious.

In 1683 the Ottoman siege of Vienna was lifted by the seminal Battle of Vienna, which was a great relief to the Pope who had helped one of the main protagonists, the Polish King John III, with massive cash injections. The Blessed Innocent was further gratified by the fall of Belgrade to the Holy League in 1688. The Holy League that had been formed in 1684 consisted initially of the Holy Roman Empire, the Polish-Lithuanian Commonwealth, and the Republic of Venice; it was possibly Pope Innocent XI's greatest legacy, and the League was strengthened immeasurably when it was joined around 1686 by a colossus in the shape of the Russian Tsardom. This would be potentially an unstoppable war machine if its theatres of operation were not too diverse.

A final bizarre note concerns the exhumation of Innocent's body in 1956 when it was retrieved for beatification. After 267 years it was found to be free from corruption (i.e. the corpse did not appear to have rotted), and so it was decorated with silver and placed in a glass and bronze sarcophagus. This unhealthy reverence for corpses and bits of corpses happened in the 20th century, and it is an apt and fitting comment on the grotesquely immutable nature of religious ideologies and their principal practitioners.

This is one more piece of evidence for the case that humanity has not advanced one jot in more than three millennia.

**Alexander VIII (1689 to 1691).** The son of the Venetian chancellor and an expert in civil law, his reign is mainly remembered for his nepotistic squandering of the Papal Treasury, the proceeds of which were directed to his own family's enrichment. Pope Alexander VII also made financial contributions to the efforts of Venice in its defence against the Ottoman, and in material terms, sent some galleys and thousands of troops for the Holy League's Albanian theatre of operations.

**Innocent XII (1691 to 1700).** From a prestigious Neapolitan family and educated by the Jesuits, he was against all nepotism and was benevolent towards those in need, even converting part of the Lateran Palace into a hospital for the poor. He banned the official post of Cardinal-nephew, and issued a Bull decreeing that a pope could raise no more than one of his own relatives to the position of Cardinal. Totally at odds with many of his predecessors, he seemed to favour the French over the Holy Roman Empire, and some of his dealings and recommendations are said to have contributed to the climate in which arose the War of the Spanish Succession.

## 16.28 Anno Domini 1700 to 1769
### 16.28.1 Context
#### 16.28.1.1 Bourbon Expansion and Wars of Succession

- Ascendancy Note: Great Britain.
- The Treaty of Union of 1706 specified the terms for the union of England and Scotland, and it was codified by two Acts of Parliament: 1706 The Union with Scotland Act in the English parliament, and 1707 The Union with England Act in the Scottish parliament.
- The Development of liberalism: François-Marie Arouet, alias Voltaire, (1694 to 1778), said: "... *the Holy Roman Empire is "neither Holy, nor Roman, nor an Empire...*"

### 16.28.1.2 The Emergence of Prussia.

In 1688 one of the Hohenzollern dynasty became Elector Frederick III of the Margraviate of Brandenburg. An Elector was a member of the Electoral College that decided who would take the title of Holy Roman Emperor – that title being, theoretically at least, an elective as opposed to a hereditary title, and conferring the three concepts of jurisdiction, sovereignty, and command, over a range of states and principalities. So, in addition to the role of Elector within the Holy Roman Empire, Frederick was now a Margrave – a centuries-old title meaning military governor – of Brandenburg, but he was also the Duke of Prussia, and Prussia was neither a part of the Holy Roman Empire nor a kingdom – it was just a Duchy of the quite separate dominion of the Polish-Lithuanian Commonwealth, although it was a colossal land area and of great significance.

Frederick's cross-border allegiance, or Personal Union, was not tenable in the long term – it had come about as a result of the Treaty of Warsaw in 1611, and possibly the complication had been overlooked in the confusion of the Thirty Year War (1618 to 1648) and the structural and demographic devastation of Brandenburg that followed that debilitating war. To satisfy Frederick's desire to be a king, the independent Kingdom of Prussia was therefore created in 1701, and the same year the title King "in" Prussia was unilaterally adopted by the Elector of Brandenburg, the erstwhile Duke becoming King Frederick I "in" Prussia so that it didn't imply any union with the Holy Roman Empire.

Now the Pope did not like this because it was his right to appoint kings, and Prussia was historically part of the old (really defunct) Teutonic Order. Additionally, his dislike of Frederick would have bordered on the fanatical, due to Frederick's father's Edict of Potsdam in 1685, by which Protestants in general, but Huguenots in particular, had been offered asylum in the territories of the Personal Union of Brandenburg and Prussia. The capital of Brandenburg at this time was a relatively unimportant city known as Berlin, and although the initially subdued Kings "in" Prussia would use that title during the period 1701 to 1772, they confirmed the emergence of what would grow by territorial aggrandisement to later become the

## The Two Thousand Year War – Papal Hegemony

dominant member, in terms of political, economic, and demographic clout, of the German Confederacy, and later Germany. Some interesting historical developments were taking place.

### 16.28.1.3 Map – The Growth of Prussia 1600 to 1795

Map from http://commons.wikimedia.org/wiki/Category:Maps released under CC-BY-SA
http://creativecommons.org/licenses/by-sa/3.0/

### 16.28.1.4 The War of Spanish Succession – Combatants

This gore-fest would spread well beyond the borders of Europe for thirteen years from 1701 to 1714.

---

#### The Grand Alliance

Holy Roman Empire; Great Britain (England and Scotland before the Act of Union of 1707); Dutch Republic; Spain loyal to the three HRE Hapsburgs Leopold I, Joseph I, and Charles VI; Duchy of Savoy; Kingdom of Prussia; Kingdom of Portugal

*versus*

#### The Two Crowns

Kingdom of France, Spain loyal to Bourbon Felipe V, Bavarian Electorate of Bavaria

---

### 16.28.1.5 The War of Spanish Succession – Background

At the end of the 17th century, despite possessing a huge empire, Spain was in decline, and Hapsburg Spanish King Carlos II, who was physically and mentally disabled (believed due to Hapsburg inbreeding) had no heir. Carlos' father, Spanish King Felipe IV (he was also Portuguese King Felipe III), had specified in his will that the succession should go to the Austrian Hapsburgs, but this would be contested. The nearest claimants by virtue of family relationships were two first cousins, the bellicose Bourbon French King Louis XIV and the Hapsburg Holy Roman Emperor Leopold I who was also King of Germany, King of Bohemia, King of Hungary, King of Croatia, and Archduke of Austria.

To complicate what might have been a simple two horse race in the year 1700, (despite HRE Leopold's long honorific title and geographic reach), French influence in internal Imperial affairs had been established by the notorious Roman Catholic Cardinal Mazarin, referred to earlier, who had played a part in the accession of Leopold and whose influence stretched to the definition of some of the diplomatic expectations of allegiance among France, Spain and the Empire. Other European powers, of course, were not ignorant of that unaffectionate triangle, and at stake was the balance of power, not just at the heart of the Western World, but potentially stretching onto the continent of the New World and to the distant settlements and spheres of influence in the Far East. The other contender for the Spanish throne was Philip, Duke of Anjou, who had been nominated in the will of the recently deceased Hapsburg Spanish King Carlos II, and who was the grandson of French King Louis XIV. The idea of a Bourbon Dynasty embracing both France and Spain, however, would have been unacceptable to those who subscribed to the absolutist mentality and wanted more clearly defined nationalism at a time when the concept of "the balance of power" was beginning to be discussed around the dinner table among politically astute power brokers. What might at one time have slipped under that table was now in focus for all to see.

### 16.28.1.6 The War of Spanish Succession – the Two Crowns

So, on one hand there were the forces of the Two Crowns: France under Louis XIV; and Spain now under the acting King Felipe V. The French State was a relatively youthful and truculent, aspiring adolescent, and the Spanish State was a greying, arthritic, but not yet toothless juggernaut.

Support for the Two Crowns also came from two components of the Holy Roman Empire: firstly, from the Electorate of Bavaria under Maximilian II. Maximilian was of changing allegiance – he had previously fought against France and against the Ottomans at Belgrade in 1688, but his personal agenda at this time was for his own dynasty, the Wittelsbach family, to replace the Hapsburgs as head of the Holy Roman Empire; and secondly, from the Electorate of Cologne under Joseph Clemens of Bavaria, the brother of Maximilian II, although given the fact that he fled to France in 1702 it's not obvious that his countrymen actually supported him.

Geographically, the Two Crowns comprised France, the French Americas, Spain, the Spanish Italian territories (Milan, Naples and Sicily), the Spanish Netherlands (various Dukedoms), the Spanish Americas, and the Spanish East Indies.

### 16.28.1.7 The War of Spanish Succession – the Grand Alliance

On the other hand, opposing the forces of the Two Crowns was the Grand Alliance consisting of: firstly, the young Dutch Republic aka United Provinces; secondly, the relatively old-established England and Scotland (soon to become Great Britain); and thirdly, the Holy Roman Empire (most of it), that was itself an uncomfortable alliance of individualist principalities as evidenced by the desertion of the Electors of Bavaria and Cologne mentioned above, but with the unlikely inclusion of some support from Spanish factions loyal to Holy Roman Emperor Charles VI, rather than to their own Spanish King Felipe V.

Complications at this time were aggravated because it was now one hundred and fifty years and eight Hapsburg Emperors since Emperor Charles V had begun the break up of his previously extensive and united empire in favour of his aristocratic descendants – further evidence of the consequences of succession issues. See detail in a previous section – *Anno Domini 1453 to 1559* – under the European stewardship of His Holiness Pope Paul IV *(1555 to 1559)*.

The Grand Alliance was joined later (1703) by the recently defined sovereign Portugal and the Duchy of Savoy; and geographically, the Grand Alliance comprised: Holland, the Dutch East Indies, England and Scotland, the English Americas, English territories in India and Africa, and the English East Indies.

### 16.28.1.8 The War of Spanish Succession – the War Itself

Ideologies and concepts that were at odds and that would lead to bigotry and atrocity, may be identified as the following with their sectarian variants: Absolutism (autocratic rule by a single head of State) and Absolute Monarchy; Constitutional Monarchy; Parliamentarianism / Republicanism (nascent democratic rule); Protestantism; and Catholicism. A foul and explosive brew – shared among allies as well as between enemies.

## The Two Thousand Year War – Papal Hegemony

The war began in 1701 in Italy when Austrian forces under Prince Eugene of Savoy attacked Milan. It quickly spread Europe-wide, and led to naval conflict in the Caribbean, and conflict in North America among regular French and English forces, but also among North American Indian tribes and settlers with unspeakable atrocities being committed there by all sides.

Of many battles, the one of most cultural significance to Britain was the victory at Blenheim by the Duke of Marlborough and Prince Eugene of Savoy in 1704. See the map below. Of strategic importance it was immense, and it saw the demise of Bavarian support for the Two Crowns, the assurance of security for Vienna – the fall of which would likely have broken the Grand Alliance – and the creation of a momentum that, with other successes, would lead to an assault on France herself.

A very brief summary is that Britain and France secretly negotiated a peace and maybe a protocol in 1711 before the war's end, and this facilitated the Peace of Utrecht. Felipe, the grandson of French King Louis XIV, was confirmed as Spanish King Felipe V, and he renounced any claim to the French throne. Some of Louis XIV's other descendants reciprocated by renouncing any claim to the Spanish throne. These dynastic demarcations satisfied some of the concerns that led to the war in the first place, but territorial aggrandisement, once stoked up, is not so easily stopped, and after Britain received a relatively simple but highly satisfactory pay-off, it would take some time to agree on the redistribution of Spain's many possessions, both in Europe and the New Worlds, among the remaining antagonists.

### 16.28.1.9 The War of Spanish Succession – The Peace of Utrecht

The war and its geographically diverse conflicts over the period 1701 to 1750 were ended by a series of treaties – Utrecht in 1713, Rastatt and Baden in 1714, and Madrid in 1750. Britain and France made peace in 1712 but war continued between France and the Holy Roman Empire until the treaties of Rastatt and Baden in 1714, and it continued between Spain and Portugal until the Treaty of Madrid in 1750. The Holy Roman Empire and Bourbon Spain concluded a peace in 1720.

Austria, then the seat of HRE Charles VI, received the Spanish Netherlands (later to become Belgium), Naples, Sardinia, and most of the Duchy of Milan.

Savoy received Sicily and some of the Duchy of Milan.

Portugal received parts of South America, notably Brazil.

Great Britain (following the Acts of Union) received Gibraltar and Minorca from Spain, and several North American territories and trading rights from France. It was some of the hype in Britain around this time that led to the madness of the South Sea Bubble, see elsewhere in the book.

The map of Europe after this war (see below) would be much closer to the one we know today, with Spain, France, and Great Britain easily recognisable, and with the birth of Italy and Germany happening in short order and fairly painlessly – although the progeny would become dysfunctional for a while. However, the agonising contraction of the Ottoman Empire towards a still distant Turkey, and in its turbulent wake the mutation of Balkan States with their impossible pedigree mix of culture, religious ideology, and ethnicity, would be very painful and mortal experiences that would be drawn out for almost another two hundred years; and there were future experimental sovereignties that would stretch around the eastern Mediterranean, but that were yet to be conceived.

So the war of Spanish Succession was brought to a conclusion by the Peace of Utrecht in 1713 that involved a series of Treaties of Utrecht among several European powers including Britain, Spain, France and others; but there was a very crafty coincidental move at this time to avoid the loss of dynastic continuity in the event of the failure to produce a male heir. That move was made when Holy Roman Emperor Charles VI issued an edict known as the Pragmatic Sanction in 1713 that provided for the inheritance of Hapsburg possessions by a daughter.

It would soon lead to trouble.

## 16.28.1.10 The War of Polish Succession – Combatants

This was a period of just five years of localised slaughter from 1733 to 1738, but it enabled some serious practice for a more sustained Poland-bashing that would continue for more than two centuries.

> Poland For Stanislaus I Leszczynski,
> Bourbon French, Bourbon Spanish,
> Kingdom of Sardinia, Bourbon Duchy of Parma
>
> *versus*
>
> Poland For Augustus III,
> Russia, Hapsburg Empire of Austria,
> Saxony, Kingdom of Prussia

The War of Polish Succession was largely due to Russia's opposition to any French-supported tenant of the Polish throne. It was also yet another excuse to wage war for possession of anything in Europe that could be gained at a time of uncertain continuity of a dynasty. It began as a conflict to decide who would succeed the King of Poland – Augustus II, who was also the Elector of Saxony. The choice of the Polish people was Stanislaus I Leszczynski, supported by France and Spain, while the hereditary successor to the elector of Saxony, Frederick Augustus II, was supported by Austria and Russia. The war was ended by the Treaty of Vienna that was begun in 1735 and eventually ratified in 1738.

### 16.28.1.11 The War of Austrian Succession – Combatants

This was an eight year period from 1740 to 1748 during which enmities could be stoked and spread before the unifications of Germany and Italy would reduce the scope for divisive intrigue. Its legacies would nevertheless add interest to the alliances and hostilities – such as the potential size of armies that could be assembled ready for the truly world-class conflicts in just over a hundred and fifty years time.

---

Kingdom of France, Kingdom of Prussia, Kingdom of Spain,
Bavaria (1741 to 1745), Saxony (1741 to 1742),
Sicily and Naples, Republic of Genoa, Sweden (1741 to 1743)

*versus*

Hapsburg Monarchy, Great Britain, Province of Hanover,
Dutch Republic, Saxony (1743 to 1745),
Kingdom of Sardinia, Russia (1741 to 1748)

---

The War of Austrian Succession was a consequence of the controversy over the eligibility (by the Pragmatic Sanction) of Maria Theresa to succeed to the Hapsburg throne that had become vacant when Emperor Charles VI died in 1740, but it was also an immediate result of the invasion of Silesia by Prussia. This War of Succession was ended by the Treaty of Aix-la-Chapelle (Aachen) in 1748.

### 16.28.1.12 The Seven Year War – Combatants

From 1756 to 1763 the Seven Year War is referred to frequently as the first Global or World War because theatres of conflict exploded in India, North America, Europe, and across the seven seas. One of the most significant outcomes was the French ceding of the vast Louisiana territory to Spain in 1762 (it was returned, initially secretly, to Napoleonic France in 1800), and what would become the second largest dominion on earth – Canada – to Britain. Instability in the Louisiana territory and the Napoleonic Wars would lead to its sale to the new United States in 1803.

Despite Britain's near bankruptcy in 1760, India also became part of the now firmly established and dominant British Empire.

---

Prussia, Great Britain,
Province of Hanover, Brunswick-Wolfenbüttel,
Iroquois Confederacy, Portugal (from 1761),
Province of Hesse Hesse-Kassel,
Province of Schaumburg-Lippe

*versus*

France, Austria, Russia (until 1762),
Spanish Empire (from 1761),
Sweden (1757 to 62), Electorate of Saxony,
Mughal Empire (from 1757)

*The Two Thousand Year War – Papal Hegemony*

## 16.28.1.13 Map – Marlborough's Victory at Blenheim 1704

Map from http://commons.wikimedia.org/wiki/Category:Maps released under CC-BY-SA
http://creativecommons.org/licenses/by-sa/3.0/ Author: Rebel Redcoat

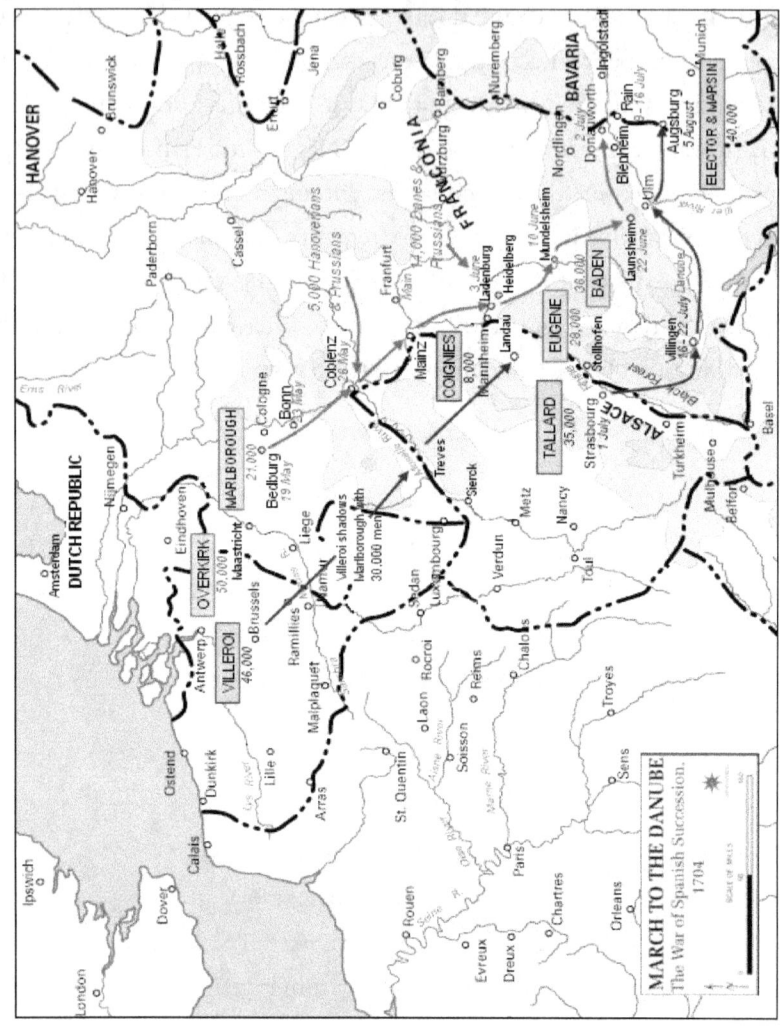

*The Two Thousand Year War – Papal Hegemony*

## 16.28.1.14 Map – Europe After the War of Spanish Succession

Map from http://commons.wikimedia.org/wiki/Category:Maps released under Creative Commons CC0 1.0 Universal Public Domain Dedication

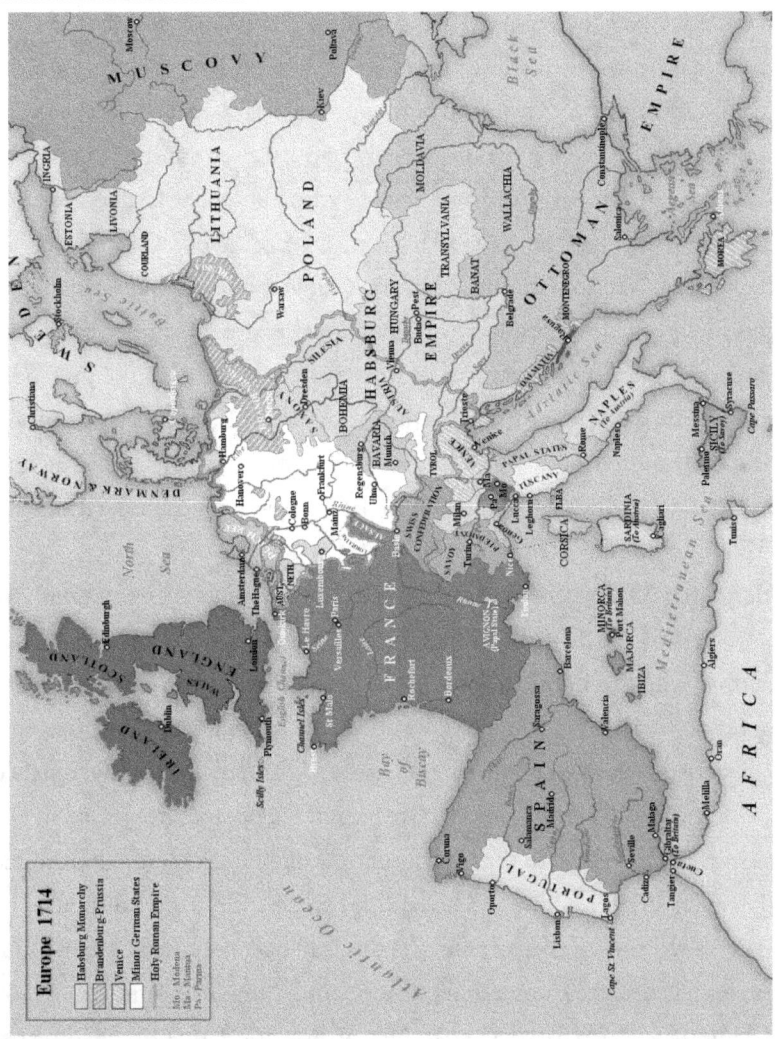

## 16.28.2 The Popes of the Period 1700 to 1769

**Clement XI (1700 to 1721).** From a noble family, with possibly Albanian military ancestry, and living in the central Italian region known as The Marches on the Adriatic coast, he is said to have been a brilliant academic and an honourable and hard-working individual, totally opposed to nepotism. His election was universally popular even among Protestants, and a meridian through Rome was named after him – The Clementina.

**Innocent XIII (1721 to 1724).** From the prestigious Conti family of Rome, he was the fourth pope from that same family; unlike many other popes he opposed the Jesuits in some matters and even sought to restrict their expansion. He gave asylum in Rome and a pension to the pretender James Stuart, son of the ousted English King James II, and offered support for a counter-revolution. With the aim of continuing papal support against the Ottoman and Muslim invasion of Europe he financed operations led by Venice on the island of Malta.

**Benedict XIII (1724 to 1730).** From the prestigious Orsini family of Rome, he was born in the Kingdom of Naples and was the third pope from that same family. He was a strict reformer though also a martinet who suppressed the public lottery. He was deceived by, among others, Cardinal Nicolò Coscia who was eventually imprisoned for ten years for his venality. Pope Benedict XIII is also said to have been weak because he was led by the nose into the elevation to the position of Cardinal of the scandalous rogue and French Prime Minister, Guillaume Dubois. On a populist note he repealed a worldwide ban on smoking that had been imposed by a previous pope, and he saw the completion of the Spanish Steps in Rome.

**Clement XII (1730 to 1740).** This aristocratic Florentine had served under three of his predecessors as a lawyer, a papal treasurer, and a High Court Prefect (a Judge surpassed only by the Pope), but he was blind after only two years of his papacy and so was obliged to make use of a host of assistants. He revived the public lottery, which along with fines imposed on those such as Cardinal Nicolò Coscia, brought in enough to fund his projects. He made several pronouncements against perceived heresies of the day such as Freemasonry and Jansenism. His papacy saw several political blunders, such as an attempt to take by force what was then, and still is, the oldest sovereign state with a written constitution, the Republic of San Marino, though this was said to have been an arbitrary act by a Cardinal Alberoni. Pope Clement XII was, however, personally responsible as commander-in-chief for failed claims on the Duchy of Parma and on the Duchy of Piacenza in north-west Italy.

**Benedict XIV (1740 to 1758).** From a noble Bologna family, he was considered one of the best educated and most wise popes, an intellectual and a scholar of good character and, unlike most of his predecessors, witty and eclectic; he was an avid reformer. Internationally, the Elector of Brandenburg was allowed the title of King of Prussia and there seems to have been some rapprochement with both the Eastern Church and with the Ottomans. However, within the Catholic Church itself, any attempt to make compromises with old religions in Pagan countries like China, even an act as simple as that of respecting one's non-Christian ancestors, was soon stamped out with a Bull. This high-handed capitulation to the wishes of the Dominican and Franciscan factions, contrary to those of the evangelising Jesuits, was manifest in 1742 in the Bull *Ex Quo Singulari*, and it cost the Church many converts and gained from the Chinese Emperor, the riposte:

> *"You destroyed your religion. You put in misery all Europeans living here in China. You desecrated the honour of all those, who died long ago."*

A similar Bull was issued in the case of missions in India with similar results. Maybe not such a wise pope after all and, by his opposition to the Jesuits, he may have unwittingly encouraged and even assisted the anti-Catholic philosopher and enlightenment movements that were about to enter (or should that be re-enter?) the scene. See the works of John Locke and Voltaire for instance.

Jesuit expulsions began in Brazil in 1754.

**Clement XIII (1758 to 1769).** From a noble Venetian family, he was of generous and good character, though something of a prude, reputedly adding fig leaves to statues in the Vatican. His reign saw: the expulsion of all Jesuits from several countries, led by France; temporarily broken diplomatic relations with Portugal; and the addition of an heretical French Encyclopaedia to the papal *Index of Forbidden Books*.

In spite of a Papal Bull in support of the Jesuits, expulsions of these meddlesome mischief-makers continued, and the anti-papal behaviour culminated in Bourbon seizures of papal territory in and around Avignon, and in the two Papal Enclave States of Benevento, and Pontecorvo, both of which were within, or bordered on, the Kingdom of Naples. This rebellion was accompanied by a demand from France, Spain, Naples, Portugal (including Brazil), and Parma, for the dissolution of the Jesuits worldwide, in response to which, after resisting for several years, Pope Clement XIII eventually called a judicial council to rule on the issue. His death the evening before the council led to unproven suspicions of poisoning, and the death of this possibly naïve but honest man caused the postponement of the issue to the next in line.

## 16.29  Anno Domini 1769 to 1800
### 16.29.1  Context
#### 16.29.1.1  Towards the French Revolution

- The War of Bavarian Succession (1778 to 1779).
- French Revolution (1787 to 1799).
- The Anglo-Corsican Kingdom (1794 to 1796).

### 16.29.1.2 The War of Bavarian Succession – Combatants

This war from 1778 to 1779 was between the Principalities of Prussia and Saxony on one side, and a nascent Austrian state on the other.

---

Archduchy of Austria

*versus*

Kingdom of Prussia, Electorate of Saxony

---

Austria at this time was in the form of a localised Hapsburg monarchy, or *Archduchy*, that wanted union with Bavaria as part of a Hapsburg expansionist programme. The northern axis of Prussia and Saxony, having their own ideas about Germanic integration and growth, manoeuvred to oppose the Austrian southern axis. Diplomacy and restricted military engagements resulted in just a short period of conflict but one in which nevertheless some tens of thousands of combatants died of disease and starvation, as a refreshing change from the more usual bullet, bayonet, or shrapnel.

### 16.29.1.3 The Fourth Anglo-Dutch War (1780 to 1784)

Against a background of weak Dutch political and military development over several decades, and following the British failure to get the Dutch Republic aka States-General on-side concerning the American revolution, during which the Dutch and Americans were major trade partners, Britain declared war just before an alliance between the Dutch, Russia, and some of the Scandinavian countries could come into force. The war was mostly fought as naval battles with the Dutch heavily outnumbered.

This global war was ended by the Treaty of Paris in May, 1784, that reaffirmed friendly relations between the nations that had previously been at peace for more than a century. It specified negotiations for maritime rights, and that all pre-war ownership of territories should be restored, except in India, where Negapatnam was ceded to the British crown.

### 16.29.1.4 The 1st Anti-Napoleonic Coalition (1792 to 1797)

Hapsburg Monarchy, Holy Roman Empire, Prussia, Great Britain, French Royalists, Spain, Portugal, Sardinia, Naples and Sicily, Misc. Italian states, Ottoman Empire, Dutch Republic.

The first coalition began with an attempt by Prussia and Austria, with marginal support from the others, to invade France with the objective of restoring the monarchy – the French King and Queen were not beheaded until 1793, at which point Britain entered the fray against the First French Republic. *The Directory,* as the revolutionary government eventually became known, was constitutionally defined in 1795.

There were successes and failures on all sides but, after initial French setbacks including the execution of some French Generals, it was Napoleon who soon emerged triumphant. First of all Prussia concluded the Peace of Basel in spring 1795 and withdrew, and then Austria signed the Treaty of Campo Formio in 1797 that, among several concessions, saw regions of present-day Belgium ceded to France, and the Republic of Venice partitioned. Britain alone remained opposed to France

### 16.29.1.5 The 2nd Anti-Napoleonic Coalition (1798 to 1802) – I

Hapsburg Monarchy, Holy Roman Empire, Great Britain, Russia, French Royalists, Portugal, Two Sicilies, Ottoman Empire.

In 1798 the Battle of the Pyramids was a milestone in Napoleon's military record when he defeated the Egyptian Mamluks. As seen in other chapters the Mamluks were slaves used by Islamic regimes to bolster their military, and the practice frequently backfired when the slave armies took control, sometimes of nation-sized regions for considerable periods. Such was the case of the Ghaznavid Dynasty that was founded by Mamluks around the year 1000 AD in the region of present-day Afghanistan and historic Transoxania east of the Caspian Sea.

The effects of the Second Anti-Napoleonic Coalition are continued into the chapter *Anno Domini 1800 to 1820.*

### 16.29.1.6 The Anglo-Corsican Kingdom

This fascinating episode in the history of the British Empire at the time of King George III involved an attempt to set up a British constitution, particularly a naval base, on the island of Corsica between the years 1794 and 1796. Such a base would have been of great strategic significance after the loss of the naval facility at Toulon.

It was during this Corsican campaign, led by Admiral Hood, that Captain Horatio Nelson (later Lord Nelson) lost an eye. Further details on the progress and demise of the attempt after Spain joined the French revolutionary axis can be read at:
http://www.jstor.org/stable/1874355?seq=1#page_scan_tab_contents

### 16.29.2 The Popes of the Period 1769 to 1800

**Clement XIV (1769 to 1774).** This Jesuit-educated Franciscan inherited a mess that hadn't been seen for many decades. Ranged against him were France, Spain, Naples, Portugal, and Parma, all with ideological demands concerning the Jesuits, and all making territorial demands. In addition, there were the Austrians with their grievance over the complicated composite Duchy of Parma and Piacenza that was Bourbon again after a temporary Hapsburg occupation from 1735 to 1748. Just about all Jesuits had been expelled from Catholic countries around the world between 1754 and 1771, but the forces against the papacy still demanded an official termination of the order; the only way forward was absolute conciliation and concession by the Pope, so accordingly the Society of Jesus was abolished by the papal brief *Dominus ac Redemptor* in 1773. Clement XIV died with symptoms of poisoning, not proved, just over a year later in 1774. The Jesuits would continue in many non-Bourbon Catholic countries in Europe, Prussia, and Russia, and unfortunately would be restored by papal licence 41 years later.

**Pius VI (1775 to 1799).** From an erstwhile wealthy, noble family in Cesena, north-east Italy, he was educated by the Jesuits and known for beginning reforms, but also for later facing difficulties with his authority and the notion of Papal Supremacy, particularly in revolutionary France from 1789. It is said by some that he was an unpleasant man and that he was extravagant on his own behalf and on that of his family, but said by others that he restored the Vatican finances and carried out many public works. Revolutionary France and an internationally developing revolutionary cadre, however, were militarily far stronger than the Pope who had few allies at this momentous time, and Napoleon Bonaparte entered Italy in 1796, brushing aside the papal troops. After provocations, Rome was taken without resistance and a Roman Republic was proclaimed in 1798. Refusing to renounce his claim to a temporal empire, Pope Pius VI was taken in ill health as far as Valence, south-eastern France, where he died in 1799.

Of particular interest at this time are the infamous activities of King Ferdinand IV of Naples who, towards the end of 1798, took advantage of Napoleon's campaigning in Egypt to attack the remaining French in Rome with a large force led by an Austrian General. The aim was to restore the Pope, but the Neapolitans were soon beaten into an undignified retreat back to Naples. Pursued by the French, Ferdinand took ship in Nelson's *HMS Vanguard* that was visiting Naples, and he fled to Palermo in Sicily from where he could only watch as Naples descended into chaos as the *Lazzaroni*, or street people, loyally continued the fight on his behalf, butchering anyone suspected of having French or anti-monarchy sympathies. To overcome the anarchy that prevailed as a sort of Italian version of France's *Terror*, so-called educated people and the nobility capitulated to the French and accepted the proclamation in late January 1799 of the Parthenopean Republic. This stop-gap republic precariously survived for six months in a state of civil war among the various republican, revolutionary, and monarchist factions, until the arrival of Cardinal Fabrizio Ruffo at the head of a Christian army of the Holy Faith.

Ruffo had been sent to Calabria by Frederick to restore the Kingdom of Naples, and his mixed band of brigands, murderers, soldiers, and peasants pillaged their way through the countryside, eventually committing unspeakable atrocities in the capital city of Naples. When King Frederick IV arrived with his vindictive Queen, the savagery continued with no quarter shown to republicans. This was not the end of the matter however, since when the French achieved their successes against Austria in 1805, they would be able to send an army to Naples again, causing the King to flee and to watch Napoleon install his own brother, Joseph Bonaparte, as King of both Naples and Sicily in 1806. Ferdinand did eventually return after Napoleon's fall from power, but in effect he was a mere puppet of the Austrian Empire, and it is said that in bitterness he violently opposed any form of liberalisation. He died in 1825, with no redeeming qualities or legacies other than the arguable one of having contributed, by his nefariousness, to the rise of the revolutionary secret society known as the Carbonari, a movement that was generally patriotic and liberal minded, though without clear aims, and which is thought to have influenced many later revolutionary movements throughout Europe, not least the power behind Italian unification that was just round the corner.

European and New World geopolitical events were impossibly convoluted for a century or more either side of the French Revolution of 1787, and it is difficult to look at any aspect of European history without considering the whole picture. In an attempt to retain the theme of historical perspectives, and in the current context of the papacy and its character over the ages, it might suffice to summarise the forces at play on the eve of the 19$^{th}$ century, without being led too far into the character of the players that are covered elsewhere.

In 1797, just a decade after the French Revolution started, the Republic of Venice had come to an end, after eleven hundred years of independence, as a result of a sequence of events that had a certain inevitability about them.

In April, 1792, following the threat of invasion by Austria and Prussia to restore the monarchy in France, the French Assembly declared war on Austria – Austria was then only just (since March) under the new Holy Roman Emperor Francis II, and he hadn't yet been crowned. By the end of 1792 the First French Republic had invaded and occupied: the Austrian southern Netherlands (Belgium); Nice; Savoy; part of the Kingdom of Sardinia; and parts of Germany in the region of the river Rhine.

During 1793 the deposed French King Louis XVI and his wife were beheaded along with many others, and France, with a huge conscript army, was at war with the anxious monarchies of Spain, Portugal, Great Britain, and the Dutch Republic.

In spite of several failures during 1793 and 1794, by the end of 1795 France had crossed the Pyrénées into northern Spain, and Spain and Prussia had sued for peace, giving up respectively, the present-day Dominican Republic (part of the island of Hispaniola), and the left bank of the Rhine. Due to its massive conscription, and with its battle experience, the French forces were now better trained, better disciplined, and more numerous than ever, though of a planned three-army attack on Vienna in 1796, only Napoleon Bonaparte's army, proceeding via Italy, was partly successful – by April, 1797, he had taken Milan and Mantua, he had isolated and extracted peace from Sardinia the previous year, and he had defeated the Austrians on more than one occasion. Acknowledging defeat, for a while at least, Austria committed to the Treaty of Leoben with secret protocols in April, 1797, and this eventually led to a peace settlement – the Peace of Campo Formio in October of that year. It should be noted that Austria and Venice had been in alliance against the Ottomans since 1684. The clandestine treaty and settlement of 1797 ceded the Austrian Netherlands and Lombardy to France, with some parts of the Venetian Republic, such as the Island of Corfu, also going to France, while Austria now ruled Venice and its eastern Adriatic territories of Istria and Dalmatia. Austria additionally recognised the northern Italian puppet republics set up by the French: the Parthenopean Republic described above; a Republic centred on Genoa; the Ligurian Republic; and the Cisalpine Republic, referred to below, which was defined during the pre-papal years of Pope Pius VII.

## 16.30 Anno Domini 1800 to 1820

### 16.30.1 Context

#### 16.30.1.1 Napoleonic Wars, Congresses and Concerts in Turmoil

The First Anti-Napoleonic Coalition (1792 to 1797) was entirely within the previous chapter of papal history – *Anno Domini 1769 to 1800*.

## The Two Thousand Year War – Papal Hegemony

The Second Anti-Napoleonic Coalition started in the previous chapter, and it is continued into this chapter. It is therefore merely referenced again below.

Three distinct phases of what was in reality a continual war are commonly identified as follows:

1. The First Barbary War (1801 to 1805).
2. The Napoleonic Wars (1803 to 1815).
3. The Peninsular War (1807 to 1814).

### 16.30.1.2 The Carbonari – a Preview of the Fascisti ?

This secret political movement is believed to have started in the early 19$^{th}$ century in France and Italy. The followers were of a patriotic and republican or modernist flavour and were opposed to the reactionary regimes that followed the French Revolution and Napoleonic Wars. They were anti-clerical and anti-Bourbon.

### 16.30.1.3 The 2$^{nd}$ Anti-Napoleonic Coalition (1798 to 1802) – II

The forces opposed to the expansionist policies of Revolutionary France at the outset were: the Hapsburg Monarchy, the Holy Roman Empire, Great Britain, Russia, French Royalists, Portugal, the Two Sicilies, and the Ottoman Empire. Details were presented in a previous chapter.

### 16.30.1.4 The 3$^{rd}$ Anti-Napoleonic Coalition (1803 to 1806)

Fatigue and changing fortunes, not least due to occupation, saw a change in the allies against what was becoming ever more obviously a Napoleonic Empire. The third allied coalition consisted of: the Holy Roman Empire, the Russian Empire, the United Kingdom (GB and Ireland), the Kingdom of Naples, the Kingdom of Sicily, the Kingdom of Portugal, and a Sweden that was destined for a reduction in prestige.

### 16.30.1.5 The 4$^{th}$ Anti-Napoleonic Coalition (1806 to 1807)

The Holy Roman Empire after nearly a thousand years had gone. Political endurance and military stamina of most of the contestants was now seriously challenged, and in a German context the divided and diverse principalities must have made German unification a most improbable concept at this time. The duration of alliances was reducing; five years, four years, three years, and this time it would be one year, with just Prussia, Russia, Saxony, Sweden, the United Kingdom, and lastly the widow, Sicily, without its old partner, Naples.

### 16.30.1.6 The 5th Anti-Napoleonic Coalition (1809)

Napoleon now had allegiances beyond the borders of France, and his Republican ideals were beginning to appeal to a significant range of candidates. Who said Imperialism was dead?

To all those arrayed against him, the French-led alliance must have seemed an intimidating adversary, especially with Russia temporarily off the field – the bout would only last for six months during the months April to October.

**Napoleonic Alliance:** French Empire, Duchy of Warsaw, Confederation of the Rhine, Bavaria, Saxony, Württemberg, Westphalia, Kingdom of Italy, Naples, Switzerland, Holland.

**Allied Coalition:** Austria, Tyrol (in rebellion against Bavaria), United Kingdom, Spain, Sicily, Sardinia, Black Brunswickers.

## 16.30.1.7 Map – Butchery of Poland – End of the 18th Century

Map from http://commons.wikimedia.org/wiki/Category:Maps released under CC-BY-SA
http://creativecommons.org/licenses/by-sa/3.0/ Author: Halibutt

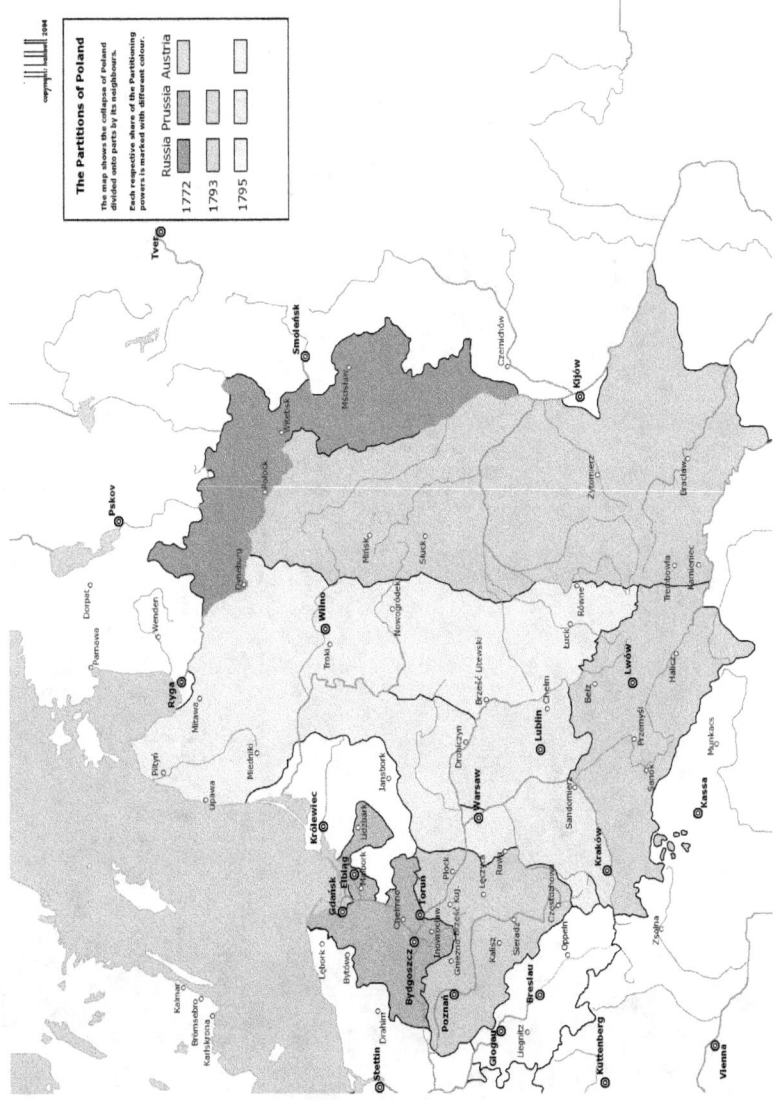

*The Two Thousand Year War – Papal Hegemony*

## 16.30.1.8 Map – Italian States 1796 – Before Campo Formio

Map from http://commons.wikimedia.org/wiki/Category:Maps released under CC-BY-SA
http://creativecommons.org/licenses/by-sa/3.0/ Author: Enok

The Kingdom of Sardinia would ultimately absorb all the states to form a united Italy.

## 16.30.1.9  Map – The Result of Campo Formio, October 1797

Map from http://commons.wikimedia.org/wiki/ Public Domain

### 16.30.1.10 The 6ᵗʰ Anti-Napoleonic Coalition (1812 to 1814)

The United States was not yet the world power that another one hundred years growth and development would provide, and so its contribution to Napoleon's Empire was not a game-changer. However, the entry on the allied side of especially Russia and Bavaria certainly would make the outcome more predictable. Napoleon's downfall was definitely much more likely after his retreat and losses of 1812 when Moscow was found by the French to be untenable after the Russians had razed it. And yet, even after the Prussian defection to the Allied side, it would still be a close-run thing, as would be seen at Waterloo.

**Napoleonic Alliance:** French Empire, Kingdom of Italy, Duchy of Warsaw, Naples, Denmark, Norway, Swiss Confederation, Confederation of the Rhine, United States of America.

**Allied Coalition:** Russia, Prussia, Austria, United Kingdom, Sweden, Spain, Portugal, Sicily, Sardinia, Saxony, Bavaria, Württemberg.

### 16.30.1.11 Maps – Developments Around the Final Conflicts

The series of maps below illustrate the changing fortunes of the belligerents and, after those maps, details are given of the settlements that followed on from the Congress of Vienna – settlements and initiatives that are collectively known by the optimistic epithet "Concert of Europe".

The Concert of Europe was certainly something of a song and dance, more a *burlesque,* that might be regarded as a conceptual rehearsal for later initiatives to contrive what would turn out to be an equally ineffective and unacclaimed stage-show – the League of Nations – and a currently toothless and unsung United Nations.

So despite that theatrical Concert of Europe, nationalistic passion and patriotism stirred up during the twenty or so years of Napoleonic warfare, together with 19ᵗʰ century revolutionary fervour, would make sure that the addiction to conflict would not be cured, and that neither would any lessons be remembered – other than how to mobilise for war.

As will be seen in the chapter in Volume Two concerning the Russian-Ottoman wars, mankind had yet to taste the delights of trench and mechanised warfare – up to the Napoleonic wars most battles had been

*The Two Thousand Year War – Papal Hegemony*

classic set pieces of infantry, artillery, and cavalry, with a few sieges of fortresses thrown in.

### 16.30.1.12 Map – Italian and Regional Powers 1810

Map from http://commons.wikimedia.org/wiki/Category:Maps released under CC-BY-SA
http://creativecommons.org/licenses/by-sa/3.0/ Author: MapMaster

## 16.30.1.13 Map – Rheinbund and Neighbours circa 1812

Map from http://commons.wikimedia.org/wiki/Category:Maps released under CC-BY-SA
http://creativecommons.org/licenses/by-sa/3.0/  Author: Ziegelbrenner

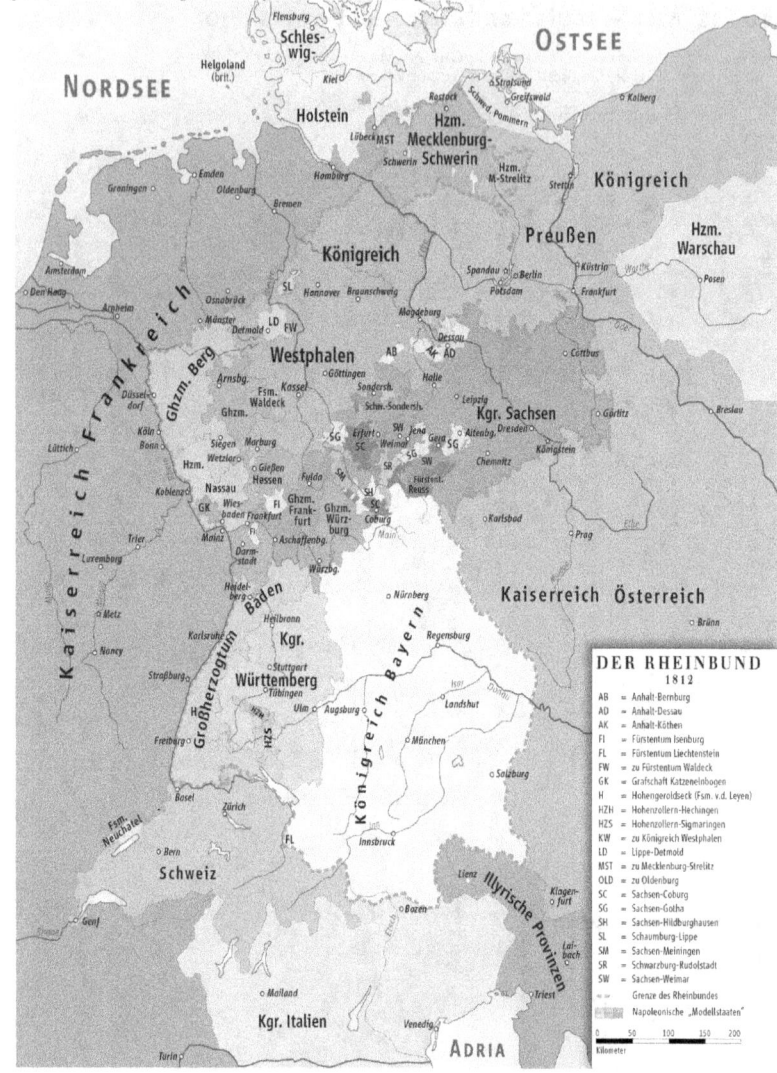

The Two Thousand Year War – Papal Hegemony

## 16.30.1.14 Map – Duchy of Warsaw & Free City of Danzig 1814
Map from http://commons.wikimedia.org/wiki/ Public Domain

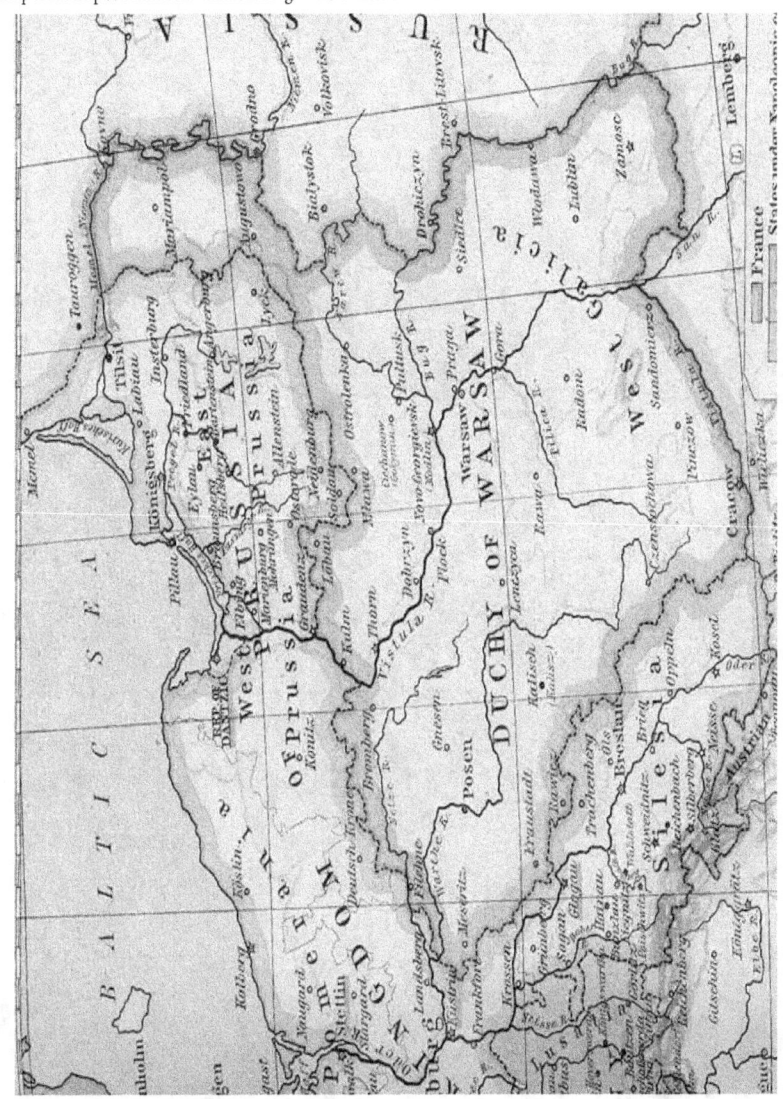

## 16.30.1.15 Map – European Powers After Congress of Vienna 1815

Map from http://commons.wikimedia.org/wiki/ Public Domain

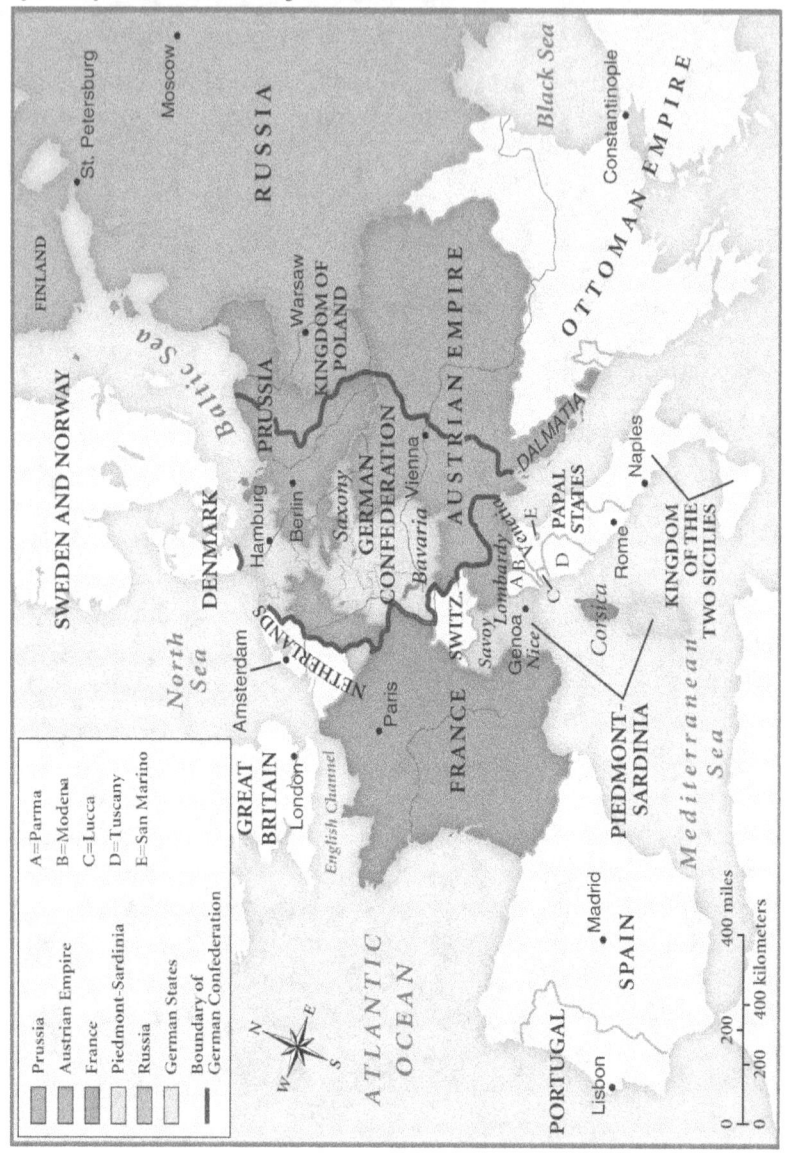

## The Two Thousand Year War – Papal Hegemony

### 16.30.1.16 Congress of Vienna and Concert of Europe After 1815

The Congress of Vienna was part of a series of treaties and agreements that were hammered out over several years, and that with an unwritten spirit of hope are referred to as the Concert of Europe. The following strategic summary is a result of the general initiatives of the time, a few years either side of the 1815 Congress.

### 16.30.1.17 The Austrian and Emerging Italian Spheres

Venice remained subject to Austria, with the Austrian Empire exercising wider hegemony over northern and central Italy and having control also of Milan, Lombardy, and of the Illyrian provinces of Carinthia (southern modern Austria), Carniola (mostly part of modern Slovenia), and Trieste (eastern Italian border with Slovenia ).

### 16.30.1.18 Map – Austrian Pretensions – Northern Adriatic Sea

Map from http://commons.wikimedia.org/wiki/ Public Domain

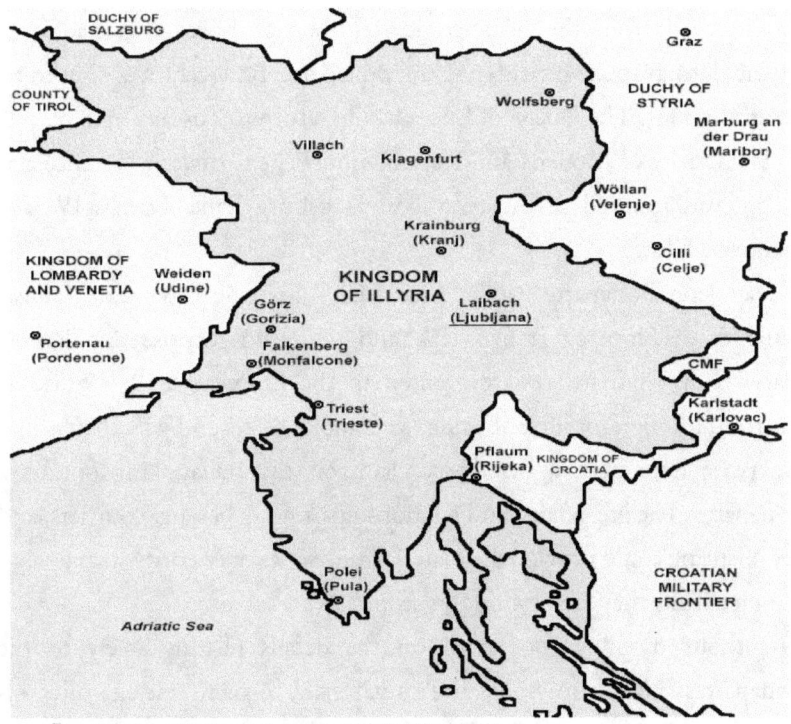

Further down the eastern coast of the Adriatic, the Austrian Empire also had dominion over Dalmatia and the seaport of Cattaro (modern Kotor in Montenegro).

The Kingdom of Sardinia very significantly now had a strong foothold in mainland Italy with the regions of Savoy, Nice, Liguria, and Piedmont, and the strategic and important city of Turin which was the capital of Piedmont, and the port of Genoa which was the capital of Liguria.

The Papal States were independent again and little changed, though the Pope did lose Avignon.

The Spanish Bourbon Dynasty in the reprehensible guise of Ferdinand IV retained the new Kingdom of the Two Sicilies that had been defined as a union of Naples and Sicily.

Tuscany remained with the Hapsburg Grand Duke of Tuscany, Ferdinand III, and the neighbouring ancient and small Duchy of Lucca was restored from the Napoleonic Republic of Lucca that had been allocated to Napoleon's sister, Elisa Bonaparte Baciocchi aka Queen of Etruria, in 1805. The Duchy of Lucca would return to Tuscany in 1847.

The Duchy of Modena and Reggio, sandwiched between Florence and Milan, was restored to the tyrannical Hapsburg Duke Francis IV (aka Francesco d'Este).

Napoleon Bonaparte had married well – his wife was Marie Louise, daughter of Emperor Francis II – and so its no surprise that Parma, Piacenza and Guastella were granted to the Empress Marie Louise of Austria, although for life only, since as Napoleon's second wife there could otherwise have been a hereditary claim on the Italian kingdom by a Bonaparte. The life, affairs, and relationships among her, her courtiers, and her offspring could provide the material for a series of celebrity soap operas, but mercifully they are beyond this scope.

Without dwelling too much on the details relating solely to the Bonapartes, Napoleon Bonaparte's final exile to Saint Helena after his defeat at the Battle of Waterloo was followed in France by a series of monarchs until the revolution of 1848 that led to the election of President Napoleon III. During that still turbulent time, the son born to Empress

## The Two Thousand Year War – Papal Hegemony

Marie Louise and Napoleon Bonaparte in 1811, Napoleon II, was briefly King of Rome (mostly in exile) and a Bohemian Duke. With promising military abilities and in an atmosphere of suspiciously Austrian imperial aspirations, to some extent he was used as a pawn as part of the posturing between Austria and France during the Concert of Europe, but he died prematurely in Vienna of tuberculosis at the age of twenty-one.

In terms of the last ruling monarchs, it was after being in exile since 1795 that the Bourbon French King Louis XVIII retook the French throne from 1814 until 1824 when he died, it is said, from a combination of obesity and gangrene. Louis XVIII was followed by his brother, the Bourbon French King Charles X, who lasted six years until he was chased out of France by an impending revolution, and the very last monarch was French King Louis-Philippe I of the House of Orléans, whose father had been a supporter of the first revolution back in 1789, and who therefore seemed to have some credentials that made him acceptable to a revolutionary movement. The reality was that he was a closet Bourgeois, and he was rumbled by the mob and, like his predecessor, the popinjay was forced to flee to England as the 1848 revolution began.

Later that year it was the turn again of the Bonaparte Dynasty, and Napoleon III who was the nephew of Napoleon I (Bonaparte) became the first elected President of the Second French Republic and a couple of years later, by his own hand, he became Emperor of the second French Empire. He took the regnal number III in recognition of his ill-fated cousin Napoleon II, and so he was the last autocratic-aristocratic head of France – as a self-styled Emperor not King. He remained in power for about twenty years.

As a footnote, the almost French King Louis XVII, the Dauphin de France, was the son of the guillotined French King Louis XVI, and for almost two hundred years he was understood to have died in suspicious circumstances at the age of ten during his confinement by the Reign of Terror in 1795. A string of conspiracy theorists claiming to be descended from him rested their case on rumours that he had escaped and not died as a child, and such claims persisted until the year 2000 when DNA testing confirmed that a preserved heart was indeed that of the child Dauphin.

### 16.30.1.19 Additional Austrian Gains

The following detail is a small part of the consequences of the partitions of Poland that started in 1772 as a result of the destruction of the Polish-Lithuanian Commonwealth by Russia, Prussia, and Austria. Poland would sadly be dismembered more than once during the next one hundred and fifty years or so, and it would see atrocities that rank among the worst known. Galicia in eastern Europe had been part of Poland and the Polish-Lithuanian Commonwealth until 1772 when it became part of the Holy Roman Empire under Empress Maria Theresa, other parts of the Commonwealth being distributed among the victors of the several conflicts at that time.

On the dissolution of the Holy Roman Empire in 1806 – the result of Napoleonic aggression – Galicia stayed with Emperor Francis II, who became Austrian Emperor Francis I of a nascent Austrian Empire instead. In present-day geography, Galicia overlaps parts of Poland and The Ukraine, but in 1815 it was part of the Kingdom of Galicia and Lodomeria that also incorporated a couple of Duchies. Another strategically important region was the Republic or Free City of Krakow in the south of present-day Poland, a neutral state uncomfortably sandwiched between Prussia, Russia, and Austria, and that was created as a tax-free zone in 1815. Nominally a Protectorate of Austria, Prussia, and Russia, Krakow would soon be annexed by Austria.

Before 1815, the Tyrol and Salzburg had been strategically important to Austria, although variously contested by internal and external interests. After 1815, those two Alpine delights were confirmed as part of Austria.

### 16.30.1.20 Great Britain

Malta became a voluntary British colony in 1800 after disillusionment with a brief French occupation, and British sovereignty was reaffirmed in 1815.

Heligoland, just off the German North Sea coast, and Frisian by culture, had been taken by Britain in 1807 and it was formally ceded by Denmark in

1814, though it would be traded later with the German Empire for various African concessions in 1890.

The loose federation of the Ionian Islands that had an older heritage of Venetian governance, and that consisted of seven principal islands with several smaller ones off the Adriatic coast of Greece, were partly taken by the British during the Napoleonic Wars. The complete group was now put under British protection where they stayed until 1864 when they were given to Greece to strengthen the authority of its monarch, the Greek King George I, who was actually an elected Danish prince of the House of Glücksburg. He reigned from 1863 to 1913.

Mauritius in the Indian Ocean was taken by the British in 1810, but the history of some of the Caribbean islands is not so straightforward: Tobago, smaller than its paired companion, Trinidad, was taken from Spain in 1797 and then contested with France; Santa Lucia similarly changed hands several times between Britain and France; and Trinidad, like Tobago, was taken from the Spanish in 1797 but was not subject to quite the same French hegemony. All were ceded to Britain in or around 1815.

Dutch coastal interests in Ceylon were ceded to Britain, and the separate inland Kingdom of Kandy was conquered.

The Cape of Good Hope, having become an outpost of the Dutch Batavian Republic in 1795 as a result of Napoleon's conquest and political manipulation of what had been the United Netherlands, was occupied by the British, and after a period of contested rule was ceded to Britain by Holland, thereby setting the scene for later British-Boer disagreements and war.

### 16.30.1.21 Switzerland

The long established Old Swiss Confederation, with its individualistic administrative canton regions, was replaced by the Helvetic Republic from 1798 to 1802 as a result of Napoleonic dominion and politicisation, but it was never stable because of internal dislike for the imposition of foreign rule. Despite a French attempt at compromise by the Act of Mediation in 1803, unrest continued with, first of all, the re-establishment of the ancient thirteen cantons, then the addition of another six, and finally, after the

Congress of Vienna, the increase to twenty-two – one of which was Geneva. The now expanded Swiss territory would be assured of its neutrality, guaranteed by the Great Powers, and it would now make itself available to host international benevolent initiatives, and at the same time prostitute itself forever, as a shelter for the ill-gotten gains of the most malignant and corrupt dictators, money-changers, and criminals the world has ever seen.

### 16.30.1.22 Spain

As mentioned above, Spain lost Trinidad to Great Britain, and its pre-Napoleonic monarch, the nefarious Ferdinand VII, was reinstated.

### 16.30.1.23 France and Portugal

In the Indian Ocean the Isle of Bourbon, east of Madagascar and southwest of Mauritius, had been taken from France by the British in 1810, but it was returned to France after the Congress and was renamed Réunion after 1848. In the Caribbean, Portuguese Guiana became French Guiana, Martinique was returned to French control after periods under British rule, and Guadeloupe, after a brief spell under Swedish-British rule in 1813 and 1814, was also returned to France.

### 16.30.1.24 Sweden, Denmark, and Norway

In 1814 Denmark had ceded Norway to Sweden, and this was confirmed by the Congress, with Denmark receiving an oddly orphaned remnant of the defunct Holy Roman Empire, Lauenburg, just east of present-day Hamburg in the Schleswig-Holstein region. This would be the cause of some very unpleasant conflicts later.

### 16.30.1.25 The Netherlands, the Batavian Republic, and Belgium

From 1581 to 1795 the Dutch Republic aka United Provinces had been a confederation of seven provinces, and following the Peace of Westphalia of 1648, its sovereignty was settled by recognition by Spain. In 1795 Napoleon invaded and proclaimed the Dutch Republic to be instead the "Batavian Republic", following it up in 1806 with the title "Kingdom of Holland" with his brother, Louis Bonaparte, as its king. This was the same Louis Bonaparte whose son Napoleon would later become Napoleon III of France.

Changes in the political culture that followed ensured that the previous *confederation* would henceforth be a single *State*, regardless of the source of dominion; although Louis' failure to deliver as had been expected led to its annexation by Napoleon as a part of France from 1810 to 1813. After the Congress, this northern lowlands region with such a challenged identity became, in combination with the lowlands of the southern Austrian Netherlands, the United Kingdom of the Netherlands, and it persisted with that name and geographical scope from 1815 to 1839.

As if there was a curse on this region that had seen such disruption ranging from the climatic inundation of Doggerland circa 6000 BC, through the Belgae and Frank occupations, yet more turmoil and revolution in 1830 eventually led to the definition of a separate Kingdom of Belgium in 1839, where the fields of Flanders quietly awaited fresh sacrifice.

After the Congress of 1815 the King of the Netherlands, being also a man of the House of Orange, received the title Grand Duke of Luxembourg, which gave him membership of, and influence within, the new German Confederation.

### 16.30.1.26 Russia

By 1795 Poland had been partitioned three times and it was no longer a sovereign entity. In 1807 the fourth coalition of forces against Napoleon had been broken, and Napoleon had created three client states: the Kingdom of Westphalia in the region of Hanover and Magdeburg that was ruled by his brother, Jerome; the Duchy of Warsaw, a shrunken version of modern Poland but important in terms of Polish continuity; and the small Free City or Republic of Danzig. After the Congress Russia was awarded the Duchy of Warsaw which would become a sort of pseudo-Kingdom of Poland which could be absorbed into the Tsardom of Russia. It would languish in that undigested condition until the chaos of 1918 would allow it to emerge and to reassert its sovereign statehood in 1922 as the Second Polish Republic under Jozef Piłsudski.

The principle of Germanic and Russian claims on Polish territory was sadly not consigned to history, as would be seen less than twenty years later in the infamous and dastardly pact between Stalin and Hitler in 1939.

Returning to 1815, Russia had taken Finland from Sweden in 1808, and retained it, and Russia similarly retained Bessarabia that had been taken from Turkey in 1812. In 2015 both are independent states again but, while Finland seems to have an assured independent future, Bessarabia remains vulnerable to the imperialistic Russian Federation.

### 16.30.1.27 Prussia

The Congress confirmed Napoleon's creation and ally, King Frederick Augustus I, as king of a shrunken southern Saxony, with Prussia receiving the northern half. Augustus (originally a Roman honorific title) had been the Elector of the state of Saxony when it was part of the Holy Roman Empire, but he had thrown his hand in with Napoleon, so he was lucky to get anything at all from the victorious coalition.

In addition to the northern half of Saxony, Prussia also received the Grand Duchy of Berg that originally had been created by Napoleon for his brother-in-law, Joachim Murat, with the intention that he would later go on to be King of Naples, making way for Napoleon's nephew, Prince Napoleon Louis Bonaparte, to become the Duke of Berg. the Duchy of Berg was a short-lived mini-state in the region of the Rhineland around Düsseldorf, Cologne, and Dortmund, very roughly the Ruhr district, and with this acquisition, Prussian lands now stretched west as far as Aachen and Trier.

Further north Prussia received Swedish Pomerania, and it retained a territory that had resulted from the last partition of Poland – Posen that became the Duchy of Posen. Finally, Prussia retained the previously gained Polish cities of Danzig and Thorn – the present-day Gdansk and Toruń respectively.

Personally, the King of Prussia was awarded the title Prince of the Swiss Canton of Neuchatel.

## 16.30.1.28 Map – Prussian Expansion 1807 to 1871

Map from http://commons.wikimedia.org/wiki/Category:Maps released under CC-BY-SA
http://creativecommons.org/licenses/by-sa/3.0/

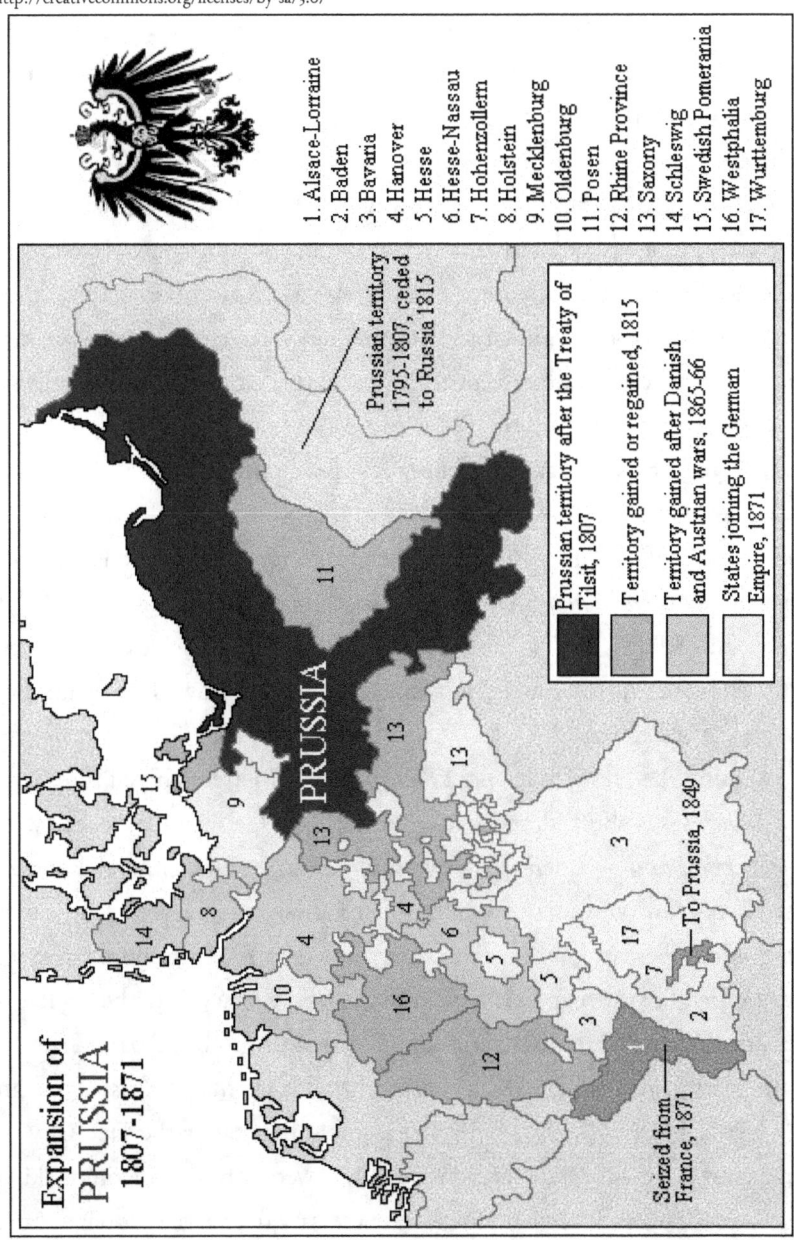

### 16.30.1.29 Turkey – The Eastern Question

Although this subject is covered in detail in the chapter on the Ottoman Empire in Volume Two it is of interest in the context of European unity at this time, and refers to how the anticipated breakup of the Ottoman Empire would be handled. In spite of centuries of conflict and thousands of lives lost and enslaved in hideous ways as a result of the invasions by the Ottomans, the Great Powers were still divided in their approach. The Russian Empire for instance was in favour of Ottoman dissolution, whereas the United Kingdom and the Austro-Hungarian Empire were considered to be in favour of its continuation – largely as a hedge against the Russian Bear. Another century would pass before the issue would be resolved after World War One. See Volume Two.

### 16.30.1.30 The German Confederacy – Seeds of Unity

Under Napoleon, the breakup of the Holy Roman Empire in 1806 had led to the unification of a number of states to form the Confederation of the Rhine or *Rheinbund* that grew to its largest extent in 1808 to consist of four kingdoms, five Grand Duchies, thirteen Duchies, seventeen Principalities, and the three Hanseatic League Free Towns of Hamburg, Lübeck, and Bremen.

Within the restrictive horizons of the Metternich culture, the *Rheinbund* was shuffled and massaged until the German Confederacy, or *Deutscher Bund*, was defined between 1815 and 1820 to include thirty-nine members – thirty-five states and four Free Cities – a reduction from 300 or so ex-Holy Roman Empire states, and more than fifteen hundred discrete authorities. See the map below. Within the Confederacy were the big five – Austria, Prussia, Saxony, Bavaria, and Württemberg – but Austria had the permanent Presidency over a Diet of delegates that consisted of an Ordinary Assembly and a General Assembly that sat at the Free City of Frankfurt. In confederate fashion, members were forbidden from making war on each other, and a consensus was necessary to engage in foreign wars.

### 16.30.1.31 The Spanish Civil War of 1820

This war of rebellion was mainly against the absolutist and tyrannical King Ferdinand VII – the revolution sought to reinstate the Spanish

*The Two Thousand Year War – Papal Hegemony*

Constitution of 1812, a modernist and liberal approach that had been defined by the Spanish Government in exile during the Peninsular Wars. It was, however, anti-papal, and the rebels briefly broke off diplomatic relations with the Pope in 1823. The revolution was eventually quashed by the French in the name and cause of the Bourbon Dynasty, and the dissolute monster King Ferdinand VII was restored to his throne to revoke the anti-papal changes made by the rebels, and to carry out vengeful atrocities that horrified even his rescuers.

The whole business of his restoration by the French, presumably with tacit approval of the pontiff, might be considered a travesty of any progress with libertarian principles that may have been made by France since its own revolution had taken place a mere thirty six years or so earlier. Such rehabilitation and restoration of tyranny in Spain should have been an affront to any humanitarian instinct that might have existed in the Vatican.

### 16.30.1.32 The Lasting Legacy of the Period – A Poisoned Chalice

The moment the French revolution overflowed the frontiers of France, physically and ideologically that is, firstly by the annexation of the papal territory of Avignon in September, 1791, and secondly by the declaration of war on Austria in April, 1792, the old Europe was destined for an unimaginable quarter century of war that, in theory, might buy an equally unimaginable century of peace.

Such wishful thinking was, of course, totally unrealistic, and the ulcers and scars left by the half-century of Napoleonic Wars and later revolutions might be judged to have set a pattern that would continue for two centuries down to the present day, gaining in degrees of abomination without significant relief other than the occasional brief *Belle Époque*.

The Holy Roman Empire that had existed for one thousand years had been abolished, and the groundwork had been laid for the formation of three European states that would complete, not an everlasting balance of power, but a formula for the maturation during the "century of peace", of animosities and jealousies that would fuel two world wars. This would be in spite of pervasive aristocratic family bonds and the integration in one of the three new states, Italy, of the beating Catholic heart – the Papal States;

but then the cosy world of privilege had not predicted the strength of disaffection that fermented and fomented in the filth that recent revolutions had failed to clean up, and that would develop into the polarised rhetoric, pathetically labelled by present-day ideologues, as "right wing" and "left wing" – simple terms that had been used to denote seating positions in the revolutionary French National Assembly, but terms that are representative of an underlying schism in human character that is possibly eternal.

Such trivial yet emotive terminology has been seized upon by politically schizophrenic and damaged minds down to the present day, and it is used in completely incorrect contexts in an attempt to achieve some measure of character assassination. Further twisted arguments and elements of *newspeak,* reminiscent of George Orwell's *1984,* have been imposed by the truly damaging ideologies, and their legacies, of demagogues, such as Stalin and Hitler, and their predecessor philosophers such as those of the Age of Enlightenment, Classical and Modern Liberalism, the Frankfurt School and present-day think tanks.

### 16.30.2 The Popes of the Period 1800 to 1820

**Pius VII (1800 to 23).** A second pope from Cesena, he was from an aristocratic family and started ecclesiastical life as a member of the Benedictine Order. He was made a Cardinal in 1785 and was only the Bishop of Imola, Bologna, when the French invaded Italy in 1797 after defeating a small Austrian force in Lombardy in 1796. To avoid the repeat of senseless slaughter seen elsewhere in Italy, the advice to his flock had been to submit to the Cisalpine Republic (1797 to 1802) that had been declared by Bonaparte as a puppet state in northern Italy. At the Papal Conclave at Venice in 1799 to elect a new pope, after months of disagreement Pope Pius VII was finally elected as a compromise among the strong feelings caused by the international events of the time. Pius managed the Concordat of 1801 agreement with Napoleon that gave the Roman Catholic Church many of the rights lost during the days of the Revolution, and he co-operated with the French over the trade embargo against Great Britain. France nevertheless annexed the Papal States and took Pius prisoner in 1809, sending him to Savona in north-west Italy.

Next, it seems that in 1813, to some extent hoodwinked by Napoleon, he apparently signed the draft version of an agreement that was supposed to be subject to further negotiations; the agreement was known as the Concordat of Fontainebleau. His uncertain compliance achieved the release from exile of himself and a number of Cardinals who then persuaded the Pope to recant, which in turn led to the rearrest of some of them for a short period until Napoleon abdicated the same year. The issues with Napoleon pushed the Pope towards Great Britain that for a while had stood alone against the French after the Peace of Lunéville in 1801. Attempts were made to settle British ecclesiastical problems in Ireland but they were to no avail, and failures and divisions in Ireland would, of course, get much worse before there would be any improvement in civil, social or religious affairs.

In 1814 the Society of Jesus – the Jesuit Order – was restored and in 1816 there was yet another declaration of heresy, this time a reiteration against an older one, Conciliarism, that favoured the authority of the Ecumenical Council over that of the Pope.

What is possibly surprising, is the almost complete reinstatement of the Papal States by the Congress of Vienna during 1814 and 1815, but that has to be viewed alongside all the provisions of that momentous accord, oddly completed nine days before Napoleon had been completely taken out of circulation by the Battle of Waterloo that took place on Sunday the eighteenth of June, 1815, after Napoleon's one hundred days on the run.

By the year 1820 any notion of temporal rule that Pope Pius VII might have entertained at the start of his papacy should have been consigned to the grave along with the many thousands of inter-denominational corpses that he was unable or unwilling to help. Despite the horror on his doorstep, the last few years of his papacy were largely concerned with the creation and settlement of Dioceses around the world, many in the Americas.

## 16.31 Anno Domini 1820 to 1914
## 16.31.1 Context
### 16.31.1.1 Napoleonic Era – Concert of Europe – World War One

The Imperial Holy Roman Empire had been wound up when its last head of state, Emperor Francis II, abdicated in 1806 and continued as the Austrian Emperor Francis I of a yet promising Austria, in the role he had invented for himself in anticipation of such a moment, in 1804. That move was hastened by Napoleon's decisive victory over Russia and Austria at the Battle of Austerlitz in 1805 that ended the Third Coalition. Keeping everything in the family, Austrian Emperor Francis I's daughter, Marie Louise of Austria, married Napoleon in 1810 and ensured that the mire and corruption of inherited and undeserved privilege would cover the entire geopolitical spectrum, and would provide oxygen for a century of revolution.

Neither the Congress of Vienna nor the ongoing Concert of Europe was in any respect driven by benevolent motives towards the people; the main architect and proponent, the Austrian Prince Clemens von Metternich, devoted his life to suppressing both nationalism and liberalism with a view to returning as far as possible to the status quo of pre-revolutionary France. Within the continental, and specifically the German, world he introduced press censorship and regulated universities to restrict intellectual expression and the publication of anything that smacked of liberalism. He further expressed his aristocratic sentiments by leading the formation of a Holy Alliance of the Crowns of Austria, Prussia and Russia, in order to give mutual aid, when and where needed, to combat political and socio-economic change that might lead to civil unrest.

In summary, the Concert of Europe lasted from 1815 to the start of the Great War in 1914, with considerable revision due to the revolutionary spring of 1848. The founders were Austria, Prussia, the Russian Empire, the United Kingdom (with constitutional reservations) and latterly France. It is sometimes referred to as the "European Restoration" due to its conservative nature and its looking back to pre-French Revolution days, and indeed the reasons for its ineffectiveness and demise related to its unwillingness and-or inability to handle: diverse nationalisms; reasonable movements for egalitarianism and reform; and the German and Italian Unification movements. Significant gatherings of the so-called Great Powers took place on six or seven occasions between 1818 and 1878, but they were powerless to prevent one or two damaging international, though localised, European conflicts. Far worse was yet to come.

### 16.31.1.2 Liberty and Emancipation – at Home and Abroad

Faced with rebellion in Ireland, the 1829 Catholic Emancipation Bill was passed in England, enabling Catholics to enter Parliament, but it would not be until the Universities Tests Act of 1871, allowing Roman Catholics into universities, that Catholic emancipation in the United Kingdom might be considered virtually complete.

The British Great Reform Act of 1832 was an albeit small milestone at this time, but it would lead to near rebellion and many deaths before real reform was achieved. This subject is covered in more detail in the section *Principal Acts of Parliament That Shaped Britain* that is within the chapter titled *The Onset of Egalitarianism and Governance by Statute*.

The Jewish Emancipation that began around 1848 was a significant part of the revolutionary changes during the second half of that turbulent 19th century, and this new freedom was the catalyst for migrations throughout Europe and into the U.S. of already wealthy Jewish bankers and merchants, and Jewish intellectuals from central Europe. Many who were not capitalists became socialists, communists and Zionists – Karl Marx; Vladimir Ilyich Lenin; Gregory Zinoviev; Lev Borisovich Kamenev; Leon Trotsky; Béla Kun; and Theodor Herzl, the Hungarian Jew credited with the popularisation, if not the foundation, of Zionism and the conception of the State of Israel. That initiative would be taken up later, towards the end of World War One, by Chaim Weizmann with the support of the Conservative British Foreign Secretary, Arthur Balfour.

Social revolutions during this period were accompanied by a churning of Empire, and the Third French Republic began after the collapse of the Second French Empire that had lasted from 1852 to 1870. As will be seen shortly, that start of the Third French Republic coincided with the start of the German Second Reich aka the German Empire which began in 1871 after the Franco-Prussian War, and which would last until 1918.

The 1870s also began the period known in France and Belgium as *La Belle Époque* that was a time of peace, optimism, and cultural and scientific development. The hopeful time was not restricted to France and it was known elsewhere in the world by names that implied a Golden Age; in a local and parochial context, 1878 saw the restoration of the Scottish Hierarchy of the Catholic Church in the spring of that year.

The optimism and the dying embers of *La Belle Époque* would, of course, be extinguished on the 28$^{th}$ July, 1914.

### 16.31.1.3 Gathering Storm Clouds

With *La Belle Époque* scarcely a decade old, the shadow of the Grim Reaper was already stirring beyond the horizon, as 1882 saw Italy enter a Triple Alliance with Germany and Austria.

In April 1904 France and Britain took the step that would effectively end any possibility of further war between the two States. They settled their outstanding colonial disputes, mainly North African, and signed up to a bi-partisan peace treaty that would last until the World War Two French Vichy Government signed a premature armistice with Germany that persisted from July 1940 to the conclusion of the allied *Liberation* during 1944. The 1904 agreement was known as *The Entente Cordiale*, and military confrontations with Germany that stopped just short of conflict began immediately during the first decade of the 20$^{th}$ century over Morocco.

By 1912 France, Britain and Russia had declared an alliance, and Germany was left with only partial support in the form of the Triple Alliance comprising itself, Austria-Hungary and Italy – the scene was thereby set for the widest and worst conflict the world had ever known.

In reality, within the preceding century-long Concert of Europe, from 1814 to 1914, the Grim Reaper and high-fatality warfare were never far away, as will be seen during the next few pages, and as may be seen in the chapter on the protracted Russian-Ottoman wars in Volume Two. That series of wars would weaken the Ottoman and Islamic threat to Europe and strengthen the position of Imperial Russia; an interesting result considering the support for the Islamic Ottomans in their struggle with the Christian Russia Bear that was given by the Christian states of Britain and France during one of the wars, the Crimean War.

Details of the principal wars (excluding the many Russian-Ottoman wars) that provided a continuous chain of conflict throughout the Concert of Europe are as follows.

### 16.31.1.4 Crimean War 1853 to 1856 – Combatants

> Russia
>
> *versus*
>
> An Alliance of the following:
> Ottoman Empire, British Empire, Second French Empire, Kingdom of Sardinia.

### The Treaty of Paris of 1856

Camillo Benso aka the Count of Cavour, who was the Prime Minister of Piedmont, managed to get France involved in the Italian *Risorgimento* during the Crimean War's Treaty of Paris of 1856.

### 16.31.1.5 The Italian Wars of Independence – An Overview

On the doorstep of Blessed Pope Pius IX (1846 to 1878), Italian unification or the *Risorgimento* (Resurgence) was about to spell the end of the Papal States, but first the Austrians had to be ousted from Italy; they were by now even more unpopular after thirty years of the anti-liberal climate engendered by the Austrian architect of the Concert of Europe, Metternich. The wars would last eighteen years from 1848 until 1866.

### 16.31.1.6 First Italian War of Independence – Combatants

The war from 1848 to 1849 had been started by an opportunistic Sardinia against Austria in the revolutionary climate of 1848.

---

Sardinia, Tuscany, Papal States, Kingdom of the Two Sicilies

*versus*

Austrian Empire

---

### Peace Treaty August 1849
### (Charles Albert abdicated to his son Victor Emmanuel II)

The armies of the Two Sicilies and the Papal States were withdrawn after the first one or two engagements and with hindsight it had been too risky a venture. Sardinia was beaten and lucky to get away with just the imposition of reparations without loss of territory.

### 16.31.1.7 Second Italian War of Independence – Combatants

---

France, Sardinia

*versus*

Austria

---

### Armistice of Villafranca July 1859 & Treaty of Zurich November 1859

## The Two Thousand Year War – Papal Hegemony

Although there was some deceit among allies and antagonists, the result of this brief war during 1859 – it lasted less than three months – was eventually as desired, starting with France receiving Lombardy from Austria and passing it straight on to Sardinia. Austria was too proud to do so directly.

The Treaty of Turin in 1860 between France and Sardinia provided for the Duchy of Savoy and the County of Nice to be ceded to France by Sardinia according to an original plan, and subject to plebiscites. The transfer of sovereignty took place but there is much speculation about the fairness of any voting that took place.

In 1860 Sardinia was forced to annex its remaining objective, the United Provinces of Central Italy, because France and Austria had met in secret and agreed that those provinces should be returned to their original owners, not to Sardinia. The United Provinces of Central Italy comprised the Duchies of Parma and Modena, the Grand Duchy of Tuscany, and the Papal States: Ferrara, Bologna, and Romagna. Again, after a plebiscite of uncertain integrity, Sardinia simply took them, and France was not prepared to go to war over the issue for fear of seeing Prussian and-or German entry into what might turn out to be a protracted conflict.

Giuseppe Garibaldi, who was originally from Nice, was unhappy at the trading of his birthplace, and he was also driven by republican aspirations for Italy's unification. The Sardinian Prime Minister, Camillo Benso, aka the Count of Cavour, was also working for Italian unification but he couldn't stand Garibaldi, and King Vittorio Emanuele II was somewhere in the middle trying to maintain unity and order.

The results after a potential civil war before the state was even complete, were: firstly, Garibaldi with his famous "one thousand red shirts" conquered the south and became military overlord of Sicily and Naples; secondly, after defeating the Papal Army at the Battle of Castelfidardo and earning the King an excommunication as a parting shot from the Pope, Prime Minister Cavour captured the Papal States of Umbria in central Italy, and The Marches in north-eastern Italy; and thirdly, the King held court at Naples to negotiate the addition of these two latest pieces to the growing Kingdom of Sardinia, now on the verge of becoming the Kingdom of Italy.

The Kingdom was officially proclaimed on March 17, 1861, and ten days later Rome was declared as the capital, even though it had not yet been taken and was still under French protection.

In June, 1862, Garibaldi unilaterally marched towards Rome intent on taking it, and he had to be prevented by armed intervention and a brief period of imprisonment. Towards the end of 1864 the King negotiated a French withdrawal of troops from Rome, to be completed within a two year period, during which the Pope would be allowed to build up his own defences. By the end of 1866 it was believed that the French had all gone, and King Vittorio Emanuele II had moved his capital to Florence, just that little bit nearer to his final objective.

### 16.31.1.8 A Link Between the German and Italian Unifications

Austria at this time still had control of Venice and the Pope had Rome, and while the current Italo-Papal centric theme is the *Risorgimento*, it isn't possible to progress further without involving German unification and its birth trauma.

At a time when the Industrial Revolution had peaked, and trade would have encouraged a rationalisation of tariffs, real German nationalism had also been kick-started by Napoleon's shake-up of Europe, so there were several reasons to want unification. The German Question, as it was known, concerned the best way to achieve unification, and the two feasible options were: a Prussian-led small solution, *Kleindeutsche Lösung*, just for northern states and without Austria; or an Austrian-led solution involving all German-speaking peoples, *Großdeutsche Lösung*.

Austria had ceded Silesia to Prussia at the Treaty of Aix-la-Chapelle aka Aachen in 1748 after the War of Austrian Succession of 1740 to 1748.

The predominant faction within the Hohenzollern Dynasty of Prussia and the states within the Prussian camp were all Protestant, whereas the Hapsburgs of Austria and the German states within the Austrian camp were Catholic.

Prussian ethnicity was German, whereas the Austrian Empire contained several non-Germanic members such as Magyars and Slavs.

Denmark had taken control of Schleswig-Holstein in a war from 1848 to 1851 mainly against Prussia, but by 1864 divisions had deepened to reveal a diminished Danish culture in Schleswig, and a wholly German culture in Holstein, so that when there were additional issues of succession, Prussia and Austria both felt they could justifiably have it – have Schleswig-Holstein that is. Which they did by nine months of war against Denmark, culminating in the ratification of the Treaty of Vienna in October, 1864. The Prussian Prime Minister and Foreign Minister since 1862 was the formidable Otto von Bismarck, and he established the partition of Schleswig-Holstein between Prussia (Schleswig) and Austria (Holstein) at the Gastein Convention in August 1865.

Bismarck's real intentions were made clear when, as a result of an administrative dispute with Austria over Schleswig-Holstein, he invaded Holstein to deliberately provoke war with Austria, and he also declared that the German Confederacy or *Deutscher Bund* was terminated.

## 16.31.1.9 Map – States of the Kingdom of Sardinia 1860s

Map from http://commons.wikimedia.org/wiki/ Public Domain

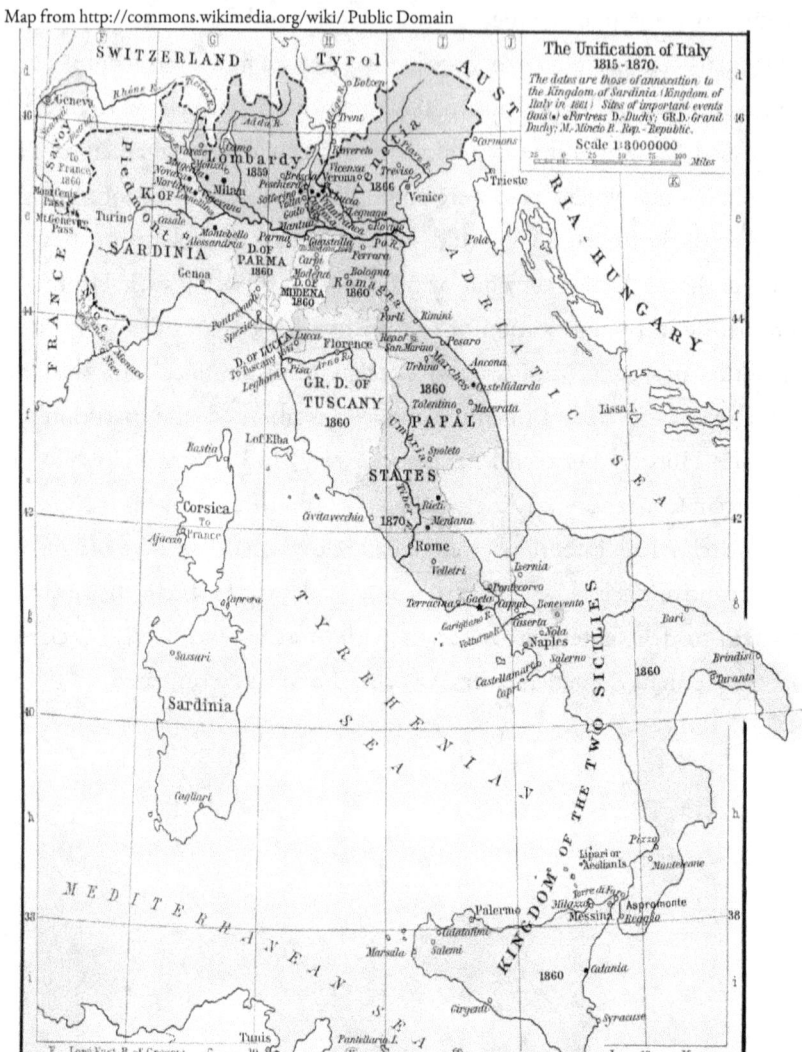

### 16.31.1.10 Austrian-Prussian or Third Italian Independence War

The Austrian-Prussian war (June-August 1866) that followed was beneficial to both German unification and the Italian *Risorgimento,* since Italy was allied to Prussia in early 1866, and at this time Austria was in decline, whereas both Prussia and Italy were experiencing growth. For the Italians it was the Third Independence War.

Battles were won by all belligerents, so a peace treaty was encouraged by Bismarck as soon as it was advantageous to him, and before either France or Russia could get involved. The Peace of Prague was agreed in August, 1866, by which France, having previously agreed with Austria to stay neutral, received control of Mantua and Venice, and by secret protocol passed them to Italy; Prussia received the province of Schleswig-Holstein and several other German states; and very significantly, Austria withdrew from any relationship with German states, which left the way free for further acquisitions by the newly defined North German Confederation.

Despite the expectation that all foreign troops would have left Rome, the Pope was still under French protection in 1867, and a second attempt to liberate the city by Garibaldi in October was repulsed.

### 16.31.1.11 Bismarck Lends a Hand

The expected balance of power among the dominions that resulted from the historical breakup of Charlemagne's empire a millennium earlier was disturbed by the Iron Chancellor Bismarck when he responded to the French declaration of war made by Emperor Napoleon III. That French declaration was originally just against Prussia, but Bismarck vigorously took up the challenge of what would become known as the Franco-Prussian war of 1870, by surprising the French when he brought in other German States. He did this faster than the French could mobilise, France being obliged to draw troops back to the motherland from Italy in August.

One of the Prussian objectives was the annexation of Alsace and Lorraine, which had been seized by France in the 17th century, but results would far exceed that modest aim.

In less than a month, at the Battle of Sedan in September, the French Emperor Napoleon III and an army of more than one hundred thousand had been captured by the Prussians who went on to lay siege to Paris from September 1870 until January 1871. A decision was made to not launch a full scale attack on the capital of the now defunct Second Empire, but to try to destroy the French army in the field, while demoralising the civil population. After several inconclusive engagements, Bismarck was at first denied the opportunity, but finally received permission to bombard Paris with heavy artillery, thus coaxing the surrender of a still defiant Paris.

A triumphal entry to Paris and a victory parade, followed by the crowning of the Hohenzollern Kaiser Wilhelm Friedrich Ludwig I in the Hall of Mirrors at the Palace of Versailles, did not endear the Germans to the French, and gave a lot of Gallic folk ideas for vengeful ceremonies over the next seventy years. The tit-for-tat would, of course, end in June 1940.

## The Two Thousand Year War – Papal Hegemony

## 16.31.1.12 Map – German States 1866 – The Deutsche Bund

Map from http://commons.wikimedia.org/wiki/Category:Maps released under CC-BY-SA
http://creativecommons.org/licenses/by-sa/3.0/  Author: Ziegelbrenner

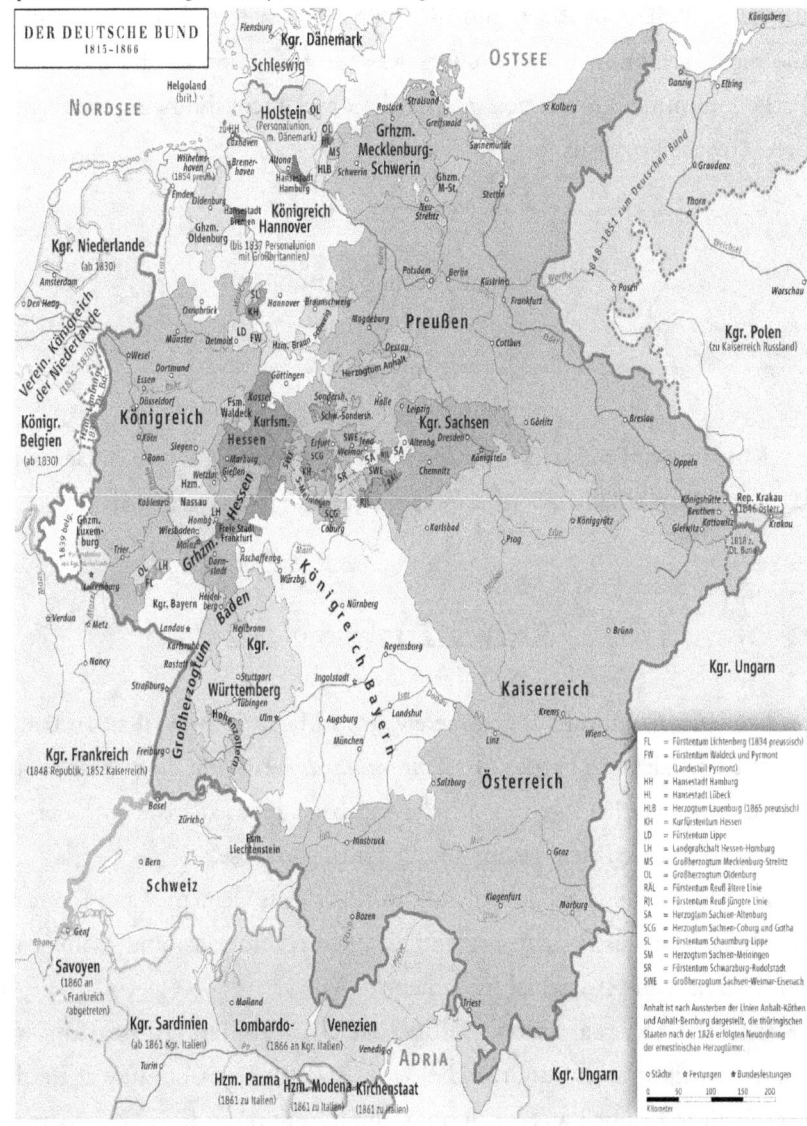

### 16.31.1.13 Franco-Prussian War – Combatants

The result of this war from July 1870 to May 1871 was the formation of the Second German Reich and the Third French Republic, but possibly the most well-known development was the formation of the short-lived Paris Commune, a revolutionary French Government following the French defeat by the Prussians.

---

French Second Republic

*versus*

Kingdom of Prussia, North German Confederation, southern German States: Baden, Württemberg, Bavaria, Hesse-Darmstadt

---

## Treaty of Frankfurt of 1871

The Paris Commune lasted merely from March to May, 1871, and after street barricades and battles, the *Communards* were brutally put down by French conservative forces, many having been released from prisoner-of-war camps by the Prussians specifically for the purpose.

That first revolution by a mainly working class element was a foretaste of the later successful Russian and Chinese revolutions, and it involved both Marxist and Anarchist movements.

### 16.31.1.14 The Papal States, Belligerent Until Italian Unification

Meanwhile, fifteen hundred kilometres away in Rome, in July, 1870, the First Vatican Council was continuing, and it went on to affirm the doctrine of papal infallibility discussed earlier. There had been many ecumenical councils, the most recent having been held at the Lateran Palace, but this was the first at the Vatican, and it had been started in 1869. That First Vatican Council would run on and on, and only be formally closed in 1960.

## The Two Thousand Year War – Papal Hegemony

In September, 1870, the Pope had, with vitriolic language, firmly rejected an honourable approach from the King of Italy that offered financial support, papal sovereignty over the Vatican, diplomatic immunity for papal nuncios and their visitors, and the façade of the entry of Italian troops solely for the protection of the papacy so that the Pope would not appear to have been drubbed and could maintain his dignity.

After a slow advance, in order to give such an honourable peace a chance, the besiegers were eventually forced to breach a wall with artillery because the Pope had ordered a defence to be made so that it would be seen that he was unwilling to surrender the city even though he was on record long before that as having indicated that he accepted the inevitable. Thanks to his callous and duplicitous reasoning and consideration, seventy or so troops were killed before the Pope scuttled away and retreated into the Vatican. There had been no need for any bloodshed at all.

The struggle had been a long one, and it was the Kings of Sardinia who had become pre-eminent, and who had been revealed as the Royal House of Italy in waiting. Sardinian King Victor Emmanuel I, aka the Duke of Aosta and of Savoy, had been part of the First Coalition against Revolutionary France during the period 1792 to 1797, but for his pains he had seen all of his dominions except for the Monarchy of Sardinia taken by the French during the Napoleonic Wars of 1802 to 1814. He got them back with the addition of Genoa after the Congress of Vienna in June 1815, but he abdicated in 1821 to appease revolutionary demands for change, and he was replaced by his brother, the Sardinian King Charles Felix, who, following the ending of the revolution with the assistance of Austrian troops, would last for ten years until 1831.

The next Sardinian king to have a go was a cousin of the outgoing childless Charles Felix, Sardinian King Charles Albert, who had previously been in the service of Napoleon, and who reputedly had liberal ideas, although in reality he seemed to vacillate and was unable to maintain any consistent managerial success. He had been part of the First Italian War of Independence, but after later defeat in his own right, he abdicated and went into voluntary exile in Portugal. His principal successes were the establishment of constitutional government that would last throughout the one hundred years of a Royalist Italy, and the production of a son – Victor Emanuel – to whom he transferred the Kingship.

So at long last Rome was entered on 20<sup>th</sup> September, 1870, and the Vatican was entered the next day, with the first king of a united Italy, King Victor Emanuel II, lasting for eight years until he died in Rome in 1878. It would be another forty years before the Italian-speaking southern Tyrolean province of Trentino was united with the new Italy; Trentino would be retained by Austria until 1919.

**Postscript:** In the Lateran Treaty of 1929 between Pope Pius XI and Benito Mussolini, the papacy finally recognised the state of Italy, with Rome as its capital, and in return the State of Italy recognised papal sovereignty over the Vatican City, an area of about one hundred acres, and with a population of less than one thousand. *A large financial sum was paid to the Pope as compensation.*

### 16.31.2 The Popes of the Period 1820 to 1914

**Leo XII (1823 to 1829).** From a noble family that had gained wealth and power from the papacy of Pope Leo XI just over two hundred years previously – the family was still resident in the Papal States – he was a prisoner for a time after Napoleon's takeover in 1798. His personal integrity has been questioned, and although he had some success with ecclesiastical matters, he is said to have been reactionary and utterly useless as a temporal leader. Pope Leo XII supported the Catholic Emancipation Bill in England but died a couple of months before its implementation.

**Pius VIII (1829 to 1830).** From a noble family in the March region of the Papal States, he was Jesuit educated and strongly against nepotism, ensuring that none of his relatives remained in clerical positions after his election as Pope. He was against any modernity in translations of the Bible, and issued a brief that required children of Catholic families to receive Catholic education.

Pope Pius VIII was troubled by the French Revolution of 1830 aka the July Revolution that saw the Bourbon French King Charles X (younger brother of Louis XVIII ) replaced by Louis-Philippe the Duke of Orléans.

The issues were as follows: firstly, the Bourbons had been a hereditary continuation of the pre-revolution dynasty, Louis-Philippe was not a Bourbon; secondly, the introduction of the death penalty in 1825 for religious hate crimes (actually described as blasphemy and sacrilege), that might backfire on Catholics; thirdly, the suggestion of financial and property returns to victims of the revolution; fourthly, the interference by Charles X in parliamentary matters and his dissolution of the National Guard of Paris; but finally, to cap it all, censorship of the press.

Three days of revolution were all that was needed to put the Bourbons to flight to England, and to see the institution of a Constitutional Monarchy under French King Louis-Philippe I, as it happened, the last King of France. Mimicking the French July uprising, there were others in Europe, notably Poland, and the southern Netherlands that saw the creation of an independent Kingdom of Belgium in July, 1831.

**Gregory XVI (1831 to 1846).** From a noble Venetian family, Pope Gregory XVI was ultra-conservative, opposing any liberal measures; he had been created Cardinal by Pope Leo XII in 1825. To combat popular uprisings following those of France, Austrian troops were employed by the Papal States to restore order, and thousands are said to have been massacred by order of this reactionary Pontiff who was against railways and gas lighting in case it promoted rebellion among the people. His Cardinals are reputed to have been behind many atrocities during a period of Roman and Papal anarchy said to have persisted for decades during the 19th century. The persistent postponement of reform and public works was believed to be partly responsible for the public's continuing rebellion and their hatred of him.

**Blessed Pius IX (1846 to 1878).** From one of the lesser noble families in the port of Senigallia on the Adriatic coast of the Papal States, his reign of thirty-one years was the longest of any pope, and to him, it almost certainly felt like it. He saw invasion of the Papal States, sweeping changes *de jure* and *de facto*, and he was close to being assassinated at times. From the start of his pontificate his behaviour attracted accusations of liberalism, and even of being a Freemason or one of the revolutionary republican

Carbonaris. In reality, as would be shown later, his liberalism was restricted to temporal matters and certainly did not reduce his spiritual and ideological dogmatism. The Catholic Encyclopaedia, with, of course, an agenda of Catholic support, and not infrequently sanitisation, breaks his reign down into four periods as follows:

1. **Conciliatory policies (1846 to 1848):** As above, characterised by political reform, release of political prisoners, and the setting up of consultative groups of people taken from the wider population. Pius IX introduced technological innovations in city infrastructure and encouraged trade – economic differences between northern and southern Italy started to become more apparent at this time. For his overall benevolent posture he was universally and internationally applauded.

2. **Failure of appeasement (1848 to 1850):** Reaping the results of his benevolence, or maybe it was just a reflection of the international climate of revolution in 1848, there were ever more demands for further concessions and radical change, and there were riots in the summer. The riots that followed the Pope's declaration of neutrality in respect of the developing conflict at Milan with Austria culminated in the assassination of the Pope's prime minister, Pellegrino Rossi, who had his throat cut in the Papal Chancellery that November. The pope fled to the Kingdom of the Two Sicilies from where he called for help from the Concert of Europe.

In the meantime, a populist Republic of Rome was declared that gave libertarian commitments, such as religious freedom and suffrage, and called for war against Austria, which country was seen as a foreign presence in Italy. Indeed the war of Italian independence and unification had already begun at Milan under King Albert of Sardinia, with the first battle being lost when the Kingdom of Sardinia was defeated by Austria at the Battle of Novara in March of 1849. Despite that bad news from the north, and incensed at their excommunication by the Pope, the Roman Republic resolved to maintain its independence, and when confronted with a besieging French and Spanish army on behalf of the Pope, the barricades went up and pleas were sent to the French reminding them of their own constitution and the right to self-determination. Support for the republicans arrived from many places including Giuseppe Garibaldi with his Italian Legion, but France, Spain, and a potential Austrian army freed in the north were too much, and the stillborn republic took the discretionary options of an agreed armistice for Rome, and retreat for Garibaldi so that he could at least fight another day.

The pope pointedly returned to Rome in his own time in 1850, and instituted a regime of his own making, but one that was favourable to France which would continue to support papal temporal governance, though with a switch to auxiliary forces after 1866 that lasted until 1870 when all French forces would finally be recalled to the motherland in response to the Franco-Prussian War of 1870 to 1871.

The Universalis Ecclesiae Papal Bull of September 1850 re-established the hierarchy of the Catholic Church in England and gave a boost to Protestant prejudice against Catholicism.

**3. His subsequent rule (1850 to 1858):** The pope was now resident in the Vatican for the first time, and all subsequent popes followed suit. Most temporal duties were allocated to a Cardinal Antonelli, and the Pope got on with spiritual matters, receiving so it is said, a favourable welcome throughout the Papal States, though there are many allegations of not just insensitivity to human rights abuses, but the active prosecution of terror, torture and execution. He had become a reactionary and embittered pope, and even his military protectors found it necessary to protest at the iniquities of the papal clergy. There may have been up to 15,000 recruits in the papal army at the time, and many are said to have been criminals. Cardinal Antonelli, eventually Secretary of State, and sanitised in the Catholic Encyclopaedia, was actually from a humble background, and yet he retired with a *personal* fortune of possibly one hundred million Lire; one brother was president of the Roman Bank, and another was the head of an office that was responsible for the regulation of grain imports.

**4. Intrigues against the Papal States (1858 to 1878):** During his later life the Pope is best remembered for the concept of Papal Infallibility that began with his initially personal assumption of infallibility when, in 1854, he issued the Bull *Ineffabilis Deus* concerning the absence of Original Sin from the Virgin Mary. The issue was that he issued the Bull himself, albeit after consulting the bishops, but that it should have been issued by the Ecumenical Council to have the full weight of Infallibility. Worse was to follow when, in 1864, he published an encyclical *Quanta Cura* (Condemning Current Errors) with an annexe, "The Syllabus of Errors Condemned by Pius IX". In the publication he claims total control of everyone, all culture and science, and all education by the Church. There is no freedom of worship or conscience for the individual, and the Church is beyond any form of State control. This was a declaration of Utramontanism meaning that absolute authority in the Church should be vested in the Pope. More astonishing than the preposterous arrogance of his statements is the fact that, in 1870, the Vatican Ecumenical Council actually proclaimed his infallibility, and added for good measure that his jurisdiction was *global*. The phrases below are verbatim examples from the publication of precisely what he was condemning; the style of the encyclical was to present the words of the offender, and then pronounce them to be heretical or unacceptable. One could be forgiven for reading the quotes below and thinking them to be quite reasonable, but that's not what the Pope thought. So, to make this very clear, the phrases below were anathema to Blessed Pius IX, and not what he would advocate – presumably he read them somewhere as part of a revolutionary manifesto or treatise perhaps (this author's guess), and he just didn't like them:

> *"liberty of conscience and worship is each man's personal right, which ought to be legally proclaimed and asserted in every rightly constituted society; and that a right resides in the citizens to an absolute liberty, which should be restrained by no authority whether ecclesiastical or civil, whereby they may be able openly and publicly to manifest and declare any of their ideas whatever, either by word of mouth, by the press, or in any other way."*

and

## The Two Thousand Year War – Papal Hegemony

*"The Roman Pontiff can, and ought to, reconcile himself, and come to terms with progress, liberalism and modern civilisation".*

This was not some shadowy remote figure in antiquity, this was modern man, only a hundred and thirty or so years ago. There's even a photograph of him. Sadly though, given the politically correct repression that has been growing during the first decade of the 21st century, and the head-in-the sand vision of politicians, he may even be ahead of his time.

In spite of telling people he was infallible, the reality was that internationally, and throughout Italy, the Church, or at least its pontiff with his temporal pretensions, was both unpopular and unsuccessful. There were issues among ecclesiastical and legal-secular authorities in Russia, Prussia, Austria, Switzerland, and the German Confederation; and in Poland the bloody January Uprising of 1863 against Russian oppression led to much collateral damage to the Catholic clergy, particularly since Pope Pius IX was outspoken in his support for Catholic Polish against Orthodox Russians. Only France, Spain, Portugal and diverse smaller South American states seemed compliant with papal pronouncements.

So in 1870, Blessed Pius IX retreated into the Vatican with the sure knowledge that whatever he pronounced was infallible and absolute, and for the next eight years there is not much more information about him other than how his length of time as pontiff was applauded.

**Leo XIII (1878 to 1903).** From an old noble family of Siena, he was Jesuit educated and a priest from 1837, seeing much of the chaos and anarchy of Italy at that time, and acting as a temporal administrator and law enforcer in the bandit country of Benevento. Pope Leo XIII was considered a reformer and more open to modernity than Pius IX, though he continued the policy of self-containment in the Vatican and advocated abstention from voting in Italian State elections. He was the first pope to appear in video photography and of whom the voice was recorded. He was outgoing internationally, and sent many encyclicals, though he couldn't resist proscribing the Anglican Church, and by implication the spiritual security of some tens of millions of church-goers, with his *Apostolicae Curae*, for example:

> "...36. Wherefore, strictly adhering, in this matter, to the decrees of the pontiffs, our predecessors, and confirming them most fully, and, as it were, renewing them by our authority, of our own initiative and certain knowledge, we pronounce and declare that ordinations carried out according to the Anglican rite have been, and are, absolutely null and utterly void."

**Saint Pius X (1903 to 1914).** The son of a postman in Venice, he was the first pope for some time without any aristocratic pretensions, and was known for benevolence and charity to the poor, and for his quick response with aid to victims of natural disasters. He made no attempt to elevate any of his family, and they received no financial assistance from him. He was no modernist though, and held to traditional ecclesiastical values, censoring books and promoting the organisation of agents to identify and report anything that smacked of Modernism, Indifferentism (the belief that other religions have value), Relativism (the belief that everything is relative and without absolutes), or any other heresy. Continuing the attitude of his immediate predecessors, he refused to accept the loss of the Papal States to Italy, and obstinately held out against foreign secular governments, even seeing a loss of diplomatic relations with France in connection with his refusal to acknowledge the Third Republic that was declared after the Franco-Prussian war disaster. Finally, he is credited with having made a contribution to the Irish Troubles by a papal decree in 1908 that complicated the issue of marriage between Protestant and Catholic.

### 16.32 Anno Domini 1914 to 1939

#### 16.32.1 Context

##### 16.32.1.1 The Great War and the Following Inter-War Years

World War One, aka the Great War as it was known at the time and before there was a second one, dragged on from 1914 to 1918 and it cannot with justice be described here. There are many approaches to its documentation, some consisting of several volumes, and they are easy to find in print and on the internet. In the context of this book, and at this point in the 20th century of Papal hegemony, detail will be restricted to a look at the causes and the results of a protracted event that to any sane mind must surely defy the existence of an all-powerful and benevolent God.

While the causes of the First World War are many and complex, there is a single explanation for the scale of the war – why it was so *Great* or widespread – as opposed to being just one or two conflicts, diverse in space and diverse in time as have been seen from time immemorial. That single explanation comes from the scale of the alliances that encircled the planet.

Furthermore, the territorial consequences of some of those alliances were exaggerated a hundredfold in respect of subsidiary colonial possessions overseas; at that time the British Empire spanned the globe and comprised dozens of what would become Nation-States after 1950. In this respect Britain was followed closely by France, and then to an increasingly lesser degree by Holland, Belgium and Germany, while other imperial powers struggled at times to remain neutral or unaligned.

Russia, of course, was the largest country on earth, and its empire embraced many republics and territories that would become better known after its 1919 revolution as the Union of Soviet Socialist Republics. Russia grew from 1721 to its largest extent in 1866, just before it sold Alaska to the U.S.A. the following year, and there is further detail on Russia's military districts that covered all of the republics in the chapter in Volume Two on the Russian Empires.

The principal alliances that drew the belligerents of World War One into uncomfortable focus were:
- Britain, France, and Belgium
- Britain and Japan
- France and Russia
- Russia and Serbia
- Germany and Austria-Hungary

The fuse that would ignite the petard, however, was not situated somewhere along the enormous vulnerable frontiers, later to feature countless miles of muddy, death trap and rat-infested trenches, meandering among France, Belgium, Germany and Russia. This particular petard, or small bomb, which was intended for a very small inter-state political doorway, was to be found secreted within the relatively tiny – almost tribal – but volatile, county-sized components of the Balkans; and in particular the target was the link between the closet bullies of Serbia and Bosnia-Herzegovina.

The background to this powder keg of unrest in the otherwise heady days of the early 20$^{th}$ century had begun in 1908 when Austria annexed Bosnia, and Serbia had threatened war; and the fast fuse would be lit by a hand from the Black Hand Gang of Slavic-Serbian nationalists who wanted the Austro-Hungarian Empire out of Bosnia in order to clear the way so that Bosnia could be absorbed by a greater Serbia. That petard would hoist not only the Serbian nationalists themselves, but much of the world as well.

The Serbian nationalists thought the best way of promoting this small-scale and very reasonable ambition would be to assassinate Archduke Franz Ferdinand of Austria-Este, heir to the position of Emperor of Austria-Hungary, who was visiting Sarajevo in Bosnia-Herzegovina on that fateful day, 28$^{th}$ June, 1914; and the Serbian, Gavrilo Princip, and others, with the support of resources supplied by Belgrade, did succeed in their immediate objective of slaying the Archduke and his wife, but the millions of deaths that were to follow were in all fairness probably beyond their worst nightmares, and the rest, as they say, is history.

In November 1918 when the armistice was called it had been four years since the balmy days when the boys had marched out of their villages under blue skies, flags waving and bands playing, as the mothers, wives and sweethearts, watched them go. And it was for four interminable years that the lions and the flower of both the Allies and the Central Powers had been sent to their deaths by the donkeys of the military High Commands, with the encouragement of the general public and, poignantly, with the acquiescence of their own friends and families. At the end of this madness Europe was blasted and devastated – the scale of losses being apocalyptic, and rarely, if ever, previously seen in such a short period.

While figures among internet websites differ, the orders of magnitude below are considered sufficient to indicate the overall horror, and a table of total dead is provided below. A simpler list of military losses alone is as follows:

- British Empire – 890,000 killed and 1,500,000 wounded.
- France – 1,400,000 killed and 2,500,000 wounded.
- Belgium – 50,000 killed.
- Italy – 600,000 killed.
- Russia – 1,700,000 killed.
- America – 116,000 killed.
- Germany – 2,000,000 killed.
- Austria-Hungary – 1,200,000 killed.
- Turkey – 325,000 killed.
- Bulgaria – 100,000 killed.

Almost nine million were killed and twenty-one million were wounded; and large parts of northern France and Belgium were wasteland.

Had anything been achieved?
Did Austria need to declare war on Serbia?
Did Russia need to mobilise to go to Serbia's aid?
Did Germany then need to declare war on a mobilising Russia?
Did France need to declare against Germany in support of Russia?
Did Germany then need to actually attack France via Belgium?
Did Britain need to send the Expeditionary Force to support Belgium?
Did Japan, Italy, and the U.S.A. need to enter the war over the next few years?

Wars as a result of the above questions or similar ones have been repeated, and the circumstances in which they arose have been re-enacted many times during the last one hundred years. They have always been associated with the same causes and with the same intent, if not with the same actors; and although they have usually been on a much smaller scale, the collateral damage to civilians in all subsequent wars has seen an ever upwards trend.

The defeated Central Powers were severely punished for their part in the Great War by a series of Treaties, Austria-Hungary also being split into two separate Nation-States. Germany was subject to the Treaty of Versailles, Austria to the Treaty of Saint Germain, and Hungary to the Treaty of Trianon. Bulgaria was subject to the Treaty of Neuilly, and the Ottoman aka Turkish Empire to the Treaty of Sèvres; all lost territory and suffered financial penalties, and in the case of Germany, the financial burden was completely unrealistic, and is commonly said to be one of the causes of the Second World War that would soon follow.

Some further events in the context of the period 1914 to 1939 are as follows:

- The German Weimar Republic lasted from 1919 to 1933.
- 1931. A republican government took power in Spain.
- January 1933. President Hindenburg appointed Adolf Hitler Chancellor of Germany.
- February 1933. The Reichstag Fire was blamed on the second largest party in Germany, the Communist Party or KPD, which was then banned, resulting in a government majority for Hitler.
- 14th July 1933. The Nazis banned all other political parties.
- 20th July 1933. The Reichskonkordat was signed between Pope Pius XI for the Vatican, and President Hindenburg and Chancellor Adolf Hitler for Germany. See below.
- 1936. Catholics in Spain who were a clear majority of the population largely supported the military coup against the Republican Government led by General Francisco Franco.

## 16.32.1.2 Map – Opposing and Neutral Forces – World War One

Map from http://commons.wikimedia.org/wiki/ Public Domain

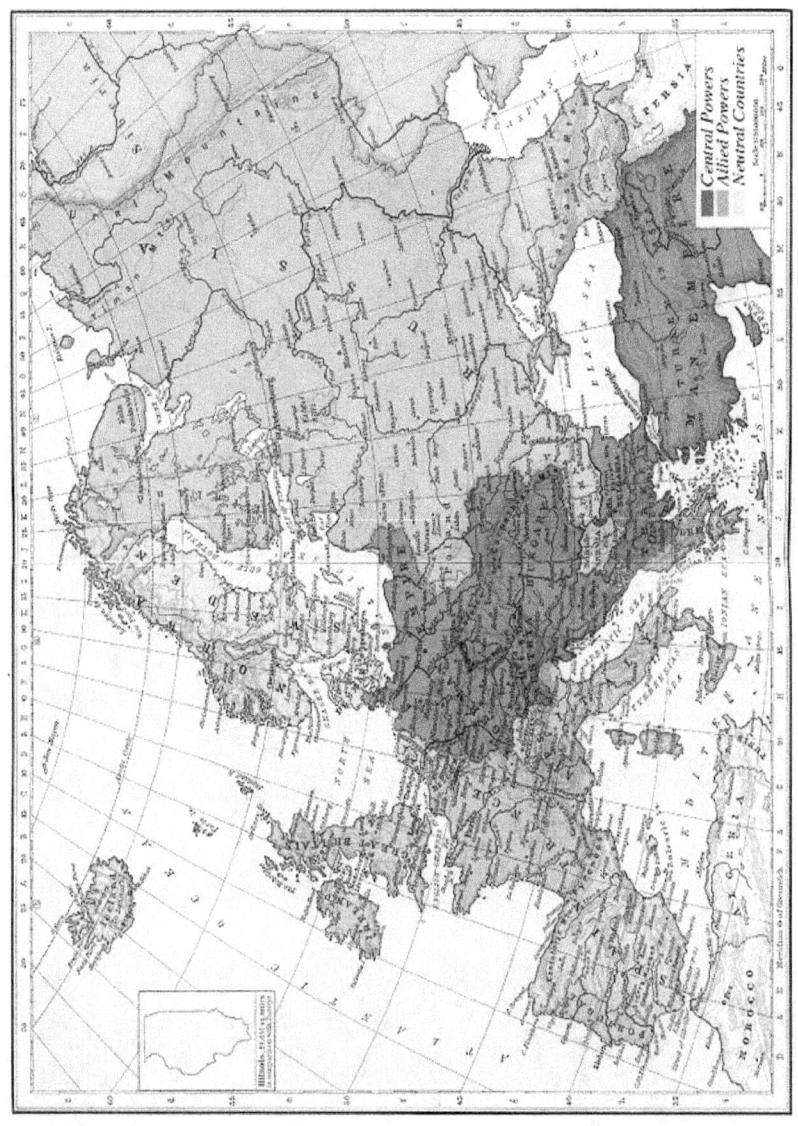

### 16.32.1.3 Map – Alliances at the Start of World War One

Map from http://commons.wikimedia.org/wiki/Category:Maps released under CC-BY-SA
http://creativecommons.org/licenses/by-sa/2.5/

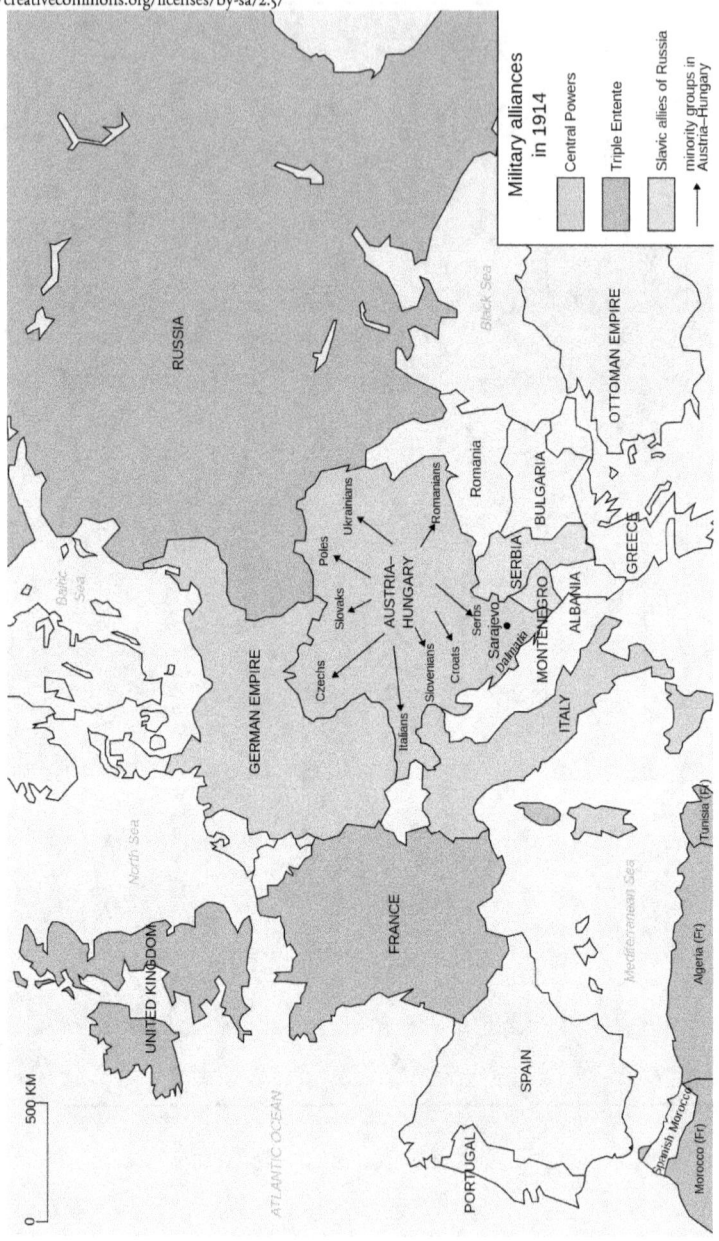

## 16.32.1.4  Map – The European Powers in 1918

Map from http://commons.wikimedia.org/wiki/ Public Domain

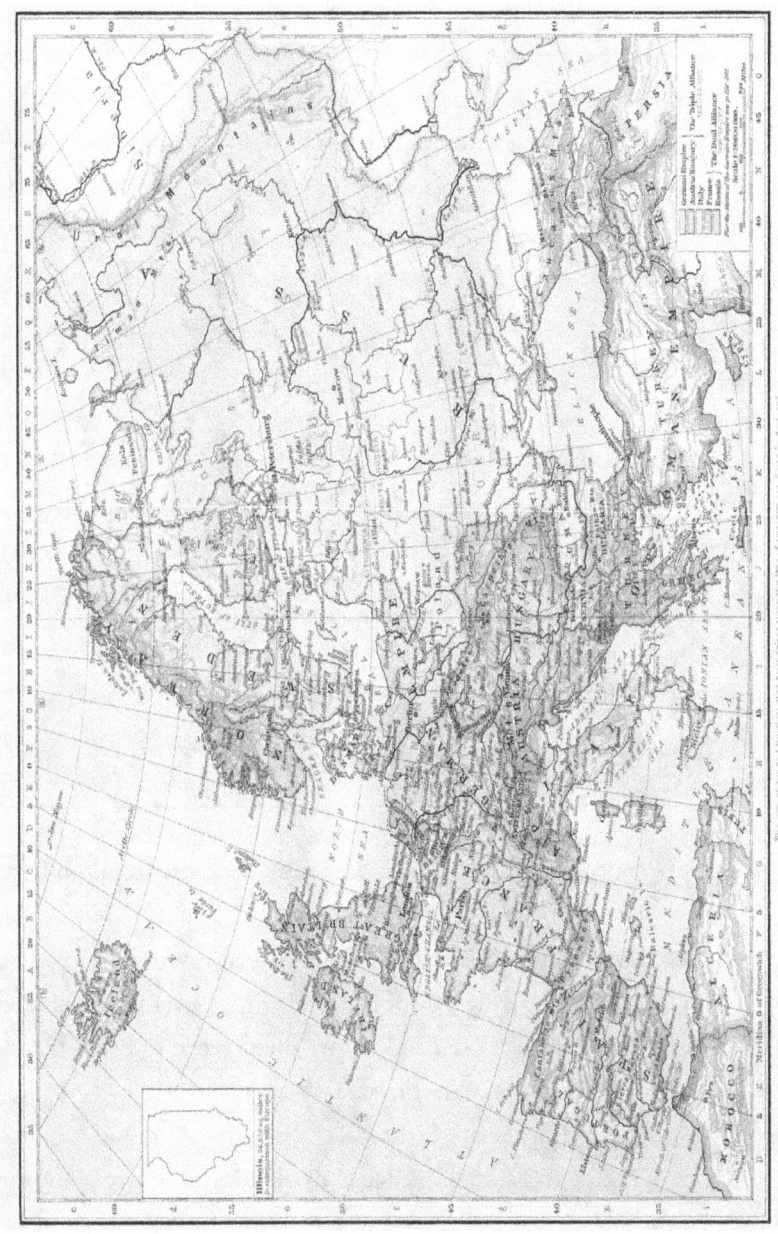

*The Two Thousand Year War – Papal Hegemony*

## 16.32.1.5 Map – German Losses by the Treaty of Versailles

Map from http://commons.wikimedia.org/wiki/Category:Maps released under CC-BY-SA
http://creativecommons.org/licenses/by-sa/2.5/  Author: 52 Pickup

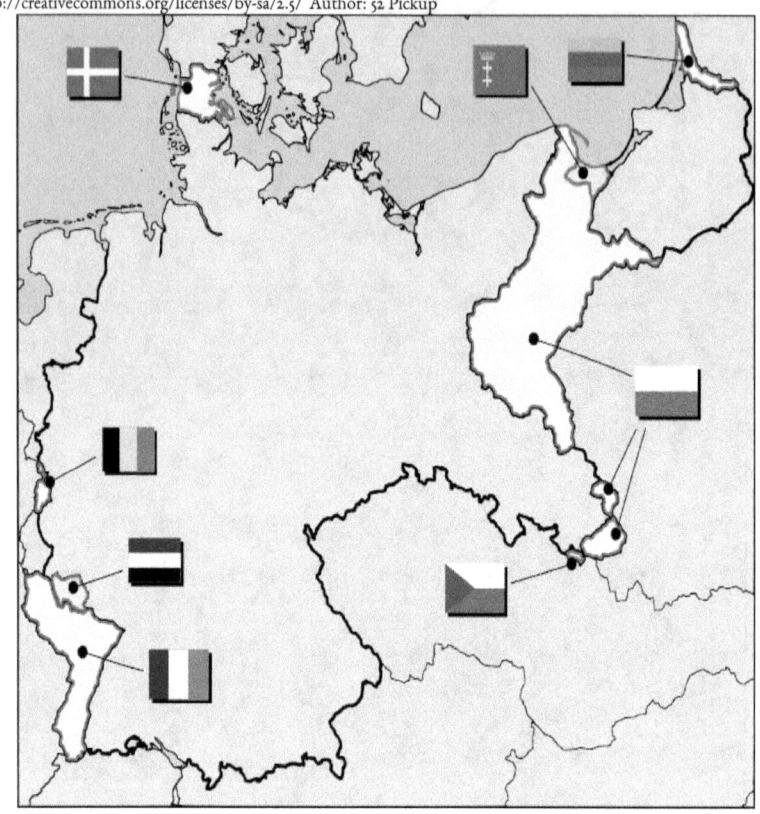

Key to Regions Ceded After World War One, Clockwise from top Left:
1. Northern Schleswig to Denmark.
2. Danzig under League of Nations control awaiting plebiscite.
3. Memel under League of Nations control awaiting plebiscite.
4. West Prussia, Posen and Upper Silesia ceded to Poland.
5. Hultschin to Czechoslovakia.
6. Alsace-Lorraine to France.
7. The Saar under League of Nations control awaiting plebiscite.
8. Eupen and Malmédy to Belgium.

*The Two Thousand Year War – Papal Hegemony*

### 16.32.1.6 Map – Interpretation of Ethnic Distribution in 1918

Map from http://commons.wikimedia.org/wiki/ Public Domain

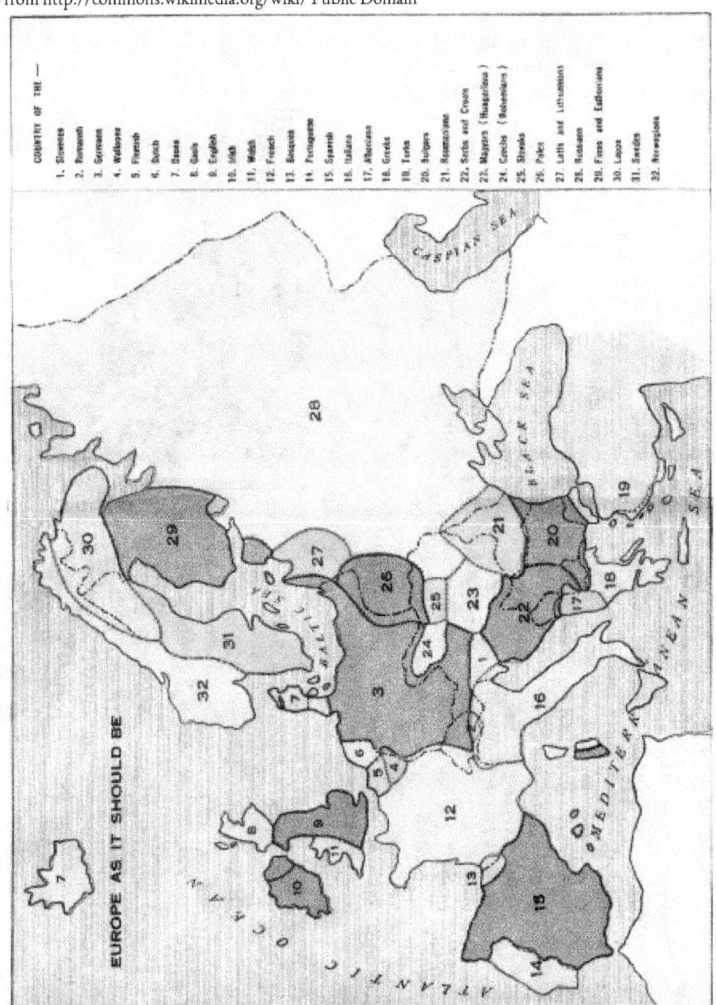

**Key**:
1.Slovenes, 2.Romansh (Swiss), 3.Germans, 4.Walloons, 5.Flemish, 6.Dutch, 7.Danes, 8.Gaels, 9.English, 10.Irish, 11.Welsh, 12.French, 13.Basques, 14.Portuguese, 15.Spanish, 16.Italians, 17.Albanians, 18.Greeks, 19.Turks, 20.Bulgars, 21.Roumanians, 22.Serbs & Croats, 23.Magyars (Hungarians), 24.Czechs (Bohemians), 25.Slovaks, 26.Poles, 27.Letts & Lithuanians, 28.Russians, 29.Finns & Estonians, 30.Lapps, 31.Swedes, 32.Norwegians.

454

*The Two Thousand Year War – Papal Hegemony*

### 16.32.1.7  Map – The Balkans from 1914 to 1992
U.S. Library of Congress, Geography and Map Division.

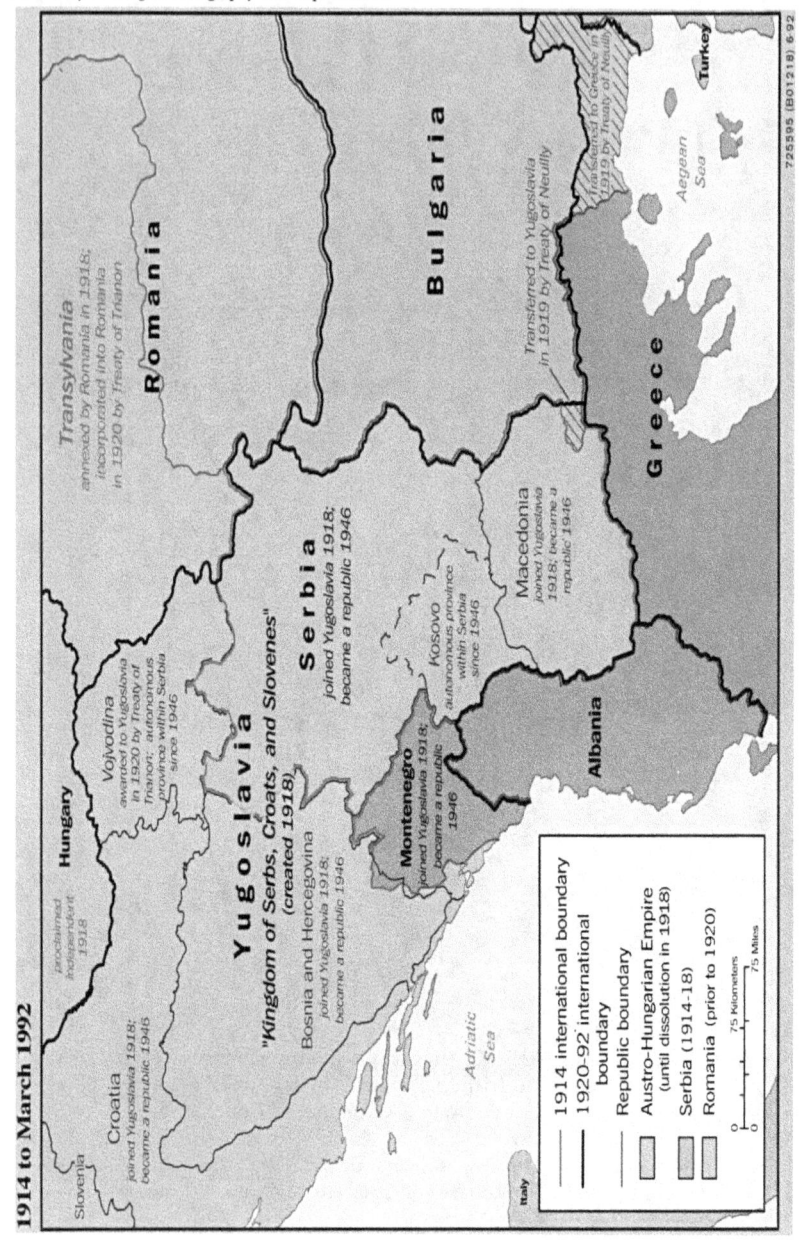

## 16.32.1.8 Table – Human Losses During World War One

http://www.bbc.co.uk/dna/ptop/plain/A2854730

| Country | Dead | Wounded | Missing | Total |
|---|---|---|---|---|
| Russia | 1,700,000 | 5,000,000 | - | 6,700,000 |
| Germany | 1,600,000 | 4,065,000 | 103,000 | 5,768,000 |
| France | 1,359,000 | 4,200,000 | 361,650 | 5,920,650 |
| Austria-Hungary | 922,000 | 3,600,000 | 855,283 | 5,377,283 |
| Italy | 689,000 | 959,100 | - | 1,424,660 |
| Britain | 658,700 | 2,032,150 | 359,150 | 3,050,000 |
| Romania | 335,706 | 120,000 | 80,000 | 535,706 |
| Turkey | 250,000 | 400,000 | - | 650,000 |
| Bulgaria | 87,500 | 152,390 | 27,029 | 266,919 |
| USA | 58,480 | 189,955 | 14,290 | 262,725 |
| Australia | 58,150 | 152,170 | - | 210,320 |
| Canada | 56,500 | 149,700 | - | 206,200 |
| Serbia | 45,000 | 133,148 | 152,958 | 331,106 |
| Belgium | 44,000 | 450,000 | - | 494,000 |
| India | 43,200 | 65,175 | 5,875 | 114,250 |
| New Zealand | 16,130 | 40,750 | - | 56,880 |
| Portugal | 7,222 | 13,751 | 12,318 | 33,291 |
| Greece | 5,000 | 21,000 | 1,000 | 27,000 |
| Montenegro | 3,000 | 10,000 | 7,000 | 20,000 |
| Japan | 300 | 907 | 3 | 1,210 |
| Totals | 7,996,888 | 21,755,196 | 1,979,556 | 31,508,200 |

### 16.32.2 The Popes of the Period 1914 to 1939

**Benedict XV (1914 to 1922).** From the nobility of Genoa, he studied law and entered the clergy in Rome. In spite of what are described as nationalistic tendencies on the part of some of the clergy, he advocated neutrality as war loomed; this was before his election as Pope. On his election in August, like his forerunners after the Italian unification, as a protest against loss of the temporal state he still would not appear on the balcony of Saint Peter's Basilica. As Pontiff he again declared papal neutrality and made unsuccessful attempts to intercede in the Great War in 1916 and 1917, describing it as *"The Suicide of Civilised Europe"* but generally being seen by all belligerents as favouring the opposition. His first papal encyclical on 1st November, 1914, *Ad Beatissimi Apostolorum*, was partly aimed at modernists and revisionists, and although it caught the mood of the time, referring to the dire European atmosphere, it would unfortunately turn out to be a huge understatement. An extract from the encyclical is as follows:

> *"...7. Far different from this is the behaviour of men today. Never perhaps was there more talking about the brotherhood of men than there is today; in fact, men do not hesitate to proclaim that striving after brotherhood is one of the greatest gifts of modern civilisation, ignoring the teaching of the Gospel, and setting aside the work of Christ and of His Church. But in reality never was there less brotherly activity amongst men than at the present moment. Race hatred has reached its climax; peoples are more divided by jealousies than by frontiers; within one and the same nation, within the same city there rages the burning envy of class against class; and amongst individuals it is self-love which is the supreme law over-ruling everything. "*

There were many more clauses bemoaning the war.

In 1915 Benedict XV tried to get both Germany and Austria-Hungary to protest to their Ottoman Turkish allies about the atrocities committed in the name of Islam against the Christian Armenians, but the one million or so civilian deaths were of no consequence to the war machine. In 1917 he continued the implementation, started by Pope Pius X, of Canon Law, which was the codification of previously used Decretals or letters from the Pope. These Decretals were used both as responses to issues and also in a pro-active sense, and up to this time they had been used to define the law; they were based on the *Corpus Juris Civilis*, the Code of Justinian dating back to the early 6th century Emperor of Eastern Rome (Constantinople) that is discussed in the chapter titled *The Eastern Roman or Byzantine Empire 330 to 1453 AD* in Volume Two. That codification process would continue for decades, and would also influence ecclesiastical law on an ecumenical scale.

Because of the Vatican's self-made isolation from mainstream Italian politics, it was not invited to the Paris Peace conference of 1919 and, in the peace that followed, the Pope was obliged to work even harder for spiritual penetration in a world that was becoming further polarised by nationalism and communism as humanity fought to decide if it is left- or right-handed.

**Pius XI (1922 to 1939).** From Milan, his father was a silk weaver (he owned the factory), and the future Pope made an initial academic career in the study of religious manuscripts and librarianship. In 1921, as nuncio to the re-defined Poland, he was expelled because he was seen as too political by both Poles and Germans, but within months he had become a Cardinal, and then Pope. The Catholic movement Catholic Action, composed of laymen (those outside of the church hierarchy and clergy), came under fire in several countries, and in 1931 the Pope was moved to issue encyclical *Non abbiamo bisogno* to refute allegations of political subterfuge in countries such as Spain and Germany, while also showing that Catholicism and Fascism were mutually exclusive. The movement's aims were to spread Catholicism throughout society and up to the seats of power, and it was criticised by conservative members of the clergy as being too activist. It is said that the Catholic Action initiative subsequently reappeared as Christian Democrat parties.

Vatican Radio was established in 1931, and Pius XI was the first pope to make a broadcast.

In 1933, on the 3rd of June, the Pope published his encyclical *Dilectissima Nobis*, condemning the new Republican Spain, and calling for Catholic Action to at least defend the Church, a call that no doubt led to even greater suspicion of Roman Catholicism and papal ambition. One clause is given below, and the full text can be found on the Vatican website:

> "...25. In a special way, We invite all the Faithful to unite in Catholic Action, which We so often have recommended and which, though not constituting a party but rather having set itself above and beyond all political parties, will serve to form the conscience of Catholics, illuminating and corroborating it in defence of the Faith against every snare."

The next month an agreement was reached with Nazi Germany that has provoked debate ever since, and which has, in fact, never been revoked; it is still in force. The Reichskonkordat, 20th July, 1933 was a treaty between the Vatican and Germany; President Hindenburg and Chancellor Adolf Hitler being the principal leaders of Germany, though German Vice-Chancellor Von Papen was the one who signed the treaty.

Looking at just one Article, it seems rather submissive when compared with the one from the encyclical above:

Article 16

> "Before bishops take possession of their dioceses they are to take an oath of loyalty either to the Reich governor of the state (Land) concerned or to the President of the Reich respectively, according to the following formula:
> Before God and on the Holy Gospels I swear and promise, as becomes a bishop, loyalty to the German Reich and to the

*State (Land) of... I swear and promise to honour the legally constituted government and to cause the clergy of my diocese to honour it. With dutiful concern for the welfare and the interests of the German state, in the performance of the ecclesiastical office entrusted to me, I will endeavour to prevent everything injurious which might threaten it."*

Other Concordats with totalitarian regimes of the time were:

Italy - Mussolini; Spain - Franco; Austria - Dollfuss; Portugal - Salazar. These have all been either revoked or substantially revised.

Two encyclicals are of interest and illuminate the Church's attitude to employer - employee rights and obligations, and to the developing philosophies and practice of communism and fascism.

*Rerum Novarum* ( On the New Things) is an encyclical issued by Pope Leo XIII, 15 May 1891.

*Quadragesimo Anno* (In the 40th Year) is an encyclical issued by Pope Pius XI, 15 May 1931 (40 years after Leo XIII's Rerum Novarum).

The two papal pronouncements have, of course, been seized by political factions of all colours and either applauded or denounced. Attempting to be objective, the first encyclical identifies the differentials in human welfare of the time, and implies that collective bargaining, ethically on both sides, is the way forward. The second covers socio-economic issues, private property, and condemns both extremes of capitalism and communism, referring to the virtues of dignity, ethics, and religion; controversially, Pius XI appears to promote measures that have been interpreted by some as conforming to contemporary fascist ideology. There have also been suggestions that the Vatican recognised the Japanese puppet Manchukuo regime in Manchuria, though this is believed to be untrue.

In his defence, it's important to be aware of his 1937 encyclical, *Mit Brennender Sorge*, that was smuggled into Germany; three of its articles are below:

"...3. When, in 1933, We consented, Venerable Brethren, to open negotiations for a concordat, which the Reich Government proposed on the basis of a scheme of several years' standing; and when, to your unanimous satisfaction, We concluded the negotiations by a solemn treaty, We were prompted by the desire, as it behoved Us, to secure for Germany the freedom of the Church's beneficent mission and the salvation of the souls in her care, as well as by the sincere wish to render the German people a service essential for its peaceful development and prosperity. Hence, despite many and grave misgivings, We then decided not to withhold Our consent for We wished to spare the Faithful of Germany, as far as it was humanly possible, the trials and difficulties they would have had to face, given the circumstances, had the negotiations fallen through. It was by acts that We wished to make it plain, Christ's interests being Our sole object, that the pacific and maternal hand of the Church would be extended to anyone who did not actually refuse it.

4. If, then, the tree of peace, which we planted on German soil with the purest intention, has not brought forth the fruit, which in the interest of your people, We had fondly hoped, no one in the world who has eyes to see and ears to hear will be able to lay the blame on the Church and on her Head. The experiences of these last years have fixed responsibilities and laid bare intrigues, which from the outset only aimed at a war of extermination. In the furrows, where We tried to sow the seed of a sincere peace, other men – the "enemy" of Holy Scripture – over-sowed the cockle of distrust, unrest, hatred, defamation, of a determined hostility overt or veiled, fed from many sources and wielding many tools, against Christ and His Church. They, and they alone with their accomplices, silent or vociferous, are today responsible, should the storm of religious

> war, instead of the rainbow of peace, blacken the German skies ...
>
> ... 8. Whoever exalts race, or the people, or the State, or a particular form of State, or the depositories of power, or any other fundamental value of the human community – however necessary and honourable be their function in worldly things – whoever raises these notions above their standard value and divinises them to an idolatrous level, distorts and perverts an order of the world planned and created by God; he is far from the true faith in God and from the concept of life which that faith upholds."

The wording is believed to be down to Cardinal Michael von Faulhaber, who ordained Pope Benedict XVI, and to the Cardinal Secretary of State, Eugenio Pacelli, who later became Pope Pius XII.

His restatement of the concept of Usury and economic exploitation is of particular significance; it was part of his encyclical *Quadragesimo Anno* from 1931, and an extract is presented below.

http://xroads.virginia.edu/~ma01/Kidd/thesis/pdf/quadragesimo.pdf

> ...
>
> *104. Accordingly, when directing Our special attention to the changes which the capitalist economic system has undergone since Leo's time, We have in mind the good not only of those who dwell in regions given over to "capital" and industry, but of all mankind.*
>
> *105. In the first place, it is obvious that not only is wealth concentrated in our times but an immense power and despotic economic dictatorship is consolidated in the hands of a few, who often are not owners but only the trustees and managing directors of invested funds which they administer according to their own arbitrary will and pleasure.*

106. *This dictatorship is being most forcibly exercised by those who, since they hold the money and completely control it, control credit also and rule the lending of money. Hence they regulate the flow, so to speak, of the life-blood whereby the entire economic system lives, and have so firmly in their grasp the soul, as it were, of economic life that no one can breathe against their will.*

107. *This concentration of power and might, the characteristic mark, as it were, of contemporary economic life, is the fruit that the unlimited freedom of struggle among competitors has of its own nature produced, and which lets only the strongest survive; and this is often the same as saying, those who fight the most violently, those who give least heed to their conscience.*

108. *This accumulation of might and of power generates in turn three kinds of conflict. First, there is the struggle for economic supremacy itself; then there is the bitter fight to gain supremacy over the State in order to use in economic struggles its resources and authority; finally there is conflict between States themselves, not only because countries employ their power and shape their policies to promote every economic advantage of their citizens, but also because they seek to decide political controversies that arise among nations through the use of their economic supremacy and strength.*

109. *The ultimate consequences of the individualist spirit in economic life are those which you yourselves, Venerable Brethren and Beloved Children, see and deplore: Free competition has destroyed itself; economic dictatorship has supplanted the free market; unbridled ambition for power has likewise succeeded greed for gain; all economic life has become tragically hard, inexorable, and cruel. To these are to be added the grave evils that have resulted from an intermingling and shameful confusion of the functions and*

*duties of public authority with those of the economic sphere - such as one of the worst, the virtual degradation of the majesty of the State, which although it ought to sit on high like a queen and supreme arbitress, free from all partiality and intent upon the one common good and justice, is become a slave, surrendered and delivered to the passions and greed of men. And as to international relations, two different streams have issued from the one fountain-head: On the one hand, economic nationalism or even economic imperialism; on the other, a no less deadly and accursed internationalism of finance or international imperialism whose country is where profit is.*

Finally, Pius XI was an addicted mountain climber, and apparently many Alpine peaks were named after him as the first to reach the top.

## 16.33 Anno Domini 1939 to 2015
### 16.33.1 Context
#### 16.33.1.1 The Approach to the Second World War

The Second World War cannot be covered in detail here, and as in the previous chapter, discussion will be restricted to the causes and consequences of the conflict that followed the previous one with a gap of only twenty-one years. Many say that, in fact, the world had been at war continuously, and some say with good cause that the world war has never ceased to the present day, although the focus and intensity may have varied.

By the mid-1930s Japan was already outside its own borders and inside China's, and Italy was similarly adventuring in Abyssinia, present-day Ethiopia. The League of Nations, an initial attempt at a United Nations, but without the membership of the U.S. or Germany, had been formed just after World War One and it was virtually toothless. It was Germany's turn to look at its borders and mull the concept of *Lebensraum* or living space; or the lack of it.

Following several incidents that with hindsight should have caused greater alarm, it was in March, 1936, that Adolf Hitler, Chancellor of the

German Third Reich since the dissolution of the Weimar Republic in 1933, confirmed Germany's resurgence by sending troops and armed police into the demilitarised region of the Rhineland that separated France from the rest of Germany. Germany had retained ownership and political control of the region, but ever since the armistice at the end of World War One, France had benefited from the security and peace of mind that the 1919 Treaty of Versailles had instituted in the form of a demilitarised buffer zone in that part of Germany. There were, however, other complications due to a treaty known as the Locarno Treaty, signed in 1925, that implied that Britain and Italy would be obliged to wage war on France if France contravened the terms of the "Rhineland Pact" that specified the demilitarised nature of that region. This naïve complexity coupled with the facts that France was politically unstable at the time and Britain was complacent, meant that no objection was raised. It was the first of a series of appeasements.

In November of the same year Germany signed the anti-Komintern pact with Japan, by which they declared their opposition to International Marxism-Communism, and by which they agreed to liaise if either was attacked by Soviet Russia. They furthermore agreed that neither would make any treaty with Russia, and Germany officially recognised Manchukuo, the Japanese puppet regime in Manchuria on the Chinese mainland, that had been established by force during 1931 and 1932. Japanese Imperial sabre-rattling had already been remarked by the U.S. at that time, ten years before the day that would "*live in infamy*" as U.S. President F.D. Roosevelt would say on 7th December, 1941 – the day of Pearl Harbour.

1937 was a relatively quiet year, and except for the rampant rearmament of the future Axis powers, and for Italy's joining Germany and Japan in the anti-Komintern pact, the European world was more or less at peace; but the road to war was now mapped out in a series of events that would happen roughly each spring and autumn until the objective was reached.

1938 – March – Germany announced its peaceful union or Anschluss with the German-speaking, neighbouring sovereign state of Austria.

1938 – September – As a result of agitation earlier in the year by Nazi activists in the German-speaking Sudetenland region of Czechoslovakia, British Prime Minister Chamberlain met with Hitler at Berchtesgaden, and after threats of war by Hitler, agreed that the Sudetenland should be ceded to Germany. Britain and France communicated this to the Czechs who were ordered to comply, but they were not satisfied with this. Hitler immediately announced that Germany would enter the Sudetenland and that the Czechs must leave and lose almost one million of their citizens, a massive industrial base, and the strategic barrier of its mainly western mountains. It was following the Czech refusal to do this – and at this juncture they believed that they had British and French support – that a crisis meeting was arranged in Munich for September 29th, where Germany, France, Britain and Italy would discuss and resolve the matter. Czechoslovakia was not invited.

The result at the end of the 1930s was that the Czechs were abandoned to a lone fate, Chamberlain received a piece of paper that said Hitler had had his fill, and Germany occupied the Sudetenland region of Czechoslovakia on October 15th without resistance. The Czech Government resigned.

1939 – March – Germany annexed the remainder of Czechoslovakia that consequently ceased to exist as a sovereign state.

1939 – May – Germany and Italy signed the Pact of Steel, a full military alliance that originally envisaged tripartite Japanese subscription, but failed in that respect because Japan wanted Russia as the focus of opposition, while Germany and Italy had Britain and France in their sights.

1939 – August – Germany and Russia signed the Ribbentrop-Molotov Non-aggression Pact that united the two countries and underscored the similarity of the two totalitarian doctrines.

In a secret protocol, the Ribbentrop-Molotov Non-aggression Pact also recorded the two predators' duplicitous agreement to dismember a list of sovereign states; not just Poland, but including Romania, Lithuania, Latvia, Estonia, Finland, and Bessarabia aka Moldavia aka the present-day Republic of Moldova. This is not something that apologists for the U.S.S.R. want us to know.

Germany and Russia were also negotiating economic ties during August, while all the time Russia was also negotiating with France and Britain to determine how best to resist any German aggression against Russia.

- 1939 – August – Britain and Poland signed a Mutual Assistance Treaty.
- 1939 – September – Germany invaded Poland.
- 1939 – September – Britain, France, Canada, Australia, New Zealand and South Africa declared war on Germany.

By the third week in September, German and Russian forces had butchered Poland and held joint victory celebrations, followed shortly by the total elimination of Polish culture and the liquidation of anyone who had previously supported Polish Sovereignty.

The reader is referred to the 1940 Katyn Massacre of many thousands of Polish servicemen that was carried out by the Russians, and that was at the time, and in a spirit of appeasement on the part of U.S. President F.D. Roosevelt, knowingly and wrongly blamed on the Germans – just one of many such examples of the true nature of the *Communazis* as the two predatory aggressors were named at the time. It also indicated the depth to which the allied administration was able to descend. One would struggle to find any difference between the two totalitarian ideologies (Stalinism and Hitlerism) whose adoption and implementation led to such brutality; and yet the causes of both are plain to see – laid out over the preceding several centuries.

## The Two Thousand Year War – Papal Hegemony

There are many books and constant documentary programmes about the course of the war and the entry and exit of combatants, with changing evidence and spin about motive and achievement. There are many revisionists and conspiracy theorists, neo-nazis and apologists, and people who deny that the Holocaust is the preserve of the Jews, and deny that it happened on the alleged scale. But possibly the most worrying issue is that as time dims the memory, and as the conflagration that lasted for six years recedes into history, the understanding of true horror also diminishes, and humanity can again entertain a taste for war, or an appetite for the behaviour that will lead to war. Evidence from history and the present shows that there is no souring of that taste, and no reduction of the appetite.

In order to compare the two world wars, the scope of losses during World War One was widened from an earlier list of figures that just applied to those killed in action, and such an increased scope was provided in an earlier table. A table indicating the tally for the whole of the Second World War adventure is included below. Note that in terms of both military and civilians, the nation with the highest percentage of losses is Poland, and that the Baltic states of Latvia and Lithuania are similarly affected. It can be no coincidence that they all fall within the predatory scope of both vengeful *Communazi* parties, thereby receiving a double dose of attrition.

War in Europe ended on the 8th May, 1945, while the war against Japan formally ended on the 2nd September, 1945, although the Japanese had indicated that they would surrender on the 15th August, 1945.

### 16.33.1.2 Table – Human Losses During World War Two

All figures are approximations, and have been simplified from sometimes distributed figures that allow for member states and colonies of the country on the left. For more accurate figures the reader should refer to any of the many sources freely available via the internet. The relative orders of magnitude shown are considered adequate for the present context.

https://en.wikipedia.org/wiki/World_War_II_casualties

| Country | Population Before WWII | Military deaths | Civilian deaths | Total deaths | Deaths % of 1939 Pop. |
|---|---|---|---|---|---|
| Albania | 1,073,000 | 30,000 | | 30,000 | 2.81 |
| Australia | 6,998,000 | 39,700 | 700 | 40,400 | 0.57 |
| Austria | 6,650,000 | 260,000 | 120,000 | 380,000 | 5.7 |
| Belgium | 8,387,000 | 12,100 | 75,900 | 88,000 | 1.05 |
| Brazil | 40,289,000 | 1,000 | 1,000 | 2,000 | 0.02 |
| Bulgaria | 6,458,000 | 22,000 | 3,000 | 25,000 | 0.38 |
| Burma (British) | 16,119,000 | 22,000 | 250,000 | 272,000 | 1.69 |
| Canada | 11,267,000 | 45,400 | | 45,400 | 0.4 |
| China | 517,568,000 | 4,000,000 | 16,000,000 | 20,000,000 | 3.86 |
| Cuba | 4,235,000 | | 100 | 100 | 0 |
| Czechoslovakia (in Nov. 1938 borders) | 10,400,000 | 25,000 | 300,000 | 325,000 | 3.15 |
| Denmark | 3,795,000 | 2,100 | 1,100 | 3,200 | 0.08 |
| Dutch East Indies | 69,435,000 | | 4,000,000 | 4,000,000 | 5.76 |
| Estonia (within 1939 borders) | 1,122,000 | Included with the Soviet, German, and Finnish Armies | 50,000 | 50,000 | 4.44 |
| Ethiopia | 17,700,000 | 5,000 | 95,000 | 100,000 | 0.6 |
| Finland | 3,700,000 | 95,000 | 2,000 | 97,000 | 2.62 |
| France | 41,700,000 | 200,000 | 350,000 | 550,000 | 1.35 |
| French Indochina | 24,600,000 | | 2,000,000 | 2,200,000 | 8.1 |
| Germany | 69,850,000 | 5,500,000 | 3,500,000 | 9,000,000 | 10.5 |
| Greece | 7,222,000 | 35,100 | 760,000 | 807,000 | 11.2 |
| Guam | 20,000 | 2,000 | | 2,000 | 10 |
| Hungary | 9,129,000 | 300,000 | 280,000 | 580,000 | 6.35 |
| Iceland | 119,000 | | 200 | 200 | 0.17 |
| India (British) | 378,000,000 | 8,7000 | 2,500,000 | 2,587,000 | 0.68 |
| Iran | 14,340,000 | 200 | | 200 | 0 |
| Iraq | 3,698,000 | 500 | | 500 | 0.01 |
| Ireland | 2,960,000 | 10,000 Irish volunteers included with UK | 200 | 200 | 0 |
| Italy | 44,394,000 | 301,400 (includes 10,000 African conscripts) | 153,200 | 454,600 | 1.03 |
| Japan | 71,380,000 | 2,120,000 | 1,000,000 | 3,120,000 | 4.37 |

## The Two Thousand Year War – Papal Hegemony

| Country | Population Before WWII | Military deaths | Civilian deaths | Total deaths | Deaths % of 1939 Pop. |
|---|---|---|---|---|---|
| Korea (Japanese Colony) | 23,400,000 | | 483,000 | 483,000 | 2.06 |
| Latvia (within 1939 borders) | 1,951,000 | Included with the Soviet and German Armies | 230,000 | 230,000 | 11.78 |
| Lithuania (within 1939 borders) | 2,442,000 | Included with the Soviet and German Armies | 350,000 | 350,000 | 14.33 |
| Luxembourg | 295,000 | | 2,000 | 2,000 | 0.68 |
| Malaya (British) | 4,391,000 | | 100,000 | 100,000 | 2.28 |
| Malta (British) | 269,000 | | 1,500 | 1,500 | 0.56 |
| Mexico | 19,320,000 | | 100 | 100 | 0 |
| Mongolia | 819,000 | 300 | | 300 | 0.04 |
| Nauru (Australian) | 3,400 | | 500 | 500 | 14.7 |
| Nepal | 6,000,000 | Included with British Indian Army | | | |
| Netherlands | 8,729,000 | 17,000 | 284,000 | 301,000 | 3.45 |
| Newfoundland (British) | 300,000 | included with the U.K. | 100 | 100 | 0.03 |
| New Zealand | 1,629,000 | 11,900 | | 11,900 | 0.73 |
| Norway | 2,945,000 | 3,000 | 6,500 | 9,500 | 0.32 |
| Papua and New Guinea (Australian) | 1,292,000 | | 15,000 | 15,000 | 1.17 |
| Philippines (U.S. Territory) | 16,000,000 | 57,000 | 1,000,000 | 1,057,000 | 6.6 |
| Poland (within 1939 borders) | 34,849,000 | 240,000 | 5,580,000 | 5,820,000 | 16.7 |
| Portuguese Timor | 500,000 | | 70,000 | 70,000 | 14 |
| Romania (within 1939 borders) | 19,934,000 | 300,000 | 500,000 | 800,000 | 4.01 |
| Ruanda-Urundi (Belgian) | 4,200,000 | | 300,000 | 300,000 | 7.1 |
| Singapore (British) | 728,000 | | 50,000 | 50,000 | 6.87 |
| South Africa | 10,160,000 | 11,900 | | 11,900 | 0.12 |
| South Pacific Mandate (Japanese) | 1,900,000 | | 57,000 | 57,000 | 3 |
| Soviet Union (within 1946 to 91 borders) | 168,524,000 | 13,850,000 | 11,000,000 | 24,000,000 | 14.2 |

| Country | Population Before WWII | Military deaths | Civilian deaths | Total deaths | Deaths % of 1939 Pop. |
|---|---|---|---|---|---|
| Spain | 25,637,000 | Included with the German Army | | | |
| Sweden | 6,341,000 | | 600 | 600 | 0.01 |
| Switzerland | 4,210,000 | | 100 | 100 | 0 |
| Thailand | 15,023,000 | 5,600 | 2,000 | 7,600 | 0.04 |
| Turkey | 17,370,000 | 200 | | 200 | 0 |
| United Kingdom | 47,760,000 | 383,800 including Overseas Territories | 67,100 | 450,900 | 0.94 |
| United States | 131,028,000 | 407,000 | 12,000 | 420,000 | 0.32 |
| Yugoslavia | 15,400,000 | 446,000 | 1,400,000 | 1,700,000 | 11 |
| Approx. Totals | 2,000,000,000 | 30,000,000 | 55,000,000 | 85,000,000 | 4 |

## 16.33.1.3 The Second World War to the Present

Most, if not all, of the disruptive socio-political issues that have arisen since the Second World War may be related to events and decisions leading up to, and occurring throughout, the many theatres of the global war that persisted from 1914 to 1945. In reality those events and the human psyche that facilitated them have been in the making for a considerable span of human generations.

Such events are firstly, the development and expression of political and social theories, such as rationalism, liberalism, fascism, and socialism; secondly, the expansion and contraction of geographic dominion such as that occurring under imperialism and communism; thirdly, the growth and recession of economic parasitism; and finally, the weariness and insecurity that is incurred during many periods of war and oppression, and that is unevenly distributed globally.

It may be deduced from these events that humanity is subconsciously scarred by a long accumulation of disturbing news, and that such damage is apparent in circumstantial behaviour ranging from the rage of British and French inner city dysfunctionality and deprivation, to the rage of Palestinian incarceration in Israeli concentration camps such as the Gaza Strip.

All of the above phenomena are acknowledged by the third hypothesis that was previewed in the Introduction to this Volume One, and they are referred to in detail in other chapters with specific reference to the way they are actually manifested in the real world.

### 16.33.1.4 Post War Germany

To complete this unambiguous real-world context section in preparation for the presentation of the popes of the period, one or two post-1945 events are noteworthy as follows:

The division of Germany led directly to a lengthy and dangerous Cold War between NATO and the U.S.S.R., but for West Germany and Japan at least, spectacular and sustained economic growth from the ashes of the Second World War as the result of disciplined and slavish hard work, while many in the so-called victor populations experienced nothing of the sort. The costly and damaging Cold War could have been avoided by different tactics during the final stages of the conquest of Germany during 1944 and 1945, by regime change in the Soviet Union, and by an allied demonstration of solidarity with both the victim peoples of the conquered nations and the Soviet Republics. Stalin and Stalinism were quite as much an enemy to everyone as Hitler and Hitlerism. That has been clearly demonstrated by the Soviet people themselves since 1990, but at the same time the lingering insecurity of the Russian Psyche as a result of the race memory of invasions over the last one thousand years ensures that there will not yet be a complete rapprochement with the West.

Germany initially rejected the notion of immigration-enhanced citizenship in favour of the employment of guest workers, principally from Turkey. In terms of political parties, the Bundesrepublik, or Federal Republic of Germany, was noted for its Christian Democrats and Green politicians, but also during the third quarter of the 20$^{th}$ century it was noted for its fanatical Red Brigades of activists and revolutionaries around 1970. Shackled to blame and guilt for having caused the Second World War, Germany, even seventy years later in the 21$^{st}$ century, rarely plays any part in international armed peace-keeping initiatives.

### 16.33.1.5 Post War Failures

Britain initially offered passports, and the right to live in Britain, to all citizens within the British Commonwealth – about one billion people in all. It is understood that this error was partially reversed when the potential consequences were realised.

There has been a proliferation of nuclear weapons; advances and reversals of civil rights; technological revolution; and enforced multiculturalism in the developed nations, while tribal polarisation, civil war, famine and strife plague the developing world.

Globalisation and migration have facilitated an increase in the frequency of pandemics, and the resurgence of diseases in nations where once they were eliminated, for example Tuberculosis and Polio is being brought back into Britain by asylum seekers from the Third World where Islamic fundamentalism opposes preventative measures.

Increased differentials of wealth are encouraging revolutionary unrest.

The United Nations, although with wider support than the League of Nations ever had (this time the U.S. is involved), is of mixed and politically susceptible utility. At the very least the U.N. is vulnerable to partisan bias in an attempt to facilitate international trade via subsidiary agencies and affiliated organisations to the benefit of its most powerful members – the U.S., for example, withholds funding when it disagrees with projects – and vetoes in the Security Council notoriously prevent egalitarian initiatives.

### 16.33.1.6 Economic Instability

The International Monetary Fund (IMF) was conceived in order to fulfil the designated role of evening out currency exchange fluctuations under a fixed rate exchange system, as long as the Bretton-Woods agreement on currency values, by which the IMF was created, held, and as long as the world observed and was restricted by the Gold Standard and by controlled exchange rates. The IMF at that time was a sort of exchange rate insurance scheme that was underwritten by the wealthier nations, but with the actuarial assumptions of working within a fixed rate system. During the post-war reconstruction period, economic recovery would also be supported by the World Bank, similarly created by Bretton-Woods, or to give the World Bank its correct title, the International Bank for Reconstruction and Development.

The reality was that the Bretton-Woods mechanism kept America on top of the pile by ensuring that the dollar was always in demand, which continuously channelled foreign currency to America, and so allowed it to run a trade deficit with no obligation to devalue the dollar. By definition, the avoidance of such a devaluation was the lynch-pin of Bretton-Woods, so it couldn't and shouldn't happen anyway. As will be seen in a later chapter, that trade deficit would continue to grow and would lead to international failures during the first decade of the 21$^{st}$ century.

### 16.33.1.7 Disagreement on Tariffs and Trade

The General Agreement on Tariffs and Trade (GATT) was a provisional, and sadly protracted, and loose agreement that specified many of the rules for international trade. After three years negotiation among 50 or so countries, concerning both a U.N. inspired International Trade Organisation (ITO) Charter that was hosted in London, and in parallel with that, separate GATT negotiations that were hosted in Geneva, a first provisional GATT was finally signed in 1947 with an initially reduced number of just eight signatories, apparently on behalf of 23 negotiating participants. GATT was put into effect in 1948, and it was only intended as a stepping stone towards a comprehensive and binding ITO that would integrate with the IMF and the World Bank under the umbrella of Bretton-Woods.

There were literally tens of thousands of tariff concessions within GATT, along with the set of agreed trade rules, but the wider intentions for the ITO appear to have been dogged by what might be regarded as ideological and socio-political aims, such as employment rights and the regulation or correction of restrictive business practice. It was unlikely ever to find acceptance among the international extremes of political posturing among those whose ratification would be required, and the dedicated proponents probably knew that, since they wanted to rush acceptance of the hard-fought GATT agreements albeit with the concession of stating that it was provisional.

Nevertheless, an ITO Draft Charter was agreed at a conference in Havana, Cuba, in 1947 just after the signing of GATT, but unlike the GATT (a relatively simple agreement), the ITO (an officious and binding U.N. Charter) needed individual nations' governmental acceptance and ratification.

Of several nations that dragged their heels, America suddenly announced that it would not be pursuing the matter through Congress further, and the U.S. thereby effectively and unilaterally vetoed the formation of an International Trade Organisation in 1950. That was three years after that hopeful inception at Havana, Cuba, in 1947, and it would be 1995 before an alternative in the form of the World Trade Organisation (WTO) would be agreed at Marrakesh that would finally, after half a century, formalise the struggling GATT that had been through several makeovers, such as unsuccessfully trying to combat trade dumping. Such makeovers are always too late, of course, to save industries that have been destroyed by nationally subsidised open trade war that was never successfully opposed by weak complacent governments, such as those that have infested Britain for many decades. The destruction of the British motor cycle industry by Japanese trade dumping is just one example. There are many more that cannot be blamed on Trade Unionists or any technological or quality deficiency.

### 16.33.1.8 Imperial Guilt Spells Gains for the US and USSR

The single most significant English development since the Second World War, however, has to be the introduction into Britain and other western countries, on such a scale, and at such a rate, of peoples, cultures, and religions that have no commonality with anything in the long history of the country, and which will not integrate within the foreseeable stretch of generations. These issues, that stem from a mixture of imperial guilt, industrial sloth, and political ideology, are covered in detail in other chapters.

It is necessary to briefly expand, and to unhappily dwell, on one of the most disgraceful and unforgivable episodes in Britain's recent post-imperial convulsions – the murder of Southern Rhodesia (aka Rhodesia) – the

## The Two Thousand Year War – Papal Hegemony

African nation with the highest literacy rate and the best health and housing across the indigenous African population, and the lowest rates of infant mortality across the whole population of Africa. Rhodesia was "the Jewel of Africa" to quote the words of Tanzania's president Nyerere.

A progressive and advanced Nation-State, Rhodesia was thrown to the dogs of the Jesuit-educated Marxist dog, Robert Mugabe, in order to satisfy some notion that "elections" and a "black majority" vote would be preferable to the present reality of outstanding welfare and gradual progression to a truly balanced and equitable society that was taking place. The retrospectively at least, evil Dr. David Owen, the socialist Foreign Secretary at the time, and the Tory buffoon Carrington, have joint responsibility for the atrocities and deaths during the Rhodesian Wars, and during the subsequent murderous Mugabe years when black and white were exterminated with a vengeance that only comes from frustrated ideological insanity, and when the Jewel of Africa was bankrupted morally as well as economically.

Possibly the worst single incident in the Rhodesian tragedy – an instance of global desertion by humanity – at this time, concerns the massacre of the survivors of a civil airliner brought down by a Russian SAM, fired by the terrorist group aligned to the Nkomo faction. Two further factors accentuate and broaden the brokers of this atrocity: firstly, the "Deafening Silence" as it became known – the failure of every single Western authority to even indicate sympathy for the victims; and secondly, the unbelievable sacking by the Church of the outspoken cleric, the Reverend John da Costa, whose sermon is referenced below.

The best that media comment could supply was the satirical parroting of the television presenter, Angela Rippon, trying to authentically and respectfully pronounce the name "Nkomo". It seems with hindsight that no-one had the least sympathy for the loss of a truly progressive and humane regime in the face of a devil whose true colours were subsequently proved beyond doubt.

Anyone with an adult awareness at that time who remained silent then, and who can remain dispassionate now, should, contrary to the author's earlier assertion that history bears no shame, hang their head in that attitude of contrition for the tens of thousands of lives of several races that were squandered at the behest of the puerile U.K. Government of the period, with hawkish American goading, and under the pressure of an insurrection led by Cuban proxies for a sterile and geriatric USSR; all under the watchful eyes of the Chinese vultures that waited with oriental patience for their carrion that was initially served up as Zambia – the erstwhile Northern Rhodesia.

The reader is cautioned against following the links below that present graphic examples of the consequences of slavish devotion to political correctness, and a harrowing response from those deserted by international morality.

http://www.viscountdown.com/

http://sarahmaidofalbion.blogspot.co.nz/2009/03/political-mightiness-in-creation-of.html

http://www.rhodesia.me.uk/AnatomyOfTerror.htm

http://www.christianaction.org.za/index.php/articles/god-and-government/164-the-deafening-silence-transcript-of-taped-broadcast

http://www.rhodesia.nl/silence.htm

*The Two Thousand Year War – Papal Hegemony*

## 16.33.1.9 Map – German Partitions in 1947 and Détente in 1990

Map from http://commons.wikimedia.org/wiki/Category:Maps released under CC-BY-SA
http://creativecommons.org/licenses/by-sa/3.0/  Author: Wiki-vr

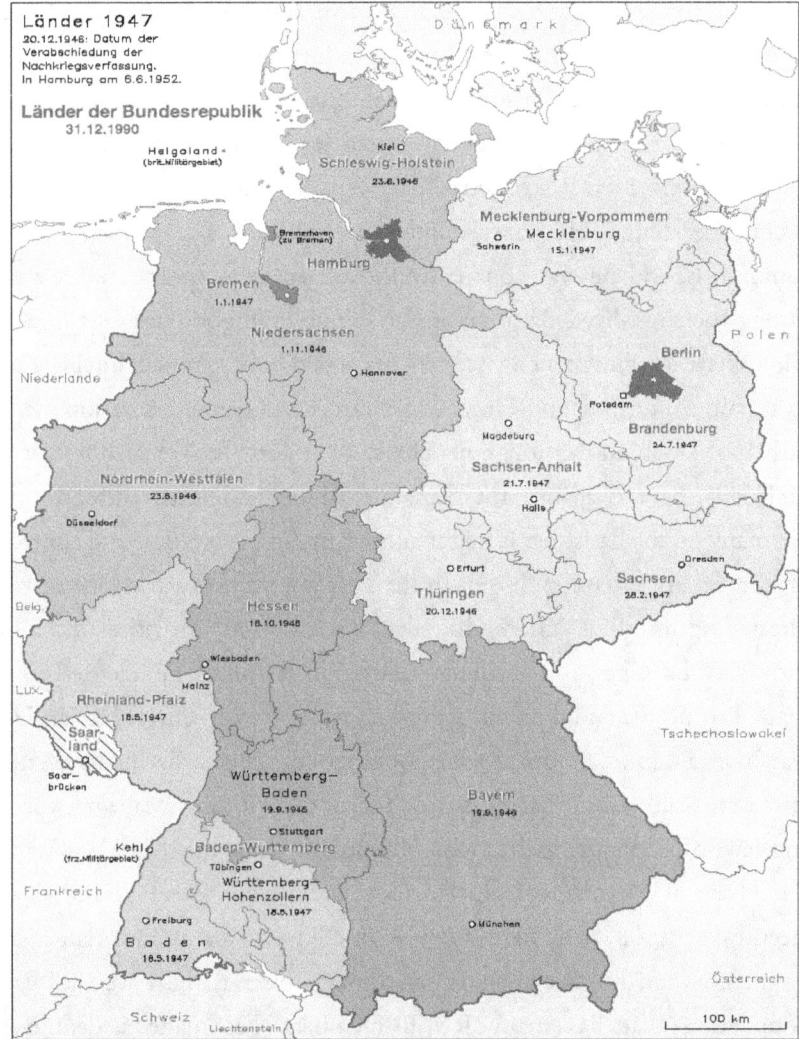

**Key to The above map:**
Dates and names relate to the adoption of the post-war constitution agreed in Hamburg in June 1952.
The names and jurisdiction of the sixteen states of the present Federal Republic are shown, and the sometimes ambiguous boundaries, particularly in the northeast, indicate differences between a partitioned Germany, extant in 1947, and the redrawn boundaries that followed reunification in 1990. The west retained its federal boundaries, while those of the old East Germany were slightly redrawn.

### 16.33.2 The Popes of the Period 1939 to 2015

**Pius XII (1939 to 1958).** From a privileged Roman family with long allegiance to the papacy, he was Jesuit educated, and was Secretary of State when elected pope. The overwhelming issues of his papacy were, and continue to be, questions of his stance and actions concerning the combatants of the Second World War and Jewish persecution. He signed the notorious 1933 Reichskonkordat, but he authored the 1937 Mit Brennender Sorge. He was certainly anti-Bolshevik and probably anti-communist, and he was apparently threatened at gunpoint by activists during the short-lived Bavarian Soviet Republic in 1919, an event that is said to have left him mentally scarred. He is said to have passed intelligence to Britain concerning anti-Hitler conspirators and German invasion plans early in the war, and although he refused to endorse the German invasion of Russia, he was against the demands for unconditional surrender of Germany on the basis that it might allow Russian penetration and control of Europe. As, of course, it did. In the post-war years much criticism was directed against Pius XII for his silence at the time, a silence that also shrouded the Allies, one of the arguments in favour of his silence being that a low profile and diplomacy made assisting Jewish refugees easier. He was, after all, in an occupied zone. Another criticism is that many of the Jews were Rabbis, but that issue would seem to be for the escape networks and Jewish people themselves who presumably made the selections. With the release of documents from the secret archives of several countries as recently as 2008 that have been examined by many historians, an ecumenical and non-sectarian organisation known as the Pave the Way Foundation that has many Jewish members, has made a definitive statement:

> "Pave the Way Foundation (PTWF), a non-sectarian organisation whose mission is to identify and eliminate non-theological obstacles between religions, announced the discovery of new documents which prove, by his actions, that Pope Pius XII was in reality a friend of the Jewish people before, during and after World War II"

PTWF gives examples of Pius XII's actions in defence of Jews against the Ottomans going back to 1917; it suggests that many thousands of Jews were helped to escape and resettle during and after the war; and it has nominated him for a listing as "Righteous among the Nations" at the Holocaust Memorial in Jerusalem.

PTWF subsequently received much criticism from historians for not being historians (though only historians are allowed into the Vatican archives where the PTWF apparently discovered much of the data), and for being duped by, among many, those trying to promote Pius XII for beatification. It's difficult to see how a partly Jewish organisation would benefit from such a misrepresentation, but maybe we just have to wait for more measured commentary from possibly less ideologically driven members of the historian community.

Finally, Pius XII began theological preparations for the Council known as Vatican II.

**Blessed John XXIII (1958 to 1963).** From Lombardy, he was one of many siblings in a family of share-croppers or tenant farmers. A priest since 1904, he served as a stretcher bearer and chaplain during World War One, rising to become a *nuncio* during the 1930s and 1940s. He was considered a genuinely good man, was known for his classless behaviour, and earned the nickname "The Good Pope".

He called the Second Vatican Council to consider relations between the Roman Catholic Church and the modern world. It opened in October, 1962, and closed under Pope Paul VI in December, 1965, and most of its results seem related to internal church affairs, though the word perfidious as a description of Jews in one of the church ceremonies was removed, and it was declared that Jews were no more responsible for the death of Christ than Christians.

**Paul VI (1963 to 1978).** From a middle-class family of lawyers in Lombardy, he was a Cardinal when elected pope, and had been the Archbishop of Milan. As Pope it became one of his first tasks to implement the results of Vatican II. His objectives were clarification of an often obscure Church, overall reform, ecumenical initiatives, and communicating with the wider world. He was seen as a progressive.

The Pilgrim Pope, as he was known, travelled more widely than any previous pope, visiting six continents. Closer to home, he visited the Orthodox Patriarchs of both Jerusalem and Constantinople – the first time in a thousand years – and he revoked the excommunications imposed during the Great Schism of 1054. In 1973 the Patriarch of the Coptic Church of Alexandria, Shenouda III, visited the Vatican and one more obstacle to common belief was removed. In 1960 the Anglican Archbishop of Canterbury, Michael Ramsey, met the Pope during a visit to Rome and opened the Anglican Centre to promote closer relations, and it seems that there was a genuine rapprochement in the air.

A thawing of hostilities even with the Protestants began around the mid 1960s. Pope Paul VI in summary did not possess any of the charisma or academic skills of his immediate predecessors, and he faced a great deal of ecclesiastical change as a consequence of Vatican II; he also faced many demands for relaxation, change, and liberalisation of centuries old norms concerning the behaviour and self-denial on the part of the clergy. Typical of the 1960s. One very significant result during his papacy was his promulgation in 1965 of a result of Vatican II, *Nostra Aetate* – the Declaration on the Relation of the Church to Non-Christian Religions. This concession to the rest of humanity sought to acknowledge the inherent spirituality of: Hindus, Buddhists, Moslems, Jews, and diverse other religions.

**John Paul I (1978).** From a working-class family in the north-east of Italy near Venice, he was much more down-to-earth than probably any pope before him; he chose an investiture instead of a coronation, and he was not crowned, opting instead for an archbishop's Pallium. He was noted for his warmth and open presentation, though this was taken by conservative hard-liners within the Vatican to be an indication of weakness and inability.

He died after only 33 days as Pope, having been found by a nun after probably dying the night before. He was sitting in bed with papers that were quickly concealed along with medication, by Secretary of State, Cardinal Jean Villot. There was no police jurisdiction, no autopsy, and naturally, conspiracy theories began to fly – never adequately dispelled by the authorities, and more recently investigated with suggested links to the collapsed clergy's bank, Banco Ambrosiano, and the suicide of the bank's chairman, Roberto Calvi aka God's Banker, in London in 1982. There were proven Mafia links, and there were proven links to the *Istituto per le Opere di Religione* – the Institute for Religious Works aka the Vatican Bank.

The case of Calvi's suicide was reopened at the end of the 20$^{th}$ century, and a forensic report in 2002 concluded that he had, in fact, been murdered. He had been a member of a secret Italian branch of the Freemasons, and his body was found hanging, with bricks in his pockets, from Blackfriars Bridge in London where he had fled. The name of the secret society that was used among the members themselves was *frati neri* that translates as "Black Friars".

Among the ranks of the *frati neri* were Silvio Berlusconi and the heads of the Italian secret services, and there are many more instances of alleged banking corruption, deaths of witnesses and suspects, and other bank failures, all beyond this scope. See the *Internet Index*.

About the charismatic Pope John Paul I, there is very little to be said, because his papacy was so short, and even the Vatican website biography is very brief and entirely factual with no subjective pleasantries. The kindest epitaph is probably due to the English Cardinal Basil Hume who is reported to have said:

> *'Seldom have I had such an experience of the presence of God... I am not one for whom the dictates of the Holy Spirit are self-evident. I'm slightly hard-boiled on that... But for me he was God's candidate.'*

**John Paul II (1978 to 2005).** From a southern Polish middle-class family, he had to endure the privations and hazards of life in Poland under the German occupation during the Second World War, having many personal close-shaves with disaster, and benevolent interaction with Jews. There can be no charges of anti-Semitism against him. He became the most widely travelled pope, and his visit to Poland in 1979 is said to have contributed to the formation in 1980 of Solidarity, the Polish trade union movement that became so much more than just a trade union, and that could be said to have led to the spread of liberty from Soviet hegemony throughout Europe. John Paul is nevertheless considered a conservative when it comes to theology and Catholic doctrine, having made no changes in respect of any of the controversial aspects of society and human behaviour. With the Orthodox Eastern Church of several eastern European states there was rapprochement for the first time in a thousand years, and in 2001, as a gesture towards Islam, he visited a mosque in Syria where he kissed the Koran. He visited Lutherans, and Soviet and U.S. leaders, but his apparently politically and spiritually eclectic vision didn't prevent three assassination attempts.

The first attempt, in 1981, resulted in him being shot and almost killed by an allegedly Soviet-KGB inspired plot via Bulgarian and Turkish agents. From archive material released in the Vatican and eastern European countries, and as a result of investigative journalism, it does seem to have been conclusively demonstrated that there were a number of KGB infiltrators in the Vatican. The second attempt, in 1982, one day before the anniversary of the first, and in Fatima, Portugal, was an attempt by a Spanish Priest to stab him with a dagger or bayonet. The attacker was prevented, spent a short period in prison, was judged to be mentally ill, and went on to become of all things, if believable, a solicitor in Belgium and-or an art expert – so it is rumoured.

In 1995, the third assassination attempt was thwarted at the preparation stage, and concerned a bomb plot by an Al-Qaeda cell in the Philippines. Of the several criticisms against him, the most serious is possibly inadequate action and lack of candour concerning the abuse of children by the clergy, though the responsibility for that has surely to be taken by all levels of the Church since papal condemnation had been made. It was said that the abuse was restricted to only about one percent of the clergy, but out of about half a million priests worldwide, that suggests there may have been as many as five thousand perpetrators, most of whom, if true, must therefore have been protected by silence on the part of their superiors. This notorious feature of the Roman Catholic Church seems to be in the news constantly.

In an age of globalisation with its technological web, a further issue that may be of concern is the number of Catholic organisations that have possibly dubious provenance, though given the fictional representation in novels and film, coupled with an explosion of conspiracy theories, any such interpretation is really down to one's personal inclination.

The following list deserves separate coverage and is given here as an example of the possibly hundreds of groups of religious activists. Dissidents themselves even, they range from orders of reclusive hermits to extroverted evangelists:

- Catholic Action (nowadays referred to in Vatican terminology as Social Action)
- Opus Dei
- Legion of Christ
- Neocatechumenal Way
- Schoenstatt
- Charismatic Movement
- Vineyard Movement
- British New Church Movement
- World Apostolate of Fátima

**Benedict XVI (2005 to 2012).** From a middle-class family in a village in Bavaria, south-eastern Germany, Joseph Ratzinger, like his predecessor, endured the lack of liberty during the Second World War, but on the other side. His father was a policeman and against Nazi ideology to the extent that the family were obliged to move. His father was retired by the time the war started, and Ratzinger had entered theological college, only to be conscripted as a child soldier in 1943 at the age of sixteen into an anti-aircraft unit, and then the infantry. It is said that in 1945, as his unit dissolved in the face of an allied advance, he deserted and went home, from where he was briefly a prisoner-of-war before re-entering theological college.

In 1951 he was ordained by Cardinal Faulhaber, one of the papal architects of the Reichskonkordat of 1939. He was a university academic during the 1960s, distancing himself from the radical movements that became revolutionary throughout France and Germany, and turning to traditional Catholicism, while still embracing the results of Vatican II, some of which involved a paradigm shift in terms of ecumenical initiatives such as the *Nostra Aetate* promulgated by Paul VI in 1965 (see above).

More recently his pronouncements regarding other religions have brought criticism. Firstly, in 2006 he gave a lecture and quoted an extract from a medieval text written in 1391 not long before the fall of Constantinople and addressed to the Ottomans; it was, he said, to illustrate *"...[the surprisingly harsh way]"* that the emperor spoke to his audience at the time. Muslims everywhere took this as, in some way, insulting, and the Pope was forced to issue an apology regardless of its relative antiquity and absolute authenticity.

In 2007 he implied that native South American Indians had always wanted to be Christianised, and that to them the process was not the imposition of a foreign culture. Those ludicrous statements were made in Brazil, but the reaction was continent-wide and he was forced later to make a statement, though not an apology. Another gaff occurred in 2009 when he lifted some excommunications, one of which had been issued against an outspoken English bishop, Richard Williamson. That excommunication had been imposed as part of a 1988 witch hunt, and had accused him of Holocaust denial. Williamson does not seem to have recanted his expression of free speech, and he continues to expound various conspiracy theories, such as U.S. intelligence service responsibility for the 9/11 New York Trade Centre atrocity.

On the subject of child abuse by the Catholic Church, it is said that before becoming Pope he was responsible for centralising the investigative processes under his predecessor, John Paul II, and that he became very familiar with all the issues. Before 2001, issues were dealt with locally, but at Ratzinger's suggestion responsibility was taken by a department within the Church, now known as the Congregation for the Doctrine of the Faith, that until 1904 had been known as "The Supreme Sacred Congregation of the Roman and Universal Inquisition" – or simply the *Inquisition*.

One final statement concerning the rump Ottoman Empire, now Turkey, is of interest. In 2004 he said that Turkey had always been different to Christian Europe and that it should look for union with other Muslim countries and not Europe. Apparently unable to sustain that position, presumably due to political pressure, whether from within or without, he has since made statements supporting Turkey's application to join the EU.

Benedict XVI was the first pope to resign since Gregory XII who resigned (as seen earlier he was actually ousted) in 1415 at the time of the three Popes fiasco. Just over two weeks notice was given by the Vatican to spare the Pope the rigours of the approaching Easter Fest. So Pope Benedict XVI, citing advanced age and deteriorating strength, gave up the honoured position on 28th February 2013, something of a surprise, since virtually all other popes had died on the job – in the vernacular, one or two literally.

He went on to live in style in the Mater Ecclesiae monastery in the Vatican Gardens, and instead of taking his old name, Joseph Ratzinger, or even a more usual Bishop Emeritus, he took the title His Holiness Benedict XVI, Pope Emeritus, which together with his decision to continue wearing the Papal white cassock, albeit without his red shoes, was considered by some to be a bit over the top; it was also the first time two Popes had co-habited in the Vatican.

As a postscript, he was said by some associates to be depressed after leaving his job, and although this is said to be common among retirees, he also seemed nostalgic for his old job as God's representative on earth.

**Francis (2013- ).** The son of an Italian railway worker and a housewife, he was born on 17th December, 1936, in Buenos Aires, Argentina, and was christened Jorge Mario Bergoglio. He is the first Jesuit to hold the position, the first Latin American, and the first from all the Americas; and although of Italian stock, he is also the first pope from outside Europe in more than 1,000 years. He chose the name Francis in honour of the 13th century monk, Saint Francis of Assisi, who was known for his kindness to animals and for his generally charitable nature.

Trained as a chemist, he is said to prefer a low profile, cooking his own food, taking public transport, and preferring more humble residences to grandiose mansions or Papal Palaces.

Within a month of becoming Pope, Francis canonised 800 saints – these were the Otranto martyrs, already beatified in 1771, and noted by the previous Pope Benedict XVI in 2007 as having been "...*killed out of hatred for their faith.*" The perpetrators of the atrocity in August, 1480, were the Ottoman Turkish Army who, at the beginning of more than two hundred years of Jihad, had been given orders to kill every man over the age of 15 who would not convert to Islam. The Skull Cathedral at Otranto has preserved the remains of the Martyrs as a reminder of the consequences of both indulging in, and resisting, the religion of the One True God.

### 16.33.3 The Centrepiece Behind the Skull Cathedral Altar, Otranto

Photo: Many examples in public domain.

## 17 Read All About It – The London Gazette

The London Gazette (online) is an excellent place to see the news associated with particular historic events during the period of the 17th to the 21st centuries. See the following online references.

Direct website – old version is:
http://www.london-gazette.co.uk/search

An updated (2014) website is:
https://www.thegazette.co.uk/history

For an option to search by publication date as far back as 1665 use:
https://www.thegazette.co.uk/all-notices/resources

Similar links can be found through Wikipedia indices at:
http://en.wikipedia.org/wiki/Wikipedia:London_Gazette_Index

National Archives can be found at:
http://discovery.nationalarchives.gov.uk/

# 18 A History of Money and Financial Empire
## 18.1 A Dissident Preface

A decade or so into the 21st century has seen the developed nations of the world at a metaphorically mixed economic and commercial crossroads and precipice combined, with common currencies failing, and erstwhile global standards such as the U.S. dollar looking fragile, while a once worthless Chinese Renminbi (meaning currency of the people) – the Yuan – is looking likely to replace it eventually, despite the odd setback along the way.

In spite of the often prejudicial nature of modern life, and the unacceptable nature of the architects of our governance, be they politicians or bankers or journalists, the desire for stability and security at any cost overrides any rebellious instincts in most of us, and results in a cowardly acquiescence and complicity – we live under a burden of debt and yet we continue to re-elect mainstream political parties that allow the greed to continue unchecked and that deny the public fair representation in Parliament.

This chapter attempts to run counter to such feeble submission, and it is necessary to state that any condemnation of the disgraceful and wretched personalities and culturally elite groups, all of which feature in the catalogue of privileged and barbarous greed that will be outlined in the following chapter, is made after a study of facts and not conspiracy, and is made without ethnocultural prejudice. Facts are more powerful than fiction, and facts take precedence over manifestations of bigotry, over faint-hearted politically correct whining, and over any attempts to mitigate what are undeniably crimes against humanity. The enumeration of facts must not be confused with narrow-minded prejudice – justified dissidence and offence to the guilty will always be the consequence of unpleasant facts, and vice versa, and the principal defendants that stand in any dissident-indicted dock must accept that, and if they have any defence at all, then they must make reasoned arguments, and not gibber weasel words or threats.

## 18.2 The Origin and Evolution of Money
### 18.2.1 Prehistoric Speculation

Speculation it may be, but it's very reasonable to imagine, hopefully without stretching credulity too much, the origins of trading or bartering in antiquity when two primitive people exchanged unwanted or excess items of some simple sort for mutual benefit. Bartering and the division of labour based on the specialisation of skills would long ago have been mutually conducive to, and also supportive of, an emerging community or corporate identity. We have seen how trade agreements can mutate into First World Statehood, in the case of the evolution of the European Union, or *United States of Europe*, from an original European Coal and Steel Community (ECSC) that was defined in 1951 among Belgium, France, West Germany, Italy, Holland, and Luxembourg.

Several millennia earlier, some obvious candidates for the earliest examples of trade would be: simple stone tools, surplus animal skins following butchery, shared items of food, and later on, shelter or hospitality, all probably taking place in circumstances where the acts of giving and receiving were fundamental elements of the bonding that was essential for the establishment of trust and the continuity of tribal cohesion. Hospitality to strangers has been a treasured feature of diverse civilisations since recorded history began, and it suggests that there may be, or was, some essential goodness in human nature, or at least a desire to increase the scope of goodwill and therefore security. This was bonding without initially a sense of bondage, and the exchange and circulation of essentials including recreational items, but excluding meaningless and misrepresented baubles. Such a concept has been described as a *gift economy*, and we still see remnants of the idea today when presents are exchanged at Christmas for instance, and the receipt of a pair of slippers may or may not quite cut the mustard, leaving a vague atavistic sense of indebtedness.

It's likely that such unconditional, consensual, and generally healthy trade exchanges took place among small groups of speechless hominins (the term *hominid* includes all the Great Apes) possibly a million years or more before the development of a spoken language enabled the timely expression of more complex deals that could involve notions of shared ownership, relative values, and the equivalence of dissimilar types and differing quantities of commodity, with the added risk of maybe deferred settlement and the inevitable evolution of debt. Perhaps it was the very need to extend trust, and to articulate equitable trade agreements, that drove the development of speech in the first place.

Although contentious among historical linguists, there is a loose acceptance that there remains in the present day a residue of an earlier replication of some common words. Those words are identified as the "Swadesh List" that covers vast geographic and language barriers, and it is suggested here that such commonality must have occurred without the whole-scale migration of peoples because the communities still remain distinct ethnically and geographically while having certain words in common. It is further suggested that such a commonality of words is due to the trade of goods and ideas, and that such etymological penetration seems to have been achieved with an otherwise undisturbed separation of the cultures through which the words passed, at least during historically remote times, and travelling merchants-salesmen in antiquity, just as much as conquerors or imperialists, may well have been responsible for spreading *the word*.

As soon as socialisation gathered pace and small tribal groups expanded, merging with others to form larger communities, hierarchies and deference of various types would have become more sophisticated, being determined by attributes ranging from the older principal ones such as physical ability and strength, to newer traits such as knowledge, intelligence, and the perceived ability to manipulate superstitious beliefs in a way that reduced fear or uncertainty; and, of course, the power to broker the exchange of commodities.

Whether or not a person was actually a broker, another difference among individuals would now be strikingly defined by the volume and type of personal trade conducted, and this would become apparent, if it was not ostentatiously flaunted, by a person's quietly accumulated disposable possessions – just a spare axe or two at first, or maybe a different animal skin covering at the time of the full moon. People even nowadays instinctively collect and hoard things and arrange *swaps* with other *collectors*.

The building blocks of envy and theft were almost certainly present from the earliest times, and any early altruistic inclination would soon have been replaced by competitively covetous tendencies towards personal advancement and security, particularly in times of hardship or threat by famine or conquest as population levels increased and land ownership claims became more necessary and enforceable. The concept of debt and obligation to the tribe as a whole and to individuals, whether in terms of goods or deeds, would have been understood long before any sort of tokens of exchange or coinage were adopted or even needed, but once bartering and the division of labour, and the concept of land ownership and rent, were established, the individual would forever be society's prisoner, with those lower down the pecking order being obliged to find solace in whatever corporate kindnesses might be bestowed by the ruling elite, or to find it in an aspiration to rise towards that elite. Ever since, it has been the fulfilment of this aspiration that is dangled as a carrot by those that have already achieved wealth and celebrity, in an attempt to justify the lottery and chicanery that is the path to membership of the State Polity or one of its subsidiaries. Excessive differentials at birth in modern societies make this a sham in all but a very few instances. To those for whom the carrot is always just out of reach, whether or not from personal laxity, the scrap heap and a life of indolence is a common consequence for many, and a life of constant struggle and uncertainty is the lot for most. To some extent it was always thus, but a question remains concerning the deliberate maintenance of debt, and the sequestration of wealth beyond reasonable limits.

### 18.2.2 Early Monetary Function and Debt

It's likely that the first monetary tokens, things with no intrinsic value, would have been used to support the recording of relative possessions and debts among members of the community, possibly when a bartering agreement was difficult to complete because of a hiatus in the coincidence of the needs of each party, or when the relative values of the items being traded needed balancing in some way, or maybe to keep a note of their entitlement as a result of success or failure at gathering or producing food and other essential resources. It's equally likely that the first writing, marks on sticks or flat stones, evolved for the same reasons, and whether sticks or stones, there would certainly have been no intrinsic value in the token, and absolutely no concept of trading the token.

Adam Smith, in his book *An Inquiry into the Nature and Causes of the Wealth of Nations* aka just *The Wealth of Nations*, uses examples of how one would equate, say, a live ox or some other large beast of burden when bartering for just a small amount of grain. Clearly, some standardised balancing commodity of exchange would be needed to prevent the bartering system from stalling. Such balancing commodities would initially have been anything that was either in constant demand or that did not deteriorate, and that could be sub-divided, e.g. smaller or larger bags of salt. Later, objects with no intrinsic value, money, would be used by common definition to facilitate the balancing of exchanges, and brokers would record any deferred payment requirement – debt. It is again likely that in primitive societies the concept of usurious interest on these balancing debts, that were of convenience to both parties, would have been far from anyone's mind. Such debt recording with strings of beads is believed to have been used by Polynesian civilisations long before money as an exchange medium was in use. This type of record keeping could have been implemented before writing was developed, and given the abstract nature of this tokenisation of essential commodities, it is highly likely that some sort of third party's definition and arbitration would have been needed to reinforce and enforce the unlikely concept of equating an inedible seashell token to a fish supper for instance. That third party in antiquity may well have been what could be termed an honest broker or proto-banker.

In order to understand how such an absurd notion as equating an intrinsically worthless seashell to food could have arisen and been popularised, it's important to remember that in some long gone simple age

## A History of Money and Financial Empire

there were few barriers to personal freedom, and that for millennia there was no money and absolutely no need for it as there is today. There was quite simply an enduring and relative abundance of everything necessary to support life without paying for it, and anything that smoothed the wheels of daily life and commodity exchange was of equal benefit to the whole community. Or was it?

Physical tasks, risk to life in the hunt, the defence of the tribe against other tribes, and the alleviation of a whole range of exigences of life would have all borne a value or incurred cost, and they could all have involved a notional payment of some sort *in lieu* from the very earliest times. Such a cost may well have been one's life, and so it can be argued that the tokenised relief from obligation and risk, as well as the acquisition of commodities and services, would therefore have been very convenient if voluntarily developed among consenting adults. One wonders how long it would have taken from the arrival of tradeable tokens, to the organisation of mercenary armies, and to the development of prostitution.

The concept of debt is synonymous with obligation and must have existed, though that debt must have been initially minimal and well managed, or the system could not have worked. The difficulty would have been allowing for the differentials of skill and ability, and of each person's needs, creating a requirement to scale and resolve transactions according to those needs. We still struggle with those concepts in the 3$^{rd}$ millennium.

Beyond the utilitarian benefits of money, however, the emergence over the centuries of agents, usurers, and bankers guaranteed the creation of a potential for exploitation of the mechanism. Weak and physically disadvantaged individuals settled into the bottom levels of society, where they would later in history become trapped as serfs, and physically stronger alpha males, such as Norman Barons, competed to reach the top of the pile, only to find perhaps that wealth and strength are not necessarily directly proportional. Within a reality comprising abstractions and illusory tokens, the cunning and sleight of hand of hunters and merchants can level the playing field, and the weedy can rival the mighty – merchant wealth could, and most certainly today does, surpass that of royalty – and some ethnocultural groups would go on to specialise in monetary sleight of hand as will be seen later.

Although the internationally organised crime of religiously sequestered wealth and temporal power that would be amassed by Papal intimidation, while acting as a proxy for a terrifying God, was still in the far future, the seeds of exploitation, crippling penury, and dissent, were sown several thousands of years ago as the concept of land ownership and rent emerged and was imposed by the strong on the weak.

It is believed by many historians that in those early primitive societies the use of tokens of exchange would have emerged independently around the world, such a trade catalyst appearing when humankind locally reached a certain sophistication that permitted choice, and at the same time reached a level of congestion that encouraged migration and necessitated the geographic portability of entitlement. Gold and silver were known to many civilisations and would have been the obvious choice for a combined intrinsically and extrinsically valued token or coin, so-called *Commodity Money*, that might be recognised as valuable quite remotely from its origin, and regardless of any design on its surface. The desire to possess such satisfying trinkets, and the achievement of success in that quest would be qualified by several factors, much the same throughout history and down to the present day:

1. The amount of one's existing disposable possessions – one's capital.
2. The extent of one's land ownership that might generate rent.
3. How hard one is prepared to work, and the nature of one's skill – one's labour.
4. The extent of one's requirement to satisfy non-essential aspirations and miserly acquisition, i.e. one's balance of leisure and thrift.

These lifestyle attributes and their relative weighting per individual have always existed in some form or other, and they are the enablers of differentials that will always result from life within a society that observes processes of governance determined by human nature – excessive debt for some, and excessive wealth and power for others. The first and second factors above are, of course, massively skewed by the inheritance of wealth and privilege, and although it may be squandered by some, it dominates all else.

### 18.2.3 The Oldest Evidence – Prehistoric and Early Classical

Bearing in mind that much archaeological evidence has been lost due to rising sea levels over the last 12,000 years, some of the very earliest known examples of monetary function or commodity exchange are:

- The existence of what is believed to have been a communal and presumably co-operative granary or seed mill almost 20,000 years ago in the region of present-day Israel – long before Hebrew invasion – the creation of an unknown autochthonous culture.
- The trading of obsidian for stone tools as long ago as 12,000 BC.
- The use of grain and cattle as exchange standards in many societies from around 9000 BC.
- The use of silver and gold bars as tokens of value from circa 4000 BC in Mesopotamia (present-day Iraq), and Egypt.

All of these examples are from the Mediterranean and surrounding regions that would have been a haven during the last glacial maximum, though they were also vulnerable to changing sea levels as the Holocene Epoch progressed and the glaciers melted, encouraging wider migration of people.

The Bronze Age Collapse of about 1200 BC, discussed earlier, affected far more than trade and monetary systems, but may nevertheless have been one of the first examples of a bust cycle following the Neolithic Revolution boom that had been occasioned by the spread of civilisation and an increase in farming settlements throughout the Mediterranean, Asia and Europe between roughly 10,000 BC and 5000 BC. When grappling with these distant times, it's essential to remember that a society that was advanced enough to leave significant markers of its presence that would survive ten or twenty millennia, did not just appear overnight. The hesitant and gradual socialising process must have begun some number of centuries or even millennia before that, and there is a school of thought that the domestication of animals and farming was such a very obvious thing to do, that it was a much more gradual and globally independent process than is often suggested – everyone would have done it without waiting to be told the obvious.

The first examples of banking, as opposed to the notion of trade exchange and monetary tokens, are believed to date back about five thousand years when banking deposits and loans in one edible form or another such as olives, dates, seeds and cattle featured in the ancient Sumerian civilisation that began circa 6000 BC in Mesopotamia. Again, two to three thousand years ago, there are examples of similar commodity storage and transactions during the eras of the Roman Republic and the Roman Empire, though banking as we now know it in terms of complex financial transactions didn't become fully established until the 18$^{th}$ century.

From Mesopotamia and Babylon there are references to primitive banking in terms of valuables being stored in temples and palaces around 3000 BC; and in legal codes that date back to about 2000 BC there are scales of monetary values in terms of fines to be paid for various offences. It is believed that some of the earliest formulations of business practice and the toleration of debt – simple economics – had their origins with the Mesopotamian and Babylonian civilisations. Further afield, between 2000 BC and 1000 BC, cowrie shells were used as currency tokens or money in China, and then from about 1000 BC, either because of a shortage of shells or to control and authenticate the token, replica cowries were made of wood, bone, stone, bronze, and possibly to give some intrinsic value, jade and semi-precious stones, gold, and silver. During the 1$^{st}$ millennium BC, precious, semi-precious, and base metals were globally used for coinage, and the combined abstract and intrinsic aspects of Commodity Money were taken for granted in just about all of the classical civilisations of Egypt,

Anatolia, Greece, Rome, the distributed Celtic tribes and cultures, and those of Asia, China, and the nomadic Arab and Turkic societies.

Sooner or later, the idea of a sweetener would have developed when a debt was repaid, possibly just as a *thank you* or alternatively it might have been paid in advance as an inducement. We have no way of knowing for sure, but the principle of obsequious ingratiation and the expectation of such by those in power, from which usury stems, is not new. However it started, the practice of paying interest, or usury as it was better known historically, became a habit and big business that has continued to reach obscene percentages (1,000%) nowadays among loan sharks. Those loan sharks are certainly not bankers, but they may well be regarded as a mutation of the proto-banker of antiquity that developed teeth during the Middle-Eastern empires and dynasties of Mesopotamia, Babylon, and Judea.

The Greek philosopher and all-round scholar, often termed a polymath, Aristotle (384 to 322 BC) had the following to say on the subject of usury:

> *"... usury is most reasonably hated, because its gain comes from money itself and not from that for the sake of which money was invented. For money was brought into existence for the purpose of exchange, but interest increases the amount of the money itself (and this is the actual origin of the Greek word: offspring resembles parent, and interest is money born of money); consequently this form of the business of getting wealth is of all forms the most contrary to nature."*

Although Aristotle didn't explicitly say so, his allusion to the fact that *"...interest increases the amount of the money itself"* is an early example of querying where the money to repay interest can come from if the money supply is some finite amount known as the principal. If no more money supply takes place, then from where does say the annual 5% of physical interest come, after one year? It can, of course, only be derived from the failure and repossession associated with one or more individuals, or by further money supply, and in the case of money that is supplied by the state, then more money supply leads to more government debt, and to public inflation.

Although this subject will be expanded later, briefly, the theory of systems that employ control of the money supply is based on a hope that economic growth will justify further money supply, but in present-day practice, the creation of government bonds against the loans that are used to generate that supply, and the trading of those bonds for profit, ensure that there is a built-in increasing debt, and a continuing reduction of money in circulation that can never be satisfied without a periodic economic collapse by one or more individuals, and also at a national-global level.

**Debt-based money and usury guarantee increasing differentials of wealth across the economic spectrum of humanity, and they ensure periodic financial collapses to allow a redistribution of finite funds. In such circumstances those finite funds always migrate upwards, never downwards – no political or mainstream economic doctrine offers any solution to this.**

In the Roman sphere of influence, interest rates were restricted to a maximum of 12% at the time of Julius Caesar around 50 BC, and a sliding scale down to 4% had been introduced by the time of the Corpus Juris Civilis in the Eastern Empire under Emperor Justinian I, circa 550 AD. In later medieval times, interest rates would be allowed to rise so high, 30% or more, that Italian bankers fell foul of the Catholic Church's proscription of usury that was reinforced at more than one Lateran Council, but which enabled Jewish groups that were not so-restricted to take over the business.

This is not some present-day issue of anti-Semitism or Jew-bashing.

With Christian blessing from the highest level, Jews had virtually monopolised the money business in the Western World by the 12th century. In Britain, Jewish administrators with their monopoly were imported by William the Conqueror. Jewish law prevented usury among Jews, but encouraged it against foreigners as prescribed in the King James Bible, Deuteronomy 23:20,

> "Unto a stranger thou mayest lend upon usury; but unto thy brother thou shalt not lend upon usury: that the LORD thy God may bless thee in all that thou settest thine hand to in the land whither thou goest to possess it."

Full advantage has been taken of this piece of international economic warfare over succeeding centuries, Christians famously turning the other cheek for another slap every time.

Before the Normans introduced such a welcome item of diversity as Jewish bankers along with their feudal system that bestowed the benefit of serfdom on a previously relatively free society, reductions in trade, and the turmoil of the re-orientation of Nation-States throughout Europe after the collapse of the Western Roman Empire had seen banking just about disappear from the West, though it had continued relatively undisturbed among the Caliphates of Arabic societies, and further afield throughout Asia and China without Jewish assistance.

### 18.2.4 1st Millennium AD and Medieval Issues

Although tally sticks or some similar mechanism may have been in use for millennia, it is generally accepted that the earliest paper money was used in China during the Tang Dynasty (618 to 907 AD), and that several centuries later in 1100 AD, under English King Henry I, the cost and rarity of paper, but more importantly, issues with his goldsmiths, again encouraged the use of tally sticks that would then stay in use from roughly the $12^{th}$ to the $19^{th}$ centuries. Tally sticks were not initially intended to be a form of every-day currency, but in the absence of circulated gold, they could be used within the population to pay for services or goods because they represented gold. They were equivalent to bills of exchange that recorded a value that could be redeemed, and they were of especial significance because they were not bound to goldsmiths who were already becoming expensive as brokers. A wooden stick would be notched to indicate value, and it would then be split lengthwise so that the matching halves could be verified later, with each party having one piece to prevent counterfeiting. In operation, an individual deposited gold with the King's Exchequer, a stick was created and split, and the part held by the Exchequer was termed the counter-foil, while the part returned to the individual was the foil. Their relative security against fraud, and the fact that they were the only currency recognised by the king for payment of taxes, encouraged their more widespread secondary use as money for payment for services and goods among citizens, reinforcing the principle of the acceptability of something with no intrinsic value as a mechanism of exchange. A similar division of a piece of wood, one piece being the stock, gave rise to the use of the word in connection with stocks and shares.

One of the earliest and most spectacular financial upsets in history, certainly in relative terms, occurred in the 1340s, and it was centred on the Lombard Banks of Tuscany in Italy. Unique conditions, due to the existence of only weakly identifiable Nation-States with, therefore, no national rescue plans, coupled with the unbelievably divisive and exploitative character of the only international organisation with any real power – the Papacy – led to reductions in trade and an increase in poverty when the populations of Europe were already vulnerable from war and plague. English King Edward III (reigned 1327 to 1377) and the Angevin King Robert of Naples were central to this early banking failure, of which more shortly, that occurred just after the start of the Hundred Year War (1337 to 1453) that involved France and Scotland on one side, and England with the Duchy of Burgundy, a remnant of the Frankish Empire, on the other. At about the same time, presumably coincidentally and not due to any global domino effect, the Chinese were forced to end the use of paper money when its over-issue led to runaway inflation in the 15$^{th}$ century AD. The mechanism of money supply and its relationship to inflation is fully covered below.

With a parochial focus a little earlier than the 14$^{th}$ century and much closer to our island home than to the exotic realms of the continental Franks or the Chinese, but about to be dragged into a huge vigorous international web of migrant Norsemen, the Anglo-Saxons in England had become very wealthy by the end of the 1st millennium, this, of course, being one of the main causes of Viking and Norman invasions. Before that increase in wealth, there had been a period immediately after the Roman withdrawal that left the native Britons without much international trade, and what there was suffered from serious piracy by both Picts and other opportunists. It would be the newly arrived Anglo-Saxons that would bring increased opportunities for successful international trade, but because they spent so much time fighting against the Scots and the Picts, and then against the Britons themselves, virtually all of the early English Expeditionary Anglo-Saxon commerce would have consisted of just supply and trade routes back to their own Saxon heartlands in northern Europe where they were known as a group by the term *Ingaevones*. Only after the subjugation of a considerable swathe of the island could the small, new England begin to spend time looking outwards for peaceful international trade again, and notwithstanding the obvious wealth that was accumulated between the reigns of Alfred the Great and Edward the Confessor during the second half of the 1st millennium, England had been somewhat commercially isolated from continental Europe.

It was following the Norman Conquest at the start of the 2nd millennium AD that English banking and trade with the rest of Europe would have been re-invigorated with a vengeance. This commercial renaissance that followed the Norman conquest of Britain was, in fact, of great Nordic significance. It relates to developments that were far more widespread than just the British Isles – it amounts to what is an untold story of the far reaching but circuitous effects of an ancient and ongoing Scandinavian diaspora, a diaspora that takes on more significance when it is remembered that the Lombard aka Langobard bankers of Italy were themselves of Scandinavian origin, as were the Vikings, and likewise the Normans via their progenitor, Rollo the Norseman, who settled in northern France circa 900 AD and gave the region the name Normandy. This Scandinavian diaspora was possibly a return journey, with a vengeance, of the very people who had migrated northwards along the

Atlantic coasts many millennia earlier, and who had ripened in a frigid northern fertility.

Further south, it was now 1000 AD, and the plethora of Italian city states in their strategic positions on the boundary between Islamic and Christian societies saw an increase in the old trades of money lending and money changing; they also saw the development of capitalism and the beginning of commercial banks with a consequent rise in Italian banking dynasties. Letters of credit to transfer funds safely were in use by the start of the 2$^{nd}$ millennium, and business loans were being made, as stated earlier, by Jews in the 12$^{th}$ century. Trade opportunities must have seemed unlimited as Vikings, who encircled the British Isles, also sailed south into the Mediterranean, and others penetrated the vastness of Russia via rivers from the Baltic to the Black and Caspian Seas. Norman adventurers established dominions as far away as Sicily, and although they were responsible for massacres and other social atrocities including ethnic cleansing throughout Britain, their longboats spread migrants and change throughout the length and breadth of Europe, facilitating and necessitating, frequently combatively, trade and communication among a multitude of states. Like the Jews, the Scandinavians were prolific financiers and merchants, but their non-proselytising Pagan culture could never compete on the global stage, and undemanding paganism could not be the basis of an enduring and insidiously condemnatory religious ideology such as Christianity that, with its Abrahamic pedigree, would complement and even promote the Abrahamic Judaic culture with its even longer pedigree and, of course, expertise in the field of banking.

At the start of the 2$^{nd}$ millennium there was a shortage of silver on which most coins were based, but there was an unsustainable and huge excess of both mints and those permitted to operate them to produce coinage, the result being an explosion of officially issued but debased coins. The widespread appearance of such debased coinage naturally led to uncertainty among the populace concerning the value of their coins, and there was a consequent increase in travelling money-changers who visited the markets and fairs swapping old coins for new, some of those new coins

## A History of Money and Financial Empire

being foreign. In spite of the foreign character of the coins, they were purveyed and accepted in a spirit of trust and gratitude for some relief from the uncertainty of value. This trade was initially monopolised by Jews, but learning fast, and aided by historical suspicion of the Jews, the Lombards of Italy had taken the lead by the 13$^{th}$ or 14$^{th}$ century, and deposits were being taken with a promise of interest on redemption. In discriminatory fashion, at various times and in some jurisdictions, such deposit taking was often denied to Jewish money traders by law, though it did nothing to prevent their inexorable progress to their current position of masters of the financial world – no doubt as presaged by Deuteronomy 23, 20.

During the period 1200 to 1500 AD a unique method of taxation based on the money in circulation was introduced into Europe. It was known as *Brakteaten* money and, with the added bonus of a reduction in hoarding, it involved the recall of coins three times a year by local towns so that gold and silver could be shaved from them. This resulted in a decrease in the absolute value of the physical tokens in circulation by as much as 25%, and it prompted people to put their money instead into physical goods, such as furniture, artworks, and even large-scale religious architecture. Coinciding with the Renaissance period, it is said that much of the lasting creativity from that age was due to a reaction by the public against the unpopular *Brakteaten* tax that had been designed to prevent people from hoarding wealth in the form of coinage, but unintentionally ensured that they hoarded finished goods instead. As will be seen many times later, maintaining money supply in the form of circulating currency is crucial to prevent an economy from stalling into a recession.

By the middle of the 14$^{th}$ century Italian banks were already using a ruse to circumvent Papal restrictions on usury; the mechanism was the Bill of Exchange – a re-discovered form of Negotiable Instrument. A Negotiable Instrument is any form of contractually defined exchange of value, in the form of a document. A Bill of Exchange was first seen, it is thought, in similar form, as early as Babylonian and Roman society, and it was a sort of international cheque involving an exchange rate, whereby the early banks made their profit from the exchange rate rather than a notional interest rate; a ludicrous fiddle due to religious doctrine, with similar semantic obscuration nowadays widely used to satisfy the dogma of Sharia Law. In Britain some of the highest usury returns (interest!) on term deposits in 2012 were from the Sharia compliant Bank of London and the Middle East (BLME), a U.K. independent Sharia'a compliant bank based in London.

Returning to corrupt practices in Medieval times, the colossal worldwide donations to the Roman Catholic Church, and the burgeoning receipts from simony (the sale of clerical appointments) and the sale of indulgences (certificates of forgiveness) were originally managed by members of the church known as the Roman Curia (managers of the Holy See), but by the middle of the 13$^{th}$ century the business was being run by bankers in Siena, Italy, the location of the present-day oldest bank in the world, the *Banca Monte dei Paschi di Siena*, formed in 1472, though before that the *Casa delle Compere di San Giorgio* had been formed in Genoa in 1407 and lasted until 1805.

In terms of early European commercial-banking empires however, it was even earlier than medieval times that Venice, Genoa, and Florence, had begun their financial ascent when, despite barbarian domination, they soared during the centuries immediately following the fall of Rome, at which time, quite coincidentally, large amounts of commodity money (intrinsically valuable hard cash!) had just disappeared from circulation. It was these Italian merchant banks, of highly questionable provenance, that were the template for virtually all subsequent banking models including that of the Bank of England.

Later, during the first half of the 13$^{th}$ century, economic development of the Republic of Genoa was facilitated by the *Banco Leccacorvo* that also extended its client base to the Pope and the King of France, but a downturn in trade in 1255 led to its collapse and pursuit by its creditors. In fact, the whole city of Siena was brought low from a banking crisis in 1298 when its largest banking house, *The Buonsignori*, failed. The banking bug was contagious however, and Florentine banking houses then took up the flag so that by 1338 Florence was home to 80 major banking institutions with hundreds of employees, and with geographic coverage of an area from

## A History of Money and Financial Empire

London to the Levant (excepting hostile Arabic controlled regions), and with most European Royal Houses on their books, many running on overdraft.

At this point it's important to bear in mind the destructive background era of the Hundred Year War from 1337 to 1453, described in detail elsewhere in this book. Just into that war, in 1345, the big three Florentine bankers, *Bardi, Peruzzi,* and *Acciaiuoli,* went bust, and this was due: firstly and principally to the default by English King Edward III to the tune of 400 million ducats that had been split as a loan of 600,000 gold florins from the *Peruzzi* and a loan of 900,000 gold florins from the *Bardi*; and secondly to the default of the Angevin King Robert of Naples on a loan of 200,000 florins. It is said that the festering memory of this financial collapse was resurrected by Mussolini during anti-British propaganda some six hundred years later. Maybe in the year 2600 someone will look back at the financial cost of conflicts and World Wars that have spanned the 19$^{th}$, 20$^{th}$, and 21$^{st}$ centuries, and it is to be hoped that someone will acknowledge the issue of the global crisis around 2010 that was so directly related to American sub-prime mortgage debt, and that adversely affected many millions of people, while immeasurably benefiting a minority of money-changers.

The perception of the liability of banks for their deposits was well-established by medieval times but, although there were no central banks and no government guarantees or health warnings, it did not stop the support of what must have seemed very risky ventures – most of the Voyages of Discovery by European navigators, such as Henry the Navigator, Cabot, and Columbus, were financed by Italian banks.

After the collapse of a whole range of banks at the same time as the *Bardi* in the middle of the 14$^{th}$ century, the next major Italian bank to emerge was that of the Medici Family who took over the previously bankrupted Papal account. On closer inspection of the behaviour and culture that pervaded the papacy for hundreds of years, it's perhaps not surprising that the Medici Bank lasted only a century from 1397 to 1494, and yet, in spite of such high-profile failures, banking and the allure of the easy money that can be made was here to stay. Notable medieval merchant banking contemporaries of the Medici Family included a Frenchman, Jacques Coeur (1395 to 1456), one or two families in the Low Countries, but most successfully the family of the German Jakob Fugger (1459 to 1525), thought by some to be one of the wealthiest individuals of all time.

Fugger bank-rolled both the Hapsburgs and the Papacy, and his successes survive him even to the present day in the form of the world's oldest philanthropic housing settlement for "Augsburgers who had fallen into hardship and who practised the Catholic faith". The intrigue surrounding all these characters is beyond the present scope, and references for further reading are included in the *Internet Index* supplied separately with this book.

### 18.2.4.1 Jewish Hegemony – True or False?

Modern western banking can loosely be said to have originated with the Italian states, and to have then spread through Germany, France and the Dutch Republic to England, where it matured for a while in London, before being adopted by American elites. As implied earlier, and as will be more conclusively demonstrated later, banking may, however, be judged to have been underpinned and quietly dominated by a Jewish presence with continuous links back to the earliest historical developments several millennia ago – this is based on objective facts and is not anti-Semitic diatribe.

Discussion in the media and throughout the internet is polluted by confusion and bigotry concerning what should be completely separate issues of, on the one hand anti-Semitism, and on the other hand valid condemnation of excessive profiteering by cultural, commercial and political elites. One controversial and often quoted source of clearly anti-Jewish opinion is a book titled *The Protocols of the Elders of Zion*, said by some to be just a plagiarism of a fictional book *Dialogue in Hell*, by Maurice Joly. The originality of the discourse, and whether it represents the fact, or the fiction of a genuine Zionist threat is hotly and chillingly debated among conspiracy theorists, Zionists, and Jewish internet activists.

For public domain texts see the chapter in Volume One titled *Internet Index of References and Other Downloads*.

Regardless of the reality of any single old manuscript or any modern discussion thread in the media or on the internet, the origins of the *manipulation* of money, as opposed to its use to assist bartering, are indisputably rooted in the mire of millennia of greed and self-interest – wherever and of whatever culture may be its provenance.

### 18.2.5 Further Medieval Developments

Banks that slowly began to resemble the functionality of high street banks that we know today began with the Bank of Barcelona (1401), the *Casa delle Compere di San Giorgio* referred to above (1407), the *Banco della Piazza di Rialto* in Venice (1587), the *Amsterdam Wisselbank* (1609), and the Bank of Hamburg (1619). Britain's oldest bank is C. Hoare & Co (1672), while Barclays was started in 1690, and the Bank of England in 1694, this being the world's second oldest central bank after the Bank of Sweden that was formed in 1668.

The Bank of England had been formed specifically to raise around £1.2 million at low rates for the Nine Year War against France and the Irish-Scottish Jacobites. From the start of the 18$^{th}$ century it set new monetary standards and practices by becoming the *de facto* central source of revenue for the government; but before this event there had been a development in 1640 that completely changed expectations, trust, and confidence among banks and the ruling Monarchy-Government within England.

The Royal Mint had been in existence since about 650 AD when *moneyers*, the men who actually fabricated coinage, had been at work in London and elsewhere in England. By the start of the 14$^{th}$ century London was the central site, and it was a seemingly obvious and secure place to store money and valuables if you didn't have your own secure storage facility. Confidence in the ability of the English Royal Mint to look after one's valuables was shattered in 1640 when the English King Charles I simply helped himself to £200,000 of private money that was stored there. Depositors now needed to find somewhere else with high security, and somewhere that was accustomed to dealing with intrinsically valuable items.

Now it so happened that during the 1600s the "Wardens and Commonalty of the Mystery of Goldsmiths of the City of London" otherwise simply known as the *Goldsmiths*, had suffered several reversals of fortune and difficulties. These setbacks comprised: falling standards of craftsmanship; excessive demands for funding and gifts by the monarchy who always saw the goldsmiths as a soft touch for gold and silver plate; excessive taxes and levies; trumped up charges and resultant fines; and finally, offers of opportunities to invest with the monarch that they couldn't refuse. The Stuart Kings from James I in 1603 up to the civil war that started in 1642, acting without the support of parliament, had become particularly notorious for such offers, one nefarious example being the Plantation of Ulster that began around 1610 under James I, whereby the long-resident Irish were ethnically cleansed, and replaced by English and Scottish Protestants – never should it be said that England's overseas exploitation was driven by race difference.

The Companies of Goldsmiths had been inveigled into financing these various exploitations and royal ventures, and they had lost money on something that could hardly be considered their core business. So, in 1640, goldsmiths were more than ready for revenge, and they were also now more aware of the risks associated with potentially unprofitable diversifications from their traditional metalworking craft, even if they were not necessarily more amenable to such. A ready made client base for such a diversification now presented itself in the shape of those that had been directly robbed by Charles I, but before that we must look at the Goldsmiths.

Goldsmiths, as rivals to the Mints, had been offering receipted safe storage of gold and silver since the start of the 2$^{nd}$ millennium when they were introduced to Britain by William the Conqueror, and they frequently found themselves guarding a hoard of coins for which there was no immediate use. It was just sitting there, and so it seemed natural to lend the coinage to merchants, to other repositories, to monarchs, to the Papacy, and to governments; the principal to be repaid to the goldsmiths with interest. Finding this such good business, the goldsmiths actively sought further deposits and offered to pay interest to depositors while maintaining a leveraged interest rate on borrowers; and we may assume that it was during a period when everything was going according to plan, and risk was the last thing on anyone's mind, that some more risky steps were taken that with hindsight amounted to a leap too far.

Firstly, in their greed, they lent such a quantity of coins that there were not enough retained to repay their depositors if those depositors all wanted their coins back – well it seemed a reasonable idea since records showed only a trickle of withdrawals, and there was a queue of people wanting to deposit even more coins.

Secondly, it was noticed by goldsmiths that people were actually using their deposit receipts, *Goldsmiths' Promissory Notes*, to trade among themselves instead of using coins so, given the public's apparent willingness to accept paper instead of hard currency, the goldsmiths began to make loans with paper instead of coins. As a result of this innovation the loan became totally detached from the reality of coins actually held by the bank. It was so easy to just print off a note, and it was almost the creation of debt from nothing. Modern banking at its worst was almost upon us.

Thirdly, and this was really naughty, the Goldsmiths began the practice of making loans against receipts for deposits that didn't exist, and they passed them into circulation as if they were *bona fide Goldsmiths' Promissory Notes* – a crafty and very risky system that extended still further their exposure due to the inequality between deposits made and funds retained to meet any demands for withdrawal of those deposits. This was now most certainly the creation of debt from nothing, and the system would only continue to work as long as the actual demand for withdrawals didn't exceed a goldsmith's reserves that he kept in his vault. *Fractional Reserve Banking* had been born. It was now a primarily debt-based economy with negative equity, and it was a system with inherent instability and inflationary tendency; and it would now get a boost from the aggrieved ex-Royal Mint depositors referred to above, who were eagerly looking for a repository secure from the King's claws, but presumably unaware of the fractional reserve risk. Some wag later suggested a link between the *"... Mystery of Goldsmiths..."* and their ability to conjure up debt-based money from nowhere.

Regardless of the actual amount of reserves held at a bank, this was a system that also only worked as long as: firstly, the concept and scope of the Negotiable Instrument was universally accepted; and secondly, that confidence in the ultimate and unconditional availability of hard coinage on demand was undisturbed. The first part was reinforced by The Promissory Notes Act of 1704, but the second part, that of the availability of coinage or the size of the Fractional Reserve and the confidence therein, was ephemeral and was based solely on trust. Betrayal of such trust continues into the 3$^{rd}$ millennium.

Stepping back fifty years however, the fact that King Charles I repaid the money he'd stolen from the Royal Mint cut no ice, and in 1642 both the goldsmiths and their client bankers would now be very happy to finance Oliver Cromwell and the Parliamentarians, and furthermore to make available the Goldsmith Company's own militia and stocks of gunpowder, muskets, and pikes. From this time on the trade in goldsmiths' promissory notes led to many artisans giving up metalwork to become full time bankers, and their promissory notes eventually became the payment on demand cheques of today – one small step having been the replacement of a named individual on a promissory note, with the word *bearer*.

Pandora's treasure-chest had been opened, and finance for war would now be so much simpler to obtain, and so very profitable for the lender. That lender was frequently one or more financiers that were derivatives of the usually Jewish Goldsmiths.

In 1557 the French Monarchy had been bankrupt, and again, as a result of colossal expenditure during the Seven Year War from 1756 to 1763 and in support of the American War of Independence from 1775 to 1783, France during the late 1780s was verging on default. Although considered to be wealthier than Britain, where the level of debt following the European and American wars was similar, it is said that it was the inability in France to service its debt by payments such as taxes levied across *all* levels of society (the aristocracy had short arms and deep pockets), coupled with France's much higher interest rates at the time, that led to revolution by the masses against King Louis in France in 1789. Similar issues in Britain led only to a grudging acceptance of financial hardship by most levels of society under King George III, the implication being that Britain was genuinely more egalitarian at the time than France – egalitarian in respect of tax liability that is.

Civil unrest, and class distinctions relating to attempts to pursue a genuine and equitable Reform Act in Britain just a few decades later, would certainly confound any suggestion of beneficial egalitarianism, as will be discussed in a later chapter.

## 18.3 The Bank of England – 1694

As noted earlier, the Bank of England was formed in 1694, and the reason for its creation at that time was very simple – it was to supply credit to the English Government at an interest rate lower than that which could be obtained from the goldsmiths. A similar arrangement had also been made in Holland by the prosperous Dutch Republic with the Bank of Amsterdam and others, and the start of the 18$^{th}$ century saw banking playing such an important role in international trade, politics and the financing of warfare that national legislation was needed to regulate it; the concept of a *National Central Bank* can be traced back to this time.

The Industrial Revolution that is generally accepted to have covered the period 1750 to 1850 saw an explosion of local banks to support the rocketing economy, and the need for some central reference helped establish the Bank of England's authority and monopoly. That monopoly of centralised deposit accounts led to the initially exclusive use of Bank of England bank notes as a means of settling accounts, and a gradual transition from the use of promissory notes to the use of cheque-based accounts. The Bank of England's exclusive right to issue bank notes (later amended) had been enshrined in its charter, and the bank's supremacy and responsibility to ensure the integrity of the British monetary system was tacitly accepted everywhere by the late 19$^{th}$ century. Conversely however, the Bank of England was initially denied the right to establish branches, and during some turbulent birth-pang economic issues in the first quarter of the 19$^{th}$ century, the separation of local banks from the central bank led to local collapses and a series of government reforms beyond the scope of this book. Further details on Joint-Stock banking, and some Acts of Parliament, such as the Bank Notes Act of 1833 and the Bank Charter Act aka Peel's Act of 1844, can all be easily found on the internet.

The British pound sterling was the world's reserve currency during the 19$^{th}$ century, but the U.S. Federal Reserve Act would take place in 1913. By remaining free to speculate and profit during most of World War One, the U.S. would rise to the prominence that it has held ever since.

The Bank of England had intimate links with government, and it enjoyed virtually exclusive control of bullion, of coinage, and of the issue of money. As a result of its experiences, both successful and during economic crises, this central bank headed the development of banking theory from the bank's formation in 1694 to the present day; and as a result of the prominence of the British Empire it influenced banking theory and exploitation around the globe. The debate concerning the wisdom of central bank authority compared to the freedom of local banks continues to the present day, with the added complexities nowadays of the International Monetary Fund, the World Bank, and the European Central Bank for instance; and in an age of globalisation, there are issues with the consequently uncertain meaning of the word *local*.

The purpose and responsibility of the Bank of England today is very different to what it was in 1694. Firstly, it is now the sole issuer of bank notes in England and Wales, and it manages the nation's gold reserves and foreign currency reserves. Secondly, it strives to ensure monetary stability, the success of which is judged by stable prices and confidence in the British Pound Sterling. In order to achieve these things, inflation has to be managed and kept to a target that is set by the Chancellor of the Exchequer. Interest rates that favour economic growth are now determined by the Bank of England Monetary Policy Committee, though any flexibility in that may well be determined by international events beyond the control of the bank. Thirdly, financial stability – the stability of the

## A History of Money and Financial Empire

UK's entire financial system including High Street banks for instance – must be ensured, if necessary by acting as a bank or lender of last resort as happened during the economic crisis of 2008 to 2011 and beyond when there was a run on certain British banks, such as Halifax-Bank of Scotland (HBOS) and Northern Rock, with some of their executives being banned for life from financial dealings as a result of investigations by the Financial Services Authority. The Financial Services Authority was itself rationalised in 2012 into the Financial Conduct Authority and the Prudential Regulation Authority, one assumes, as a result of its own shortcomings and complicity in one of the greatest economic disasters ever seen.

It is necessary, however, to return to the events and the greed immediately following the formation of the Bank of England, since it is such events that may be said to have been major contributory factors to the separation by revolution of the North American colonies from Britain. Firstly, the Bank of England was set up by collecting Tally Sticks as payment for bank shares that would then be held by a small number of secret subscribers. Tally Sticks, as described earlier, were an ancient concept. In England they had been adopted by English King Henry I, circa 1100 AD, as a means of keeping the mechanisms of monetary exchange and the raising of finance out of the clutches of usurious lenders. Circa 1671, however, they had been seriously abused by English King Charles II when he ordered their over-production without collateral, and now, circa 1700, they were set to be replaced by the Bank's own paper bank note system, thereby taking control away from the King. After their adoption around 1100 AD, Tally Sticks would eventually be completely superseded by about 1850.

The initial intention for the Bank of England's first issue of £1.2 million was that it should attract interest at 8% with an annual management fee of £4,000. In the event, however, only about £750,000 was actually invested, and even this was based only on Tally Sticks that were abundant at the time that the private bank received its Royal Charter. Nevertheless, in 1694 the government somehow received its £1.2m loan from the Bank of England, the loan being secured by direct national taxation, and the public became liable to pay back the £1.2m via taxes. The spending spree that drove the industrial revolution and the build-up of the British Navy to its world supremacy had begun, and it was all based on the mysterious transmutation of inanimate Tally Sticks into public debt.

Four years later the national debt had risen to £16m, and fifty years later it was about £140m – a debt owed by the public at large to the private banks in an era of unparalleled poverty for most but fabulous industrial wealth for a minority.

It was during this climate of national insolvency that attempts were made from the 1760s onwards to raise taxes in the American colonies as a contribution to the defence of those colonies during and after the Seven Year War that lasted from 1756 to 1763, but the attempts were seen as interference in the thirteen colonies' financial affairs without the colonies' parliamentary representation, and the War of Independence from 1775 to 1783 ensued, during which period almost half of all prison inmates in England were commercial debt defaulters. The only real winners were the secret shareholders of the Bank of England .

## 18.4 The Gold Standard – A Quarter Millennium of Indecision

Gold has been used for many millennia as a convenient means of exchange within closed societies, and also because of its unmistakable allure, across cultural boundaries and between communities of strangers. In the modern age it has been sorely tried and tested with some of the most exacting international regulations and it has been found wanting, although there are today both fanatical proponents and opponents of the idea of a Gold Standard.

Among trading nations a Gold Standard is of most use if they all set the price of their currencies in terms of a defined quantity of gold, but there are three different viewpoints of the concept of gold exchange. Within a single country, coinage has an exchange value in gold termed *Gold Specie Standard*, whether or not the coin is pure gold. Internationally, coins of different nations are valued against each other according to the term *Gold Exchange Standard*, while gold bullion that is not coinage is traded internationally according to a *Gold Bullion Standard*.

## 18.4.1 Table – Milestones – The Gold Standard Since 1717

| Year | Notes |
|---|---|
| 1717 | England *de facto* more or less adopted a Gold Standard when Sir Isaac Newton, in one of his many illustrious roles, in this case as Master of the Royal Mint, modified the Mint Ratio of silver and gold during an assay of the coinage. Mint Ratio is the price of an ounce of gold in terms of ounces of silver. His valuation was such as to deter the use of silver and put Britain onto a Gold Standard, though silver coinage remained in use. |
| 1799 | By now there had been a silver shortage due to wars, and there were shortages of both silver and copper coins. That shortage would worsen during the next century. |
| 1816 | The Gold Sovereign was introduced as part of a re-coinage programme aimed at stopping counterfeit production of coins, and bringing greater stability. Gold, silver and copper coins were all affected. |
| 1819 | The U.K. Act for the Resumption of Cash Payments (notes could be redeemed for gold) effectively planned for the more formal *de facto* adoption of the Gold Standard. |
| 1821 | The restoration of convertibility of Bank of England notes happened two years earlier than anticipated in the Act of 1819. |
| 1833 | Bank of England notes became legal tender. |
| 1834 | Although the U.S. formally had a bimetallic standard of gold and silver, some sources say that this was the year that it *de facto* moved to gold, while others say 1873. The U.S. now fixed gold at $20.67 per ounce, and it would remain at that value until 1933 – virtually one hundred years. |
| 1844 | The Bank Charter Act made Bank of England notes 100% backed by gold. The notes were now the *de jure* currency standard, and money was regulated according to a Gold Standard. |
| 1870s | Several more major countries, many of them in the British Empire, joined the Gold Standard. |
| 1873 | In the U.S. the demonetisation of silver became known as the Crime of '73. This was the year that some sources say the U.S. adopted the Gold Standard *de facto*, others say 1834. |
| 1880 | This began the Classical Gold Standard period during which most countries' currencies were based on gold. International tariffs were minimised, leading to free trade and widespread economic growth. Inflation in the U.S. was a tiny 0.1% average per annum. There would be 34 years of relative stability until 1914, and then World War One would destroy everything. |
| 1900 | U.S. *de jure* adoption of Gold Standard. |
| 1914 to 1918 | Inflation and war costs put paid to the Gold Standard. |

| Year | Notes |
|---|---|
| 1925 to 1931 | There was a brief period of what was known as the Gold Exchange Standard, by which countries other than the U.S. and the U.K. could hold their choice of reserves not directly as gold, which was in short global supply, but as dollars or pounds that were fixed against gold. The U.S. and U.K. held only gold reserves. |
| 1931 | The Gold Exchange Standard fell apart after Britain experienced large outflows of gold and left the Gold Standard. |
| 1933 | The U.S. under President Franklin D. Roosevelt imposed the nationalisation of all gold held by private citizens. |
| 1946 to 1971 | The Bretton Woods system is described elsewhere in this book. It was a Gold Standard that massively favoured the U.S. dollar, but one that gave some stability to the post-war years. French President de Gaulle indicated unhappiness with the system in 1965. |
| 1971 | U.S. gold reserves had been decreasing for some time and, coupled with the effects of America's repeated balance-of-payments deficits, confidence in the continuity of a U.S. capability to convert dollars to gold was eroded. This prompted France's President Pompidou to attempt to redeem all of France's dollar reserves for gold – in American eyes a step too far – and after secession by Germany, and rebellion by other nations, the *Nixon Shock of 1971* – the statement that America would no longer redeem U.S. dollars for gold – ended the world's Gold Standard. |

## 18.5 The Rise (and Fall ?) of the American Economy
### 18.5.1 Introduction

In 1965 the U.S. was the largest creditor nation in the world, that is to say the wealthiest on paper, but by 2013 it was the world's largest debtor nation. Although by no means dead, it is living on borrowed money and, without any solution to its massive national debt, it is living on borrowed time.

The true meaning and significance of debt-based, usurious, and interest-laden money, and whether there is any alternative, may be illustrated by looking at the phenomenon of the United States of America that began in relatively recent historical times and, conveniently for this discussion, started with relatively little essential elitism and was truly founded on egalitarianism – relatively that is.

This assessment is valid for the pioneering period of that nation when land ownership and exploited division of labour were minimal, and while usury was essentially minimised because commodity exchange at the frontier of the civilised world was often in terms of barter and not monetary tokens. The new nation had no long history of hegemony or violent conquest – that would come later against the native Americans, against Canada where a U.S. invasion failed, and against the Spanish in the southern territories and Mexico where many southern and south-western states would be quite simply appropriated by an expansionist United States of America. Neither was there anything to cloud its origins other than a little religious fundamentalism and its participation in the slave trade between Africa and America, which was no more than just one sector of an evil global slave trade that involved the kidnapping of members of all races, and the repression and deaths of maybe a billion or more serfs in all countries worldwide over a millennium or so. Slavery continues into the $3^{rd}$ millennium and is not the preserve of any one race or nation.

Aspects of the U.S. phenomenon that are convenient to study comprise: firstly, events either side of both the American war of Independence (1775 to 1783) and the American Civil War (1861 to 1865); secondly, the birth and ceaseless growth of the U.S. economy; and thirdly, a raft of changes to the

U.S. banking system and financial industry that have been globally prejudicial.

## 18.5.2 Colonial Scrip and Independence

In the Euro-American revolutionary climate towards the end of the 18th century, Adam Smith wrote his seminal work on the subject of the wealth of nations, and there was significant debate and open critical commentary concerning monetary theory and the predatory nature of banking, particularly in the new U.S.A. In a world with far fewer personal bank accounts than nowadays, it's possible that more was questioned and understood about the subject by influential people of the 18th century, than by the whole population of today.

Before the advent of its central bank – the Federal Reserve – early American bills of credit were issued not by banks or by the Federal Government, but by individual States, and those bills were usually though not always intended for payment of both taxes and private trade transactions. They were known as *fiat* currency, which means that they could not be exchanged for gold or silver bullion that was in short supply (which is why such notes were introduced), and they were under state control, not bank control. These bills of credit were based and issued on the creditworthiness of the government not as a result of its debt or *bond* to a bank. Colonial America was new and without the baggage of centuries of European bank burden.

These bills of credit or Colonial Scrip bore no interest because they were not raised by a loan from any bank, and they did not add to the state's tax burden because no government bonds needed to be issued to cover them. Any such government-issued bond would have needed revenue to come to the government so it could be used to make the repayment, and that could only have come from taxation of the population. So, in a new and developing nation where naturally primitive and restrictive trade circumstances had previously needed barter to see any circulation of goods and trade of any sort, the refreshingly simple convention of debt-free and widely recognised tickets or scrips were a component that helped to see a massive increase in economic development. The government's ability to withdraw some of these scrips from circulation as tax payments when needed also controlled inflation and ensured relatively, though not exclusively, smooth growth.

The Pennsylvania Scrip that had been developed with the help of Benjamin Franklin was one of the most successful and stable of those throughout the thirteen colonies, and it was Franklin who was called to explain the principle of its success to the British Board of Trade in London in 1763.

British Currency Acts had begun in 1751 with the objective of controlling fluctuations in the value of colonial paper money that was susceptible to depreciation. It was such fluctuations in value that had made the American scrip, quite reasonably, undesirable to British trade partners, and following Franklin's possibly naïve revelations in England, the Currency Acts were extended in 1764. Their restriction on the scope of Colonial Scrip and therefore on trade among the colonies was effective within months, and the resulting depression and economic difficulties throughout most of the colonies was seen as being due to British intervention. It was this perception and blame, even if it was not a reality, that is believed by many to have been a major contribution to the moves for independence.

The Bank of North America, a private business, was chartered in 1781, but the First U.S. Central Bank, opposed by Benjamin Franklin until he died in 1790, was finally chartered for twenty years from 1791 to 1811 after much debate about whether or not it was constitutional. It was heavily funded by the Jewish magnate, Nathan Mayer Rothschild, who is often quoted as saying:

> "Give me control of a nation's money and I care not who makes the laws".

The New York Stock Exchange was also started at this time – in 1792.

### 18.5.3 Freemasonry, Illuminati, and Jewish Influence

The Rothschild Empire is covered elsewhere in this book in detail, but briefly, in the present context, it was in 1798 that the eminent scientist,

Professor John Robison of the University of Edinburgh, who was also general secretary of the respected Royal Society of Edinburgh, published a book titled, *Proofs of a Conspiracy Against All the Religions and Governments of Europe Carried on in the Secret Meetings of Freemasons, Illuminati and Reading Societies.* In that book he gave details of a shadowy Rothschild-Illuminati plot that linked French Jacobins, Freemasons, Jews, and the new Americans, and which anticipated the revolutionary movements over the next century. It implied that within centuries there could be a New World Order that would exert financial and political domination without accountability. Regardless of the extent to which his particular theory may have been true then or now, present-day events and statistics might be interpreted to give him at least some credit for foresight. Returning to the first years of the 19$^{th}$ century, a very real Rothschild shadow would indeed be cast very shortly. John Robison's book is in the public domain.

There are many quotes by the leading lights of the developing U.S. on the subject of central banking in general, and on the specific events that they were witnessing, two of the many arguments against the formation of a U.S. Central Bank at the time being as follows:

> "History records that the money changers have used every form of abuse, intrigue, deceit, and violent means possible to maintain their control over governments by controlling money and its issuance."
> — President James Madison

and

> "I wish it were possible to obtain a single amendment to our Constitution - taking from the federal government their power of borrowing."
> — President Thomas Jefferson

## A History of Money and Financial Empire

Jefferson is further quoted as having said, although the original source is obscure:

> *"I believe that banking institutions are more dangerous to our liberties than standing armies. If the American people ever allow private banks to control the issue of their currency, first by inflation, then by deflation, the banks and corporations that will grow up around [the banks] will deprive the people of all property until their children wake-up homeless on the continent their fathers conquered. The issuing power should be taken from the banks and restored to the people, to whom it properly belongs."*

From many of his other more assuredly citable quotes he would certainly have endorsed this sentiment.

It was Jefferson who refused to renew the charter of the First Central Bank in 1811, largely because it was seventy percent foreign owned, and this is said by some to have contributed to the causes of the war between America and England at that time. There is considerable controversy and conspiracy theory accusation surrounding events at this time as to whether it was, in fact, the loss of the charter for the Rothschild's Bank of the United States that spurred Nathan Mayer Rothschild to remark from England:

> *"Either the application for renewal of the charter is granted, or the United States will find itself involved in a most disastrous war."*
>
> ...
>
> *"Teach those impudent Americans a lesson. Bring them back to colonial status."*

War between the U.S. and Britain began within a year – in 1812.

### 18.5.4 From Revolution to Civil War – the Greenback Dollar

The Second U.S. Central Bank was also chartered for twenty years from 1817 to 1836, and it was soon involved in the first U.S. internal economic crisis, termed the Panic of 1819, seen by some as the first manifestation of the boom and bust phenomenon. There had been an earlier Panic of 1797 but that was due to international issues. It was during this second bank charter, in 1835, that President Andrew Jackson paid off the whole of the national debt, but by 1838 it had returned to more than $3 million and has grown ever since. President Andrew Jackson was totally opposed to the principle of central banks and their remit to print paper currency. He was responsible for preventing the renewal of the U.S. Central Bank after 1836, but there would be a further, more prolonged financial crisis in the U.S. from 1837 until 1844, with classic unemployment, bankruptcies, and company failures.

The debate over the wisdom of employing a central bank would continue, and egalitarian rhetoric would accumulate for decades to provide a deep and rich litter that often obscures and confuses any attempt to identify real human value from ideological pomp.

Abraham Lincoln in his State of the Union Address of December, 1861, spoke in favour of the rights of labour over capital thus:

> "...Labor [sic] is prior to and independent of capital. Capital is only the fruit of labor, and could never have existed if labor had not first existed. Labor is the superior of capital, and deserves much the higher consideration..."

Adam Smith would write similar words in *An Inquiry into the Nature and Causes of the Wealth of Nations* in 1776, the whole of which book seems to be contradictory in places, and ideologically chaotic, even though it is regarded as enlightened by many.

The U.S. National Banking Act of 1863 was an attempt to promote national banks above local and private state banks by backing national bank note issues with government securities, and taxing just the state bank

## A History of Money and Financial Empire

issues, but although the federal currency became regulated, private bank state issues continued, and in 1864 Lincoln is reputed to have said, though it is denied by some:

> *"The money powers prey upon the nation in times of peace and conspire against it in times of adversity. The banking powers are more despotic than a monarchy, more insolent than autocracy, more selfish than bureaucracy. They denounce as public enemies all who question their methods or throw light upon their crimes. I have two great enemies, the Southern Army in front of me and the bankers in the rear. Of the two, the one at my rear is my greatest foe ... I see in the near future a crisis approaching that unnerves me and causes me to tremble for the safety of my country; corporations have been enthroned, an era of corruption in High Places will follow, and the Money Power of the country will endeavour to prolong its reign by working upon the prejudices of the People, until the wealth is aggregated in a few hands, and the Republic destroyed."*

However accurate that quotation may be, he certainly did further resist the attempts by bankers to impose interest rate-burdened loans on the U.S. in connection with the funding of the American Civil War that lasted from 1861 to 1865. He did this by issuing via the U.S. Treasury almost half a billion greenback dollars that were free of debt and interest. These notes, green on one side, were used to pay state employees, the military, and for the purchase of war supplies, though there are conflicting opinions on the success of that policy. Lincoln was, of course, assassinated, but periodic issue of the greenbacks continued until 1971, after which they remained as legal tender but in diminishing numbers until the last decade of the 20$^{th}$ century. Almost one hundred years after Lincoln's murder, another U.S. president was assassinated, one who was also associated with the issue of

U.S. Treasury notes instead of those from the Federal Reserve, John F. Kennedy. Conspiracy theories abound concerning both murders.

It is suggested by some that throughout this period in U.S. history, the mid-19th century that is, external influences were at work to encourage a U.S. civil war, the objective being to create two separate and weaker nations that would be susceptible to international, and implicitly European, banking manipulation. Some support for this notion comes from the earlier words of Nathan Mayer Rothschild in 1811, and also from the response by the banking fraternity to Abraham Lincoln's issue of greenbacks that may be represented by the words, reported in 1865 in the Times newspaper, London, of businessman Lord Goschen (also variously an English MP, First Lord of the Admiralty, and Chancellor of the Duchy of Lancaster). Those words are taken from the book *Lincoln Money Martyred*, written in 1935 by Dr. R. E. Search, and Goschen said:

> *"If this mischievous financial policy which has had its origin in the North American Republic (greenback issue of money) during the late (civil) war should become endurated down to a fixture, then that government will furnish its own money without cost. It will pay off its debts and be without debts. It will have all the money necessary to carry on its commerce. It will become prosperous beyond precedent in the history of the world. The brains and wealth of all countries will go to North America. That government must be destroyed or it will destroy every monarchy on the globe."*

Historians have assumed that by "monarchy" he meant the monarchy of the money lenders. In the same book, *Lincoln Money Martyred*, Dr. R. E. Search goes on to state:

> *"... So we should not be surprised when we find that ...*
> - *When the government of old Egypt fell, four per cent of the people owned all the wealth.*

- *When the Babylonian civilisation collapsed, three per cent of the people owned all the wealth.*
- *When old Persia went down to destruction two per cent of the people owned all the wealth.*
- *When ancient Greece went down to ruin one-half of one percent of the people owned all the wealth.*
- *When the Roman Empire fell by the wayside, two thousand people owned the wealth of the civilised world and then followed the Dark Ages from which they did not recover until wealth was scattered by continuous wars, a great share of it being therein destroyed.*
- *It is said at this time that less than two (2) per cent of the people control ninety (90) per cent of the wealth of America."*

### 18.5.5 Unstoppable Growth by Attrition – At Home and Abroad

1907 was the year of one of the U.S.'s early economic crises – before there was a central bank. It was short-lived, about ten weeks, but halved stock values. The causes were failing Market Liquidity, and loss of confidence in the banking system. Such would be seen time and again over the next one hundred years.

In 1907 the severity was reduced by voluntary action by several banks including the celebrated J.P. Morgan, and the impact was to pave the way for the Federal Reserve Bank in 1913 – just ready for the immensely profitable World War One.

Following the betrayal of his election manifesto by the signing into law of the Federal Reserve Act that led to the creation of the Federal Reserve Bank, President Woodrow Wilson (in office 1913 to 1921) said:

*"I am a most unhappy man. I have unwittingly ruined my country ... A great industrial nation is controlled by its system of credit. Our system of credit is concentrated. The growth of the nation therefore, and all our activities, are in the hands of a few men. We have come to be one of the worst ruled, one of*

*the most completely controlled and dominated governments in the civilized world. No longer a government by free opinion, no longer a government by conviction and the vote of the majority, but a government by the opinion and duress of a small group of dominant men."*

The first head of the private Federal Reserve Bank was Paul Warburg, an Ashkenazi German Jewish immigrant who was part of the family firm of M.M. Warburg, founded in 1798. This privately owned German bank exists to the present day. The 20th century English private bank, S. G. Warburg, that sprouted among the ruins of the Second World War, was also part of the Warburg family empire. Paul Warburg had previously worked at Samuel Montague & Company, bankers, in London, and a French bank in Paris and, as will be seen in the last part of this section, networking among Jewish banking interests, even before the age of the internet and social networks, was prodigious.

Outside of central banking circles, opinion of central bankers is frequently hostile. For example, Milton Friedman, Nobel Prize winning economist, said:

*"The Federal Reserve definitely caused the Great depression by contracting the amount of currency in circulation by one-third from 1929 to 1933."*

Many such quotes exist, and in addition to a host of destructive conspiracy theories, much compelling footage of real Senate hearings is freely available for anyone to see on the internet.

### 18.5.6 Wall Street – a Forgotten Lesson

As part of the response to the Wall Street crash of October 24th 1929, known as Black Thursday, and to the deepening Great Depression, it was in 1932 and 1933 that two U.S. democrats, Carter Glass and Henry Steagall, sponsored various initiatives to regulate certain activities of the Federal Reserve Bank in particular, and to define permitted relationships among

## A History of Money and Financial Empire

Commercial Banks, Investment Banks, and Securities Firms. The complex results were the Glass-Steagall Act of 1932, and the 1933 Banking Act. Simplistically, the intention was to impose restrictions on inter-bank connivance, and to regulate what banks could do with customers' money. Eighty years later there is again talk of the wisdom of such firewalls in the banking industry to restrain the irresponsible behaviour of arrogant and narcissistic banking buffoons.

There was controversy about the effectiveness of the Glass-Steagall Act, and much whining, though mainly, of course, from its victims, the banking community, and in the climate of the boom years of the 1990s when a lot of the industry was already acting outside of the restrictions of the Acts, Glass-Steagall was dismantled in 1999 by the Gramm-Leach-Bliley Act under the presidency of Bill Clinton. A mere sixteen months later a recession began in March, 2001, and within another seven years the toxic debt created by mainly U.S. financial institutions, disproportionately Jewish, had poisoned the globe, and caused financial disaster to many thousands, and considerable discomfort to hundreds of millions of deposit account and pension fund holders.

U.S. sub-prime mortgages and their sale into the secondary mortgage market were the direct cause of the 2008-2011 ongoing economic crisis. The "N.I.N.J.A. mortgage", responsible at source for most of the damage, was a *No-Income-No-Job-or-Assets* loan, freely given for reasons of political correctness, but doomed to failure from the start. It resulted in the massive transfer ($trillions) of wealth from greedy and naïve European banks, and by association, the European tax-paying public, into some U.S. financial black hole that may never be brought to account.

## 18.6 Parliamentary and Royal Sequestration of Britain's Wealth

This is a timeline of the steady erosion of the common wealth of the people over the last one thousand years or so. That erosion has been accomplished by those who have been, and still are, revered and worshipped by many – the English and British Royal Families with their many aristocratic tentacles – and by those who may not be so revered – government and establishment bodies and individuals.

It is an indication of the theft of wealth from the common purse by Royal and elite sequestration.

### 18.6.1 Saxon Autonomy, Norman Tyranny, and Liberal Irony

After circa 500 AD there was a steady British rationalisation and integration of tribes and national resources, including Anglo-Saxon dominated culture, wealth, and land ownership, all at some cost to the enfeebled Romano-British strands of civilisation. As described elsewhere, that older British culture was either physically pushed or became more focussed in the western parts of Britain – Cornwall, Wales, and Scotland, while among an unknown blend of older British tribes and newer Anglo-Saxon settlers, all of whom remained in the core and eastern regions, there was a commensurate half millennium's worth of increase in national unity and defensive strength in the face of Viking depredation until Britain was suddenly the subject of a disastrous Norman Conquest. Britain at that time had become used to the folk moot that was a democratic system of ensuring truly popular leadership, but the changes about to unfold were apocalyptic.

An initially ruthless statutory tyranny or dictatorship of William I ("The Conqueror") was steadily replaced by a fragmented, distributed oligarchy led by heinous Norman robber cum butcher Barons that would be perpetuated via aristocratic inheritance of wealth and honorific title. That vile and undeserving "blue-blooded" oligarchy has persisted in reality to the present day, passing through an even lower period of feudal oppression that arguably lasted for some six hundred years until the onset of a different form of repressive ambivalence known as liberalism. Sometimes sponsored in high places, liberalism would initially raise its malleable body in an attempt to push back against the legacy of Norman tyranny, only to fall victim to human fallibility in a socio-political environment that had become so highly toxic after centuries of Norman pollution.

Characterised by several Acts of Parliament, such as the Habeas Corpus Act of 1679, the Bill of Rights of 1689, and the Great Reform Act of 1832, liberalism gives an illusion of equal rights and freedom, but those rights and freedoms can be bypassed whenever necessary by the State, and they can be bypassed by the unelected power brokers of the "fourth estate" – the modern media.

One example of the irony of liberalism begins with the Star Chamber that will be covered later, but which was, in summary, a closed court of judgement that dealt out arbitrary punishments, including mutilation, that were unarguably extra-judicial whatever their claimed aristocratic provenance. The Star Chamber was used from about the 14$^{th}$ until the 17$^{th}$ centuries and, although its origins were associated with an attempt to move forward from the medieval and hideously non-judicial *trial by fire*, and *trial by combat*, it was discontinued for good reason in the spirit of liberalism. And yet in more recent times that same "liberalism" has exhibited its own unsavoury side through the extra-judicial and undemocratic ideological bias of our liberal mainstream media with its *trial by headline*, and its *trial by editorial* – character assassination in public instead of physical mutilation.

Long before there could be any "liberal" irony however, from the arrival of William the Conqueror Britain was the scene of more than five hundred years of civil war and turmoil, during which wealth was accumulated by the ruling elite at the expense of the masses – an inheritance of fabulous wealth and comfort for a small few, and the inheritance of grinding disadvantage and penury for the majority. Interest bearing loans were introduced and exploited from this time onwards, their management being the sole preserve of the capable, and in this respect highly experienced, Jewish community that was brought to England by William I, and that was imposed on the English with the specific mandate of ensuring the maximum ongoing extraction of wealth from the island's defeated and downtrodden population into the pockets of the Normans – with a good percentage going to the Jewish silversmiths, goldsmiths, and money-changers.

### 18.6.2 Medieval and Post Medieval Changes

King Edward I (aka Longshanks, aka the Hammer of the Scots) confiscated lands from the Welsh during the last quarter of the 13$^{th}$ century. He failed to subdue the Scots but, by the Edict of Expulsion in 1290, he removed from the population at large, the Jewish elite in England who, from their uncontested position, could raise money by usury, something that their Hebrew religion, as expressed in the Biblical book of Deuteronomy, prevented them from imposing on their own cultural Jewish compatriots. These issues are described elsewhere in this book.

English King James I (reign 1603 to 1625), who had already become Scottish King James VI in 1587, introduced a hesitant geographic expansion, but little real wealth – Scotland was still predominantly rural and impoverished in English terms, though free of the predations of the English Barons. It's likely that loyalty within the Scottish clan system gave at least an illusion of freedom at this time.

Although King James introduced no significant wealth, he did introduce financial issues in the form of difficulties that he faced when it came to raising finance. He was used to having what he wanted as a younger man in Scotland and he was constantly at odds with the English parliament when he wanted more. The Ulster Plantations were underway by 1610, and they involved the appropriation of Irish land by English-speaking Protestants who had been shipped in from both Scotland and England. This was grand larceny that would haunt not only the thieves and their grasping spawn, but the whole population into the 3$^{rd}$ millennium. Around the same time, King James disbanded Parliament on several occasions for failing to provide him with money to repay his debts, and because it would not fund his ongoing court extravagance of more than £500,000 per annum in early 17$^{th}$ century money. An attempt to settle on an allowance of £200,000, negotiated under the name of "The Great Contract" of 1610, failed, and again, Parliament was dissolved.

Inevitably, concessions were made at the public expense and aristocratic titles were sold by the Crown, thereby increasing the number of elite predators. In spite of the efforts of present-day historians to rehabilitate the reputation of English King James I, the facts of his legacy are the character of his arrogant and selfish son, English King Charles I, more decades of futile and failed international warfare, and the English Civil War that in reality was spread in time either side of the obviously hot and armed conflict that took place between 1642 and 1646, and that saw losses by death and exile, on both sides, of possibly nobler men of principle than some of those that took their place. That contention certainly seems demonstrated by some of the features of the Restoration, and by events that occurred during the next two centuries that would see the introduction of another predatory class of humanity – the rise of the privileged private landowner through parliamentary membership and the possession of judicial seats. This was sometimes in connection with "Rotten Boroughs", and the whole rotten private edifice would rival the miserly monarchs, the Church, and the robber barons that had violently retained ascendancy since 1066.

The Restoration of English King Charles II in 1660 led to many consequences that were not in the public interest: obscene public spectacles of hanging, drawing, and quartering of the erstwhile Republicans and egalitarians who had been involved in the execution of the profligate English King Charles I; tax raising benefits for the monarchy that introduced indirect taxation in the form of excise duty on alcoholic beverages, thereby disproportionately hitting the poorer members of society; destructive divisions of revenue and responsibility; and deterioration through ill-judged warfare that would be a common feature through to the time of King George III, who had the throne from 1760 to 1820 and who would preside over the separation of the American colonies from the rest of the British Empire.

Like his ancestors, George III had extravagant tastes, and an initiative to contain his excesses, coupled with the fact that the monarchy up to this time was responsible for much of the cost of the civil administration, required the introduction of major changes to the mechanisms of Treasury and Exchequer. King George III surrendered some relatively small revenues, including in 1793 those from Ireland, but he was the first monarch to receive money from the Civil List, and he was also allowed to keep the income from the Duchy of Lancaster. His Civil List entitlement began with an annual amount equivalent to something in excess of £110 million in present-day terms, plus the odd capital grant during his lifetime that amounted overall to the equivalent then of more than £200 million.

All this, of course, had to come from the purse of the tax-payer and, despite earlier social and egalitarian successes of the English Civil War, both actual and envisaged, we have been left instead with the eternal infamy of iniquitous government coupled with the parasitism of a greedy lesser aristocracy – descendants of robber barons – nominally overseen by a weak dysfunctional monarchy.

The Civil List was finally abolished by the Sovereign Grant Act of 2011 that instead awards the monarch a fixed percentage of the net revenue of the Crown Estate, starting with 15% in 2012.

### 18.6.3 Land Grabbing – the Exploitation of Ireland

One among many notorious examples of land-grabbing occurred between the years 1834 and 1847, and it is referred to as the Irish Ballykilcline removals and assisted New World emigration. These evictions were the culmination of a rent protest that was staged by peasants who, since the English-Scottish plantation period, had been forced to live in squalid and inadequately landed conditions. Their protest began when the principal leaseholder became infirm or insane in 1834, after which it passed through a period of haphazard rent defaults until the onset of the debilitating Great Irish Potato Famine in 1845 that created even greater stress and misery for the community. At this low point, instead of receiving humanitarian aid that might be expected in any decent civilisation, they were confronted by police, dragoons, and infantry, that were sent in during

May, 1847, to demolish the homesteads and evict the already starving residents who were to be effectively transported against their wishes to the New World. Such was the expression of liberalism in the *Age of Enlightenment*.

The Great Famine persisted until 1852, and the widespread demographic hit on Ireland in terms of emigration and deaths is legendary.

### 18.6.4 Land Grabbing – English Acts of Enclosure

Although the iniquitous theft of land from common ownership is perhaps best seen in the form of the thousands of Enclosure Acts – see the chapter titled *Enclosure aka Inclosure Acts 1773 to 1882* – of which those during the one hundred year period from about 1750 to 1850 represent a peak, the practice had begun much earlier. Since the reign of English King Henry III (1216 to 1272), who was the son of the duplicitous English King John (aka King John Lackland) who reneged on the Magna Carta, Statutes were passed, starting during the early 13$^{th}$ century, that enabled the conversion of common land into royal and baronial deer parks. Thereafter, anyone caught stealing the King's deer would be summarily executed or mutilated by having their hands cut off. Aristocratic inheritance retains such lands to the present day.

In Tudor times (1485 to 1603) spanning the reigns of English King Henry VII, King Henry VIII, King Edward VI, English Queen Mary I and Queen Elizabeth I, wool was much more profitable than grain production, and vast arable lands were turned over to grazing. Peasants were evicted from common land to wander from the outset as not just paupers (people with no income) but, following the loss of their homes, as vagrants – and vagrants were regarded as criminals, and associated with vagabonds.

Following the theft of their hereditary lands, sometimes by the Abbots of religious orders, thousands were hunted down by a vengeful and psychopathic elite, and subjected to an imaginative range of mistreatments and exile, all under the guise of lawful punishment. It had been an exceedingly painful transition for many – from home-owner to pauper, to vagrant, to hunted vagabond, and finally into exile – while the elite grew fatter. The unfortunate victims of such elite predation suffered terribly at the Petty Sessions Courts.

Henry VIII's dissolution of the monasteries had the complex effect of the annexation of land to not royal ownership but to mean-minded private ownership. This led to an increase in the unemployed and a massive reduction in the erstwhile principal source of aid and refuge for the poor – the monasteries and the several communities of monks.

It has been estimated that more than a fifth of England's approximately 50,000 square miles, some 10,000 square miles or around seven million acres, was annexed from common ownership by elite prerogative through Acts of Parliament, and it has been suggested that a similar area was also stolen without parliamentary approval. Fourteen million acres or twenty thousand square miles. That alone is a damning indictment without questioning the morality or credibility of the historic claims of entitlement that were made by an elite minority to the profits and enjoyment of the vast majority of the land in the first place, that land being part of a nation that depended on the farming population before the Enclosures for its very existence and defence. Even if these figures are in error by 50%, the culpability of those behind the appropriation of this formally common land is mitigated by not a jot.

### 18.6.5 Land Grabbing – Highland Clearances in Scotland

The appalling barbarity during the period known as the Highland clearances can only be alluded to in the limited space here, and although the Scots as a whole fully deserve their combative reputation for major contributions to the military victories of the British Empire, serious fault lines divided Highlander from Lowland Scot. Highlanders in particular were part of a clan system that was based on loyalty and the expectation of protection by the clan chief, and they retained their Gaelic cultural characteristics of language, dress, and a rural, often subsistence farming way of life, although the traditional Scottish kilt and trappings are said to have been romanticised and possibly exaggerated somewhat by Sir Walter Scott.

Lowland Scots were ethnically and culturally very similar to Highlanders, but with possibly more of an Anglo-Saxon influence and a tendency to regard Highlanders as barbarians, while Highlanders are believed to have deferred to their religious ministers more readily than did Lowlanders. The result was that corrupt Lairds and other pillars of Scottish society, particularly other Lowland Scots, were able to effect the round-up of Highlanders like the sheep that would occupy their vacated highlands and homesteads.

The development of docility to such a fatal extent in the Highland culture was perhaps a prime consequence of the defeat of the Jacobite Highland army at Culloden in 1746, and the vengeful pacification under the son of English King George II, the "butcher" Duke of Cumberland, that quickly followed. Piecemeal ethnic cleansing began within a couple of decades, and continued through the 19$^{th}$ century until about 1880. Figures quoted for total emigrations are of the order of 200,000, and the reader is directed to the internet for many examples of the abhorrent behaviour of authorities at all levels of the Union of England and Scotland that had been forged in 1707. Links are provided in the *Internet Index*.

### 18.6.6 Present-day Privatisation and Retraction of Responsibility

Privatisations of what were already publicly owned utilities during the last quarter of the 20$^{th}$ century created the opportunity for the transfer of many current and future £billions from public hands to a minority.

This was done under the guise of making ownership available to the public-at-large that in reality already had ownership via the State; the result being that shortly after purchase, individuals would sell their shares and see them become concentrated in the hands of corporations. The public experience would then be characterised by firstly increased unemployment within the privatised utilities with its consequent cost of unemployment benefit to the State and taxpayer, and secondly higher costs for the services at the hands of the new owners of the utilities. Attempts to justify the original privatisations had, of course, involved the utter nonsense of citing a supposed historical inefficiency and the need for de-regulation and technological improvement to incentivise the introduction of self-interested shareholders, on the basis that investment would not otherwise be found, while the real objectives were firstly, the transfer of dividend streams into private hands – a shameless theft exactly comparable with the Acts of Enclosure – and secondly, the reduction of government accountability – commercial cowardice.

There is, of course, absolutely no reason why a publicly owned utility should not be efficiently managed; there is no reason why one of the objectives of publicly owned utilities should not be the employment and training of the nation's engineers; and there is no reason why a publicly owned utility cannot incorporate the best technical infrastructure.

Publicly owned utilities see all profits retained for the benefit of the utility and the nation. France and Germany, for instance, do this very well and they have extended that capability to dominate British utilities, with the result that at a time of enormous "pension-stress" in the U.K., revenue streams from British utilities are flooding into other countries' pension funds.

Perhaps the loss of employment – employment being a secondary benefit of public utilities – was not foreseen, or perhaps it was of no consequence to the Conservative Government of 1979 when the first privatisations began, but the practice was continued with a vengeance across the political divide, until 2014 saw the majority of public utilities in Britain owned outright by foreign corporations, or held by a majority interest of such corporations. As noted above, this involves net, regular losses of what would otherwise be the United Kingdom's revenue, or do we believe that the foreign investors became involved for charitable reasons?

Abandonment of home produced coal in favour of gas that can be terminated without notice by potentially hostile adversaries was another legacy of the lunacy of late 20th century governments.

Characterised as they were by fecklessness, and by the utter personal greed of individuals at all levels, governments have become vulnerable to global lobbies that select such soft and disreputable targets – primarily the states that afford them a platform in the first place. Lobbies such as the locally minority "Green Party" make vociferous attacks and demand judicial inquiries into such issues as the nation's right to take pre-emptive action against terrorists that are planning attacks on British soil, and the nation's right to determine energy policies that, alone, offer the opportunity to meet the requirements of the 21st century.

## 18.6.7 The Crown Estates Today

By the 21st century the English Royal Family's wealth was defined, in the public eye, by the Crown Estate that consists of urban and rural properties ranging from shopping centres and race courses to farms. However, they also personally own: governmental and public buildings in the capital city, London; the royal residences of Balmoral and Sandringham with their extensive park lands; and they also have title to vast tracts of Forestry and more than half of the nation's foreshore. Mineral and marine rights extending to the limits of the continental shelf complete the portfolio, all of which had an overall capital value of more than £8 billions in 2012.

Taxable income from the revenues of the Duchies of Lancaster and Cornwall are drawn by the monarch and the Prince of Wales respectively, but their avoidance of tax on other revenue streams is a matter of contention.

In addition to the above holdings it must be remembered that the monarch has ownership of any naturally occurring gold and silver, regardless of whose land within which it lies, and all of the nation's swans, again regardless of their migration routes or nesting habitat.

Many other so-called royal possessions to which the nation has token access such as Buckingham Palace, Windsor Castle, the crown jewels and other works of art, all with a combined value of several £Tens of billions, are in fact owned by the nation, which enables an accountant's assessment to state that the personal worth of the entire royal family is only around £1 billion. Given the far from transparent nature of royal finances, that figure must be regarded as very conservative, and it excludes the capital values of the Duchies, and the value of other national treasures that are held in trust but nevertheless available solely for royal pleasure.

## 18.7 Catastrophic Financial Reversals
### 18.7.1 The Great Tulip Mania 1637

Brought from Ottoman Turkey during the 17th century and grown in the Dutch provinces, prices for these exotic and desirable flowers peaked at thousands of florins for rare types during the years 1634 and 1635 as speculation fever caused buyers to commit to contracts based on future production. Such prices equated to possibly ten or more times the annual income of a craftsman. The tulip craze collapsed abruptly, leaving a differential that has been repeated many times with different commodities over the few hundred years since then, without any lesson being learned, and whereby investors were left with a valueless asset that had been bought with borrowed money, while producers were left with something equivalent to just a bunch of flowers, and a lucky few disappeared with huge profits that were gained from transactions on paper that involved no substance whatsoever.

### 18.7.2 The South Sea Bubble
#### 18.7.2.1 Introduction

The almost unbelievable story of the South Sea Bubble, that painfully dragged out from 1711 to 1720, began when Queen Anne, the last of the Stuarts, was on the thrones of England, Scotland and Ireland. Queen Anne reigned from 1702 to 1707 over England, Scotland and Ireland; then, following the 1706-1707 Acts of Union of England & Scotland, over Great Britain and Ireland until she died in 1714.

This was a time when the events of the Glorious Revolution, by which Prince William of Orange became English King William III in a bloodless coup, were a recent memory, and it is suggested by analysts of socio-political trends that a major change happened at this time in England's and subsequently Great Britain's political and economic ideology. This change concerned the perception of worldly wealth as having either a finite or an infinite nature; and the resultant drive for empire and the need for conquest is said by some to have arisen from a belief, sub-consciously or otherwise, that it was finite and up for grabs. It is said that Adam Smith's philosophy and writings that were set down just after the time of the South

Sea Bubble affair, during the third quarter of the 18th century, implied a contrary view – a view that all wealth is created by human labour, and that in a growing nation, as opposed to a nation in a state of stagnation such as China was at that time, the acquisition of wealth was therefore potentially limitless.

Insensitive to such theoretical notions of economic empire that would later be liberally and tritely expressed as globalisation, there were already murmurings by the time of the early 18th century of what, in just a few decades, would become the pounding cacophony of the Industrial Revolution; and among the middle-classes there were the mental stirrings of what would harden into a mindset of capital investment and an increase in personal fortune that would dwarf anything that had gone before. With its own armies, the East India Company had been successfully trading with enormous profits and territorial acquisitions since it received its Royal Charter from Queen Elizabeth I in 1600, and it was so powerful that any onlookers who had been excluded from initial investment there, might well be enthusiastic for any chance to repeat the formula of unprecedented success, and to build up an overseas interest and revenue. This was the first quarter of the 18th century, and it would be another fifty years before Captain James Cooke would bring back images of a balmy, blue South Pacific – the South Sea Bubble was going to be more characteristic of the much colder, grey waters of the South Atlantic, and particularly the east coast of the Americas where most of the action would take place. See the map below.

## 18.7.2.2 Map – Spanish Lands in the 18th Century New World

Map from http://commons.wikimedia.org/wiki/Category:Maps released under CC-BY-SA
http://creativecommons.org/licenses/by-sa/3.0/

### 18.7.2.3 The Bubble Inflates and Bursts Spectacularly

The South Sea Company was founded by a group of merchants in 1711 who were led by the Earl of Oxford who, as Lord Robert Harley, was also leader of the Tory party. Lord Harley was the last leader of Parliament before the title "Prime Minister" came into use. The company was incorporated by an Act of Parliament as a joint-stock company with transferable shares, the Act bearing the title An Act for Making Good Deficiencies and Satisfying the Publick Debts; and for Erecting a Corporation to Carry On a Trade to the South Seas.... Its premise was that the War of Spanish Succession, discussed earlier, would soon end, and that concessions by the Spanish would provide huge business opportunities among the Spanish colonies. Although Harley was proved correct regarding the end of the war that was concluded in 1713-1714 as a result of a series of treaties – the Treaties of Utrecht – the anticipated Spanish business capitulation did not materialise, and there were only one or two trade concessions – for slaves and woollens. Even this was offset by the resumption of war with Spain in 1718, known as the War of the Quadruple Alliance, that lasted until 1720. This latest war saw the uncomfortable bedfellows, Britain, France, the Dutch Republic, the Holy Roman Empire, and the Duchy of Savoy, as allies, raging against the Spanish and Jacobite movement throughout the Mediterranean Sea, Europe, and the Americas.

Back in 1711 however, a recently unified Great Britain was in debt to the tune of about £10 million after ten years of warfare, and so, with his merchant consortium backing him, Harley's offer to pay off that debt in return for 6% per annum on the sum advanced seemed heaven-sent; and the government had no hesitation in also giving the proposed company exclusive trading rights with the Spanish South American colonies. A government guaranteed 6% would have been very attractive to prospective investors who also had the expectation of massive capital growth. To service the £600,000 annual interest payment, the usual victim was thrust into the equation – the taxpayer – and new and permanent taxes were announced on items, such as wine, tobacco and other popular commodities of the time, a practice that continues to the present day, and which effectively puts the public's money into the pockets of speculators and illusory financiers of frequently corrupt or inept government whim and ambition; but then the taxpayer has voted them in, and so it must be acceptable and, by supporting mainstream political parties today, voters willingly penalise themselves.

In a climate of unprecedented hype in the early 18$^{th}$ century the franchise was very limited and there were few "voters". Lavish company offices, false representation of expectations such as the certainty of payments in gold and silver from newly found mines in Peru, and assisted by the fortuitous growth of a pompous fashion for just holding its shares, the company had managed to survive, although it only actually began shipping produce in 1717. After the years of waiting however, the awful reality was that only one ship per year was allowed by the Spanish, and to cap it all, its cargo would be taxed at 5% by the Spanish King Felipe V.

This was not at all what had been vaunted and so, in order to raise more money, and in competition with the Bank of England that was just another private company and not a national central bank at this time, the South Sea Company applied to take on more of the nation's debt. A further £2 million was promised to the government, to be repaid at 5%, and a similar deal was struck between the Bank of England and the Government. These deals were incorporated by three Acts of Parliament in 1717, the South Sea Act, the Bank Act, and the General Fund Act; the first two incorporating the deals with the two lenders, and the third providing some general explanations. There is much interesting comment from the time in William Cobbett's *The Parliamentary History of England...*, volume 7, freely downloadable from the internet. Cobbett's recordings of parliamentary process became what we now know as *Hansard* in 1803.

Trading with the Spanish colonies ceased the following year, 1718, when war began but, undaunted and as bullish as ever despite being insolvent, the company still competed with the Bank of England for the award of yet another government bond for the repayment of the remainder of the national debt, almost £31 million this time, and at 5%. Horse trading with the government towards the definition of the Act to incorporate this latest loan commenced in 1720, and if the South Sea Company could be the winner, it would attract an effective endorsement or vote of confidence from the government that would bolster its reputation in the eyes of the public, and attract even more cash investment to pay off those wanting to cash in their shares. The cash was also needed by the doomed company to be able to satisfy its obligation to redeem the government's debt since it had misrepresented its position to just about everyone. It was effectively a *Ponzi* scheme, long before the term had been invented, but the writing was now beginning to appear on the wall.

From 1711 the South Sea Company share price had been around £125 and flat until 1720. In January, 1720, it was about £130, but by the start of June, after the government had eventually chosen the South Sea Company in preference to the Bank of England to eliminate that £31 million of national debt, and after the two contenders had gone through a process akin to a Dutch auction, the South Sea Company shares had passed £500. By August the price had peaked at £1,000, a fortune in those times, and this was where the bubble burst. Within a month it was back down to £150, and by the end of the year £100.

The nation had seen a period of insanity during which fortunes were made and lost by hundreds of people in all walks of life: some in domestic service, members of the clergy, merchants and literary figures, polymaths, such as Sir Isaac Newton, the Master of the Mint, and many of the aristocracy including the English King George I and the Prince of Wales. Many of the willing and naïve victims could weather the losses, but hundreds more were bankrupt and suicides were commonplace. Some of the officers of the company and some politicians were indicted, and some fled the country with their huge profits. Harley, who had occupied the government post of First Lord of the Treasury, had already been impeached on a separate issue and had dropped out of sight, leaving the mess to be sorted out by Britain's first officially titled Prime Minister, Sir Robert Walpole, in 1721.

Following the collapse of the company a series of Acts starting in 1721 were passed with titles totally at variance with the one ten years earlier in

1711, such as *"... An Act for Making Several Provisions to Restore the Publick Credit Which Suffers by the Frauds and Mismanagements of the Late Directors of the South-Sea Company and Others ..."*.

The extent of the foolishness however, went far beyond the South Sea Company; the nation had been swept by a mania for shares in speculative ventures such as *Distilling Sunshine From Vegetables, Buying the Irish Bogs*, and incredibly, a scheme *...to carry out an undertaking of great advantage but no-one to know what it was...* They all received thousands of pounds, as said, fortunes at the time.

### 18.7.3 Ponzi Schemes and Massacres in Palestine

There have been many Ponzi schemes throughout recent history and two of the best-known examples are covered here.

The first occurred in 1919 when Charles Ponzi, a clerk in the city of Boston in the United States, ran an investment scheme that was similar to pyramid selling, in that it used later investors' deposit money to repay the earlier investors - with apparently huge gains. As more and more people were sucked in, the gains seemingly were solid and reliable, but it was, of course, a form of fractional reserve, meaning that, with everyone wanting their profits, it would only take a small number of demands for the return of original deposits to bring the whole system down, leaving the vast majority unable to even get a respectable fraction of their deposit money back.

With impunity and with government support, U.K. banks in the 3$^{rd}$ millennium ran, and continue to run, Ponzi schemes in the form of Fractional Reserve Banking; and they use taxpayers' money to pay bankers' bonuses; but then the government was given a mandate by being voted in by the taxpayer so it must be acceptable.

The second specific example of a Ponzi scheme is the largest ever, with international implications and historical anecdotal connections. It involved a gentleman named Bernard Madoff, and this tale of *chutzpah* was also centred in the United States. Chairman of the NASDAQ stock market, and an Ashkenazi Jew, Madoff was convicted in 2009 of running a Ponzi scheme that took in at least $65 billion - he was sentenced to 150 years in prison, with a court order to return as much as $17 billion in misappropriated funds. Madoff had identifiable personal assets of only around $1 billion when he was convicted, although it is estimated that many $billions are distributed in off-shore accounts and that they will never be traced unless he has a change of heart.

There are two footnotes to the story; firstly, Madoff's oldest son hanged himself in 2010, and his youngest son died of cancer in 2014 – both had reportedly exposed their father's Ponzi scheme to the authorities, and both owed millions of dollars to their father, although along with their uncle, Bernard Madoff's younger brother, the three family members had allegedly withdrawn something approaching $20 million each from associated businesses for personal consumption.

The second footnote concerns an organisation named *Hadassah* – the Women's Zionist Organization of America, the one-time Chief Financial Officer of which, Sheryl Weinstein, had an affair with Bernard Madoff. It was alleged that the organisation that underwrites the Hadassah Medical Centre and the Hebrew University, both in Jerusalem, Israel, lost as much as $90 million during 2008 because of Madoff's Ponzi scheme, and that as a result, after a long struggle, the Hadassah Medical Centre was facing bankruptcy in 2014. Weinstein also is said to have personally lost money, and she has been described as a victim.

The reality at least in respect of Hadassah however, is just a little different. In January, 2009, the president of Hadassah in the U.S. confirmed that in fact $130 million had been withdrawn from their *"Bernard Madoff facility"*, and that they had *"done quite well"* since 1987; but she did also say that the organisation was still short of finances, and would the public please dig deep to help them out, because over the past five years it had sent $91 million in cash every year to projects run by Hadassah in Israel, and that the organisation was committed to send another $91 million in 2009 to pay for various essentials such as salaries at the Hadassah Hospital in Jerusalem. That's more than half a billion dollars, so the issues faced at home by the Women's Zionist Organization of America do not seem to entirely explain the Israeli Medical Centre's shortage of funds, and in fact the near insolvency has been attributed to several reasons by the Israeli authorities who are bailing it out during 2014, not least to "extravagant salaries".

The Hadassah Medical Centre in Israel has a long history – it had been established as a few diverse clinics from 1912 to 1918, absorbing the site of an older hospital named the Meir Rothschild Hospital that dated back to its original foundation in 1854 by Baron Rothschild, and the present-day Medical Centre was further integrated and rebuilt in 1939. There was, however, a dark time for the medical facility in 1948 during the Jewish (re)conquest of Palestine when it was the focus of an incident known as the Hadassah Convoy Massacre.

Hadassah Hospital is strategically located on Mount Scopus, and it was believed by Arab forces to have been a base used five days earlier by the Israelis who had committed the Deir Yassin massacre, slaughtering more than one hundred Palestinian Arab villagers. The Arab force claimed that they attacked a military convoy that was in fact a mixed military and humanitarian mission composed of Jewish *Haganah* paramilitary militia, and hospital staff and patients, all on their way to relieve the strategic hospital that was in fact also a base for the Haganah. Seventy-seven Israeli medical staff, patients, and paramilitaries, and one British soldier died.

In 2005 Hadassah – the Women's Zionist Organization of America – was nominated for the Nobel Peace Prize in acknowledgement of its multicultural work in Jerusalem among all ethnic groups, much of which was no doubt funded as a result of the calls in the U.S. for donations to make up for the partial predations of Bernard Madoff, though the collections cannot have been enough according to the state of the Hospital's finances in 2014; but then, of course, the 2007-2008 failures of organisations like Lehman Brothers, and the allegedly criminal conspiracy of Goldman Sachs with consequent multi-billion dollar gains for hedge fund management company Paulson & Co. had not occurred at the time that Hadassah was passing round the hat.

### 18.7.4 Enron and British Collusion

Enron was a Houston, Texas, based American energy company that shamelessly exploited customers internationally by hiking prices in a newly de-regulated market – one of the benefits that results from the privatisation of national utilities that deal in the essentials of life as opposed to luxuries. It is said that from about 1997 until 2001 when the company became the biggest bankruptcy in U.S. history at that time, all high-level business efforts were directed into deception concerning cash flow, asset value, and liabilities. Many employees of Arthur Andersen (Accountants), Merrill Lynch (Financial Consultants), and RBS-Natwest (Bankers), were convicted, although some are thought to have been possibly victims of miscarriages of justice and forced confessions. Around twenty-one thousand Enron employees, and eighty-five thousand employees of Arthur Andersen became jobless, Enron shareholders lost more than $70 billion, and as many as one and a half million individuals were affected by issues such as pension fund reduction. This was damage on a scale with which Timur-the-lame and Chinggis Khan would have been familiar.

In the U.K. there were allegations that the Labour Government's energy policies had been "tuned" in inappropriate ways to favour Enron, who were one of the Labour Party's sponsors, and that via corporate cronyism, the Arthur Andersen company had been rehabilitated and readmitted to the United Kingdom's services supplier lists after being banned for its connivance in the De Lorean car scandal during the 1980s. To demonstrate that cronyism is not the sole province of the Labour Party, from the other side of The House, Lord Wakeham, a previous Conservative energy minister, had joined Enron's board as a non-executive director in 1994, and questions were asked as to why he did not see anything amiss. In 2008 the British Joint Disciplinary Scheme enquired into his involvement that had been described as: *"a key role ... he was the only professional accountant on Enron's audit committee,* but it stated *...It does not appear that Lord Wakeham had a sufficient understanding of these transactions..."* and that it was "not practicable" to pursue Wakeham over the Enron débâcle. One has to ask why he was on an audit committee for something about which he was ignorant, and precisely what he did contribute, either directly or by omission.

Enron's record bankruptcy lasted only a year because in 2002 WorldCom, the U.S. second largest telephone provider, filed for bankruptcy with $41 billion debts, and it admitted improperly claiming $3.8 billion expenses, but that's another story, and would itself be eclipsed the same decade when Lehman Brothers would file for bankruptcy with more than $750 billion debts, and whose nefarious and profligate practices would lead to a projection by the official receivers of the need for investigations that will take decades in order to unravel the entirety of its dealings.

### 18.7.5 U.S. Monopolisation – the Death of Bretton-Woods

World War One, if any single event ever really warrants particular attention among complex economic evolutionary phenomena, signalled the apparent beginning of the end for Britain and the other European colonial powers in respect of financial world dominance. The qualifier apparent has to be added because it is said by some that most of the world's wealth, whether on paper or in gold, still resides to this day in European banks or repositories in the names of elite corporations such as the Rothschilds that are effectively stateless – ignoring any cultural affinity and loyalty that is contentiously assumed to exist in respect of the State of Israel of course. It is certain that, after two world wars, relative wealth in terms of consumerism for the masses in Europe compared to the masses in the U.S. changed massively in favour of the U.S. during the 20$^{th}$ century, although the view of the level of U.S. debt and budget deficit in the 21$^{st}$ century is truly alarming for any prospect of global stability.

Differentials within Nation-States, both in terms of absolute wealth and the equitable distribution of the effective tax burden, are also believed to have changed in favour of the wealthier members of society over the last century, and whether America has more or less poverty than Europe is now a moot point, especially in light of economic migration and globalisation. Whatever the differences in poverty, the distribution of wealth is actively managed by governments through non-income related aka indirect taxes such as VAT that disproportionately benefit the wealthy, and this is despite the rise in so-called liberalism and egalitarian state morality. These issues are the nub of much dissident activity such as the Occupy Movement, and they deserve much greater expansion than the scope here permits. See the chapter below titled *What the People Say*.

A notable blow to the stability, integrity, and morality of international finance was struck by the United States in 1971, partly due to the cost of the Vietnam war and the growing U.S. trade deficit, and partly cynically, in response to an anticipated French attempt to exercise its rights and redeem dollars for gold under the administration of the Gaullist President Georges Pompidou following de Gaulle's earlier statements on the subject in 1965. This blow was dealt by the ultimately disgraced U.S. President, Richard Nixon, at the time when the government unilaterally cancelled the Bretton-Woods agreement that had been in force since 1944, and thereby severed the link between the dollar and gold, plunging the whole world into an age typified by the limitless issuance of worthless Fiat Money, and the limitless creation of debt. In 1944 the Bretton-Woods agreement had fixed the value of thirty-five U.S. dollars to one ounce of gold, and pegged other currencies to the dollar at fixed rates with a promise to repay gold against dollars to other nations' central banks. Within that regulatory framework, any imbalances in international trade were corrected by either or both of IMF loans and gold bullion exchanges. Without the Bretton-Woods controls the price of gold could now speculatively spiral to unimaginable heights, and international exchange rates could now be a plaything of speculators; all of which exacerbated fluctuations. Trade deficits and money supply, particularly in America, could now be unconstrained, and rampant inflationary and bust cycles were inevitable, with equally inevitable bankruptcies and debt defaulters. And so it proved to be – to the obscene advantages of the obese and parasitic money-changers.

### 18.7.6 European Defaulters

As an alternative to an outright declaration of bankruptcy, that is expected to wipe clean the slate and allow a fresh start, debt defaulting has been a regular occurrence in Europe.

Spain has defaulted no less than thirteen times since 1500, and Portugal and Greece five times each since 1800. It is almost one thousand years since Britain defaulted on international debt, and the younger offshoot nations such as Australia, the U.S., and Canada have never defaulted. Greece is of particular concern given its membership of the Euro, since it has spent about half of its recent historical independent existence in a state of default. That's not far off one hundred years of default. Greece became completely free from Ottoman rule in 1832, largely due to the intervention in its war of independence that lasted from 1821 to 1829, and with subsequent support by Britain, France and Russia after many atrocities had been committed by both Turks and Greeks. Greek sensitivities after independence were only cursorily considered when the convening powers dubiously imposed on the fledgling Greek Orthodox nation a Roman Catholic Bavarian, King Otto of the House of Wittelsbach, along with a harsh regime of absolute monarchy. He reigned from 1833 to 1862.

In spite of taxes said to have been worse than those imposed by the Ottomans, it may well be that a series of corrupt and disadvantageously mean bank loans from money-changers based in Britain and France during its early years were responsible for setting the scene for two hundred years of poor economic performance that, coupled with its own misrepresentation of its books when it got into bed with the Euro, has served to exclude Greece from access to many international capital markets.

It may well be therefore, that the anti-Merkel rhetoric and caricature of the years 2012 and 2013 may actually be traced back via Greek race memory to the imposition of a Nordic monarch perhaps, rather than the more obvious invasion by Nazi Germany during the Second World War. Angela Merkel is the German Chancellor at the time of writing in 2015.

On the very day that this book goes to press Greece, yet again, is hovering on the brink of default on its eye-watering debts and of a possible

*A History of Money and Financial Empire*

exit from not just the European Monetary Union, but also from the European Union itself – a step that, should it happen, will call into question some of the wisdom of globalisation and of ideological attempts to forcibly merge, in political terms, the disparate economies and cultures of North and South, and of East and West. A trading union and a slower approach to confederation might well have made more sense.

### 18.7.7 Global Corporate Collapse – the Great Crash of 2008

Mechanisms, that cynically or conspiratorially might be said to support an attempt to concentrate wealth in the hands of an ever decreasing elite group of bankers, are nevertheless undeniably involved in the creation of debt and economic collapse. This may be inferred from media reporting through the 2008 economic crisis, often referred to as the *Credit Crunch*.

Four steps in such a sequence are as follows:

1. A loan by a central bank to the government is supported by the issue of a bond from the government to the central bank, and that bond is then scheduled to be repaid by taxes raised from the public. The actual amount of such tax received will be dependent on the number of people in employment and the volume of trade.
2. Interest rates and money supply set by the central bank can be controlled according to the wishes of fiscal policy-makers in order to affect the volume of trade and inflation rates. This may, however, make repayment of loans in general and the conduct of business difficult if not impossible. Banks may therefore refuse loans, and cash-flow in difficult times will lead to company closures and crashes. Whether maliciously intentioned or not, austerity measures have this effect – but – the opposite policy of abundant unsecured credit may adversely affect the balance of payments (exports-imports) and also have this effect.
3. Subsequent transfer of money and assets among survivors of crashes proceeds according to any timing-plan that is defined by those controlling the money supply. In some cases this monetary crisis will be exacerbated by loan defaults that become an expense

(a loss) of diverse smaller banks that will then fail if there is a run on the available but insufficient money that is being held at such banks against deposits that had been made in good faith, the bank failure being in reality due to the inadequate, and only *fractional* reserve of monies retained. Yet further expenses (losses) are incurred by the depositors who were not quick enough to get to the withdrawals counter at the bank before it ceased operations.

4. The monetary crisis that is on the verge of becoming an economic collapse is now aggravated by loss of public confidence and the consequent retention in private hands across the public of even more of the money supply. An economic collapse is now imminent, and a recession is likely to be just around the corner.

### 18.7.7.1 Minsky-Kindleberger Perspective, Financial Crisis 2008

This section is based on the work of:

J. Barkley Rosser, Jr. Professor of Economics, James Madison University
Marina V. Rosser, Professor of Economics James Madison University
Mauro Gallegati, Professor of Economics Università Politecnica delle Marche, Ancona, Italy. January, 2012

Mechanisms such as the four step process above are not new. They have been formalised in theories developed since the 1970s, and specifically further proposed in 1996 by two eminent economists, Hyman Minsky and Charles Kindleberger. All the components in the theories leading up to their 1996 paper are to some extent or other based on the underlying concept that:

> *"...credit is intrinsically unstable and thus naturally prone to crashes".*

The 1996 paper links the unsurprising aspects that are obvious to us all, with hindsight anyway, of speculation and then panic when it all falls apart – it's been going on at least since medieval times, and even in modern discussions on the subject it is considered to be a self-fulfilling prophecy when coupled with entrepreneurial spunk and bullish confidence.

## A History of Money and Financial Empire

With a fondness for exotic Teutonic or German terminology, *bank rush* is rendered in their paper on the subject, as *Torschlusspanik – gate closure panic*. Their 1996 paper united the ideas of the rate of price rises as a result of speculative bubbles and subsequent market collapse in the form of three possible profiles. In summary, those three profiles reflect the rate of price changes in terms of increases and decreases including any interleaved periods of stability. Such rates are determined by the perception of the market; that is to say, by the reactions by brokers, by agents, and by a diverse overall collection of people whose control of sales and purchases further affects the situation. Those perceptions and reactions may be drawn out, or they may be sudden and catastrophic, with all the attendant profits for the astute minority, and with crashes and losses being the lot of the peripheral and often naïve gamblers. The three profiles have been described as follows:

> *"... One is when price rises in an accelerating way and then crashes very sharply after reaching its peak. Another is when price rises and is followed by a more similar decline after reaching its peak. The third is when price rises to a peak, which is then followed by a period of gradual decline known as the period of financial distress, to be followed by a much sharper crash at some later time."*
> 
> – A Minsky-Kindleberger *Perspective on the Financial Crisis.*

That 1996 paper was referred to in 2012 as part of an investigation into the global recession that followed the economic crisis of 2008-9. The investigation was made by three Professors of Economics: J. Barkley Rosser, Marina V. Rosser, and Mauro Gallegati, who identified the occurrence of all three profiles of speculation and collapse across the sectors:

1. Oil.
2. Housing (real estate).
3. Stock Market.

Analogous to the combined effect of three natural disasters: a tsunami during a severe volcanic earthquake, the *coincidence* of the above three economic pressures during the years 2006 to 2009 were impossible to contain, and so it is no surprise that the terminology and commentary on that period is extreme though not over-emotional when we talk of: *"The Great Financial Crisis of 2008 to 2009 and the consequent Great Recession that persisted to 2013, and for some nations, persists to 2015"*.

The Minsky-Kindleberger model is based on the following five steps:

1. An exogenous (external cause or origin) shock modifies the incentive system the economy is based upon.
2. These new incentives channel credit toward a given sector and produce a localised economic boom.
3. Euphoria leads to the overestimation of the Return on Investment (ROI) and to over-trading.
4. Fundamentals are reconsidered and credit dries up.
5. Torschlusspanik, or bank rush.

*A History of Money and Financial Empire*

### 18.7.7.2 Bubble and Profile One – Oil

The first type of bubble was oil:

Oil Prices ($) showing June 2008 peak in red:

| | |
|---|---|
| Feb 2008 | 94.82 |
| Mar 2008 | 103.28 |
| Apr 2008 | 110.44 |
| May 2008 | 123.94 |
| Jun 2008 | 133.05 |
| Jul 2008 | 133.90 |
| Aug 2008 | 113.85 |
| Sep 2008 | 99.06 |

Data (above):
http://www.indexmundi.com/commodities/?commodity=crude-oil-brent&months=300

Oil Price Chart (below):
http://www.freedomtofiefdom.com

The first type of profile, being in respect of the above oil price movements, is shown in the graph below:

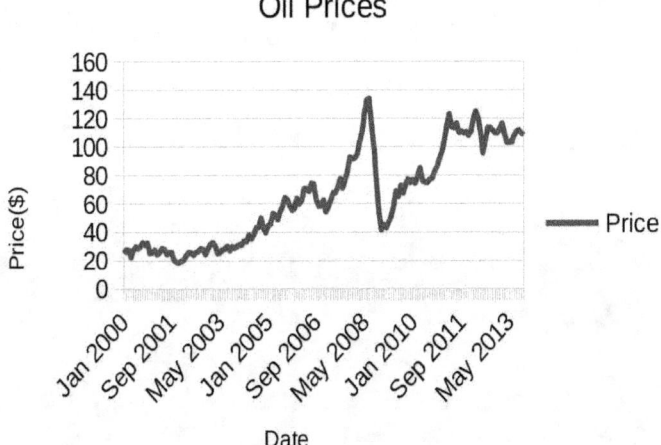

Summarising the words of the economists referred to above, finances related to oil do not work in the same way as most financial assets, and so it is not possible to say with certainty that the oil price changes were really a speculative bubble. What is undeniable, however, is that after a long period of gradual price rises from 2000 to 2007 or so, prices accelerated in early 2008 and peaked as shown above (the peak was actually $147.29 on 11$^{th}$ July), falling in short order to around $30 by the end of 2008. The rapid return to a high level that is not much short of the previous peak, and a level that has been sustained for close to five years at the end of 2013 is a phenomenon that to most people beggars belief.

### 18.7.7.3 Bubble and Profile Two – House Prices

The second type of bubble was in respect of average house prices that had already peaked in the U.K. in November, 2007. The peak in the U.S. had been some months earlier in the second quarter of 2006, with a decline that continued through 2007, and in fact was continuing five years later:

| | |
|---|---|
| June 2007 | 177985 |
| July 2007 | 179320 |
| August 2007 | 180243 |
| September 2007 | 180875 |
| October 2007 | 181556 |
| November 2007 | 181796 |
| December 2007 | 181369 |
| January 2008 | 181455 |
| February 2008 | 181608 |
| March 2008 | 179489 |
| April 2008 | 179169 |
| May 2008 | 178432 |
| June 2008 | 175098 |

Data (above):
http://www.landregistry.gov.uk/public/house-prices-and-sales/search-the-index#sthash.E4DCFLnS.dpuf

House Price Chart (below):
http://www.freedomtofiefdom.com
The second type of profile in respect of average house prices was as follows:

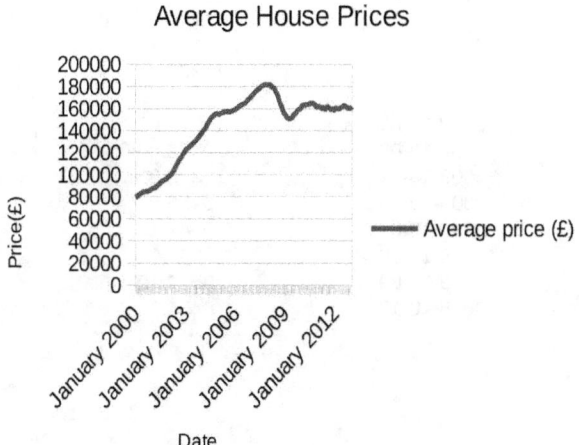

Again summarising the words of the economists referred to above, the second type of bubble was in real estate, particularly in connection with domestic housing. It is common practice to use relationships between rental costs and income to get an indication of the reality of whether a bubble mechanism is driving the market, and 2005 in the U.S. saw these metrics exceed anything seen since 1890. The housing price crisis was indeed judged to have been a speculative bubble with prices rising and decreasing at roughly the same rate. More than five years later bank lending for house purchase was still judged to be inadequate and unfair to first time buyers, with consequent impact on the building industry and therefore employment in that respect.

### 18.7.7.4 Bubble and Profile Three – the Global Stock Markets

The third and lagging bubble was the stock market, typified by the U.S. Dow Jones Industrial Average that is considered representative of worldwide stock-markets:

The Dow Jones was initially apparently unaffected by either the housing downturn after its peak or the oil peak, but a few months later in 2008 there was a marked drop:

| | |
|---|---|
| 2008-09-19 | 11388.44 |
| 2008-09-22 | 11015.69 |
| 2008-09-23 | 10854.17 |
| 2008-09-24 | 10825.17 |
| 2008-09-25 | 11022.06 |
| 2008-09-26 | 11143.13 |
| 2008-09-29 | 10365.45 |
| 2008-09-30 | 10850.66 |
| 2008-10-01 | 10831.07 |
| 2008-10-02 | 10482.85 |
| 2008-10-03 | 10325.38 |
| 2008-10-06 | 9955.50 |
| 2008-10-07 | 9447.11 |
| 2008-10-08 | 9258.10 |
| 2008-10-09 | 8579.19 |
| 2008-10-10 | 8451.19 |

*A History of Money and Financial Empire*

And then the Dow Jones fell to a Minimum circa 9th March, 2009, from which it has recovered, but from which time business confidence and banking stability has not, even into 2014.

| | |
|---|---|
| 2009-02-26 | 7182.08 |
| 2009-02-27 | 7062.93 |
| 2009-03-02 | 6763.29 |
| 2009-03-03 | 6726.02 |
| 2009-03-04 | 6875.84 |
| 2009-03-05 | 6594.44 |
| 2009-03-06 | 6626.94 |
| 2009-03-09 | 6547.05 |
| 2009-03-10 | 6926.49 |
| 2009-03-11 | 6930.40 |
| 2009-03-12 | 7170.06 |
| 2009-03-13 | 7223.98 |

Data (above):
http://research.stlouisfed.org/fred2/series/DJIA/downloaddata

Dow Jones Chart (below):
http://www.freedomtofiefdom.com

The third type of profile, in respect of stock market value was as follows:

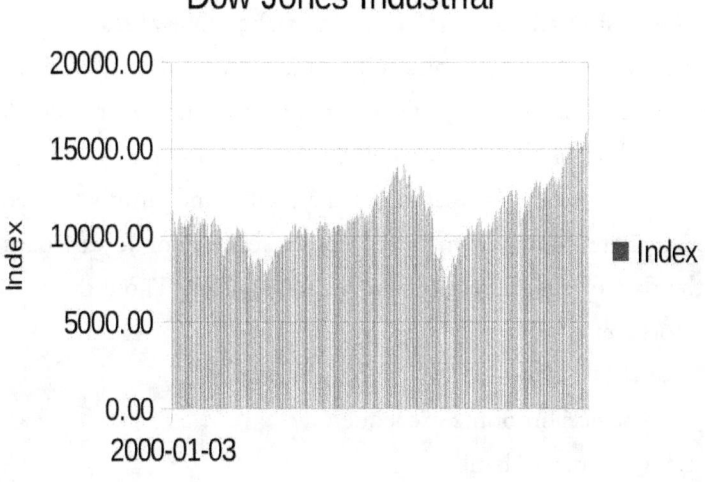

The economists referred to earlier were in no doubt about the third and the most common type of bubble that was seen worldwide. In July, 2007, markets in more complicated and fragile tradeable financial products peaked – the examples given in the economists' paper were "Credit Default Swaps" and "Collateralised Debt Obligations". Iniquitous traps such as these, for both the wary and the unwary, can also have consequences for totally innocent parties and are described elsewhere in this book. The collapse of those markets was followed by the Dow Jones Industrial Average peaking in October 2007 after a gradual increase in spite of ongoing fluctuations. The Dow Jones then went into free-fall after a severe crisis in mid September 2008, hitting rock bottom in March 2009, from which, of course, it has rebounded with enormous gains for the canny, and no doubt deep regrets for those who sold at the wrong time. See these references:

http://www.philstockworld.com/tag/credit-default-swaps/?gclid=CJbDkJDlisgCFQ63GwodizoPNA

http://www.philstockworld.com/tag/collateralized-debt-obligations/?gclid=CMDYvc3kisgCFcZuGwodqpkHwg

## 18.8 Recession an Ancient Peril - Inflation a New One

This is a necessarily complex subject therefore a roadmap of this chapter may be useful. The overall objectives are: firstly, to develop an understanding of the issues; secondly, to see if anything is being missed when the subjects are presented in the media; and thirdly, to determine whether there is any reason to suspect malfeasance or at least buffoonery on the part of the three principal fiscal operators. Those three principal operators are:

1. Chancellors of the Exchequer.
2. Commercial banks.
3. Governors of central banks - in Britain's case the Governor of the Bank of England.

**Firstly**, some present-day economic viewpoints and definitions will be examined.

**Secondly**, one or two observations and speculations from history will be identified.

**Thirdly**, examples of present-day alternative and dissident views will be cited.

For the benefit of readers with an uncertain grasp of algebraic principles, throughout the following discourse the use of equations should be regarded as a physical balance, where each side of the = symbol must be the same weight to keep the expression level. If one term is reduced, then a term on the other side of the expression must also be reduced to maintain balance. If one term is increased, then a term on the other side must increase to maintain the balance and to conform to the relationship expressed by the overall expression.

### 18.8.1 The Keynesian Viewpoint

After many years involvement with economic theory the Cambridge mathematician, John Maynard Keynes, proposed in his 1936 book, *The General Theory of Employment, Interest and Money*, that the causes and solution of economic crises can be approached in a scientific way and that such crises can be resolved by government intervention. The book can be read on the internet, in of all places, the Marxist website:

https://www.marxists.org/reference/subject/economics/keynes/general-theory/index.htm

Keynes's approach identifies the symptoms of recession, and he suggests a fiscal policy involving manipulation of: the money supply; interest rates; and public spending. The objective of such manipulation is to boost demand, employment, and production.

However, he also issues a caution that tinkering with such things can, in fact, lead to worse conditions; one example being that too much state intervention in respect of grand infrastructure schemes, for instance, can be a deterrent to private investment in such schemes. In a capitalist society it is growth of the private sector and not state sponsored schemes that represent progress. Another critical requirement for his theory to work properly in the long-term is that in boom times the government must in some way pay back what it had borrowed to support its previous intervention; and there is a huge risk here because, in reality, boom times have seldom, if ever, resulted in such an adequate payback. Each recession, therefore, begins with an underlying discrepancy that is worse than the previous one.

Further risks associated with Keynesian policies are, firstly, that an expectation develops on the part of the general public that government can resolve all economic issues by measures such as tax cuts, public spending and employment incentives – individual and private sector innovation, therefore, becomes watered down. Increased national debt is the only way that such illusions of social security can be serviced, and this leads to the second risk, which is that financiers (the international money-changers) can, with little risk to themselves, get their usurious returns from government lending. Those usurious returns, of course, come from repayments made by the taxpayer – it may be remembered that the Bank of England was formed on that very premise. Therefore investment that would otherwise have gone to the private sector becomes unavailable – it goes instead to servicing loans to pay unemployment benefit for instance. This was one of the main *public benefits* (!) to come from the privatisations under Prime Minister Thatcher; an outcome surely never imagined by Thatcher's idol John Maynard Keynes.

Another extreme variation of economic hiatus may occur during a policy of austerity measures when, despite Quantitative Easing (Q.E., see more detail later), we see a Credit Crunch during which money intended for consumers stays in commercial banks' coffers. Q.E. philosophy involves an illusory movement of available money into what should be a proactive bank that is just waiting to sponsor a spending spree. There is, however, at least one ghastly government and H.M. Treasury oversight – there is no pressure of any sort on the banks to conform to expectations.

Keynes's theories have been the mainstay of chancellors of the exchequer or their equivalents in just about every western democracy for more than 70 years, and coincidentally, many such democracies now have a much greater debt as a percentage of GDP than some emergent nations, the U.S. being the leader in the debt ratings. Global as well as individual national growth followed by recession has become an expected pattern, and the cry is, or was, *"...bring on the debt, we can go on like this forever, and anyway, we all die sometime..."*. This was an actual declared mindset throughout the financial industry during the 1980s, and there is small evidence of any change of mind since.

For any given Nation-State, the pseudo-mathematical representation of Keynesian Theory for the overall behaviour of the economy on the Demand aka consumer side is:

Output = Consumer Spend + Investment + Government Spend + (Exports-Imports)

Output aka Demand aka Aggregate Demand (AD) is a sort of indication of society's total disposal of all its available revenue, and the items on the right of the equation represent the various sources of that revenue.

The relationship above is often shown symbolically as:

$Y=C+I+G+NX$ where $NX$ = net exports.

The symbolism of this is useful when comparing inferences that are made from the monetarist's point of view below.

### 18.8.2 The Monetarist Viewpoint – e.g. Milton Friedman

Monetarist policies, as exemplified more recently by the ideas of Milton Friedman, are less scientific than those of the opposing Keynesians, and they are described by some as being philosophical. They suggest that money is really neutral and does not promote an increase in production, it only encourages inflation; they say that economies have inherent stability, and that markets work best without intervention – something also suggested by Adam Smith two centuries earlier. The risky possibility of instability and disaster as a result of intervention is accepted by both Keynesians and Monetarists.

The monetarist approach is to ensure that the increase in the supply of money tracks GDP and that its issuing authority, the central bank, whether the Federal Reserve of the U.S. or the Bank of England for instance, should operate against fixed fiscal rules and not with some sort of discretionary ability that might worsen the situation. That does, of course, assume that the fiscal rules are valid in the first place, any risks presumably being mitigated by the fact that minimum intervention is the motto.

The pseudo-mathematical representation of Monetarists' Theory for the relationship between money and real output aka revenue available to be taken as income is:

(Money) x (Velocity) = (Price) x (Real Output)

or in shortened symbolic form:

$M \times V = P \times Y$

Where:
M is the amount of Money in the economy.
V is Velocity of spend in £ aka annual activity or turnover – we might visualise it as the number of Pounds Sterling passing through the point-of-sale tills (U.S. "cash registers") every year.
P is Price level.
Y is aggregate Real Output (aka Real Available Income).

From the above relationship monetarists say that if output is to increase while velocity and prices are constant, then the money supply must increase.

### 18.8.3 Monetarists and Keynesians Crossover

Keynesians also recognise the above relationship ($M \times V = P \times Y$), and they make further inferences using their own relationship ($Y = C + I + G + NX$); so that they conclude from the two relationships that:

$$\frac{M \times V}{P} = C + I + G + NX$$

Which says that, if Prices (P) fall while the physical amount of Money in circulation (M) is constant (and if we assume that the Velocity (V) has not yet had a chance to change), then real purchasing power (the overall value of the left side of the equation) is increased which increases the value of the right side of the equation and therefore increases Consumer Spend (C) and Investment (I).

Therefore, if Government Spend (G) and NX are constant, then Y aka Output will increase.

We then have to assume that the Velocity (V) picks up and reinforces the growth of Real Available Income (Y).

Contrived international exchange rate depreciation can also increase Exports (because they become cheaper abroad) and therefore increase Output. Tax cuts also increase Output because of the extra Money that becomes available for Consumer Spend.

**In summary, *Keynesians are strongly in favour of fiscal policies*.**

NB. International exchange rate depreciation may be brought about if the central bank reduces the nominal interest rate, but it depends on the national inflation rate and other factors perceived by an international investor. The real interest rate to an investor = nominal rate − inflation rate, but the desirability of a currency is also determined with reference to expectations of its close competitors.

Monetarists would go along with some of the above, particularly that an increase in the Money supply would increase Consumer Spend and therefore Output. Their reluctance, however, would centre on issues of deeper tinkering with taxes and interest rates. Such reluctance would be due: firstly, to the fact that lost revenue from taxes has to be recouped from somewhere else by more borrowing and debt, possibly by the sale of government bonds; and secondly, because interest rate changes are viewed very differently by savers and borrowers. See below − "The Thrift Paradox".

**In summary, *Monetarists are strongly against fiscal policies*.**

### 18.8.4 Recession in Theory

Recession is defined just about everywhere in very few simple words, such as "a significant decline in economic activity over periods of the order of months". The period is usually two quarters and, in present-day terms, the economic activity is usually measured by concepts such as:

1. Industrial production. (Service sector output is more difficult but nevertheless relevant).
2. Employment – reduced order books lead to layoffs.
3. The relative performance of a merchant's notions of separate wholesale and retail operations.

The causes of recession, as opposed to its perception and definition, are, of course, far more complex, and although personal income might be compromised during a recession, money *per se* is not necessarily involved in either the causes or the comprehension of a hiatus in economic performance. We might, therefore, expect to see examples of recession in remote history before money was a part of life, but more of that later.

Causes of recession are described by economists as "Shocks or Disturbances" upon the two categories of Supply and Demand, both of which latter terms require clarification. We can take them as being personified respectively, on the one hand by the Producer, that is to say the economics of factory production, and on the other hand by the Consumer. The Consumer is the general public, and it experiences changes in the economy, and then forms a world-view that will influence its behaviour and its Demand for goods. In 2007-8, the change in the consumer's world-view from a state of blissful credit addiction to one of grave alarm as banks locked their doors and appeared to be on the point of collapse, was indeed a long overdue shock.

Ideally for growth we want both Supply and Demand to increase in a sustainable way and with exports exceeding imports, but it is arguably the worst outcome if Demand aka Aggregate Demand (as seen above, AD in economist-speak) falls off, since that would mean over-production and then in unregulated circumstances a corrective fall in production or Supply anyway. It is difficult to force an increase in consumption.

A fall in Supply, however, can have unambiguous if draconian solutions as seen in wartime when a nation's survival is more obviously at stake, and we might see a Ministry of Supply that can overcome personal liberties and take measures to force an increase in production.

### 18.8.4.1 Supply Side Shock – Economics of Factory Production

Resource and energy cost increases will raise the cost of production – the classic single factor being the price of oil. However, the costs of all other raw material imports and the costs of sub-component supplies are also a risk, as are wages and interest payments on loans and capital. Supply Side Shock will therefore reduce GDP because we must subtract all these cost increases from national output. Prices to consumers will need to be increased to cover those extra costs, and increasing prices are known by the dreaded term "inflation" which, if uncontrolled, will lead to the feedback of further problems, for example wage demands and industrial action – strikes that reduce production even further – and the result will be even greater instability.

Historically, during times of inflation, monetary policy that involves tinkering with interest rates alone has failed to repair lower output and has failed to put an end to recessions. *Keynesian theories are said to be inadequate in respect of Supply Shocks*.

### 18.8.4.2 Demand Side Shock – World-view of the General Public

Aggregate Demand (AD) referred to above embraces the complex element of a consumer's Consumption with its implied linkage to Imports, plus one or two other revenue streams. Overall, AD can be expressed from the Keynesian formula above as the sum of those streams as follows:

AD = Consumption + Investment + Government Spending + (Exports – Imports).

These components of AD may reduce for a number of reasons and, if they do, then AD may also reduce and be a cause of recession because reduced AD means reduced Supply and therefore reduced GDP. Some of the reasons for a reduction in AD in respect of Consumption alone are:

1. Loss of consumer confidence due to the world-view of current affairs issues such as struggling banks, wars, and unemployment.
2. Higher interest rates mean that borrowing is expensive.
3. Savers will be tempted to keep their money instead of spending it or investing it.
4. Reduced purchasing power due to increased prices (inflation).
5. Poor international exchange rates make imports more expensive.
6. Non-intuitively, reducing prices (deflation) may encourage people to wait for a market to bottom out, so again they sit on their money instead of spending it or investing it.

So both inflation and deflation can encourage recession.

Debtors can be doubly hit by increased interest rates and reducing prices because it means that they had paid more than they needed to for whatever purchase the money was borrowed, and the biggest loan most people ever take is their mortgage, so debtors may even be in negative equity.

There are many debtors after the ongoing 2007-8 economic collapse that was immediately followed by recession and a credit crunch, and all of those debtors are where they are because of mismanagement by: commercial banks, the central bank of England, H.M. Government, the media and H.M. Treasury – but – not least themselves by their own failure to exercise discretion in the irresistible cultural climate of greed that is characterised by the 1980s, but which persisted for over three decades.

There can be long term consequences of sustained recession that may not be immediately obvious. It has been estimated by the UK Treasury that an economy growing at 2% per year will double its size after 35 years. If the growth rate had been just 0.5% more, then it would have doubled in size 7 years sooner – which means that there could have been an extra 7 years of trading and growth – growth that would furthermore have been based on a stronger economy.

### 18.8.5 Inflation in Theory

Inflation, like recession, is defined in a few simple words. It is said to manifest as "an increase in the cost of living that is characterised by prices that are rising faster than some arbitrarily low and desired rate". Its opposite, deflation, is the case when prices are falling. Causes of inflation, again like those of recession, are defined in terms of "Shocks" to the two conceptual areas of the economy, Supply and Demand, but unlike recession, inflation has a couple of specific measures or indices with which we are mostly familiar:

The *CPI* – the Consumer Price Index which excludes mortgage interest payments.

The *RPI* – the Retail Price Index which includes mortgage interest payments and is consequently more volatile. Cuts in interest rates might therefore reduce RPI and appear to be welcome.

### 18.8.5.1 Cost-push Inflation

This occurs when there are increasing costs in the production supply chain. A wide variety of sources call this a negative cost shock, and the result is increased costs to the consumer and, likely though not necessarily, a reduction of AD.

The causes are the same as some of those associated with a Supply Side Shock that may lead to recession as discussed earlier, but this time there is the addition of food costs and other essentials that affect domestic life, as opposed to just those that affect specifically the industrial production line, such as raw materials and other component parts.

Falling international exchange rates are something of a paradox, since although they may help exports, they will raise the CPI since a large percentage of its basket are imports which become more expensive – an inflationary effect.

### 18.8.5.2 Demand-pull Inflation

This is perhaps more difficult to grasp than all the above cases, and it centres on the premise that the Aggregate Demand may increase due to one or more of its component increases, but that the Supply (aka Aggregate Supply or AS) does not respond quickly enough and cannot keep up. The problem is more than that however, and it shows itself by the presence of unused money (not necessarily hard currency) washing about the economy with nothing to buy. The causes, again, have an economist-speak label of Demand Shock, and examples are:

1. Equity release when house prices rise sharply – home owners give themselves a treat.
2. Reduced cost of borrowing after interest rates are reduced – again people want a treat.
3. Both the above effects would show up in the Savings Ratio – see below.
4. Wages rise faster than productivity – a productivity increase is needed to raise the Aggregate Supply.
5. Imprudent government borrowing and spending.

With regards to the last point, the government should always borrow prudently, and only as far as is needed to make up for the difference between essential costs and income from taxes. Some Public Sector Spend is unavoidable and would, therefore, be classed as essential. However, if money raised by borrowing from banks – it's usually borrowed by issuing government bonds – goes beyond the Public Sector Borrowing Requirement (PSBR), then this can lead to excessive Aggregate Money and become a Demand Shock. At the end of 2014, Britain's public sector finances were not well-managed, and the PSBR is unhealthily large despite the start of an apparent economic recovery. The large PSBR was said to be partly due to poor tax receipts because of wage restraints, all of which illustrates the complexity of economic management in unstable periods.

### 18.8.6 Deflation in Theory

Manifested as falling prices, deflation occurs when the Aggregate Demand is falling behind Aggregate Supply. The result is a requirement to generate sales in a sluggish environment, and the production industry is obliged to sell off its excess stocks at low prices.

### 18.8.7 The Savings Ratio and the Paradox of Thrift

There is one more lesser-known measure concerning inflation, and it is known as the "Savings Ratio", which broadly expresses the percentage of an individual's disposable income that is put into savings. Sudden changes in the Savings Ratio are said to be indicative of a possibly impending recession, or a period of either inflation or deflation; the changes might be regarded as an almost subconscious expression of the world-view of the general public.

As indicated above, savings can be prejudicial to Aggregate Demand by keeping *currency* out of circulation, and this gives rise to the phenomenon termed the "Paradox of Thrift", a Keynesian concept of recent times that implies that the saver may benefit in the short term, but that long term losses of production due to investment starvation will ultimately degrade the savings. It is an idea that is said to date back to antiquity, which prompts a consideration of the different forms of *currency* that may be saved (given that banks were rare in antiquity), though as seen earlier, the Goldsmiths traditionally fulfilled that role before banks.

The answer, of course, concerns the difference between, on the one hand intrinsically valued currency, that is, *Commodity Money* such as gold or silver coinage, and on the other hand *Fiat Money* that is money that has a value only because of some sort of guarantee or "Promise to Pay the Bearer". So there is another consideration when examining the Paradox of Thrift, in that if Fiat Money savings are committed to a bank, then those savings may be lent to someone else and promote spending by that other person, whereas if intrinsically valuable Commodity Money is saved as cash under the bed, then that really does remove currency from the economy. Yet another spin on all this is the indictment that banks operate only fractional reserves, and so any saved money that is banked, Fiat or otherwise, will just enable the banks to increase even further the risk to the whole community, and also to create a larger number of vulnerable debtors. The "Paradox of Thrift" is clearly a well-named conundrum.

### 18.8.8 Summary of Present-Day Economic Definitions

It seems that recession can only be lifted in a way that supports future stable growth when the right productive areas of the economy receive targeted resources; sadly house prices and sales are too often the lead item in mainstream media news broadcasts. Property turnover is seen as an easy way out, and blinkered government and bank initiatives are started, for which increased house prices and sales are seen as some sort of cure-all or gold medal. This is a bad solution because house price rises involve the creation of more borrowing and debt, certainly lower down the property ladder, and house sales require no increase in real production other than a very small increase in house building that can only be brought about later in the cycle as requirements and borrowing ability reach all parts of society as opposed to just the wealthy sectors. Those wealthier sectors are frequently over-populated by overseas investors, who are always first in line, and whose contribution is usually restricted to the large cities, such as London, New York, San Francisco, Vancouver, Sydney and Auckland. The British banks' unwillingness to lend, and a lack of State pressure on those banks to release funds meant that there was minimal change anywhere outside London in these respects circa 2010.

Without doubt, there is a real issue of malfeasance, naïvety, or buffoonery – or all three – somewhere in the present-day estates of governance – unless, of course, we can bring ourselves to admit that there has been an uncontrollable and an unavoidable historical transition from Freedom to anarchic Fiefdom in the world of banking, economics and fiscal policy, and that the blame lies somewhere in the past.

Fiscal policy, referred to several times above, is the expression of government decisions on how to spend and set interest rates in order to:

- Control inflation.
- Reduce unemployment.
- Eliminate boom and bust extremes that create business cycles instead of steady growth.

The tools that the nation's managing economists have at their disposal to implement fiscal policy are based on either a Keynsian approach or a Monetarist approach, and both are strongly advocated by acknowledged international experts in the field of economics, but how can they both be right?

The simple answer, of course, is that they cannot possibly both be right at the same time.

So the experts do their best and they present all of the *complex effects* mentioned in the several sections above in graphical form involving the *simple concepts* such as Aggregate Demand and Aggregate Supply. These graphs cover the long-term, but they also illustrate short term effects.

Graphical techniques show the real interactions among prices, GDP, input costs, and input resource utilisation, but further such detail is beyond the scope of this section. References are provided for access to that level of detail, and the last note here is that, despite the availability of copious theory, none of the elements of our governance has yet managed the British economy in a way that benefits Britain in both a consistent way and in the long term – far more questions need to be asked about the integrity, the political will, and the opposing forces of political restraint versus political pragmatism among elected members of Parliament and the Central Bank. One might well question their agenda and their fitness for purpose – unless their apparent incompetence is mitigated by some other factor affecting global economics that is either uncontrollable or that is being missed altogether. Many such suggestions of "alternative agenda" abound on the internet – frequently concerning cultural elites that are both fanciful and credible – but they are usually dismissed by the mainstream media as conspiracy theory or bigoted prejudice, and they are beyond the scope of this book. Trite as it may be to say it, something nevertheless stinks.

### 18.8.9 Historical Observation and Speculation
### 18.8.9.1 Recession in Antiquity

From the very earliest times, well before money was invented but after a degree of division of labour or specialisation of skills had been recognised as useful, it is not difficult to understand that bartering and the rate or *velocity* of bartering, might be affected by several causes: by shortages of hunted quarry or resources; by difficulties due to poor climate in obtaining commodities, regardless of whether those commodities would normally be randomly gathered or harvested to plan; by spontaneous tribal movements; by tribal conflicts; and by sickness. Our ancestors would not have called it *recession*, but a reduction in the rate of normal bartering and its consequences would indeed have been a recession, and the effects would have been stark – hunger and other life-threatening privations.

By contrast with the complexities of life today, both the manifestation and the causes of recession in such an ancient and innocent environment are simple to comprehend. If there were no raw animal skins for instance, and these were the principal items that were traded with a neighbouring tribe for salt perhaps, or if there was no demand by that neighbouring tribe for whatever reason, then inter-tribal trade would stall, and there might be consequences for trade among other tribes as well, with a reduction in the movement of finished products, such as clothing and tools. A break in the movement of one type of commodity or natural resource would then conceivably result in further reductions in the movement of other goods – the seriousness of the situation being determined by the extent to which division of labour had increased dependency, and the extent to which recognised land claims had reduced the right to forage – both of which factors would determine the resilience of a group in terms of its ability to be self-sufficient.

Even in a very simple society without any notion of money, the problem could quickly become complex, and exchanges could become more difficult to resume particularly if anyone had taken umbrage or become debilitated. Neolithic consumer confidence, trust, and tolerance in that remote and presumably unregulated time would likely have resulted in drastic and violent remedy. We only have to look at the violence that erupted in response to runs on banks in Cyprus and elsewhere during the period from 2007 to 2013 to imagine the response to shortages of essential commodities 10,000 years ago.

Although the use of the term "recession" in an economics context is thought to have originated around the middle of the 17$^{th}$ century, it was suggested earlier that the Bronze Age Collapse during the 2$^{nd}$ millennium BC, may have involved aspects of recession following the Neolithic Revolution boom that had lasted for some millennia and that had seen expansions of technology and agriculture. It has also been suggested by academics that Britain may have experienced an early recession during the transition from the Bronze Age to the Iron Age, as a result of the over-valuation or over-veneration of Bronze, at a time when it was becoming ceremonial and sentimental by comparison with the superior qualities of durability and sharpness of iron.

More recently than the Bronze Age, it was seen earlier in this chapter that there had been a financial upset involving the Lombard Banks of Tuscany in Italy during the 1340s that had resulted in reductions in trade and an increase in poverty. Other problems a little later were due to defaulters, so they do not count in any tally of recessions. It was also noted earlier that the Chinese were forced to end the use of paper money when its over-issue led to runaway inflation in the 15$^{th}$ century AD.

### 18.8.9.2 Inflation in the Western Isles

It is clear from the foregoing that aspects of inflation are more difficult to comprehend than recession, and that the problem cannot be addressed without the assumption of not just the existence of money, but the assumption of notions of exchange rates, availability of product, money supply, and possibly most importantly, an understanding of the difference between *Commodity Money* and *Fiat Money*, the latter making money supply so very easy. Inflation is on the one hand related to the value of money when it is compared to gold, a relationship that affects purchasing power, and quite separately to rising prices that are added to the mix by traders when the quantity of money in circulation is increased.

## A History of Money and Financial Empire

One anecdotal example of an historical observation concerning Aggregate Demand and Aggregate Supply that also introduces the effect of the volume of money in circulation can be turned into a useful conceptual aid. The observation was made before present-day financial psychology became so complex and it comes from the travels of Samuel Johnson and James Boswell who went from Edinburgh to the Inner Hebrides in 1773. In the book *A Journey to the Western Isles of Scotland* there is a passage concerning a sale of eggs that had been made some years previously.

> "[...when told that] a hundred hen eggs, new laid, were sold in the Islands for a penny, he supposed that no inference could possibly follow, but that eggs were in great abundance. Posterity has since grown wiser; and having learned, that nominal and real value may differ, they now tell no such stories, lest the foreigner should happen to collect, not that eggs are many, but that pence are few."

It is an interesting slant on the view of price versus product and the money supply, and if we reverse the normal perception and consider the situation from the point of view of the person owning the eggs, we can interpret the eggs as currency and the pennies as product. With only a very small number of pennies in circulation within the closed environment of the island, the egg seller has to make a good offer to get a penny because pennies are rare. Hence the egg seller will give many eggs to get a penny. Now, if by some means there are suddenly several hundred times more pennies in circulation on the island, but only 100 or so eggs, and the people with the money really want eggs while the egg seller lusts for pennies, then the egg seller can offer say 20 eggs for a penny – take it or leave it. There are now many more people with pennies than previously, and there is a good chance that someone will be desperate, and wealthy enough to cough up. The result is that the price of eggs has rocketed, and there is roaring inflation just because the money supply was increased. In such a simple example where currency can be regarded as pennies or eggs, the egg seller's price hike is not quite such a bad example of racketeering if we consider that everyone simply wants the best deal they can get. The example is, of course, a fictitious extension from the original tale in Samuel Johnson's book.

### 18.8.9.3 Recession – Old, Inflation – New

It is suggested that although there have been many recessions throughout history, inflation is a very recent phenomenon, and does coincide with an increase in the use of money and grovelling obeisance to central banks and money-changers. Grain prices were once free of inflation for centuries as can be seen from the graph below of the variation in the price per quarter (8 bushels) of wheat. For nearly three centuries, from 1287 to 1562, although there were at times some sharp deviations from the mean value of about 125 pence per quarter, it is highly significant that there was no sustained upward trend that could be related to irreversible inflation like that seen during the last century. In medieval times and the Middle Ages there simply was no such thing as inflation in the way we know it today when prices of essentials increase but never reduce appreciably. Price increases due to extraordinary events, such as wars, the Black Death, and occasional racketeering, may have occurred, but there was no irreversible underlying upward trend, and unlike modern improvements to enable food production to keep pace with population growth, agrarian practices were largely unchanged for hundreds of years, almost up to the 19th century.

## 18.8.9.4 Graph – the Historical Lack of Inflation in Grain Prices

Data from: *An Inquiry into the Nature and Causes of the Wealth of Nations*. By Adam Smith
Graph: Copyright © William Neil Beverley 2015 Freedom to Fiefdom.

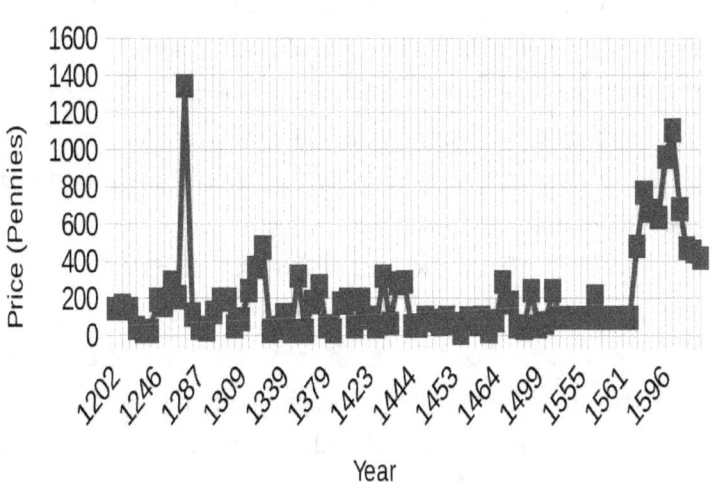

Three possible explanations (and there may well be more) for the arrival of irreversible inflation may be:

**Firstly**, that in a supposedly egalitarian age, wage increases for the working classes enabled the spread of consumerism and therefore increased the chances of the Shocks that damage stable Supply and Demand that were described above. In 1688 about 75% of the population were still employed on the land, so that represents a lot of potential change as society approached the beginning of the Industrial Revolution that roughly lasted from 1750 to 1850. This is the least contentious of the three explanations suggested here, and the dates have an interesting close correlation with those associated with the next two possible explanations.

**Secondly**, the Bank of England was formed in 1694 by secret subscription – nothing contentious there – but, in addition to the realisation of profit from its core business of lending to H.M. Government at more attractive rates than the goldsmiths, there was nothing to stop it from profiteering from its relationships with other private banks and by the issue of *financial instruments*. According to the Bank of England's website, the issue of customised banknotes began around 1725, but it wasn't until a few decades after the Napoleonic Wars, about 1853, that impersonal and freely usable printed banknotes appeared. This was just after the Bank Charter Act of 1844 that gave the Bank of England a massive advantage over provincial banks in terms of who could print money. This was just about the time – 1852 – that Disraeli became Chancellor of the Exchequer in the Earl of Derby's Conservative Government.

The Bank of England, with its secret subscribers, had been handed a monopoly to print money.

Printing money, tinkering with fiscal policy, and trading in *financial instruments*, yet more usury, contribute nothing to the production of life's true necessities, and yet the lessons from economic crises and busts are that they are directly responsible for life's disruptions, for the upward migration of wealth, and for the increase of welfare differentials. Central banks facilitate and encourage all these issues.

**Thirdly**, A significant number of *individuals* of great influence and partisan cultural bias emerged during a period that coincided with the Industrial Revolution and the revolutionary fervour of the second half of the 19$^{th}$ century. As descendants of the frequently self-made pioneer of a financial empire, this new class of Moghuls and Magnates were born with an inheritance of wealth and influence that is unimaginable to most of the world's population. They controlled commercial dominions that were more powerful than some aristocracies and nations of the period – economic imperialism came of age at this time, circa 1800.

In the case of one of the wealthiest of these empires, it was immediately after the Battle of Waterloo, which finally ended the Napoleonic Wars in 1815, that the Rothschild European Dynasty took control of Britain's gold reserves after having been in charge of gold shipments during the war, and after having been well placed to capitalise on changing markets at the end of hostilities. Rothschild was the first to know the result of hostilities via his extensive web of continental agents, and it is said that by his mere deportment at the time of Waterloo, he contributed to uncertainty while clandestinely buying massively at low prices, while other traders sold stocks under the impression that the war had been lost. Within days the stocks had rocketed in value. Neither the first nor the last to benefit from the adversity and suffering of others, such is the obscene face of unrestrained capitalism.

Manipulation of the nation's stock values by a widely acknowledged cold and bloated plutocrat with little, if any, national allegiance, and with influence over both the money supply and the value of gold at the heart of the British Empire, was the equivalent of the power of divine intervention. Rothschild domination was not just restricted to England's fiscal policy. In the form of a brotherly cabal throughout Europe, the Rothschild Dynasty could influence the global economy and take profit from all the European wars at least into the 20$^{th}$ century.

As referred to earlier, there are convincing allegations that, with a display of fiscal hostility, the Rothschild Dynasty had already managed to foment war against the central bank-resistant United States in 1812. There is a further compelling mixture of fact, vitriol and, no doubt, some conspiracy theory concerning later actions by the dynasty as a whole, and by certain individuals.

The first alleges that financial assistance was given by the Rothschilds during the birth of the Soviet Union; if true, then this may well have been in order to gain influence in any "central bank" of which the new U.S.S.R. would have need. At the level of the individual, there are later allegations that the 3$^{rd}$ Baron Rothschild – Victor Rothschild – was the so-called "fifth man" who was associated with Kim Philby, Donald Maclean, Guy Burgess and Anthony Blunt from the 1930s to at least the 1950s.

References concerning some of the above allegations, possibly the result of extreme viewpoints, are:

http://www.independent.co.uk/news/uk/home-news/rothschild-spied-as-the-fifth-man-1444440.html

http://henrymakow.com/2013/07/Was-Victor-Rothschild-a-Soviet-Agent.html#sthash.DlIckYfF.dpuf

https://en.wikipedia.org/wiki/Victor_Rothschild,_3rd_Baron_Rothschild

http://www.telegraph.co.uk/culture/books/3591716/All-the-gifts-but-contentment.html

http://www.spyculture.com/profile-victor-rothschild/

In summary, three specific factors that may be responsible for the frequency of economic disruptions since 1800 are: an increasingly affluent and financially capricious "middle-class"; central bank influence; and sequestration of wealth by partisan cultural elites and persons – some of whom may be unfit for their honorific positions in the State Polity.

## 18.8.10  Present-Day Innovation and Monetary Reform
### 18.8.10.1  Quantitative Easing

Quantitative Easing is a relatively new way of injecting money into the economy to promote spending instead of saving; it is invoked in response to the fact that interest rates are already low, and so the usual tinkering by lowering interest rates to encourage spending will no longer work. It is an unconventional monetary policy first tried in Japan circa 1990, and employed by the U.S. and U.K central banks since 2009. The word Quantitative refers to the quantity of assets purchased, see below, and it is really a semantic fiddle to get around the fact that, by the terms of the Maastricht Treaty, members of the European Union are prohibited from printing money to alleviate public debt.

The central bank first of all defines the new money electronically – that money hasn't actually come from anywhere at all, *it is just said to exist* (hence *Fiat*) on its balance sheet after getting permission to do so from the Treasury. The central bank now has to transfer that virtual money to some institution that will actually start to use it to combat recession, without enabling the criticism from Maastricht-Brussels that it is printing money. The central bank also has to get something back to show against the huge deficit it is about to introduce to its balance sheet, so, instead of buying *new* bonds from the government which is the way governments normally

## A History of Money and Financial Empire

get their money for public spending, the central bank buys bonds and various other securities that *already exist* and that are held as assets by financial institutions, such as commercial banks, pension funds, insurance companies, and by other private sector firms. Those financial institutions and firms are cashing in their saved assets – their bond reserves – in order to spend the money they will receive by buying new assets. It is said that this cashing in or increase in liquidity is beneficial because it enables the commercial banks, that are in receipt of such new liquidity, to replace the assets they have just sold to the central bank with new assets in the form of more loans to businesses. Such cashing in also enables businesses that sold their bond assets to the central bank to invest in new assets that may be aligned to increased production. Apart from the worrying fact that the new money has actually come from nowhere, and that it has left an enormous debt behind, the idea sounds fine in theory if we are just looking in one direction.

There are, in fact, several immediate issues here, and they are presented below as four "Q.E. Issues".

**Q.E. Issue 1.** All of that new money in an economy that has not yet increased production can lead to inflation.

**Q.E. Issue 2.** Many of the banks that theoretically have increased their liquidity have done no such thing because they were previously ruined and in a state of what might be termed negative liquidity before they were bailed out in this way.

**Q.E. Issue 3.** Banks quite simply did not increase lending as a result of Q.E. They kept the money to bring back up their reserves and even attempted to pay increased bonuses to their top employees. The following extracts from the Executive Summary of seven of the Bank of England reports titled *Trends on Lending*, from 2009 to 2015, paint a dismal picture, and irrefutably prove the assertion that they sat on Q.E. funds:

> *The flow of net lending to UK businesses **remained negative** in September and lending to companies fell across all the main sectors of the economy in **2009** ... The flow of total net*

> mortgage lending **slowed** in September though the annual rate of lending growth remained broadly unchanged.

> The flow of net lending to UK businesses **remained negative** in February [**2010**], though less so than in January ... The flow of net mortgage lending by all UK-resident mortgage lenders was **little changed** in February.

An agreement in February, 2011, between H.M. Government and Barclays Bank, Lloyds Banking Group, the Royal Bank of Scotland and HSBC was given the name, "Project Merlin", and it was intended to promote lending and regulate bank bonuses. Despite the agreement however, Bank of England figures show that total net lending from the five main UK banks actually fell in every quarter of 2011.

Continuing the *Trends on Lending* extracts:

> The stock of lending to UK businesses overall **contracted** in the three months to February [**2011**], as did the stock of lending to small and medium-sized enterprises ... The flow of net mortgage lending by UK-resident mortgage lenders **picked up** in January and February ... UK lenders, **though remained subdued**.

> The annual rate of growth in the stock of lending to UK businesses **was negative** in the three months to February [**2012**] ... The stock of lending to small and medium-sized enterprises **continued to contract** ... Mortgage approvals by all UK-resident mortgage lenders for house purchase **fell** over the three months to February, though were higher than the same period last year.

> The annual rate of growth in the stock of lending to UK businesses **was negative** in the three months to August [**2013**]

> ... The stock of lending to small and medium-sized enterprises and to large businesses also **contracted** over this period ... Approvals by all UK-resident mortgage lenders for house purchase and remortgaging rose over the three months to August.

> Over the past six months [October **2014**], the monthly net lending flow to UK businesses has been volatile on a month-to-month basis but, on average, was **broadly close to zero**. Mortgage approvals by all UK-resident mortgage lenders for house purchase **picked up** in June, **before easing back** slightly in August.

> The rate of growth in **some measures** of the stock of lending to UK businesses **picked up** in the three months to February [**2015**] ... Mortgage approvals by all UK-resident mortgage lenders for house purchase **rose slightly** in the three months to February compared to the previous period.

In other words, significant lending only began again during 2015 – several years after Q.E. and "Project Merlin" !

**Q.E. Issue 4.** The market price of government bonds has risen because of Q.E., and this reduces the yield to investors which has had a major negative effect on Company Pensions. According to the Pension Protection Fund, UK pension schemes have experienced colossal deficits because final-salary schemes are normally estimated with the expectation that all assets are held as secure government bonds. As a part of the Q.E. process, many of those bonds have in fact been sold off, which means that they must be replaced by some other form of stock that is less secure. Coupled with that, the fall in bond yields on those bonds that remain in the pension funds means that the value of annuities on offer to new pensioners has dropped, and such losses that are incurred by the purchaser of a contractual annuity after Q.E. was introduced, will never be recovered. The government and central bank money-changers have dipped into the nation's private pension pot. This surely deserves the accusation of malfeasance and rank buffoonery, if not blatant theft.

By 2014 the U.S. Federal Reserve had thus far incurred more than $4 trillion of *extra* debt in pursuit of Q.E., and the U.K. something less than £500 billion. The expectation is that this debt will be re-sold to industry when good times return, but as alluded to above, the historical record of the government making restitution during boom times is not good. The future is not rosy.

### 18.8.10.2 The Reform Movement

Virtually all dissident organisations air their views nowadays via websites and blogs as well as the more traditional avenues of books and lecture tours, and there are for many such links in the *Internet Index* with this book. A survey of these organisations suggests that the most forceful demands for monetary reform have three very simple clarion calls:

**Firstly**, it is the government that should issue money and currency – most definitely not central banks. Those central bank organisations need the government's Treasury authority to make the issue anyway. The habit of using a proxy such as a central bank is a historic one from a time when physical gold was needed from the people who had the most – the goldsmiths – in order to pay for war. The Central Bank (Bank of England), although originally a private institution with not necessarily any more integrity or generosity or state allegiance than the thieving goldsmiths, was chartered so that it might at least give better terms than the goldsmiths. Nowadays in an age of mainly electronic currency, less than 3% of the nation's wealth is actually in the form of hard currency – notes and coins. The government might just as well initiate the electronic transactions itself and avoid the central bank's interest levy. Just like Abraham Lincoln tried to do.

**Secondly**, banks whether central or commercial, should never lend on a fractional reserve basis, and all loans must be secured loans so that in theory although all depositors might not be able to withdraw all their funds simultaneously as hard cash, at least the banks' books balance in terms of assets and liabilities. Any depositor can always have an electronic transaction to return their original deposit with whatever interest is due which is no worse than present-day practice. In an age of electronic transactions, the concept of fractional reserve should be replaced by an electronic bottom line. We already see deficits of trillions of pounds and dollars, therefore a possibly temporary negative bottom line is of no greater significance than it is with the present system, and with no interest payments to a central bank that negative bottom line would be expected to move more readily towards the black.

**Thirdly**, a less universal though very common call is that failed banks should be exactly that. No bail-outs – this is because it seems reasonable to believe that the money used so far to bail out the banks could have compensated the banks' clients for their losses if the bank had been allowed to go under, and, if that is not the case, then we have to ask for what purpose was the "bail-out" so far, and how much more will be needed to complete that purpose. In other words, the target for compensation should be the general public, not the banks.

Currently, money is created electronically from nowhere by central banks and given to the government in the form of a debt that must be redeemed with interest. In Britain, *bonds* are actually sold to customers by the Bank of England's UK Debt Management Office (DMO), the great majority being named *gilts*, though some other instruments are sold at a *discount* which means that the *gain* on redemption can be called something other than *interest*; the word interest will be used here for all types of financial instrument associated with the creation of government money because it is still *usury* whatever semantic fiddle is used.

A "Government Bond" is just that – it is a *bond* that is made between the central bank and the government. It commits the government to extract the interest and capital from the tax payer and to return it to the bank – or to its investors. Historically however, it has been seen that U.S. colonial scrip and the later greenback dollar of Abraham Lincoln could be issued debt-free and with no interest, directly by the government without any central bank involvement at all. And it worked. It worked because there was confidence that the government would redeem the currency – the scrips – for gold if necessary, and that it would accept such "scrip currency" for payments of Inland Revenue.

Britain once had such a government-issue interest-free currency named the Bradbury Pound. It was an H.M. Treasury-issued bank note produced in August, 1914, at the start of World War One when it was found that Bank of England gold reserves were perilously low. The purpose of the Bradbury Pound was to stave off any run on the banks, and its strength was its ability to create consumer confidence because it was underwritten by the British Nation.

In summary, given the reduced impact of the fractional reserve principal in an electronic age, the single largest area for reform would seem to be the issue of money – not so much the quantity, but *who* issues the money, and *who* gets paid for doing so.

## 19 Finance, Politics, and the Media – Hegemony or Conspiracy?

Conspiracy theories and imaginative flummery have eaten into the body of all dissident commentary throughout the internet, but nowhere more deeply and thoroughly than into the subjects of money and banking, and its control (and therefore State tolerated control) by a frequently secretive elite. That elite is invariably a blend of ancient Chivalric Orders, Freemasonry, Secret Societies both old and new, and surpassing all, and reaching its grim tentacles across all of recorded history, the Semitic peoples of Mesopotamia and Babylon, and their later cultural and religious derivatives, commonly known as the Jews.

It is true that some of the oldest evidence for possibly co-operative commodity exchange dates back 20,000 years or so to a site in Israel, although that pre-dates the arrival of the Hebrew people, with later pre-eminent Jewish money-changers being active throughout the several civilisations of Mesopotamia and the Levant, and it is also true that usury was prohibited by the Catholic Church for Christians, but that it was allowed for Jews because it was recorded as so in the Old Testament of the Bible. Maybe as a consequence of those deep-rooted, possibly circumstantial issues, goldsmiths (many of whom were Jewish) were the obvious original source of well-qualified and well-equipped, if not well-intentioned, bankers; but what is the actual evidence, if any, for Jewish hegemony in the world's finances, and does that extend to politics and the media – a logical extension of power that is often attributed to Jews by a vociferous dissident community?

That question has to be addressed with a survey of Jewish history since their diaspora that started circa 6th century BC. A presentation of such facts that cannot just be dismissed with the familiar rants of racism or anti-Semitism may then form a body of evidence that can be judged by any reader – the chapter in Volume Two titled *The Empire of the Hebrews* is essential reading.

Quite apart from any historical precedent, the extent of present-day control of the Western World's finances seems to be totally disproportionate to the world's Jewish population. This can only be due to a combination of the weakness, gullibility, and financial ineptitude on the part of Gentiles aka Goyim, and the superior guile, planning, and loyalty to their own kin that is to be found amongst the Jewish people. Tightly focussed unity of purpose versus naïvety. Jewish merchants have a pervasive, culturally reinforced expectation of dominance over a Gentile Scaramouch that is already burdened with complex feelings of guilt and insecurity. Wherever nourishment flows to a living destination from a living source, the only fitting analogy is the parasite and its complacent host.

All banking cultures, whether Jewish or not, that are based on the fractional reserve principle, and that are buoyed up by ephemeral debt-based balance sheets, are parasitic. State support for these banks in times of trouble is a problematic mix of public defence and capitulation to the bank's shareholders and dividend takers.

## 19.1 The Rothschilds and Zionism

Obscuration and the defence of inter-twined financial empires and influence has reputedly been repeated by many predominantly Jewish financial interests with great success. Frequently inter-related by marriage, a few familiar examples are the Rothschilds, Bischoffsheims, Pereires, Seligmans, Goldsmiths, Warburgs, Lehmans, Paulsons, and Lazards.

In the face of such overwhelming financial strength, the perception, real or imagined, of global control conducted by a quiet Jewish super-elite has given rise throughout history to pogroms and anti-Jewish sentiment. 20th century holocaust-guilt founded on indisputable horror, but arguably exaggerated numbers, now prevents many from even discussing the *possibility* of Zionist economic, political and media persuasion and domination seventy years after the events of a World War that slaughtered around eighty million people worldwide.

In the internet age there are countless blogs and websites attacking Zionism, frequently with identical and obviously plagiarised rhetoric, and there are equally bellicose and threatening ripostes from combative organisations such as the Jewish Defence League, and the Anti-Defamation League.

## Finance, Politics, and the Media – Hegemony or Conspiracy?

When taken together, the vitriolic and murderous outpourings of Nationalist, Socialist, Marxist, Zionist, Christian, Supremacist and Islamic internet activists are a devoted dissident's nightmare when it comes to deciding wherein lies one's own inclination. The range of such ill-feeling and discontent is indicative of zero progress towards global co-existence and is suggestive of the absence of even the minutest maturation of human nature over the last few millennia. Probably the reverse is true, and that may be taken as evidence to support this book's proposition that any "Golden Age" of humanity lies in the distant past or distant future, but certainly not within the current inappropriately named *epoch of enlightenment and rationalism*. Vitriolic resentment of obscene differentials, and intolerance of the exploitation of the many by the few is not envy it is a rightful expression of justifiable anger, and many of the murderous outpourings by all sides in a debate about surreptitious governance are only unacceptable in a legal framework, not in a moral one.

The Rothschild financial empire is possibly the wealthiest corporate, but now diversely distributed, entity ever seen. It began around the second half of the 18th century in what was then the Free State or City of Frankfurt-am-Main, Germany, and it was first of all under the guidance of the descendants of an Ashkenazi Jewish money-changer, Moses Amschel Bauer. As shown in detail in Volume Two, Ashkenazi Jews, that today are believed to represent the vast majority of world Jewry, were apparently originally from the Caucasus region named Khazaria, and they adopted the Hebrew religion during the 8th century in preference to Christianity or Islam. They were neither members of the original tribes of Israel that contributed to the Jewish Diaspora that began circa 500 BC, nor were they ethnically Semitic. This view is sometimes the one put forward by obviously anti-Semitic critics, but it is also proposed by many Jews themselves. Another explanation is that they are descended from originally Middle-Eastern Hebrews that migrated north into Germany, from where they then spread in all directions. Although that view is reputedly supported by some DNA evidence, it cannot refute the very real Khazarian conversion that produced so many obviously non-Semitic cultural members of the worldwide Jewish community.

From among the often harsh and envious references on the internet, compounded by half-truths and mystery, only a limited range of undeniable facts about the Rothschilds emerge. There is a suggestion by many that the complex relationships concerning the origins and propagation of the family, and the diverse nature of the Rothschild's financial base, were deliberately contrived and maintained to ensure immunity to attack by Gentiles who are sometimes contemptuously referred to by Jews as *Goyim* or cattle. Such alleged arrogant bigotry is often quoted in support of attacks on Jewish culture.

The family name Rothschild derives from the German for "red shield", a symbol displayed on the Rothschilds' original shop-front and that had been preceded by a green one. Its use in connection with several generations of family members dates back to the 16$^{th}$ century, though it is understood to have been adopted by Mayer Amschel Bauer, son of Moses Bauer, during the 1760s when he took over the family business.

Before entering the family business, Mayer Amschel Bauer had risen through the ranks of the Jewish-owned Oppenheimer Bank in Hanover to become a junior partner, and it was through contacts established at that time that he gained access to the court of Prince William of Hanau, so that by 1770 he could profess royal patronage and display the Coat of Arms of Hess-Hanau outside the family shop on Judenstrasse aka Judengasse – Jew Street – in Frankfurt. He then married and raised the sons who would spread the family business throughout Europe.

Starting in 1798 with Nathan Mayer Rothschild who went to England, five brothers rapidly created the trading and banking empire with bases in Frankfurt, London, Paris, Vienna and Naples, taking significant profits from diverse sources: the Napoleonic Wars; the rush for worldwide gold and diamonds in connection with figures such as Cecil Rhodes, and organisations such as De Beers and Anglo-American Corporation; and through commercial ventures, such as the Suez Canal, the expansion of railways, and oil exploration.

## Finance, Politics, and the Media – Hegemony or Conspiracy?

In 1806, and in his fully inherited and finally matured role as William IX Prince-Elector of Hesse, the erstwhile Prince William of Hanau was obliged to flee to Denmark when his kingdom was absorbed into the Napoleonic Dynasty by Napoleon's brother Jérôme, ruler of the puppet Kingdom of Westphalia. By now William had amassed an immense fortune, some of which he left with the Rothschilds. William's ancestor, Charles I, had begun the business of renting out the Hessian army during the War of Spanish Succession (1701 to 1714), and that massive revenue generator was continued by Landgrave Frederick II, the father of William IX, notably supplying the British against the Americans during the American War of Independence – just one transaction alone being equivalent to almost £500 million in today's money. By the time of William's tenure, the family fortune is estimated to have been the largest in Europe, and it was to this wealth that the Rothschilds and other Jewish bankers were attracted.

The Rothschilds were closely rivalled for some time by a banking family, the Bethmanns, who were also based in Frankfurt and who began business in 1748. There is some controversy about whether they were Christian, Jewish, or Christian-practising Jewish. The Bethmanns bank seems to have been ultimately eclipsed completely by the Rothschilds, and was eventually absorbed into ABN AMRO Bank of the Netherlands that had to be nationalised as a consequence of the economic crisis that began in 2007.

The wealth of the Rothschilds has become less obvious since the middle of the 19th century, and the obscurity of their financial power conveniently masks what has been estimated as many trillions of pounds, which if true would make them the undisputed pinnacle of world wealth, against which the debts of not just the Third World, but also the entire Western World, would be dwarfed.

## 19.2 More and Yet More Money Changers of Questionable Loyalty

### 19.2.1 Frankfurt-am-Main

In 1694 more than a quarter of Frankfurt-based Jewish families were money lenders or pawn-brokers – that makes more than one hundred potential sources of future bankers.

### 19.2.2 Warburg, Swiss Bank Corporation, UBS

The English private bank, S. G. Warburg, was founded in 1946 but was acquired by the Swiss Bank Corporation in 1995 which evolved by also absorbing several U.S. investment banks into UBS AG in 1998. The Swiss Bank Corporation had been formed originally in 1854 and was linked at that time with a similar consortium of bankers-underwriters that were based in Frankfurt.

### 19.2.3 BNP-Paribas, Bichoffsheim, Goldschmidt

In the early 1800s two Jewish brothers of the Bichoffsheim family formed banks in Amsterdam, Antwerp, and Brussels. By 1860, after marrying the daughter of a Jewish banker, Hayum-Salomon Goldschmidt, who was based in Frankfurt, the brother Louis-Raphaël had established the Bischoffsheim-Goldschmidt bank in Paris and London. Louis-Raphaël had additionally served his banking apprenticeship as a clerk in Frankfurt-am-Main. By 1863 their banking empire extended across Holland, Belgium, France and Britain.

By 1869 the Bischoffsheim-Goldschmidt Empire was rivalled by other banks, including the Banque de Paris, that had been formed by the merging of about ten separate investment and banking concerns.

French banks were nationalised in 1946, then privatised in 1993. BNP Paribas suffered minimal damage during the economic crisis of 2007 to 2012, and was Bank of the Year in 2012 by which time it had become the third largest in the world. From a state-owned bank to a privately owned global super-elite in less than fifty years. It would be interesting to identify the changes to the sources and destinations of revenue flows over that period.

### 19.2.4 Samuel Montague and Company

Foreign Bankers, in Leadenhall Street, London. Founded in 1853, Samuel Montagu's company financed much Jewish cultural and educational development from Jerusalem to Russia, and in England and America; some of the work was in connection with the Rothschilds. He was an Orthodox Jew, and was involved in the Gold and Silver Commission (work published 1890). He was made a Baronet on the recommendation of Gladstone's government in 1894. Interestingly his son, Edwin Samuel Montagu, a British MP, Privy Councillor, and cabinet member, was strongly opposed to Zionism and its racist policies that would eventually become a part of the modern state of Israel.

### 19.2.5 Sir Edgar Speyer, 1st Baronet 1862 to 1932

A U.S. born Ashkenazi Jew with roots in Frankfurt-am-Main, he was naturalised British in 1892. Speyer was involved in international finance, and he was Chairman of the nascent London Underground company between 1906 and 1915, its period of massive growth. In 1915 he was obliged to return to the U.S. when, in spite of his resignation from both U.S. and German affiliated companies, he became the object of anti-German attacks, and in 1921 his naturalisation was revoked by the British Government following an investigation into allegations that he had traded with the enemy during World War One. Having been also a member of the Privy Council, he was eventually struck off that as well. He strongly denied all allegations, and, it is said, maintained his dignity throughout, despite compelling evidence of duplicity.

### 19.2.6 George Blumenthal 1858 to 1941

Jewish, and yet again born in Frankfurt-am-Main, Blumenthal was one of a small group of bankers that in 1896 shored up U.S. Government gold reserves to the extent of about $60 million during the presidency of Grover Cleveland. Cleveland was reputedly one of the most honest U.S. presidents, and he helped create the climate that would see the U.S. economy recover from a crisis, the panic of 1893, that at that time was the worst in its history.

George Blumenthal was related to the Ashkenazi Jew, Levi Strauss, by whom much of the world's population has been bejeaned, and he was the brother-in-law of Eugene Isaac Meyer (1875 to 1959), a U.S. financier, publisher of the Washington Post, Chairman of the U.S. Federal Reserve Bank (1930 to 1933), and the first President of the World Bank Group in 1945 following the Bretton Woods agreement that fixed the dollar-gold link. Eugene Isaac Meyer's daughter, Katharine Graham, was the editor of the Washington Post at the time of the Watergate scandal that resulted in the impeachment of U.S. President Richard Nixon.

### 19.2.7 Lazard Brothers

George Blumenthal had been the U.S. representative of the German-based Jewish bankers, Speyer & Co., that also had branches in London and Paris, but he became prominent as the American head of a company in which he was initially a partner in France – the Jewish firm of Lazard Frères – which was a financial firm with diverse interests that originally had been founded by two French Jewish immigrants in 1848 in the southern U.S.

### 19.2.8 Lazard Group LLC.

A descendant of Lazard Frères from the revolutionary year of 1848, it is today a major global financial institution controlling assets of $100 billions.

### 19.2.9 Sir James Goldsmith 1933 to 1997

This billionaire, born in Paris, was the son of Franck Adolphe Benedict Goldschmidt (1878 to 1967) who had been born in Frankfurt, and who became a Hotel tycoon. He had diplomatic and banking ancestors within the principalities of the Holy Roman Empire and the pre-unification Italian states, and he was related by marriage to the Rothschild dynasty.

Sir James Goldsmith's life is a caricature of privileged aggression and dissidence associated with a host of friends and enemies, all of them, of whatever cultural roots, cast from a similar mould. They all lived on a different planet to the millions from whose labour their profits were derived, and their estates continue to be derived.

Goldsmith was a host and intimate member of the circle within which moved the dysfunctional elite such as Lord Lucan, indicted but never brought to trial for the alleged murder of his family's nanny. One of the most plausible explanations for Lucan's disappearance is that to eliminate any embarrassment, he was disposed of by members of his own "law-abiding" (!) circle – the cream of society – alleged by one investigative media documentary to have included those at the very top.

### 19.2.10 Helbert Wagg & Co.

Acquired by Schroders PLC between 1959 and 1962 under the direction of Gordon Richardson (later Lord) and his godfather, Lionel Fraser, who was chairman of the issuing house Helbert Wagg. Schroders was of London and Hamburg origins – a Hamburg Jew, Johann Heinrich Schroder (John Henry), founded the bank in 1818 in London after working there since 1804 with his brother Johann Friedrich (John Fredrick). Schroders plc. is among the one hundred largest companies listed on the London Stock Exchange. During the 1860s, J. Henry Schroder Wagg & Co. went on to become one of the largest merchant banks – they specialised in international finance.

See the document *HelbertWagg1939Letter.pdf* which illustrates the bank's interest in potential change at the start of the Second World War. It is available for download – see the chapter in Volume One titled *Internet Index of References and Other Downloads*.

From the Palgrave Dictionary of Anglo-Jewish History:

The German Jewish immigrant, John Wagg (1793 to 1878), founded a stockbroking firm, "Helbert, Wagg & Co.", around 1823 with his uncle John Helbert who was related to the Rothschild family. They were the Rothschild's stockbroker.

Between the years 1842 and 1933 the Wagg family, in the form of John's sons Arthur and Edward, increased the firm's scope to that of a Merchant Bank, focussing on arbitrage transactions – profiteering from no-risk trading that takes advantage of the difference between bid and offer (buy and sell) prices in diverse markets. This was a lofty and unnecessary intermediary making money simply from money – usury – by taking a slice from *transactions* concerning other folks' essential commodities that quite separately involve notions of profit taken by a retailer.

Whilst the Wagg family was becoming Anglicised a substantial legacy to the Jewish Board of Guardians was made from the estate of Edward Wagg in 1933.

### 19.2.11 Schroders, President of the World Bank, and Gordon Brown

Gordon Richardson (later of the Group of Thirty – G30) left Schroders to become Governor of the Bank of England in 1973, and Michael John Verey succeeded him. Verey's chief executive at Schroders was James Wolfensohn, the Jewish-Australian son of English emigrants who in 1980 adopted U.S. citizenship in order to become eligible for the post of President of the World Bank. Initially failing in this quest, he formed his own international bank, and finally became president of the World Bank for the period 1995 to 2005. He was a financier and a Bilderberger, who had previously been an executive partner of the disgraced Salomon Brothers in New York.

In 2011 Wolfensohn said of ex-British Chancellor and ex-Prime Minister, Gordon Brown, that there was no-one better for the role of Managing Director of the International Monetary Fund. Brown's successor as Prime Minister, David Cameron, said, on the contrary:

> "It does seem to me that, if you have someone who didn't think we had a debt problem in the UK when we self-evidently do have a debt problem, then they might not be the most appropriate person to work out whether other countries around the world have debt and deficit problems ... Above all what matters is: is the person running the IMF someone who understands the dangers of excessive debt, excessive deficit? ... it really must be someone who gets that rather than someone who says that they don't see a problem".

This was just before the incumbent Jewish Managing Director of the IMF, Dominique Strauss-Kahn, one-time activist member of the French Union of Communist Students, hit the headlines in a sex scandal in which diverse complainants brought charges, including statements of intent to bring civil actions if there was no public prosecution. Despite admissions by him, and some compelling forensic evidence, there does not seem to have been any persistent prosecution against him, though he became separated from his wife, who is heiress to her Jewish grandfather Paul Rosenberg's art dealership fortune.

Among other commentators on Gordon Brown's fitness for the post was a financial blogger, Felix Salmon, who said that Brown:

> *"...comes with way too much baggage: he'll never be able to admit that enormous chunks of what he did as Chancellor turned out, in hindsight, to be disastrous", and in respect of Brown's delivery of guidance, "... Brown simply has no credibility on that front ... His diplomatic skills leave something to be desired as well".*

During the insane British asset disposals under Prime Minister Margaret Thatcher, for which Schroders was the principal agent, Winfried Bischoff while CEO of Schroders increased its value from £30 million in 1984 to £1.3 billion in 2000 when he was knighted, and after which the investment banking division of Schroders was sold to Citigroup of which he then became chairman in 2007.

Sir Winfried Franz Wilhen Bischoff (born in Aachen, Germany in 1941) is an Anglo-German banker, and currently (2013) chairman of Lloyds Banking Group plc. There does not seem to be any detail of his early life in any of the regular internet archives, and so, his meteoric rise is a mystery at the time of writing this, though he was Chairman of the hard-hit Citigroup when the economic crisis deepened in 2008.

### 19.2.12 Salomon Brothers

Founded in 1910 by three brothers and a clerk, Ben Levy, it was at one time one of the largest financial service companies on Wall Street, becoming part of Citigroup by the end of the 20th century after a passage of association and incorporation via an unhelpful web of names, such as Morgan Stanley, Smith Barney, Phibro Corporation, Travelers Group, and

Citicorp. Salomon's growth through all its guises, and with all its ugly bedfellows was significantly derived from Treasury Bond and mortgage backed security trading. In other words, money derived from other money that was derived all along merely from debt, and encouraged by the U.S. Government via schemes such as the Government National Mortgage Association (GNMA), or Ginnie Mae. In the early nineteen nineties Salomon was fined for trying to acquire more than the permitted allowance of Treasury Bonds.

### 19.2.13 Bear Stearns, Lehman Brothers, Merrill Lynch

Bear Stearns was the principal purveyor of toxic U.S. sub-prime mortgage debt to the world in the first decade of the 3$^{rd}$ millennium.

Lehman Brothers and Merrill Lynch are similarly regarded as predatory and now extinct blood-suckers of the world's wealth, a process that can be traced back to the beginnings of such eventually toxic trading, that was innovated and elevated by figures such as John Gutfreund, also Jewish, who was Salomon's managing partner in 1978. Gutfreund left the company in 1991 at the time of the "Treasury Bond" scandal referred to above, and was personally fined and barred from holding the position of CEO in such a company again. Within a short five years the economic crisis that persisted to 2013 had occurred, the crisis being due in large part to the greed and profligate practices of Salomon and its compatriots.

### 19.2.14 John Key – Prime Minister of New Zealand

In the present context of *"Finance, Politics, and the Media"* an unlikely connection exists with the antipodean nation of 4 millions, New Zealand. John Key, the Prime Minister of that nation in 2015, was once one of the most ruthless currency traders at Merrill Lynch where he made himself tens of £millions.

Like so many of his fellow Jews in international finance, he does not seem to have any loyalty to any country except maybe Israel. One example might be his attempts to change New Zealand's flag because it *"...means nothing..."* to him.

Anecdotal?, circumstantial?, conspiracy theory?, there are many references to the subject on the internet and in literature. A few references that also connect with other aspects of the present context are:

http://www.thevinnyeastwoodshow.com/vinny-mr-news-eastwoods-blog/john-keys-real-past-exposed-must-see-please-share-6mins

http://www.postmanproductions.org/?p=2885

https://aotearoaawiderperspective.wordpress.com/tag/merrill-lynch/

### 19.2.15 Oppenheimer, De Beers, Anglo-American Corporation

At first sight the Oppenheimer family gave up its interest in diamonds in November 2011 when it sold its 40% share of De Beers to the multi-national Anglo-American Corporation, the largest producer of platinum among many other minerals – diamonds included. On closer inspection, the deal was nothing more than a juggling of family interests, no doubt to enhance a blend of security, control and tax-efficiency, and a distancing from the controversy of blood diamonds. Anglo-American Corporation was founded in 1917, jointly by Ernest Oppenheimer who was born near Frankfurt-am-Main, Germany, to Jewish parents; and by the American bank J.P. Morgan & Co.

Ernest Oppenheimer, later Sir Ernest, was chairman of De Beers in 1929, and Anglo-American Corporation is still part-controlled by Nicholas Oppenheimer, Sir Ernest's grandson, keeping diamonds well and truly in the family despite media reporting.

### 19.2.16 Goldman-Sachs, J.P. Morgan, Rothschild – Again

In 1848 Marcus Goldman, an Ashkenazi Jew, left Frankfurt-am-Main and settled in the U.S. Goldman joined with his son-in-law, Samuel Sachs, who was born in the U.S. of German Jewish immigrants, and Goldman's company became Goldman-Sachs in 1904. Samuel Sachs was also a friend of Philip Lehman who was born in the U.S. of German Jewish immigrants, Lehman Brothers having the dubious honour of accounting for the largest bankruptcy in U.S. history in 2008, and being the first failure that led to the global economic crisis and world recession that continued for at least five years.

*Finance, Politics, and the Media – Hegemony or Conspiracy?*

When J.P. Morgan's father died in 1890, he inherited the family business, originally dry goods retailing (a U.S. term for textiles and clothing), that was worth about $10 million. In 1901 the first $billion company, U.S. Steel was created with Morgan finance, and when J.P. died in 1913 his business empire and controlling interests after little more than twenty years had rocketed to involve more than 40 major international corporations in fields such as banking, steel, mining, electrical, shipping, and railways; it was worth many billions of dollars even at that time.

In 1895, using their own personal gold reserves, the J.P. Morgan and Rothschild banks bought bonds from the U.S. Government that was attempting to defend the nation's plummeting gold reserves and the Gold Standard. Those banks, comprising major European representation, then sold them on for enormous profits.

In 1913 as a result of J.P. Morgan's direct action to halt the economic crisis of 1907 that occurred during the presidency of Theodore "Teddy" Roosevelt, the climate was right for a more permanent solution that would not be so reliant on the enthusiasm and charisma of an individual. Accordingly, J.P. Morgan with others were instrumental in persuading President Woodrow Wilson to sign into law the creation of the Federal Reserve network of 12 private banks – the Rothschilds being among the principal stockholders of those banks. Around this time it is understood that the Rothschilds had a 20% share of J.P. Morgan.

In 2008 J.P. Morgan Chase bought Bear Stearns (previously $130 per share) for just $2 per share – the deal being guaranteed by government money via the U.S. Federal Reserve for $30 billions.

*Finance, Politics, and the Media – Hegemony or Conspiracy?*

In 2013 J.P. Morgan Chase hit the headlines when more than $6 billion were lost as a result of allegedly inept and negligent management, followed by an attempted cover-up:

http://www.prlog.org/10058722-morgan-chase-buyout-of-bear-stearns-trillionaires-delight.html

> *'The buyout of Bear Stearns by Morgan is the culmination of two centuries of persistent work by the families of Rothschild, Morgan and Rockefeller to effectively control the Federal Reserve. This article highlights the history of the quest..'*

### 19.2.17 Jacob Schiff

The final reference in this section is to another U.S. Jewish immigrant from Frankfurt-am-Main, Jacob Schiff, who was intimately connected with the Rothschilds and who is considered by some to be the most prominent and politically effective individual in respect of the advancement of Jewish influence in America to the present day, and in early 20$^{th}$ century Russia until Stalin distanced himself from the original Jewish-dominated revolutionaries.

Schiff arrived in the U.S. in 1865 and became the principal of the investment banking firm, Kuhn, Loeb & Co., seen as a rival to J.P. Morgan. He was also a director of many well-known companies, such as Wells Fargo and the Equitable Life Assurance Society, and in 1892 he was the principal driver of the "Hebrew Free Loan Society" that lends only to Jews and, according to their website, *"....has helped more than 875,000 borrowers..."* down to the present day. Around this time his daughter married into the Warburg dynasty, from which family Paul Warburg would become a member of the new Federal Reserve Bank in 1914.

It is said that Schiff's greatest socio-political achievements concerned his hatred of Imperial Russia that was a supporter of the young United States, and his assistance to the enemies of the Russian Tsar. Schiff financed Japan in its successful war against Russia in the early 20$^{th}$ century, and certainly by the time of the Russian revolution he was making loans to the new Soviet regime.

Russian Jewish emigration to the U.S. is said to have been massively increased by Schiff's lobbying of President Grover Cleveland to veto the Immigration Bill of 1897 that would have imposed literacy tests for new immigrants. If passed, it would have barred hundreds of thousands from a new life in the booming U.S.

Despite one or two secular charitable donations, Schiff's massive philanthropic contributions favoured only those of his own Jewish culture.

## 19.3 The Aga Khan

Isma'ilism is a branch of Shi'a Islam; they are also distinguished as the Severners. The Aga Khan is the Imam or head of the sect that traces its roots back to the Fatimid Caliphate. Acceptance in the West of this fabulously wealthy person was assured by the assistance given by one of his ancestors to the British during the Afghan war of 1841 and 1842.

A British passport holder, the Aga Khan is a multi-billionaire with a vast estate in France (among many worldwide properties) and at the same time he is the spiritual leader of a sect of around 15,000,000 Muslims who pay him an annual retainer – some as much as around one tenth of their annual income. Although considered a philanthropist, the absurdity of the whole phenomenon beggars belief.

## 19.4 A Food Scam – the Hebrew-Islamic Alliance

As far as it appears from the British side of the Atlantic, the Kosher Nostra money-making schemes, likened by some to a protection racket, are effectively a tax on American consumers, more than those in Europe. In order to realise sales of product to Jewish consumers, the products of many high-profile food and other consumables producers, such as Heinz, General Foods, Proctor and Gamble, have to be labelled with a certification of Kosher origin – frequently marks such as (U) or (K), and Jewish congregations are instructed to avoid products that do not display these marks of Kosher certification. There is a small per-unit payment, but massive overall annual payment to Jewish organisations, or Rabbinical Councils, that levy the certification cost, such as the Union of Orthodox Jewish Congregations that has its headquarters in New York. Annual receipts have been estimated to be in the $millions, and accumulated sums in the $billions. The response by Jewish cultural organisations such as the aggressive Anti-Defamation League when questioned about the fairness of such a multi-cultural tax is not just restricted to the riposte that the unit cost is small, which entirely misses the point of the massive accumulated benefits, but is accompanied by a mindless and vitriolic accusation that any questioning of this racket is the result of anti-Semitic, far-right bigotry.

More information can be found under the internet search tags: *Hekhsher Tzedek*, and *Magen Tzedek*, and the results show that this is big business under the banner of social justice – for one elite group.

Similar money-making Halal schemes abound to serve the growing Muslim populations of western and southern hemisphere countries that previously did not require notification, principally, of the barbarous nature of animal slaughter practised by the Islamic and Hebrew religions. The responses again, are bullish, evasive and aggressive, with diversionary red-herring statements about the benefits of job-creation to serve their industry of greed and deceit.

Halal foods are now predominant in many British schools, and no posturing by Islamic apologists will reverse the fact that some of the funds that are derived from the imposition of this horror on the non-Islamic population, will most certainly arrive in the pockets of Jihadists. Reference, *Zakat* and *Khums* tax requirements under Islamic religious tradition, and Sharia Law.

## 19.5 Political Hegemony
### 19.5.1 Jacobins, the Illuminati, Winston Churchill

The Illuminati was a real organisation founded during the Age of Enlightenment in the style of the even older and also very real Freemasonry movement, but it should not be confused with internet references to older movements such as "The Illuminati of Zwickau" – a Lutheran sect of Anabaptists who were active at Wittenberg in 1522. The Illuminati movement of interest here was formed in 1776 in Bavaria by the Jewish-born, Jesuit-educated Adam Weishaupt, known within their own circle as *Spartacus*. Weishaupt also became a Freemason in 1777 in an attempt, it is said, to take over that movement and make it conform to his more rational and modern Illuminati agenda – Illuminated Freemasonry. His world-view and subversive objectives are associated with those of a group including Voltaire (aka François-Marie Arouet) who became a Freemason in the year of his own death 1778, along with his friend, Benjamin Franklin. Other celebrated figures of similar persuasion included the French illuminists Diderot and Rousseau, and the Anglo-American revolutionary, Thomas Paine.

It is Diderot who is remembered for the famous remark:

> *"Man will never be free until the last king is strangled with the entrails of the last priest".*

Within such a circle of luminaries, Weishaupt was reputedly patronised by the Rothschilds and commissioned by them to ensure the development of the Illuminati society as an underground Kabbalist movement to destabilise mainstream governments and Christian churches – Kabbalism being a mystical interpretation of the Old Testament by Hebrew Rabbis, and comprising books that are not part of the Authorised Bible.

Regardless of whether the Rothschild connection is speculative conspiracy theory or fact, subversive and anarchistic motives throughout Europe at all levels of society were real, and they were discussed at length in a contemporary book, referred to in a previous chapter, by a respected

*Finance, Politics, and the Media – Hegemony or Conspiracy?*

Scottish academic, John Robison, who was Professor of Natural Philosophy, and Secretary to the Royal Society of Edinburgh. His book, *Proofs of a Conspiracy Against all the Religions and Governments in Europe*, is in the *Internet Index* accompanying this book. There are present-day Freemasons who dispute the assertions by Robison, but similar assertions were made by his contemporary French commentator, Abbé Barruel; those dissenting Freemasons in fact deny any link whatsoever between the German (Bavarian) Illuminati, French Freemasonry and the French Revolution.

Weishaupt was not a Christian and was probably either an atheist or a Pagan, with fashionable esoteric and mystic leanings, similar to the developments of Theosophy and Spiritualism later in the 19$^{th}$ century. This propensity is alleged to have developed into a blend of occult, political, and sociological doctrines that pre-empted the later anarchy movements by a century or so, with the following set of proscriptive objectives or ideals:

1. Abolition of monarchy and all ordered governments.
2. Abolition of private property and inheritance.
3. Abolition of patriotism.
4. Abolition of the family and marriage, and the institution of communal education for children.
5. Abolition of all Christian morality and of all religion.

These views anticipated the imminent culture of seminal anarchists, such as Proudhon, Bakunin, and Kropotkin, and a legacy of ambitions that were partially adopted by Marxism and later embraced by what many believe to be an aspiring present-day New World Order.

Freemasonry is believed to have arrived in France and Germany from England during the 1770s, and it has been seen as influential in the revolutionary movements, of which Jacobinism was only one, that culminated in the French Revolution during the summer of 1789, behind which the Royalists believed that the gold of the Duke of Orleans was involved, while some revolutionary Jacobins believed British gold was involved. Given the state of the French economy at the time, it was almost certainly not French gold, and it is difficult to believe that anyone claiming to be British would have been behind it.

If gold there was, then its source remains a mystery, unless it came from Freemasons who were well represented in the Jacobin Club, and it is a reasonable assumption that members of the Illuminati were among them.

The widespread effects and reality of subversive movements such as the Illuminati was confirmed by the abolitionist Anglican Bishop Porteus, Bishop of both Chester and London, and a Privy Councillor, who at the end of the 18th century observed to the clergy of his diocese:

> *"It now appears from undoubted evidence, collected from the most authentic sources, and produced about the same time, by two different authors, of different countries and religions, and writing without the least concert or communication with each other, that there have in fact subsisted in the heart of Europe certain sects of men, distinguished by various fanciful names, and various mysterious rites and ceremonies, but all concurring in one common object, namely, the gradual overthrow, not merely of all religion, but of all civil government and social order throughout the world."*
> *– A Dictionary of All Religions and Religious Denominations*
> *Jewish, Heathen, Mahometan, Christian, Ancient and Modern.*
> By Hannah Adams, 1784.
> (Fourth Edition 1817, entry under Illuminati, or Illuminees.)

It is the contention of many that some of the principal figures in that diverse subversive movement were the wealthiest in the land, and that they were inherently culturally and spiritually distinct from the aristocratic status quo. Warfare and any adversity that increased government borrowing was an economic windfall for this elite super-stratum; they were and are the super-financiers and, by implication, they are mainly Jewish.

On this topic, like many other contentious issues, there is much contradiction and venom among internet blogs and media commentary concerning historical fact or hysterical fiction.

Further commentary concerning subversive activity was reputedly made by Sir Walter Scott in his book, *The Life of Napoleon*, although a search through the book for anything on the Illuminati revealed nothing to this writer, the closest references being to the initially egalitarian and reclusive nature of the Jacobin movement that was to burst into the open in France revealing its basely bigoted and dark psychopathy so horrifically during "The Terror".

Searching through Scott's book did turn up references to the leading lights of the enlightenment – Voltaire and Rousseau – but even within the community of these French *Enlightened Ones*, Jews were reviled by Voltaire but venerated by Rousseau, who, for that reason, is sometimes wrongly classified as Jewish.

On page 12 of Volume II of Scott's book there is an interesting foretaste of 20th century mainstream media control, and on page 13 references to Papal hegemony. Page 33 contains references to the Jacobins and Duke d'Orleans and the nature of the Illuminati, but nowhere in *The Life of Napoleon* does that organisation seem to be actually named by Scott.

The full story of Adam Weishaupt and his many international Illuminati associates who were seemingly interested in improving the lot of humanity, according to their ideology by ridding it of conventional religious and state shackles, is beyond the current scope; likewise, the circumstances of the Illuminati's ostracism and downfall.

So, it must suffice to note that there were links of some sort between Illuminati and Jacobins, both of whom might charitably be said to have originated from pure principles. Both movements were known to the leading lights of the emerging American nation, among whom George Washington is quoted as distancing himself and his Freemasonry affiliation from their "*...diabolical tenets... and ...pernicious principles...*".

*Finance, Politics, and the Media – Hegemony or Conspiracy?*

Winston Churchill in 1920, linking the French and Russian revolutions, and also some revolutionary and anarchic personalities, said of the Illuminati:

> "This movement among the Jews is not new. From the days of Spartacus-Weishaupt to those of Karl Marx, and down to Trotsky (Russia), Bela Kun (Hungary), Rosa Luxembourg (Germany), and Emma Goldman (United States), this worldwide conspiracy for the overthrow of civilization and for the reconstitution of society on the basis of arrested development, of envious malevolence, and impossible equality, has been steadily growing. It played, as a modern writer, Mrs. Webster, has so ably shown, a definitely recognizable part in the tragedy of the French Revolution. It has been the mainspring of every subversive movement during the Nineteenth Century; and now at last this band of extraordinary personalities from the underworld of the great cities of Europe and America have gripped the Russian people by the hair of their heads and have become practically the undisputed masters of that enormous empire."

Winston Churchill also confirmed the prevalence of Jewish influence in the development of Soviet Russia in the same article in the Illustrated Sunday Herald of 8th February, 1920. The full article may be read at: http://www.fpp.co.uk/bookchapters/WSC/WSCwrote1920.html

With some further commentary at:

http://jewishcurrents.org/february-8-churchill-on-jews-communism-and-zionism-3849

## 19.5.2 The Bolshevik, Fabian, and Jewish Connection

Lenin (Vladimir Ilyich Ulyanov, 1870 to 1924) was of Jewish descent on his maternal side, though he was baptised into the Russian Orthodox Church by his pious father. It is said that his mother's generally lax attitude to religion contributed to Lenin's conversion to atheism shortly after his father died, and after his brother was executed for plotting against the Czar. However, Lenin was also heavily influenced by Mikhail Bakunin, an indefatigable and charismatic revolutionary who was notably anti-Semitic, and who was also an adherent of the tenets of the Illuminati movement of Adam Weishaupt, of Anarchism, and some say, of Satanism. Furthermore, Bakunin was vigorously anti-Marxist. Both Lenin (compellingly alleged by several sources) and Bakunin were Freemasons.

Lenin, with such a bizarrely eclectic background and *curriculum vitae* of political thought, was, of course, the leader of the Bolshevik faction during and after the various stages of the Russian revolution, and funding for the Bolshevik cause is an interesting component, or sidebar of any history of money and banking hegemony. It is unbelievably conspiratorial, but fact.

The modern-day Fabian Society was founded in 1884 by, among several other well-known names, George Bernard Shaw, who fawningly said of Lenin:

> *"It is a real comfort to me, an old man, to be able to step into my grave with the knowledge that the civilisation of the world will be saved ... it is here in Russia that I have actually been convinced that the new Communist system is capable of leading mankind out of its present crisis, and saving it from complete anarchy and ruin."*

The Fabian Society was named after the Roman General Fabius Maximus, whose softly softly tactics were admired by socialists who were surreptitiously trying to move government and society towards communism as espoused by Marx, Engels, and many others. Two of the most notable Fabians of recent times are the late ex-Labour Cabinet

Minister, Anthony Wedgwood Benn, and former British Prime Minister, Tony Blair, whose cabal has done so much to destabilise British culture, and promote foreign wars of mass destruction among civil populations. An early Fabian epithet was written down as:

> "For the right moment you must wait, as Fabius did most patiently, when warring against Hannibal, though many censured his delays; but when the time comes you must strike hard, as Fabius did, or your waiting will be in vain, and fruitless."

A few leading figures that are usually just represented in history as a part of the Russian revolution are believed by some (Sir Winston Churchill included) to have been members of activist organisations other than the obvious revolutionary parties, seemingly at odds with Soviet ideology and ambition. A book that could not be authenticated, but which is cited in many references as having been published in 1932 by one Nikolai Svitkov – *About Freemasonry in Russian Exile* – is said to have identified among many post-revolutionary exiles, the names of the following significant Russian Freemasons, several of whom were also Jewish, as being part of Soviet evolution from the start, through to the middle of the 20th century:

| Vladimir Ulyanov-Lenin | Possibly the most well-known Soviet leadership figure. Jewish*. *See note below. |
|---|---|
| Leon Trotsky | Founder and head of the Red Army. Jewish. |
| Grigori Zinoviev | Head of the Comintern international communist evangelical arm. Stalin's opponent, by whom he was eventually executed. Jewish*. |
| Leon Kamenev | Lenin's deputy, but executed by Stalin. Jewish. |
| Maxim Litvinov | Ambassador to both Britain and U.S. and an international fixer; favoured by both Lenin and Stalin. Jewish. |
| Yakov Sverdlov | Chairman of the Central Executive Committee. He ordered the execution of Tsar Nicholas II and his family on July 16, 1918. Jewish*. |
| Maxim Gorky | Writer and close friend and colleague of Stalin. Moscow Gorky Park was named after him. |
| Karl Radek | Secretary of the Comintern; his mercurial allegiances led to his eventual execution in a labour camp. Jewish*. |

Note: Jewish* – Some of these people such as Lenin, Zinoviev, Radek and Sverdlov also reputedly belonged to the organisation *B'nai B'rith*, aka Sons of the Covenant, said to be the oldest Jewish-Israeli solidarity movement, founded in New York in 1843, and a component of the rise of Zionism. It is nowadays a very non-mysterious secular global organisation with $multi-million budgets and international aid involvement.

Other references that are citable, such as "*The Rulers of Russia*", first published in 1938 by the Catholic writer, the Reverend Denis Fahey, categorically list the significant revolutionaries, by origin, and state that:

"... of the 556 important functionaries of the Bolshevik State, ... there were in 1918-1919, ... 457 Jews."

If true, then there is an indisputable link between Zionism and Bolshevism.

The fascinating, wide and eclectic associations of many of the late 19th and early 20th century revolutionary leading lights in fashionable international literary and philosophical circles during *La Belle Époque*, as well as in the more expected political and revolutionary-governmental movements are not in doubt, but they are beyond the scope of this book except to note that in connection with the overall idea that the Russian revolutionary movement and subsequent years were maybe not exactly what was originally intended, and that they were even dysfunctional, it is alleged that many of those leading lights – the apparently socialist and communist-inspired celebrated leaders of the early Russian Soviet experiment – were in fact closet capitalists, and that they were ultimately overturned by an irresistible cadre of despotic and anarchic proletarian psychopaths to whom a person such as Stalin was a natural leader, and totally at odds with Lenin and his adherents. Later history certainly bears out some of that assertion, particularly in respect of Stalin being the persistently dark and murderous one.

Outside the more obvious and immediate circle of assuredly Russian operators, a remarkable U.S. German-Jewish immigrant and philanthropist named Joseph Fels was a Fabian by nature, and he supported many experiments and initiatives to alleviate labour issues, and to promote the welfare of disadvantaged social groups, predominantly Jewish ones. His parents had emigrated to America during the troublesome European revolutionary mid-19th century, but he was particularly active in Britain after initially arriving in the country to expand his soap empire.

Joseph Fels made many contributions to Russian revolutionary progress, notably in 1907 when, in Britain, he funded the destitute delegates of the Fifth Congress of the Social Democratic Party. That Congress saw the conclusive emergence of Bolshevik supremacy, and the definition of revolutionary tactics, and it had been repeatedly banned in countries bordering Russia, hence its arrival in London. Many principal players including Lenin, Stalin, and Litvinov were present at this Congress, and shortly afterwards these three with others organised what became a notorious bank robbery in Georgia (U.S.S.R.) to gain funds for the Bolshevik cause. Nearly one hundred people were killed or injured during that fund-raising event.

For details of a book written by Fels' wife, Mary, (maiden name Rothschild), see:

## Finance, Politics, and the Media – Hegemony or Conspiracy?

http://archive.org/details/josephfelshislifoofels

That book, *Joseph Fels: His Life-Work* (1916), might be regarded as a practical account of reality, of which Adam Smith's *Wealth of Nations* might be considered an allegory. It is a true account of the often benevolent implementation of capital for the exploitation of labour in order to make profit, and it unashamedly promotes the objective of preserving Jewish cultural integrity and racial purity, a motive denied to others in an era of multicultural ideological servitude. Its interest in the context of the present book lies in its infinitely simpler background and innocent acceptance of what, in a politically correct Britain today, would most certainly be considered bigotry; such extreme judgement being mitigated by the fact that Fels' philosophy and expression is the product of a culture that is seen to be a minority and a victim, and by Fels' undoubted, if racially prejudiced, philanthropy. In other words, dual standards for some are fine if the betrayal suits the ideology.

1907 was also the year when what is now known as the Anglo-Dutch Shell Oil Company was formed by a merger of the Royal Dutch Oil Company and the British Shell Transport and Trading Company Ltd., founded by the Jewish Sir Marcus Samuel in association with his brother, Samuel Samuel. One of the principal drivers for the creation of the European-centred oil company was the growth of the U.S. Standard Oil Company, led by John Rockefeller. These two companies were the early 20$^{th}$ century equivalents of the present-day IT giants, with turnovers of around one percent of their host nations' GDP.

Standard Oil gave financial support to the Russian revolutionaries in exchange for oil rights in the U.S.S.R. after coveting the notable profits made there by Marcus Samuel, and many say that the early growth of the Soviet economy was largely due to American finance from, and investment by, a range of its biggest corporations and banks. Names, such as Rockefeller, J.P. Morgan, Warburg, R.C.A., Chase Manhattan and Westinghouse among many others, have been credited with funding the regime which rapidly became Stalin's personal tyranny – responsible for quite as much misery as any despotic state throughout history – an ugly example of the benefits of private enterprise and free capital markets.

Yet another Jewish-American entrepreneur, Armand Hammer of Ukrainian origin, whose father was heavily involved with the American Socialist Labour Party and later the Communist Party, was actively trading with the U.S.S.R. during its early period, starting on a small scale circa 1921 and increasing through to the Second World War, and then building up again afterwards and continuing through the Cold War period. He had brief dealings with Lenin at first, and he was continuously under FBI surveillance. His business interests ranged from small-scale pharmaceutical and consumer goods, through philanthropic grain missions to Russia, to his largest $billion U.S. company, Occidental Petroleum.

## 19.6 Dodgy Dealing U.K. Style

### 19.6.1 Introduction

In addition to the undisputed benefits to disadvantaged individuals and groups, charities facilitate the immoral abdication of responsibility by government and the exploitation of a naïve population by criminal and terrorist organisations. It would be instructive to consider the real root causes of the need for external aid in the first place, and why charitable organisations are necessary. Natural disasters are one thing, but ongoing famine as a result of the attempted occupation of uninhabitable regions of the world are quite another, as are cases of criminal cruelty to children and animals. Geopolitical hegemony and primitive tribal behaviour with automatic weapons should be controlled by the United Nations; a United Nations free of animosity and petulance, and without the coveting of natural resources and the strategic duplicity so often seen among its members. It can be done, but it is not done.

*Finance, Politics, and the Media – Hegemony or Conspiracy?*

## 19.6.2  Carbon Credit Trading

How much nonsense will we tolerate? – See:
http://fca.org.uk/consumers/scams/investment-scams/carbon-credit-trading

From the Financial Conduct Authority:

> *"A carbon credit is a certificate or permit which represents the right to emit one tonne of carbon dioxide ($CO_2$) and they can be traded for money.*
> *However, many investors have told us they are not able to sell or trade the carbon credits they have bought. None of these investors reported making a profit.*
> *This supports our view that there is not a viable secondary market for ordinary investors to sell or trade carbon credits, despite claims and promises made by many firms, advisers and brokers promoting and selling them as an investment.*
> *We have also received reports that an increasing number of firms are using dubious, high-pressure sales tactics to sell carbon credits to investors."*

## 19.6.3  Charities

There are more than 160,000 charities registered in Britain and one has to wonder how China and the Soviet Union for instance survive without such "benevolence".

Charities can be investigated via many key words in internet searches, but one or two starting links for further research might be:

https://www.gov.uk/government/organisations/charity-commission

http://en.wikipedia.org/wiki/Charity_Commission_for_England_and_Wales

http://en.wikipedia.org/wiki/List_of_charities_accused_of_ties_to_terrorism

### 19.6.4 Quasi Autonomous Government Organisations – Quangos

The promotion of Quangos is a clear statement of the inability of central government to cope with fiscal and social management. It may be represented as democratic devolution, and may be an unavoidable phenomenon when a nation reaches a certain tipping point.

While it is only a snapshot of a changing monster, the purpose of including this list is to give an idea of some of the less-well buried, hidden costs of government that are open to abuse, such as the direct or indirect funding of proscribed organisations, and the provision of aid to some foreign governments that have industrial, space and nuclear programmes in excess of our own. These are frequently, though not always, driven by ideology, and are often altered when governments change, that is to say that without doubt, some Quangos are undemocratic, and they facilitate entry into the fringes of the political arena of potentially corrupt bodies of activists and extremists.

Some references are:

http://www.theguardian.com/news/datablog/2009/jul/07/public-finance-regulators

http://www.taxpayersalliance.com/

http://www.taxpayersalliance.com/quangos_the_unseen_government_of_the_uk

http://www.telegraph.co.uk/news/politics/8063628/Quango-reform-full-list.html

*Finance, Politics, and the Media – Hegemony or Conspiracy?*

### 19.6.5 Think Tanks

These variously powerful and influential moguls represent a significant degree of outsourcing of political theory to unelected and unaccountable bodies. To whom are they responsible? What chains of extra-parliamentary lobbying do they facilitate? Who pays for them? Who benefits?

Some references are:

http://www.telegraph.co.uk/news/politics/1576447/The-top-twelve-think-tanks-in-Britain.html

https://en.wikipedia.org/wiki/List_of_think_tanks_in_the_United_Kingdom

http://www.theguardian.com/politics/2013/sep/30/list-thinktanks-uk

http://www.careers.ox.ac.uk/options-and-occupations/sectors-and-occupations/think-tanks/

http://www.theguardian.com/politics/thinktanks

### 19.6.6 Gordon Brown, and Think Tank and Charity Exploitation

This waster of British wealth betrayed some of his underlying motives in power when he added to a funding row that became news in January, 2008.

A *Daily Telegraph* newspaper article revealed plans backed by Brown that would politicise Britain's think-tanks, opening the way for them to become fronts for secret political donations. Additionally, the proposed changes were expected to allow and encourage charities to spend much of their time campaigning on contentious political issues, and yet the director of the think-tank Policy Exchange seemed most concerned that some philanthropists would take their money elsewhere, not that democracy might be undermined by yet more non-governmental and partisan lobbying according to financial clout – especially given the fact that, unlike political parties, charities are not obliged to make the sources of their funding known to the public; they are clearly beyond public scrutiny, and as warned by the Tories, charities could turn into lobbies that raise political funds with the objective of gaining influence by a back door.

### 19.6.7 Lobbyists

Definitions in this section are taken from the Public Affairs Council website: http://www.publicaffairscouncil.org.uk

#### 19.6.7.1 Definition of Lobbying and Related Matters

**Lobbying** means, in a professional capacity, attempting to influence, or advising those who wish to influence, the UK Government, Parliament, the devolved legislatures or administrations, regional or local government or other public bodies on any matter within their competence.

**Lobbyists** are those who, in a professional capacity, work to influence, or advise those who wish to influence, the institutions of government in the UK, with respect to:

- the formulation, modification or adoption of any legislative measure (including the development of proposals for legislation);
- the formulation, modification or adoption of a rule, regulation or any other programme, policy or position;
- the administration or execution of a governmental or other public programme or policy within the UK (including the negotiation, award or administration of a public contract, grant, loan, permit or licence).

**Institutions of government** means the UK Government, Parliament, the devolved legislatures or administrations, regional or local government or other public bodies.

**Public Affairs services** means the provision of:

- lobbying or advice on lobbying as defined above;
- services with intent to assist lobbying, including the provision of monitoring, public affairs and programme support, strategic communications advice, profile raising, decision-making analyses and perception auditing services.

**Public Affairs practitioner** means any individual who, in a professional capacity, provides, as a substantive and sustained part of their responsibilities, public affairs services as defined above.

### 19.6.7.2 Introduction to the Problem

The scandal of public servants taking payment in the form of bribes to represent partisan interests and to give clients preferential access to, and even influence over the decision making process of Parliament exploded into the news between 2009 and 2013, but the issue is not a new one.

The clients of the faithless and untrustworthy public servants are frequently professional lobbyists though many individuals seeking advantage are also involved in the scam.

The very first lobbyist was Charles Weller Kent who represented the National Farmers' Union from 1913 to 1916. His job title was Parliamentary Lobbyist, though he was principally a barrister and a journalist, and commentary on his life and role seems to make the arrogant assumption that parliamentary lobbying is an honourable vocation.

As may be seen in the two following references, many lobbying websites, as might be expected, give the impression of moneyed Management Consultancies, whereas at least one U.K. presence is something entirely different, and one example below (a blogsite not a website) betrays an attitude of presumptuous (*"...Lobbying is an essential part of a healthy democracy..."*) carping, though with an implied underlying tendency towards academia rather than commercialism.

In order to inflate their own egos and to create an impression of importance in the mind of the public, lobbying organisations sometimes use the pseudonyms *Public Affairs*, *Public Relations*, and *Interest Groups*.

### U.S. Style:
http://www.carmengroup.com/?gclid=CKinjeD8wrcCFQ3KtAodpz8ApA

### U.K. Style:
http://www.bell-pottinger.com/

http://www.unlockdemocracy.org.uk/pages/open-up-lobbying

http://standup4lobbying.wordpress.com

**Trans-Atlantic Style:**
http://www.conormcgrathpa.com/

### 19.6.7.3 A Handful of Betrayals

In 1994 a number of Conservative party members agreed to submit questions to Parliament in exchange for money. This became known as the Cash-For-Questions Scandal and seriously damaged the John Major Conservative Government. The main gamesters were Conservative MPs Neil Hamilton and Tim Smith who allegedly took cash from Mohamed Al Fayed, who owned Harrods at the time, to ask questions in Parliament in Al Fayed's interest. Al Fayed supported the story.

Ian Greer Associates, a firm of lobbyists was allegedly the broker of the bribes.

Smith owned up and resigned immediately, but Hamilton said he was innocent although he was forced to resign as corporate affairs minister and lost his seat in Parliament in 1997. Hamilton and Greer issued libel writs against the *Guardian*, but dropped them, and Hamilton also sued Al Fayed for libel and lost.

As a result of the scandal John Major established the "Committee on Standards in Public Life" to investigate overall declining standards in Parliament and in public life – it didn't stop the "Expenses Scandal" a decade later.

In January, 2009, four Labour Lords – Truscott, Taylor of Blackburn, Snape, and Moonie – were caught by an undercover investigation by the *Sunday Times* that claimed its reporters approached the men in the guise of lobbyists acting on behalf of a company interested in getting an exemption from business rates. All four socialist Peers of the Realm were alleged to have offered to help pass amendments to proposed legislation if they were paid something like £120,000.

Taylor and Truscott were found to have breached the Lords Code of Conduct by *"failing to act on their personal honour"*, although Snape and Moonie were cleared – Taylor and Truscott thereby becoming the first members of the House of Lords to be suspended since 1642.

## Finance, Politics, and the Media – Hegemony or Conspiracy?

In March, 2010, the *Sunday Times* and the Channel 4 Dispatches programme alleged that three former Labour cabinet ministers had indicated that they were willing to help a lobbying firm if they were paid cash. Former Transport Secretary, Stephen Byers, was filmed saying that he was like a *"cab for hire"*, and that he would work for up to £5,000 a day; former Defence Secretary, Geoff Hoon, said he would make use of his knowledge and contacts and that his fee was £3,000 a day; and the last allegation involved the former Health Secretary Patricia Hewitt, said to have claimed that she helped obtain a seat on a government advisory group for a client who paid her £3,000 a day.

For *"bringing the Parliamentary Labour Party into disrepute"*, all three were suspended, and Byers and Hoon were later found guilty of a *"serious breach of parliamentary rules"*, but Hewitt was cleared. David Cameron who was Leader of the Opposition said at the time that the revelations would make the public think all MPs were *"sleazy pigs"*.

October 2011 saw the resignation of Cameron's own Defence Secretary, Liam Fox, following pressure concerning his working relationship with a friend and adviser, Adam Werritty, who was a former flatmate of Fox, and who had been Fox's best man at his wedding.

Werritty had apparently visited Fox several times at the Ministry of Defence, had accompanied him on foreign trips where he met diplomats and contractors in the defence industry, and had even given his own business card to defence staff in a way that suggested he was an official adviser to Fox. All this with no official government role.

An investigation found that Fox had breached the Ministerial Code, but he was cleared of gaining financially or having breached national security; he brazenly said there had been no impropriety.

## Finance, Politics, and the Media – Hegemony or Conspiracy?

In December, 2011, undercover reporters with the *Independent* newspaper allegedly found that a former Conservative MP and Bell Pottinger executive, Tim Collins, had boasted that the *"public affairs company"* (Lobbyists) had access to government. Collins had apparently told reporters:

> *'I've been working with people like Steve Hilton, David Cameron, and George Osborne for 20 years-plus. There is not a problem getting the messages through."*

Downing Street, of course, said the reported claims were a *"gross exaggeration"*.

Peter Cruddas, Conservative Party co-treasurer, resigned in March, 2012, after being secretly filmed apparently offering access to the P.M., David Cameron, in exchange for a party donation of £250,000 a year.

The claim was made to *Sunday Times* reporters who were posing as possible donors. Cruddas said that £250,000 would give "premier league" access, and dinner with David Cameron *"...with the possibility of influencing government policy"*.

A *Daily Telegraph* investigation in March, 2013, disclosed that councillors across the country were offering themselves for hire to property developers. This line up at the trough was prompted because imminent new and relaxed planning laws would allow all local authorities that did not have a plan for development in their area would be expected to approve any application which could be said to be a "sustainable development". Since it isn't illegal for councillors to work as paid consultants, and due to almost half of all councils having failed to agree local plans, the councillors expected, and presumably got, a bonanza – fees of up to £20,000 for advice on getting developments approved are believed to have been common, this despite an apparent conflict of interest.

June, 2013, saw Patrick Mercer, Conservative MP for Newark, quit his post after a *Daily Telegraph* and BBC Panorama programme found he had tabled questions and motions in Parliament after taking thousands of pounds from fake lobbyists who claimed interests in Fiji.

Mercer apparently tabled several questions to ministers and lodged a parliamentary motion after receiving an advance payment of £4,000 for what he thought would bring him a regular £24,000 a year. Mercer is accused merely of failing to declare payments received after signing a contract with what he believed to be a lobbying firm.

### 19.6.7.4 Lobby Bill – the Passage Through Parliament

Given the small selection above that is only an example of the few who have been caught, and there are doubtless many who have not been and who will never be exposed, one might think that a Bill to stop the rampant corruption would be welcomed.

The reverse seems to be the case given some of the outrageous filibustering attempted by the MPs debating a Bill to introduce legislation that would require lobbying companies and individuals to be registered. From Hansard, one of the respondent's words are as follows:

Thomas Docherty (Dunfermline and West Fife) (Lab): I beg to move, that the Bill be now read a Second time.

... and later – Thomas Docherty was obliged to respond:

> *I am surprised that Ministers are reluctant to have a code of conduct, and I hope the Minister responding to this debate will set out why they are reluctant. The hon. Gentleman is right that it would be helpful to have a code of conduct. If it helps provide reassurance, perhaps I should give a guarantee that I would bring forward a draft code of conduct prior to any Committee stage of this Bill.*

### 19.6.7.5 Lobby Bill – Progress and Prognosis

In April, 2013:

According to the *Guardian* newspaper, more than 100 lobbying professionals still held parliamentary passes that they received from the House of Lords, and senior managers of "Interest Groups" and of some businesses still have passes despite Coalition Government promises to change the perception and practice of lobbying.

### 19.6.8 The Most Corrupt British Public Figures in Living Memory

Although clouded by some dubious and vitriolic conspiracy theorists, and frequently a taboo subject, there is clear evidence that often by invitation of the host nations, the money trade has been continuously exploited by a culture that has international and historical continuity – the Jews – who are part of all societies and who often take inconspicuous names but high profile credits for infamy. A couple of the most notorious exploiters of the wider public, who just happen to be Jews, are said to be Dame Shirley Porter, once Conservative leader of Westminster City Council, and Robert Maxwell MP, one time owner of Mirror Group Newspapers. Both have been described in the press as:

> "... the most corrupt British public figure[s] in living memory..."

Reference:
http://www.theguardian.com/books/2007/mar/24/politicalbooks.biography

Maxwell, at least, exploited countless thousands of the British working class, and Porter virtually gave away public assets and caused working class misery in order to support Conservative Party objectives. Porter allegedly continues to benefit financially from her privileged position as an heiress of her father Sir Jack Cohen's Tesco supermarket fortune, and every time a meek and milked member of the public makes a purchase from Tesco they are lining the pockets of the dynasty of which Porter is, at least, a part.

Porter lived in Israel for a while and continued to direct profits, allegedly, in part at least, from her interest in Tesco to philanthropic causes in Israel. She returned to London in August, 2008, after some years in a state of self-imposed exile, and a quote from *The Insider* is as follows:

Reference:

http://www.theinsider.org/news/article.asp?id=2138

> *"Dame Shirley Porter, the corrupt Jewish politician who was caught rigging an election and manipulating the political system, has returned to London today from her self-imposed exile in Israel. The shamed "Dame" is a billionaire heiress of the major international retail corporation, Tesco. Her most famous scams include selling properties owned by the local authority to loyal voters, selling local graveyards owned by the local authority to speculators for 5 pence each (about 2 cents) – without even informing any of the people whose loves ones were buried there, and forcing poor and homeless residents out of the area – openly describing it as an "expulsion" and "good riddance".*

Original sources of the detail were:

http://www.independent.co.uk/news/uk/this-britain/after-12-years-dame-shirley-is-back-in-westminster-411001.html

and

http://www.theguardian.com/uk/2006/aug/07/conservatives.politics

Porter's opinion of herself might be inferred from the website:
http://www.dameshirleyporter.net/

Maxwell, who in 1971 had been the subject of a British Board of Trade inquiry, and had been declared unfit to run a public company, was buried with the equivalent of a state funeral on the Mount of Olives in Jerusalem. This abominably selfish and greedy pig is best remembered in Britain for defrauding the Mirror Group pension Fund to the extent of almost half a billion pounds, and consigning thousands of English pensioners to a miserable existence on about half of what they were due in pension payments. Much of this money was channelled to Israel.

The list of such international thieves appears to have increased still further during 2016 – to the detriment of yet more English pensioners.

### 19.6.8.1 The Unique Case of Switzerland

Starting as the likely source of Celtic culture in the $1^{st}$ millennium BC, developing an identity by the $13^{th}$ or $14^{th}$ century, and becoming independent of the Holy Roman Empire in 1499, Switzerland adopted a federal constitution in 1848 and is currently ranked as the world's largest private banking centre. The country is host to more than 500 major banks, and it is estimated that as much as 35% of global private wealth is held in Switzerland. On $24^{th}$ August, 2010, a deadline was set for UBS AG to provide the U.S. Internal Revenue Service with the names of more than four thousand Americans with Swiss offshore accounts – the U.S. Department of Justice had issued Switzerland with the deadline which, if missed, could have led to UBS losing its US operating licence. The harvest from this clamp-down is unclear, but on-going.

## 20 The Onset of Egalitarianism and Governance by Statute
### 20.1 Introduction

This chapter looks at increasing involvement and intervention in geopolitical events by the Commoner, and changes to the imposition of the rule of law made by the governing body.

There was a strengthening over the $2^{nd}$ millennium of traditional European-wide Medieval *Estates*, and in Britain, the three usual divisions were reinforced by the concept of Norman feudalism. In France in 1789, the *Estates General* marked the end of multi-class councils, and it was the predecessor of a series of embittered revolutionary councils that descended into the "Reign of Terror", from which France would deliver itself just before Napoleon arrived on the scene in 1799.

Although there were small variations throughout Europe and Imperial Russia, three principal estates formed the following hierarchy, being headed by the agents of God:

1. The Clergy.
2. The Nobility.
3. The Commoner.

In addition to the above three principal estates, there was often an even lower level of humanity – Serfs and Peasants – and coincidentally, it was in 1787 that the term "fourth estate" came into use in Britain to denote the press, or in modern times, the media.

Returning to the Post Medieval Age, there would be regular conflict and jockeying among the first two estates, Clergy and Nobility, and occasional revolutionary leapfrogging from the bottom – Commoner, and Serf or Peasant. The French Estates General at the time of the revolution of 1789 was a general assembly of the first three estates in an attempt to resolve the crippling economic collapse and famine of the time.

In the present-day British Parliament, the estates are manifest as two houses:

- The Upper – The Lords Spiritual and Temporal – a combination of Estates 1 and 2.
- The Lower – The Commons.

The rest of us in $3^{rd}$ millennium reality have no representation once a Member of Parliament has been elected, and the likelihood of the raising of a constituent's real interests in parliament may be somewhat better than the probability of winning the lottery, but it is nevertheless negligible. See the comment concerning the result of the 2015 General Election in the sub-section below titled *The Great Reform Act 1832 and the Chartist Movement*.

Other than Parliament, modern conceptual branches of the United Kingdom Government, can be listed as:

- The Legislature (law making).
- The Judiciary (law application and decision making).
- The Executive (law enforcement).

In order to achieve day-to-day governance, the formal branches above are supported by Banks (both private and Central), the Media, and theoretically (because the United Kingdom is effectively a secular nation) by the Church of England; although the Church also has active representatives in the Upper House in the persons of Lords as seen above. Further extra-governmental support comes from Quangos and Think Tanks.

Politicians court favours from all these estates, and entertain lobbyists for both strategic and personal gains – gains that usually remain confidential, but which are sometimes revealed as scandals, as seen in the United Kingdom in the spring of 2013. See the chapter in Volume Two titled *Rotten to the Core – A Feral Host*.

In non-secular and non-monarchical nations the Church might be one of the estates, for example Iran and other nations that live under Sharia Law, and to an increasing extent Turkey and Egypt in 2013, although a backlash kept Egypt under a secular military dictatorship in 2014.

In the 3$^{rd}$ millennium the introduction of Sharia courts into Britain is a reality – increasingly so with the increasing Islamic population of Britain, and the burgeoning distribution of mosques – and this represents the greatest threat to Egalitarianism that Britain has seen for possibly a millennium. There are estimated to be between 1,000 and 2,000 mosques in 2013. An online database resource that refers to around 1,444 of that number can be found at:

http://www.salaam.co.uk/mosques/index.php.

## 20.2 Parliament and the Judiciary - Evolution and Divergence

When and by what authority do customs become laws?

### 20.2.1 From Antiquity

Before the Royal House of Wessex that began with the reign of King Cerdic, who arrived in Hampshire circa 495 AD, early forms of government or parliamentary sessions or councils around England differed according to the cultural roots of the local community. Nordic tribes held a *Thing*, and Germanic tribes held a *Folkmoot*. From the 6$^{th}$ century to the 11$^{th}$ century, the evolving and ascendant Anglo-Saxon culture held a *Witenagemot* also known as a *Witan*. All such councils had their roots in the ancient and laudable tribal principle of sitting round the fire to strengthen the tribe's identity and authority in whatever way seemed appropriate and in context at the time, and according to customs that originated in a forgotten antiquity.

In that antiquity it seems reasonable to believe that early human societies would have seen their governance as a single process that shaped customary behaviour into an obligation both to and by the group, and that assumed a reasonable or at least honourable benevolence from the alpha males, much as happens elsewhere in the animal kingdom. The degree of retribution towards those that departed from custom was not entirely predictable, but it was expected, understood, and would have been applauded by any innocent bystanders whenever it happened – especially because it was happening to someone else, making the innocents feel more inclusive. Perhaps such circumstances were related to the concepts of, on the one hand *schadenfreude*, and on the other hand an active attempt to become surrounded by a crowd in the case of trouble – a bit like the instinctive bait-ball behaviour of fish under attack by a predator.

The precise role of the Saxon Witan is unclear, but in addition to supporting the King, it is believed to have had considerable powers that included the ability to choose and terminate a King's rule. This happened in the case of Sigeberht of Wessex (756 to 757) who was ultimately killed, and also in the case of the reinstatement in 1014 of Æthelred the Unready, on whom were placed conditions that he "*must do better*". No doubt the extent to which power was wielded would have depended on the relative strengths of character of all involved – much as during subsequent centuries.

Other powers of the Witan would have included the setting of taxation, the issuing of Charters and Statutes, the facilitation of appeals and petitions to the King, grants of land, legal matters, church matters, and military policy both domestic and foreign; although it should be noted that the division of authority between the King and his subjects, and the importance of the consent of each within the Witan, is a contentious subject and is open to present-day interpretation.

One such source of information is: *English Constitutional History From The Teutonic Conquest to the Present Time* by Taswell-Langmead, Thomas Pitt. Third Edition 1886.

Reference:

https://archive.org/details/ed3englishconstiootasw


Witan sessions were called by the King as necessary, but at least annually, and they were attended by nobles, aldermen, thanes, abbots and bishops. The exact composition also varied according to need and the convenience of its location, but it has been said that every freeman had a right to attend.

## The Onset of Egalitarianism and Governance by Statute

Locally, *Shire Moots* were regularly convened in each county to hear and try legal cases under age-old Common Law, and to discuss local issues; they were attended by local lords and bishops, the sheriff, and four representatives of each village.

Superstition and social deference were and are slow to change – they governed reason 10,000 years ago at a tribal level and they still do today. Over the millennia, however, and by common acquiescence, customs gradually became law and, growing in importance, they suited the ambitions of those who were otherwise unable or unwilling to materially benefit society – informers and lawyers were born, and there was profit and power to be gained by ensuring a level of sophistication and mystery that could not easily be penetrated by the masses. In law as in religion, and the two were frequently linked, elitism and pompous cronyism ruled, and a proliferation of legal and ecclesiastical councils made life that much sweeter and lucrative for the enlightened elite.

In the more sophisticated times that followed the Medieval Age (1066 and later) when it came to the administration of justice as a consequence of the enforcement of laws and customs, that is to say, the formal correction and punishment within the Nation-State, it was the *source* of the laws – the particular administrative body that made the laws – that mainly determined the differentiation of evolving councils and courts; and that tendency continued until the end of the 19th century. From the start of the 20th century things changed, and court structure became defined more by the *subject and severity of cases*, rather than by the *sources of the laws*.

Those older judicial sources have become obfuscated, and knowledge of them has become ever more esoteric; and that obfuscation, combined with a stupefying accumulation of Statutes and Acts over one thousand years, has confounded the ancient precepts of Common Law, the loss of which, just like the loss of Common Land, most certainly does not favour the Common Man.

### 20.2.2 The Corporation of the City of London

According to an article in the *New Statesman* on 24th February, 2011, a 19th century reformer described the City of London Corporation as a:

> "...prehistoric monster which had mysteriously survived into the modern world."

Geographically, the Corporation occupies the site of an ancient settlement that was known during the Roman occupation as Londinium, but which is acknowledged on the Corporation's own website as being of older Celtic origin – Londinion. The site is also described in Geoffrey of Monmouth's work *History of the Kings of Britain* as being the seat of King Lud who was an Ancient Briton-Welshman with an even older pedigree. Ludgate and Ludgate Hill, on which stands St. Paul's Cathedral, are named after him.

Usually known simply as the City or the Square Mile, it covers about 1.2-square-miles of the centre of London, and it hosts the Bank of England and many other British public and private financial institutions, plus many foreign-owned global corporations. From Medieval times until 2006 it was known as the Corporation of London, and it has its own Member of Parliament with an additional parliamentary observer known as *The Remembrancer*, an unelected lobbyist who sits next to the Speaker in the Commons, and who has a similar seat in the House of Lords – a sort of spy in both Houses of Parliament – and who is an extra representative of the interests of the Corporation, but who is frequently described by critics as a representative specifically of the bankers.

The City of London Corporation has its own administrative centre known as Guildhall, it has its own Lord Mayor of London that is quite distinct from the Mayor of London, and it has its own Police Authority.

Its origins as a totally independent authority within Britain go back to the Norman Conquest when William the Conqueror introduced Jewish money-changers to Britain to manage the nation's finances, and the

## The Onset of Egalitarianism and Governance by Statute

isolated and elitist ceremonies and practices began then and have not ceased.

It is said that the principal business of the Corporation nowadays is the management of large financial interests, for the beneficiaries of those interests, across a raft of international tax havens – mostly British overseas territories of some description – ranging from the Channel Islands to such dichotomies of welfare as the islands of the Caribbean – but also including non-British repositories of black money such as Switzerland. In that respect the City of London Corporation is the hub of global tax evasion, and a paragon of the lack of accountability to the general public.

The blatant public relations glitz of the Corporation's website, coupled with the fact that the voters in that Authority's local elections who send a Member of Parliament to the English Palace of Westminster include alien corporate bodies such as the U.S. Goldman Sachs Corporation and Chinese Banks, only makes the Corporation more sinister in terms of the welfare of the general British public as opposed to the welfare of corporate institutions and the cultural elite that has the greatest share in those international organisations.

Why should Goldman Sachs, for instance, have a voice in the English parliament?

The Corporation's system of Livery Companies, and the truly esoteric processes of gaining membership of the Corporation as a Freeman are beyond the scope of this book. Suffice to say that, despite exposés and popular movements, and despite declarations of intent by some Prime Ministers, all efforts to remove the inequitable governance and to rectify the illegitimate provenance of this pompous and predatory maverick over the last several decades have failed. The Corporation's budget is large enough to convert any doubters, and the heads of all mainstream political parties are mired with *benefits* of one sort or another from its continuation.

References:
http://www.newstatesman.com/economy/2011/02/london-corporation-city

http://www.cityoflondon.gov.uk/Pages/default.aspx

### 20.2.3 Norman Change

Immediately after the Norman Conquest in 1066 a feudal system that was defined by the possession of land was introduced, and Anglo-Saxon systems were replaced by Norman systems; the Shire Moot evolved into the County Court – the beginning of local government – and centuries later, the Witan and the Shire Moot would manifest themselves as the two Houses of Parliament, the application of the law being separated out and administered in the Courts of Justice.

Under the feudal system land was granted, and in return, services and labour were provided to the landlord; the granting of land relied on the identification of Lord and Vassal, and the establishment of a binding relationship between them. This binding relationship was ratified by a formal Commendation Ceremony at which there was an act of Homage (submission) and the swearing of an Oath of Fealty. From older traditions of Vassalage it was said that *"...The lord's man might be born unfree, but the Commendation Ceremony freed him"*. Some freedom!

Descriptions of Norman councils vary among historical sources.

The "Norman Curia Regis" – the King's or Royal Court – was a permanent inner council of advisers and officials and persisted until circa 1215, in many ways replacing the Witan. It was composed of Tenants-in-Chief who held land granted directly from the King. During the 13th century it was referred to as the "King's Council in Parliament", and was the basis for the first true parliament, or Model Parliament of 1295. (This was largely a result of the earlier and illegal parliament called by Simon de Montfort in 1265). The Curia Regis was, at the very least, an assembly of courtiers that would be in attendance at all times.

The "Norman Magnum Concilium" – Great Council or House of Lords – was a larger group of noble advisers especially summoned from time to time to support the Curia Regis (though considered inferior to it) and it comprised lay and ecclesiastical magnates. It was last called in 1640 and then became extinct.

The "Norman Commune Concilium" was composed of baronial councillors bound to the King by feudal ties; of this council, William

Stubbs (1825 to 1901) says in his book, *The Constitutional History of England in its Origin and Development*, that *"...Qualification for membership was [no longer] official wisdom, but [possession of land]"*, and its decisions of a judicial, civil, or military type were considered binding on the vassals. It was known in later medieval times within the Corporation of the City of London as the "Court of Common Council", and was used, for example, to regulate various traders and brokers in food, and commodity markets.

According to Sir Edward Coke (1552 to 1634), Magnum Concilium, Commune Concilium, Commune Concilium Regis, and Commune Concilium Regni were all essentially the same council. Coke was a lawyer, a renowned judge, and an MP; he was one of the foremost supporters of the Common Law, and he defended it against assaults by the "Courts of Equity" and by the Stuarts, particularly James I (1603 to 1625).

In summary, regardless of the label given to any one of the Norman councils, they carried out judicial and executive functions entirely on the basis of advice from a landed gentry that was increasingly Norman, and decreasingly Anglo-Saxon-English in character. Unsurprisingly, in the face of such attrition, a diaspora of Anglo-Saxon talent took place that reached the limits of the western civilised world, for example as far as taking mercenary employment in the elite regiments that guarded the emperors of the Byzantine Empire, regiments that were known as the Varengian aka Varangian Guard.

### 20.2.4 Keepers and Justices of the Peace

Keepers of the Peace were commissioned from among the knights in 1195 by King Richard I, and they were answerable to him; their job was to ensure the King's Peace in unlawful areas.

From 1199 Grants of official positions, land, and commissions were made by the Monarch as Letters Patent – open letters – and were issued under the Great Seal.

In 1327 an Act (1 Edw. 3 Stat. 2 ...Justices of the Peace c. 16) had referred to *"...good and lawful men"* to be appointed in every county to guard the Peace, and subsequently, Justices of the Peace were appointed in every county by Edward III from 1361. From 1361 to the early 19th century when the present system of local government was introduced, Justices of the Peace, on behalf of the Monarch, did most of the judicial work of England and Wales. During that period they also headed local administration, set wage levels, oversaw infrastructure development (roads, bridges and developing water and sewerage systems), and managed all local services that the Monarch and Parliament deemed necessary for the nation's well-being. More detail may be found in a 1938 book by B. H. Putnam titled *Proceedings Before The Justices Of The Peace In The 14th And 15th Centuries*.

### 20.2.5 Commission of the Peace – County Level

As a consequence of this statutory recognition of the need for micro-management at a county level, there was a Commission of the Peace for each county, and JPs were and still are inscribed on it to enshrine their duties, at a local level, to the nation – both Monarch and subjects. Of the Commission of the Peace, Blackstone says:

> *"But it is not as a juror only that the English gentleman is called upon to determine questions of right, and distribute justice to his fellow-subjects: it is principally with this order of men that the commission of the peace is filled. And here a very ample field is opened for a gentleman to exert his talents, by maintaining good order in his neighbourhood; by punishing the dissolute and idle; by protecting the peaceable and industrious; and, above all, by healing petty differences, and preventing vexatious prosecutions. But, in order to attain these desirable ends, it is necessary that the magistrate should understand his business; and have not only the will, but the power also, (under which must be included the knowledge,) of administering legal and effectual justice. Else, when he has mistaken his authority, through passion, through ignorance, or absurdity, he will be the object of contempt from his*

*inferiors, and of censure from those to whom he is accountable for his conduct."*

Nowadays, apart from judicial work, JPs are best known for their responsibilities for the licensing of premises selling alcohol. JPs were appointed on the basis of their undisputed local power in socio-economic terms; they were either land owners or prominent merchants, and then and now, no accountable certification was or is involved as a pre-requisite, though some magistrates are qualified lawyers.

### 20.2.6 Quarter Sessions

The Justice of the Peace Act of 1361 (34 Edw. III Justices of the Peace c. 1) provided that JPs should meet four times a year to conduct local business. These Quarter Sessions were later (1388) named as *Epiphany* (Jan–Mar), *Easter* (Apr–Jun), *Midsummer* (Jul–Sept) and *Michaelmas* (Oct–Dec), and they survived until they were replaced by Crown Courts in January 1972, as part of the 1971 Courts Act.

Under an Act of 1389 (13 Ric. II Justice of the Peace Act c. 7), JPs received a subsistence allowance of four shillings a day. This was rarely historically paid, and has not been paid in recent times, but it was in the same year, 1389, that the first Game Law was passed, and disfigurement and other harsh penal revenge by JPs themselves and other landlords was legalised. JPs frequently found themselves passing sentence on poachers who were their own tenants, and who might have been merely trying to feed their families in the face of variable harvests due to weather, increased taxes and capped wages. Taxes, price fixing, and wages were also a subject of Acts in this year, and they were also enforced by the same JPs. These administrative duties of JPs continued until 1888, and during the middle and late 19th century they often found themselves in competition with other landowners for labour and markets particularly in the wool industry. (see Cobbett, Coke and Blackstone).

By 1600 more than 50 editions of works for the guidance of JPs had been published, but in terms of welfare it was definitely a case of one law for the rich and one for the poor, and Sir Edward Coke commented on the judicial system in the following terms:

> "... such a form of subordinate government for security and quiet of the realm as no part of the Christian world hath the like."

From his writings he does seem to have been, if not a philanthropist, at least an original thinker at a time of huge differentials, and although it may not have been particularly his own intention, subordination and silencing of the populace was the clear result, if not the immediate objective, of many Acts of Parliament.

### 20.2.7 Parish and Village Constables and Religious Loyalty

Parish Constables and village constables appeared in 1576. These were unpaid parishioners who were conscripted for annual service, but religious and sovereign turbulence during the 16$^{th}$ and 17$^{th}$ centuries, and rivalry among proponents of Protestantism and Catholicism led to much unrest at all levels of the realm, and to an understandable spread of a lack of faith and a leaning towards secularism. Some JPs were also considered neglectful and incapable, and the justice system was under threat and in danger of fragmentation to such an extent that there was even a suggestion that the judicial system might be privatised, as alluded to by Queen Elizabeth I's Lord Keeper:

> "Her Majesty may be driven, clean contrary to her most gracious nature and inclination, to appoint and assign private men for profit and gain sake to see her penal laws to be executed".

This wake-up call, together with the inquisition-related attention of bishops from 1564, led to a requirement in 1579 for JPs to swear an oath of fidelity to the religion of the time, and so restored order and some stability just in time to help present a unified response to the Spanish Armada in 1588.

## 20.2.8 The Poor Laws and the Marriage Ceremony

The duties of JPs were redefined in 1590 by a new Commission, and in 1597 they became responsible for administering the Poor Law by an Act for the Relief of the Poor that obliged JPs to build and administer Houses of Correction where unruly elements of society like thieves, rogues, and vagabonds could be detained. The JPs would usually appoint unwilling Overseers of the Poor from among landowners, and from employees of the Church such as churchwardens to do the work, and a series of refinements to the Poor Laws were made during the next few centuries.

An Act of 1652 empowered JPs to perform marriages, and made all other forms of the marriage ceremony illegal.

Up to the Restoration of the Monarchy in 1660 there was a shift in the balance of JPs, with nobles being reduced in favour of esquires. This was reversed after the Restoration, with James II actively attempting to establish a majority of his cronies among JPs, these JPs being responsible for the repression of dissenters who had become more vociferous and varied after the heady days of the British Republic.

The Glorious Revolution of 1688, that saw William of Orange replace James II, led to a less enlightened shift backwards towards feudalism when in 1700, as a result of increased emphasis on property qualification rather than religious or political allegiances, 74 JPs in Middlesex were removed from the Commission of the Peace. Additionally, the property qualification had not been changed since 1439, and so it was raised, and this shift in emphasis was introduced into statute in 1732; twelve years later it was declared that it was *"...of the utmost consequence to provide against persons of mean estates"* being appointed. *"Only men of substance"* were then appointed by the Lord Lieutenant, and this was effectively on the recommendation of the Crown.

Not such a Glorious Revolution after all for *"...persons of mean estates"*.

### 20.2.9 Petty Sessions

Courts of Petty Sessions originated in the 16<sup>th</sup> century when local groups of JPs gathered to deal with *petty* issues, such as vagrancy (victims could be branded with a "V"), minor crimes, routine grants of licenses, poor relief, and anything that could reduce the load on the Quarter Sessions that were becoming overwhelmed. They gradually became more formalised, and in 1605 an order of the Privy Council identified and acknowledged Local Sessions that could be held without a jury; these became known as Petty Sessions with two or more JPs and a local attorney acting as clerk, and they were eventually enshrined in statute in 1828 (9 Geo. IV c.43) when County Justices were authorised to divide their counties into Petty Sessional Districts.

### 20.2.10 Municipal Corporations Act 1835

From 1829 to 1888 some of the JPs' administrative duties were transferred to the growing local government authority. Before the Municipal Corporations Act 1835 JPs had derived their office by Charter, but after the Act, they were nominated for the boroughs by the Lord Chancellor in consultation with local advisers, and for the county benches, by the Lord Lieutenants, and then confirmed by the Lord Chancellor; the ultimate appointment of both was made by the Crown with the advice of the Lord Chancellor. In the Duchy of Lancaster alone, both county and borough magistrates were nominated by the Chancellor of the Duchy.

### 20.2.11 Social Darwinism 1870

At home and abroad this was an era of very significant changes, both philosophically and politically. There was the emergence of Germany and Italy as unified Nation-States, and the continuing appearance of revolutionary movements throughout Europe; the European empires continued their expansion into Africa against a background of slavery that had been abolished by most European nations, but that was continued by Arab slavers; and last but certainly not least, there was the consolidation of the U.S. Federal Empire in the Americas following its cathartic Civil War of 1861 to 1865 – an enormous refuge for any and all dissidents and refugees of persecution in Europe.

### 20.2.12 The Rise of Liberalism

A few of the principal actors on this stage, warming the audience for the main act – Liberalism – were Thomas Henry Huxley, Jean-Baptiste Lamarck, Joseph Fisher, Herbert Spencer, Thomas Malthus, Francis Galton, and Richard Hofstadter. Their specific mindset and their contributions for good or bad are beyond the current scope, but they can be identified easily via search engines on the internet.

In 1906 in Britain the Liberals challenged the appointment system which favoured Conservatives, and for county magistrates the property qualification was abolished which led to an increase in Liberal JPs to almost 50% of the Commission. This was ratified in 1910 by a Royal Commission on the Appointment of Justices of the Peace which recommended an Advisory Committee system, and by the end of 1911, Advisory Committees with usually balanced Liberal and Conservative representation had been set up in most counties to advise Lords Lieutenants on nominations. A decade or so later Advisory Committees were in place for the boroughs as well. Until 1925, appointment to these committees was for life, but after 1925 a system of six year appointments and enforced retirement was introduced. Around this time, in 1920, a Magistrates' Association was formed to formalise the dissemination of guidelines and knowledge necessary for fair and consistent justice. Women JPs began to appear, and membership of the association grew from an initial 563 to 27,000 in about 80 years.

The Criminal Justice Act 1948 and the Justices of the Peace Act 1949 gave the Petty Sessions more autonomy and local accountability, and focussed attention on the progress of voluntary magistrate training (or lack of it), leading in 1966 to the introduction by the Lord Chancellor of compulsory training for all newly appointed magistrates.

The Justices of the Peace Act 1968 formalised the relationship between the Court Clerk who had the legal knowledge, and the Justice of the Peace who had no formal qualification, but who took responsibility for assessing facts and witnesses and pronouncing sentence, or deferring to a higher court. More than 90% of cases in the criminal courts are handled in this way today. The age of retirement for JPs was also reduced from 75 to 70.

## 20.2.13 The End of the Courts of Assizes and Quarter Sessions

As a result of The Courts Act 1971, 600 years of legal practice was amended when the courts of Assizes and Quarter Sessions were replaced by a single new Crown Court. The Act also increased the powers of JPs by giving them full jurisdiction over England and Wales, and it was described by Lord Hailsham (Quintin Hogg) in the following superlative terms:

> "...by far the biggest measure of law reform in this particular field for at least a century and, in some respects, since the institution of the assize system in the reign of Henry II".

The Criminal Justice Act 1972 and Local Government Act 1972 formalised the division of central and local funding.

In 1974 Courts of Petty Sessions were replaced by Magistrates' Courts with the following formalised administrative duties: licensing of public houses, licensed victuallers, clubs, restaurants, cinemas, lodging houses, premises licensed for liquor, music, dancing, and premises registered for the storage of explosives.

On 1st April, 1992, the Lord Chancellor assumed responsibility for the administration of Magistrates' Courts.

Police and Magistrates' Courts Act 1994 – despite initial criticisms that the Act represented an attack on democratic accountability, an independent study concluded that local police authorities were actually being re-invigorated. It replaced an earlier Police Act of 1964 and defined police authority areas, and the relationship with the government in the person of the Home Secretary. Magistrates' Court Committees were also rationalised to improve performance and accountability all the way to the Lord Chancellor.

The Police Act 1996 amended the above Act, and a series of Courts Acts deriving from various reviews, white papers, and the 2001 publication named *Review of the Criminal Courts of England and Wales*, led to the demise of Magistrates' Court Committees, and the creation in 2005, of Her Majesty's Courts Service that was responsible for the Court Service (that embraced County and Crown Courts), and the roles of the defunct Magistrates' Court Committees.

Part 3 of The Constitutional Reform Act 2005 established the "Supreme Court" that would become the interface between the European Union judiciary and the U.K. judiciary, and on the first day of October 2009, the Supreme Court replaced the Appellate Committee of the House of Lords as the highest court in the United Kingdom. This was a significant milestone in the constitutional history of Britain – the highest Court of Justice for Britons was now in Brussels.

Finally, in 2011 Her Majesty's Courts Service merged with the Tribunals Service to form Her Majesty's Courts and Tribunals Service.

**Conclusion**: There has indeed been *some considerable change* from the presumed, simple system of sitting round the camp-fire and getting a kicking, biting and scratching from one's tribal peers as a penalty for any misdemeanour.

## 20.3 The Court Structure Now – Buried Within the EU

The two diagrammes below show how the United Kingdom's Supreme Court is now embedded within the European Court of Justice, where it has the role of negotiating any discrepancies between federal and state judicial processes.

With acknowledgement of the copyright of the website of the Supreme Court (see link below) it is proposed to present extracts that summarise the latest developments, and that put them in a historical context according to the Supreme Court itself.

The first President of The Supreme Court, from October 2009 to September 2012, was Nicholas Addison Phillips, Baron Phillips of Worth Matravers KG PC. He had followed a career in the Royal Navy and the Judiciary.

The second and current (2015) President from 2012 is The Right Hon. Lord Neuberger of Abbotsbury, previously Master of the Rolls from 1st October, 2009. He worked as a Merchant Banker at N M Rothschild & Sons and then in the Judiciary.

### 20.3.1 www.supremecourt.uk – Terms and Conditions

Terms and Conditions for the use of material are as follows:

> *The material featured on this site is subject to Crown copyright protection unless otherwise indicated. The Crown copyright protected material (other than the Royal Arms and departmental or agency logos) may be reproduced free of charge in any format or medium provided it is reproduced accurately and not used in a misleading context.*
> *Where any of the Crown copyright items on this site are being republished or copied to others, the source of the material must be identified and the copyright status acknowledged.*

That copyright is hereby acknowledged.

### 20.3.2 Appellate Committee of The House of Lords

https://www.supremecourt.uk/about/appellate-committee.html

> *The judicial role of the House of Lords evolved over more than 600 years: originally from the work of the royal court, the "Curia Regis", which advised the sovereign, passed laws and dispensed justice at the highest level.*
> *Until 1399, both Houses of Parliament heard petitions for the judgments [sic] of lower courts to be reversed. After this date, the House of Commons stopped considering such cases, leaving the House of Lords as the highest court of appeal. (By custom, the whole House of Lords could sit as a court on special occasions, such as the trial of one of their own members).*
> *In 1876, the Appellate Jurisdiction Act was passed to regulate how appeals were heard. It also appointed Lords of Appeal in Ordinary: highly qualified professional judges working full time on the judicial business of the House. These Law Lords*

were able to vote on legislation as full Members of the House of Lords, but in practice rarely did so.

Before the second world war, the Law Lords used to hear appeals each day in the chamber of the House of Lords.

After the House of Commons was bombed, the Law Lords moved their hearings to a nearby committee room to escape the noise of the building repairs, constituting themselves as an Appellate Committee for the purpose. In fact, this temporary arrangement proved so successful that it became permanent, and continued for the remainder of the Appellate Committee's life.

On the commencement of the Supreme Court in October 2009, all current Law Lords became its first Justices.

The first Justices remain Members of the House of Lords, but are unable to sit and vote in the House. All new Justices appointed after October 2009 will be directly appointed to The Supreme Court on the recommendation of a selection commission.

### 20.3.3 Supreme Court History

https://www.supremecourt.uk/about/history.html

*1 October 2009 marks a defining moment in the constitutional history of the United Kingdom: transferring judicial authority away from the House of Lords, and creating a Supreme Court for the United Kingdom in the historic setting of the former Middlesex Guildhall on Parliament Square.*

*In this location, The Supreme Court forms part of a pre-existing quadrangle made up of the Houses of Parliament, Westminster Abbey and Treasury.*

*As civil administration developed, it tended to be conducted by the Justices of the Peace and its offices were often co-located with the first tier of the courts.*

*The Onset of Egalitarianism and Governance by Statute*

*This close association reached a peak in the latter half of the nineteenth century, since when the two activities have tended to separate. In April 2005, all Magistrates' Court houses were transferred from the care of County Councils to the Department of Constitutional Affairs (DCA).*

### 20.3.3.1 Supreme Court – Middlesex Guildhall

https://www.supremecourt.uk/about/middlesex-guildhall.html

*The home of the new Supreme Court will be an impressive building in an historic location directly linked with the law for nearly a millennium.*

### 20.3.4 Supreme Court References to the EU Court of Justice

https://www.supremecourt.uk/about/the-supreme-court-and-europe.html

*Like other final courts, the UKSC is, in the areas of European law in which the United Kingdom has accepted the jurisdiction of the Court of Justice of the European Union (CJEU), under the duty imposed by Article 267 of the Treaty on the Functioning of the European Union to ask the CJEU to give preliminary rulings concerning:*

1. *the interpretation of the Treaties; and*
2. *the validity and interpretation of acts of the institutions, bodies, offices or agencies of the Union;*

*where such a question is raised in proceedings before it and it considers that a decision on the question is necessary to enable it to give judgment [sic].*

*Where an application for permission to appeal raises such a question, the UKSC does not, when considering whether in the light of that question to grant permission or to make a reference to the CJEU, apply a test of whether the question is of general public importance.*

*The Onset of Egalitarianism and Governance by Statute*

*The Supreme Court of the United Kingdom is a member of the Network of the Presidents of the Supreme Judicial Courts of the European Union.*

That network of Presidents has its own website: http://www.networkpresidents.eu/

This link leads to another 28 national Supreme Court websites, plus three observer states, two of which have yet further websites. This literal web of complexity relates solely to the judicial aspects of the EU.

## 20.3.5 Diagramme – Secular Estates of the EU

From http://commons.wikimedia.org/wiki/Category:Maps released under CC-BY-SA
http://creativecommons.org/licenses/by-sa/3.0/ Author: 111Alleskönner

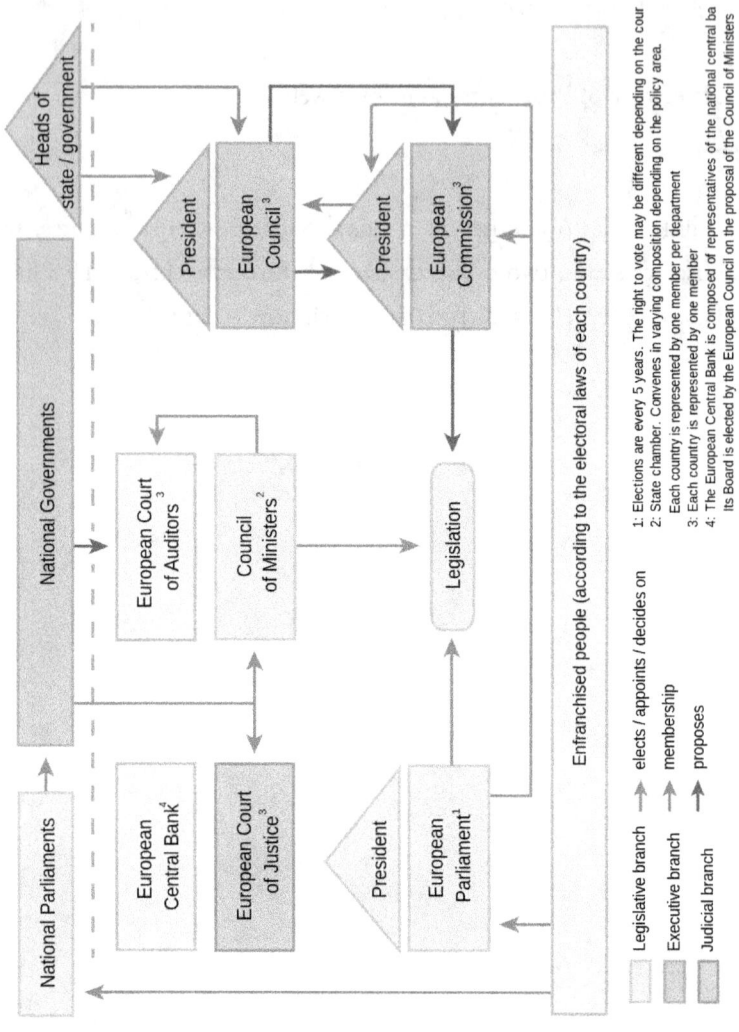

*The Onset of Egalitarianism and Governance by Statute*

## 20.3.6 Diagramme – UK Judiciary and New UK Supreme Court

The Supreme Court of the United Kingdom feeds into the European Court of Justice in the diagramme above

From http://commons.wikimedia.org/wiki/ Public Domain

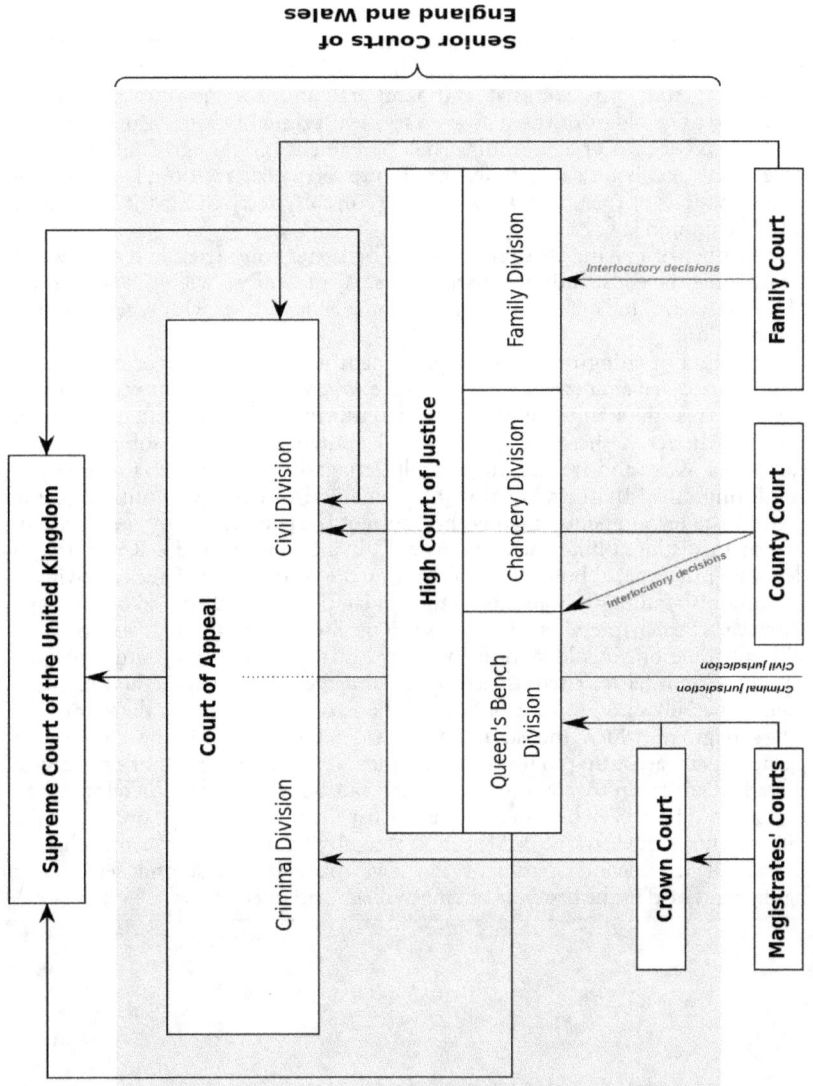

## 20.4 Principal Acts of Parliament that Shaped Britain

Sir William Blackstone, in his book *Commentaries on the Laws of England*, describes the method of naming Acts as follows:

> ### Method of Naming Acts
>
> "Let us next proceed to the leges scriptae, the written laws of the kingdom, which are statutes, acts, or edicts, made by the king's majesty by and with the advice and content of the lords spiritual and temporal and commons in parliament assembled. The oldest of these now extant, and printed in our statute books, is the famous Magna Carta, as confirmed in parliament [...] though doubtless there were many acts before that time, the records of which are now lost, and the determinations of them perhaps at present currently received for the maxims of the old common law.
>
> The manner of making these statutes will be better considered hereafter, when we examine the constitution of parliaments. At present we will only take notice of the different kinds of statutes; and of some general rules with regard to their construction.
>
> The method of citing these acts of parliament is various. Many of our antient statutes are called after the name of the place, where the parliament was held that made them: as the statutes of Merton and Marlbridge, of Westminster, Glocester, and Winchester. Others are denominated entirely from their subject; as the statutes of Wales and Ireland, the articuli cleri, and the praerogativa regis. Some are distinguished by their initial words, a method of citing very antient; being used by the Jews in denominating the books of the pentateuch; by the Christian church in distinguishing their hymns and divine offices; by the Romanists in describing their papal bulles; and in short by the whole body of antient civilians and canonists, among whom this method of citation generally prevailed, not only with regard to chapters, but inferior sections also: in imitation of all which we still call some of our old statutes by their initial words, as the statute of quia emptores, and that of circumspecte agatis. But the most usual method of citing them, especially since the time of Edward the second, is by naming the year of the king's reign in which the statute was made, together with the chapter, or particular act, according to it's numeral order [...]. For all the acts of one session of parliament taken together make properly but one statute; and therefore when two sessions have been held in one year, we usually mention stat. 1. or 2. Thus the bill of rights is cited, as 1 W. & M. st. 2. c. 2. signifying that it is the second chapter or act, of the second statute or the laws made in the second sessions of parliament, held in the first year of king William and queen Mary."

## The Onset of Egalitarianism and Governance by Statute

### 20.4.1 Charter of Liberties aka Coronation Charter

Proclaimed by English King Henry I in writing at his accession in 1100, this charter was an olive branch to the earls and barons to compensate for abuses of power by his predecessor, English King William II aka Rufus.

Rufus was considered a tyrant who indulged in abuses, such as over-taxation, the exploitation of church lands and finances, and interference in religious practices. Over the next 100 years the charter was little used, but it was very significant as a lead-in to Magna Carta.

### 20.4.2 The Magna Carta(s) of 1215 and 1225.

Issued in 1215 under King John Lackland, it passed into law under English King Henry III in 1225, but it was re-issued in its most enduring form by King Edward I in 1297.

Magna Carta was described by the Master of the Rolls, Lord Denning (1899 to 1999), as:

> "...the greatest constitutional document of all times, the foundation of the freedom of the individual against the arbitrary authority of the despot".

#### 20.4.2.1 Image of an Original Magna Carta

Illustration from http://commons.wikimedia.org/wiki/ Public Domain

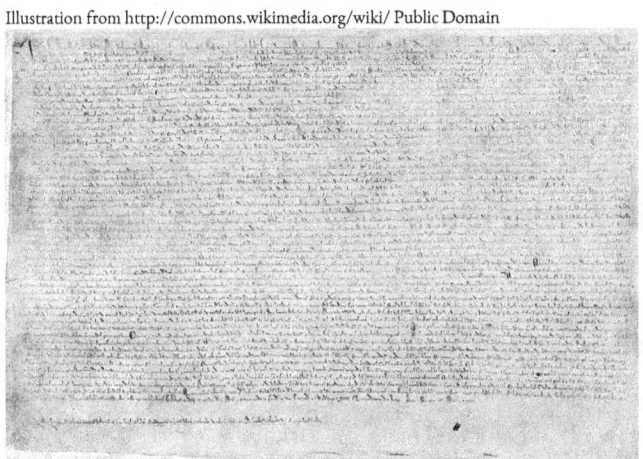

### 20.4.3 The Treason Act 1351

There is a distinction between High Treason against the Crown, and Petty Treason which concerns disloyalty to a subject. The following extract concerns High Treason, and is taken from:

http://www.legislation.gov.uk/aep/Edw3Stat5/25/2/section/II

> **Title: Treason Act 1351 – 1351 CHAPTER 2 25 Edw 3 Stat 5.**
>
> A STATUTE made at WESTMINSTER; In the Parliament holden in the Feast of Saint Hilary; In the Twenty-fifth Year of the Reign of K. EDWARD the Third
>
> II Declaration what Offences shall be adjudged Treason. Compassing the Death of the King, Queen, or their eldest Son; violating the Queen, or the King's eldest Daughter unmarried, or his eldest Son's Wife; levying War; adhering to the King's Enemies; killing the Chancellor, Treasurer, or Judges in Execution of their Duty.
>
> ITEM, Whereas divers Opinions have been before this Time in what Case Treason shall be said, and in what not; the King, at the Request of the Lords and of the Commons, hath made a Declaration in the Manner as hereafter followeth, that is to say; When a Man doth compass or imagine the Death of our Lord the King, or of our Lady his Queen or of their eldest Son and Heir; or if a Man do violate the King's Companion, or the King's eldest Daughter unmarried, or the Wife the King's eldest Son and Heir; or if a Man do levy War against our Lord the King in his Realm, or be adherent to the King's Enemies in his Realm, giving to them Aid and Comfort in the Realm, or elsewhere, and thereof be probably attainted of open Deed by the People of their Condition: ... , and if a Man slea the Chancellor, Treasurer, or the King's Justices of the one Bench or the other, Justices in Eyre, or Justices of Assise, and all other Justices assigned to hear and determine, being in their Places, doing their Offices: And it is to be understood, that in the Cases above rehearsed, that ought to be judged Treason which extends to our Lord the King, and his Royal Majesty.

There have been many Treason Acts since the first one in 1351, revisions usually being driven by some event or other of the time. The 1848 Act, for instance, criminalised the advocacy of republicanism, and it was brought in at the time of the revolutionary fervour that swept through Europe after the Napoleonic Wars – a time when memories of the French Jacobin *Terror* were still fresh in everyone's minds.

The last Treason Act was in 1945, the only changes being procedural. Trials of one or two traitors from the Second World War such as William Joyce aka Lord Haw Haw, benefited from these changes.

## 20.4.4 The Act of Supremacy 1534

Title: Act of Supremacy, Public Act, 26 Henry VIII, c. 1.

The 1534 Act of Supremacy that was passed by parliament defined the right of King Henry VIII to be the Supreme Head on Earth of the Church of England. This created an unbridgeable schism between Henry's England and the Catholic Church of Rome and the Pope.

## 20.4.5 The Petition of Right 1628

Considered by many to be as significant as was Magna Carta in 1215, and as binding as the Bill of Rights would become in 1689, the Petition of Right *was not an Act of Parliament and so was not a Statute*. It was forced, after a struggle and hitherto rare co-operation between the upper and lower Parliamentary Houses, upon a greedy and self-centred King Charles I who, since his accession in 1625, had taken money by unauthorised taxation and by enforced loans, had imposed martial law, and as a consequence of the latter had forced the billeting of soldiers on private households.

The petition demanded:

1. that no freeman should be forced to pay any tax, loan, or benevolence, unless in accordance with an Act of Parliament;
2. that no freeman should be imprisoned contrary to the laws of the land;
3. that soldiers and sailors should not be billeted on private persons;
4. commissions to punish soldiers and sailors by martial law should be abolished.

Reference:

http://www.luminarium.org/encyclopedia/petitionofright.htm

The text may also be read at the following additional websites:

http://www.nationalarchives.gov.uk/pathways/citizenship/rise_parliament/transcripts/petition_right.htm

http://www.constitution.org/eng/petright.htm

The preamble and first two clauses as an example are as follows:

> **The Petition of Right**
>
> The Petition exhibited to his Majesty by the Lords Spiritual and Temporal, and Commons, in this present Parliament assembled, concerning divers Rights and Liberties of the Subjects, with the King's Majesty's royal answer thereunto in full Parliament.
>
> To the King's most excellent Majesty.
>
> Soit droit fait come est desire
> 'HUMBLY shew unto our Sovereign Lord the King, the Lords Spiritual and Temporal, and Commons, in Parliament assembled, That whereas it is declared and enacted by a Statute made in the time of the Reign of King Edward the First, commonly called Statutum de Tallagio non concedendo, that no Tallage or Aid shall be laid or levied by the King or his Heirs in this Realm, without the good Will and Assent of the Archbishops, Bishops, Earls, Barons, Knights, Burgesses and other the Freemen of the Commonalty of this Realm; and by the Authority of Parliament holden in the Five and twentieth Year of the Reign of King Edward the Third, it is declared and enacted, that from thenceforth no Person should be compelled to make any Loans to the King against his Will, because such Loans were against Reason and the Franchise of the Land; and by other Laws of this Realm it is provided, that none should be charged by any Charge or Imposition called a Benevolence, nor by such like Charge; by which the Statutes before mentioned, and other the good Laws and Statutes of this Realm, Your Subjects have inherited this Freedom, that they should not be compelled to contribute to any Tax, Tallage, Aid or other like Charge not set by Common Consent in Parliament.
>
> 'II.Yet nevertheless, of late divers Commissions directed to sundry Commissioners in several Counties, with Instructions, have issued; by means whereof Your People have been in divers Places assembled, and required to lend certain Sums of Money unto Your Majesty, and many of them, upon their Refusal so to do, have had an Oath administered unto them not warrantable by the Laws or Statutes of this Realm; and have been constrained to become bound to make Appearance and give Attendance before Your Privy Council and in other Places; and others of them have been therefore imprisoned, confined, and sundry other Ways molested and disquieted; and divers other Charges have been laid and levied upon Your People in several Counties by Lord Lieutenants, Deputy Lieutenants, Commissioners for Musters, Justices of Peace and others, by Command or Direction from Your Majesty, or Your Privy Council, against the Laws and Free Customs of the Realm.

There are nine further obsequious yet accusatory clauses.

*The Onset of Egalitarianism and Governance by Statute*

## 20.4.6 The Habeas Corpus Act 1679

The background to this Act of 1679 begins with an intimation in Magna Carta in 1215, in which is contained an article that, although not an exact basis for a writ of *habeas corpus*, nevertheless states:

> *"No freeman shall be taken or imprisoned or disseised or exiled or in any way destroyed, nor will we go upon him nor will we send upon him except upon the lawful judgement of his peers or the law of the land."*

A petition for *habeas corpus* can be made by anyone on behalf of a prisoner, and a writ of *habeas corpus* can then be issued from a higher legal authority to a lower one. Writs of *habeas corpus* that force an imprisoning authority, such as a Sheriff, to release a prisoner to a Court where the legality of detention can be examined, had been in use *de facto* since the reigns of English King Henry II and King Edward I, around the time of the 13th and early 14th centuries.

After some 350 years, it was during the reign of English King Charles I that it was felt necessary to formalise the area of the law concerning apprehension and arraignment, and an Act that was passed in 1640 was titled *An Act for the Regulating the Privie Councell and for taking away the Court commonly called the Star Chamber*.

Reference:
http://www.british-history.ac.uk/report.aspx?compid=47221

That 1640 Act ensured that a petition or writ of *habeas corpus* could not be overruled by either the King or the Privy Council, and it abolished the extra-judicial and arbitrary Star Chamber that had been in active use since English King Henry VII circa 1485, though as a separate Court it had been conceived almost a century before that. There was clearly a perceived abuse of the individual of all levels of society, and an assumed further misuse of the Star Chamber which was mainly used against aristocratic peers who might otherwise escape justice, and in cases where the law may not have actually been broken but where some sort of obnoxious privileged misdemeanour had occurred.

The Habeas Corpus Act of 1679, that was passed during the reign of English King Charles II, enshrined in law *(codified)* the use of petitions and writs, and thereby forced the Courts to take full notice and consideration of the legality of detaining a person as a prisoner. If its provisions could be enjoyed by all members of society – literate or illiterate – then it would be a massive leap forward for the principles of liberty and justice.

> **Title: Habeas Corpus Act 1679 – 1679 CHAPTER 2 31 Cha 2.**
>
> An Act for the better secureing the Liberty of the Subject and for Prevention of Imprisonments beyond the Seas.
>
> Recital that Delays had been used by Sheriffs in making Returns of Writs of Habeas Corpus, &c.
> WHEREAS great Delayes have beene used by Sheriffes Goalers and other Officers to whose Custody any of the Kings Subjects have beene committed for criminall or supposed criminall Matters in makeing Returnes of Writts of Habeas Corpus to them directed by standing out an Alias and Pluries Habeas Corpus and sometimes more and by other shifts to avoid their yeilding Obedience to such Writts contrary to their Duty and the knowne Lawes of the Land whereby many of the Kings Subjects have beene and hereafter may be long detained in Prison in such Cases where by Law they are baylable to their great charge and vexation.
>
> [I.] Sheriff, &c. within Three Days after Service of Habeas Corpus, with the Exception of Treason and Felony, as and under the Regulations herein mentioned, to bring up the Body before the Court to which the Writ is returnable; and certify the true Causes of Imprisonment. Exceptions in respect of Distance.
>
> For the prevention whereof and the more speedy Releife of all persons imprisoned for any such criminall or supposed criminall Matters whensoever any person or persons shall bring any Habeas Corpus directed unto any Sheriffe or Sheriffes Goaler Minister or other Person whatsoever for any person in his or their Custody and the said Writt shall be served upon the said Officer or left at the Goale or Prison with any of the Under Officers Underkeepers or Deputy of the said Officers or Keepers that the said Officer or Officers his or their Under Officers Under-Keepers or Deputyes shall within Three dayes after the Service thereof as aforesaid (unlesse the Committment aforesaid were for Treason plainely and specially expressed in the Warrant of Committment) upon Payment or Tender of the Charges of bringing the said Prissoner to be ascertained by the Judge or Court that awarded the same and endorsed upon the said Writt not exceeding Twelve pence per Mile and upon Security given by his owne Bond to pay the Charges of carrying backe the Prisoner if he shall bee remanded by the Court or Judge to which he shall be brought according to the true intent of this

> present Act and that he will not make any escape by the way make Returne of such Writt or bring or cause to be brought the Body of the Partie soe committed or restrained unto or before the Judges or Barons of the said Court from whence the said Writt shall issue or unto and before such other person and persons before whome the said Writt is made returnable according to the Command thereof, and shall likewise then certifie the true causes of his Detainer or Imprisonment unlesse the Committment of the said Partie be in any place beyond the distance of Twenty miles from the place or places where such Court or Person is or shall be resideing and if beyond the distance of Twenty miles and not above One hundred miles then within the space of Ten dayes and if beyond the distance of One hundred miles then within the space of Twenty dayes after such delivery aforesaid and not longer.

There are two more provisions in the full wording of the Act.

### 20.4.7 The Bill aka The Declaration of Rights 1688-1689

This declarative Act was a condemnation of English King James II, and a statement that justified his ousting during the Glorious Revolution of 1688 that replaced him with William of Orange. The Bill or Declaration also purports to state the rights of the general public and the rights of the successors to the throne – it was of particular significance given the hiatus in the royal family at the time.

In this respect the Bill directed that, if William of Orange had any children by a second marriage, then first in-line to the throne would be any children born to Mary or Anne – the two daughters of ex-King James II. A further restriction was that no Catholic, or anyone married to a Catholic, would be permitted to succeed to the throne.

First of all, the Bill made a number of indictments against English King James II justifying his forced abdication, and that was followed by a list of rights of the individual.

Reference:
http://www.legislation.gov.uk/aep/WillandMarSess2/1/2/introduction

> **Title: Bill of Rights 1688 – 1688 CHAPTER 2 1 Will and Mar Sess 2.**
>
> An Act declareing the Rights and Liberties of the Subject and Setleing the Succession of the Crowne.
>
> Whereas the Lords Spirituall and Temporall and Comons assembled at Westminster lawfully fully and freely representing all the Estates of the People of this Realme did upon the thirteenth day of February in the yeare of our Lord one thousand six hundred eighty eight present unto their Majesties then called and known by the Names and Stile of William and Mary Prince and Princesse of Orange being present in their proper Persons a certaine Declaration in Writing made by the said Lords and Comons in the Words following viz
>
> The Heads of Declaration of Lords and Commons, recited.
> Whereas the late King James the Second by the Assistance of diverse evill Councellors Judges and Ministers imployed by him did endeavour to subvert and extirpate the Protestant Religion and the Lawes and Liberties of this Kingdome.
>
> **Dispensing and Suspending Power.**
> By Assumeing and Exerciseing a Power of Dispensing with and Suspending of Lawes and the Execution of Lawes without Consent of Parlyament.
>
> **Committing Prelates.**
> By Committing and Prosecuting diverse Worthy Prelates for humbly Petitioning to be excused from Concurring to the said Assumed Power.
>
> **Ecclesiastical Commission.**
> By issueing and causeing to be executed a Commission under the Great Seale for Erecting a Court called The Court of Commissioners for Ecclesiasticall Causes.
>
> **Levying Money.**
> By Levying Money for and to the Use of the Crowne by pretence of Prerogative for other time and in other manner then the same was granted by Parlyament.

Following the item above – Levying Money – there are several more indictments in the Act, and then a statement concerning the abdication of James II as follows – this was, remember, the lead-in to what would become known, rather over-optimistically, as *"The Glorious Revolution"*:

## The Onset of Egalitarianism and Governance by Statute

... Continuation of Bill of Rights 1688 in Respect of King James II

Recital that the late King James II. had abdicated the Government, and that the Throne was vacant, and that the Prince of Orange had written Letters to the Lords and Commons for the choosing Representatives in Parliament.

And whereas the said late King James the Second haveing Abdicated the Government and the Throne being thereby Vacant His Hignesse the Prince of Orange (whome it hath pleased Almighty God to make the glorious Instrument of Delivering this Kingdome from Popery and Arbitrary Power) did (by the Advice of the Lords Spirituall and Temporall and diverse principall Persons of the Commons) cause Letters to be written to the Lords Spirituall and Temporall being Protestants and other Letters to the severall Countyes Cityes Universities Burroughs and Cinque Ports for the Choosing of such Persons to represent them as were of right to be sent to Parlyament to meete and sitt at Westminster upon the two and twentyeth day of January in this Yeare one thousand six hundred eighty and eight in order to such an Establishment as that their Religion Lawes and Liberties might not againe be in danger of being Subverted, Upon which Letters Elections haveing beene accordingly made.

### The Subject's Rights.
And thereupon the said Lords Spirituall and Temporall and Commons pursuant to their respective Letters and Elections being now assembled in a full and free Representative of this Nation takeing into their most serious Consideration the best meanes for attaining the Ends aforesaid Doe in the first place (as their Auncestors in like Case have usually done) for the Vindicating and Asserting their auntient Rights and Liberties, Declare

### Dispensing Power.
That the pretended Power of Suspending of Laws or the Execution of Laws by Regall Authority without Consent of Parlyament is illegall.

### Late dispensing Power.
That the pretended Power of Dispensing with Laws or the Execution of Laws by Regall Authoritie as it hath beene assumed and exercised of late is illegall.

### Ecclesiastical Courts illegal.
That the Commission for erecting the late Court of Commissioners for Ecclesiasticall Causes and all other Commissions and Courts of like nature are Illegall and Pernicious.

### Levying Money.
That levying Money for or to the Use of the Crowne by pretence of Prerogative without Grant of Parlyament for longer time or in other manner then the same is or shall be granted is Illegall.

### Right to petition.
That it is the Right of the Subjects to petition the King and all Commitments and Prosecutions for such Petitioning are Illegall.

...

Several more rights are identified in the full wording of the Act, though the reality, as seen so much later in 1832 at the time of the still inadequate first Reform Act, leaves no doubt concerning the class-distinctive practical rights, and the cramped real liberty of the people.

### 20.4.8 The Act of Settlement 1701

The Act of Settlement became necessary as a consequence of the requirements in the Bill of Rights of 1689 in respect of the parliament-mandated Protestant succession to the throne.

As a brief recap of the dynastic upheavals that had riven the House of Stuart during the previous half century: English King Charles I had been executed during the English Civil War, and yet following the demise of the Commonwealth (of England, Scotland and Ireland), the Restoration had taken the retrograde step of returning Charles' son Charles II to the throne. English King Charles II died without legitimate heir, so his brother became English King James II, and Scottish King James VII.

After the barbarous and cavalier recriminations that followed the death of Lord Protector Oliver Cromwell in 1658, parliamentary power was increasing again, and the Glorious Revolution of 1688 forced the abdication of English King James II, whose two daughters, Mary and Anne, became heirs to the throne; and it was Mary who became English Queen Mary II, while her husband, the Dutch Prince William of Orange, became English King William III.

However, Queen Mary II died childless in late 1694 and she was succeeded by her husband English King William III, of whom any children by a second marriage would be denied the throne by the Bill of Rights. Therefore, in 1700 a potential dilemma was recognised by parliament when the reserve option for monarch was eliminated due to the death of the young Duke of Gloucester, who was the only surviving child of the Princess Anne (Queen Mary's sister). This meant that eventually Anne's half-brother, James, could be King unless someone else could be found. The parliamentary horror was palpable because this James, who had been born in 1688, was Catholic, and it was his birth as a possible successor that

## The Onset of Egalitarianism and Governance by Statute

had been one of the main reasons for the Glorious Revolution in the first place.

In reality, English King William III would die in 1702, and the throne would pass to the Princess Anne as English Queen Anne I, who would continue on the throne until 1714, after which a George would arrive in England – English King George I – the first Hanoverian and a Protestant; but Parliament had to do something first in order to ensure this would happen.

As seen below in the wording of the Act, the nominee was Sophia, the granddaughter of the English King James I by his daughter, Elizabeth, the latter having married Frederic V, Elector Palatine and King of Bohemia. Sophia was therefore a first cousin of the previous English King Charles II and English King James II, and she was also the Electress of the Principality of Hanover in Germany. Her German son would become the English (Anglicised) King George I, who would also rule over Scotland – a German Protestant being preferable to an English Catholic it seems.

The full text of the Act of Settlement may be read at the following website:

http://www.legislation.gov.uk/aep/Will3/12-13/2/introduction

> **Title: Act of Settlement 1700 – 1700 CHAPTER 2 12 and 13 Will 3.**
>
> An Act for the further Limitation of the Crown and better securing the Rights and Liberties of the Subject
>
> I Recital of Stat. 1 W. & M. Sess. 2. c. 2. §2. and that the late Queen and Duke of Gloucester are dead; and that His Majesty had recommended from the Throne a further Provision for the Succession of the Crown in the Protestant Line. The Princess Sophia, Electress and Duchess Dowager of Hanover, Daughter of the late Queen of Bohemia, Daughter of King James the First, to inherit after the King and the Princess Anne, in Default of Issue of the said Princess and His Majesty, respectively and the Heirs of her Body, being Protestants.
>
> Whereas in the First Year of the Reign of Your Majesty and of our late most gracious Sovereign Lady Queen Mary (of blessed Memory) An Act of Parliament was made intituled [An Act for declaring the Rights and Liberties of the Subject and for setling the Succession of the Crown] wherein it was (amongst other things) enacted established and declared That the Crown and Regall Government of the Kingdoms of England France and Ireland and the Dominions thereunto belonging should be and continue to Your Majestie and the said late Queen during the joynt Lives of Your Majesty and the said Queen and to the Survivor And that after the Decease of Your Majesty and of the said Queen the said Crown and Regall Government should be and remain to the Heirs of the Body of the said late Queen And for Default of such Issue to Her Royall Highness the Princess Ann of Denmark and the Heirs of Her Body And for Default of such Issue to the Heirs of the Body of Your Majesty And it was thereby further enacted That all and every Person and Persons that then were or afterwards should be reconciled to or shall hold Communion with the See or Church of Rome or should professe the Popish Religion or marry a Papist should be excluded and are by that Act made for ever incapable to inherit possess or enjoy the Crown and Government of this Realm and Ireland and the Dominions thereunto belonging or any part of the same or to have use or exercise any regall Power Authority or Jurisdiction within the same And in all and every such Case and Cases the People of these Realms shall be and are thereby absolved of their Allegiance And that the said Crown and Government shall from time to time descend to and be enjoyed by such Person or Persons being Protestants as should have inherited and enjoyed the same in case the said Person or Persons so reconciled holding Communion professing or marrying as aforesaid were naturally dead After the making of which Statute and the Settlement therein contained Your Majesties good Subjects who were restored to the full and free Possession and Enjoyment of their Religion Rights and Liberties by the Providence of God giving Success to Your Majesties just Undertakings and unwearied Endeavours for that Purpose had no greater temporall Felicity to hope or wish for then to see a Royall Progeny descending from Your Majesty to whom (under God) they owe their Tranquility and whose Ancestors have for many Years been principall Assertors of the reformed Religion and the Liberties of Europe...

The first clause or provision above continues, and there are four in all.

## 20.4.9 Enclosure aka Inclosure Acts 1773 to 1882

Caveat: There is frequent reference throughout the internet to parliamentary Statutes concerning Enclosure Acts from 1604 to 1914, but commonly available detail seems to be restricted to the date range 1773 to 1882, though increasing digitisation of old records, and-or a search more diligent than the author's may alter that observation.

As indicated earlier, land ownership is considered key to the descent of mankind from Freedom to Fiefdom, and his captivity therein.

The series of Enclosure Acts that were perpetrated by Statute from 1604 or earlier, down to the years of World War One, typically 1914, were only a part of the story of the transition to Fiefdom for the majority of the British people. Some sources identify the beginning of enclosures by Statute to a time as early as the 13th century, but regardless, the expectation of immunity against any successful opposition from the common people has been embedded in the calloused minds of the ruling elite by the excesses of their ancestors, the Normans, and by over half a millennium of immunity to prosecution by any sort of moral ombudsman. There can be no such reckoning, or natural justice, because no such higher authority exists – neither temporal nor spiritual.

An arrogant omission of even the smallest sense of humanity led to a contempt among the ruling elite that was reinforced by an almost effortless survival in the face of rebellion – any insurrection in Britain always being crushed or averted without excessive drama – and any concessions that were made were therefore made with bad grace, and minimally. This is an important part of our history that has been neglected and all too often ignored.

On the website of the United Kingdom Parliament there is an expected dearth of any sort of recognition of the centuries of misery caused by the indisputable theft of land, and the consequent creation of artificial and inequitable social and economic differentials. The site even makes a candid suggestion that enclosure was good for productivity, though it does not make the obvious connection between *productivity* and *return on privileged capital* – or more appropriately *return on stolen property*.

Reference:
http://www.parliament.uk

In Parliament's own words:

> *Overall, between 1604 and 1914 over 5,200 enclosure Bills were enacted by Parliament which related to just over a fifth of the total area of England, amounting to some 6.8 million acres.*

And:

> *There is little doubt that enclosure greatly improved the agricultural productivity of farms from the late 18th century by bringing more land into effective agricultural use. It also brought considerable change to the local landscape.*

There is a frank admission on the website of the United Kingdom National Archives of the lack of complete information on the scale of enclosures.

Reference:
http://www.nationalarchives.gov.uk

In the archive's own words:

> *Only after 1845 are the enclosure awards held at The National Archives comprehensive.*

And:

> *Many early enclosures of common lands, pastures and manorial wastes, whether made by popular agreement or by compulsion, have left no formal record.*

*The Onset of Egalitarianism and Governance by Statute*

As indicated in an earlier section it has been estimated that, including the land taken by unauthorised actions – theft – some twenty thousand square miles overall was stolen from public ownership. This is a terrible milestone in our history.

Use of the Star Chamber was made by the ruling elite to enforce judgements if necessary, and such determinations pre-dated the use of the modern series of Statutes that begin either in 1604 or with The Inclosure Act 1773, and that end with The Commonable Rights Compensation Act 1882, or later. STAC in the extract below from the National Archives is a reference to a specific Star Chamber case, and, overall, a vast number are listed, though they do include issues other than contentious and resisted enclosures. From the National Archives:

> *Controversial enclosures, particularly those which were resisted by force, may have resulted in legal proceedings before local or central law courts, such as the Court of Requests or Star Chamber. For example, STAC 3/6/32 relates to the enclosure of commons at Shebbear in Devon in the mid 16th century.*

Most commoners, of course, could not read and would have been totally ignorant of the robbery about to take place – there are even records in the archives of pardons being issued in cases of illegal enclosure, which implies that the thief was allowed to keep the ill-gotten gains with the blessing of the Courts.

A single example of an Act is presented below.

> **Title: Inclosure Act 1773 – 1773 CHAPTER 81 13 Geo 3**
>
> An Act for the better Cultivation, Improvement, and Regulation of the Common Arable Fields, Wastes, and Commons of Pasture in this Kingdom.
>
> **Preamble.**
> Whereas there are in several parishes and places in this kingdom several wastes and commons, and several open and common fields, which, by reason of the different interests the several land owners and occupiers, or persons having right of common, have in such wastes, commons and fields, cannot be improved, cultivated or enjoyed to such great advantage for the owners and occupiers thereof, and persons having right of common, as they might be and are capable of if an improved course of husbandry was to be pursued respecting such open and common fields in each parish respectively, and such wastes or commons of pasture were to be properly drained or otherwise amended:
>
> **[I.] How arable lands shall be fenced.**
>
> In every parish or place in this kingdom where there are open or common field lands, all the tillage or arable lands lying in the said open or common fields shall be ordered, fenced, cultivated and improved in such manner by the respective occupiers thereof, and shall be kept, ordered and continued in such course of husbandry, and be cultivated under such rules, regulations and restrictions, as three-fourths in number and value of the occupiers of such open or common field lands in each parish or place, cultivating and taking the crops of the same, and having the consent of the owners in manner hereinafter mentioned, and likewise the consent of the rector, impropriator or tithe owner, or the lessee of either of them respectively, first had in writing, shall, at a meeting (in pursuance of notice for that purpose in writing under the hands of one-third of such occupiers, to be affixed on one of the principal doors of the parish church, chapel or place where meetings have been usually held for such parish or place respectively, twenty one days at least before such meeting, specifying the time and place of such meeting), by writing under their hands, constitute, direct and appoint, and which notice any of such occupiers are hereby authorised and impowered to give.

There are several more sections of the 1773 Act, and other Acts, all accessible at the references given above.

## 20.4.10 The Great Reform Act 1832 and the Chartist Movement

Always only grudgingly relaxing its stranglehold, and with hesitant and faltering steps towards liberty and away from the Norman feudal bondage in which it still held the general public, the British elite's measures introduced by the first Act of parliamentary reform – The 1832 Representation of the People Act (2 & 3 Wm. IV, c. 45) aka The Reform Act 1832 aka The Great Reform Act – failed to significantly address the totally undemocratic nature of the British Parliament, and the same was true for the parliaments of Scotland and Ireland, where separate Reform Bills were passed in the same year.

Most of the Rotten Boroughs, such as Old Sarum that consisted of just three houses with seven franchised residents, were abolished by the Act, along with other travesties, so that in all, 56 boroughs in England and Wales were disenfranchised, and 31 others were reduced to only one MP, while 67 new constituencies were created. Expressed in other terms, around 143 faulty borough seats were abolished, and 130 were created; but there was still no secret ballot, and the restriction of the franchise to male householders – a restriction that was couched in certain monetary terms – meant that women and 80% of working men still had no vote.

The result of the failure to address the concerns of a general public that, some say, was on the edge of another Civil War or at least rebellion, led to the founding of the Chartist Movement in 1838, and in the same year the issue of a People's Charter identifying grievances. The Charter was phrased by twelve members of a group comprising six representatives from the London Working Men's Association, and six radical Members of Parliament, and it made the following six demands:

1. All men to have the vote (universal manhood suffrage).
2. Voting should take place by secret ballot.
3. Parliamentary elections every year, not once every five years.
4. Constituencies should be of equal size.
5. Members of Parliament should be paid.

6. The property qualification for becoming a Member of Parliament should be abolished.

Those six demands were issued in the form of a leaflet, to which was appended a note of the list of responsible promoters as below:

Reference:

http://www.parliament.uk/

> *Subjoined are the names of the gentlemen who embodied these principles into the document called the "People's Charter" at an influential meeting held at the British Coffee House, London, on the 7th of June, 1837:–*
> Daniel O'Connell, Esq., M.P.
> Mr Henry Hetherington.
> John Arthur Roebuck, Esq., M.P.
> Mr John Cleave.
> John Temple Leader, Esq., M.P.
> Mr James Watson.
> Charles Hindley, Esq., M.P.
> Mr Richard Moore.
> Thomas Perronet Thompson, Esq., M.P.
> Mr William Lovett.
> William Sharman Crawford, Esq., M.P.
> Mr Henry Vincent.
> – Reference: *British Working Class Movements: Select Documents 1789-1875*, edited by GDH Cole and AW Filson (Macmillan, 1951).

Parliament's failure to respond to this and subsequent submissions led to national unrest in the form of strikes and armed conflict; there were dozens of deaths, and for many, transportation to the colonies, while all along, spies in the ranks of the Chartists had kept the authorities informed

## The Onset of Egalitarianism and Governance by Statute

of virtually all of the plots. By about 1858 the movement was all but burned out, and its critics label it a failure.

Reform Acts were repeated in the context of parliamentary reform until 1928, although by 1918, the only continuing omission concerning implementation of the People's Charter of 1837/1838 was the demand for annual parliamentary elections, and that demand remains unfulfilled to the present day, although Reform-related Acts have continued into the 3rd millennium with no end in sight.

The 1832 Act is only partly digitised at the National Archive, and the small example detail below may be supplemented from the following U.S. source:

http://www.princeton.edu/~achaney/tmve/wiki100k/docs/Reform_Act_1832.html

### Title: Great Reform Act, 1832 – 1832 2&3W4n147.

Whereas it is expedient to take effectual measures for correcting divers abuses that have long prevailed in the choice of members to serve in the commons' house of parliament to deprive many inconsiderable places of the right of returning members to grant such privilege to large populous and wealthy towns to increase the number of knights of the shire to extend the elective franchise to many of his majesty's subjects who have not heretofore enjoyed the same and to diminish the expense of elections Be it therefore enacted by the king's most excellent majesty by and with the advice and consent of the lords spiritual and temporal and commons in this present parliament assembled and by the authority of the same That each of the boroughs enumerated in the schedule marked (A) to this act annexed ^ shall from and after the end of this present parliament cease to return any member or members to serve in parliament in And be it enacted that each of the boroughs enumerated in the schedule marked (B) to this act annexed shall from and after the [.....]

(that is to say) Old Sarum Newtown St Michaels or Midshall Gatton Bramber Bossiney Dunwich Ludgershall St Mawes Beeralston West Looe St German's Newport Blechingley Aldborough Camelford Hindon East Looe Corfe Castle Great Bedwin Yarmouth Queenborough Castle Rising East Grinstead Higham Ferrers Wendover Weobly Winchelsea Tregoney Haslemere Saltash Orford Gallington Newton Ilchester Boroughbridge Stockbridge New Romney Hedon Plympton Seaford Heytesbury Steyning Whitchurch Wootton Bassett Downton Fowey Milborne Port Aldeburgh Minehead Bishop's Castle Okehampton Appleby Lostwithiel Brackley and Amersham

In words taken from the National Archives concerning *"Democracy in Britain"*:

> ***"By the time of the third Reform Act in 1884, Britain was less democratic than many other countries in Europe".***

In the 2015 General Election in Britain 1,454,436 Scottish National Party voters gained 56 seats in parliament, while a combined total of 5,038,712 UKIP and Green Party voters gained just one seat each, and so that statement concerning the state of parliamentary representation of the people in 1884 is just as true of today's parlous and risible, so-called *"British Democracy"*.

### 20.4.11 The Acts of Union – Scotland 1706 & 1707, Ireland 1800

The extracts below give an indication of the parliamentary initiatives, virtually a century apart, that sought to unify the British Isles that for centuries had seen bloodshed due to territorial aggrandisement by forces ranging from tribal raiding parties to Nation-States. It was England that drove the processes for unification, and it was conflict among religious, aristocratic, and nationalist factions and ideologies that would keep the blood-feuds active into the 3$^{rd}$ millennium. The Irish Acts of Union were finally prompted by the Irish Rebellion of 1798.

### 20.4.12 Act of Union – Scotland 1706

The first Act was passed in the English Parliament and it was followed by a similar Act in the Scottish Parliament.

There are 25 Articles in total and the full detail can be seen online at:

http://www.legislation.gov.uk/aep/Ann/6/11/introduction

See the extract below.

*The Onset of Egalitarianism and Governance by Statute*

**Title: Union with Scotland Act 1706 – 1706 CHAPTER 11 6 Ann.**

An Act for an Union of the Two Kingdoms of England and Scotland

Most gracious Sovereign
Recital of Articles of Union, dated 22d July, 5 Ann.; and of an Act of Parliament passed in Scotland, 16th January, 5 Ann.
Whereas Articles of Union were agreed on the Twenty Second day of July in the Fifth year of Your Majesties reign by the Commissioners nominated on behalf of the Kingdom of England under Your Majesties Great Seal of England bearing date at Westminster the Tenth day of April then last past in pursuance of an Act of Parliament made in England in the Third year of Your Majesties reign and the Commissioners nominated on the behalf of the Kingdom of Scotland under Your Majesties Great Seal of Scotland bearing date the Twenty Seventh day of February in the Fourth year of Your Majesties Reign in pursuance of the Fourth Act of the Third Session of the present Parliament of Scotland to treat of and concerning an Union of the said Kingdoms
And Whereas an Act hath passed in the Parliament of Scotland at Edinburgh the Sixteenth day of January in the Fifth year of Your Majesties reign wherein 'tis mentioned that the Estates of Parliament considering the said Articles of Union of the two Kingdoms had agreed to and approved of the said Articles of Union with some Additions and Explanations And that Your Majesty with Advice and Consent of the Estates of Parliament for establishing the Protestant Religion and Presbyterian Church Government within the Kingdom of Scotland had passed in the same Session of Parliament an Act intituled Act for securing of the Protestant Religion and Presbyterian Church Government which by the Tenor thereof was appointed to be inserted in any Act ratifying the Treaty and expressly declared to be a fundamental and essential Condition of the said Treaty or Union in all times coming the Tenor of which Articles as ratified and approved of with Additions and Explanations by the said Act of Parliament of Scotland follows

ARTICLE I.
The Kingdoms United; Ensigns Armorial

That the two Kingdoms of England and Scotland shall upon the First day of May which shall be in the year One thousand seven hundred and seven and for ever after be united into one Kingdom by the name of Great Britain And that the Ensigns Armorial of the said United Kingdom be such as Her Majesty shall appoint and the Crosses of St. George and St. Andrew be conjoyned in such manner as Her Majesty shall think fit and used in all Flags Banners Standards and Ensigns both at Sea and Land.

ARTICLE II.
Succession to the Monarchy.

That the Succession to the Monarchy of the United Kingdom of Great Britain and of the Dominions thereto belonging after Her most Sacred Majesty and in default of Issue of Her Majesty be remain and continue to the most Excellent Princess Sophia Electoress and Dutchess Dowager of Hanover and the Heirs of her body being Protestants upon whom the Crown of England is settled by an Act of Parliament made in England in the Twelfth year of the reign of His late Majesty King William the Third intituled an Act for the further Limitation of the Crown and better securing the rights and Liberites of the Subject And that all

> Papists and persons marrying Papists shall be excluded from and for ever incapable to inherit possess or enjoy the Imperial Crown of Great Britain and the Dominions thereunto belonging or any part thereof and in every such Case the Crown and Government shall from time to time descend to and be enjoyed by such person being a Protestant as should have inherited and enjoyed the same in case such Papist or person marrying a Papist was naturally dead according to the Provision for the descent of the Crown of England made by another Act of Parliament in England in the first year of the reign of Their late Majesties King William and Queen Mary intituled an Act declaring the Rights and Liberites of the Subject and settling the Succession of the Crown.

## 20.4.13 Union with England Act 1707

This was the second Act. It was held in the Scottish Parliament.

> **Title: Union with England Act 1707 – 1707 c. 7.**
>
> Act Ratifying and Approving the Treaty of Union of the Two Kingdoms of SCOTLAND and ENGLAND
>
> The Estates of Parliament Considering that Articles of Union of the Kingdoms of Scotland and England were agreed on the twenty second of July One thousand seven hundred and six years by the Commissioners nominated on behalf of this Kingdom under Her Majesties Great Seal of Scotland bearing date the twenty seventh of February last past in pursuance of the fourth Act of the third Session of this Parliament and the Commissioners nominated on behalf of the Kingdom of England under Her Majesties Great Seal of England bearing date at Westminster the tenth day of April last past in pursuance of an Act of Parliament made in England the third year of Her Majesties Reign to treat of and concerning an Union of the said Kingdoms Which Articles were in all humility presented to Her Majesty upon the twenty third of the said Month of July and were Recommended to this Parliament by Her Majesties Royal Letter of the date the thirty one day of July One thousand seven hundred and six And that the said Estates of Parliament have agreed to and approven of the saids Articles of Union with some Additions and Explanations as is contained in the Articles hereafter insert And sicklyke Her Majesty with advice and consent of the Estates of Parliament Resolving to Establish the Protestant Religion and Presbyterian Church Government within this Kingdom has past in this Session of Parliament an Act entituled Act for secureing of the Protestant Religion and Presbyterian Church Government which by the Tenor thereof is appointed to be insert in any Act ratifying the Treaty and expressly declared to be a fundamentall and essentiall Condition of the said Treaty or Union in all time coming Therefore Her Majesty with advice and consent of the Estates of Parliament in fortification of the Approbation of the Articles as above mentioned And for their further and better Establishment of the same upon full and mature deliberation upon the forsaids Articles of Union and Act of Parliament Doth Ratifie Approve and Confirm the same with the Additions and Explanations contained in the saids Articles in manner and under the provision aftermentioned whereof the Tenor follows
> I
> That the Two Kingdoms of Scotland and England shall upon the first day of May next ensuing the date hereof and forever after be United into One Kingdom

> by the Name of Great Britain And that the Ensigns Armorial of the said United Kingdom be such as Her Majesty shall appoint and the Crosses of St Andrew and St George be conjoined in such manner as Her Majesty shall think fit and used in all Flags Banners Standards and Ensigns both at Sea and Land
> II
> That the Succession to the Monarchy of the United Kingdom of Great Britain and of the Dominions thereunto belonging after Her Most Sacred Majesty and in default of Issue of Her Majesty be, remain and continue to the Most Excellent Princess Sophia Electoress and Dutchess Dowager of Hanover and the Heirs of Her body being Protestants upon whom the Crown of England is settled by an Act of Parliament made in England in the twelfth year of the Reign of His late Majesty King William the Third entituled An Act for the further Limitation of the Crown and better securing the Rights and Liberties of the Subject And that all Papists and persons marrying Papists shall be excluded from and for ever incapable to inherit possess or enjoy the Imperial Crown of Great Britain and the Dominions thereunto belonging or any part thereof And in every such case the Crown and Government shall from time to time descend to and be enjoyed by such person being a Protestant as should have inherited and enjoyed the same in case such Papists or person marrying a Papist was naturally dead according to the provision for the Descent of the Crown of England made by another Act of Parliament in England in the first year of the Reign of their late Majesties King William and Queen Mary entituled An Act declaring the Rights and Liberties of the Subject and settling the Succession of the Crown v

There are again, as with the 1706 Act, 25 Articles in total, and the full detail can be seen online at:

http://www.legislation.gov.uk/aosp/1707/7/introduction

There was an additional amendment to the last Act:

> **Title: Union with Scotland (Amendment ) Act 1707 – 1707 CHAPTER 40 6 Ann.**
>
> An Act for rendring the Union of the Two Kingdoms more intire and complete.

There are six parts and the detail can be seen online at:

http://www.legislation.gov.uk/apgb/Ann/6/40/introduction

## 20.4.14 Union with Ireland Act 1800

The first Act was passed in the English Parliament and it was followed by a similar Act in the Irish Parliament.

> **Title: Union with Ireland Act 1800 – 1800 CHAPTER 67 39 and 40 Geo 3.**
>
> An Act for the Union of Great Britain and Ireland.
>
> Preamble.
> Whereas in pursuance of his Majesty's most gracious recommendation to the two Houses of Parliament in Great Britain and Ireland respectively, to consider of such measures as might best tend to strengthen and consolidate the connection between the two kingdoms, the two Houses of the Parliament of Great Britain and the two Houses of the Parliament of Ireland have severally agreed and resolved, that, in order to promote and secure the essential interests of Great Britain and Ireland, and to consolidate the strength, power and resources of the British Empire, it will be adviseable to concur in such measures as may best tend to unite the two kingdoms of Great Britain and Ireland into one kingdom, in such manner, and on such terms and conditions, as may be established by the Acts of the respective Parliaments of Great Britain and Ireland:
>
> [1.] The Parliaments of England and Ireland have agreed upon the articles following:
>
> And whereas, in furtherance of the said resolution, both Houses of the said two Parliaments respectively have likewise agreed upon certain Articles for effectuating and establishing the said purposes, in the tenor following:
>
> Article First
> That Great Britain and Ireland shall upon Jan. 1, 1801, be united into one kingdom; and that the titles appertaining to the crown, &c. shall be such as his Majesty shall be pleased to appoint.
>
> That it be the First Article of the Union of the kingdoms of Great Britain and Ireland, that the said kingdoms of Great Britain and Ireland shall, upon the first day of January which shall be in the year of our Lord one thousand eight hundred and one, and for ever after, be united into one kingdom, by the name of the United Kingdom of Great Britain and Ireland, and that the royal stile and titles appertaining to the imperial crown of the said United Kingdom and its dependencies, and also the ensigns, armorial flags and banners thereof, shall be such as his Majesty, by his royal proclamation under the Great Seal of the United Kingdom, shall be pleased to appoint.
>
> Article Second
> That the succession to the crown shall continue limited and settled as at present.
>
> That it be the Second Article of Union, that the succession to the imperial crown of the said United Kingdom, and of the dominions thereunto belonging, shall continue limited and settled in the same manner as the succession to the imperial crown of the said kingdoms of Great Britain and Ireland now stands limited and

> settled, according to the existing laws and to the terms of union between England and Scotland.

There are eight Articles in all, and the detail can be seen online at:
http://www.legislation.gov.uk/apgb/Geo3/39-40/67/introduction

### 20.4.15 Act of Union – Ireland 1800

This was the second Act. It was held in the Irish Parliament.

> **Title: Act of Union (Ireland) 1800 – 1800 CHAPTER 38 40 Geo 3.**
>
> An Act for the Union of Great Britain and Ireland.
>
> The parliaments of Great Britain and Ireland have resolved to concur in measures for uniting the two kingdoms:
>
> Whereas in pursuance of his Majesty's most gracious recommendation to the two houses of parliament in Great Britain and Ireland respectively, to consider of such measures as might best tend to strengthen and consolidate the connexion between the two kingdoms, the two houses of the parliament of Great Britain, and the two houses of the parliament of Ireland have severally agreed and resolved, that in order to promote and secure the essential interests of Great Britain and Ireland, and to consolidate the strength, power, and resources of the British empire, it will be adviseable to concur in such measures as may best tend to unite the two kingdoms of Great Britain and Ireland, into one kingdom, in such manner, and on such terms and conditions, as may be established by the acts of the respective parliaments of Great Britain and Ireland.
>
> said parliaments have agreed upon following articles:
>
> And whereas in furtherance of the said resolution, both houses of the said two parliaments respectively have likewise agreed upon certain articles for effectuating and establishing the said purposes in the tenor following:
>
> Article First.
> Great Britain and Ireland to be united for ever from 1 Jan. 1801.
>
> That it be first article of the union of the kingdoms of Great Britain and Ireland, that the said kingdoms of Great Britain and Ireland shall, upon the first day of January, which shall be in the year of our lord one thousand eight hundred and one, and for ever, be united into one kingdom, by the name of "the united kingdom of Great Britain and Ireland," and that the royal stile and titles appertaining to the imperial crown of the said united kingdom and its dependencies, and also the ensigns, armourial flags and banners thereof, shall be such as his Majesty by his royal proclamation under the great seal of the united kingdom shall be pleased to appoint.
>
> Article Second.

> Succession to the crown to continue as at present.
>
> That it be the second article of union, that the succession to the imperial crown of the said united kingdom, and of the dominions thereunto belonging, shall continue limited and settled in the same manner as the succession to the imperial crown of the said kingdoms of Great Britain and Ireland now stands limited and settled, according to the existing laws, and to the terms of union between England and Scotland.

Again, there are eight Articles in all, and the detail can be seen online at: http://www.legislation.gov.uk/aip/Geo3/40/38/introduction

### 20.4.16 The Human Rights Act 1998

This lengthy and complex Act can be seen online at:
http://www.legislation.gov.uk/ukpga/1998/42/introduction/enacted

> **Title: Human Rights Act 1998 – 1998 CHAPTER 42.**
>
> An Act to give further effect to rights and freedoms guaranteed under the European Convention on Human Rights; to make provision with respect to holders of certain judicial offices who become judges of the European Court of Human Rights; and for connected purposes.
>
> [9th November 1998]
>
> Be it enacted by the Queen's most Excellent Majesty, by and with the advice and consent of the Lords Spiritual and Temporal, and Commons, in this present Parliament assembled, and by the authority of the same, as follows:—
>
> **Introduction**
>
> **1 The Convention Rights**
>
> (1) In this Act "the Convention rights" means the rights and fundamental freedoms set out in—
>
> > (a) Articles 2 to 12 and 14 of the Convention,
> > (b) Articles 1 to 3 of the First Protocol, and
> > (c) Articles 1 and 2 of the Sixth Protocol,
>
> as read with Articles 16 to 18 of the Convention.
>
> (2) Those Articles are to have effect for the purposes of this Act subject to any designated derogation or reservation (as to which see sections 14 and 15).
>
> (3) The Articles are set out in Schedule 1.
>
> (4) The Secretary of State may by order make such amendments to this Act as he considers appropriate to reflect the effect, in relation to the United Kingdom,

of a protocol.

(5) In subsection (4) "protocol" means a protocol to the Convention—

(a) which the United Kingdom has ratified; or
(b) which the United Kingdom has signed with a view to ratification.

(6) No amendment may be made by an order under subsection (4) so as to come into force before the protocol concerned is in force in relation to the United Kingdom.

## 2 Interpretation of Convention rights

(1) A court or tribunal determining a question which has arisen in connection with a Convention right must take into account any—

(a) judgment, decision, declaration or advisory opinion of the European Court of Human Rights,
(b) opinion of the Commission given in a report adopted under Article 31 of the Convention,
(c) decision of the Commission in connection with Article 26 or 27(2) of the Convention, or
(d) decision of the Committee of Ministers taken under Article 46 of the Convention,

whenever made or given, so far as, in the opinion of the court or tribunal, it is relevant to the proceedings in which that question has arisen.

(2) Evidence of any judgment, decision, declaration or opinion of which account may have to be taken under this section is to be given in proceedings before any court or tribunal in such manner as may be provided by rules.

(3) In this section "rules" means rules of court or, in the case of proceedings before a tribunal, rules made for the purposes of this section—

(a) by the Lord Chancellor or the Secretary of State, in relation to any proceedings outside Scotland;
(b) by the Secretary of State, in relation to proceedings in Scotland; or
(c) by a Northern Ireland department, in relation to proceedings before a tribunal in Northern Ireland-
　(i) which deals with transferred matters; and
　(ii) for which no rules made under paragraph (a) are in force.

Legislation

## 3　Interpretation of legislation

(1) So far as it is possible to do so, primary legislation and subordinate legislation must be read and given effect in a way which is compatible with the Convention rights.

(2) This section—

(a) applies to primary legislation and subordinate legislation whenever enacted;
(b) does not affect the validity, continuing operation or enforcement of any incompatible primary legislation; and
(c) does not affect the validity, continuing operation or enforcement of any incompatible subordinate legislation if (disregarding any possibility of revocation) primary legislation prevents removal of the incompatibility.

## 4  Declaration of incompatibility

(1) Subsection (2) applies in any proceedings in which a court determines whether a provision of primary legislation is compatible with a Convention right.

(2) If the court is satisfied that the provision is incompatible with a Convention right, it may make a declaration of that incompatibility.

(3) Subsection (4) applies in any proceedings in which a court determines whether a provision of subordinate legislation, made in the exercise of a power conferred by primary legislation, is compatible with a Convention right.

(4) If the court is satisfied—

(a) that the provision is incompatible with a Convention right, and
(b) that (disregarding any possibility of revocation) the primary legislation concerned prevents removal of the incompatibility,

it may make a declaration of that incompatibility.

(5) In this section "court" means—

(a) the House of Lords;
(b) the Judicial Committee of the Privy Council;
(c) the Courts-Martial Appeal Court;
(d) in Scotland, the High Court of Justiciary sitting otherwise than as a trial court or the Court of Session;
(e) in England and Wales or Northern Ireland, the High Court or the Court of Appeal.

(6) A declaration under this section ("a declaration of incompatibility")—

(a) does not affect the validity, continuing operation or enforcement of the provision in respect of which it is given; and
(b) is not binding on the parties to the proceedings in which it is made.

## 5  Right of Crown to intervene

(1) Where a court is considering whether to make a declaration of incompatibility, the Crown is entitled to notice in accordance with rules of court.

(2) In any case to which subsection (1) applies—

(a) a Minister of the Crown (or a person nominated by him),
(b) a member of the Scottish Executive,

> (c) a Northern Ireland Minister,
> (d) a Northern Ireland department,
>
> is entitled, on giving notice in accordance with rules of court, to be joined as a party to the proceedings.
>
> (3) Notice under subsection (2) may be given at any time during the proceedings.
>
> (4) A person who has been made a party to criminal proceedings (other than in Scotland) as the result of a notice under subsection (2) may, with leave, appeal to the House of Lords against any declaration of incompatibility made in the proceedings.
>
> (5) In subsection (4)—
>
> "criminal proceedings" includes all proceedings before the Courts-Martial Appeal Court; and
> "leave" means leave granted by the court making the declaration of incompatibility or by the House of Lords.
>
> ...

There are several more sections concerning the methodology and the processes of the Act, and that is followed by a series of Schedules that identify specific Human Rights, and the way they relate to the European Court of Human Rights (ECHR). One or two examples of Schedules are as follows:

## Human Rights Act 1998 – Exaxmples of Schedules

SCHEDULES

**SCHEDULE 1 The Articles**

### Part I The Convention

### Rights and Freedoms

### Article 2

**Right to life**

1    Everyone's right to life shall be protected by law. No one shall be deprived of his life intentionally save in the execution of a sentence of a court following his conviction of a crime for which this penalty is provided by law.

2    Deprivation of life shall not be regarded as inflicted in contravention of this Article when it results from the use of force which is no more than absolutely necessary:

    (a)    in defence of any person from unlawful violence;
    (b)    in order to effect a lawful arrest or to prevent the escape of a person lawfully detained;
    (c)    in action lawfully taken for the purpose of quelling a riot or insurrection.

### Article 3
**Prohibition of torture**

No one shall be subjected to torture or to inhuman or degrading treatment or punishment.

### Article 4
**Prohibition of slavery and forced labour**

1    No one shall be held in slavery or servitude.

2    No one shall be required to perform forced or compulsory labour.

3    For the purpose of this Article the term "forced or compulsory labour" shall not include:
    (a)    any work required to be done in the ordinary course of detention imposed according to the provisions of Article 5 of this Convention or during conditional release from such detention;
    (b)    any service of a military character or, in case of conscientious objectors in countries where they are recognised, service exacted instead of compulsory military service;
    (c)    any service exacted in case of an emergency or calamity threatening the life or well-being of the community;
    (d)    any work or service which forms part of normal civic obligations.

## Article 5
### Right to liberty and security

1   Everyone has the right to liberty and security of person. No one shall be deprived of his liberty save in the following cases and in accordance with a procedure prescribed by law:
    (a)   the lawful detention of a person after conviction by a competent court;
    (b)   the lawful arrest or detention of a person for non-compliance with the lawful order of a court or in order to secure the fulfilment of any obligation prescribed by law;
    (c)   the lawful arrest or detention of a person effected for the purpose of bringing him before the competent legal authority on reasonable suspicion of having committed an offence or when it is reasonably considered necessary to prevent his committing an offence or fleeing after having done so;
    (d)   the detention of a minor by lawful order for the purpose of educational supervision or his lawful detention for the purpose of bringing him before the competent legal authority;
    (e)   the lawful detention of persons for the prevention of the spreading of infectious diseases, of persons of unsound mind, alcoholics or drug addicts or vagrants;
    (f)   the lawful arrest or detention of a person to prevent his effecting an unauthorised entry into the country or of a person against whom action is being taken with a view to deportation or extradition.

2   Everyone who is arrested shall be informed promptly, in a language which he understands, of the reasons for his arrest and of any charge against him.

3   Everyone arrested or detained in accordance with the provisions of paragraph 1(c) of this Article shall be brought promptly before a judge or other officer authorised by law to exercise judicial power and shall be entitled to trial within a reasonable time or to release pending trial. Release may be conditioned by guarantees to appear for trial.

4   Everyone who is deprived of his liberty by arrest or detention shall be entitled to take proceedings by which the lawfulness of his detention shall be decided speedily by a court and his release ordered if the detention is not lawful.

5   Everyone who has been the victim of arrest or detention in contravention of the provisions of this Article   shall have an enforceable right to compensation.

## Article 6
### Right to a fair trial

1   In the determination of his civil rights and obligations or of any criminal charge against him, everyone is entitled to a fair and public hearing within a reasonable time by an independent and impartial tribunal established by law. Judgment shall be pronounced publicly but the press and public may be excluded from all or part of the trial in the interest of morals, public order or national security in a democratic society, where the interests of juveniles or the protection of the private life of the parties so require, or to the extent strictly

necessary in the opinion of the court in special circumstances where publicity would prejudice the interests of justice.

2   Everyone charged with a criminal offence shall be presumed innocent until proved guilty according to law.

3   Everyone charged with a criminal offence has the following minimum rights:

> (a)   to be informed promptly, in a language which he understands and in detail, of the nature and cause of the accusation against him;
> (b)   to have adequate time and facilities for the preparation of his defence;
> (c)   to defend himself in person or through legal assistance of his own choosing or, if he has not sufficient means to pay for legal assistance, to be given it free when the interests of justice so require;
> (d)   to examine or have examined witnesses against him and to obtain the attendance and examination of witnesses on his behalf under the same conditions as witnesses against him;
> (e)   to have the free assistance of an interpreter if he cannot understand or speak the language used in court.

## Article 7
### No punishment without law

1   No one shall be held guilty of any criminal offence on account of any act or omission which did not constitute a criminal offence under national or international law at the time when it was committed. Nor shall a heavier penalty be imposed than the one that was applicable at the time the criminal offence was committed.

2   This Article shall not prejudice the trial and punishment of any person for any act or omission which, at the time when it was committed, was criminal according to the general principles of law recognised by civilised nations.

## Article 8
### Right to respect for private and family life

1   Everyone has the right to respect for his private and family life, his home and his correspondence.

2   There shall be no interference by a public authority with the exercise of this right except such as is in accordance with the law and is necessary in a democratic society in the interests of national security, public safety or the economic well-being of the country, for the prevention of disorder or crime, for the protection of health or morals, or for the protection of the rights and freedoms of others.

## Article 9
### Freedom of thought, conscience and religion

1   Everyone has the right to freedom of thought, conscience and religion; this right includes freedom to change his religion or belief and freedom, either alone or in community with others and in public or private, to manifest his religion or belief, in worship, teaching, practice and observance.

2   Freedom to manifest one's religion or beliefs shall be subject only to such limitations as are prescribed by law and are necessary in a democratic society in the interests of public safety, for the protection of public order, health or morals, or for the protection of the rights and freedoms of others.

## Article 10
### Freedom of expression

1   Everyone has the right to freedom of expression. This right shall include freedom to hold opinions and to receive and impart information and ideas without interference by public authority and regardless of frontiers. This Article shall not prevent States from requiring the licensing of broadcasting, television or cinema enterprises.

2   The exercise of these freedoms, since it carries with it duties and responsibilities, may be subject to such formalities, conditions, restrictions or penalties as are prescribed by law and are necessary in a democratic society, in the interests of national security, territorial integrity or public safety, for the prevention of disorder or crime, for the protection of health or morals, for the protection of the reputation or rights of others, for preventing the disclosure of information received in confidence, or for maintaining the authority and impartiality of the judiciary.

## Article 11
### Freedom of assembly and association

1   Everyone has the right to freedom of peaceful assembly and to freedom of association with others, including the right to form and to join trade unions for the protection of his interests.

2   No restrictions shall be placed on the exercise of these rights other than such as are prescribed by law and are necessary in a democratic society in the interests of national security or public safety, for the prevention of disorder or crime, for the protection of health or morals or for the protection of the rights and freedoms of others. This Article shall not prevent the imposition of lawful restrictions on the exercise of these rights by members of the armed forces, of the police or of the administration of the State.

## Article 12
### Right to marry

Men and women of marriageable age have the right to marry and to found a family, according to the national laws governing the exercise of this right.

## Article 14
### Prohibition of discrimination

The enjoyment of the rights and freedoms set forth in this Convention shall be secured without discrimination on any ground such as sex, race, colour, language, religion, political or other opinion, national or social origin, association with a national minority, property, birth or other status.

### Article 16
### Restrictions on political activity of aliens

Nothing in Articles 10, 11 and 14 shall be regarded as preventing the High Contracting Parties from imposing restrictions on the political activity of aliens.

### Article 17
### Prohibition of abuse of rights

Nothing in this Convention may be interpreted as implying for any State, group or person any right to engage in any activity or perform any act aimed at the destruction of any of the rights and freedoms set forth herein or at their limitation to a greater extent than is provided for in the Convention.

### Article 18
### Limitation on use of restrictions on rights

The restrictions permitted under this Convention to the said rights and freedoms shall not be applied for any purpose other than those for which they have been prescribed.

## Part II The First Protocol

### Article 1
### Protection of property

Every natural or legal person is entitled to the peaceful enjoyment of his possessions. No one shall be deprived of his possessions except in the public interest and subject to the conditions provided for by law and by the general principles of international law.

The preceding provisions shall not, however, in any way impair the right of a State to enforce such laws as it deems necessary to control the use of property in accordance with the general interest or to secure the payment of taxes or other contributions or penalties.

### Article 2
### Right to education

No person shall be denied the right to education. In the exercise of any functions which it assumes in relation to education and to teaching, the State shall respect the right of parents to ensure such education and teaching in conformity with their own religious and philosophical convictions.

### Article 3
### Right to free elections

The High Contracting Parties undertake to hold free elections at reasonable intervals by secret ballot, under conditions which will ensure the free expression of the opinion of the people in the choice of the legislature.

### Part III The Sixth Protocol

#### Article 1
#### Abolition of the death penalty

The death penalty shall be abolished. No one shall be condemned to such penalty or executed.

#### Article 2
#### Death penalty in time of war

A State may make provision in its law for the death penalty in respect of acts committed in time of war or of imminent threat of war; such penalty shall be applied only in the instances laid down in the law and in accordance with its provisions. The State shall communicate to the Secretary General of the Council of Europe the relevant provisions of that law.

The overall "Human Rights" initiative is an attempt to micro-manage human nature in the context of the *individual* while allowing Nation-States and religions to pick and choose the parts that suit them; and the reinforcement of the right to kill during times of war might be seen as an admission of the futility of any attempt to moralise when faced with the impossible complexity of primeval and capricious human *Corporate Empathy*.

For sheer elitism and unashamed self-advancement, however, the next extract concerning the interests of ECHR judges surely deserves a rosette.

### 20.4.16.1 The ECHR Judges Look After Themselves !

There are three more Schedules to the Human Rights Act 1998, making four in total, but it is possibly surprising – outrageous perhaps – to note that the fourth and final Schedule concerns protection of pensions for judges involved with the ECHR.

One might incredulously ask why the judges should have put their own interests forward in this way. It is quite reasonable that their interests should be represented *somewhere*, but the appropriateness of embedding those interests in a Human Rights Act while no other category of citizen is so protected suggests that there has been no reduction in the exasperating greed, arrogance and presumption of superiority made by those who just happen to find themselves in a position to do so. No other person's pension is protected by the ECHR in such a fashion.

> ### ... Judges Enshrine Their Own Comfort
>
> ### SCHEDULE 4
> ### Judicial Pensions
> **Duty to make orders about pensions**
>
> **1**
> (1) The appropriate Minister must by order make provision with respect to pensions payable to or in respect of any holder of a judicial office who serves as an ECHR judge.
>
> (2) A pensions order must include such provision as the Minister making it considers is necessary to secure that—
>
>> (a) an ECHR judge who was, immediately before his appointment as an ECHR judge, a member of a judicial pension scheme is entitled to remain as a member of that scheme;
>> (b) the terms on which he remains a member of the scheme are those which would have been applicable had he not been appointed as an ECHR judge; and
>> (c) entitlement to benefits payable in accordance with the scheme continues to be determined as if, while serving as an ECHR judge, his salary was that which would (but for section 18(4)) have been payable to him in respect of his continuing service as the holder of his judicial office.

There is even more concerning their contributions, and as noted above, one might wonder why pensions for the judges alone should be included in such an Act.

## 21 What the People Say

Several tables that are indicative of well-being in terms of prosperity or poverty, and of life expectancy for instance, along with other quite separate tables that are indicative of good governance are available on the internet. See references in the *Internet Index*. A couple of examples below illustrate such a mixture of real and abstract concepts, and they contain some surprises. See also the following link:
http://info.worldbank.org/governance/wgi/index.aspx#home

### 21.1 The People's View of Governance

That World Bank initiative defines Governance as:

> *"Governance consists of the traditions and institutions by which authority in a country is exercised. This includes the process by which governments are selected, monitored and replaced; the capacity of the government to effectively formulate and implement sound policies; and the respect of citizens and the state for the institutions that govern economic and social interactions among them."*

The same World Bank initiative covers the following categories:

- Voice and Accountability.
- Political Stability and Absence of Violence.
- Government Effectiveness.
- Regulatory Quality.
- Rule of Law.
- Control of Corruption.

The online source above is interactive and beyond further expansion here, but another international representation of the public's confidence in government is presented below as a *Table – of Confidence in Governments Internationally*, derived from data collected by Gallup, best known for their public opinion polls, and provided by the OECD (Organisation for Economic Co-operation and Development).

## 21.2 The People's View of Personal Well-being

An example of the perception of well-being internationally, has been developed from other data also collected by Gallup, and the same data is represented in reports by several different organisations to indicate peoples' perception of themselves in terms of whether they are *Thriving*, or *Struggling*, or *Suffering*, and finally to show their *Daily Experience*. One such report shows 155 countries, with the United Kingdom in 17$^{th}$ place as below, and with 44% of its population *Struggling*. Other countries that are lower in the list have been omitted, but the full report is available as indicated, and with the full report there is also a detailed explanation of the approach taken to gather the data:

http://www.geographic.org/country_ranks/global_wellbeing_index_2010_country_ranks.html

1. Denmark.
2. Finland.
3. Norway.
4. Sweden.
5. Netherlands.
6. Costa Rica.
7. New Zealand.
8. Canada.
9. Israel.
10. Australia.
11. Switzerland.
12. Panama.
13. Brazil.
14. United States.
15. Austria.
16. Belgium.
17. United Kingdom.
18. Further countries omitted.

## 21.3 The Happy Planet Index

A final reference in this chapter of the book is to a similar report from an organisation representing its data on the internet as:
http://www.happyplanetindex.org/data/

It uses the following categories to derive a Happy Planet Index – the higher the score the happier:

- Life Expectancy (Data taken from the United Nations Development Programme).
- Experienced Well-being (Data taken from Gallup).
- Ecological Footprint (Data taken from the World Wildlife Fund).

The Happy Planet Index pushes the U.K. down to 39th., and the U.S.A. to 104th, out of 151.

The surprising entry of two developed nations, the U.K. and the U.S.A., way below countries that occupy the top four places – Costa Rica, Vietnam, Jamaica, and Belize – is possibly a consequence of ecological footprint.

The bottom five entries, positions 147 to 151, are:

- The Central African Republic
- Niger
- Mali
- Botswana
- Chad.

So it's not just a simple case of some sort of ideological inversion of expectations due to the report's design by a statistician with some sort of grudge.

The mathematical calculation of the Happy Planet Index is as follows:
HPI = (Experienced Well-being x Life Expectancy) / EcoFootprint

Any assessment of the value of such league tables, and whether we can draw any conclusions about the worth of life in the developed world is left to the reader.

## 21.4 Table – Confidence in Governments Internationally

http://www.oecd-ilibrary.org/governance/government-at-a-glance-2013/trust-in-government-policy-effectiveness-and-the-governance-agenda_gov_glance-2013-6-en

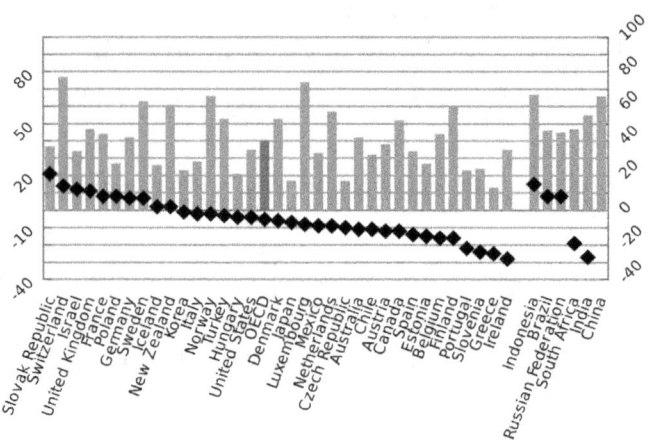

**Source: Gallup World Poll**

Data for Chile, Germany and the United Kingdom are for 2011 rather than 2012. Data for Iceland and Luxembourg are for 2008 rather than 2007. Data for Austria, Finland, Ireland, Norway, Portugal, Slovakia, Slovenia and Switzerland are for 2006 rather than 2007.

Information on data for Israel may be found at the following website: http://dx.doi.org/10.1787/888932315602

Columns above refer to the percentage who answered 'yes' to the question: "Do you have confidence in national government?". The black diamond points indicate the percentage change (fall in confidence) between 2007 and 2012.

## 22 From Freedom to Fiefdom – Summary and Conclusions
## 22.1 Increasing Sophistication

Sophistication:

1. To make less natural and more "worldly".
2. To use Sophistry – subtly plausible but false argument.

All of the examples of betrayal and genocide among increasingly dense and decreasingly diverse communities from the Migration or Early Medieval Age, circa 450 AD, down to the modern age, such as those identified in other chapters of both volumes of this book, are impossibly removed from the prehistoric liberty and unsophisticated choice that pertained in a context of low population levels and true ethnic diversity. Cyclical predations by elites, and reactive revolutions of variable success by the masses, seem to be the norm when human congestion and social sophistication reaches a certain level – a level that was reached long before even the Early Medieval Age. Even then, no doubt, sophistication and divisions provoked an amount of cognitive dissonance, or plain frustration, at times.

In fact noticeably raised population levels, if not exactly congestion, were already apparent to the early Greeks who were driven to attempt and, likely after some failures, eventually were able to settle their expanding and more remote Poleis or Greek City States circa 1000 BC (see Volume Two). So it would seem reasonable to place a definite absence of congestion at a time some millennia before the Greeks.

That presumption is reinforced by at least three considerations: Firstly, we do not know the density of surrounding Mediterranean peoples as the Greeks expanded – they are known to have displaced at least one weaker existing community of the three known earlier cultures on Sicily, and displacement is at least suggestive of congestion; Secondly, in a geographically more distant region, bronze casting was already common by the $2^{nd}$ millennium BC in China – it is noted in Volume Two of this book that by this time China might be considered a mega-civilisation because of its academic references to an *ancient* jurisdiction of *ten thousand states*; Thirdly, back in the Ancient Middle East, we saw the Bronze Age Collapse, circa 1200 BC, that was due to some sort of predatory contention for resources, or to a series of conflicts that were unsustainable by a number of apparently well-established cultures.

On these bases, therefore, it seems reasonable to suggest some millennia BC for the onset of a significant, albeit a still tolerable, density of population and divisive sophistication if not congestion. See also the estimates for population levels at the start of the Holocene Epoch in the section below titled *Hypothesis 1 – A Tower of Babel*, sub-section *Some Real Figures*.

## 22.2 Increasing Governance

The ancient inclusive Pagan spiritualities and superstitious belief systems of the world were overturned by the appearance of the fearsome three Abrahamic faiths (Judaism, Christianity, and Islam) as recently as the start of the Common Era, as population, empires, and communications increased. That notorious and related trinity, with its many prophets in common, represents the world's principal surviving "theism", which, together with Hinduism and Buddhism, has seen religious demands and exploitation increase in proportion to population, as sophisticated ecclesiastical leaders are gratified by their intimidated and unsophisticated slavish flocks – two thousand years of secular Papal Hegemony are typical. Lower population levels and cultural diversity most certainly favoured individual beliefs and an immunity to proselytism.

An environment of low population levels also would have ensured that, despite the concept of debt, there would have been a natural cap on the extent to which personal greed could contrive the bondage of another person without them simply walking away into the wild blue yonder where there could be no pursuit by bailiffs or bands of retainers. Tribal and community honour too, within later growing communities, must surely have been originally a two-way process in which exploitation would be intolerable. Such expectations were recorded in the Anglo-Saxon Chronicles where traditional deliberations of the Folk Moot included the right, that was reserved to the subjects, to renounce their leaders and monarchy.

The exhortation of King Alfred the Great to his successors that is mentioned in Volume Two of this book in the context of the sadly lost *Dome-Book* or *Liber Judicialis* is repeated here:

> *'To all who are charged with the administration of public affairs I give the express command that they show themselves in all things to be just judges precisely as in the Liber Judicialis it is written; nor shall any of them fear to declare the common law freely and courageously."*

Lamentably, at the start of the 2nd millennium in Britain, Norman greed and brutality would introduce a monstrous feudal system and royal prerogative that was designed to keep the majority in serfdom, that majority being the culturally different and vanquished Old British and Anglo-Saxon population. This regime of subjugation was infinitely worse than anything seen under Roman rule, and as recorded throughout subsequent history, the outrage of repression and slavery was maintained for another millennium, and money has literally become, instead of the token of freedom and choice, the root of, if not *all* evil, then certainly by its association with the growth of debt, theft, and usury, a large part of it.

The catalyst for such bondage is, of course, the civilised and deceptively digestible, but ultimately nefarious, notion of employment on the basis of the division of labour while beholden to some notional Capital that must be fed. The money-employment axis is probably the sharpest and most inescapable barb on the tricorn hat of governance, described later, which is taken for granted and accepted by everyone as a necessity; exploited without fair reward throughout recent history by a minority exemplified by and beginning with the Norman Barons; perpetuated by usurious banking mechanisms run by a cultural elite; and opposed only by the futility of an ill-timed and malformed Marxist ideology at one extreme, and a now defunct, impotent, and vilified miscellany of trade unions of workers at another.

For much of the modern period, remuneration for work was made with Fiat Money, Fiat meaning *"let it be done"*, which is interpreted as both the definition of its creation, and a statement of the obligation of its acceptance as legal tender. It is illegal to refuse to accept Fiat Money – a government-sponsored sheet of printed paper with no intrinsic value, but with an implied abstract Government I.O.U. or guarantee, that in Britain was historically equivalent to, or worth, one pound weight of sterling silver.

Strictly, Fiat Money is equivalent to absolutely nothing, since by its definition it cannot be exchanged for any bullion at all. To make matters worse, increasingly over the last twenty or so years, the remuneration for work has been made by an even more abstract electronic transfer of what what might be called *Accounting Units* (£) as credit, and this has obliged everyone to have a bank account, thereby extending the clutches of banks, and introducing some interesting Keynesian changes to the dynamics of the national economy such as those described earlier concerning the *money supply*. Further inequitable drains on personal wealth during this period have been introduced by punitive indirect taxation on essentials, significantly energy, and by the revenue-raising scam related to climate change.

Monetary and commercial system changes that herald a return to the bondage of the Wild West "company store", which was the only outlet for one's wages, and which operated at hyper-inflated prices, are apparent in: firstly, the encapsulation of debt within a facility for its reduction by deductions at the source of one's remuneration; secondly, the amount of actual money tokens in circulation and their availability for economical use; thirdly, rampant and seductive media advertising of consumer products linked to loans for their immediate acquisition; and fourthly, the coupling among credit and savings agencies with resultant effects on contrived inflation and deflation.

Overall, such developments encourage credit obesity at the level of the individual and, at the institutional level, the risk of fund poaching by different arms of a given bank or financial institution as a consequence of the homogenisation of electronic accounts. It is credit obesity and unregulated financial markets that promote instability across the world's markets.

During the second decade of the 3rd millennium the latter peril of fund poaching is scheduled for attention by the introduction of firewalls within financial institutions to separate commercial and domestic departments of the same bank, in the same way that brokers and dealers have, or theoretically had, been separated for decades since the principle of the U.S. Glass-Steagall Act, that was referred to in the earlier section *A History of Money and Financial Empire*. Revisiting the subject, that Act was passed in 1933 by the U.S. Congress as the Banking Act, and it prohibited the participation of commercial banks in investment activities. Its name derives from the two Senators who sponsored it, and it was an emergency response during the Great Depression when around 5,000 banks collapsed.

For what are said to have been symptoms of its "reduced effectiveness", the Glass-Steagall Act was totally repealed in 1999. This was during the Federal Reserve Bank's leadership by Alan Greenspan (1987 to 2006) who presided over a few initially successful active interventions by the "Fed", following the diligence of his predecessor, Paul Volcker (1978 to 1987). Greenspan however, later presided over total anarchy when his policy was based on the assumption that any financial crashes should be allowed to happen because they could be corrected after the event, and that the continuing complexity of financial instruments, such as "derivatives", should be allowed to proceed.

The repeal of the Glass-Steagall Act removed control of many aspects of financial trading, and enabled the even greater proliferation of two types of passive money parasites:

Firstly there were the *brokers* – commission receiving agents dealing on behalf of *clients* to buy and sell securities, such as bonds, stocks, commodities and options – and derivatives.

Secondly, and encouraged by the success of the brokers, there was an explosion of *dealers* – individuals and firms acting on *their own behalf* to trade the same sorts of securities as brokers.

The rise of this trading in abstract financial instruments, mainly those complex derivatives, as opposed to, and at the expense of real industrial product, was the basis for the creation of an abstract system that could be destroyed by the push of a few electronic buttons.

So at the start of humanity's 3rd millennium in the common era, money was now increasingly being made from money, and not from any sort of productive employment or labour; and despite the digitisation and automation of finance, central banks were still permitted by governments to *issue* money against bonds that would reap entirely unearned rewards from interest that would have to be paid eventually by the tax-paying public. And all this in an industry with the power to cripple the global economy.

It would take less than a decade for such a crippling event to occur, and this book suggests that in 1999 it was a most undesirable pair – President Bill Clinton and Alan Greenspan – that were instrumental in creating the conditions that would lead to financial melt-down in 2008.

## 22.3 Humanity's Empirical Phenomena

Empirical: Deduced by experimentation and observation rather than theory.

The historical themes of oppression and resistance laid out in the chapters throughout Volume One, and reinforced by those in Volume Two, are clearly the result of humanity's experimentation upon itself, and those themes now permit some observations and conjectures that will assist the presentation of five specific hypotheses that have enabled the author to come to terms with the present – to find closure concerning the death of true freedom.

## 22.4 Seven Conjectures

### 22.4.1 Conjecture 1 The Equivalence of Feudalism and Imperialism

A first point is that there is an equivalence between Feudalism and Imperialism, in that both involve an hierarchy of deference and obligation based on notional ownership or dominion concerning territory – both the Feudal Lord and the Imperial Conqueror require tribute in some form from the vassal or colony. One difference, however, is in the persistence of obligation or enslavement after the hegemony is apparently lifted, in the case of Imperialism by independence, and in the case of Feudalism by reform.

Historically, Feudalism is terminated piecemeal, though never entirely, over a lengthy period of time, and the travesty of notional land ownership by a small minority to the disadvantage and exclusion of a majority continues without end, whereas following the end of Empire, any remaining notional ownership or bond between the old imperial nation and the newly independent one usually relates to trading rights, language, and culture.

Complete and consensual independence, as distinct from liberation by a war of independence, is a modern imperial concept, and after such agreed independence of a vassal state, memories of ownership on the part of the post-imperial power often change to politically correct contrition and an obligation of support for the ex-vassal state's infrastructure and possibly national defence – if the vassal state needs and wants it. There are numerous examples of both ex-colonial support and neglect throughout the Third World where premature independence, that was enforced by envious and self-interested third party predators such as the U.S. and the U.S.S.R., took no account of civil, tribal, or racial stability.

The analogous case of the individual's transition from feudal subservience to the status of "freeman" carries no such hope of contrition or concession for most definite past evils on the part of the ruling elite, nor any expectation of ongoing maternal support or concern. In fact, the reality is quite the reverse, given the retention by the elite of such a vast and inequitable tract of land that was sequestered by enclosure and contrary to any notion of natural justice. The only concessions ever made by the controlling owners of a community – the various estates of governance – were historically gained as the result of force, or the threat of force on the part of the downtrodden, such governmental generosity commonly being elicited by means of minor insurrection and dissidence, by open rebellion, or as a last resort by armed revolution. Nowadays some concessions are cynically drip-fed under extreme duress by governments in order to buy votes while seeking a mandate for office, but reform of the disparate hoarding of property and land is a taboo that ensures a continuation of the dysfunctional mindset of the majority of the disadvantaged population.

One of the very few known older historical cases of putative obligation to an ex-vassal state, where an attempt may have been made to fulfil the obligation, might be the single and final attempt at the defence of Britain when, after the usurper Emperor Magnus Maximus had left in 388 AD, the Romans under General Flavius Stilicho returned sometime during the period 396 to 398. They conducted a brief naval campaign against the Picts, and on land made a futile attempt to quell invasions by the Scotti and the Saxons. The half Vandal - half Roman General Stilicho actually failed and was executed for his trouble.

### 22.4.2 Conjecture 2 Imperial Slipstreaming

A second point is that many empires seem to have evolved in the wake of an earlier collapsed or weakened empire, and to have derived their power from a vigour arising and maturing because of, not in spite of, an originally raw primitiveness, or "barbarian" state. The new rising empire frequently achieved this evolution through federation and confederation, leading to opportunistic geographical settlements and integration that supported the consolidation of capability and potential. Certainly in earlier administrations, the employment by the imperial power of mercenaries that were raised in vassal states was seen to enhance the military organisation and prowess of the vassal states, and frequently, that employment was expected by the vassal state to advance its stature by penetration of the ranks of the ruling hierarchy so that they might take, maybe Fabian-style, some of the reigns of power.

Such ascent to imperial status by erstwhile disadvantaged and relatively primitive barbarian tribes might be used as an argument in favour of the principle of Empire, given its availability to anyone capable of stepping forward to take the advantage. There is documentary evidence for such advancement of *foederati* in the case of the Western Roman Empire, and there are many examples of both the Huns and the Mongols forming confederations with their victims. This observation leads to the next two related, though expanded, viewpoints.

### 22.4.3 Conjecture 3 Imperial Start and Endgame Issues

A third point concerns the recognition of start and endgame issues. Controlling powers have been seen to arise suddenly from obscure origins, and to be of both short and very long duration, but the decline of an exhausted empire is commonly accompanied by a reverse flow of colonisation leading to the eventual dilution of the identity and culture of the old imperial power, and its mutation into the character of a new empire. Time and again this has corresponded with the forced elevation and modernisation of sometimes innocently primitive and naïve tribes and peoples by conquest and colonisation, only to be followed by their eventual de-colonisation, desertion, and destitution – Southern Rhodesia aka Zimbabwe being the most notorious example which, along with South Africa, has seen the murder of several thousands of both black natives and descendants of earlier colonists who saw themselves as responsible "natives of the land" – white farmers – on a scale that far exceeds any injustice that might have been meted out to the indigenous black population under colonial rule. Those two African nations utterly fail to attract the same criticism by the Western community as that given to the erstwhile dictatorial regimes in Libya and Iraq for instance, and the ongoing absurdity of North Korea – all three of which have been indicted for crimes against their populations, the first two having been subjected to enforced regime change by war. *Realpolitik* will be addressed again later.

End-of-empire syndrome consists, variously, of fatigue and decadence, over-extension, political bullying from peer imperialists, and demographic pressure from within and without. In more remote historical times, as suggested throughout Volumes One and Two, independence has rarely if ever been granted without a struggle or the spontaneous collapse of the imperial power; whereas in the last one hundred years many African nations for instance have been simply abandoned to their fate after independence was encouraged by the international community, leading to economic collapse, genocide, grinding poverty, millions of deaths, and millions of stateless refugees.

As if to underscore the two concepts of repetitive history and the callous discounting of any lessons that might be learned, the original "scramble for Africa" that involved the European powers of the Old World has been simply replaced by a cynical and exploitative dash by the United States, Russia, and China, all of which new-age imperialists use an element of aid to disguise their real motive of the acquisition of natural resources and influence.

Alongside post-imperial obligations in a modern, enlightened, and liberal world there now develops a perceived responsibility for previous exploitation that occurred during the days of colonialism, and a natural consequence of that is a sense of guilt – whether deserved or not – that is reinforced by international peer pressure from without, and from within by a Liberal *meme* that is fostered by well-spoken Marxist historians (see earlier examples concerning the CPHG), and by a cacophony of confused bleating from other quarters, notably the air-headed and superficial journalists who dominate the media. Such divisive social conscience leads to further cultural anarchy and dissolution of the ex-imperial power that in reality favours and benefits absolutely no-one.

## 22.4.4 Conjecture 4 Imperial Legacies

Fourthly, concerning economies and legacies, the prospect of purely economic empires is relatively new. Whispers of economic warfare possibly only gained a raised voice, with increasing technology, as recently as World Wars One and Two, although that quiet beginning has increased to a deafening blast of antagonistic globalisation ever since.

Rather less severe than warfare, aspects of taxation and tribute, however, were significant in antiquity, and are well documented in the Roman,

*From Freedom to Fiefdom – Summary and Conclusions*

Chinese, and Papal Empires, for instance. More recently, there have been satisfying dividend harvests in the cases of the Hanseatic League, the British Empire's East India Company, and in similar Empire-oriented Companies of other European colonial nations. Most of these tributes and harvests were in connection with an incentive to colonise and to influence or proselytise, but in spite of inexcusable blunders that sometimes amounted to atrocities, and despite the imposition of an unwelcome religious ideology, the extraction of natural resources and profits were often associated with at least some sort of economic or socially beneficial return to the vassal states. Such returns are always muted by the bleating referred to above.

Examples of legacies bequeathed by colonial powers to vassal states include: standards of governance where there were none; infrastructure, education, and health standards, where there were none; but regrettably, religious bigotry where there was little or none. Related to the last-mentioned of these legacies are the many ethnically-enhanced sectarian conflicts among tribes who previously had independence, and in line with several themes in this discourse, *the space to remain separate*. In the 3$^{rd}$ millennium specific cases of sectarian nightmare are: the Muslim-Christian atrocities of Nigeria and the Middle East; the Christian-Muslim atrocities of the Balkans and the Middle East; and the Hebrew-Gentile and Hebrew-Muslim atrocities of the Middle East. The common factor, of course, is the multi-coloured Abrahamic cult.

Throughout history without exception the above factors have led to post-colonial fragmentation, civil decay, and internecine strife that for some period of readjustment is far worse than any perceived exploitation under colonial rule. In some circumstances, typified by several African and Middle-Eastern States, it seems beyond recovery in the near future despite the paternal overtures by both ex-colonial powers and the so-called United Nations. Similarly, and in something of a unique position, the symptoms of continuing and increasing Israeli imperialism, and the consequences of an undiminished desire for revenge around all of its borders, are much the same as the negative issues above, and there does not seem to be any mitigating factor or reason for optimism relating to some sort of settlement in the foreseeable future in that arena. The prognosis is quite the reverse.

One final example of unrest following the end of empire concerns the successful attempts by the ethnic minority of Māoris in New Zealand to reverse the Treaty of Waitangi that was signed on 6th February, 1840, by the British Crown and leading Māori chiefs. The Treaty unambiguously ceded sovereignty to Britain in return for citizenship and equal protection under the law for all – including Māori slaves and those who were even lower than slaves that were awaiting a fate in the cooking pot of various cannibalistic Māori factions. That jewel in the South Pacific, the seed of what should have developed over an acceptable timespan into a truly balanced multicultural society, and that appeared for many years to be doing so, is being poisoned by uncontrolled immigration, and by the fulfilled demands by an ethnic minority of very pale-faced part-Māoris for exclusive control of vast tracts of forestry, seashore, and sea and seabed resources. Had the demands for exclusivity of possession been fulfilled in favour of the European majority, then relegation to the status of "Pariah State" might have been expected, followed by trade sanctions and an invasion by the United States of America, confident of victory in the absence of any nuclear defence capability in the small nation of New Zealand.

## 22.4.5 Conjecture 5 Imperial Morality and Stamina

A fifth point concerns the maintenance of an appetite for war, and the prevalence of barbarous behaviour exhibited by some empires. Without doubt many empires are in close contention for the mantle of "Most Undesirable", but it is suggested that those associated with rapacious ideologies, such as Communism, Judaism, Christianity, and Islam, feature towards the top of the list.

Internal barbarity was especially common in the Eastern Roman Empire with its mutilations, and the Mongols and Turks spread terror and murder on a genocidal scale when they were resisted, but the atrocities committed by the Crusaders and Muslims, and later by the Ottomans, did not require provocation. Ripples of Turkish barbarity were also seen in relatively

*From Freedom to Fiefdom – Summary and Conclusions*

recent times, circa 1915, in the form of the genocide involving between one and two million Armenian Christian victims around the time of the demise of the Ottoman Empire, although the Turkish spirit of bestiality continues into the 3$^{rd}$ millennium in like fashion with the oppression of the Kurdish culture and people, and most recently as Turkish complicity and accommodation concerning the 2014 manifestation of ISIL on the south-eastern Turkish border. Turkish assaults on neutral journalists were even televised.

The Imperial Russian Empire of the Czars was land-hungry, and the Soviet Russian Empire wanted to conquer the world for communism. The current empires of the Russian Federation, the United States, and China are resource-hungry, but all are now ideologically ambivalent except for their intense nationalism. One caveat to this concerns the immensely powerful American Jewish lobby – an empire in itself – that has the power to prolong the destabilisation of the Middle East in order to increase the short-term security of Israel. All four of these present-day juggernauts have the most stamina for empire in the 3$^{rd}$ millennium because they all have most, if not all, of the following five attributes:

- Adequate population-demographic profile.
- Rigid political control of their population.
- Colossal natural resources.
- Economic strength.
- A pervasive culture of intense Nationalism.

No other Nation, Federation, or Union compares to Russia, America, and China in the combination of these strengths.

From a close and partisan English perspective, it might be said that England was drawn by religious indoctrination and by cultural links into the Crusades, and that it was drawn by a militant Norman dictatorship into an opposition to any and all examples of recurring European ascendancy. That opposition to any other ascendant Nation-State, noticeably absent during the Anglo-Saxon Early Medieval Age, exceeded the requirements for self-defence for 1,000 years, and it encouraged the development of a bombastic and confident spirit that would see the rise of the British Empire, and England being drawn into World War I by the obligation of a geopolitical alliance despite Victorian familial dynastic links among the European monarchies.

It was arguably only the addition of an anti-fascist ideology to an already ageing spirit that added enough weight in favour of the fulfilment of the Polish and French alliance against Germany at the beginning of World War II. Britain's initial appeasement would, of course, be replaced by a furious resistance and prolonged defiance that was possibly due to two main factors – Sir Winston Churchill and the English Channel.

### 22.4.6 Conjecture 6 Social Maturity, Confidence, Survivability

After some threshold of community development was reached in the distant past, the nature of that threshold being some elusive measure of population density and social conformance and complexity, there would have been a sudden and marked sharpening of cultural awareness and tribal bonding akin to maturity – a virtually physical sense of community and benevolent patriotism that favoured tribal increase and not extinction, and that might be compared to other evolutionary step-changes or later socio-political revolutions. After that seminal moment that made cultural survival more likely, it is suggested here that interactions among such similar tribal communities have been much the same throughout subsequent historical time and geographical space, the only variations being the size of the communities, and the technology that was available to accentuate the differences and advantages of one over another.

Some minimal set of subconscious lessons had been learned, and a steadily thickening carapace of patriotic nationalism was a necessary shield against aggressors for many centuries. However, that shield has now become both a cause of street-thuggery and a target for the bile of simple-minded though devious elitist-socialist-thuggery, the latter being vomited increasingly onto the streets of cities worldwide, as the aggressive evils of fascism are ignorantly conflated with defensive nationalism.

The atavistic preserve of nationalism has been brought into undeserved disrepute by two recent world wars, the second of which at least was more the result of the clash of two uninhibited and belligerent political ideologies than of simple nationalisms. It was the survival in undiminished potency of one of those ideologies, Stalinist Communism, nominally on the side of the victors, that ensured its propagation like a cancer throughout many of the weakest parts of the social infrastructure of the winning side, particularly academia, the media and journalism, and the entertainment industry. An early result was an over-reaction in the form of McCarthyism in the United States, but just a heavy-lidded, blinking obtuseness in Britain and the rest of Europe; and the later outcome everywhere has been that traditional culture has been dragged down with the disposal of the respectability of nationalism.

It may be that, in spite of the posited social threshold that was reached in the distant past, society could yet be, or maybe already has been, plunged sideways towards chaotic disorder with loss of corporate balance – the *Koyaanisqatsi* of the Hopi Indians – a vast humiliation of at least language, as the syndrome was so eloquently described by the film director, Francis Ford Coppola when commenting on the film *Koyaanisqatsi* – a voiceless photo-montage of both stunningly natural and nauseously industrial images of the U.S.

A vast humiliation of language in the form of political correctness would certainly seem to be one of the troubling symptoms affecting Britain, Europe, ex-colonies, and their cultures in the 3$^{rd}$ millennium.

## 22.4.7 Conjecture 7 Perpetual Warfare

Nowhere does peace last forever, and a constant recourse to war may be signified by any combination of social, civil, cultural, or international issues.

It is suggested that human nature and the fundamental imperatives of greed and security, that are often referred to as *Realpolitik*, are unalloyed by technology, time, and geography, and that in reality it is only our perception and confidence – our assessment of risks, and our willingness to gamble – that vary. As a species we are compulsive gamblers, devoid of the concept of loss.

All of the above is, of course, just another way of saying that historical records of empires really do suggest that history inexorably and unfailingly repeats itself, but each time with a vengeance, and with increased human collateral damage. We ignore the very obvious lessons at our peril.

## 22.5 Five Hypotheses

A Review:

1. Global welfare and social integrity in our age is less than that pertaining at the dawn of civilisation, and the downward spiral is marked by a series of tipping points, the first of which was the development of the faculty of speech.

2. The descent of man is a consequence of humanity's social evolution and *social natural selection* – a counterpart to, and a counter-productive consequence of, biological mutation and Darwinian natural selection.

3. Belligerent posturing remains a fundamental and determining trait of humanity at both individual and group levels. Enhanced by the faculty of speech, and hampered by ideology, human behaviour can be represented by a very simple syndrome that derives from the ancient theme of the seven deadly sins. As portrayed in many nature films, we inherit belligerence and posturing in undiluted measure from our anthropological ancestors.

4. The paradigm of governance today is corrupt and threadbare, and worldwide it can be reduced to just three aspects: National Government, Corporate Spirituality, and a Currency Mechanism. Unfortunately, as will be shown, these three concepts derive directly from the practical social consequences of the previous two hypotheses concerning social natural selection and belligerent posturing, the provenance of which guarantees their fallibility and the inevitable shortcomings of all forms of governance.

5. Lessons from history are rarely learned because perception from a comfortable perspective fails to capture essential dynamics, and cannot capture horror. Group Psychopathy compounds the problem.

*From Freedom to Fiefdom – Summary and Conclusions*

### 22.5.1 Hypothesis 1 – A Tower of Babel
### 22.5.1.1 Introduction – This Book's Front Page Questions

The simple answer to the questions on the front cover of this book, and an explanation that might perhaps be related in a small way to the story of the Tower of Babel in the Book of *Genesis* in the Hebrew Bible, is that early humans developed the faculty of speech in a remote age – in an anthropological age of belligerence and bellicosity possibly a million or more years ago – and in a culture that was not far removed from that of the apes. In that intellectually immature human phase, rhetoric and verbal bullying developed before adequate ethical instincts became part of the human psyche.

The examples below of potentially timeless "Global News Headlines" are the consequence of such rhetoric, and they illustrate the issues that this author has sought to fully explore within the pages of Volumes One and Two.

Speech can be either a "one to one" or a "one to many" linkage among the participants in a verbal exchange, as opposed to the concept of a corporate, unspoken or subconscious linkage that is reinforced by limited but respected habit among a speechless group of lesser beings. See the earlier discussions on Synchronicity and corporate behaviour in the section titled *Speculative Mechanisms*. In addition to open intention, words can be whispered, they can be overheard when they were not meant to be, they can be the agents of disinformation, and they can be misinterpreted and misappropriated – wilfully or by accident.

Compared to the restrictions imposed by limited speechless habits, with their quietly implicit and ritualistic self-regulation, the cacophonous explosion of an infinitude of nouns, verbs, adjectives, and pronouns that followed the development of speech has become as much a part of natural selection as biological mutation, see also below. Such an explosion of potential duplicity is a recipe for seriously enhanced social disaster, and the liberal expression of speech by those who could shout the loudest, perversely, would soon lead to the suppression of free speech, and it would enable the coercion of a weak heretical majority by a ruthless dogmatic minority that would continually seek ways to maintain its own favoured status quo.

Loud speech and words destroy muted consensus, and they enable "dictatorship" – the very word says it all – and global inequity today is directly proportional to population growth and the sophistication of a vocal "civilisation". In the present day there are daily reminders of ill-conceived and foolish attempts at dictatorship through some forms of social networking that elicit "followers" and provide a platform for bad-mouthed autocrats.

When comparing the origin and destiny of humanity all these issues can only suggest the fall of mankind not an ascent.

### 22.5.1.2 Global Front Page News Headlines

The following sound-bites might well be the consequence of social, financial, and geopolitical empire and tyranny throughout history, and they bemoan the paradox of progress.

*Division and Specialisation of Labour Exploited by Predatory Intermediaries!*

*Direct Barter Replaced by Bankers Peddling Interest-laden Debt!*

*Land Claims on Free and Common Land Produce Notional Identity for only a Minority!*

*Refugees in Their Own Society – the Majority of Humanity Will Never Have Roots or Rights of Tenure!*

*Religious Ideology Replaces Instinct – Now Parasitic On Human Endeavour!*

*Abracadabra – In nomine Patris, et Filii, et Spiritus Sancti – Allahu Akbar – God is Greatest!*

*War Promotes National Unity, Peace Promotes Division and Complacency!*

### 22.5.1.3 Widening the Hypothesis

Although all these issues – a speech-inspired nemesis – are presented as hypothesis one, they might more correctly be regarded as comprising a recursive hypothesis that gains strength as a result of appraising the earlier

*From Freedom to Fiefdom – Summary and Conclusions*

seven conjectures in conjunction with the four following hypotheses. It is a proposal that will hopefully become fully credible to the reader after all the imperial sagas in both volumes of the book have been read in their entirety.

This first hypothesis is the result of an extended contemplation of the consequences of all examples of humanity's evolution – being a series of noisy and noisome adventures down the millennia, more often than not involving abhorrent acts that truly defy the notion of civilised behaviour, and that continue to the present day with undiminished horror.

### 22.5.1.4 More is Less

In support of the first hypothesis it is suggested that if it were possible to derive a measure of the net global well-being and social integrity in the present day, and to compare it with the same measure made at the dawn of civilisation, then we would probably find that the measure today is far inferior to that pertaining at the dawn of civilisation.

Let us look, for instance, at just one aspect of our current experience – debt-slavery – that is to say, the obligation to redeem "original debt", as if it were some sort of doctrinal equivalent to the imagined "original sin" of Christianity. A measure of the need to redeem such debt, or at least to avoid it, in the only way possible as an independent adult – by providing one's labour to someone else for most of one's life – has become incomparably higher since the ancient innovation of the principle of the "Division of Labour". Indeed such exploitation by its definition could not have occurred in "prehistoric" times, and modern times have refined the enslavement.

The appeal of such a broad first hypothesis, a hypothesis centred on spoken language, can best be strengthened by personal reflection on the worldwide historical record of ideologically-related increasing subservience, mutilation, and slaughter over the centuries; and by a serious look at the differentials of wealth nowadays that are only made possible by dogmatic ideology reinforced by recent technology. More than half of the world's population live in relative poverty, and possibly a quarter in life-threatening circumstances.

To support a personal reflection, and in order to give one's mind and powers of conception some sort of datum, it might be helpful to substitute for the rather nebulous "dawn of civilisation", an arbitrary, more recent but nevertheless early date for which we have some academic estimates, and to consider one or two of the "achievements" of humanity.

### 22.5.1.5 Some Real Figures

Total world population of Homo sapiens of all ethnicities at the start of the Holocene Epoch, that is circa 10,000 BC, is estimated by several academics to have been between one and ten millions, but with a higher probability of it being less than five millions (5,000,000) in that vast and open world. For the rest of this section we will assume the figure of five millions as a worst case in respect of the following illustrations.

In 2015 – that is twelve millennia later – the world population is more than seven thousand millions (7,000,000,000), most being in close confinement, burdened with inflexible obligation and legislation, and frustrated by restricted movement; these restrictions being due to man-made reasons of liberty and-or affordability.

Next, looking for some human achievements:

### 22.5.1.6 Wealth Then and Now

Firstly in terms of wealth, it is suggested that it would not have been possible for 1% of the early Holocene population (50,000 people) to have controlled 50% of the world's riches – such is the degree of wealth differential that we see today by 2015 estimates.

Another way of looking at this is to consider whether, spread across the whole open world, devoid of infrastructure, it would have been likely or even possible for one person in every one hundred persons to possess and control more than that controlled by the other ninety-nine – that would be to suggest that 4,950,000 people would have submitted to containment in a world with no barriers to freedom of movement when the physical odds were 99 to 1 in favour of successful escape from bondage. Furthermore, such successful escape or release would have been encouraged because the concepts of enforceable land-ownership, debt, and money, did not exist.

### 22.5.1.7 War and Genocide Then and Now

Secondly, in terms of the ability to cause deaths by conflict, in 1940 the world population was about 2,300 millions. Deaths during the Second World War were about 85 millions, which gives a global death rate of 3.6% of the world's population. In 10,000 BC the population was likely to have been a maximum of 5 millions, of which 3.6% gives a figure of 180,000. It is most unlikely that such a thinly scattered population could have contrived the deaths of such a host with such a space in which to disperse, and in the absence of ideological baggage.

### 22.5.1.8 Life Expectancy Then and Now

Thirdly, the myth of poor life expectancy is a matter of interpretation and sensitivity. Often quoted figures that indicate something like an average longevity of 35 years for an adult at the start of the Holocene are derived by averaging adult survival, as implied by archaeological evidence, with infant mortality. Infant deaths were much higher historically, although they were no barrier to survival of the species, and they did not stop an increase to the unacceptable population levels of today. Statistics resulting from ten adults surviving to the age of 70, in a society where ten infants were still-born, would be presented as a life expectancy of 35, which is artful and bogus if one really wants an indication of the quality and expectation of life by mature individuals. Additionally, the demographics of poverty stricken and drought-blighted regions of the world today suggest that infant mortality is of little real significance to national survival.

### 22.5.1.9 Pandemic Then and Now

Fourthly, in terms of health and serious diseases like the plague, epidemics and pandemics have occurred throughout history, and they continue to occur due to increased trade – globalisation – and due to congested living conditions. Many other present-day afflictions such as cancer and obesity are exacerbated by modern lifestyle. Therefore, any argument that ill-health was greater in antiquity is fatuous and more likely to be the reverse.

Two references on this subject are as follows:

http://www.ancient-origins.net/news-evolution-human-origins/life-expectancy-myth-and-why-many-ancient-humans-lived-long-077889

http://longevity.about.com/od/longevitystatsandnumbers/a/Longevity-Throughout-History.htm

### 22.5.1.10 Quality of Life Then and Now

Finally, it is suggested that a debate concerning quality of life would also be won in favour of the inhabitants of antiquity, as might be implied by the results of some present-day surveys, the results of which depress the U.S.A. and the U.K. for instance, far below countries, such as Costa Rica and Vietnam. See the previous chapter in this volume titled *What the People Say* for further detail on this.

If the reader suspects that he or she is languishing a victim of the fifth hypothesis, to be discussed shortly, then it is suggested that further contemplation of any of the periods in the chapter *The Two Thousand Year War – Papal Hegemony* might help with a fresh reality shock.

### 22.5.2 Hypothesis 2 – Four Social Mutations and Squalor

It is the author's second hypothesis that the *descent of man* is a consequence of humanity's social evolution over many millennia, from a state of freedom, that was once as complete as that of any animal in the wild, to a condition of multi-faceted fiefdom – the descent having been driven by bullying, consensual deference, unopposed bondage, and one-sided obligation; all as a result of *social natural selection* – a process that in scale at least, is unique to *homo sapiens* – whereas Darwinian natural selection is considered to apply to all living forms.

Via social natural selection, class stratification becomes almost unavoidably hereditary and accepted by those of all tiers – loyal, self-effacing monarchists are found everywhere from hovel to palace. No revolutionary reversal has ever persisted, and one need look no further than the billionaires of the ex-Soviet Union and China for confirmation – where oligarchs were born overnight from the ranks of the previously equal *apparatchiks*.

It is suggested that as an augmentation of the brute force that regulates the lower orders of animals, this form of natural selection has been occasioned by four very specific universal *social mutations*.

### 22.5.2.1 The Origins of Governance

Four universal social mutations, being of ancient origin, can be found in most civilisations around the world, and they may be summarised as:

**1. The Division of Labour**, or specialisation of work skills, and its later exploitation by a possessive social stratum that has accumulated produce while others have merely consumed it without a second thought.

Surplus produce might be considered as one type of capital, and in equitable conditions its accumulation is an option available to all.

Specialisation within the limited range of skills necessary for life in antiquity may have begun with or just before the development of the faculty of speech, but the ability to take advantage of one's successfully accumulated produce must have required some increased level of communication and social cohesion. Therefore it is suggested that two "tipping points", possibly separated in time, are associated with this first social mutation – specialisation, and exploitation.

**2. Land Ownership**, as distinct from territorial occupation by lower animals.

This is exemplified in Britain by Norman hegemony and the imposition of feudalism at the start of the $2^{nd}$ millennium; and by later thefts of historical common land by privileged Norman descendants – both aristocratic and judicial.

Land is another type of capital, and all capital taken together is self-sustaining. Profiteering or taking dividends, through enforceable land ownership, must have required the faculty of speech and some level of congestion in an established society or there could have been no "customer" base.

**3. The Imposition of religious ideologies**, with their corrupt ecclesiastical elites and militia, in place of instinctive superstition and Pagan spirituality.

The ascent of ecclesiastic-minded bullies is enabled by the intimidation of the masses: by the fear of eternal damnation or immediate physical beheading; and by the creation of a climate in which apostasy is a worse blasphemy than agnosticism – gang membership of Islam, for instance, is for life.

The vast capital and fabulous wealth accumulated by members of the Abrahamic League such as the Christian Pope, Jewish-International financiers, and the Muslim Aga Khan exceeds by far the GDP of many of the world's Nation-States.

**4. Contamination, by usury** and intermediaries, of originally simple balancing mechanisms that evolved to support the bartering of resources and commodities, and in very recent times the contamination of entire economies by contrived inflation.

All these corruptions assist the differential accumulation of capital.

It is the need for management of the first two of the above developments – two developments that only with abuse become particularly divisive – that gives rise to notions of the requirement for some form of governance to regulate and perpetuate a status quo – the "haves" and the "have nots". The last two of the above developments – the inventions of religion and usury – then become defensive weapons of the emerging elite – an elite that will form the central government. Three resultant corporate manifestations that comprise overall governance will be identified later.

The reality of all four of the above concepts have become apparent as history unfolded with bewilderingly repetitive indignities and horrific undertone, and these concepts are not the author's, they have all been alluded to by many socio-political commentators, ranging in more modern times from Thomas Paine and his many peers, through Karl Marx, to Adolf Hitler, and they are both undeniably factual and perfectly to be expected in societies that have exceeded some threshold of population size and sophistication that was crossed many millennia ago. Many repellent ideological absurdities have followed that sophistication, but to label imperialism and capitalism *per se*, as evil, is like accusing a predatory carnivore of murder when it kills for food, or like blaming a bullet that kills someone.

A harsh but suitable allegory of our over-developed global society, with all of its psychological garbage, might be the case of a newly urbanised society, embraced by all, but without the ability to adequately process and manage the disposal of its own ideological and physical excreta. Resulting conditions would be cultural and physical squalor, in which the imperative to survive at any cost, and to take pleasure at any expense, could only lead to worsening and dysfunctional behaviour, loss of all dignity, and corruption.

The next section presents evidence of precisely that type of squalor.

### 22.5.2.2 A Social Nadir in Modern Britain

Demeaning examples of the results of the concepts described above appeared in gargantuan quantity throughout the upper echelons of society, and among councillors, during the parliamentary expenses scandal in Britain at the end of the first decade of the $3^{rd}$ millennium. It is clear that equivalent scandals have been recurring features for several centuries in many financial, cultural, and commercial initiatives, and also in public life where Machiavellian principles are sanctioned for the rulers, and straight and narrow strictures are prescribed for the ruled. However, by the start of the second decade of the present millennium when it might have been supposed that a lesson had been learned during the first decade, even further distasteful characteristics emerged, and continue to emerge and to defy any belief in the advancement of human ethics in the modern age.

Socio-political developments so far during the $3^{rd}$ millennium fully support the concept of leveraged degradation of mankind. Just three specific examples are as follows:

**Firstly**, the lobbying scandals during which politicians prostituted themselves at the hands of those seeking privileged access to parliament and undeserved influence.

**Secondly**, the hacking scandals – driven by journalistic greed – that reached into the mire of mainstream media and law enforcement agencies with no regard for an individual's entitlement to privacy and grief in times of loss.

**Thirdly**, the large-scale racially organised sexual abuse of white children by Muslim Pakistani men in, at the last count, at least seven British cities – Reading, Oxford, Birmingham, Rotherham, Rochdale, Aylesbury, and London. There are thousands of known cases.

All of the many distasteful episodes associated with just these three examples left ever widening ripples of disgust, as they exposed, particularly in connection with the third case of ideologically-driven sexual abuse, complicit and corrupt social and council workers, and even law enforcement officers, all of whom denied the very real responsibility for the crimes that they had committed in the trusted roles that they had perverted in pursuit of some sort of gain.

There are constant examples of depravity and corrupt practice by those in positions of trust in every single area of society, and although the concept of human depravity is not a new one, it is both the cause of, and the consequence of, humanity's historical loss of liberty, and the transition for most of us from freedom to fiefdom, albeit with the occasional palliative of relative social and financial success – there is always someone worse off, and many shamelessly look the other way.

The next section is an attempt to identify the characteristics of human nature that produce the squalid and deviant actors that have created such a broken nation in the British Isles, and conveniently it will be found that the characteristics apply equally well to the corporate Nation-State.

### 22.5.3 Hypothesis 3 – Human Nature and Corporate State Nature

In order to expand the notions of human nature, both at the level of the individual, and in the case of corporate groups, an examination of "posturing" must be made, and this third hypothesis proposes that a very simple syndrome defines such posturing or behaviour over time.

A synopsis of this posturing can be completely represented by conflicting collisions among the following extremes of both individual and corporate group behaviour. The corporate group may be any conglomerate of human beings from a "mob", to a tribe, or to a sovereign Nation-State.

The concept of defining non-judgemental extremes, within which character may fluctuate, is derived from the age-old concept of the entirely judgemental seven deadly sins that have been proscribed by historical figures ranging from King Solomon three thousand years ago, to monks and popes of the so-called common era.

It is proposed that the entirety of the behavioural boundaries suggested in this book are sufficient to explain all of the aberrations and expressions of an ambitious human nature in its socio-political roles, as it negotiates the steep *psychological slalom* of life from top to bottom, and with relentless repetition from birth to death; the onerous cycle being further burdened with conflicting musky urges and social mores.

The perception of oneself, one's adversaries, and one's allies, is affected by the relative positions of all three within such boundaries, and the course for many will involve a willing or unwilling brush with the extremes, and in some cases will even lead to a preference for ideological extremism. Simplified and incomplete symptoms at any instant might be naïvety or extreme ego for example, but the third hypothesis in this book suggests that all seven extremes of posture are necessary and sufficient to characterise the subject in a useful way for historical comparisons. That subject may equally be an individual or a Nation-State.

The schematic representation below should really be a continuous circular course since the duration of a lifetime may expose us to changing influences that drive us to different postures as we careen among these sometimes difficult-to-avoid boundary markers; nobody can pass this obstacle course without some loss of points. In the case of an individual, a bad line through these extremes of posture may be taken without any conscious decision but purely as a result of inherent character and possibly radicalising peer pressure, and in the case of a corporate state the line may result from historical achievements or failures that have led to either excessive zeal after victory, or to lack of security after defeat.

Therefore, there may be a built-in compromised attitude, and this can lead to the very same circumstances at a corporate level as at the level of an individual member of society. In the case of the former these aberrations and extremes may favour a Nadir of Governance that is comparable with the sort of individual dysfunctionality that leads to social pariahs and pariah States as exemplified in the earlier section titled *A Social Nadir in Modern Britain.*

This admittedly pseudo-scientific representation is the author's attempt to categorise both people and empires in respect of their development and behaviour over time. It was designed to focus thought, and to help to combine the concept of the four social mutations listed above, with the concept of the three corporate takeovers that are exercised by an evolving government, and that will be described shortly.

The intention is to show a sequence of pairs of extremes of posture between which individuals and Nation-States or empires will pass during their lifetime from conception to death. Other pairs of extreme attitude might be added to, or substituted for the author's choice, but the principle should be clear; and other concepts, such as pragmatism, altruism, and integrity, might be subsidiary within the set below, as would the traditional seven deadly sins.

## From Freedom to Fiefdom – Summary and Conclusions

Susceptibility to the extremes is repeated endlessly, and an affinity may be influenced by:

- For an individual – *personal epiphany*.
- For the corporate Nation-State – *reform or tyranny*.
- For groups within the Nation-State – *revolution*.

Recognition of the need to condition and control the capricious individual among these extremes for the good of society has been demonstrated throughout history and diverse cultures, and we see it evolving and expressed as:

- Superstition and Taboo.
- Custom.
- Commandments.
- Laws.

Recognition of the need to condition and regulate the internal and extra-territorial behaviour of Nation-States is evidenced by:

- National Constitutions.
- International Conventions and Treaties.

Attempts to implement these controls and regulations have resulted in a kaleidoscope of national and international primitive councils and Courts of Justice over several millennia.

A schematic illustrating individual and corporate posturing is below.

### 22.5.3.1 Schematic Showing Individual and Corporate Posturing

**Instinct** *versus* **Ideology**

**Hubris** *versus* **Humility**

**Benevolence** *versus* **Avarice**

**Prudence** *versus* **Indolence**

**Anonymity** *versus* **Identity**

**Treachery** *versus* **Fidelity**

**Celebrity** *versus* **Infamy**

The analogy is intended to be viewed as a slalom course through which a contestant has to pass as quickly as possible, and repeatedly, while remaining within the extremes.

For reference, the historical seven deadly sins are:

1. **Pride**
2. **Envy**
3. **Gluttony**
4. **Lust**
5. **Anger**
6. **Greed**
7. **Sloth**

The next section relates features of present-day governance to our ancient past using some of the above conjecture.

## 22.5.4 Hypothesis 4 Part One: Mechanisms of Governance

The fourth hypothesis proposes that just three principles of governance of the Nation-State are sufficient to understand the management of present-day Society; and that, from four universal social mutations suggested earlier, they evolve over time and under the influence of rhetoric. They are nothing short of three "Corporate Takeovers" of the individual, and have evolved from the prudent and ancient folklore that pertained when speech was a novelty.

These three principles of governance have become self-sustaining and corrupt behemoths that are identifiable today regardless of culture or political regime; and individuals that used to be an inclusive part of a corporation of speechless hominins – guided by instinct and common habit – are now decoupled from their fellow-subjects except for language-specific spoken words. The dictatorial principles are as follows:

### 22.5.4.1 A System for National Government

Arising from the need to manage an increasingly complex society that results from abuse of the first two social mutations of convenience listed above – *Division of Labour* and *Land Ownership* – this control mechanism comprises Central and Local Government and all of their enforcement and policy agencies and operatives that are spread across notional Legislative, Judicial, and Executive branches, with the support of Quangos and Think Tanks. Central and subsidiary banks complete the physical mechanisms, and public opinion is strongly influenced through the complicity and partisan publicity that governments derive from most mainstream media organisations, sometimes referred to as the "fourth estate". The very obvious symbiosis among political parties and moguls of the media and business needs no further indictment here. It is apparent every day.

### 22.5.4.2 Corporate Spirituality

Corporate Religions, Churches, Charities, and Sects have evolved over the millennia – frequently as one of the estates of governance – and they gain their oppressive dominance by the hijacking and mutation of originally healthy and defensive primal superstition. The hijackers are elite ecclesiastical superintendents – the clergy – often possessed with a dubious spirituality. Nourishment of their sometimes militaristic organisations takes, among this clergy, the form of dedication to spiritual promotion; and among the congregation: obligatory financial donations; a fear of death; and blind faith in an alternative to oblivion.

All the exploitative doctrine and sacraments guarantee a healthy revenue and lifestyle for the higher clerical elite, while some of the laity – religious activists seized with missionary zeal – will become victims of their own delusion and they will happily kill and-or be killed.

### 22.5.4.3 A Resource Exchange Mechanism

The main characteristic of money-changers through the ages that is adopted in support of the imposition of governance is usurious and debt-based money. This binds a population to a lifetime of graft. In more recent times, corrupt and exploitative fiscal policy facilitates the upward migration of wealth nationally, and internationally, the payment to capital-rich bodies of remote and unaccountable domicile. The tax-paying public becomes obliged to make these payments through yet more graft; and globalisation dramatically increases both the yield and the robustness of such corrupt practices by the introduction of layers of international obscurity.

The next section re-introduces the concept of exploitation and proselytising that inevitably arise when a government takes extreme positions among the boundaries suggested by the *Schematic Showing Individual and Corporate Posturing* above.

### 22.5.5 Hypothesis 4 Part Two: Maintaining the Grip

Once true democratic freedoms have been lost to the oligarchy that is the real beast behind all governments, then ownership as opposed to leadership of mankind must be maintained by constant evangelism and exploitation within the three fields of endeavour detailed below.

### 22.5.5.1 Political Evangelism

Combining deliberate misrepresentation of facts, or disinformation that is sometimes issued by both allies and enemies, with the anxiety of daily existence under objectionable, devious, and corrupt leadership or employment, can lead to unfortunate consequences for a mindset that is already ill at ease because of the above psychological syndrome. When unmitigated by reason, many individuals and Nation-States have thereby been driven from a position of mild dissent to the development and the pursuit of ideologies that have frequently led to misery, civil unrest, war, and death for millions.

Such a wrong line can be taken as easily by someone born with a silver spoon in their mouth as by a pauper, and this worldly aspect can lead to:

*political evangelism and fanatical control that mercilessly brooks no dissent.*

### 22.5.5.2 Religious Evangelism

Another less tangible manifestation of a slip-up in this slalom cum psychological syndrome derives from a blend of superstition, fear of death, and the abdication of individual responsibility by the escalation of all personal issues to a higher guardian authority – God. This leads to blind faith in the invisible, and the vice of unfettered imagination that creates the fear of, and submission to God. Additionally, personal frustrations and perversions that are inevitably associated with insecurity, with dysfunctional feeble-mindedness, or with an unhealthily obsessive need to bond with others of the same flimsy persuasion, encourage contradictory senses of superiority, invincibility, and self-righteous pious mission. This other-worldly aspect can lead to:

*religious evangelism and fanatical proselytism that mercilessly brooks no dissent.*

### 22.5.5.3 Monetary Evangelism

Finally, outside the confines of political or religious doctrine, and initially conceived to satisfy a laudable desire for personal resource or commodity security in connection with both storage of goods and bartering transactions, bankers and banking practices based on usury (interest bearing loans) have been expanded and perfected to an extreme during a recent period of just over four hundred years, although banking originated at least two millennia ago in the classical world of Mesopotamia, specifically among the Semitic Babylonians. Some historians suggest an even more remote time.

It is these relatively recent bankers – mutant Goldsmiths – that have inveigled governments into the support for an unsustainable system of generating money through debt – the Fractional Reserve Banking System and Fiat money, all of which were described earlier in the book. The refinement of bank structure and banking methodologies, with the resultant cancerous accumulation of fabulous wealth by a usurious banking elite, and with that elite's realisation of national and global monetary domination over a multitude of lesser mortals that actually bear the debt, has become an end in itself that even attracts bonuses. Usury and bonuses – insatiable greed with no moral or rational objective can lead to:

*monetary evangelism and fanatical exploitation that mercilessly brooks no dissent.*

### 22.5.5.4 The Tricorn Hat Caricature

In a momentary caricature, this evangelising trio of worldwide exploitative mechanisms takes on the semblance of a gigantic, battered, and threadbare tricorn hat in a hideously deceptive chameleon livery. It is the obligatory ideological top-knot nowadays truculently sported by any political popinjay, be they reactionary or revolutionary; a badge of office of the coxcomb or Jacobin that aspires to celebrity and leadership, and one that is also sheepishly worn by many small-time buffoons. This satirical abstraction of governance is nowadays an odious and an invidious icon, doffed at will, and to which it is assumed we will all defer. It is otherwise held in place by an ancient chinstrap of social division and exclusion. The complete and ludicrous triple-barbed assembly is a result of the four timeless universal social mutations alluded to above, and it will become apparent that much of what we accept to be self-evident truths about such a trinity of notoriety as represented by the tricorn hat caricature, are at best naïve distortion, and at worst calculated deception.

In the search for hard historical evidence of the origins of the above dilemma, and during the presentation of that evidence, there are many traps in the form of: firstly, mischievous conspiracy theorists' wilful misinterpretations of fact; secondly, the social conformists' myopic greyness and apocalyptic amnesia; and thirdly, overt charlatans and closet supremacists galore. The evidence is there, and this book is about facts – however unpalatable and indigestible they may be. It is presented without sympathy for whomever this literary digest may cause nausea.

### 22.5.5.5 A Nadir of Western Governance

Reckless and unconscionable political coercion, multi-cultural religious intimidation, and monetary exploitation is demonstrably the form and fabric of the tricorn hat. It graces the heads of society and governance today, and it is made worse by individual cowardice, ignorance, and inexperience – all of which can be found within venal central government executives worldwide.

There is always a very real danger that political leadership and individual spirituality can turn despotic and become corrupt, and there is always a very real danger that the drive for financial security can become all-consuming, with an insatiable drive towards monetary obesity for some at the expense of financial famine for others. Political, Religious, and Financial-Fiscal evangelism, without integrity or credibility – the tricorn hat of bad governance throughout at least recent history.

Similarly tainted, aristocratic and royal privilege are too frequently associated with merely inherited celebrity and wealth, and the current performance of the recipients of the Civil List in Britain often demonstrates what should result in a disqualification, rather than applause, veneration, and the undeserved eligibility for the mantle of a far earlier ancestral ability and achievement. Parliamentary and local council representatives of the people, of whatever political flavour, are similarly just as vulnerable to corruption in spite of what should be the honour to serve as democratically elected icons.

This book was about global history, socio-political accidents and habits, and about their effects on human nature – and vice versa. It was also, however, specifically about the life of a one-time aspirational and inspirational giant of the world stage, and about the psychotic melodrama and chaotic complexity into which that now faded and jaded, hopelessly naïve giant has been compressed. Treacherously beset and derided nowadays by its own kin and its own addled ego, the tragedy of Britain today might have been lessened had that nation been possessed with a more equitable social conscience towards its own populace, and if there had been a fashion for greater reverence by a battered and now fragmented populace for national achievements. The abiding dilemma is that a civil majority will always be exploited and willingly sacrificed by a disreputable civil or military minority that becomes identified with the corporate state and thereby attracts resentment – national schizophrenia is a perfectly natural consequence for all nations, but in a modern multicultural society it will be exaggerated by differences that never had time to ameliorate.

Precisely when and why the label "Perfidious Albion" became deserved and-or justifiably persistent may or may not have become apparent during the chapters of Volume One and Volume Two, but rot and corporate senility that would invite criticism from without and within most definitely began some hundreds of years ago – even if brief periods and acts of remission, enlightenment, and reform may be identified since. The same may be said of all nations.

### 22.5.5.6 Dissident Postures Within a Governed Population

Putting the individual and the corporate state together, it is suggested that there are three principal dissident postures within the governed population:

Firstly, and only represented by a minuscule minority of the global population, we have the individual, strongly stated dissident posture.

Secondly, there is the passive compliant posture taken by the silent and by the near-silent majority. Unless an individual takes some minimal action to assert his or her opposition to a demonstrably flawed regime, then that individual must be a part of the hushed and complacent support base of the regime; the difficulty is in identifying and commencing that minimal action. Placing a cross on a piece of paper on polling day is simply not enough.

Thirdly, this book is not about conspiracy theories, but it emphatically supports the assertion that the individual is often misinformed and ill-

## From Freedom to Fiefdom – Summary and Conclusions

informed about the reality of day to day life as portrayed by the media, and that the individual is actively dissuaded and at times dis-informed concerning his rights and entitlements in law. Such disinformation is to be found not only directly within the English State system of government, but throughout the mainstream media, and as an undertone among the hundreds of quasi-autonomous doctrinaire organisations – Think Tanks and Charities – and among self-confessed Quangos. It is found at both individual and corporate levels. The term quasi-autonomous is used for all three of the above aspects of governance since there are always links, even if only sub-conscious ideological ones, among their media publications, blogs, websites, institutions, societies, and their membership. That totality of concerted partisan posture in England, that is so different to the very obvious murderous secret police organisations of many totalitarian regimes around the world, can be represented as a leashed attack dog, sometimes reposing in a not too menacing way, dreamily sleeping by a homely fire maybe, but at other times as a launched beast, snarling and foaming on an elastic leash to intimidate anyone not of the same ideology. There have been just a few publicised blatantly obvious establishment-supported outrages, and only a few suspicious deaths as far as we know in Britain and its allied neighbours, but there is nevertheless an anti-democratic crushing control mechanism, fostered by a seance-like elite, and foisted on its dumb congregation, the majority of instances usually and euphemistically being written off as political expediency or political correctness.

The same attack dog analogy also applies to those platforms for the dogma of many activist organisations of the people who would like to consider themselves a government in waiting. The factor that unites the corporate faces of the state and these organisations of the people is the nature of the person holding the attack dog's leash – someone possessed with a politically ambitious or just plain vicious variety of human nature – that long-term immutable, but short-term corruptible human attribute that at the level of the individual can be any combination of the attributes identified in the section titled *Schematic Showing Individual and*

*Corporate Posturing*, and which on a corporate or Nation-State level is just the same.

### 22.5.6 Hypothesis 5 – Armchair Historians

The fifth hypothesis, as a final point of caution, concerns the perception of history.

It is proposed that the mere comfort of reading a book, or engaging in armchair socio-political debate, creates a subconscious disconnect from reality, and induces in its place a sense of relief verging on *schadenfreude*, as described earlier, a German word meaning "taking relief or even pleasure from the discomfort of others." That possibly ancient superstitious and head-in-the-sand feeling, that what has happened to others cannot therefore happen to ourselves, can act as a barrier to achieving a state of historiographical nirvana that is necessary to enable complete sympathetic understanding, and to generate a real conviction of belief – a conviction that is essential in order to build a determination to avoid the unpleasantness of the past.

Just as an elapsed-time photograph of a busy street will fail to capture any human dynamics – it will show instead only an empty, static, and lifeless infrastructure – so a less than rigorous study of even several of the most horrendous, historical reality shock-waves can seem irrelevant and forgettable from our comfortable and painless perspective. After a brief and inadequate study, unpleasant episodes in history may be dismissed by some as being just that – history and not reality – and the only way to progress beyond such a short-sighted impasse, or false horizon, is to broaden that horizon to include the whole of known history, or as much as possible, in all of its repetitive and undiminished savage detail. Then, and only then, and with an open and receptive mind, will the lessons become obvious.

Unfortunately, the myopic and deaf Principals of national and world governance also have very comfortable armchairs, and a demonstrable susceptibility to corruption in their partisan sponsored positions, so it is really no surprise that we see no lessons taken from the screams of an ecumenical and multi-cultural host of literally billions of victims of human barbarity. The reader is invited to reflect for a while on the magnitude of that suffering, past and present, and to search for some proof of human progress.

# 23 A Glossary of Contentious Terms

| Term | Meaning |
|---|---|
| Nasty | Malicious, spiteful, morally offensive, indecent. |
| Bigot | A person who is intolerant of any ideas other than their own. |
| Fool | Someone who has been tricked and made to appear ridiculous. |
| Anarchism | A movement for social justice through freedom. Possibly an oxymoron. |
| Acerbic | Sharp or biting, as in character or expression. |
| Activism | Policy of taking direct, often militant action to achieve an end – political or social. |
| Aggressive | Inclined to behave in an actively hostile, unthinking fashion. |
| Authoritarian | Characterised by, or favouring absolute obedience to authority, as against individual freedom; favouring, denoting, or relating to government by a small elite with wide powers. In reality, it may apply to any part of the political spectrum. |
| Avarice | Extreme greed. |
| Behemoth | An apocryphal beast from Hebrew folklore. An uncontrollable, chaotic force. |
| Bellicose | Warlike or hostile in respect of an individual. |
| Belligerent | Warlike or hostile in respect of a national or political entity. |
| Benevolence | Compassionate generosity. |
| Bolshevik | Often Pejorative. Derived from the Russian for "big" or "more", it is just the name of the larger faction of the Second Congress of the Russian Social Democratic Workers' Party in 1903, the "smaller" faction being the Mensheviks. |
| Celebrity | Fame; renown. Too often bestowed for triviality. |
| Chutzpah | Yiddish: audacious, shameless effrontery, arrogance. |
| Cognitive Dissonance | Confusion due to one's conflicting instincts, beliefs, and opinions. Leon Festinger, 1956. |

## A Glossary of Contentious Terms

| Term | Meaning |
|---|---|
| Communism | A system of government in which the state plans and controls the economy, and a single, often authoritarian party holds power, claiming to make progress toward a higher social order in which all goods are equally shared by the people. Now tainted by its association with crimes against civil populations, the suppression of opposition through terror and censorship, and declared policies of belligerent self-aggrandisement. |
| Conservative | Preserving the Status Quo; or to restore traditional values, and to limit change. |
| Decadence | Moral degeneration or decay, depravity, excessive self-indulgence. |
| de facto | In practice. |
| de jure | In law. |
| Doctrine | The body of the teachings of a religion, or a religious leader, organisation, or social group; or the text thereof. |
| Dogma | Considered to be absolutely true regardless of evidence. The adjective therefore implies: in a superior or arrogant way; opinionated; dictatorial. |

## A Glossary of Contentious Terms

| Term | Meaning |
|---|---|
| Ethnogenesis | The process of the emergence of an ethnic identity. Contentious and frightening for some, and associated by some with the Soviet era, and particularly with Russian philosophers who turned away from the Atlantic Perspective towards a Pan-Asian one. Possibly of renewed interest in connection with the self-imposed ideology of western multiculturalism. The concept of ethnogenesis embraces and integrates two distinct processes: Firstly, the early and initial integration of indigenous, or more correctly autochthonous (of the very soil, not just a first arrival), but diverse ethnic components into a single ethnic identity; and Secondly, and after a period of the maturation of that initial ethnic identity, the inclusion of immigrant cultures and immigrants themselves in the process of ethnogenesis. It is a recursive concept, and another classic dialectic from the largest land-empire on earth. If interrupted or disrupted, ethnogenesis can lead to civil war, inter-tribal atrocities, and ethnic cleansing, all of which were seen in the Balkans and Africa in the late 20th century. See also race riots elsewhere in this book. As a concrete example, the emergence of a Turkic identity may be a result of this process. |
| Eugenics | The concept, study, or belief, that humanity can be improved by contrived and controlled breeding, and by extension, policies to achieve this. Usually employed for ideological reasons, and by non-consensual imposition. Arguably an essential part of Ethnogenesis. |
| Fabian | Relating to caution and the avoidance of direct confrontation, typical of the Roman general Quintus Fabius Maximus. Nowadays: committed to gradual rather than revolutionary means for spreading socialist principles. |

## A Glossary of Contentious Terms

| Term | Meaning |
|---|---|
| Fascism | A system of government, or an organisation with centralisation of authority under a dictator, but with a corporate economy and classless social structure, differing from socialism only in its nationalistic ideology. Now tainted by its association with war and civil crimes, and the suppression of opposition through terror and censorship, and policies of belligerent self-aggrandisement. |
| Federation and Confederation | A federation is a more permanent union of self-governing states with something at least in the way of a central, common constitution. A confederation is more of a union of convenience, usually for international representation and the furtherance of common causes with respect to other states. |
| Fidelity | Loyalty; faithfulness in a relationship. |
| Fundamentalism | Often Pejorative. Characterised by a return to original principles; not necessarily a bad thing. Often confused with *radicalism* that is said to have resulted from doctrinal abrogation by extremists, but which is often just a politically correct mitigation of Islamic terrorism. |
| Globalism | A national geopolitical policy in which the entire world is regarded as the appropriate sphere for a state or organisation's influence; desirous of world government or dominance. |
| Hubris | Excessive pride or self-confidence; arrogance. |
| Humility | Modest opinion or estimate of one's own importance; timidity |
| Ideology | Doctrine, philosophy, body of beliefs or principles belonging to an individual or group. Again, the adjective can imply arrogance. |
| Indolence | Habitual laziness; sloth. |
| Insidious | Subtle, cunning, and treacherous. |
| Instinct | A natural or inherent impulse or behaviour. |
| Invidious | Having embedded implications of hatred, resentment, and offensive discrimination. |

# A Glossary of Contentious Terms

| Term | Meaning |
|---|---|
| Left and Right Wing: | The terms Right and Left originated during the French Revolution, and they referred to where, relative to the chair of the President, people sat in the French parliament. They have no logical relevance to present-day political or social movements, especially when prefixed by "far". These terms are now entirely pejorative, and they are the weapon of choice of the nasty bigots of the mainstream media and certain other pugnacious organisations. Use with caution. |
| Left Wing | The liberal or radical faction of a group. Naïvely interpreted as socialist or communist. |
| Liberal | Not traditional. Can imply *without principles*; timidity in the face of adversity. |
| Mainstream | The default; Self–maintaining and prevailing current of thought, influence, or activity. Not necessarily virtuous or desirable but liberally assumed so. |
| Marxist–Leninist version of Communism | Advocates the overthrow of capitalism by the revolution of the proletariat. See Bolshevik. |
| Menshevik | The moderate smaller wing of the Russian Social Democratic Party advocating gradual reform to achieve socialism. See Bolshevik. |
| Multiculturalism | The ideology that cultures and races should be intermixed within national boundaries by specific policies and by accelerated design and implementation. In practice, it is the application, with Liberal approbation, of eugenics policies. |
| Nationalism | Devotion to the interests or culture of one's nation. Naïvely and-or ideologically interpreted as racist, and deprecated by the mainstream in favour of supra-nationalism or the New World Order (NWO). |
| Pejorative | A disparaging or belittling word or expression, often used incorrectly and in ignorance. |
| Pernicious | Dangerous, deadly, and malign by stealth. |
| Prudence | Wise in handling practical matters; exercising good judgement or common sense. |
| Pugnacious | Combative and belligerent, inclined to disagree regardless of facts. |

## A Glossary of Contentious Terms

| Term | Meaning |
|---|---|
| Racism / Racist | The belief that races have distinctive cultural and physical characteristics that are determined by hereditary factors, and that this endows some races with an intrinsic superiority over others in some respect. These terms now, are always pejorative and a weapon of choice of the mainstream media and certain other pugnacious organisations. The objective of their use is frequently to achieve character assassination without further dialogue, and to close down political debate. |
| Radical | Departing markedly from the usual, traditional, or customary; extreme. May be constructive or destructive. Often misused as an excuse for terrorism. |
| Reactionary | A person opposed to radical change. May be constructive or destructive. |
| Right Wing | The conservative or reactionary faction of a group. Naïvely interpreted as nationalist. |
| Self–aggrandisement : | An act undertaken to increase power and influence. |
| Socialism | The stage in Marxist–Leninist theory that is intermediate between capitalism and communism, and in which collective ownership of the economy under the dictatorship of the proletariat has not yet been successfully achieved. It is a revolutionary pause for breath that is too often seen by liberals as an end in itself, and at which point ideologies lose focus and become distorted. |
| Status Quo | The existing condition or state of affairs. By colloquial extension – the ruling elite. |
| Totalitarian | Of, relating to, being, or imposing a form of government in which the political authority exercises absolute and centralised control over all aspects of life; the individual is subordinated to the state, and opposing political and cultural expression is suppressed. |
| Treason | Disloyalty; a betrayal of trust or confidence – a legal concept of the Status Quo. |

| Term | Meaning |
|---|---|
| Treachery | Wilful and inexcusable betrayal of fidelity, confidence, or trust. |
| Tribalism | The organisation, culture, or beliefs of a tribe; a strong feeling of identity with, and loyalty to one's tribe, to one's type or to one's group. |
| Venal | Mercenary, susceptible to bribery and corruption. |

## 24 Bibliography

Many of the following sources were read in their entirety, and all to some extent were referred to for the purposes of assisting the verification of propositions in abstractions that were encountered elsewhere. The sources are mostly in the public domain, and they are easily accessible from the internet.

| Category | Title | Author |
| --- | --- | --- |
| Biographical | Pyrrhus. | Abbott, J. |
| Biographical | The Discourses of Epictetus. | Matheson, P.E. (Translator). |
| Biographical | The Life of King Alfred. | Asser, Bishop of Sherborne. |
| Chronicle | British History in Twelve Books. | Geoffrey of Monmouth. |
| Chronicle | Bulfinch's Mythology | Bulfinch, Thomas |
| Chronicle | Chronicles of Eusebius. | Bedrosian, Robert. (Translator). |
| Chronicle | Chronicles of Froissart. | Macaulay, G.C. (Editor). |
| Chronicle | Chronicles of the Picts and Scots. | Skene, W. (Editor). |
| Chronicle | De Bello Gallico and Other Commentaries. | Caesar, Caius Julius. |
| Chronicle | Historia Anglorum (English Comments, Main Text Latin). | Henry of Huntingdon. |
| Chronicle | Historia Britonum of Nennius. | Giles, J.A. (Translator). |
| Chronicle | Historia Britonum of Nennius, Irish Version. | Todd, James Henthorn (Translator). |
| Chronicle | History of the English People, Volume I. (Bulfinch) | Green, J.R. |
| Chronicle | Liber Landavensis (The Book of Teilo). | Rees, W.J. (Translator). |
| Chronicle | Millennium | Holland, Tom |
| Chronicle | Pausanias' Description of Greece (10 Original Books). | Various. (Translators). |

| Category | Title | Author |
|---|---|---|
| Chronicle | Ptolemy, Tacitus, and the Tribes of North Britain. | Mann, J.C. and D.J.Breeze. |
| Chronicle | Anglo-Saxon Britain. | Allen, Grant. |
| Chronicle | The Anglo-Saxon Chronicle. | Various – unknown. |
| Chronicle | The Annals. | Tacitus. |
| Chronicle | The Chronicle of Florence of Worcester. | Forester, Thomas. (Translator). |
| Chronicle | The Chronicle of The Early Britons Latin/Welsh Name Rendering. | Geoffrey of Monmouth. |
| Chronicle | The Chronicle of The Early Britons MS LXI *Brut y Bryttaniait*. | W.R.Cooper (Translator). |
| Chronicle | Not a Chronicle, a Paper (it belongs with the two above) – Neglected British History. | W. M. Flinders Petrie, F.R.S. |
| Chronicle | Not a Chronicle, a recent book (it belongs with the titles above) – The Phoenician Origin of Britons Scots and Anglo-Saxons. | L.A. Waddell. |
| Chronicle | The Chronicle of The Isle of Man. | Church Historians of England Series. |
| Chronicle | The Chronicle of The Kings of England. | William of Malmesbury. |
| Chronicle | The Description of Wales. | Giraldus Cambrensis. |
| Chronicle | The Geography of Ptolemy Elucidated. | Rylands, T.G. |
| Chronicle | The Geography of Ptolemy, Online Resources. | See browser links. |
| Chronicle | The Geography of Strabo (3 Volumes). | Hamilton and Falconer. |
| Chronicle | The Historical Library of Diodorus the Sicilian. | Diodorus Siculus. |
| Chronicle | The Historical Works of Giraldus Cambrensis. | Forester, Thomas. (Translator). |
| Chronicle | The Historical Works of Simeon of Durham. | Stevenson, Rev. J. (Translator). |

*Bibliography*

| Category | Title | Author |
|---|---|---|
| Chronicle | The Historical Works of the Venerable Beda (5 Books). | Stevenson, Rev. J. (Translator). |
| Chronicle | The History Of Herodotus (2 Volumes). | Macaulay, G.C. (Translator). |
| Chronicle | The History of the Peloponnesian War by Thucydides (8 Books). | Crawley, R. (Translator). |
| Chronicle | The Itinerary of Archbishop Baldwin Through Wales. | Giraldus Cambrensis. |
| Chronicle | The Itinerary of John Leland in England. | Leland, John. |
| Chronicle | The Life of Gildas. | Caradoc of Llancarfan. |
| Chronicle | The Magna Carta. | King John and The Barons. |
| Chronicle | The Meditations of Marcus Aurelius Antoninus. | Casaubon, Meric (1634). (Translator). |
| Chronicle | The Natural History of Pliny (36 Books in 6 Volumes). | Bostock and Riley. (Translator). |
| Chronicle | The Oera Linda Book. | Sandbach, William R. (Translator). |
| Chronicle | The Prophecies of the Brahan Seer, Coinneach Odhar Fiosaiche. | Mackenzie, Alexander. |
| Chronicle | The Thoughts of Marcus Aurelius Antoninus. | Long, George (1862). (Translator). |
| Chronicle | The Works of Gildas and Nennius. | Giles, J.A. (Translator). |
| Chronicle | Unearthing Structure in Ptolemy's Geographia. | Isaksen, Leif. |
| Chronicle | Various Other Chronicles. | Church Historians of England. |
| Geographical | The History of the Kingdom of Ireland. | Burton, Richard (aka Nathaniel Crouch). |
| Geographical | The History of Wales. | Jones, John. |
| Geographical | The Island of Formosa Past and Present. | Davidson, J.W. |

| Category | Title | Author |
|---|---|---|
| Imperial / War | A History of the Later Roman Empire (2 Volumes). | Bury, J.B. |
| Imperial / War | A Short History of Spain and Portugal. | Stanford University. |
| Imperial / War | A Study of History Volume 6. | Toynbee, Arnold. |
| Imperial / War | A Tour Up the Straits From Gibraltar to Constantinople. | Sutherland, Capt. D. |
| Imperial / War | Bulgarian Horrors. | Gladstone, W.E. |
| Imperial / War | History Of Greece (12 Volumes). | Grote, George. |
| Imperial / War | History of Greece to the Death of Alexander the Great. | Bury, J.B. |
| Imperial / War | History of Rome (3 Volumes of 36 books). | Livius, Titus (Livy). |
| Imperial / War | History Of The Decline And Fall Of The Roman Empire. | Gibbon, Edward. |
| Imperial / War | History of the Langobards. | Paul The Deacon. |
| Imperial / War | History of the Ottoman Turks. | Creasy, Sir Edward. |
| Imperial / War | History of the Wars (Procopius 8 Books). | Dewing, H.B. (Translator). |
| Imperial / War | The Controversy of Zion. | Reed, Douglas. |
| Imperial / War | The Downfall of Napoleon Buonaparte. | Scott, Sir Walter. |
| Imperial / War | The Empire of the Khazars. | Bury, J.B. |
| Imperial / War | The Empresses of Constantinople. | McCabe, Joseph. |
| Imperial / War | The Fifteen Decisive Battles of The World. | Creasy, E. |
| Imperial / War | The Invasion of Europe by the Barbarians. | Bury, J.B. |

## Bibliography

| Category | Title | Author |
| --- | --- | --- |
| Imperial / War | The Life of Napoleon Buonaparte (9 Volumes, 1827). | Scott, Sir Walter. |
| Imperial / War | The Murderous Tyranny of the Turks. | Toynbee, Arnold. |
| Imperial / War | The Origin and Deeds of the Goths, by Jordanes. | Mierow, C. (Translator). |
| Imperial / War | The Origin of the English Nation. | Chadwick, H. Munro. |
| Imperial / War | The Ottoman Power in Europe. | Freeman, E.A. |
| Imperial / War | The Prince. | Machiavelli. |
| Imperial / War | The Russians in Bulgaria and Rumelia. | Moltke, Baron Von. |
| Imperial / War | The Russo Turkish War. | Barnwell, R.G. |
| Imperial / War | The Secret History of the Mongols (Volume 1). | Cleaves, F.W. (Translator). |
| Imperial / War | The Story of the Greeks. | Guerber, H. A. |
| Imperial / War | The Thirteenth Tribe. | Koestler, Arthur. |
| Imperial / War | Turkey: A Past and a Future. | Toynbee, Arnold. |
| Imperial / War | Two Great Retreats. | Grote, George. |
| Imperial / War | William the Conqueror and the Rule of the Normans. | Stenton, Frank Merry. |
| Money | A Treatise on Money. | Nicholson, J.S. |
| Money | About J.S. Nicholson. | Groenewegen, P. |
| Money | An Inquiry into the Nature and Causes of the Wealth of Nations. | Smith, Adam. |
| Money | Lincoln Money Martyred. | Search, Dr.R.E. |
| Money | Modern Money Mechanics. | Federal Reserve Bank Chicago. |

| Category | Title | Author |
|---|---|---|
| Money | Sovereign and Quasi-Sovereign States: Their Debts To Foreign Countries. | Clarke, Hyde. |
| Money | The Dialogue Concerning the Exchequer, circa 1180. | Unknown. |
| Money | The Economic Consequences of the Peace (WWI) 1920. | Keynes, J.M. |
| Money | The Financiers and the Nation. | Johnston, T. |
| Money | The Gospel of Wealth and Other Timely Essays 1900. | Carnegie, A. |
| Money | The Royal Commission on Gold and Silver 1889. | Gairdner, C. |
| Money | The South Sea Bubble. | McKay, Charles. |
| Money | Treatises and Essays on Subjects Connected with Economical Policy (1853). | McCulloch, J.R. |
| Religious Ideology | A Candid History of the Jesuits. | McCabe, Joseph. |
| Religious Ideology | A Dictionary of Christian Biography and Literature to the End of the Sixth Century AD, with an Account of the Principal Sects and Heresies. | Wace, Henry. |
| Religious Ideology | A History of the Popes. | McCabe, Joseph. |
| Religious Ideology | Against the Robbing and Murdering Hordes of Peasants. | Luther, Martin. |
| Religious Ideology | Book of Martyrs (aka The Acts and Monuments of John Foxe). | Fox, Rev. J. and Rev. C.Goodrich. |
| Religious Ideology | Book of Martyrs http://www.exclassics.com/foxe/foxintro.htm. | Fox, Rev. J. |
| Religious Ideology | Crises in the History of the Papacy. | McCabe, Joseph. |
| Religious Ideology | Heretics. | Chesterton, Gilbert K. |

# Bibliography

| Category | Title | Author |
|---|---|---|
| Religious Ideology | History of Christian Church (1st Edition 2 Volumes) with Waldenses and Albigenses. | Jones, William. |
| Religious Ideology | History of Christian Church (5th Edition 2 Volumes) with Waldenses and Albigenses. | Jones, William. |
| Religious Ideology | History of the Catholic Church from the Renaissance to the French Revolution (2 Volumes). | MacCaffrey, Rev. J. |
| Religious Ideology | How The Cross Courted the Swastika For Eight Years. | McCabe, Joseph. |
| Religious Ideology | How The Pope Of Peace Traded In Blood. | McCabe, Joseph. |
| Religious Ideology | Liber Pontificalis (The Book of the Popes). | Loomis, L.R. (Translator). |
| Religious Ideology | Nicene Fathers, AnteNicene (10 Volumes). | Schaff, Philip (1885). |
| Religious Ideology | Nicene Fathers, PostNicene (28 Volumes). | Schaff, Philip (1885). |
| Religious Ideology | Pagan and Christian Rome. | Lanciani, R. |
| Religious Ideology | Philosophumena, or The Refutation of All Heresies (2 Volumes). | Hippolytus. |
| Religious Ideology | Quanta Cura (Condemning Current Errors). | Pope Pius IX Encyclical, 1864. |
| Religious Ideology | Quod Nunquam (On the Church in Prussia). | Pope Pius IX Encyclical, 1875. |
| Religious Ideology | Religion and the State in Islam: From Medieval Caliphate to the Muslim Brotherhood. | Bulliet, Richard. |
| Religious Ideology | The 95 Theses. | Luther, Martin. |
| Religious Ideology | The Anti-Papal Manual. | Nortwick, William H. Van. |
| Religious Ideology | The Apostolic Tradition of Hippolytus. | Easton, Burton Scott. (Translator). |

| Category | Title | Author |
|---|---|---|
| Religious Ideology | The Lies And Fallacies Of The Encyclopedia Britanica. | McCabe, Joseph. |
| Religious Ideology | The Malleus Maleficarum 1487 (Hammer of the Witches). | Summers, Rev. M. (Translator). |
| Religious Ideology | The Popes and Their Church. | McCabe, Joseph. |
| Religious Ideology | The Ritual Murder Libel and the Jew (Original by Pope Clement XIV). | Roth, C. (Editor). |
| Religious Ideology | The Sacred Congregation de Propaganda Fide (1622-1922). | Guilday, Peter. |
| Religious Ideology | The Secret Societies of All Ages and Countries. | Heckethorn, Charles William. |
| Religious Ideology | The Story of Evolution. | McCabe, Joseph. |
| Religious Ideology | The Syllabus of Errors Condemned. | Pope Pius IX (Issued with Quanta Cura). |
| Religious Ideology | The Totalitarian Church Of Rome. | McCabe, Joseph. |
| Religious Ideology | The Vatican's Last Crime. | McCabe, Joseph. |
| Religious Ideology | The War [WWI] and the Churches. | McCabe, Joseph. |
| Religious Ideology | The Writings of Irenaeus (2 Volumes). | Roberts, Rev. A. and Rev. W.Rambaut. (Translator). |
| Religious Ideology | The Writings of Tertullian (Founder of Early Church). | Dodgson, Rev. C. (Translator) |
| Religious Ideology | Waters Flowing Eastward, The War Against the Kingship of Christ. | Fry, L. |
| Religious Ideology | Works of Martin Luther (2 Volumes). | Luther, Martin. |
| Socio-political | A History of Wales. | Lloyd, John Edward. |
| Socio-political | A Journal Of The Plague Year. | Defoe, Daniel. |

*Bibliography*

| Category | Title | Author |
|---|---|---|
| Socio-political | A Selection of Discourses of Epictetus with the Encheiridion. | Epictetus. |
| Socio-political | An Encyclopedist of the Dark Ages, Isidore of Seville. | Brehaut, Ernest. |
| Socio-political | An Introduction to the Political Thought of John Locke. | Mack, Eric. |
| Socio-political | Commentaries on the Laws of England. | Blackstone, William. |
| Socio-political | Common Sense. | Paine, Thomas. |
| Socio-political | Critias. | Plato. |
| Socio-political | Dialogue in Hell Between Machiavelli and Montesquieu. | Joly, Maurice. |
| Socio-political | Essays. | Bacon, Francis. |
| Socio-political | Eugenics in Evolutionary Perspective. | Huxley, Sir Julian. |
| Socio-political | Eusebius of Caesarea's Ecclesiastical History. | McGiffert, Arthur Cushman. (Translator). |
| Socio-political | Exchange of Goods and Ideas Along the Silk Roads. | Educational. |
| Socio-political | Historical Essays and Studies | Dalberg-Acton, John Emerich Edward. |
| Socio-political | History Of The Plague In London. | Defoe, Daniel. |
| Socio-political | Joseph Fels, His Life Work. | Fels, Mary. |
| Socio-political | Mein Kampf. | Hitler. |
| Socio-political | Memoirs of Napoleon (3 Volumes). | de Bourrienne. |
| Socio-political | Nachtrag von Weitern Originalschriften. | Weishaupt, Adam. |
| Socio-political | On Heroes, Hero Worship, and the Heroic in History. | Carlyle, Thomas. |

| Category | Title | Author |
|---|---|---|
| Socio-political | Proceedings Before The Justices Of The Peace In The 14$^{th}$ And 15$^{th}$ Centuries | Putnam, B. H. |
| Socio-political | Proofs of a Conspiracy Against All the Religions and Governments of Europe. | Robison, John. |
| Socio-political | Putney Debates and More. | Lilburne, John and Many Others. |
| Socio-political | Red Symphony. | Landowsky, J. |
| Socio-political | Ridpath's Universal History. | Ridpath, J.C. |
| Socio-political | Roman Britain in 1914. | Haverfield, F. |
| Socio-political | Selected Writings and Speeches (3 Volumes). | Coke, Sir Edward. |
| Socio-political | The Acts and Monuments of John Foxe (8 Abridged Volumes). | Cattley, Rev. S. (Editor). |
| Socio-political | The Ancient Greek Historians (Harvard Lectures). | Bury, J.B. |
| Socio-political | The Art of War. | Machiavelli. |
| Socio-political | The Balkans. | Forbes, Toynbee et Al. |
| Socio-political | The Cambridge Ancient History (Misc. Volumes). | Edited by Bury, J.B. and Others. |
| Socio-political | The Cambridge Medieval History (Misc. Volumes). | Edited by Bury, J.B. and Others. |
| Socio-political | The Communist Manifesto. | Karl Marx and Friedrich Engels. |
| Socio-political | The Constitutional History of England. | Stubbs, William. |
| Socio-political | The Divine Right of Kings or Regal Tyranny (Comparison Text). | Lilburne, John and Thomas Hobbes. |
| Socio-political | The English Revolution, 1640 | Hill, Christopher. |

## Bibliography

| Category | Title | Author |
|---|---|---|
| Socio-political | The Fraud of Human Rights | Stanmore, Robert |
| Socio-political | The French Revolution, A History (3 Volumes). | Carlyle, Thomas. |
| Socio-political | The Geographical Journal Vol. 66, No. 6 (Dec., 1925), Prehistoric Routes Between Northern Europe And Italy Defined By The Amber Trade. | J.M. de Navarro. |
| Socio-political | The History of England from the Accession of JamesII. | Macaulay, Thomas Babington. |
| Socio-political | The History of English Law Before the Time of Edward I | Sir Frederick Pollock and F. W. Maitland |
| Socio-political | The History of Freedom. | Dalberg-Acton, John Emerich Edward. |
| Socio-political | The History of Napoleon Buonaparte. | Lockhart, John Gibson. |
| Socio-political | The History of Rome (5 Volumes). | Mommsen. |
| Socio-political | The Hoax of the Twentieth Century. | Butz, Arthur R. |
| Socio-political | The Idea of Progress An Inquiry Into Its Origin And Growth. | Bury, J.B. |
| Socio-political | The Legacy of Greece. | Livingstone, R.W. (Editor). |
| Socio-political | The London Gazette, 1665 to the Present. | The Gazette Official Public Record. |
| Socio-political | The Military Writings and Speeches of Leon Trotsky. | Leon Trotsky aka Lev Davidovich Bronstein. |
| Socio-political | The Parliamentary History of England (36 Volumes) Later Hansard. | Cobbett, William. |
| Socio-political | The Problem of China. | Russell, Bertrand. |
| Socio-political | The Protocols of the Learned Elders of Zion. | Marsden, V.E. (Translator). |

| Category | Title | Author |
|---|---|---|
| Socio-political | The Protocols of the Learned Elders of Zion: Between history and Fiction. | Hagemeister, Michael. |
| Socio-political | The Protocols of Zion Tool-kit. | Meyers, P. |
| Socio-political | The Two Treatises of Civil Government. | Locke, John. |
| Socio-political | The Works of John Locke in Nine Volumes (1689). | Locke, John. |
| Socio-political | The Works of John Locke in Ten Volumes (revised 1823). | Locke, John. |
| Socio-political | The Writings of Thomas Paine (4 Volumes including *Age of Reason*). | Conway, M.D. (Editor). |
| Socio-political | Theodoric the Goth. | Hodgkin, Thomas. |
| Socio-political | Utopia. | More, Thomas. |
| Socio-political | Warrant For Genocide. | Cohn, Norman. |

## 25 Internet Index of References and Other Downloads

It is essential to consult as many sources as reasonably practicable when looking for pointers and lessons from history. Internet search engines can give biased results - Google for instance, often points to commercially associated websites, and frequently and extensively to Wikipedia, although, in mitigation, Wikipedia can itself be used as a portal to many independent and primary sources and websites.

At least three other search engines were used in the compilation of data for this book – Microsoft's Bing.com, the lesser known Duckduckgo.com, but of great use to suppress Google-inspired unsolicited adverts and personal data harvesting, the apparently admirable Startpage.com which acts as a proxy for Google, and theoretically at least, filters and blocks spying by both commercial and governmental agencies:

https://startpage.com/

In addition to the use of multiple search engines, multiple websites and as many original texts as was practicable were consulted to cross-reference historical, financial, and socio-political detail. Sanitised and politically correct ideological mainstream news sources were avoided where possible, but have been accessed with caution.

An extensive list of internet websites that were referenced to help verify the detail in this book is available as part of a separate eBook titled *"Freedom to Fiefdom, A Dissident's Internet Index"*, which may be opened in PDF Reaader Applications, such as Linux Okular, Adobe Acrobat, or a PDF Reader on a tablet.

Whichever option is chosen, links will be available to click and visit the associated website, and greater resolution of maps for instance might be obtained with a tablet or PC alongside the printed book.

A link to download *"Freedom to Fiefdom, A Dissident's Internet Index"* – free of charge for purchasers of this book – may be obtained by emailing to info@freedomtofiefdom.com the precise subject line as follows:

REQUEST V3F2F

## 26 A Very English End – Nennius' Wonders of Britain.

The very last word, originally at the end of the single book hardback version of Volume One, goes to Nennius for a fascinating insight into some of the tourist attractions of Britain in a not-too-distant antiquity. Documented in a chapter of the *Historia Brittonum* titled *de mirabilibus britanniae*, these delightfully Romantic, sometimes mystical accounts, are an example of a mindset that seems to survive all other pernicious ideologies and repressions throughout history, being represented as a mixture of fact and Pagan beliefs and superstitions from the remotest times to present-day fringe beliefs. The observers of the "Wonders" were part of a culture that has almost certainly been here for more than twelve thousand years, and long may they, and their spirit of place and people, continue to survive the imposition of alien cultures and ideological extremes.

### 26.1 Loch Lomond – River Leven

> *"The first wonder is the lake Lumonoy. In there are sixty islands, and men dwell there, and sixty rocks encircle it, with an eagle's nest on each rock. There are also sixty rivers flowing into that place, and nothing goes out of there to the sea except one river, which is called Lenm/Lenin."*

### 26.2 River Severn – Severn Bore

After further writings during the 16th century, this is believed by some to refer to the river Test in Hampshire and not the well-known river Severn Bore..

> *"Wonder two: the mouth of the river Trahannon, because one wave like a mountain at The Teared [the bore] covers the banks and it ebbs like all the other seas."*

## 26.3 The Hot Springs at Bath

The Ancient British deity *Sul*, preceded the Roman-named adoption as Minerva, and was (is) in the territory of the post-Roman Saxon tribe called the *Hwicce*.

> *'Wonder three – the hot pool, which is in the region of the Huich and encircled by a wall made of brick and stone and to that place men go during all seasons to be washed and to each, as it may have pleased them, the bath thus may be made according to his own will: if he may have willed, the bath will be cold, if warm, it will be warm."*

## 26.4 Salt Springs at Droitwich

In the same recent Saxon territory as above – that of the *Hwicce*.

> *'The fourth wonder is: the fountains discovered in the same [place] of salt, from which fountains salt is cooked: from that place diverse plain-foods are salted and they are not near the sea, but from the earth they emerge."*

## 26.5 Extra Turbulent Severn Bore Locations

Possible locations: Nowadays near Frampton-on-Severn. Historically, before modern waterways imposed constrictions, it could be seen at Upper Parting, where the river divided into two near Gloucester. The reference by Nennius is to excessive turbulence when the bore would have reflected off surrounding banks and collided with itself.

> *"Another wonder is the Duo Rig Habren, that is the two kings of the Severn. When the sea is flooded to The Teared [the bore] within the mouth of the Severn, two waves of spume separately convene and make war between themselves in the manner of sea-rams and each proceeds to the other and they collide at one another and again withdraw one from another and again they proceed on each Teared [bore]. This they do*

*A Very English End – Nennius' Wonders of Britain.*

*from the initiation of the world all the way to the present day."*

## 26.6 Whirlpools Resulting From Severn Bore

Locations now unknown, but believed to be somewhere on the Welsh coastline upstream from Newport, South Wales. Coastal erosion, silting, and human intervention has altered much of the region.

> *'There is another wonder: it is the confluence of Linn Liuan; the mouth of that river flows into the Severn, and when both the Severn is flooded to The Teared [the bore], and the sea is flooded similarly into the aforementioned mouth of the river, both it is received into the lake/pool of the mouth in the mode of a whirlpool and the sea does not advance up. And a bank/shore exists near the river, and so long as the Severn is flooded to The Teared [the bore] that bank/shore is not covered, and when the sea and Severn ebbs, at that time lake Liuan vomits all that it has devoured from the sea and both that bank/shore is covered and in the likeness of a mountain in one wave it spews and bursts. And if there was the army of the whole region, in the midst of where it is, and it directed its face against the wave, even the army the wave carries off through the force, by fluid full clothes. If, on the other hand, the backs of the army were turned against it, the same wave doesn't harm, and when the sea may have ebbed, then the entire bank, which the wave covers, backwards is bared and the sea recedes from it."*

## 26.7 Mysterious Source of Fish – Location Now Unknown

Possibly a man-made ancient fish-farm, or containment pool. Possible locations include the area between the rivers Severn and Wye, a spot now beneath a major road intersection in Cardiff, and two historic wells in diverse parts of South Wales.

*A Very English End – Nennius' Wonders of Britain.*

"There is another wonder in the region of Cinlipiuc. There is in that place a spring called the Well-pool of Guur Helic. No stream flows out of it or into it. Men go to the spring to fish – some go to the eastern part of the spring and draw out fish from that part, some to the right, some to the left, and the west, and fish are drawn from those parts, and different types of fish are drawn from each part. It is a great wonder to find fish in the spring while there is no stream flowing in and none out of it, and in there they find four types of fish, and by no means is it deep! The depth is at every point to the knees; it is twenty foot in length and breadth; the bank is high that holds it from each direction."

## 26.8 An Apple-like Fruit Growing on an Ash-like Tree

A nationally rare tree called the True Service Tree (*Sorbus domestica*), also known as the Whitty Pear, does grow more commonly in Worcestershire, the Welsh borders, and Wyre Forest. The river Wye (Gwy) is therefore a prime contender for this tree, the fruits of which (called Sorbs) have at times been used to make a cider-like beverage. Its foliage is similar to the Mountain Ash.

"Near the river, which is named the Guoy, apples are found upon Ash trees in a sloping woodland [or pass], at the mouth of the river."

## 26.9 Continuous Wind Emitted by a Cave

Location now unknown, but it was probably somewhere in Gwent.

"There is another wonderful thing in the area which is called Guent. There is, in that place, a pit, from which blows out a wind the whole time without intermission. And when no wind blows in the season of summer, from that pit it incessantly blows, such that no one is able to put up with it nor

*A Very English End – Nennius' Wonders of Britain.*

face the pit's depths. And the name of it is 'Vith Guint' in the Briton's speech, and in Latin also 'The Blowing Wind'. It is a great wonder this wind blows from the earth."

## 26.10 The Levitating Altar

This phenomenon is generally accepted as being centred in the region of the Mumbles, or Oystermouth, on the Gower peninsula.

> "There is another wonder in Guyr – the altar, which is in the place, which is called Loyngarth, which is held up by the will of god. It seems better to me to narrate the history of that altar than to keep silent. But the fact is, while Saint Iltut was worshipping in the cave, which is next to the sea, which laps against the ground at the said place, (the mouth of the cave, also, is on the sea), and, behold, a ship was sailing towards him and two men sailing her and the corpse of a holy man was with them in the boat and the altar over the face of it, which was held up by the will of god and the man of god [Iltut] has advanced in their way and the corpse of the holy man and the altar remained inseparably above/before the face of the holy body. And they have said to saint Iltut: "that man of god has entrusted to us, in order that we might draw that person to you and we might bury him with you, and the name of him you may not reveal to any person, that men may not swear by him." Those two men returned to the ship and they have sailed. But that saint Iltut has established a church around/near the corpse of the holy man and around/near the altar and it continues all the time to this present day the altar is held up by the will of god. A certain minor king has come, in order that he might test, carrying a twig in his hand; he has formed a curve around the altar and he has held the twig by both hands from both sides and he has drawn it to himself in such a way the truth of that thing he has proved and that

*A Very English End – Nennius' Wonders of Britain.*

*person afterwards during the month uninjured/untouched died. Another in truth [?for the truth] under the altar has looked and the sight of the eyes he has lost and before the month uninjured/untouched his life he has ended."*

## 26.11 The Returning Plank

Believed to have been situated in the area of Mathern near Chepstow where the rivers Wye and Severn converge.

*'There is another wonderful thing in the above oft-mentioned region of Guent. There is there a spring near to the wall of the well of Mouric, and timber in the middle of the spring, and men wash their hands together with their faces, and they have the timber beneath their feet when they wash – for instance I have both tried and seen it. When it is inundated by the sea, until the worst the Severn is extended over everything coastal, and covers, and all the way to the spring it is stretched out, and the spring is filled from the teared Severn, and draws the wood with itself all the way to the great sea, and throughout the space of three days on the sea it is turned upside-down, and on day four, in the above mentioned spring, it is found. It is also a fact that one from the countryside might have buried it in the earth to require it proved, and on day four it was found in the spring and the former rustic, he who concealed and buried it, was dead before the end of the month."*

## 26.12 Cabal's Cairn

Believed to relate to a physical property of the local geology on a mountain in the Elan Valley. The local rock is a sort of aggregate of pebbles that might crumble and be interpreted as imprints. The cultural significance of the area is enhanced by the presence of possibly Bronze Age burial mounds

*A Very English End – Nennius' Wonders of Britain.*

*There is another wonderful thing in the region which is called Bucit. There is there a mound of stones and one stone placed on top has a footprint of a dog on it. When hunting the porker Troynt, stamped Cabal (who was the dog of the soldier Arthur) the step in the stone, and afterward Arthur gathered together stones under the stone on which was the track of his dog, and it is called Carn Cabal. And men come, and they take the stone in their hands through the space of the day and night, even so, in the daylight of the following day it is come upon on top of his collection."*

## 26.13 Amr's Tomb

Believed located some miles west of Ross-on-Wye, and south-west of Hereford.

*"There is another miracle in the region which is called Ercing. A sepulcra is shown near a spring which is given the name Licat Amr, and the name of the hero who's grave is in the tumulus, it follows, was called Amr. He was the son of Arthur the soldier, and he himself has killed him in that very place and done the burying. And men come to measure the tumulus in length: sometimes it is six feet; sometimes nine; sometimes twelve; sometimes fifteen. For whatever the measurement you will measure it in such a succession, again you will not find it with the same measurement; and even I have made confirmation on my own."*

## 26.14 Cruc Mawr Tomb

Believed to have been near Cardigan.

*"There is another wonder in the region which is called Cereticiaun. There is there a mountain, which is given the name Cruc Maur, and there is a grave on the summit of it,*

## *A Very English End – Nennius' Wonders of Britain.*

*and every man whosoever that will come to the grave and stretch himself out next to it, however short they will be, the grave and the man have been found within one length, and, if it will be that the man is short and small, similarly also it is found the length of the grave is like the height of the man, and, if he will be long and tall, even if he might be of length four cubits near the height of every man so the tumulus is discovered.* ***And every wanderer who's up to weariness, the man will bow three bows near that, he will not be beyond himself up to his day of death, and he will not be weighted down again by any weariness, even if he will go alone to the boundaries of the cosmos."***

## End of Volume One

## 27 Index to Volume One

The index has the following sections and (sub-classes):

- Cultures
- Dominions
- Ideology & Evolution (Religious, Monetary, Political, Socio-Political, Speculative, Islam)
- People: HRE = Holy Roman Emperor, RE = Roman Emperor
- Time Periods (Archaeological, Cultural, Geological)
- War & Genocide (Papal Atrocity, Battles, Wars, Outrages)

# Alphabetical Index

## Cultures

Angle 4, 79, 116, 120-122, 132

Anglo-Saxon 4, 26, 34, 60, 87, 114, 115, 122-124, 126-129, 131-133, 136-141, 143, 148, 207, 286, 293, 298, 501, 528, 534, 631, 636, 637, 694, 695, 705, 740

Ashkenazi 526, 544, 591, 595, 596, 601

Assyrian 9, 20, 280, 302

Babylonian 227, 302, 496, 503, 525, 726

Beaker 40, 55, 56, 58

Belgae 71, 75, 78, 417

British 5, 7, 10, -19, 26-28, 31-33, 36, 40-44, 46, 47, 53-55, 58, 60, 63-65, 68-75, 77, 80-82, 87-92, 94-98, 101-105, 109-111, 115, 122, 124, 127, 128, 131, 132, 138, 144-148, 151, 152, 159-161, 163, 165, 169-171, 177, 186, 196, 198-201, 207, 225, 249, 307, 325, 389, 395-397, 414-416, 423, 425, 427, 445, 447, 465, 468-470, 472, 474, 483, 501, 502, 505, 511-515, 519, 528, 531, 534, 536, 537, 546, 547, 572, 573, 581, 588, 593, 595, 598, 599, 604, 605, 607, 608, 612, 615, 619, 626, 627, 630, 634, 635, 641, 665, 669, 670, 672, 676, 677, 695, 703, 704, 706, 718, 739, 740, 753

Briton 28, 34, 40, 41, 61, 63, 69, 72, 83, 89, 91, 96, 105, 111, 114, 118, 126, 128, 132, 143, 148, 175, 195, 199, 501, 634, 645, 739, 740, 756

Bulgar 178, 281, 336, 447, 448, 453, 455, 468, 482, 742, 743

Burgundian 104, 106, 257, 307

Carthaginian 82

Celtic 3, 41, 42, 45, 49, 50, 55, 58, 60, 61, 63-66, 68, 70, 80-82, 94-96, 207, 278, 497, 628, 634

Chinese 66, 150, 180, 186, 323, 393, 436, 464, 476, 488, 500, 576, 635, 703

Corded Ware 55, 56

Cro-Magnon 31, 32, 207

Danish 122-127, 129, 138, 207, 285, 293, 415, 431, 453

Egyptian 44, 93, 229, 396

Frisian 120-122, 132, 414

Gentile 210, 211, 590, 592, 703

Goth 9, 10, 48, 93, 94, 100, 104, 253, 257-260, 263, 264, 267-271, 274, 743, 750

Greek 9, 46, 50, 64, 65, 71, 72, 82, 84, 88, 223, 224, 228, 234, 243, 245, 248-250, 252, 253, 269, 270, 277, 279, 280, 298, 301, 302, 313, 320, 322, 334, 335, 346, 347, 415, 453, 497, 550, 693, 743, 748

Hebrew 9, 223, 243, 495, 530, 545, 589, 591, 603-606, 703, 709, 732

Hellenic 56

Hessian 593

## Index to Volume One

Hittite 59, 302

Homo Sapiens 29

Homo-sapien Cro-Magnonensis 31

Homo-sapien neanderthalensis 31

Homo-sapien-sapien 31

Hun 103, 104, 107, 210, 260, 262, 701

Ingaevone 120, 148, 501

Ionian 415

Irish 31, 60, 64, 65, 71, 79, 81, 114, 116, 117, 124, 145, 207, 278, 279, 371, 444, 453, 468, 507, 508, 530, 532, 544, 672, 676, 677, 739

Jewish 33, 83, 144-146, 183, 211, 246, 328, 335, 358, 365, 425, 467, 478-480, 482, 498, 502, 503, 520, 544, 589, 591, 592, 595-597, 600, 601, 603, 609, 610, 613, 626, 652, 746

Jute 4, 116, 120-122, 132

Lithuanian 333, 373, 378, 380, 414, 453

Lombard 51, 105, 146, 269-272, 274, 275, 279-282, 304, 313, 317, 362, 364, 377, 400, 411, 422, 429, 479, 500, 501, 503, 576

Magyar 48, 289, 298, 431, 453

Mamluk 396

Megalithic Folk 53

Minoan 46

Mongol 9, 227, 318-323, 325, 469, 701, 704, 743

Norman 26, 32, 34, 114, 122, 123, 131-133, 135-141, 143, 144, 207, 208, 287, 290, 293, 300-305, 307, 308, 311-314, 493, 499, 501, 502, 528-530, 629, 634, 636, 637, 665, 669, 695, 705, 715, 743, 750

Ostrogoth 102, 104-108, 264, 267-270

Ottoman 87, 333, 334, 336, 337, 346, 349, 352, 353, 355, 356, 359, 362, 363, 366, 367, 373, 376-379, 383, 386, 392, 393, 396, 400, 401, 406, 420, 426, 427, 448, 457, 479, 484-486, 538, 550, 704, 705, 742, 743

Phoenician 9, 28, 41, 42, 73, 82, 278, 740

Pict 32, 60-62, 66, 78, 81, 97, 102, 105, 114, 115, 128, 132, 207, 501, 700, 739

Polish 150, 160, 333, 336, 373, 377, 378, 380, 387, 414, 417, 418, 443, 453, 457, 466, 481, 482, 706

Prussian 15, 309, 310, 406, 418, 419, 426, 429-431, 433, 434, 436, 441, 444

Ripuarian 100

Roman 7, -11, 20, 24, 26, 27, 32, 34, 42, 48, 50, 60-65, 68, 69, 71, 72, 74, 76-83, 86-91, 99, 101-113, 128, 131, 143, 146, 208, 210, 212, 213, 215, 216, 220, 223-225, 227, 228, 240, 243, 245, 246, 248, 249, 251-253, 255-258, 260-265, 268, 270, 271, 274, 276-291, 295, 297-301, 303, 307-309, 311, 312, 314-323, 325, 327-330, 332, 335, 337, 339, 343, 347, 349, 350, 352-359, 361, 364, 366, 367, 369-371, 377-380, 382-386, 396, 398, 399, 401, 414, 416, 418, 420-422, 424, 425, 439-441, 443, 457, 458, 478, 479, 483, 485, 496, 498, 499, 501, 503, 504, 525, 541, 550, 596, 611, 628, 634, 695, 700-702, 704, 734, 742, 748, 753, 760

Salian 100, 266, 289

Sarmatian 66

Saxon 26, 27, 34, 60, 79, 87, 92, 95, 102, 114-116, 119-129, 131-133, 135-141, 143, 148, 207, 286, 289, 290, 293, 298, 501, 528, 534, 631, 632, 636, 637, 694, 695, 700, 705, 740, 753

Scot 32, 60, 61, 114, 115, 128, 132, 207, 319, 362, 501, 530, 534, 535, 739, 740

Scotti 76, 81, 102, 105, 114, 700

Scythian 61, 66

Sea People 59

Slav 56, 69, 277, 287, 363, 446

Swede 122, 123, 311, 338, 367, 369-371, 376, 388, 389, 401, 402, 406, 416, 418, 453, 470, 507, 690

Tatar 319, 322, 323

Thuringian 309

Trojan 28, 60, 169

Turk 9, 328, 329, 334, 336, 346, 347, 356, 359, 361, 453, 550, 704, 742, 743

Urnfield 58

Uyghur 65

Viking 34, 122-126, 129, 131, 132, 134, 136, 207, 501, 502, 528

Visigoth 100, 102-107, 259, 262, 264, 270

## Dominions

American Empire (US) 171, 389, 406, 470, 489, 517, 521, 544, 549, 581, 603, 610, 690, 702, 704, 705, 707

Angevin Empire 320

Austrian Empire 399, 411, 412, 414, 428, 431

Austro-Hungarian Empire 420, 446

Ayyubid Dynasty 314

Britannic Empire 95, 96

British Commonwealth 472

British Empire 33, 389, 397, 427, 445, 447, 512, 515, 531, 534, 581, 676, 703, 706

Byzantine Empire 84, 87, 88, 99, 134, 225, 269, 274, 279-281, 302, 304, 333, 457, 637

English Commonwealth 367

Frankish Empire 135, 275, 284, 286, 500

Gallic Empire 94

Latin Empire 320, 322

Manchukuo Puppet State 459, 464

Mongol Empire 321

Mughal Empire 389

Ottoman Empire 333, 337, 356, 367, 373, 376, 386, 396, 401, 420, 427, 485, 705

Russian Empire (Imperial) 401, 420, 424, 705

Sassanid, Persian Dynasty 100, 335

Second French Empire 425, 427

Second Reich 309, 415, 426

Spanish Empire 367, 389

Tang Dynasty 499

Vichy Puppet State 426

Weimar Republic 448, 464

## Ideology & Evolution

Acacian Schism (Religious) 219, 263, 266, 267

Aggregate Demand (Monetary) 563, 566, 567, 570, 571, 573, 577

Aggregate Supply (Monetary) 570, 571, 573, 577

Amber Trade (Monetary) 47, 48, 50, 52, 749

Anarchism (Political) 18, 24, 32, 92, 144, 195, 215, 255, 269, 354, 398, 436, 439, 443, 606, 607, 611, 697, 702

Barter (Monetary) 13, 489, 491, 492, 507, 517, 518, 575, 710, 716, 725

Bill of Rights (Socio-Political) 529, 655, 660-662

Blasphemy (Religious) 5, 24, 233-239, 316, 439, 716

Bonds (Monetary) 600

Bretton-Woods (Monetary) 472, 473, 548, 549

Bronze Age Collapse (Socio-Political) 32, 59, 495, 576, 694

Calvinism (Religious) 365

Canossa (Socio-Political) 290, 291, 295, 306

Central Bank (Monetary) 11, 511, 512, 519-522, 573, 586

Colonial Scrip (Monetary) 518, 519

Commodity Money (Monetary) 494, 496, 571, 576

## Index to Volume One

Common Law 131, 238, 633, 637

Communism (Political) 10, 16, 425, 448, 457, 459, 464, 470, 478, 598, 610, 611, 613, 614, 616, 704, 705, 707, 733, 736, 737, 748

Communist Manifesto (Political) 748

Corporate Empathy (Speculative) 15, 16, 23, 687

Council of Trent (Religious) 355, 358, 361, 362

Credit Crunch (Monetary) 551, 562, 568

Crusades and Crusaders (Religious) 14, 137, 213, 225, 302, 304, 305, 308, 312, 314, 317-322, 329, 336, 347, 348, 704, 705

Debt (Monetary) 488, 490-493, 495-498, 505, 509, 510, 514, 517, 518, 522, 523, 527, 541-543, 548-551, 560, 562, 563, 565, 572, 582, 583, 586, 587, 590, 598, 600, 694-696, 710-712, 724, 726

Deflation (Monetary) 571

Democracy in Britain in 1884 (Political) 672

Divine Right of Kings (Religious) 232, 748

Dome-Book – King Alfred's Common Law 695

Ethnogenesis (Speculative) 7, 9, 734

Fabian Society (Political) 611

Fascism (Political) 110, 401, 457, 459, 470, 706, 735

Fiat money (Monetary) 518, 549, 571, 576, 582, 696, 726

Fractional Reserve (Monetary) 146, 509, 510, 544, 552, 571, 586-588, 590, 726

French Revolution – The Terror (Socio-Political) 609

French Revolution (Socio-Political) 394, 399, 401, 424, 438, 607, 610, 736, 745, 749

Friedman (Monetary) 526, 563

Glorious Revolution (Socio-Political) 233, 367, 371, 378, 538, 641, 659, 660, 662, 663

Gregorian Calendar (Socio-Political) 362

Group Psychopathy (Speculative) 17, 22, 23, 708

Halal (Religious) 605

Heresy and Heretics (Religious) 9, 212, 218, 224-227, 229-232, 239, 241, 243, 244, 248-250, 253, 254, 258, 259, 261, 262, 265, 268-270, 272, 277-279, 283, 309, 314-316, 319, 325-327, 329, 333-335, 363, 365, 373, 375-377, 392, 394, 423, 442, 444, 709, 744, 745

Huguenot (Religious) 147, 233, 361, 363, 364, 374, 377, 380

Human Rights (Socio-Political) 153, 164, 166, 168, 678, 679, 681, 682, 687, 749

Hussite (Political) 333, 348

Hypothesis 1 (Speculative) 694, 709

Hypothesis 2 (Speculative) 714

Hypothesis 3 (Speculative) 719

Hypothesis 4 (Speculative) 723, 724

Hypothesis 5 (Speculative) 730

Independence (Socio-Political) 16, 148, 151, 360, 366, 374, 427, 428, 433, 437, 510, 514, 517, 518, 593

Inflation (Monetary) 515, 560, 569, 570, 576, 578, 579

Islam – Abbasid Caliphate 281

Islam – Fatima 237, 482

Islam – Fatimid Caliphate 299, 604

Islam – Ismaili 604

Islam – Jihad 14, 486, 605

Islam – Koran 211, 482

Islam – Madrasah 364

Islam – Moslem 480

Islam – Muhammad 24, 227, 235, 237, 316

Islam – Muslim 24, 179, 180, 210, 211, 229, 234-238, 280, 281, 283, 303, 320, 321, 323, 325, 356, 373, 392, 484, 485, 604, 605, 703, 704, 716, 718, 745

Islam – Qur'an 211, 234-236

Islam – Rashidun Caliphate 278

Islam – Severner 604

Islam – Shi'a 237, 604

Islam – Sunni 237

Islam – Twelver 237

Julian Calendar (Socio-Political) 362

Keynes (Monetary) 561, 562, 744

Knights Hospitaller (Religious) 307, 315, 324, 325

Knights Templar (Religious) 308, 315, 324, 325

Kosher (Religious) 604

Liber Judicialis – King Alfred's Common Law 695

Liberalism (Political) 221, 379, 422, 424, 439, 440, 443, 470, 528, 529, 533, 549, 643

Lollard (Political) 326, 329

Magna Carta (Socio-Political) 20, 23, 131, 315, 533, 652, 653, 655, 657, 741

Matter (Socio-Political) 218

Megalithic Yard (Speculative) 53

New World Order (Political) 36, 520, 607, 736

Ninety-Five Theses (Religious) 352

Out of Africa Hypothesis (Speculative) 8

Papal Supremacy (Religious) 291, 292, 303, 324, 397

Paradox of Thrift (Monetary) 571, 572

Peace of Cateau-Cambrésis 343, 359

Pogrom (Socio-Political) 145, 590

Privatisation 535, 536, 547, 562

Quantitative Easing (Monetary) 562, 582

Recession (Monetary) 59, 470, 503, 527, 552, 554, 560-563, 566-569, 571, 572, 575, 576, 578, 582, 601

Reform Act (Socio-Political) 425, 511, 529, 630, 645, 662, 669, 671, 672

Ridolfi Plot (Socio-Political) 362

Riot (Socio-Political) 7, 24, 171, 181-186, 286, 440, 682, 734

Rotten Boroughs 531, 669

Synchronicity (Speculative) 14, 15, 709

Synod of Whitby (Religious) 278, 279

The Investiture Controversy (Religious) 290

Usury (Monetary) 146, 461, 492, 497-499, 503, 504, 513, 517, 530, 562, 580, 587, 589, 597, 695, 716, 724-726

Wealth of Nations (Monetary) 492, 522, 579, 615, 743

Western Schism (Religious) 221, 326, 327, 329

## People

A.J.P. Taylor (Historian-Chronicler) 10

Abraham Lincoln (US) 522, 524, 586, 587

Adam Weishaupt (Socio-Political) 606, 609, 611

Adeodatus I (Pope) 277

Adolf (HRE) 448, 458, 463, 716

Adrian I (Pope) 281

Adrian II (Pope) 285

Adrian III (Pope) 286

Adrian IV (Pope) 308, 312, 313, 321

Adrian V (Pope) 321

Adrian VI (Pope) 353

Aemilian (RE – West) 94

Agapetus I (Pope) 268

Agapetus II (Pope) 288

Agapitus (Pope) 268

Agatho (Pope) 278

Alexander I (Pope – Saint) 248

## Index to Volume One

Alexander II (Pope) 303

Alexander III (Pope) 313, 315

Alexander IV (Pope) 319

Alexander Nevsky (Novgorod – Rus) 316

Alexander Severus (RE – West) 91

Alexander V (Pope) 327, 332

Alexander VI (Pope) 348-350, 374

Alexander VII (Pope) 376, 379

Alexander VIII (Pope) 371

Alfred the Great (Anglo-Saxon) 127-129, 285, 286, 501, 695

Allectus (RE – West) 95, 96

Anacletus (Pope) 20, 246, 311

Anastasius I (Pope – Saint) 258

Anastasius I (RE – East) 84

Anastasius II (Pope) 266

Anastasius III (Pope) 287

Anastasius IV (Pope) 312

Anicetus (Pope) 249

Anicius Olybrius (RE – West) 104, 106

Anne (English Queen) 148, 538, 663

Anterus (Pope) 252

Antoninus Pius (RE – West) 90, 231

Arcadius (RE – East) 102, 257-259

Aristotle (Historian-Chronicler) 497

Arthur (Ancient British King) 79

Attila (Hun) 103, 104, 107, 260, 262

Augustus (RE – West) 83, 84, 88, 96-102, 105, 107, 254, 264, 387, 418

Aurelian (RE – West) 93-95

Aureolus (RE – West) 94

Avidius Cassius (RE – West) 90

Balbinus (RE – West) 92

Basiliscus (RE – East) 261, 263, 265

Benedict I (Pope) 270

Benedict II (Pope) 279

Benedict III (Pope) 285

Benedict IV (Pope) 287, 288

Benedict IX (Pope) 300, 301

Benedict V (Pope) 297

Benedict VI (Pope) 297

Benedict VII (Pope) 297

Benedict VIII (Pope) 299

Benedict X (Pope) 302

Benedict XI (Pope) 324

Benedict XII (Pope) 325, 327

Benedict XIII (Pope) 304, 326, 332, 333, 392

Benedict XIV (Pope) 333, 334, 393

Benedict XV (Pope) 456, 457

Benedict XVI (Pope) 311, 461, 483, 485, 486

Benjamin Franklin (US) 519, 606

Black Prince (English) 328, 329

Boadicea (Iceni – Ancient British) 68, 69, 89

Boniface I (Pope) 261

Boniface II (Pope) 268

Boniface III (Pope) 274

Boniface IV (Pope) 277

Boniface IX (Pope) 330, 331

Boniface V (Pope) 277

Boniface VI (Pope) 286

Boniface VII (Pope) 297

Boniface VIII (Pope) 232, 323

Bonosus (RE – West) 94

Brennus (Celtish) 82, 259

Caius (Pope) 128, 255, 739

Caligula (RE – West) 80, 89, 245

Calvin (Socio-Political) 356

Caracalla (RE – West) 91

Caratacus (Catuvellaunian – Ancient British) 88, 89

Carausius (RE – West) 95, 96

Carinus (RE – West) 93

Carlos I (Spanish King, HRE Charles/Karl V) 343, 352

Carlos II (Spanish) 367, 382, 383

Carus (RE – West) 93

Celestine I (Pope) 261

Celestine II (Pope) 307, 311

Celestine III (Pope) 315

Celestine IV (Pope) 316

Celestine V (Pope) 323

Cerdic (Anglo-Saxon) 132, 631

Charlemagne (HRE) 7, 27, 275, 282-284, 286, 289, 353, 433

Charles Albert (Sardinian-Italian King) 437

Charles Felix (Sardinian-Italian King) 437

Charles I (English King) 33, 507, 531, 657, 662

Charles II (English King) 368, 370, 513, 531, 658, 662, 663

Charles IV (HRE) 327, 328

Charles of Anjou (French) 318, 320, 322

Charles V (French King) 328

Charles V (HRE, Karl V, Spanish Carlos I) 318, 343, 344, 352, 354-359, 384

Charles VI (HRE) 384, 386, 388

Charles VIII (French King) 338, 348-350

Charles X (French King) 413, 438

Christopher Hill (Historian-Chronicler) 10

Claudius (RE – West) 89, 93, 94

Claudius Ptolemaeus (Historian-Chronicler) 72

Clement I (Pope) 246

Clement II (Pope) 300, 301

Clement III (Pope) 303-305, 314

Clement IV (Pope) 320

Clement IX (Pope) 376

Clement V (Pope) 324

Clement VI (Pope) 327

Clement VII (Pope) 326, 329, 330, 343, 353, 355

Clement VIII (Pope) 333, 365

Clement X (Pope) 377

Clement XI (Pope) 392

Clement XII (Pope) 392, 393

Clement XIII (Pope) 394

Clement XIV (Pope) 397, 746

Cletus (Pope) 246

Clodius Albinus (RE – West) 91

Cnut (Danish) 133

Commodus (RE – West) 90, 247, 250

Conon (Pope) 279

Conrad I (Sicilian King) 318

Conrad II (HRE) 300

Conrad II (Sicilian King) 318

Conrad IV (German King) 309, 317

Constans I (RE – West & East) 99, 242, 254

Constans II (RE – East) 103, 277, 278

Constans II (RE – West) 103

Constantine (Pope) 280, 281

Constantine II (RE – West) 99, 242, 254, 281

Constantine III (RE – West & East) 103

Constantine the Great (RE – West) 98, 99, 223, 227, 239, 242, 253, 254, 256, 257, 263, 276

Constantius Chlorus (RE – West) 95, 97

## Index to Volume One

Constantius Chlorus (Western Region Tetrarchy – Caesar) 96

Constantius II (RE – West) 99, 100, 242

Constantius III (RE – West) 103

Cornelius (Pope) 227, 252, 375

Damasus I (Pope) 243, 257, 258

Damasus II (Pope) 301

Deusdedit (Pope) 277

Diadumenian (RE – West) 91

Didius Julianus (RE – West) 90

Diocletian (Eastern Region Tetrarchy – Augustus) 96

Diocletian (RE – West) 84, 93, 96, 97, 251

Diodorus Siculus (Historian-Chronicler) 72, 740

Dionysius (Pope) 253

Domitian (RE – West) 89, 245, 246

Domitianus II (RE – West) 95

Domitius Alexander (RE – West) 98

Donus (Pope) 278

Duke of Aosta (Italian) 437

E.P. Thompson (Historian-Chronicler) 10

Edgar the Ætheling (Anglo-Saxon) 133

Edmund Ironside (Anglo-Saxon) 133

Edward Gibbon (Historian-Chronicler) 20, 91

Edward I (English King) 144, 319, 323, 325, 530, 653, 657, 749

Edward II (English King) 325

Edward III (English King) 327, 328, 500, 505, 638

Edward the Confessor (Anglo-Saxon) 132-135, 501

Edward VI (English King) 337, 358, 533

Edwin of Mercia (Anglo-Saxon) 135

Egbert (Anglo-Saxon) 27, 126

Elagabalus (RE – West) 91

Elizabeth I (English Queen) 337, 354, 358-360, 362-364, 533, 539, 640

Eparchius Avitus (RE – West) 104, 106

Eric Hobsbawm (Historian-Chronicler) 10

Eugene I (Pope) 278

Eugene II (Pope) 284

Eugene III (Pope) 312

Eugene IV (Pope) 334-336, 346

Eugenius (RE – West) 101

Eusebius (Pope) 219, 239, 240, 243, 245, 247, 256, 739, 747

Eutychian (Pope) 232, 253

Evaristus (Pope) 248

Fabian (Pope – Saint) 252

Felipe II (Spanish) 344, 355, 359, 361, 364

Felipe III (Portuguese King) 382

Felipe III (Spanish King) 374

Felipe IV (Spanish) 367, 368, 382

Felipe V (Spanish) 382-385, 542

Felix I (Pope) 253

Felix II (Pope) 256

Felix III (Pope) 265

Felix IV (Pope) 267

Ferdinand I (HRE) 344, 359

Flavius Glycerius (RE – West) 105-107

Flavius Majorian (RE – West) 104, 106-108, 260

Flavius Victor (RE – West) 101

Flavius Zeno (RE – East) 105, 107, 263, 264

Florianus (RE – West) 94

Formosus (Pope) 286, 287

Francis I (Austro-Hungarian Emperor) 414, 424

Francis I (French King) 343, 351-356, 358

Francis II (HRE) 399, 412, 414, 424

Francis of Assisi (Roman Catholic Saint) 486

Franz Ferdinand (Austro-Hungarian Archduke) 446

Frederick I (Sicilian King) 317

Frederick I (HRE) 308, 312-314

Frederick II (HRE) 309, 315-318, 325

Frederick III (HRE) 346, 380

Friedrich Engels (Socio-Political) 611, 748

Gaiseric (Vandal) 259-262

Gaius Julius Caesar (Roman Republic) 83, 88

Gaius Octavian Augustus (RE – West) 83, 84, 88

Galba (RE – West) 89

Galerius (Eastern Region Tetrarchy – Caesar) 96

Galerius (RE – West) 97, 254

Gallienus (RE – West) 92, 253

Gallus (RE – West) 92, 252

Garibaldi (Italian Revolutionary) 429, 430, 433, 441

Gelasius I (Pope) 266

Gelasius II (Pope) 307

Genghis Khan (Mongol) 208, 547

Geoffrey of Monmouth (Historian-Chronicler) 72, 634, 739, 740

George I (English King) 543, 663

George I (Greek King) 415

George II (English King) 535

George III (English King) 397, 511, 531, 532

George Washington (Socio-Political) 609

Geta (RE – West) 91

Gildas (Historian-Chronicler) 72, 116, 118, 741

Gnaeus Pompeius Magnus (Roman Republic) 88

Gordian I (RE – West) 92

Gordian II (RE – West) 92

Gordian III (RE – West) 92

Gordon Brown (Socio-Political) 169, 598, 599, 619

Gratian (RE – West & East) 101, 102, 257

Gregory I (Pope) 269, 271

Gregory II (Pope) 280

Gregory III (Pope) 280

Gregory IV (Pope) 284

Gregory IX (Pope) 316, 319

Gregory the Great (Pope) 272

Gregory V (Pope) 298

Gregory VI (Pope) 299-301

Gregory VII (Pope) 232, 290, 291, 295, 303, 304, 306

Gregory VIII (Pope) 307, 314

Gregory X (Pope) 321

Gregory XI (Pope) 329

Gregory XII (Pope) 332, 485

Gregory XIII (Pope) 304, 362, 363

Gregory XIV (Pope) 364, 365

Gregory XV (Pope) 373

Gregory XVI (Pope) 439

Hadrian (RE – West) 78, 85, 90, 231, 298

Harold Godwinson (Anglo-Saxon) 129, 133-136

Harold Harefoot (Danish) 133

Harthacnut (Danish) 133

Hector Munro Chadwick (Historian-Chronicler) 120

Henri I (French King) 135

Henri II (French King) 358, 359, 361

Henry I (Sicilian King) 317

Henry I (English King) 290, 499, 513, 653

Henry II (English King) 146, 312, 313, 657

Henry II (HRE) 299, 300

Henry II (Sicilian King) 317

Henry II (Spanish King) 329

## Index to Volume One

Henry III (English King) 146, 318, 319, 325, 533, 653

Henry III (HRE) 300-302

Henry IV (HRE) 290, 291, 295, 302-305

Henry of Huntingdon (Historian-Chronicler) 739

Henry of Navarre aka King Henri IV (French King) 363, 364

Henry Raspe (HRE) 309

Henry the Navigator (Portuguese Prince) 505

Henry V (HRE) 291, 306-308

Henry VI (HRE) 314, 315, 317

Henry VII (English King) 348, 350, 533, 657

Henry VII (German King) 317, 325

Henry VII (HRE) 317, 325

Henry VIII (English King) 312, 337, 338, 350, 352, 354, 356, 357, 363, 533, 534, 655

Heraclius (RE – East) 255, 273, 277

Herennius Etruscus (RE – West) 92, 94

Hereward the Wake (Anglo-Saxon Resistance) 293

Hilarius (Pope) 263

Hitler (German Chancellor – Third Reich) 417, 422, 448, 458, 463, 465, 471, 478, 716, 747

Honorius (RE – West) 102, 103, 106, 257, 259, 261

Honorius I (Pope) 229, 277, 278

Honorius II (Pope) 303, 307

Honorius III (Pope) 316, 322

Honorius IV (Pope) 322

Hormisdas (Pope) 267, 268

Hostilian (RE – West) 94

Hyginus (Pope) 248

Ingenuus (RE – West) 94

Innocent I (Pope) 259, 261

Innocent II (Pope) 311

Innocent III (Pope) 225, 313, 315, 319

Innocent IV (Pope) 309, 316-319

Innocent IX (Pope) 365

Innocent V (Pope) 321

Innocent VI (Pope) 328

Innocent VII (Pope) 331

Innocent VIII (Pope) 347

Innocent X (Pope) 374, 375

Innocent XI (Pope) 371, 377, 378

Innocent XII (Pope) 371, 379

Innocent XIII (Pope) 348, 392

James I (English King) 360, 530, 531, 663

James II (English King) 378, 392, 659, 662, 663

James II (Spanish King) 323

James Stuart (Scots, Irish, & Welsh) 392

James VI (Scots, Irish, & Welsh) 360, 530

James VII (Scots, Irish, & Welsh) 662

Joannes (RE – West) 103

John Hunyadi (Hungarian) 336

John I (Pope) 267

John II (Pope) 268

John III (Polish King) 378

John III (Pope) 270

John IV (Pope) 277

John IV (Portuguese King) 374

John IX (Pope) 287

John Lackland (English King) 533, 653

John Locke (Historian-Chronicler) 367, 393, 747, 750

John of Gaunt (English) 328

John of Salisbury (Historian-Chronicler) 312

John Paul I (Pope) 480, 481

John Paul II (Pope) 220, 481, 485

John V (Pope) 279

John VI (Pope) 279
John VII (Pope) 279
John VIII (Pope) 285, 286
John X (Pope) 288
John XI (Pope) 287, 288
John XII (Pope) 288, 289, 297
John XIII (Pope) 297
John XIV (Pope) 297, 298, 321
John XIX (Pope) 300
John XV (Pope) 298
John XVI (Pope) 298
John XVII (Pope) 299
John XVIII (Pope) 299
John XX (Pope) 298, 321
John XXI (Pope) 298, 321
John XXII (Pope) 325, 326
John XXIII (Pope) 330-333, 479
Joseph I (HRE) 382
Jotapianus (RE – West) 94
Jovian (RE – West & East) 100, 242, 253
Jovinus (RE – West) 103
Julian aka Julian the Apostate (RE – West) 100, 242, 253, 255
Julius Caesar (Roman Republic) 63, 80, 82, 83, 88, 498
Julius I (Pope) 256
Julius II (Pope) 350
Julius III (Pope) 357
Julius Nepos (RE – West) 105, 106, 264
Julius Saturninus (RE – West) 94
Justin I (RE – East) 84, 267
Justinian II the Slit-nosed (RE – East) 280
Karl Marx (Socio-Political) 425, 610, 716, 748

Karl V (HRE, Charles V, Spanish Carlos I) 343, 352
King Charles I (Naples & Sicily) 318, 322
King Charles III (Naples & Sicily) 330
Lady Jane Grey (Nine Day Queen – English) 337
Laelianus (RE – West) 94
Lando (Pope) 287
Lenin (Soviet Russian) 425, 611, 613, 614, 616, 752
Leo I (Pope – Saint) 260, 262, 263
Leo II (Pope – Saint) 278
Leo III (Pope – Saint) 282
Leo III the Isaurian (RE – East) 280
Leo IV (Pope – Saint) 285
Leo IX (Pope – Saint) 301
Leo IX (Pope) 301, 302, 304
Leo V (Pope) 287
Leo VI (Pope) 288
Leo VII (Pope) 288
Leo VIII (Pope) 289, 297
Leo X (Pope) 351-353
Leo XI (Pope) 366, 438
Leo XII (Pope) 438, 439
Leo XIII (Pope) 443, 459
Leopold (Medieval Duke of Austria) 315
Leopold I (HRE) 382
Liberius (Pope) 256, 258
Libius Severus (RE – West) 104, 106
Licinianus (RE – West) 94
Licinius (RE – West) 88, 98, 99, 254
Linus (Pope) 246
Lord Acton (Historian-Chronicler) 19
Lothair I (HRE) 283, 284
Louis II (HRE) 285
Louis II of Anjou (French) 330

## Index to Volume One

Louis IV of Bavaria (HRE) 325, 327

Louis VIII (French King) 320

Louis XII (French King) 339, 349, 351

Louis XIV (French King) 368, 370, 375-378, 382, 383, 385

Louis XVI (French King) 400, 413

Louis-Philippe I (French King) 413, 439

Lucius I (Pope) 252

Lucius II (Pope) 312

Lucius III (Pope) 314

Lucius Verus (RE – West) 90

Luther (Socio-Political) 233, 352, 375, 744-746

Macrianus Major (RE – West) 94

Macrianus Minor (RE – West) 94

Macrinus (RE – West) 91

Magnentius (RE – West) 99, 100, 254

Magnus Maximus (RE – West) 101, 700

Manfred (Naples & Sicily) 318-320, 322

Marcellinus (Pope) 255

Marcellus I (Pope) 255

Marcellus II (Pope) 358

Marcian (RE – East) 104

Marcus Aemilius Lepidus (RE – West) 88

Marcus Antonius aka Mark Antony. (RE – West) 88

Marcus Aurelius (RE – West) 90, 245-247, 741

Marcus Claudius Tacitus (RE – West) 93

Margaret Thatcher (British P.M.) 562, 599

Maria Theresa (Holy Roman Empire Empress) 414

Marinus I (Pope) 286

Marinus II (Pope) 288

Marius (RE – West) 94

Mark (Pope) 83, 88, 240

Martin I (Pope) 277

Martin IV (Pope) 322

Martin V (Pope) 332, 333

Mary I (English Queen) 337, 358, 361, 363, 533

Mary II (English Queen) 662

Maurice (RE – East) 271-273

Maxentius (RE – West) 97, 98, 255, 256

Maximian (RE – West) 95, 97

Maximian (Western Region Tetrarchy – Augustus) 96

Maximilian I (HRE) 352

Maximilian II (HRE) 383

Maximinus I aka Maximinus Thrax (RE – West) 92, 251

Maximinus II (RE – West) 97, 98, 241

Maximus (RE – West) 97, 101, 103, 104, 611, 700, 734

Mazarin, Cardinal 374, 375, 382

Michael IV (RE – East) 134

Miltiades (Pope) 256

Morcar of Northumbria (Anglo-Saxon) 135

Mussius Aemilianus (RE – West) 94

Mussolini (Italian) 438, 459, 505

Napoleon (French) 396, 398-400, 402, 406, 412, 413, 415-418, 420, 422-424, 430, 433, 437, 438, 593, 609, 629, 742, 743, 747, 749

Nennius (Historian-Chronicler) 60, 72, 249, 739, 741, 752, 753

Nepotianus (RE – West) 100

Nero (RE – West) 89, 245, 246

Nerva (RE – West) 90, 245, 246

Nicholas I (Pope) 285

Nicholas II (Pope) 302, 303, 613

Nicholas III (Pope) 322

Nicholas IV (Pope) 323

Nicholas V (Pope) 325, 326, 346

Numerian (RE – West) 93, 97

Offa (Anglo-Saxon) 282

Oliver Cromwell (English) 367, 510, 662

Otho (RE – West) 89

Otto II (HRE) 297

Otto III (HRE) 297-299

Pacatianus (RE – West) 94

Paschal I (Pope) 283

Paschal II (Pope) 306

Paul I (Pope) 281, 480, 481

Paul II (Pope) 220, 346, 481, 485

Paul III (Pope) 355, 357, 363

Paul IV (Pope) 358, 361, 363, 384

Paul V (Pope) 372, 375

Paul VI (Pope) 280, 479, 480, 484

Pausanius aka Pausanias (Historian-Chronicler) 739

Pelagius I (Pope) 270, 271

Pelagius II (Pope) 270, 271

Pertinax (RE – West) 90, 91

Pescennius Niger (RE – West) 91

Peter (Pope – Saint) 212, 232, 245, 246, 263, 275, 279, 282, 284, 285, 303-306, 323, 456

Philip the Arab (RE – West) 92

Philippe IV (French King) 323, 324

Philippe VI (French King) 327

Phocas (RE – East) 273, 274

Pius I (Pope) 248

Pius II (Pope) 346

Pius III (Pope) 350

Pius IV (Pope) 361

Pius IX (Pope) 221, 427, 439, 440, 442, 443, 745, 746

Pius V (Pope) 362, 365

Pius VI (Pope) 281, 397, 398

Pius VII (Pope) 400, 422, 423

Pius VIII (Pope) 438

Pius X (Pope) 220, 444, 457

Pius XI (Pope) 438, 448, 457-459, 463

Pius XII (Pope) 461, 478, 479

Plato (Historian-Chronicler) 224, 747

Postumus (RE – West) 94

Prince of Wales (English) 537, 543

Priscus (RE – West) 94, 103

Priscus Attalus (RE – West) 103

Probus (RE – West) 93

Procopius (6th century Historian) (Historian-Chronicler) 103

Procopius (RE – West) 100, 104

Procopius Anthemius (RE – West) 104, 106

Proculus (RE – West) 94

Pupienus (RE – West) 92

Quietus (RE – West) 94

Quintillus (RE – West) 93, 94

Regalianus (RE – West) 94

Richard I (English King) 315, 637

Richard III (English King) 348

Richard of Cornwall (HRE) 318, 319

Robert the Bruce (Scots, Irish, & Welsh) 325

Rollo (Normandy – Viking Settler) 134, 287, 501

Romanus (Pope) 82, 272, 287

Sabinian (Pope) 274

Sabinianus (RE – West) 94, 274

## Index to Volume One

Saloninus (RE – West) 94

Sebastianus (RE – West) 103

Septimius Severus (RE – West) 90, 91, 240

Sergius I (Pope) 279

Sergius II (Pope) 285

Sergius III (Pope) 287, 288

Sergius IV (Pope) 299

Severinus (Pope) 277

Severus II (RE – West) 97

Severus, Alexander (RE – West) 91

Severus, Septimius (RE – West) 90, 91, 240

Sextus Martinianus (RE – West) 99

Sigeberht (Anglo-Saxon) 632

Silbannacus (RE – West) 94

Silverius (Pope) 268

Silvio Berlusconi (Socio-Political) 481

Simeon of Durham (Historian-Chronicler) 123, 125, 740

Simplicius (Pope) 265

Sir Edward Coke (Historian-Chronicler) 637, 640

Sir Isaac Newton (Historian-Chronicler) 515, 543

Sir William Blackstone (Historian-Chronicler) 652

Siricius (Pope) 258

Sisinnius (Pope) 280

Sixtus I (Pope) 248

Sixtus II (Pope) 253

Sixtus III (Pope) 262

Sixtus IV (Pope) 347

Sixtus V (Pope) 363, 364

Soter (Pope) 249

Stalin (Soviet Russian) 417, 422, 471, 603, 613-615

Stephen I (Pope – Saint) 252

Stephen IV (Pope) 281

Stephen IX (Pope) 288

Stephen of Blois (English) 311

Stephen V (Pope) 283

Stephen VI (Pope) 286

Stephen VII (Pope) 286, 287

Stephen VIII (Pope) 288

Stephen X (Pope) 302

Stilicho (Roman General – Half Vandal) 101, 102, 106, 258, 259, 700

Strabo (Historian-Chronicler) 740

Sweyn Forkbeard (Danish) 133

Sylvester I (Pope) 256

Sylvester II (Pope) 299

Sylvester III (Pope) 300

Symmachus (Pope) 267

Tacitus, The Annals circa 100 AD (Historian-Chronicler) 20

Telesphorus (Pope) 248, 252

Tetricus I (RE – West) 95

The Venerable Bede (Historian-Chronicler) 114, 123, 218, 231, 255, 277, 741

Theoderic I (Visigoth – Ostrogoth King) 104, 262

Theoderic II aka Theoderic The Great (Visigoth – Ostrogoth King) 104, 106

Theodora (RE – East) 268

Theodore I (Pope) 277

Theodore II (Pope) 287

Theodosius I the Great (RE – West & East) 101-103, 244, 257

Theodosius II (RE – East) 103, 104, 229

Titus (RE – West) 89

Titus Livius aka Livy (Historian-Chronicler) 72, 742

Tony Blair (Socio-Political) 169, 187, 238, 612

Trajan (RE – West) 240, 246-248

Trajan Decius (RE – West) 90, 92

Trotsky (Soviet Russian) 425, 610, 613, 749

Urban I (Pope) 251

Urban II (Pope) 305

Urban III (Pope) 314

Urban IV (Pope) 320, 322

Urban V (Pope) 328, 329

Urban VI (Pope) 329, 330

Urban VII (Pope) 364

Urban VIII (Pope) 373, 374

Valens (RE – East) 100, 101, 242

Valentine (Pope) 284

Valentinian I (RE – West) 100, 101, 244

Valentinian II (RE – West) 101

Valentinian III (RE – West) 103, 104, 260

Valerian (RE – West) 92, 227, 252, 253

Valerius Valens (RE – West) 98

Vespasian (RE – West) 89, 245

Vetranio (RE – West) 100

Victor Emanuel II (Italian King) 438

Victor Emmanuel I (Sardinian-Italian King) 437

Victor I (Pope) 250

Victor II (Pope) 302, 303

Victor III (Pope) 304

Victorinus (RE – West) 95

Vigilius (Pope) 268, 270, 271

Vitalian (Pope) 278

Vitellius (RE – West) 89

Volusianus (RE – West) 94

Wilhelm Friedrich Ludwig I (German Kaiser) 434

William Cobbett (Historian-Chronicler) 542

William II (English King) 305, 653

William III (English King) 538, 662, 663

William of Malmesbury (Historian-Chronicler) 740

William of Ockham (Historian-Chronicler) 221, 309, 326

William Stubbs (Historian-Chronicler) 636

Winston Churchill (British – G.B.) 606, 610, 612, 706

Zachary (Pope) 280

Zephyrinus (Pope) 250

Zosimus (Pope) 261

Æthelred (Anglo-Saxon) 133, 298, 632

Æthelred the Unready (Anglo-Saxon) 133, 632

## Places

Aachen 320, 376, 388, 418, 430, 599

Africa 8, 41, 42, 44, 58, 59, 68, 92, 98, 103, 123, 142, 152, 154, 155, 174, 207, 259-261, 268, 272, 276, 356, 368, 384, 466, 469, 475, 517, 642, 701, 702, 734

Aix-la-Chapelle 369, 388, 430

Alexandria 83, 93, 99, 102, 212, 213, 216, 219, 231, 241, 242, 254, 258, 276, 480

Alsace 301, 433, 452

Anatolia 56, 59, 70, 497

Antioch 212, 213, 216, 219, 240, 243, 247, 276

Aquitaine 106, 231, 324

Armenia 56, 128, 129, 212, 255, 319, 334

Armorica 79, 129

Asia 56, 154, 225, 226, 229, 232, 239, 245, 276, 327, 495, 497, 499

Atlantic 26, 37, 40-44, 47, 55, 64, 81, 123, 142, 207, 502, 539, 604, 622, 734

Augusta Treverorum 96

## Index to Volume One

Austria 63, 315, 319, 337, 344, 359, 367, 382, 386, 387, 389, 395, 396, 399, 400, 402, 406, 411-414, 420, 421, 424, 426, 428-431, 433, 438, 440, 443, 445-448, 455, 457, 459, 464, 468, 690, 692

Avignon 256, 321, 324-333, 365, 378, 394, 412, 421

Bavaria 284, 325-327, 382-384, 388, 395, 402, 406, 420, 436, 483, 606

Belgium 78, 95, 352, 359, 369, 376, 386, 396, 399, 416, 417, 426, 439, 445-447, 452, 455, 468, 482, 489, 594, 690

Berlin 380

Black Sea 48, 55, 59, 66, 123, 246, 336

Bosnia 446

Brittany 54, 64, 65, 68, 70, 79, 92, 95, 129, 135, 308

Byzantium 99, 123

Carthage 68, 71, 92, 227, 240, 241, 244, 248, 260

Caspian Sea 55, 59, 81, 123, 396

Caucasus 49, 591

China 24, 29, 56, 65, 66, 150, 152, 269, 322, 328, 363, 373, 393, 463, 468, 496, 497, 499, 539, 617, 693, 702, 705, 714, 749

Constantinople 99, 103, 123, 212, 213, 216, 219, 228, 229, 232, 253, 254, 258, 261, 263, 264, 266-268, 270, 274, 276-278, 280, 288, 297, 300, 320, 322, 336, 346, 356, 457, 480, 484, 742

Crete 59, 376

Crimea 278

Cyprus 59, 178, 317, 576

Danube River 48-50, 64, 353

Denmark 122, 132, 133, 238, 307, 308, 311, 367, 406, 414, 416, 431, 452, 468, 593, 664, 690

Don River 49

Ephesus 229, 231, 261, 263, 279

Europe 7, -14, 16, 28, 31, 38-41, 44, 46-50, 53, 55, 56, 58, 63, 65, 70, 80, 82, 84, 100, 101, 105, 123, 124, 130, 131, 137, 150, 152-155, 177, 207, 210-212, 215, 233, 238, 267, 270, 284, 285, 288, 290, 298, 305, 306, 318, 320, 327, 329, 330, 336, 346, 352, 353, 355-363, 366, 376, 377, 382, 385-387, 389, 391, 392, 397, 399, 406, 411, 413, 414, 421, 424-427, 430, 439, 440, 447, 456, 467, 478, 482, 485, 486, 489, 495, 499-503, 520, 541, 548, 550, 581, 592, 593, 604, 606-608, 610, 629, 642, 654, 664, 672, 687, 707, 742, 743, 748, 749

Flanders 135, 352, 359, 369, 417

France 37, 40, 54-56, 61, 92, 94, 106, 115, 122, 123, 137, 147, 150, 152, 155, 174, 180, 221, 225, 240, 260, 280, 282, 284, 290, 297, 302, 305-308, 318, 319, 321, 322, 324-329, 331, 332, 337, 339, 340, 343, 344, 347, 349-353, 355-357, 360, 361, 364-371, 374-377, 382, 383, 385-389, 394, 396-402, 412, 413, 415-417, 421, 423, 424, 426-429, 433, 437, 439, 441, 443-447, 452, 455, 464-466, 468, 484, 489, 500, 501, 504, 506, 507, 510, 511, 516, 536, 541, 550, 594, 596, 604, 607, 609, 629, 664

Francia 284, 285

Gdansk 50, 418

Genoa 304, 314, 318, 321, 330, 343-347, 349, 350, 354, 388, 400, 412, 437, 456, 504

Germany 24, 50, 75, 94, 96, 123, 146, 174, 180, 238, 280, 284, 289-291, 297, 301, 302, 307-309, 311, 312, 317, 319-321, 330, 331, 346, 347, 352, 360, 381, 382, 386, 388, 399, 426, 445-448, 455, 457-460, 463-466, 468, 471, 477, 478, 483, 484, 489, 506, 516, 536, 550, 591, 599, 601, 607, 610, 642, 663, 692, 706

Golgotha 299

## Index to Volume One

Greece 50, 56, 61, 115, 238, 261, 276, 362, 415, 455, 468, 497, 525, 550, 739, 742, 749

Greek City State 693

Hungary 178, 262, 289, 319, 328, 330, 337, 346, 359, 362, 367, 382, 426, 445-448, 455, 457, 468, 610

India 56, 66, 147, 151, 152, 174, 179, 363, 367, 384, 389, 393, 396, 455, 468, 539, 703

Inundation of Doggerland 40, 45, 46, 417

Iran 56, 468, 631

Iraq 56, 59, 152-154, 468, 495, 701

Israel 145, 152, 425, 495, 545, 546, 548, 589, 591, 595, 600, 627, 628, 690, 692, 705

Italy 47, 50, 51, 56, 64, 82, 101, 105, 107, 123, 146, 214, 238, 259, 262-265, 269-271, 274-277, 281, 283-285, 288, 289, 291, 295, 299-302, 306, 307, 312-314, 316, 317, 320, 321, 323-326, 329-331, 334, 338, 339, 343, 344, 347, 349-352, 354, 359-361, 365, 375, 385, 386, 388, 393, 397, 398, 400-402, 404, 406, 411, 412, 421-423, 426, 427, 429, 430, 433, 437, 438, 440, 443, 444, 447, 455, 459, 463-465, 468, 480, 489, 500, 501, 503, 504, 552, 576, 642, 749

Jerusalem 212, 213, 216, 219, 246, 247, 276, 277, 299, 305, 307, 317, 318, 330, 479, 480, 545, 546, 595, 627

Judea 276, 497

Kazakhstan 66

Kiev 123

Lake Peipus 310, 316

Levant 505, 589

London 10, 37, 61, 81, 114, 128, 136, 137, 145-147, 175, 185, 192, 194, 204, 277, 329, 337, 473, 481, 487, 504-508, 519, 524, 526, 537, 572, 592, 594-597, 608, 614, 627, 634, 635, 637, 669, 670, 718, 747, 749

Lorraine 284, 302, 433, 452

Maeshowe 41

Mediolanum 96

Mediterranean Sea 26, 40, 41, 43, 44, 46-48, 53, 56, 59, 64, 103, 142, 154, 208, 226, 274, 284, 299, 302, 320, 322, 353, 362, 386, 495, 502, 541, 693

Mercia 124, 135, 279, 282

Mesopotamia 40, 59, 495-497, 589, 725

Mongolia 319, 469

Moscow 406, 613

Naples 270, 277, 280, 285, 303, 304, 318, 320, 323, 330, 331, 338, 344, 346, 348-351, 353, 354, 356, 359, 360, 383, 386, 388, 392, 394, 396-399, 401, 402, 406, 412, 418, 429, 500, 505, 592

Netherlands 177, 238, 359, 363, 368, 370, 374-376, 384, 386, 399, 400, 415-417, 439, 469, 593, 690

Newgrange 41

Nicomedia 96, 99

Norway 122, 134, 311, 367, 406, 416, 469, 690, 692

Orkneys 37, 41, 61, 207

Pacific 469, 539, 704

Pangea 35

Pannonia 243, 262

Papal States 223, 272, 275, 276, 281, 299, 302, 314, 316, 317, 331, 338-340, 343, 355, 358, 363, 374, 412, 421, 423, 427-429, 436, 438, 439, 441, 444

Paris 24, 134, 262, 313, 332, 374, 395, 427, 434, 436, 439, 457, 526, 592, 594, 596

Persia 100, 320-322, 525

Poland 50, 55, 64, 123, 174, 178, 238, 300, 319, 330, 338, 377, 387, 403, 414, 417, 418, 439, 443, 452, 457, 466, 467, 469, 481, 482

Prague 433

## Index to Volume One

Rhine 38, 39, 46, 64, 101, 106, 121, 148, 399, 400, 402, 406, 420

Rome 20, 50, 64, 68, 78, 82, 83, 88, 89, 92, 96, 99, 100, 102, 104, 106, 115, 123, 212, 213, 216, 217, 219, 220, 223, 229, 232, 240, 243, 245, 246, 248, 250, 252, 253, 258-264, 266, 268, 269, 271, 272, 274-280, 282, 283, 285, 286, 288, 289, 291, 297-302, 304-307, 312-315, 318, 320, 322, 324, 326-331, 333, 346, 347, 349, 350, 354, 361, 362, 364, 365, 372-374, 377, 392, 398, 413, 430, 433, 436, 438, 440, 441, 456, 457, 480, 497, 504, 655, 664, 742, 745, 746, 749

Russia 24, 50, 56, 122, 123, 319, 338, 387-389, 395-397, 401, 402, 406, 414, 417, 418, 424, 426, 427, 433, 443, 445-447, 455, 464-466, 478, 502, 550, 595, 603, 610, 611, 613, 614, 616, 629, 702, 705

Sardinia 26, 98, 250, 251, 274, 285, 299, 343, 344, 386-388, 396, 399, 400, 402, 404, 406, 412, 427-430, 432, 437, 440

Seine 134

Serbia 96, 445-447, 455

Siberia 29

Sicily 53, 256, 260, 274, 299, 303, 305, 308, 311-315, 317, 318, 320, 322, 323, 344, 346, 383, 386, 388, 396, 398, 399, 401, 402, 406, 412, 429, 502, 693

Silesia 388, 430, 452

Sirmium 96

Spain 40, 42, 43, 54-56, 61, 65, 94, 103, 106, 259, 280, 283, 308, 311, 329, 339, 340, 343, 344, 346, 348, 349, 351, 352, 359-361, 363, 365, 366, 368-371, 374, 376, 382, 383, 385-389, 394, 396, 397, 400, 402, 406, 415, 416, 421, 441, 443, 448, 457-459, 470, 541, 550, 742

Sweden 122, 311, 338, 367, 369-371, 376, 388, 389, 401, 402, 406, 416, 418, 470, 507, 690

Syria 90, 152, 228, 229, 232, 240, 334, 482

Thames 38, 39, 46

The Balkans 49, 56, 152, 154, 261, 304, 446, 454, 703, 734, 748

Tibet 66

Tin Islands 42, 73, 80

Transoxania 396

Turkey 55, 56, 59, 64, 65, 70, 96, 226, 278, 279, 386, 418, 420, 447, 455, 470, 471, 485, 538, 631, 743

Venice 146, 262, 281, 313, 332, 338-340, 343, 344, 346, 347, 349, 350, 352, 353, 355, 356, 363, 372, 376, 378, 379, 392, 396, 399, 400, 411, 422, 430, 433, 444, 480, 504, 507

Vladimir 425, 611, 613

Volga River 49, 55, 123

Wales 32, 45, 60, 70, 71, 75, 79, 89, 114-117, 123, 132, 173, 179, 182, 238, 307, 308, 312, 512, 528, 537, 543, 617, 638, 644, 652, 669, 680, 740, 741, 746, 754

Wessex 27, 124-127, 129, 132, 133, 277, 279, 631, 632

Xinjiang 56, 65, 66

## Time Periods

Archaeological – Bronze Age 32, 42, 58, 59, 63, 126, 495, 576, 694, 757

Archaeological – Early Medieval Age 693, 705

Archaeological – Iron Age 7, 28, 58, 60, 63, 68, 71, 74, 576

Archaeological – Lower Palaeolithic 28, 29

Archaeological – Medieval Age 629, 633, 693, 705

Archaeological – Mesolithic 32, 37, 41, 42, 53, 114, 207, 208, 274

Archaeological – Middle Palaeolithic 29

Archaeological – Modern Age 143

*Index to Volume One*

Archaeological – Neolithic 32, 46, 50, 53, 207, 208, 495, 575, 576

Archaeological – Upper Palaeolithic 29

Cultural – Basilika 84

Cultural – Caroline Era 34

Cultural – Classical 422, 495, 515

Cultural – Corpus Juris Civilis 84, 457, 498

Cultural – Dominate 84

Cultural – Edwardian Era 34

Cultural – Elizabethan Era 34

Cultural – Georgian Era 34

Cultural – Hellenistic 228

Cultural – Inter-war Period 34

Cultural – Jacobean Era 34

Cultural – La Belle Époque 426, 613

Cultural – Modern Britain 34, 717, 720

Cultural – Norman Conquest Period 34

Cultural – Plantagenet Period 34

Cultural – Principate 84

Cultural – Regency Period – English King George III 34

Cultural – Restoration Era 34

Cultural – Roman Britain 34, 113, 748

Cultural – Stuart Period 34

Cultural – Tudor Period 34

Cultural – Victorian Era 34

Cultural – Viking Incursions 34

Geological – Holocene Epoch 29, 30, 32, 37, 44, 495, 694, 712

Geological – Jurassic 35

Geological – Mesozoic Era 35

Geological – Pleistocene Epoch 28, 29

Geological – Triassic 35

**War & Genocide**

Afghan war 604

American Civil War 517, 523

Battle of Austerlitz 424

Battle of Bossenden Wood 184

Battle of Bow Street 184

Battle of Cable Street 184

Battle of Civitate 301, 304

Battle of Civitella 301

Battle of Ethandun 126

Battle of Fulford Gate 135

Battle of George Square 184

Battle of Hastings 136, 137

Battle of Hattin 314

Battle of Lechfeld 298

Battle of Lepanto 362

Battle of Lewisham 184

Battle of Nedao 262

Battle of Novara 440

Battle of Ostia 285

Battle of Pavia 343, 353

Battle of Phoenix 278

Battle of Preveza 356

Battle of Sedan 433

Battle of Stamford Bridge 136

Battle of the Catalaunian Plains 107, 260, 262

Battle of the Pyramids 396

Battle of Varna 336

Battle of Vienna 378

Battle of Waterloo 412, 423, 580

Battle of Watling Street 89

Crimean War 427

Duke of Cumberland 535

## Index to Volume One

English Barons' Wars 315, 319

English Civil War 33, 233, 531, 532, 662

First Anglo-Dutch War 367, 368

Fourth Anglo-Dutch War 395

Franco-Dutch War 367, 369, 370

Gothic War 269, 270

Hapsburg-Valois War 358

Hundred Year War 12, 326, 328, 338, 366, 500, 505

Hussite Wars 333

Italian Wars 338-340, 355, 358, 427

Mary Rose 337, 357

Napoleonic Wars 400, 401

Nine Year War 367, 371, 507

Northern Wars 338

Opium Wars 150

Papal Atrocity – Albigenses 315, 316, 745

Papal Atrocity – Battle of Benevento 320

Papal Atrocity – Battle of Castelfidardo 429

Papal Atrocity – Battle of Foggia 319

Papal Atrocity – Battle of Legnano 313

Papal Atrocity – Battle of Monte Porzio 313, 315

Papal Atrocity – Battle of Tagliacozzo 320

Papal Atrocity – Cathars 224, 225, 227, 314, 325

Papal Atrocity – Cesena 329, 397, 422

Papal Atrocity – Jacques Fournier 325

Papal Atrocity – War of the Eight Saints 329

Papal Atrocity – Wars of Castro 374

Rhodesian Wars 475

Second Anglo-Dutch War 368

Second Punic War 68

Seven Year War 389, 510, 514

Spanish Civil War 420

Third Anglo-Dutch War 369, 370

Thirty Year War 366, 367, 373, 374, 380

Vietnam War 549

War of Austrian Succession 388, 430

War of Bavarian Succession 394, 395

War of Devolution 368, 376

War of Saluzzo 366

War of Spanish Succession 382-385, 391, 541, 593

War of the League of Cognac 343

War of the Quadruple Alliance 541

War of the Sicilian Vespers 321, 322

War of Urbino 351

Wars of the Guelphs and Ghibellines 313

World War One 15, 34, 148, 344, 420, 424, 425, 444, 445, 448-450, 452, 455, 456, 463, 464, 467, 479, 512, 515, 525, 548, 588, 595, 665, 706, 744, 746

World War Two 5, 7, 10, 33, 34, 69, 144, 145, 151, 154, 426, 448, 463, 467, 468, 470, 471, 474, 478, 481, 483, 526, 550, 597, 616, 654, 706, 713

www.ingramcontent.com/pod-product-compliance
Lightning Source LLC
Chambersburg PA
CBHW051531230426
43669CB00015B/2559